Great Truths by Great Authors.

I have somewhere seen it observed, that we should make the same use of a Book that the Bee does of a Flower; she steals sweets from it, but does not injure it.

Colton.

Great Truths

BY

Great Authors.

A

DICTIONARY

OF

Aids to Reflection,

QUOTATIONS OF MAXIMS, METAPHORS, COUNSELS, CAUTIONS, APHORISMS, PROVERBS, &c. &c.

FROM

Writers of all Ages and both Hemispheres.

PHILADELPHIA:
J. B. LIPPINCOTT & CO.
1856.

STEREOTYPED BY L. JOHNSON & CO.
PHILADELPHIA.

Preface to the American Edition.

Great truths bear to great men the relation at once of cause and effect. A sublime truth, once uttered and made a part of standard literature, becomes thereafter a perpetual spur to noble deeds. The maxims of the wise form part of a nation's intellectual coin, and, like other coin, serve both as the measure and the prolific source of intellectual wealth. Alexander the Great, it is said, constantly slept with Homer under his pillow. The ideal hero of the Iliad helped to make the real heroes of later Greece. Great ideas, in fact, usually precede and cause illustrious achievements. Hence it is that the literature of a people invariably contains within it that which has made the people what it is.

The object of the compiler of the present work was to collect into a narrow compass, and to arrange in a form convenient for reference and consultation, a choice collection of the remarkable utterances of the great among all nations, but chiefly of the great men among the Anglo-Saxon race. The American Edition has been enlarged and enriched by numerous extracts from the writings of our own distinguished men. Among those eminent Americans whose choicest sayings have here been garnered, may be mentioned the names of Washington, Adams, Jefferson, Franklin, Hamilton, Ames, Wirt, Clay, Calhoun, Webster, Story, Jonathan Edwards, Archibald Alexander, Wayland, Channing, Irving, Cooper, Bryant, Longfellow, Everett, Prescott, Bancroft, Emerson, and many others.

The work, as thus enlarged and enriched, forms a mine of thought of inestimable value to every one. To the young, particularly, it is of special value, as furnishing the means of storing the youthful mind with a fund of high and ennobling thoughts, such as have shaped the destinies of the great and good who have preceded them.

ILLUSTRATIONS OF TRUTH;

OR,

THINGS NEW AND OLD.

Abuse of Power. — *Shakspeare.*

THAT Man, that sits within a Monarch's heart,
And ripens in the sunshine of his favour,
Would he abuse the countenance of the King,
Alack, what mischiefs might he set abroach,
In shadow of such Greatness!

Accusation. — *Shakspeare.*

I would, I could
Quit all offences with as clear excuse,
As well as, I am doubtless, I can purge
Myself of many I am charged withal:
Yet such extenuation let me beg,
As, in reproof of many tales devised,
By smiling Pick-thanks and base Newsmongers,
I may, for some things true, wherein my youth
Hath faulty wander'd and irregular,
Find pardon on my true submission.

Acquaintance. — *Seneca.*

IT is safer to affront some People than to oblige them; for the better a Man deserves, the worse they will speak of him.

Acquaintance. — *Cowley.*

IF we engage into a large Acquaintance and various familiarities. we set open our gates to the Invaders of most of our time: we expose our Life to a quotidian Ague of frigid Impertinences, which would make a wise Man tremble to think of. Now, as for being known much by sight, and pointed at, I cannot comprehend the Honour that lies in that: whatsoever it be, every Mountebank has it more than the best Doctor.

Acquaintance. — *Lord Bacon.*

IT is good discretion not to make too much of any man at the first; because one cannot hold out that proportion.

Acquaintance. — *La Rochefoucauld.*

WHAT makes us like new Acquaintances is not so much any weariness of our old ones, or the pleasure of change, as disgust at not being sufficiently admired by those who know us too well, and the hope of being more so by those who do not know so much of us.

Acquirement. — *Colton.*

THAT which we acquire with the most difficulty we retain the longest; as those who have earned a fortune are usually more careful than those who have inherited one.

Acting. — *From the French.*

THERE is no secret in the heart which our Actions do not disclose. The most consummate hypocrite cannot at all times conceal the workings of the Mind.

Acting. — *Tillotson.*

IT is hard to personate and act a part along; for where Truth is not at the bottom, Nature will always be endeavouring to return, and will peep out and betray herself one time or other.

Action. — *Colton.*

DELIBERATE with Caution, but act with Decision; and yield with Graciousness, or oppose with Firmness.

Activity. — *Longfellow.*

LIVES of great men all remind us
We can make our lives sublime,
And, departing, leave behind us
Footprints on the sands of Time.
Let us then be up and doing;
With a heart for any fate,
Still achieving, still pursuing,
Learn to labour and to wait.

Adaptation. — *Lord Greville.*

AS we should adapt the style of our writing to the Capacity of the Person it is addressed to, so should we our manner of *acting;* for as Persons of inferior *Understandings* will misconceive, and perhaps suspect some sophistry from an Elegance of Expression which they cannot *comprehend,* so Persons of inferior *Sentiment* will probably mistake the intention, or even suspect a fraud from a delicacy of acting which they want capacity to *feel.*

Adaptation. — *From the Latin.*

HE alone is wise who can accommodate himself to all the contingencies of Life; but the fool contends, and is struggling, like a swimmer against the stream.

Adaptation. — *Shakspeare.*

To the latter end of a Fray, and the beginning of a Feast,
Fits a dull Fighter, and a keen Guest.

Adaptation. — *St. Evremond.*

AS long as you are engaged in the World, you must comply with its maxims; because nothing is more unprofitable, than the Wisdom of those persons who set up for Reformers of the Age. 'Tis a part a man cannot act long, without offending his friends and rendering himself ridiculous.

Adaptation. — *Gresset.*

THE Eagle of one House is the Fool in another.

Address. — *Colton.*

A MAN who knows the World, will not only make the most of every thing he does know, but of many things he does not know, and will gain more credit by his adroit mode of hiding his Ignorance, than the Pedant by his awkward attempt to exhibit his Erudition.

Adoration. — *Shakspeare.*

RELIGIOUS in mine error, I adore
The Sun, that looks upon his worshipper,
But knows of him no more.

Adversity. — *Horace.*

ADVERSITY has the effect of eliciting Talents, which, in prosperous Circumstances, would have lain dormant.

Adversity. — *Shakspeare.*

You were used
To say, Extremity was the trier of Spirits;
That common chances common men could bear;
That, when the Sea was calm, all boats alike
Show'd mastership in floating: Fortune's blows,
When most struck home, being gentle wounded, crave
A noble cunning.

Adversity. — *Byron.*

SOME, bow'd and bent,
Wax gray and ghastly, withering ere their time,
And perish with the reed on which they leant;
Some seek Devotion, Toil, War, Good or Crime,
According as their Souls were form'd to sink or climb.

Adversity.—*Crabbe.*

In this wild world the fondest and the best
Are the most tried, most troubled, and distress'd.

Adversity.—*Thomson.*

Ye good distress'd!
Ye noble few! who here unbending stand
Beneath Life's pressure, yet bear up awhile,
And what your bounded view, which only saw
A little part, deem'd evil, is no more;
The storms of wintry Time will quickly pass,
And one unbounded Spring encircle all.

Adversity.—*Rogers.*

The good are better made by ill:—
As odours crush'd are sweeter still!

Adversity.—*Byron.*

A THOUSAND years scarce serve to form a State;
An hour may lay it in the dust; and when
Can Man its shatter'd splendour renovate,
Recall its virtues back, and vanquish Time and Fate?

Adversity.—*Lord Greville.*

ASK the Man of Adversity, how other men *act* towards him: ask those others, how he *acts* towards them. Adversity is the true touchstone of Merit in both; happy if it does not produce the dishonesty of Meanness in one, and that of Insolence and Pride in the other.

Adversity.—*Shakspeare.*

Sweet are the uses of Adversity;
Which, like the toad, ugly and venomous,
Wears yet a precious jewel in his head.

Adversity.—*Addison.*

THE Gods in bounty work up Storms about us,
That give Mankind occasion to exert
Their hidden Strength, and throw out into practice
Virtues that shun the day, and lie conceal'd
In the smooth seasons and the calms of Life.

Adversity.—*Young.*

Affliction is the good Man's shining scene:
Prosperity conceals his brightest ray;
As Night to Stars, Woe lustre gives to Man.

Advice.—*Von Knebel.*

HE who can take Advice, is sometimes suverior to him who can give it.

Affability. — *From the French.*

AFFABILITY in a Prince is the magnet of Truth.

Affectation. — *Cowper.*

IN Man or Woman, but far most in Man,
And most of all in Man that ministers
And serves the Altar, in my Soul I loathe
All Affectation. 'Tis my perfect Scorn;
Object of my implacable disgust.

Affectation. — *From the French.*

WE are never rendered so ridiculous by Qualities which we possess, as by those which we aim at, or affect to have.

Affectation. — *Saville.*

I WILL not call Vanity and Affectation twins, because, more properly, Vanity is the Mother, and Affectation is the darling Daughter; Vanity is the Sin, and Affectation is the Punishment; the first may be called the Root of Self-love, the other the Fruit. Vanity is never at its full growth, till it spreadeth into Affectation; and then it is complete.

Affectation. — *St. Evremond.*

AFFECTATION is a greater enemy to the Face than the small-pox.

Affectation. — *Goldsmith.*

THE unaffected of every Country nearly resemble each other, and a page of our Confucius and your Tillotson have scarce any material difference. Paltry Affectation, strained Allusions, and disgusting Finery, are easily attained by those who choose to wear them; they are but too frequently the badges of Ignorance, or of Stupidity, whenever it would endeavour to please.

Affection. — *Shakspeare.*

UNREASONABLE Creatures feed their young:
And though Man's face be fearful to their eyes,
Yet, in Protection of their tender ones,
Who hath not seen them (even with those wings
Which sometimes they have used with fearful flight)
Make war with him that climb'd unto their nest,
Offering their own lives in their young's defence?

Affection. — *Rogers.*

GENEROUS as brave,
Affection, Kindness, the sweet offices
Of Love and Duty, were to him as needful
As his daily bread.

Affection. — *Shakspeare.*

I HAVE given suck: and know
How tender 'tis, to love the babe that milks me.

Affection. — *Anon.*

IN the Intercourse of social Life, it is by little acts of watchful Kindness, recurring daily and hourly,—and opportunities of doing Kindnesses, if sought for, are for ever starting up,—it is by Words, by Tones, by Gestures, by Looks, that Affection is won and preserved. He who neglects these trifles, yet boasts that, whenever a great sacrifice is called for, he shall be ready to make it, will rarely be loved. The likelihood is, he will not make it: and if he does, it will be much rather for his own sake, than for his Neighbour's.

Affection. — *Shakspeare.*

THE poor Wren,
The most diminutive of birds, will fight,
Her young ones in her nest, against the Owl.

Affection. — *Shakspeare.*

A GRANDAM's name is little less in Love
Than is the doting title of a Mother.
They are as Children, but one step below.

Age. — *Shakspeare.*

O, SIR, you are old;
Nature in you stands on the very verge
Of her confine; you should be ruled and led
By some discretion, that discerns your state
Better than you yourself.

Age. — *Shakspeare.*

THE aim of all is but to nurse the Life
With Honour, Wealth and Ease, in waning Age:
And in this aim there is such thwarting strife,
That one for all, or all for one we gage:
As Life for Honour in fell Battles rage,
Honour for Wealth, and oft that Wealth doth cost
The death of all, and altogether lost.
So that in vent'ring all, we leave to be
The things we are for that which we expect:
And this ambitious foul Infirmity,
In having much, torments us with defect
Of that we have: so then we do neglect
The thing we have, and all for want of Wit,
Make something nothing by augmenting it.

Ambition. — *Shakspeare.*

I HAVE ventur'd,
Like little wanton boys that swim on bladders,
This many summers in a Sea of Glory:
But far beyond my depth: my high-blown Pride
At length broke under me; and now has left me,
Weary, and old with service, to the mercy
Of a rude stream, that must for ever hide me.

Ambition. — *Byron.*

BUT quiet to quick bosoms is a Hell,
And there hath been thy bane; there is a Fire
And motion of the Soul which will not dwell
In its own narrow Being, but aspire
Beyond the fitting medium of Desire;
And, but once kindled, quenchless evermore,
Preys upon high adventure, nor can tire
Of aught but rest; a Fever at the core,
Fatal to him who bears, to all who ever bore.
This makes the Madmen who have made men mad
By their contagion; Conquerors and Kings,
Founders of Sects and Systems, to whom add
Sophists, Bards, Statesmen, all unquiet Things
Which stir too strongly the Soul's secret Springs,
And are themselves the Fools to those they fool;
Envied, yet how unenviable! what stings
Are theirs! One breast laid open were a School
Which would unteach Mankind the Lust to shine or rule.

Ambition. — *Shakspeare.*

DREAMS, indeed, are Ambition; for the very substance of the ambitious is merely the shadow of a Dream. And I hold Ambition of so airy and light a quality, that it is but a shadow's shadow.

Ambition. — *La Bruyere.*

A SLAVE has but one Master, the ambitious Man has as many Masters as there are persons whose aid may contribute to the advancement of his Fortune.

Amusements. — *Burton.*

LET the World have their May-games, Wakes, Whitsunales; their Dancings and Concerts; their Puppet-shows, Hobby-horses, Tabors, Bagpipes, Balls, Barley-breaks, and whatever sports and recreations please them best, provided they be followed with discretion.

Anathema. — *Shakspeare.*

If she must teem,
Create her child of Spleen, that it may live,
And be a thwart disnatur'd torment to her!
Let it stamp wrinkles in her brow of Youth;
With cadent tears fret channels in her Cheeks;
Turn all her Mother's pains, and benefits,
To laughter and contempt; that she may feel,
How sharper than a serpent's tooth it is,
To have a thankless child!

Anathema. — *Shakspeare.*

O VILLAINS, Vipers, damn'd without redemption;
Dogs, easily won to fawn on any man;
Snakes in my heart-blood warm'd, that sting my heart;
Three Judasses, each one thrice worse than Judas!

Anatomy. — *Melancthon.*

IT is shameful for Man to rest in ignorance of the structure of his own Body, especially when the knowledge of it mainly conduces to his welfare, and directs his application of his own Powers.

Ancestry. — *Colton.*

IT is with Antiquity as with Ancestry, Nations are proud of the one, and Individuals of the other; but if they are nothing in themselves, that which is their pride ought to be their humiliation.

Ancestry. — *Percival.*

I am one,
Who finds within me a nobility,
That spurns the idle pratings of the great,
And their mean boast of what their fathers were,
While they themselves are fools effeminate,
The scorn of all who know the worth of mind
And virtue.

Ancestry. — *Daniel Webster.*

THERE may be, and there often is, indeed a regard for ancestry, which nourishes only a weak pride; as there is also a care for posterity, which only disguises an habitual avarice, or hides the workings of a low and grovelling vanity. But there is also a moral and philosophical respect for our ancestors, which elevates the character and improves the heart.

Anger. — *Shakspeare.*

Must I give way and room to your rash Choler?
Shall I be frighted, when a Madman stares?

Anger. — *Shakspeare.*

FRET, till your proud heart break;
Go, show your Slaves how choleric you are,
And make your Bondsmen tremble. Must I budge?
Must I observe you? Must I stand and crouch
Under your testy humour? By the Gods,
You shall digest the venom of your Spleen,
Though it do split you: for, from this day forth,
I'll use you for my Mirth, yea, for my Laughter,
When you are waspish.

Anger. — *Plutarch.*

THE continuance and frequent fits of Anger produce an evil habit in the Soul, called Wrathfulness, or a propensity to be angry; which ofttimes ends in Choler, Bitterness, and Morosity; when the Mind becomes ulcerated, peevish, and querulous, and like a thin, weak plate of iron, receives impression, and is wounded by the least occurrence.

Anger. — *Pope.*

THEN flash'd the living Lightning from her eyes,
And screams of horror rend th' affrighted skies.
Not louder shrieks to pitying Heaven are cast,
When husbands, or when lap-dogs, breathe their last;
Or when rich china vessels, fall'n from high,
In glitt'ring dust and painted fragments lie!

Anger. — *Spenser.*

AND him beside rides fierce revenging Wrath
Upon a Lion loth for to be led;
And in his hand a burning Brond he hath,
The which he brandisheth about his hed;
His eies did hurle forth sparcles fiery red,
And stared sterne on all that him beheld;
As ashes pale of hew and seeming ded;
And on his dagger still his hand he held
Trembling through hasty Rage when Choler in him sweld.

Anger. — *Savage.*

WHEN Anger rushes, unrestrain'd to action,
Like a hot steed, it stumbles in its way.
The Man of Thought strikes deepest, and strikes safely.

Anger. — *Colton.*

THE Sun should not set upon our Anger, neither should he rise upon our Confidence. We should forgive freely, but forget rarely. I will not be revenged, and this I owe to my Enemy; but I will remember, and this I owe to myself

Anger. — *Clarendon.*

ANGRY and choleric Men are as ungrateful and unsociable as Thunder and Lightning, being in themselves all Storm and Tempests; but quiet and easy Natures are like fair Weather, welcome to all, and acceptable to all Men; they gather together what the other disperses, and reconcile all whom the other incenses: as they have the good will and the good wishes of all other Men, so they have the full possession of themselves, have all their own thoughts at peace, and enjoy quiet and ease in their own fortunes, how strait soever it may be.

Anger. — *Shakspeare.*

LET your Reason with your Choler question
What 'tis you go about. To climb steep hills
Requires slow pace at first. Anger is like
A full hot horse; who being allow'd his way,
Self-mettle tires him.

Anger. — *Plutarch.*

LAMENTATION is the only musician that always, like a screech-owl, alights and sits on the roof of an angry Man.

Anger. — *Plutarch.*

HAD I a careful and pleasant companion, that should show me my angry face in a glass, I should not at all take it ill; to behold a Man's self so unnaturally disguised and disordered, will conduce not a little to the Impeachment of Anger.

Antagonism. — *Lord Greville.*

SOME Characters are like some bodies in Chemistry; very good perhaps in themselves, yet fly off and refuse the least conjunction with each other.

The Antiquary. — *Peter Pindar.*

RARE are the Buttons of a Roman's breeches,
In Antiquarian eyes surpassing riches:
Rare is each crack'd, black, rotten, earthen dish,
That held of ancient Rome the flesh and fish.

Antiquity. — *Chesterfield.*

I DO by no means advise you to throw away your Time, in ransacking, like a dull Antiquarian, the minute and unimportant parts of remote and fabulous times. Let blockheads read, what blockheads wrote.

Antiquity. — *Tacitus.*

ALL those things which are now held to be of the greatest Antiquity, were, at one time, new; and what we to-day hold up by Example, will rank hereafter as a Precedent.

Antiquity. — *Colton.*

IT has been observed, that a Dwarf standing on the shoulders of a Giant, will see farther than the Giant himself; and the Moderns, standing as they do on the vantage-ground of former discoveries, and uniting all the fruits of the experience of their forefathers, with their own actual observation, may be admitted to enjoy a more enlarged and comprehensive view of things than the Ancients themselves; for that alone is *true Antiquity*, which embraces the Antiquity of the *World*, and not that which would refer us back to a period when the *World was young*. But by whom is this *true* Antiquity enjoyed? Not by the Ancients who did live in the infancy, but by the Moderns who *do* live in the maturity of things.

Antiquity. — *Burke.*

WHEN ancient Opinions and Rules of Life are taken away, the loss cannot possibly be estimated. From that moment we have no compass to govern us; nor can we know distinctly to what port to steer.

Appearances. — *Shakspeare.*

THE World is still deceived with Ornament.
In *Law*, what Plea so tainted and corrupt,
But, being season'd with a gracious Voice,
Obscures the Show of Evil? In *Religion*,
What damned Error, but some sober Brow
Will bless it, and approve it with a text,
Hiding the grossness with fair Ornament?
There is no Vice so simple, but assumes
Some mark of Virtue on its outward parts.
How many *Cowards*, whose hearts are all as false
As stairs of sand, wear yet upon their chins
The beards of Hercules, and frowning Mars;
Who, inward search'd, have livers white as milk?
And these assume but Valour's excrement,
To render them redoubted. Look on *Beauty*,
And you shall see 'tis purchased by the weight;
Which therein works a miracle in Nature,
Making them lightest that wear most of it:
So are those crisped snaky golden locks,
Which make such wanton gambols with the wind,
Upon supposed Fairness, often known
To be the dowry of a second head,
The skull that bred them, in the sepulchre.
Thus Ornament is but the guiled shore
To the most dangerous sea; the beauteous scarf

Vailing an Indian beauty; in a word,
The seeming Truth which cunning Times put on
To entrap the wisest.

Appearances. — *La Rochefoucauld.*

IN all the professions every one affects a particular look and exterior, in order to appear what he wishes to be thought; so that it may be said the World is made up of Appearances.

Appearances. — *Churchill.*

APPEARANCES to save his only care;
So things seem right, no matter what they are.

Appearances. — *Shakspeare.*

THERE is a fair Behaviour in thee, Captain;
And though that Nature with a beauteous wall
Doth often close in pollution, yet of thee
I will believe, thou hast a Mind that suits
With this thy fair and outward Character.

Appreciation. — *Lord Greville.*

YOU may fail to shine, in the opinion of others, both in your Conversation and Actions, from being superior, as well as inferior, to them.

Apprehension. — *Burke.*

BETTER to be despised for too anxious apprehensions, than ruined by too confident a security.

Argument. — *Butler.*

It is vain
(I see) to argue 'gainst the grain,
Or like the stars, incline men to
What they're averse themselves to do;
For when disputes are wearied out,
'Tis inter'st still resolves the doubt.

Aristocracy. — *Eward Everett.*

WHAT subsists to-day by violence, continues to-morrow by acquiescence, and is perpetuated by tradition; till at last the hoary abuse shakes the gray hairs of antiquity at us, and gives itself out as the wisdom of ages. Thus the clearest dictates of reason are made to yield to a long succession of follies.

And this is the foundation of the aristocratic system at the present day. Its stronghold, with all those not immediately interested in it, is the reverence of antiquity.

Art. — *From the Latin.*

It is the Height of Art to conceal Art.

Art. — *Lavater.*

THE enemy of Art is the enemy of Nature; Art is nothing but the highest sagacity and exertions of Human Nature; and what Nature will he honour who honours not the Human?

Artifice. — *La Rochefoucauld.*

THE ordinary employment of Artifice is the mark of a petty Mind; and it almost always happens that he who uses it to cover himself in one place, uncovers himself in another.

Artifice. — *Washington Irving.*

THERE is a certain artificial polish—a common-place vivacity acquired by perpetually mingling in the *beau Monde*, which, in the commerce of the World, supplies the place of natural suavity and good humour, but is purchased at the expense of all original and sterling traits of Character: by a kind of fashionable discipline, the Eye is taught to brighten, the Lip to smile, and the whole Countenance to emanate with the semblance of friendly Welcome, while the Bosom is unwarmed by a single Spark of genuine Kindness and good-will.

Ascendency. — *Lord Greville.*

WHATEVER natural Right Men may have to Freedom and Independency, it is manifest that some Men have *a natural* Ascendency over others.

Asking. — *Fuller.*

IF thou canst not obtain a Kindness which thou desirest, put a good face on it, show no Discontent nor Surliness: an hour may come, when thy request may be granted.

Associates. — *From the Latin.*

IF you always live with those who are lame, you will yourself learn to limp.

Associates. — *La Bruyere.*

IF Men wish to be held in Esteem, they must associate with those only who are estimable.

Associates. — *Lavater.*

HE who comes from the Kitchen smells of its smoke; he who adheres to a Sect has something of its Cant; the College-Air pursues the Student, and dry Inhumanity him who herds with literary Pedants.

Associates. — *Lord Chesterfield.*

CHOOSE the company of your superiors, whenever you can have it; that is the right and true Pride.

Assuming. — *De Moy.*

ASSUMED Qualities may catch the Affections of some, but one must possess Qualities really good, to fix the heart.

Associates. — *Fuller.*

ASSOCIATE with Men of good Judgment: for Judgment is found in Conversation. And we make another Man's Judgment ours, by frequenting his Company.

Associates. — *Shakspeare.*

THOU art noble; yet, I see,
Thy honourable Metal may be wrought
From that it is disposed. Therefore 'tis meet
That noble Minds keep ever with their Likes:
For who so firm, that cannot be seduced?

Astronomy. — *Cicero.*

THE contemplation of Celestial Things will make a Man both speak and think more sublimely and magnificently when he descends to human affairs.

Atheism. — *Hare.*

THERE is no being eloquent for Atheism. In that exhausted receiver the Mind cannot use its wings,—the clearest proof that it is out of its element.

Atheism. — *Lord Herbert of Cherbury.*

WHOEVER considers the Study of Anatomy, I believe, will never be an Atheist; the frame of Man's Body, and Coherence of his Parts, being so strange and paradoxical, that I hold it to be the greatest Miracle of Nature.

Atheism. — *Washington Allston.*

THE atheist may speculate, and go on speculating till he is brought up by annihilation; he may then return to life, and reason away the difference between good and evil; he may even go further, and imagine to himself the perpetration of the most atrocious acts; and still he may eat his bread with relish, and sleep soundly in his bed; for his sins, wanting as it were substance, having no actual solidity to leave their traces in his memory, all future retribution may seem to him a thing with which, in any event, he can have no concern; but let him once turn his theory to practice—let him make crime palpable—in an instant he feels its hot impress on his soul.

Authority. — *Shakspeare.*

THOUGH Authority be a stubborn bear, yet he is oft led by the nose with gold.

Authority. — *Shakspeare.*

AUTHORITY, though it err like others,
Hath yet a kind of Med'cine in itself,
That skins the vice o' the top.

Authority. — *Shakspeare.*

O Place! O Form!
How often dost thou with thy case, thy habit,
Wrench awe from fools, and tie the wiser souls
To thy false seeming?

Authority. — *Shakspeare.*

Authority bears a credent bulk,
That no particular scandal one can touch,
But it confounds the breather.

Authors. — *Johnson.*

PEOPLE may be taken in *once*, who imagine that an Author is greater in private life than other Men.

Authors. — *Longfellow.*

THE motives and purposes of authors are not always so pure and high, as, in the enthusiasm of youth, we sometimes imagine. To many the trumpet of fame is nothing but a tin horn to call them home, like laborers from the field, at dinner-time, and they think themselves lucky to get the dinner.

Authors. — *Colton.*

IT is a doubt whether Mankind are most indebted to those who, like Bacon and Butler, dig the gold from the mine of Literature, or to those who, like Paley, purify it, stamp it, fix its real value, and give it currency and utility. For all the practical purposes of Life, Truth might as well be in a prison as in the folio of a Schoolman, and those who release her from her cobwebbed shelf, and teach her to live with Men, have the merit of *liberating*, if not of *discovering* her.

Authors. — *Sir Egerton Brydges.*

AUTHORS have not always the power or habit of throwing their talents into conversation. There are some very just and well-expressed observations on this point in Johnson's Life of Dryden, who was said not at all to answer in this respect the Character of his Genius. I have observed that vulgar readers almost always lose their veneration for the writings of the Genius with whom they have had personal intercourse.

Authors. — *Colton.*

THE Society of dead Authors has this advantage over that of the living; they never flatter us to our faces, nor slander us behind our backs, nor intrude upon our privacy, nor quit their shelves until we take them down. Besides, it is always easy to shut a Book, but not quite so easy to get rid of a lettered Coxcomb.

Authors. — *Byron.*

BUT every Fool describes in these bright days
His wondrous Journey to some foreign Court,
And spawns his Quarto, and demands your praise.

Authors. — *Young.*

SOME write, confined by Physic; some, by Debt;
Some, for 'tis Sunday; some, because 'tis wet;
Another writes because his Father writ,
And proves himself a Bastard by his Wit.

Authors. — *Byron.*

HE had written Praises of a Regicide;
He had written Praises of all Kings whatever;
He had written for Republics far and wide,
And then against them bitterer than ever.

Authors. — *Butler.*

MUCH thou hast said, which I know when
And where thou stol'st from other Men;
Whereby 'tis plain thy Light and Gifts
Are all but plagiary Shifts.

Authors. — *Cowper.*

AND Novels (witness every Month's Review)
Belie their Name and offer nothing new.

Authors. — *Johnson.*

SUCCESS and Miscarriage have the same effects in all conditions. The prosperous are feared, hated, and flattered; and the unfortunate avoided, pitied, and despised. No sooner is a Book published, than the Writer may judge of the opinion of the World. If his Acquaintance press round him in public Places, or salute him from the other side of the Street; if Invitations to dinner come thick upon him, and those with whom he dines keep him to Supper; if the Ladies turn to him when his coat is plain, and the Footmen serve him with attention and alacrity; he may be sure that his Work has been praised by some Leader of literary Fashions.

Authors. — *Byron.*

ONE hates an Author that's *all Author*, Fellows
In Foolscap uniforms turn'd up with ink,
So very anxious, clever, fine, and jealous,
One don't know what to say to them, or think,
Unless to puff them with a pair of bellows:
Of Coxcombry's worst Coxcombs, e'en the Pink
Are preferable to these shreds of paper,
These unquench'd snuffings of the midnight taper.

Authors. — *Spenser.*

HOW many great Ones may remember'd be,
Which in their days most famously did flourish,
Of whom no word we hear, nor Sign now see,
But as things wip'd out with a spunge do perish,
Because the living cared not to cherish
No gentle Wits, through pride or covetize,
Which might their Names for ever memorize!

Authors. — *Cowper.*

NONE but an Author knows an Author's cares,
Or Fancy's fondness for the child she bears.

Autumn. — *Spenser.*

THEN came the Autumne, all in Yellow clad,
As though he joyed in his plenteous store,
Laden with Fruits that made him laugh, full glad
That he bad banisht Hunger, which to-fore
Had by the belly oft him pinched sore;
Upon his Head a Wreath, that was enrold
With ears of Corne of every sort, he bore,
And in his Hand a Sickle he did holde,
To reape the ripened Fruit the which the Earth had yold.

Autumn. — *Thomson.*

FLED is the blasted Verdure of the Fields;
And shrunk into their Beds, the flowery Race
Their sunny robes resign. Even what remain'd
Of stronger Fruits falls from the naked Tree;
And Woods, Fields, Gardens, Orchards, all around
The desolated prospect thrills the soul.

Avarice. — *Hughes.*

IT may be remarked for the comfort of honest Poverty, that Avarice reigns most in those who have but few good Qualities to recommend them. This is a Weed that will grow in a barren Soil.

Avarice. — *Moore.*

THE Love of Gold, that meanest rage,
And latest folly of Man's sinking age,
Which, rarely venturing in the van of life,
While nobler passions wage their heated strife,
Comes skulking last, with Selfishness and Fear,
And dies, collecting lumber in the rear!

Avarice. — *Pope.*

RICHES, like Insects, when conceal'd they lie,
Wait but for wings, and in their season fly.
Who sees pale Mammon pine amidst his store,

Sees but a backward steward for the poor;
This year, a reservoir, to keep and spare;
The next, a fountain, spouting through his heir,
In lavish Streams to quench a Country's thirst,
And men and dogs shall drink him till they burst.

Avarice. — *Pope.*

WEALTH in the gross is death, but Life diffused;
As Poison heals, in just proportion used:
In Heaps, like Ambergris, a Stink it lies,
But well dispersed, is Incense to the Skies.

Avarice. — *Blair.*

O CURSED Lust of Gold: when for thy sake
The Fool throws up his interest in both worlds,
First starved in this, then damn'd in that to come.

Avarice. — *Spenser.*

AND greedy Avarice by him did ride
Upon a Camell loaden all with Gold:
Two Iron Coffers hong on either side,
With precious Metall full as they might hold,
And in his Lap an Heap of Coine he told;
For of his wicked Pelf his God he made,
And unto Hell him selfe for Money sold;
Accursed Usury was all his Trade,
And Right and Wrong ylike in equall Ballaunce waide.
His Life was nigh unto Death's Dore yplaste;
And thred-bare Cote and cobled Shoes he ware,
Ne scarse good Morsell all his Life did taste,
But both from Backe and Belly still did spare,
To fill his bags, and Richesse to compare:
Yet Childe nor Kinsman living had he none
To leave them to; but, thorough daily care
To get, and nightly feare to loose his owne,
He led a wretched life unto himself unknowne.

Avarice. — *La Rochefoucauld.*

AVARICE often produces opposite effects; there is an infinite number of People who sacrifice all their property to doubtful and distant Expectations; others despise great future Advantages to obtain present Interests of a trifling nature.

Avarice. — *La Rochefoucauld.*

EXTREME Avarice almost always mistakes itself; there is no Passion which more often deprives itself of its Object, nor on which the Present exercises so much Power to the prejudice of the Future.

Avarice. — *Colton.*

THE Avarice of the Miser may be termed the grand Sepulchre of all his other Passions, as they successively decay. But, unlike other Tombs, it is enlarged by *Repletion,* and strengthened by *Age.*

Awkwardness. — *Churchill.*

WHAT'S a fine Person, or a beauteous Face,
Unless Deportment gives them decent Grace?
Bless'd with all other requisites to please,
Some want the striking Elegance of Ease;
The curious eye their awkward movement tires;
They seem like Puppets led about by wires.

Badinage. — *Zimmerman.*

IN the sallies of Badinage a polite fool shines; but in Gravity he is as awkward as an elephant disporting.

Bashfulness. — *Fuller.*

CONCEIT not so high a notion of any, as to be bashful and impotent in their presence.

Bashfulness. — *Plutarch.*

AS those that pull down private houses adjoining to the Temples of the Gods, prop up such parts as are contiguous to them; so, in undermining Bashfulness, due regard is to be had to adjacent Modesty, Good-nature, and Humanity.

Bashfulness. — *Mackenzie.*

THERE are two distinct Sorts of what we call Bashfulness: this, the awkwardness of a Booby, which a few steps into the world will convert into the pertness of a Coxcomb: that a Consciousness, which the most delicate Feelings produce, and the most extensive Knowledge cannot always remove.

Beauty. — *Shakspeare.*

For her own Person,
It beggar'd all Description; she did lie
In her pavilion,
O'erpicturing that Venus, where we see,
The Fancy out-work Nature.

Beauty. — *Byron.*

AN Eye's an Eye, and whether black or blue,
Is no great matter, so 'tis in request;
'Tis Nonsense to dispute about a Hue—
The kindest may be taken as a Test.
The fair Sex should be always fair; and no Man,
Till thirty, should perceive there's a plain Woman.

Beauty. — *Sir A. Hunt.*

WHAT is Beauty? Not the Show
Of shapely Limbs and Features. No.
These are but flowers
That have their dated hours
To breathe their momentary Sweets, then go.
'Tis the stainless Soul within
That outshines the fairest Skin.

Beauty. — *Rogers.*

But then her Face,
So lovely, yet so arch, so full of mirth,
The overflowings of an innocent Heart.

Beauty. — *Byron.*

WHO hath not proved how feebly Words essay
To fix one spark of Beauty's heavenly ray?
Who doth not feel, until his failing sight
Faints into dimness with its own delight,
His changing cheek, his sinking heart confess
The Might—the Majesty of Loveliness?

Beauty. — *Spenser.*

LONG while I sought to what I might compare
Those powerful Eyes, which lighten my dark Spirit;
Yet found I nought on Earth, to which I dare
Resemble the Image of their goodly light.
Not to the Sun, for they do shine by Night;
Nor to the Moon, for they are changed never;
Nor to the Stars, for they have purer Sight;
Nor to the Fire, for they consume not ever;
Nor to the Lightning, for they still presever;
Nor to the Diamond, for they are more tender;
Nor unto Chrystal, for nought may them sever;
Nor unto Glass, such Baseness mought offend her;
Then to the Maker's Self they likest be;
Whose light doth lighten all that here we see.

Beauty. — *Byron.*

SHE gazed upon a World she scarcely knew
As seeking not to know it; silent, lone,
As grows a Flower, thus quietly she grew,
And kept her Heart serene within its Zone.
There was Awe in the Homage which she drew;
Her Spirit seem'd as seated on a throne
Apart from the surrounding World, and strong
In its own strength—most strange in one so young!

Beauty. — *Milton.*

BEAUTY, like the fair Hesperian Tree
Laden with blooming Gold, had need the guard
Of Dragon-watch with unenchanted eye,
To save her Blossoms and defend her Fruit
From the rash hand of bold Incontinence.

Beauty. — *Spenser.*

FOR shee was full of amiable Grace,
And manly Terror mixed therewithal;
That as the one stirr'd up Affections base,
So th'other did Men's rash Desires apall,
And hold them backe, that would in error fall:
As he that hath espide a vermeill Rose,
To which sharpe Thornes, and Breeres the way forstall,
Dare not for Dread his hardy Hand expose,
But wishing it farr off his ydle Wish doth lose.

Beauty. — *Shakspeare.*

How like Eve's Apple doth thy Beauty grow,
If thy sweet Virtue answer not thy Show!

Beauty. — *Shakspeare.*

COULD Beauty have better commerce than with Honesty?

Beauty. — *Spenser.*

HER Looks were like beams of the morning Sun,
Forth-looking through the window of the East,
When first the fleecie Cattle have begun
Upon their perled grass to make their feast.

Beauty. — *Rochester.*

OH! she is the Pride and Glory of the World:
Without her, all the rest is worthless dross:
Life, a base slavery; Empire but a mock;
And Love, the Soul of all, a bitter curse.

Beauty. — *Byron.*

HER glossy Hair was cluster'd o'er a Brow
Bright with intelligence, and fair and smooth;
Her Eyebrow's Shape was like the aërial Bows,
Her Cheek all purple with the beam of Youth,
Mounting at times to a transparent glow,
As if her Veins ran lightning.

Beauty. — *Lee.*

Is she not brighter than a Summer's Morn,
When all the Heaven is streak'd with dappled Fires,
And fleck'd with Blushes like a rifled Maid?

Beauty. — *Shakspeare.*

All Orators are dumb, when Beauty pleadeth.

Beauty. — *Shakspeare.*

The Roman Dame,
Within whose face Beauty and Virtue strived
Which of them both should underprop her Fame:
When Virtue bragg'd Beauty would blush for Shame;
When Beauty boasted Blushes, in despite
Virtue would stain that o'er with Silver White.
But Beauty, in that White intituled,
From Venus' Doves doth challenge that fair field;
Then Virtue claims from Beauty Beauty's Red,
Which Virtue gave the Golden Age to gild
Their Silver Cheeks, and call'd it then their shield;
Teaching them thus to use it in the fight,—
When Shame assail'd, the Red should fence the White.

Beauty. — *Milton.*

BEAUTY is Nature's Coin, must not be hoarded,
But must be current, and the Good thereof
Consists in mutual and partaken Bliss,
Unsavoury in th' enjoyment of itself:
If you let slip Time, like a neglected rose,
It withers on the stalk with languish'd head.

Beauty. — *Byron.*

HER Glance how wildly beautiful! how much
Hath Phœbus woo'd in vain to spoil her Cheek,
Which glows yet smoother from his amorous clutch!
Who round the North for paler dames would seek?
How poor their forms appear! how languid, wan, and weak!

Beauty. — *Spenser.*

YE tradeful Merchants! that with weary toil
Do seek most precious things to make your gain;
And both the Indias of their treasure spoil,
What needeth you to seek so far in vain?
For lo! my Love doth in herself contain
All this World's Riches that may far be found;
If Saphyrs, lo! her Eyes be Saphyrs plain;
If Rubies, lo! her Lips be Rubies sound;
If Pearls, her Teeth be Pearls, both pure and round;
If Ivory, her Forehead Ivory ween;
If Gold, her locks are finest Gold on Ground;
If Silver, her fair Hands are Silver Sheen:
But that which fairest is, but few behold,
Her mind, adorn'd with Vertues manifold.

Beauty. — *Spenser.*

THE Fairness of her Face no tongue can tell,
For she the Daughters of all Women's Race,
And Angels eke, in Beautie doth excell,
Sparkled on her from God's owne glorious Face,
And more increast by her owne goodly Grace,
That it doth farre exceed all human Thought,
Ne can on Earth compared be to ought.

Beauty. — *Shakspeare.*

BEAUTY lives with Kindness.

Beauty. — *Crabbe.*

LO! when the Buds expand the Leaves are green,
Then the first opening of the Flower is seen;
Then come the honied breath and rosy smile,
That with their sweets the willing sense beguile;
But as we look, and love, and taste, and praise,
And the Fruit grows, the charming Flower decays;
Till all is gather'd, and the wintry blast
Moans o'er the place of love and pleasure past.

So 'tis with Beauty,—such the opening grace
And dawn of glory in the youthful face;
Then are the charms unfolded to the sight,
Then all is loveliness and all delight;
The nuptial tie succeeds, the genial hour,
And, lo! the falling off of Beauty's flower;
So through all Nature is the progress made,—
The Bud, the Bloom, the Fruit,—and then we fade.

Beauty. — *Spenser.*

FOR Beauty is the bait which with delight
Doth Man allure, for to enlarge his kind;
Beauty, the burning lamp of Heaven's light,
Darting her beams into each feeble Mind,
Against whose power nor God nor Man can find
Defence, reward the daunger of the wound;
But being hurt, seek to be medicin'd
Of her that first did stir that mortal stownd.

Beauty. — *Byron.*

HEART on her Lips, and Soul within her Eyes.
Soft as her clime, and sunny as her skies.

Beauty. — *Shakspeare.*

THAT whiter skin of her's than snow,
And smooth as monumental alabaster.

Beauty. — *Spenser.*

FOR sure of all that in this mortal frame
Contained is, nought more Divine doth seem,
Or that resembleth more th' immortal flame
Of heavenly light, than Beauty's glorious beam.
What wonder then if with such rage extreme
Frail men, whose eyes seek heavenly things to see,
At sight thereof so much enravish'd be?

Beauty. — *Mrs. Tighe.*

OH! how refreshing seem'd the breathing wind
To her faint limbs! and while her snowy hands
From her fair brow her golden hair unbind,
And of her zone unloose the silken bands,
More passing bright unveil'd her Beauty stands;
For faultless was her Form as Beauty's Queen,
And every winning grace that Love demands,
With wild attemper'd dignity was seen
Play o'er each lovely limb, and deck her angel mien.

Beauty. — *Byron.*

SUCH was ——— !—such around her shone
The nameless Charms unmark'd by her alone;
The Light of Love, the Purity of Grace,
The Mind, the Music breathing from her Face,
The Heart whose softness harmonized the whole—
And, oh! that Eye was in itself a Soul!

Beauty. — *Shakspeare.*

FAIR Ladies, mask'd, are Roses in their Bud:
Dismask'd, their damask sweet commixture shown,
Are Angels vailing Clouds, or Roses blown.

Beauty. — *Scott.*

THERE was a soft and pensive Grace,
A cast of thought upon her Face,
That suited well the Forehead high,
The Eye-lash dark, and downcast Eye:
The mild Expression spoke a mind
In duty firm, composed, resign'd.

Beauty. — *Spenser.*

EVERY Spirit as it is most pure,
And hath in it the more of heavenly light,
So it the fairer Body doth procure
To habit in ——
For of the Soul the Body form doth take,
For Soul is form and doth the Body make.

Beauty. — *Byron.*

SHE was a Form of Life and Light,
That, seen, became a part of sight,
And rose, where'er I turn'd mine eye,
The Morning-star of Memory!

Beauty. — *Shakspeare.*

My Beauty, though but mean,
Needs not the painted flourish of your praise;
Beauty is bought by judgment of the eye,
Not utter'd by base sale of chapmen's tongues.

Beauty. — *Moore.*

WHILE she, who sang so gently to the lute
Her dream of home, steals timidly away,
Shrinking as violets do in summer's ray,
But takes with her from Azim's heart that sigh
We sometimes give to forms that pass us by
In the world's crowd, too lovely to remain,
Creatures of light we never see again!

Beauty. — *Byron.*

BUT Virtue's self, with all her tightest laces,
Has not the natural stays of strict old age;
And Socrates, that model of all duty,
Own'd to a penchant, though discreet, for Beauty.

Beauty. — *Shakspeare.*

SINCE brass nor stone, nor earth nor boundless sea,
But sad Mortality o'er-sways their power,
How with this rage shall Beauty hold a plea,
Whose action is no stronger than a flower?
O, how shall Summer's honey breath hold out
Against the wreckful siege of battering days,
When rocks impregnable are not so stout,
Nor gates of steel so strong, but Time decays?
O fearful Meditation! where, alack,
Shall Time's best jewel from Time's chest lie hid?
Or what strong hand can hold his swift foot back?
Or who his spoil of Beauty can forbid?

Beauty. — *Shakspeare.*

'TIS Beauty truly blent, whose red and white
Nature's own sweet and cunning hand laid on:
Lady, you are the cruell'st She alive,
If you will lead these graces to the grave,
And leave the world no copy.

Beauty. — *Milton.*

He on his side
Leaning half rais'd, with looks of cordial love
Hung over her enamour'd, and beheld
Beauty, which whether waking or asleep,
Shot forth peculiar graces.

Beauty. — *Moore.*

EV'N then, her Presence had the power
To soothe, to warm,—nay, ev'n to bless—
If ever bliss could graft its flower
On stem so full of bitterness—
Ev'n then her glorious Smile to me
Brought warmth and radiance, if not balm,
Like Moonlight on a troubled sea,
Brightening the storm it cannot calm.

Beauty. — *Pope.*

YET graceful Ease, and Sweetness void of Pride,
Might hide her faults, if Belles had faults to hide:
If to her share some female errors fall,
Look on her Face, and you'll forget 'em all.

Beauty. — *Shakspeare.*

I saw sweet Beauty in her Face,
Such as the daughter of Agenor had,
That made great Jove to humble him to her hand,
When with his knees he kiss'd the Cretan strand.
. . . I saw her coral Lips to move,
And with her Breath she did perfume the air:
Sacred and sweet, was all I saw in her.

Beauty. — *Ben Jonson.*

GIVE me a Look, give me a Face,
That makes Simplicity a Grace;
Robes loosely flowing, Hair as free!
Such sweet neglect more taketh me,
Than all the adulteries of art;
That strike mine eyes, but not my heart.

Beauty. — *Rowe.*

From every blush that kindles in thy Cheeks,
Ten thousand little Loves and Graces spring
To revel in the Roses.

Beauty. — *Shakspeare.*

OH, She doth teach the torches to burn bright!
Her Beauty hangs upon the cheek of Night
Like a rich jewel in an Ethiop's ear:
Beauty too rich for use, for Earth too dear.

Beauty. — *Shakspeare,*

Move these eyes?
Or whether, riding on the balls of mine,
Seem they in motion? Here are sever'd Lips,
Parted with sugar breath; so sweet a bar
Should sunder such sweet friends: Here in her Hairs
The painter plays the spider; and hath woven
A golden mesh to entrap the hearts of men,
Faster than gnats in cobwebs: but her Eyes,—
How could he see to do them? having made one,
Methinks it should have power to steal both his,
And leave itself unfinish'd.

Beauty. — *Joanna Baillie.*

TO make the cunning artless, tame the rude,
Subdue the haughty, shake th' undaunted soul;
Yea, put a bridle in the lion's mouth,
And lead him forth as a domestic cur,
These are the triumphs of all-powerful Beauty!

Beauty. — *Shakspeare.*

HER Stature, as wand-like straight,
As silver-voiced; her Eyes as Jewel-like,
And cased as richly; in pace another Juno;
Who starves the ears she feeds, and makes them hungry,
The more she gives them speech.

Beauty. — *Shakspeare.*

BEAUTY is but a vain and doubtful Good,
A shining Glass, that fadeth suddenly;
A flower that dies, when first it 'gins to bud;
A brittle glass, that's broken presently;
A doubtful Good, a Gloss, a Glass, a flower,
Lost, faded, broken, dead within an hour.

And as Good lost, is seld or never found,
As fading Gloss no rubbing will refresh,
As flowers dead, lie wither'd on the ground,
As broken Glass no Cement can redress,
So Beauty blemish'd once, for ever's lost,
In spite of physic, painting, pain and cost.

Beauty. — *Joanna Baillie.*

WITH Goddess-like demeanor forth she went,
Not unattended, for on her as Queen
A pomp of winning Graces waited still,
And from about her shot darts of desire
Into all eyes to wish her still in sight.

Beauty. — *Addison.*

'TIS not a set of Features, or Complexion,
The tincture of a Skin, that I admire:
Beauty soon grows familiar to the Lover,
Fades in his eye, and palls upon the sense.

Beauty. — *Thomson.*

HER form was fresher than the morning Rose,
When the dew wets its leaves; unstain'd and pure,
As is the Lily, or the mountain Snow.

Beauty. — *Shakspeare.*

HER lily Hand her rosy Cheek lies under,
Cozening the pillow of a lawful kiss:
Without the bed her other fair Hand was,
On the green coverlet: whose perfect white
Show'd like an April daisy on the grass,
With pearly sweat, resembling dew of Night.
Her Eyes, like marigolds, had sheathed their light;
And, canopied in darkness, sweetly lay,
Till they might open to adorn the day.

Beauty. — *Thomson.*

A NATIVE Grace
Sat fair-proportion'd on her polish'd Limbs,
Veil'd in a simple robe, their best attire,
Beyond the pomp of dress: for Loveliness
Needs not the foreign aid of Ornament,
But is when unadorn'd adorn'd the most.

Beauty. — *Shakspeare.*

SHE looks as clear
As morning Roses newly wash'd with Dew.

Beauty. — *Joanna Baillie.*

WHEN I approach
Her Loveliness, so absolute she seems
And in herself complete, so well to know
Her own, that what she wills to do or say,
Seems wisest, virtuousest, discreetest, best;
All higher knowledge in her Presence falls
Degraded, Wisdom in discourse with her
Lose discount'nanc'd, and like Folly shows.

Beauty. — *Young.*

WHAT tender force, what dignity divine,
What virtue consecrating every Feature;
Around that Neck what dross are gold and pearl!

Beauty.—*Blair.*

BEAUTY! thou pretty plaything! dear deceit!
That steals so softly o'er the stripling's heart,
And gives it a new pulse unknown before.
The grave discredits thee: thy Charms expunged,
Thy Roses faded, and thy Lilies soil'd,
What hast thou more to boast of? Will thy lovers
Flock round thee now, to gaze and do thee homage?
Methinks I see thee with thy Head laid low;
Whilst surfeited upon thy damask Cheek,
The high-fed worm, in lazy volumes roll'd,
Riots unscar'd. For this was all thy caution?
For this thy painful labours at thy glass,
T' improve those Charms, and keep them in repair,
For which the spoiler thanks thee not? Foul feeder!
Coarse fare and carrion please thee full as well,
And leave as keen a relish on the sense.

Beauty.—*Jeffrey.*

BEAUTY
That transitory Flower: e'en while it lasts
Palls on the roving sense, when held too near,
Or dwelling there too long: by fits it pleases;
And smells at distance best: its sweets, familiar
By frequent converse, soon grow dull and cloy you.

Beauty.—*Moore.*

OH, what a pure and sacred thing
Is Beauty, curtain'd from the sight
Of the gross World, illumining
One only mansion with her light:
Unseen by Man's disturbing eye—
The Flower, that blooms beneath the Sea
Too deep for sun-beams, doth not lie
Hid in more chaste obscurity!

Beauty.—*Lansdowne.*

SHE seizes hearts, not waiting for consent,
Like sudden death, that snatches unprepared;
Like fire from Heav'n, scarce seen so soon as felt.

Beauty.—*Otway.*

ANGELS were painted fair to look like you:
There's in you all that we believe of Heav'n—
Amazing Brightness, Purity, and Truth,
Eternal Joy, and everlasting Peace.

Beauty. — *Rowe.*

THE Bloom of op'ning Flowers, unsullied Beauty,
Softness, and sweetest Innocence she wears,
And looks like Nature in the World's first Spring.

Beauty. — *Southern.*

O HOW I grudge the grave this heav'nly Form!
Thy Beauties will inspire the arms of Death,
And warm the pale cold tyrant into life.

Beauty. — *Rowe.*

Is she not more than painting can express,
Or youthful Poets fancy, when they love.

Beauty. — *Patterson.*

O FATAL Beauty! why art thou bestow'd
On hapless Woman still to make her wretched!
Betray'd by thee, how many are undone!

Beauty. — *Lee.*

A LAVISH planet reign'd when she was born,
And made her of such kindred mould to Heav'n,
She seems more Heav'n's than ours.

Beauty. — *Dryden.*

ONE who would change the worship of all climates,
And make a new Religion where'er she comes,
Unite the differing faiths of all the World,
To idolize her Face.

Beauty. — *From the French.*

BEAUTY, unaccompanied by Virtue, is as a Flower without Perfume.

Beauty. — *St. Pierre.*

EVERY trait of Beauty may be referred to some virtue, as to Innocence, Candour, Generosity, Modesty, and Heroism.

Beauty. — *From the Italian.*

SOCRATES called Beauty a short-lived Tyranny; Plato, a Privilege of Nature; Theophrastus, a silent Cheat; Theocritus, a delightful Prejudice; Carneades, a solitary Kingdom; Domitian said, that nothing was more grateful; Aristotle affirmed that Beauty was better than all the letters of recommendation in the World; Homer, that 'twas a glorious gift of Nature; and Ovid, alluding to him, calls it a favour bestowed by the Gods.

Beauty. — *Lord Greville.*

THE Criterion of true Beauty is, that it increases on examination; of false, that it lessens. There is something, therefore, in true Beauty that corresponds with right reason, and is not merely the creature of Fancy.

Beauty. — *Dryden.*

MARK her majestic Fabrick; she's a Temple
Sacred by birth, and built by hands Divine:
Her Soul's the Deity that lodges there;
Nor is the Pile unworthy of the God.

Beauty. — *Anonymous.*

BEAUTY is spread abroad through earth and sea and sky, and dwells on the face and form, and in the heart of Man; and he will shrink from the thought of its being a thing which he, or any one else, could monopolize. He will deem that the highest and most blessed privilege of his genius is, that it enables him to cherish the widest and fullest sympathy with the hearts and thoughts of his brethren.

Beauty. — *Dryden.*

HER Eyes, her Lips, her Cheeks, her Shapes, her Features,
Seem to be drawn by Love's own hand; by Love
Himself in love.

Beauty. — *Lee.*

O SHE is all Perfections!
All that the blooming Earth can send forth fair;
All that the gaudy Heavens could drop down glorious.

Beauty. — *Otway.*

OH! she has Beauty might ensnare
A Conqueror's soul, and make him leave his crown
At random, to be scuffled for by slaves.

Beauty. — *Colton.*

THAT is not the most perfect Beauty, which, in public, would attract the greatest observation; nor even that which the Statuary would admit to be a faultless piece of clay, kneaded up with blood. But that is true Beauty, which has not only a Substance, but a Spirit,—a Beauty that we must intimately know, justly to appreciate,—a Beauty lighted up in conversation, where the Mind shines as it were through its casket, where, in the language of the Poet, "the eloquent blood spoke in her Cheeks, and so distinctly wrought, that we might almost say her Body thought." An order and a mode of Beauty which, the more we know, the more we accuse ourselves for not having before discovered those thousand Graces which bespeak that their owner has a Soul. This is that Beauty which never cloys, possessing Charms as resistless as those of the fascinating Egyptian, for which Antony wisely paid the bauble of a World,—a Beauty like the rising of his own Italian Suns, always enchanting, never the same.

Beauty.—*Clarendon.*

IT was a very proper answer to him who asked, why any man should be delighted with Beauty? that it was a question that none but a blind man could ask; since any beautiful object doth so much attract the sight of all men, that it is in no man's power not to be pleased with it.

Beauty.—*Steele.*

TO give pain is the tyranny, to make happy the true empire, of Beauty.

Beauty.—*Ralph Waldo Emerson.*

BEAUTY is the mark God sets on virtue. Every natural action is graceful. Every heroic act is also decent, and causes the place and the bystanders to shine. When a noble act is done—perchance in a scene of great natural beauty; when Leonidas and his three hundred martyrs consume one day in dying, and the sun and moon come each and look at them once in the steep defile of Thermopylæ; when Arnold Winkelried, in the high Alps, under the shadow of the avalanche, gathers in his side a sheaf of Austrian spears to break the line for his comrades; are not these heroes entitled to add the beauty of the scene to the beauty of the deed?

Beauty of Nature.—*Dwight.*

THE beauty and splendour of the objects around us, it is ever to be remarked, are not necessary to their existence, nor to what we commonly intend their usefulness. It is therefore to be regarded as a source of pleasure gratuitously superinduced upon the general nature of the objects themselves, and in this light as a testimony of the Divine Goodness peculiarly affecting.

Becoming our own Master.—*Anonymous.*

EVERYBODY is impatient for the time when he shall be his own Master; and if coming of Age were to make one so, if Years could indeed "bring the philosophic Mind," it would rightly be a day of rejoicing to a whole household and neighbourhood. But too often he who is impatient to become his own Master, when the outward checks are removed, merely becomes his own Slave.

Behaviour.—*La Bruyere.*

A COLDNESS or an Incivility manifested towards us by a Superior, makes us hate him; but no sooner does he condescend to honour us with a Salute or a Smile, than we forget the former Indignity, and become perfectly reconciled to him.

Being Alone.—*Byron.*

To view alone
The fairest scenes of land and deep,
With None to listen and reply
To thoughts with which my heart beat high,
Were irksome.

The Village Bells.—*Cowper.*

HOW soft the Music of those Village Bells.
Falling at intervals upon the Ear
In Cadence sweet! now dying all away,
Now pealing loud again and louder still,
Clear and sonorous as the gale comes on.
With easy force it opens all the cells
Where Mem'ry slept.

Benevolence.—*Shakspeare.*

'TIS pity, Bounty had not eyes behind;
That Man might ne'er be wretched for his Mind.

Benevolence.—*Mackenzie.*

THERE is no use of money equal to that of Beneficence; here the enjoyment grows on reflection.

Benevolence.—*Colton.*

THERE is nothing that requires so strict an Economy as our Benevolence. We should husband our Means as the Agriculturist his manure, which if he spread over too large a superficies produces no crop, if over too small a surface, exuberates in rankness and in weeds.

Benevolence.—*Kant.*

BENEFICENCE is a duty. He who frequently practises it, and sees his benevolent intentions realized, at length comes really to love him to whom he has done Good. When, therefore, it is said, "Thou shalt love thy neighbour as thyself," it is not meant, thou shalt love him first, and do him Good in consequence of that Love, but, thou shalt do Good to thy neighbour; and this thy Beneficence will engender in thee that Love to Mankind which is the fulness and consummation of the Inclination to do Good.

Benevolence.—*Cicero.*

MEN resemble the gods in nothing so much as in doing Good to their fellow-creatures.

Benevolence.—*From the French.*

THE Conqueror is regarded with awe, the wise Man commands our esteem; but it is the benevolent Man who wins our affections.

Benevolence. — *Howels.*

THE disposition to give a cup of cold water to a disciple is a far nobler property than the finest intellect. Satan has a fine intellect, but not the image of God.

Benevolence. — *Seneca.*

THERE will ever be a place for Virtue.

Benevolence. — *Shakspeare.*

FOR his Bounty,
There was no Winter in't; an Autumn 'twas,
That grew the more by reaping.

Bewilderment. — *Shakspeare.*

THERE was Speech in their Dumbness, Language in their very Gesture; they looked, as they had heard of a World ransomed, or one destroyed: a notable passion of Wonder appeared in them; but the wisest beholder, that knew no more but seeing, could not say, if the importance were Joy, or Sorrow; but in the extremity of the one it must needs be.

The Bible. — *Wayland.*

THAT the truths of the Bible have the power of awakening an intense moral feeling in Man under every variety of character, learned, or ignorant, civilized or savage; that they make bad men good, and send a pulse of healthful feeling through all the domestic, civil, and social relations; that they teach men to love right, to hate wrong, and to seek each other's welfare, as the children of one common Parent; that they control the baleful passions of the human heart, and thus make men proficient in the science of self-government; and, finally, that they teach him to aspire after a conformity to a Being of infinite holiness, and fill him with hopes infinitely more purifying, more exalted, more suited to his nature, than any other which this world has ever known, are facts as incontrovertible as the laws of philosophy, or the demonstrations of mathematics.

Bigotry. — *Dryden.*

THE good old Man, too eager in Dispute,
Flew high; and as his Christian Fury rose,
Damn'd all for Heretics who durst oppose.

Bigotry. — *Feltham.*

SHOW me the Man who would go to Heaven alone if he could, and in that Man I will show you one who will never be admitted into Heaven.

Bigotry. — *Prior.*

SOON their crude Notions with each other fought;
The adverse Sect denied what this had taught;
And he at length the ampliest triumph gain'd,
Who contradicted what the last maintain'd.

Biography. — *Terence.*

MY advice is, to consult the Lives of other Men, as he would a looking-glass, and from thence fetch examples for his own imitation.

The Love of Birds. — *Thomson.*

'TIS Love creates their Melody, and all
This waste of Music is the Voice of Love;
That even to Birds, and Beasts, the tender arts
Of pleasing teaches. Hence the glossy kind
Try every winning way inventive Love
Can dictate, and in courtship to their mates
Pour forth their little souls.

Birth. — *Charron.*

THOSE who have nothing else to recommend them to the respect of others, but only their Blood, cry it up at a great rate, and have their mouths perpetually full of it. They swell and vapour, and you are sure to hear of their families and relations every third word. By this mark they commonly distinguish themselves; you may depend upon it there is no good bottom, nothing of true worth of their own when they insist so much, and set their credit upon that of others.

Birth. — *Lord Greville.*

WHEN real Nobleness accompanies that imaginary one of Birth, the imaginary seems to mix with real, and becomes real too.

The Birthday. — *Young.*

ALAS! this Day
First gave me Birth, and (which is strange to tell)
The Fates e'er since, as watching its return,
Have caught it as it flew, and mark'd it deep
With something great; extremes of good or ill.

Blindness. — *Milton.*

THUS with the year
Seasons return, but not to me returns
Day, or the sweet approach of Ev'n or Morn,
Or sight of vernal Bloom, or summer's Rose,
Or Flocks, or Herds, or human Face divine;
But Cloud instead, and ever-during Dark,
Surrounds me, from the cheerful ways of Men
Cut off, and for the Book of Knowledge fair
Presented with a universal Blank
Of Nature's Works, to me expung'd and ras'd,
And Wisdom at one entrance quite shut out.

Blindness. — *Milton.*

O DARK, dark, dark, amid the blaze of Noon,
Irrevocably dark, total Eclipse
Without all hope of Day!
O first created Beam, and thou great Word,
Let there be Light, and Light was over all;
Why am I thus bereav'd thy prime decree?

Blood. — *Shakspeare.*

HIGH-stomach'd are they both, and full of Ire,
In rage deaf as the Sea, hasty as Fire.

Bluntness. — *Shakspeare.*

HE speaks home; you may relish him more in the Soldier, than in the Scholar.

Blushing. — *Spenser.*

THE doubtful Mayd, seeing herself descryde,
Was all abasht, and her pure Yvory
Into a clear Carnation suddeine dyde;
As fayre Aurora rysing hastily
Doth by her Blushing tell that she did lye
All night in old Tithonus' frozen bed,
Whereof she seemes ashamed inwardly.

Blushing. — *Scott.*

WITH every change his Features play'd,
As Aspens show the Light and Shade.

Boasting. — *Young.*

WE rise in Glory, as we sink in Pride;
Where Boasting ends, there Dignity begins.

Boasting. — *Shakspeare.*

CONCEIT, more rich in Matter than in Words,
Brags of his Substance, not of Ornament:
They are but Beggars that can count their Worth.

Boasting. — *Shakspeare.*

I'LL turn two mincing steps
Into a manly stride: and speak of Frays
Like a fine bragging Youth: and tell quaint Lies,
How honourable Ladies sought my Love,
Which I denying they fell sick and died:
I could not do with all:—then I will repent,
And wish for all that, that I had not kill'd them:
And twenty of these puny Lies I'll tell,
That Men shall swear, I have discontinued school
Above a twelvemonth.

Boasting. — *Shakspeare.*

Who knows himself a Braggart,
Let him fear this; for it will come to pass,
That every Braggart shall be found an Ass.

Book-Making. — *Edward H. Everett.*

IT is remarkable that many of the best Books of all sorts have been written by persons who, at the time of writing them, had no intention of becoming authors. Indeed, with slight inclination to systemize and exaggerate, one might be almost tempted to maintain the position—however paradoxical it may at the first blush appear—that no good Book can be written in any other way; that the only literature of any value is that which grows indirectly out of the real action of society, intended directly to affect some other purpose; and that when a man sits doggedly in his study and says to himself "I mean to write a good Book" it is certain, from the necessity of the case, that the result will be a bad one.

Books. — *Fuller.*

THOU mayst as well expect to grow stronger by always eating as wiser by always reading. Too much overcharges Nature, and turns more into disease than nourishment. 'Tis thought and digestion which makes Books serviceable, and gives health and vigour to the mind.

Books. — *Fuller.*

TO divert at any time a troublesome fancy, run to thy Books: they presently fix thee to them, and drive the other out of thy thoughts. They always receive thee with the same kindness.

Books. — *Tom Brown.*

PLAYS and Romances sell as well as Books of Devotion; but with this difference; more people read the former than buy them; and more buy the latter than read them.

Books. — *Anon.*

I HAVE ever gained the most profit, and the most pleasure also, from the Books which have made me think the most; and, when the difficulties have once been overcome, these are the Books which have struck the deepest root, not only in my memory and understanding, but likewise in my affections.

Books. — *Hare.*

BOOKS, as Dryden has aptly termed them, are spectacles to read Nature. Eschylus and Aristotle, Shakspeare and Bacon, are Priests who preach and expound the mysteries of Man and the Universe. They teach us to understand and feel what we see, to decipher and syllable the hieroglyphics of the senses.

Books. — *Joineriana.*

Books, like Friends, should be few and well chosen.

Books. — *Milton.*

As good almost kill a Man as kill a good Book. Many a man lives a burden to the Earth; but a good Book is the precious Life-blood of a Master-spirit, embalmed and treasured up on purpose, to a life beyond life.

Books. — *Clarendon.*

He who loves not Books before he comes to thirty years of age, will hardly love them enough afterward to understand them.

Books. — *Colton.*

Many Books require no thought from those who read them, and for a very simple reason;—they made no such demand upon those who wrote them. Those Works, therefore, are the most valuable, that set our thinking faculties in the fullest operation. For as the solar light calls forth all the latent powers and dormant principles of vegetation contained in the kernel, but which, without such a stimulus, would neither have struck root downward, nor borne fruit upward, so it is with the light that is intellectual; it calls forth and awakens into energy those latent principles of thought in the minds of others, which, without this stimulus, reflection would not have matured, nor examination improved, nor action embodied.

Books. — *Shenstone.*

When self-interest inclines a man to print, he should consider that the purchaser expects a penny-worth for his penny, and has reason to asperse his honesty if he finds himself deceived; also, that it is possible to publish a Book of no value, which is too frequently the product of such mercenary people.

Books. — *Channing.*

God be thanked for Books. They are the voices of the distant and the dead, and make us heirs of the spiritual life of past ages. Books are the true levellers. They give to all, who will faithfully use them, the society, the spiritual presence of the best and greatest of our race. No matter how poor I am. No matter though the prosperous of my own time will not enter my obscure dwelling. If the sacred writers will enter and take up their abode under my roof, if Milton will cross my threshold to sing to me of Paradise, and Shakspeare to open to me the worlds of imagination and the workings of the human heart, and Franklin to enrich me with his practical wisdom, I shall not pine for want of intellectual companionship, and I may become a cultivated man though excluded from what is called the best society in the place where I live.

Books. — *Lord Greville.*

THE man who only relates what he has heard or read, or talks of sensible men and sensible Books in general terms, or of celebrated passages in celebrated Authors, may talk *about sense;* but he alone, who speaks the sentiments that arise from the force of his own mind employed upon the subjects before him, can talk sense.

Books. — *Longfellow.*

MANY readers judge of the power of a Book by the shock it gives their feelings—as some savage tribes determine the power of muskets by their recoil; that being considered best which fairly prostrates the purchaser.

Borrowing. — *Shakspeare.*

NEITHER a Borrower, nor a Lender be:
For loan oft loses both itself and friend;
And borrowing dulls the edge of husbandry.

The Bottle. — *Johnson.*

IN the Bottle discontent seeks for comfort, cowardice for courage, and bashfulness for confidence.

The Braggart. — *Shakspeare.*

HERE'S a Stay,
That shakes the rotten carcase of old Death
Out of his rags! Here's a large Mouth, indeed,
That spits forth Death, and Mountains, Rocks and Seas;
Talk as familiarly of roaring Lions,
As Maids of thirteen do of Puppy-Dogs!
What Cannoneer begot this lusty Blood?
He speaks plain Cannon, Fire, and Smoke, and Bounce;
He gives the Bastinado with his Tongue;
Our ears are cudgel'd.

Brilliancy. — *Longfellow.*

WITH many readers Brilliancy of style passes for affluence of thought; they mistake buttercups in the grass for immensurable gold mines under the ground.

Building. — *Kett.*

NEVER build after you are five-and-forty; have five years income in hand before you lay a Brick, and always calculate the expense at double the estimate.

Business. — *Saville.*

A MAN who cannot mind his own Business, is not to be trusted with the King's.

Business. — *Steele.*

TO men addicted to delights, Business is an interruption; to such as are cold to delights, Business is an entertainment. For which reason it was said to one who commended a dull man for his Application, "No thanks to him; if he had no Business, he would have nothing to do."

Business. — *Shakspeare.*

To Business that we love, we rise betime,
And go to it with delight.

Business. — *Swift.*

MEN of great parts are often unfortunate in the management of public Business, because they are apt to go out of the common road by the quickness of their imagination.

Buying. — *Franklin.*

BUY what thou hast no need of, and ere long thou shalt sell thy necessaries.

Calling. — *Shakspeare.*

VIRTUE's office never breaks men's troth.

Calm. — *Moore.*

HOW calm, how beautiful comes on
The stilly Hour, when Storms are gone;
When warring Winds have died away,
And Clouds, beneath the glancing ray,
Melt off, and leave the Land and Sea
Sleeping in bright Tranquillity,—
When the blue Waters rise and fall,
In sleepy Sunshine mantling all;
And ev'n that Swell the Tempest leaves,
Is like the full and silent heaves
Of Lovers' Hearts, when newly blest,
Too newly to be quite at rest!

Calm. — *Moore.*

'TWAS one of those ambrosial eves
A day of storm so often leaves
At its calm setting—when the West
Opens her golden Bowers of Rest,
And a moist radiance from the skies
Shoots trembling down, as from the eyes
Of some meek penitent, whose last
Bright hours atone for dark ones past,
And whose sweet tears, o'er wrong forgiven,
Shine, as they fall with light from Heaven!

Calumny. — *Shakspeare.*

BE thou as chaste as ice, as pure as snow, thou shalt not escape Calumny.

Candour. — *Shakspeare.*

I HOLD it cowardice,
To rest mistrustful where a noble Heart
Hath pawn'd an open Hand in sign of Love.

Cant. — *Burns.*

LEARN three-mile Pray'rs, an' half-mile Graces,
Wi' weel-spread Looves, an' lang wry Faces;
Grunt up a solemn, lengthen'd Groan,
And damn a' parties but your own;
I'll warrant then, ye're nae Deceiver,
A steady, sturdy, staunch Believer.

Cant. — *Shakspeare.*

'TIS too much proved,—that, with Devotion's Visage,
And pious Action, we do sugar o'er
The Devil himself.

Captiousness. — *Chesterfield.*

A VULGAR Man is captious and jealous; eager and impetuous about trifles. He suspects himself to be slighted, and thinks every thing that is said meant at him.

Care. — *Shakspeare.*

CARE keeps his Watch in every old Man's eye,
And where Care lodges, Sleep will never lie;
But where unbruised Youth with unstuff'd brain
Doth couch his limbs, there golden Sleep doth reign.

Care. — *Spenser.*

RUDE was his garment, and to rags all rent,
Ne better had he, ne for better car'd;
With blistred hands emongst the cinders brent,
And fingers filthie, with long nayles unpar'd,
Right fit to rend the food on which he far'd:
His name was Care; a blacksmith by his trade,
That neither day nor night from working spar'd,
But to small purpose yron wedges made:
Those be unquiet thoughts that careful Minds invade.

Care. — *Shakspeare.*

O POLISH'D Perturbation! golden Care!
That keep'st the ports of Slumber open wide
To many a watchful night!—he sleeps with 't now,
Yet not so sound, and half so deeply sweet,
As he, whose brow, with homely biggin bound,
Snores out the watch of Night.

Care. — *Burns.*

BUT human bodies are sic fools,
For a' their colleges and schools,
That when nae real ills perplex them,
They mak enow themsels to vex them.

Care. — *Shakspeare.*

CARE is no cure, but rather corrosive,
For things that are not to be remedied.

Kingly Cares. — *Shakspeare.*

GIVES not the hawthorn bush a sweeter shade
To shepherds, looking on their silly sheep,
Than doth a rich embroider'd canopy
To Kings, that fear their subjects' treachery?
O, yes, it doth; a thousand-fold it doth.
The shepherd's homely curds,
His cold thin drink out of his leather bottle,
His wonted sleep under a fresh tree's shade,
All which secure and sweetly he enjoys,
Is far beyond a Prince's delicates,
His viands sparkling in a golden cup,
His body couched in a curious bed,
When Care, Mistrust, and Treason, wait on him.

Cause of all Causes. — *Shakspeare.*

HE that of greatest works is Finisher
Oft does them by the weakest minister:
So Holy Writ in babes hath judgment shown,
When judges have been babes. Great floods have flown
From simple sources; and great seas have dried,
When miracles have by the greatest been denied.
Oft Expectation fails, and most oft there
Where most it promises; and oft it hits,
Where Hope is coldest, and Despair most sits.
It is not so with Him that all things knows,
As 'tis with us that square our guess by shows:
But most it is presumptuous in us, when
The help of Heaven we count the act of Men.

Cause and Effect. — *Shakspeare.*

MAD let us grant him then; and now remains,
That we find out the Cause of this Effect;
Or, rather say, the Cause of this Defect;
For this Effect, defective, comes by Cause.

Caution. — *Publius Syrius.*

IT is a good thing to learn Caution by the misfortunes of others.

Caution. — *Shakspeare.*

THINGS, done well,
And with a Care, exempt themselves from fear:
Things, done without Example, in their issue
Are to be fear'd.

Celestial Objects. — *Cicero.*

I PERCEIVE you contemplate the seat and habitation of men; which, if it appears as little to you as it really is, fix you eyes perpetually upon heavenly Objects, and despise earthly.

Censure. — *Pope.*

WE ought in humanity no more to despise a man for the misfortunes of the mind than for those of the body, when they are such as he cannot help.

Censure. — *La Rochefoucauld.*

FEW persons have sufficient wisdom to prefer Censure which is useful to them, to Praise which deceives them.

Censure. — *Young.*

HORACE appears in good humour while he censures, and therefore his Censure has the more weight, as supposed to proceed from Judgment, not from Passion.

Ceremony. — *Shakspeare.*

CEREMONY
Was devised at first to set a gloss
On faint deeds, hollow welcomes,
But where there is true friendship, there needs none.

Ceremony. — *Hare.*

FORMS and Regularity of Proceeding, if they are not justice, partake much of the nature of justice, which, in its highest sense, is the spirit of distributive Order.

Ceremony. — *Selden.*

CEREMONY keeps up things; 'tis like a penny glass to a rich spirit, or some excellent water; without it the water were spilt, and the spirit lost.

Ceremony. — *Steele.*

AS Ceremony is the invention of wise men to keep fools at a distance, so Good-breeding is an expedient to make fools and wise men equals.

Ceremony. — *Shakspeare.*

O HARD condition, and twin-born with greatness,
Subject to breath of ev'ry fool, whose sense
No more can feel but his own wringing.
What infinite heart-ease must Kings neglect,

That private Men enjoy? and what have Kings,
That Privates have not too, save Ceremony?
Save gen'ral Ceremony?——
And what art thou, thou idol Ceremony?
What kind of God art thou? that suffer'st more
Of mortal griefs, than do thy worshippers.
What are thy rents? what are thy comings-in?
O Ceremony, show me but thy worth:
What is thy toll, O Adoration?
Art thou aught else but Place, Degree and Form,
Creating awe and fear in other men?
Wherein thou art less happy, being fear'd,
Than they in fearing.
What drink'st thou oft, instead of Homage sweet,
But poison'd Flatt'ry? O be sick, great Greatness,
And bid thy Ceremony give thee cure.
Think'st thou, the fiery fever will go out
With Titles blown from Adulation?
Will it give place to flexure and low bending?
Can'st thou, when thou command'st the beggar's knee,
Command the health of it? no, thou proud dream,
That playst so subtly with a King's repose.

Ceremony.—*Chesterfield.*

ALL Ceremonies are in themselves very silly things: but yet a man of the world should know them. They are the outworks of manners and decency, which would be too often broken in upon, if it were not for that defence, which keeps the enemy at a proper distance. It is for that reason that I always treat fools and coxcombs with great Ceremony; true Good-breeding not being a sufficient barrier against them.

Chance.—*La Rochefoucauld.*

THE generality of men have, like plants, latent properties, which Chance brings to light.

Chance.—*Terence.*

HOW often events, by Chance, and unexpectedly come to pass, which you had not dared even to hope for!

Change.—*Johnson.*

SUCH are the vicissitudes of the World, through all its parts, that day and night, labour and rest, hurry and retirement, endear each other: such are the Changes that keep the mind in action: we desire, we pursue, we obtain, we are satiated; we desire something else, and begin a new pursuit.

Chaos. — *Shakspeare.*

LET Order die,
And let this World no longer be a stage,
To feed contention in a lingering act;
But let one spirit of the first-born Cain
Reign in all bosoms, that each heart being set
On bloody courses, the rude scene may end,
And Darkness be the burier of the Dead!

Character. — *Shakspeare.*

HIS real Habitude gave life and grace
To appertainings and to ornament,
Accomplish'd in himself, not in his case:
All aids themselves made fairer by their place;
Came for additions, yet their purpos'd trim
Piec'd not his grace, but were all grac'd by him.
So on the tip of his subduing tongue
All kinds of arguments and question deep,
All replication prompt, and reason strong,
For his advantage still did wake and sleep:
To make the weeper laugh, the laugher weep,
He had the dialect and different skill,
Catching all passions in his craft of will;
That he did in the general bosom reign
Of young, of old; and sexes both enchanted.

Character. — *Sir William Temple.*

THE best rules to form a young Man are, to talk little, to hear much, to reflect alone upon what has passed in company, to distrust one's own opinions, and value others that deserve it.

Character. — *Merkel.*

ORDINARY people regard a man of a certain force and inflexibility of Character as they do a lion. They look at him with a sort of wonder—perhaps they admire him; but they will on no account house with him. The lap-dog, who wags his tail and licks the hand, and cringes at the nod of every stranger, is a much more acceptable companion to them.

Character. — *Chesterfield.*

WHEN upon a trial a man calls witnesses to his Character, and those witnesses only say, that they never heard, nor do not know any thing ill of him, it intimates at best a neutral and insignificant Character.

Character. — *Lavater.*

ACTIONS, looks, words, steps, form the alphabet by which you may spell Characters.

Character. — *Fitzosborne.*

WERE I to make trial of any person's qualifications for an union of so much delicacy, there is no part of his conduct I would sooner single out, than to observe him in his resentments. And this not upon the maxim frequently advanced, "that the best friends make the bitterest enemies;" but on the contrary, because I am persuaded that he who is capable of being a bitter enemy, can never possess the necessary virtues that constitute a true friend.

Character. — *Shakspeare.*

He sits 'mongst men, like a descended God:
He hath a kind of honour sets him off,
More than a mortal seeming.

Character. — *Shakspeare.*

THERE are a sort of men, whose visages
Do cream and mantle like a standing pond;
And do a wilful stillness entertain,
With purpose to be dress'd in an opinion
Of wisdom, gravity, profound conceit;
As who should say, "I am Sir Oracle,
And, when I ope my lips, let no dog bark!"
I do know of these,
That therefore only are reputed wise,
For saying nothing; who, I am very sure,
If they should speak, would almost damn those ears,
Which, hearing them, would call their brothers fools.

Character. — *Shakspeare.*

Thou art full of love and honesty,
And weigh'st thy words before thou giv'st them breath,—
Therefore these stops of thine fright me the more:
For such things, in a false, disloyal knave,
Are tricks of custom; but, in a man that's just,
They are close denotements working from the heart,
That passion cannot rule.

Character. — *Shakspeare.*

I WILL no more trust him when he leers, than I will a serpent when he hisses: he will spend his mouth, and promise, like Brabler the hound: but when he performs, astronomers foretell it: it is prodigious, there will come some change; the sun borrows of the moon, when he keeps his word.

Character. — *Bruyere.*

THERE are peculiar ways in men, which discover what they are through the most subtle feints and closest disguises.

Character. — *Shakspeare.*

NATURE hath fram'd strange fellows in her time:
Some, that will evermore peep through their eyes,
And laugh, like parrots, at a bag-piper;
And other of such vinegar aspéct,
That they'll not show their teeth in way of smile,
Though Nestor swear the jest be laughable.

Character. — *Shakspeare.*

O, HE'S as tedious
As is a tir'd horse, a railing wife;
Worse than a smoky house:—I had rather live
With cheese and garlic, in a windmill, far,
Than feed on cates, and have him talk to me,
In any summer-house in Christendom.

Character. — *Lavater.*

YOU may depend upon it that he is a good man whose intimate friends are all good.

Character. — *Shakspeare.*

REPUTATION, reputation, reputation! O, I have lost my reputation! I have lost the immortal part of myself; and what remains is bestial.

Character. — *Shakspeare.*

REPUTATION;—oft got without merit, and lost without deserving.

Character. — *Socrates.*

THE way to gain a good Reputation is to endeavour to be what you desire to appear.

Character. — *Novalis.*

CHARACTER is a perfectly educated will.

Character. — *Shakspeare.*

THIS is he
That kiss'd away his hand in courtesy;
This is the ape of form, monsieur the nice,
That, when he plays at tables, chides the dice
In honourable terms; nay, he can sing
A mean most meanly; and in ushering,
Mend him who can; the ladies call him, sweet;
The stairs as he treads on them kiss his feet.

Character. — *Shakspeare.*

HE will steal himself into a man's favor, and, for a week, escape a great deal of discoveries; but when you find him out, you have him ever after.

Character. — *Colton.*

THE two most precious things this side the grave are our Reputation and our Life. But it is to be lamented that the most contemptible whisper may deprive us of the one, and the weakest weapon of the other. A wise man, therefore, will be more anxious to deserve a fair name than to possess it, and this will teach him so to live, as not to be afraid to die.

Character. — *Shakspeare.*

THIS fellow's wise enough to play the fool;
And, to do that well, craves a kind of wit:
He must observe their mood on whom he jests,
The quality of persons and the time;
And, like the haggard, check at every feather
That comes before his eye. This is a practice,
As full of labour as a wise man's art;
For folly, that he wisely shows, is fit;
But wise men, folly fallen, quite taint their wit.

Character. — *Fuller.*

GET and preserve a good name, if it were but for the public service: for one of a deserved Reputation hath oftentimes an opportunity to do that good, which another cannot that wants it. And he may practise it with more security and success.

Character. — *Shakspeare.*

THOU wilt quarrel with a man that hath a hair more, or a hair less, in his beard than thou hast. Thou wilt quarrel with a man for cracking nuts, having no other reason but because thou hast hazel eyes; what eye, but such an eye, would spy out such a quarrel? Thy head is as full of quarrels, as an egg is full of meat.

Character. — *Lavater.*

AVOID connecting yourself with Characters whose good and bad sides are unmixed, and have not fermented together; they resemble vials of vinegar and oil; or palettes set with colours; they are either excellent at home and intolerable abroad, or insufferable within doors and excellent in public: they are unfit for friendship merely because their stamina, their ingredients of character are too single, too much apart; let them be finely ground up with each other, and they will be incomparable.

Character. — *Colton.*

DUKE Chartres used to boast that no man could have less real value for Character than himself, yet he would gladly give twenty thousand pounds for a good one, because he could immediately make double that sum by means of it.

Character. — *Addison.*

PEOPLE of gloomy, uncheerful imaginations, or of envious, malignant tempers, whatever kind of life they are engaged in, will discover their natural tincture of mind in all their thoughts, words, and actions. As the finest wines have often the taste of the soil, so even the most religious thoughts often draw something that is particular from the constitution of the mind in which they arise. When folly or superstition strikes in with this natural depravity of temper, it is not in the power even of religion itself to preserve the Character of the person who is possessed with it from appearing highly absurd and ridiculous.

Character. — *Shakspeare.*

THIS man hath robbed many beasts of their particular additions; he is as valiant as a lion, churlish as a bear, slow as the elephant: a man, into whom nature hath so crowded humours, that his valour is crushed into folly, his folly sauced with discretion: there is no man hath a virtue, that he hath not a glimpse of; nor any man an attaint, but he carries some stain of it: he is melancholy without cause, and merry against the hair: he hath the joints of every thing; but every thing so out of joint, that he is a gouty Briareus, many hands and no use; or purblind Argus, all eyes and no sight.

Character. — *Shakspeare.*

SPARE in diet;
Free from gross passion, or of mirth, or anger;
Constant in spirit, not swerving with the blood;
Garnish'd and deck'd with modest compliment;
Not working with the eye, without the ear,
And, but in purged judgment, trusting neither.

Character. — *Anon.*

MANY persons carry about their Characters in their hands; not a few under their feet.

Character. — *Shakspeare.*

BEING not propp'd by ancestry, (whose grace
Chalks successors their way,) neither allied
To eminent assistants, but spider-like,
Out of his self-drawing web, he gives us note,
The force of his own merit makes his way;
A gift that Heaven gives for him.

Character. — *From the French.*

A MAN'S Character is like his Shadow, which sometimes follows, and sometimes precedes him, and which is occasionally longer, occasionally shorter than he is.

Character. — *Hare.*

THERE is a glare about worldly success, which is very apt to dazzle men's eyes. When we see a man rising in the world; thriving in business; successful in his speculations; if he be a man out of our own line, who does not come into competition with us, so as to make us jealous of him, we are too apt to form a foolishly high opinion of his merits. We are apt to say within ourselves, "What a wonderful man this must be, to rise so rapidly?" forgetting that dust and straw, and feathers, things with neither weight nor value in them, rise the soonest and the easiest. In like manner, it is not the truly great and good man, generally speaking, who rises the most rapidly into wealth and notice. A man may be sharp, active, quick, dexterous, cunning; he may be ever on the watch for opportunities to push his fortunes; a man of this kind can hardly fail of getting on in the world: yet with all this, he may not have a grain of real Greatness about him. He may be all I have described, and yet have no Greatness of Mind, no Greatness of Soul. He may be utterly without Sympathy and fellow-feeling for others; he may be utterly devoid of all true Wisdom; he may be without Piety and without Charity; without Love, that is, either for God or Man.

Character. — *Shakspeare.*

THERE can be no kernel in this light nut; the Soul of this Man is his Clothes.

Character. — *Shakspeare.*

He has been bred i' the wars
Since he could draw a sword, and is ill-school'd
In boulted language; meal and bran together
He throws without distinction.

Character. — *Shakspeare.*

TO be generous, guiltless, and of free disposition, is to take those things for bird-bolts, that you deem cannon-bullets. There is no slander in an allowed Fool, though he do nothing but rail: nor no railing in a known Discreet Man, though he do nothing but reprove.

Character. — *Shakspeare.*

He that trusts you
Where he should find you Lions, finds you Hares:
Where Foxes, Geese. You are no surer, no,
Than is the Coal of Fire upon the Ice,
Or Hailstone in the Sun.

Character. — *Shakspeare.*

Best Men are moulded out of Faults.

Character. — *Bulwer Lytton.*

NEVER get a Reputation for a small perfection, if you are trying for fame in a loftier area. The world can only judge by generals, and it sees that those who pay considerable attention to minutiæ, seldom have their Minds occupied with great things. There are, it is true, exceptions; but to exceptions the world does not attend.

Character. — *Colton.*

THE most consistent men are not more unlike to others than they are at times to themselves; therefore, it is ridiculous to see Character-mongers drawing a full-length Likeness of some great man, and perplexing themselves and their readers by making every feature of his Conduct strictly Conform to those lines and lineaments which they have laid down; they generally find or make for him some Ruling Passion the rudder of his course; but with all this pother about Ruling Passions, the fact is, that all men and all women have but one *apparent Good.* Those, indeed, are the strongest Minds, and are capable of the greatest actions, who possess a telescopic power of intellectual vision, enabling them to ascertain the real magnitude and importance of distant goods, and to despise those which are indebted for all their grandeur solely to their contiguity.

Character. — *Shakspeare.*

THE purest treasure mortal times afford,
Is—spotless Reputation; that away,
Men are but gilded loam, or painted clay.
A jewel in a ten-times-barr'd-up chest
Is—a bold Spirit in a loyal Breast.

Character. — *Franklin.*

THE most trifling actions that affect a man's Credit are to be regarded. The sound of your hammer at five in the morning, or nine at night, heard by a Creditor, makes him easy six months longer; but if he sees you at a Billiard table, or hears your voice at a Tavern, when you should be at work, he sends for his money the next day.

Character. — *La Rochefoucauld.*

WHATEVER Disgrace we have merited, it is almost always in our power to re-establish our Reputation.

Character. — *Shakspeare.*

LET me have Men about me that are fat;
Sleek-headed Men, and such as sleep o' nights:
Yond' Cassius has a lean and hungry look;
He thinks too much: such Men are dangerous.

Character. — *S. T. Coleridge.*

HOW wonderfully beautiful is the delineation of the Characters of the three Patriarchs in Genesis! To be sure, if ever man could, without impropriety, be called, or supposed to be, "the friend of God," Abraham was that man. We are not surprised that Abimelech and Ephron seem to reverence him so profoundly. He was peaceful, because of his conscious relation to God.

Character. — *Shakspeare.*

LOOK, as I blow this feather from my face,
And as the air blows it to me again,
Obeying with my wind when I do blow,
And yielding to another when it blows,
Commanded always by the greater gust;
Such is the Lightness of you Common Men.

Character. — *Shakspeare.*

IN war was never Lion raged so fierce,
In peace was never gentle Lamb more mild.

Character. — *Shakspeare.*

GOOD Name, in man, and woman,
Is the immediate jewel of their souls.
Who steals my purse, steals trash; 'tis something, nothing;
'Twas mine, 'tis his, and has been slave to thousands:
But he, that filches from me my Good Name,
Robs me of that, which not enriches him,
And makes me poor indeed.

Character. — *Pope.*

SELF-LOVE thus push'd to social, to divine,
Gives thee to make thy neighbour's blessing thine.
Is this too little for the boundless heart?
Extend it, let thy enemies have part.
Grasp the whole world of Reason, Life, and Sense,
In one close system of benevolence:
Happier as kinder, in whate'er degree,
And height of Bliss but height of Charity.

Character. — *Shakspeare.*

A HUNGRY lean-fac'd Villain,
A mere Anatomy, a Mountebank,
A thread-bare Juggler, and a Fortune-teller;
A needy, hollow-ey'd, sharp-looking Wretch,
A living dead Man; this pernicious Slave,
Forsooth, took on him as a Conjurer;
And gazing in mine eyes, feeling my pulse,
And with no face, as 'twere, out-facing me.

Character. — *Shakspeare.*

In the Reproof of Chance
Lies the true Proof of Men. The sea being smooth,
How many shallow bauble boats dare sail
Upon her patient breast, making their way
With those of nobler bulk?
But let the ruffian Boreas once enrage
The gentle Thetis, and anon, behold
The strong-ribb'd bark through liquid mountains cut,
Bounding between the two moist elements,
Like Perseus' horse: Where's then the saucy boat,
Whose weak untimber'd sides but even now
Co-rivall'd greatness? Either to harbour fled,
Or made a toast for Neptune. Even so
Doth Valour's Show, and Valour's Worth, divide,
In storms of Fortune: For, in her ray and brightness,
The herd hath more annoyance by the brize,
Than by the tiger; but when the splitting wind
Makes flexible the knees of knotted oaks,
And flies fled under shade, why, then the Thing of Courage,
As roused with rage, with rage doth sympathize,
And with an accent tuned in self-same key,
Returns to chiding Fortune.

Character. — *Shakspeare.*

I know him a notorious Liar,
Think him a great way Fool, solely a Coward;
Yet these fix'd evils sit so fit in him,
That they take place, when Virtue's steely bones
Look bleak in the cold wind: withal, full oft we see
Cold Wisdom waiting on superfluous Folly.

Character. — *Shakspeare.*

He reads much:
He is a great Observer, and he looks
Quite through the deeds of men: he loves no plays;
He hears no music:
Seldom he smiles; and smiles in such a sort,
As if he mock'd himself, and scorn'd his spirit
That could be mov'd to smile at any thing.

Character. — *Shakspeare.*

HE'S truly valiant, that can wisely suffer
The worst that man can breathe; and make his wrongs
His outsides; to wear them like his raiment, carelessly;
And ne'er prefer his Injuries to his Heart,
To bring it into danger.

Charity.—*Pope.*

IN Faith and Hope the world will disagree,
But all mankind's concerned in Charity:
All must be false that thwart this one great end;
And all of God, that bless mankind, or mend.

Charity.—*Spenser.*

GOOD is no good but if it be spend:
God giveth good for none other end.

Charity.—*Byron.*

THE drying up a single tear has more
Of honest fame, than shedding seas of gore.

Charity.—*Pope.*

IS there a variance? enter but his door,
Balk'd are the courts, and contest is no more.
Despairing quacks with curses left the place,
And vile attorneys, now a useless race.

Charity.—*Colton.*

POSTHUMOUS Charities are the very essence of Selfishness, when bequeathed by those who, when alive, would part with nothing.

Charity.—*Seneca.*

A PHYSICIAN is not angry at the intemperance of a mad patient, nor does he take it ill to be railed at by a man in a fever. Just so should a wise man treat all mankind, as a physician does his patient, and look upon them only as sick and extravagant.

Charity.—*Shakspeare.*

GENTLY to hear, kindly to judge.

Public Charities.—*Colton.*

PUBLIC Charities and benevolent Associations for the gratuitous Relief of every species of Distress, are peculiar to Christianity; no other system of civil or religious policy has *originated* them; they form its highest praise and characteristic feature.

The Charlatan.—*Shakspeare.*

HE now, forsooth, takes on him to reform
Some certain edicts, and some strait decrees,
That lie too heavy on the Commonwealth:
Cries out upon abuses, seems to weep
Over his country's wrongs; and, by this Face,
This seeming Brow of Justice, did he win
The hearts of all that he did angle for.

Chastity. — *Shakspeare.*

The Heavens hold firm
The walls of thy dear Honour; keep unshak'd
That Temple, thy fair Mind.

Chastity. — *Saville.*

A CLOSE Behaviour is the fittest to receive Virtue for its constant guest, because there, and there only, it can be secure. Proper Reserves are the outworks, and must never be deserted by those who intend to keep the place; they keep off the possibilities not only of being taken, but of being attempted; and if a woman seeth danger, though at never so remote a distance, she is for that time to shorten her line of liberty. She, who will allow herself to go to the utmost extent of every thing that is lawful, is so very near going further, that those who lie at watch will begin to count upon her.

Cheerfulness. — *Pope.*

WHAT then remains, but well our power to use,
And keep Good Humour still, whate'er we lose?
And trust me, dear Good Humour can prevail,
When airs, and flights, and screams, and scolding fail;
Beauties in vain their pretty eyes may roll;
Charms strike the sight, but merit wins the soul.

Cheerfulness. — *Collins.*

WHEN Cheerfulness, a nymph of healthiest hue,
Her bow across her shoulders flung,
Her buskins gemm'd with morning dew,
Blew an inspiring air, that dale and thicket rung.

Cheerfulness. — *Montaigne.*

THE most manifest sign of Wisdom is continued Cheerfulness.

Cheerfulness. — *Lord Bolingbroke.*

I HAVE observed, that in comedies the best actor plays the droll, while some scrub rogue is made the fine gentleman or hero. Thus it is in the farce of Life,—wise men spend their time in Mirth, 'tis only fools who are serious.

Cheerfulness. — *Steele.*

CHEERFULNESS is always to be supported if a man is out of pain, but Mirth to a prudent man should always be accidental. It should naturally arise out of the occasion, and the occasion seldom be laid for it; for those tempers who want Mirth to be pleased, are like the constitutions which flag without the use of brandy. Therefore, I say, let your precept be, "be easy." That mind is dissolute and ungoverned, which must be hurried out of itself by loud laughter or sensual pleasure, or else be wholly in active.

Cheerfulness. — *Colton.*

CHEERFULNESS ought to be the *viaticum vitæ* of their life to the old; age without Cheerfulness, is a Lapland winter without a sun; and this spirit of Cheerfulness should be encouraged in our youth, if we would wish to have the benefit of it in our old age; time will make a generous wine more mellow; but it will turn that which is early on the fret, to vinegar.

Cheerfulness. — *Seneca.*

TRUE Joy is a serene and sober motion: and they are miserably out, that take Laughing for rejoicing: the seat of it is within, and there is no Cheerfulness like the resolutions of a brave mind.

Cheerfulness. — *Horace.*

THE Mind that is cheerful in its present state, will be averse to all solicitude as to the future, and will meet the bitter occurrences of Life with a placid Smile.

Cheerfulness. — *Pliny.*

AS in our lives so also in our studies, it is most becoming and most wise, so to temper Gravity with Cheerfulness, that the former may not imbue our minds with Melancholy, nor the latter degenerate into Licentiousness.

Cheerfulness. — *Massinger.*

CHEERFUL looks make every dish a feast,
And 'tis that crowns a welcome.

Cheerfulness. — *Spenser.*

AND her against sweet Cheerfulnesse was placed,
Whose eyes like twinkling stars in evening cleare,
Were deckt with smyles, and all Sad Humors chased,
And darted forth Delights, the which her goodly grac'd.

Chiding. — *Shakspeare.*

THOSE, that do teach young babes,
Do it with gentle means, and easy tasks;
He might have Chid me so: for, in good faith,
I am a child to Chiding.

The Child. — *Byron.*

BUT thou wilt burst this transient sleep,
And thou wilt wake, my Babe, to weep;
The tenant of a frail abode,
Thy tears must flow, as mine have flow'd:
Beguil'd by follies every day,
Sorrow must wash the faults away,
And thou may'st wake perchance to prove
The pang of unrequited love.

The Child. — *Byron.*

SWEET be thy cradled slumbers! O'er the sea,
And from the mountains where I now respire,
Fain would I waft such blessing upon thee,
As, with a sigh, I deem thou might'st have been to me!

The Child. — *Campbell.*

LO! at the couch where Infant Beauty sleeps,
Her silent watch the mournful Mother keeps:
She, while the lovely Babe unconscious lies,
Smiles on her slumbering Child with pensive eyes,
And weaves a song of melancholy joy—
"Sleep, image of thy father, sleep, my boy:
No lingering hour of sorrow shall be thine;
No sigh that rends thy Father's heart and mine;
Bright as his manly Sire the Son shall be
In form and soul; but, ah! more blessed than he!
Thy fame, thy worth, thy filial love, at last,
Shall soothe this aching heart for all the past—
With many a smile my solitude repay,
And chase the world's ungenerous scorn away."

The Child. — *Rogers.*

THE hour arrives, the moment wish'd and fear'd;
The Child is born, by many a pang endear'd.
And now the Mother's ear has caught his cry;
Oh grant the Cherub to her asking eye!
He comes . . . she clasps him. To her bosom press'd,
He drinks the balm of life, and drops to rest.

The Child. — *Rogers.*

THEN, gathering round his bed, they climb to share
His kisses, and with gentle violence there,
Break in upon a dream not half so fair.

The Child. — *Byron.*

TO aid thy Mind's Developments,—to watch
Thy Dawn of little Joys,—to sit and see
Almost thy very Growth,—to view thee catch
Knowledge of objects,—wonders yet to thee!
To hold thee lightly on a gentle knee,
And print on thy soft cheek a Parent's kiss;—
This, it should seem, was not reserved for me!
Yet this was in my nature:—as it is,
I know not what is there, yet something like to this.

Childhood. — *Bishop Erle.*

A CHILD is man in a small letter, yet the best copy of Adam, before he tasted of Eve or the apple; and he is happy whose small practice in the world can only write his character. His soul is yet a white paper unscribbled with observations of the world, wherewith, at length, it becomes a blurred note-book. He is purely happy, because he knows no evil, nor hath made means by sin to be acquainted with misery. He arrives not at the mischief of being wise, nor endures evils to come, by foreseeing them. He kisses and loves all, and, when the smart of the rod is past, smiles on his beater. The elder he grows, he is a stair lower from God. He is the Christian's example, and the old man's relapse; the one imitates his pureness, and the other falls into his simplicity. Could he put off his body with his little coat, he had got eternity without a burden, and exchanged but one heaven for another.

Children. — *Byron.*

YET a fine Family is a fine thing
(Provided they don't come in after dinner;)
'Tis beautiful to see a Matron bring
Her Children up, (if nursing them don't thin her.)

Children. — *Byron.*

HE smiles, and sleeps!—sleep on
And smile, thou little, young Inheritor
Of a world scarce less young: sleep on, and smile!
Thine are the hours and days when both are cheering
And innocent!

Children. — *Thomson.*

LOOK here and weep with tenderness and transport
What is all tasteless luxury to this?
To these best joys, which holy Love bestows?
Oh Nature, parent Nature, thou alone
Art the true judge of what can make us happy.

Children. — *Greville.*

I HARDLY know so melancholy a reflection, as that Parents are necessarily the sole directors of the management of Children; whether they have, or have not, judgment, penetration, or taste, to perform the task.

Children. — *Cicero.*

WHAT gift has Providence bestowed on Man, that is so dear to him as his Children?

Children. — *Byron.*

LOOK! how he laughs and stretches out his arms,
And opens wide his blue eyes upon thine,
To hail his Father: while his little form
Flutters as wing'd with joy. Talk not of pain!
The childless cherubs well might envy thee
The pleasures of a Parent! Bless him!
As yet he hath no words to thank thee, but
His heart will, and thine own too.

Children. — *Oehlenschläger.*

THE plays of natural lively Children are the infancy of art. Children live in the world of imagination and feeling. They invest the most insignificant object with any form they please, and see in it whatever they wish to see.

Children. — *Thomson.*

MEANTIME a smiling Offspring rises round,
And mingles both their graces. By degrees,
The Human Blossom blows; and every day,
Soft as it rolls along, shows some new charm.

Choice of Life. — *Cicero.*

THE number is small of those persons, who, either by extraordinary pre-eminence of genius, or by superior erudition and knowledge, or who, endowed with either of these, have enjoyed the privilege of deliberately deciding what Mode of Life they would the most wish to embrace.

The Choleric. — *Fuller.*

THOSE Passionate Persons who carry their heart in their mouth are rather to be pitied than feared; their threatenings serving no other purpose than to forearm him that is threatened.

Christianity. — *Anon.*

THERE is only one way in which Philosophy can truly become popular, that which Socrates tried, and which centuries after was perfected in the Gospel,—that which tells men of their Divine Origin and Destiny, of their Heavenly Duties and Calling. This comes home to men's hearts and bosoms, and, instead of puffing them up, humbles them. But to be efficient, this should flow down straight from a higher sphere. Even in its Socratic form, it was supported by those higher principles, which we find set forth with such power and beauty by Plato. In Christian Philosophy, on the other hand, the ladder has come down from heaven, and the angels are continually descending and ascending along it.

Christianity. — *Channing.*

SINCE its introduction, human nature has made great progress, and society experienced great changes; and in this advanced condition of the world, Christianity, instead of losing its application and importance, is found to be more and more congenial and adapted to man's nature and wants. Men have outgrown the other institutions of that period when Christianity appeared, its philosophy, its modes of warfare, its policy, its public and private economy; but Christianity has never shrunk as intellect has opened, but has always kept in advance of men's faculties, and unfolded nobler views in proportion as they have ascended. The highest powers and affections which our nature has developed, find more than adequate objects in this religion. Christianity is indeed peculiarly fitted to the more improved stages of society, to the more delicate sensibilities of refined minds, and especially to that dissatisfaction with the present state, which always grows with the growth of our moral powers and affections.

Church. — *Burns.*

HERE some are thinkin' on their sins,
  An' some upo' their claes;
Ane curses feet that fyl'd his shins,
  Anither sighs an' prays:
On this hand sits a chosen swatch,
  Wi' screw'd-up, grace-proud faces;
On that, a set o' chaps, at watch,
  Thrang winkin' on the lasses.

The Citizen. — *Cowper.*

SUBURBAN villas, highway-side retreats,
  That dread th' encroachment of our growing streets,
Tight boxes, neatly sash'd, and in a blaze
With all a July sun's collected rays,
Delight the citizen, who gasping there
Breathes clouds of dust, and calls it country air.

The Citizen. — *Churchill.*

OR at some Banker's desk, like many more,
  Content to tell that two and two make four,
His name had stood in City annals fair,
And prudent dulness mark'd him for a Mayor.

Civility. — *Chesterfield.*

THE insolent Civility of a proud man is, if possible, more shocking than his Rudeness could be; because he shows you, by his Manner, that he thinks it mere Condescension in him; and that his goodness alone bestows upon you what you have no pretence to claim.

Civility. — *Tillotson.*

A GOOD Word is an easy Obligation; but not to speak ill, requires only our silence, which costs us nothing.

Civilization. — *Burke.*

WE are but too apt to consider things in the state in which we find them, without sufficiently adverting to the causes by which they have been produced, and possibly may be upheld. Nothing is more certain than that our Manners, our Civilization, and all the good things which are connected with Civilization, have, in this European world of ours, depended for ages upon two principles; and were indeed the result of both combined; I mean the spirit of a Gentleman and the spirit of Religion. The Nobility and the Clergy, the one by profession, the other by patronage, kept learning in existence even in the midst of arms and confusion, and whilst governments were rather in their causes than formed. Learning paid back what it received to Nobility and Priesthood, and paid it with usury, by enlarging their ideas and by furnishing their minds.

Civilization. — *Anon.*

IN the Bible the Body is said to be more than Raiment. But many people still read the Bible Hebrew-wise, backward: and thus the general conviction now is that Raiment is more than the Body. There is so much to gaze and stare at in the Dress, one's eyes are quite dazzled and weary, and can hardly pierce through to that which is clothed upon. So too is it with the mind and heart, scarcely less than with the body.

Civilization. — *Hare.*

THE ultimate tendency of Civilization, is toward Barbarism.

Civilization. — *Colton.*

ALL nations that have reached the highest point of Civilization, may from that hour assume for their motto, *videri quam esse.* And whenever and wherever we see Ostentation substituted for Happiness, Profession for Friendship, Formality for Religion, Pedantry for Learning, Buffoonry for Wit, Artifice for Nature, and Hypocrisy for every thing; these are the signs of the times which he that runs may read, and which will enable the Philosopher to date the commencement of National Decay, from the consummation of National Refinement.

Civilization. — *Hare.*

CHRISTIANITY has carried Civilization along with it, whithersoever it has gone: and, as if to show that the latter does not depend on physical causes, some of the countries the most civilized in the days of Augustus are now in a state of hopeless Barbarism.

Civilization. — *Colton.*

A SEMI-CIVILIZED state of Society, equally removed from the extremes of Barbarity and of Refinement, seems to be that particular meridian under which all the reciprocities and gratuities of hospitality do most really flourish and abound. For it so happens that the ease, the luxury, and the abundance of the *highest* state of Civilization, are as productive of *selfishness*, as the difficulties, the privations, and the sterilities of the *lowest.*

Classical Studies. — *Story.*

IT is no exaggeration to declare that he who proposes to abolish classical studies proposes to render, in a great measure, inert and unedifying the mass of English literature for three centuries; to rob us of the glory of the past, and much of the instruction of future ages; to blind us to excellences which few may hope to equal and none to surpass; to annihilate associations which are interwoven withour best sentiments, and give to distant times and countries a presence and reality as if they were in fact his own.

Cleanliness. — *Thomson.*

EVEN from the Body's Purity, the Mind
Receives a secret sympathetic aid.

Climate. — *Sir W. Temple.*

OUR Country must be confessed to be, what a great foreign physician called it, the region of spleen; which may arise a good deal from the great uncertainty and many sudden changes of our weather in all seasons of the year: and how much these affect the heads and hearts, especially of the finest tempers, is hard to be believed by men whose thoughts are not turned to such speculations.

Climate. — *Justus Möser.*

THE institutions of a Country depend in great measure on the Nature of its Soil and Situation. Many of the wants of man are awakened or supplied by these circumstances. To these wants, manners, laws, and religion must shape and accommodate themselves. The division of Land, and the rights attached to it, alter with the Soil; the laws relating to its Produce, with its Fertility. The manners of its inhabitants are in various ways modified by its Position. The religion of a miner is not the same as the faith of a shepherd, nor is the character of the ploughman so warlike as that of the hunter. The observant legislator follows the direction of all these various circumstances. The knowledge of the Natural Advantages or Defects of a Country thus form an essential part of political science and history.

Club Gossip.—*Shakspeare.*

THEY'LL sit by the fire, and presume to know
What's done i' the Capitol: who's like to rise,
Who thrives, and who declines; side factions, and give out
Conjectural marriages; making parties strong,
And feebling such as stand not in their liking.

Commendation.—*Fielding.*

COMMEND a Fool for his Wit, or a Knave for his Honesty, and they will receive you into their bosom.

Commerce.—*Addison.*

A WELL-REGULATED Commerce is not, like law, physic, or divinity, to be over-stocked with hands; but, on the contrary, flourishes by multitudes, and gives employment to all its professors.

Commerce.—*Anon.*

A STATESMAN may do much for Commerce, most by leaving it alone. A river never flows so smoothly, as when it follows its own course, without either aid or check. Let it make its own bed: it will do so better than you can.

The Comet.—*Thomson.*

LO! from the dread immensity of space
Returning, with accelerated course,
The rushing Comet to the sun descends:
And as he sinks below the shading earth,
With awful train projected o'er the heavens,
The guilty nations tremble.

Companionship.—*Greville.*

OUR Companions please us less from the charms we find in their conversation, than from those they find in ours.

Companionship.—*Lessing.*

THE most agreeable of all Companions is a simple, frank man, without any high pretensions to an oppressive greatness: one who loves life, and understands the use of it; obliging, alike at all hours; above all, of a golden temper, and steadfast as an anchor. For such an one we gladly exchange the greatest genius, the most brilliant wit, the profoundest thinker.

Company.—*Chesterfield.*

NO man can possibly improve in any Company, for which he has not respect enough to be under some degree of restraint.

Company.—*Lavater.*

THE freer you feel yourself in the presence of another, the more free is he.

Company. — *Chesterfield.*

TAKE, rather than give, the tone of the Company you are in. If you have parts, you will show them, more or less, upon every subject; and if you have not, you had better talk sillily upon a subject of other people's than your own choosing.

Company. — *Swift.*

NATURE has left every man a capacity of being agreeable, though not of shining in Company; and there are a hundred men sufficiently qualified for both who, by a very few faults, that they might correct in half an hour, are not so much as tolerable.

Comparison. — *Shakspeare.*

WHEN the Moon shone, we did not see the Candle.
So doth the greater glory dim the less;
A Substitute shines brightly as a King,
Until a King be by; and then his state
Empties itself, as doth an inland Brook
Into the Main of Waters.

Comparison. — *Johnson.*

THE Superiority of some men is merely local. They are great, because their associates are little.

Comparisons. — *Addison.*

NOTWITHSTANDING man's essential Perfection is but very little, his comparative Perfection may be very considerable. If he looks upon himself in an abstracted light, he has not much to boast of; but if he considers himself with regard to others, he may find occasion of glorying, if not in his own Virtues, at least in the absence of another's Imperfections. This gives a different turn to the reflections of the Wise man and the Fool. The first endeavours to shine in himself, and the last to outshine others. The first is humbled by the sense of his own infirmities, the last is lifted up by the discovery of those which he observes in other men. The Wise Man considers what he wants, and the Fool what he abounds in. The Wise man is happy when he gains his own approbation, and the Fool when he recommends himself to the applause of those about him.

Complaining. — *Shakspeare.*

I WILL chide no breather in the world, but myself; against whom I know most faults.

Compliments. — *Chesterfield.*

COMPLIMENTS of Congratulation are always kindly taken, and cost one nothing but pen, ink, and paper. I consider them as draughts upon Good Breeding, where the exchange is always greatly in favour of the drawer.

Composition. — *Colton.*

THE great cause of that delight we receive from a fine Composition, whether it be in Prose or in Verse, I conceive to be this: the marvellous and magic power it confers upon the reader; enabling an inferior mind at one glance, and almost without an effort, to seize, to embrace, and to enjoy those remote Combinations of Wit, melting Harmonies of Sound, and vigorous Condensations of Sense, that cost a superior mind so much perseverance, labour, and time.

Conceit. — *Colton.*

NONE are so seldom found alone, and are so soon tired of their own company, as those Coxcombs who are on the best terms with themselves.

Conceit. — *Pope.*

CONCEIT is to nature what paint is to beauty; it is not only needless, but impairs what it would improve.

Conceit. — *Shakspeare.*

CONCEIT in weakest bodies strongest works.

Conciliation.—*Cicero.*

IT is the part of a prudent man to conciliate the minds of others, and to turn them to his own advantage.

Conduct. — *Shakspeare.*

GIVE every man thine ear, but few thy voice:
Take each man's censure, but reserve thy judgment.

Conduct. — *Shakspeare.*

DEFECT of Manners, want of Government,
Pride, Haughtiness, Opinion, and Disdain
The least of which,
Loseth men's hearts; and leaves behind a stain
Upon the beauty of all parts besides,
Beguiling them of commendation.

Conduct. — *Greville.*

IT is not enough that you form, nay, and follow, the most ex cellent Rules for Conducting yourself in the world; you must also know when to deviate from them, and where lies the exception.

Conduct. — *Clarendon.*

IF we do not weigh and consider to what end this life is given us, and thereupon order and dispose it right, pretend what we will to the arithmetic, we do not, we cannot, so much as number our days in they narrowest and most limited signification.

Conduct. — *Shakspeare.*

HAVE more than thou showest,
Speak less than thou knowest,
Lend less than thou owest,
Learn more than thou trowest,
Set less than than thou throwest.

Conduct. — *Epictetus.*

UPON every fresh accident, turn your eyes inward and examine how your are qualified to encounter it. If you see any very beautiful person, you will find Continence to oppose against the temptation. If labour and difficulty come in your way, you will find a remedy in Hardiness and Resolution. If you lie under the obloquy of an ill tongue, Patience and Meekness are the proper fences against it.

Conduct. — *Shakspeare.*

THINGS ill got had ever bad success.

Conduct. — *Seneca.*

I WILL govern my life, and my thoughts, as if the whole world were to see the one, and to read the other; for what does it signify, to make any thing a secret to my neighbour, when to God (who is the searcher of our hearts) all our privacies are open?

Conduct. — *Fuller.*

ALL the while thou livest ill, thou hast the trouble, distraction, inconveniences of life, but not the sweets and true use of it.

Conduct. —*Epictetus.*

AS in walking it is your great care not to run your foot upon a nail, or to tread awry, and strain your leg; so let it be in all the Affairs of Human Life, not to hurt your Mind, or offend your Judgment. And this rule, if observed carefully in all your deportment, will be a mighty security to you in your undertakings.

Conduct. — *Shakspeare.*

OBEY thy parents, keep thy word justly; swear not; commit not with man's sworn spouse; set not thy sweet heart on proud array. . . . Keep thy foot out of brothels, thy pen from lenders' books.

Conduct. — *Joanna Baillie.*

I WOULD, God knows, in a poor woodman's hut
Have spent my peaceful days, and shared my crust
With her who would have cheer'd me, rather far
Than on this throne; but being what I am,
I'll be it nobly.

Conduct. —*Joanna Baillie.*

I TAKE of worthy men whate'er they give:
Their Heart I gladly take, if not their Hand;
If that too is withheld, a courteous Word,
Or the Civility of placid Looks.

Conduct. —*Pope.*

WHEN we are young, we are slavishly employed in procuring something whereby we may live comfortably when we grow old; and when we are old, we perceive it is too late to live as we proposed.

Conduct. — *Cowper.*

Disgust conceal'd
Is oft-times proof of Wisdom, when the fault
Is obstinate, and cure beyond our reach.

Conduct. — *Shakspeare.*

Self-love is not so vile a sin
As self-neglecting.

Conduct. — *Byron.*

To what gulphs
A single deviation from the track
Of Human Duties leads even those who claim
The homage of mankind as their born due,
And find it, till they forfeit it themselves!

Conduct. — *Cowper.*

HE that negotiates between God and Man,
As God's Ambassador, the grand concerns
Of Judgment and of Mercy, should beware
Of lightness in his speech. 'Tis pitiful
To court a grin, when you should woo a soul;
To break a jest, when pity would inspire
Pathetic exhortation; and address
The skittish fancy with facetious tales,
When sent with God's commission to the heart!

Conduct. —*Joanna Baillie.*

TO whom do lions cast their gentle looks?
Not to the beast that would usurp their den.
Whose hand is that the forest bear doth lick?
Not his that spoils her young before her face.
Who 'scapes the lurking serpent's mortal sting?
Not he that sets his foot upon her back.
The smallest worm will turn, being trodden on;
And doves will peck, in safeguard of their brood.

Conduct. — *Milton.*

ONLY add
Deeds to thy Knowledge answerable, add Faith,
Add Virtue, Patience, Temperance, add Love,
By name to come call'd Charity, the soul
Of all the rest: then wilt thou not be loath
To leave this Paradise, but shalt possess
A Paradise within thee, happier far.

Conduct. — *Milton.*

SON of Heav'n and Earth,
Attend: that tnou art happy, owe to God;
That thou continuest such, owe to thyself,
That is, to thy Obedience; therein stand.

Confession. — *Pope.*

A MAN should never be ashamed to own he has been in the wrong, which is but saying in other words, that he is wiser to-day than he was yesterday.

Confidence. — *Shakspeare.*

TRUST not him that hath once broken Faith.

Confidence. — *Colton.*

WHEN young, we trust ourselves too much, and we trust others too little when old. Rashness is the error of Youth, timid caution of Age. Manhood is the isthmus between the two extremes; the ripe and fertile season of Action, when alone we can hope to find the head to contrive, united with the hand to execute.

Confidence. — *Lavater.*

TRUST him little who praises all, him less who censures all, and him least who is indifferent about all.

Conscience. — *Addison.*

A MAN'S first care should be to avoid the reproaches of his own Heart; his next, to escape the censures of the World. If the last interferes with the former, it ought to be entirely neglected; but otherwise there cannot be a greater satisfaction to an honest mind, than to see those approbations which it gives itself seconded by the applauses of the public.

Conscience. — *Colton.*

WE should have all our communications with men, as in the presence of God; and with God, as in the presence of men.

Conscience. — *Colton.*

THE Breast of a good man is a little heaven commencing on earth; where the Deity sits enthroned with unrivalled influence, every subjugated passion, "like the wind and storm, fulfilling his word."

Conscience. — *Fichte.*

THE most reckless Sinner against his own Conscience has always in the background the consolation, that he will go on in this course only this time, or only so long, but that at such a time he will amend. We may be assured that we do not stand clear with our own Consciences, so long as we determine, or project, or even hold it possible, at some future time to alter our course of action.

Conscience. — *South.*

A PALSY may as well shake an oak, or a fever dry up a fountain, as either of them shake, dry up, or impair the delight of Conscience. For it lies within, it centres in the heart, it grows into the very substance of the soul, so that it accompanies a man to his grave; he never outlives it, and that for this cause only, because he cannot outlive himself.

Conscience. — *Horace.*

NOT even for an hour can you bear to be alone, nor can you advantageously apply your leisure time, but you endeavour, a fugitive and wanderer, to escape from yourself, now vainly seeking to banish Remorse by wine, and now by sleep; but the gloomy companion presses on you, and pursues you as you fly.

Conscience. — *Shakspeare.*

UNNATURAL deeds
Do breed unnatural troubles: Infected minds
To their deaf pillows will discharge their secrets.

Conscience. — *South.*

NO man ever offended his own Conscience, but first or last it was revenged upon him for it.

Conscience. — *Shakspeare.*

CONSCIENCE, it makes a man a coward; a man cannot steal, but it accuseth him; a man cannot swear, but it checks him; a man cannot lie with his neighbour's wife, but it detects him.

Conscience. — *Fuller.*

IF thou wouldst be informed what God has written concerning thee in Heaven, look into thine own Bosom, and see what graces he hath there wrought in thee.

Conscience. — *S. T. Coleridge.*

CAN any thing be more dreadful than the Thought, that an innocent child has inherited from you a disease, or a weakness, the penalty in yourself of sin, or want of caution?

Conscience. — *Fuller.*

A GUILTY Conscience is like a whirlpool, drawing in all to itself which would otherwise pass by.

Conscience. — *Shakspeare.*

WHO would bear the whips and scorns of Time,
The Oppressor's wrong, the Proud Man's contumely,
The pangs of despised Love, the Law's delay,
The insolence of Office, and the spurns
That patient Merit of the unworthy takes,
When he himself might his quietus make
With a bare bodkin? who would fardels bear,
To grunt and sweat under a weary life;
But that the dread of something after death,—
The undiscover'd country, from whose bourn
No traveller returns,—puzzles the will;
And makes us rather bear those ills we have,
Than fly to others that we know not of?
Thus Conscience doth make cowards of us all;
And thus the native hue of Resolution
Is sicklied o'er with the pale cast of Thought;
And enterprises of great pith and moment,
With this regard, their currents turn awry,
And lose the name of Action.

Conscience. — *Mason.*

'TIS ever thus
With noble minds, if chance they slide to folly;
Remorse stings deeper, and relentless Conscience,
Pours more of gall into the bitter cup
Of their severe Repentance.

Conscience. — *Shakspeare.*

TRY what Repentance can. What can it not?
Yet what can it, when one cannot repent?
O wretched state! O bosom, black as death!
O limed soul, that, struggling to be free,
Art more engaged!

Conscience. — *Colton.*

TO be satisfied with the Acquittal of the World, though accompanied with the secret Condemnation of Conscience, this is the mark of a little mind; but it requires a soul of no common stamp to be satisfied with its *own* Acquittal, and to despise the Condemnation of the World.

Conscience. — *Shakspeare.*

WHAT stronger breast-plate than a Heart untainted?
Thrice is he arm'd, that hath his quarrel just;
And he but naked, though lock'd up in steel,
Whose Conscience with Injustice is corrupted.

Conscience. — *Dryden.*

HERE, here it lies: a lump of lead by day;
And in my short, distracted, nightly slumbers,
The hag that rides my dreams.

Conscience. — *Steele.*

THE World will never be in any manner of order or tranquillity, until men are firmly convinced, that Conscience, Honour, and Credit are all in one interest; and that without the concurrence of the former, the latter are but impositions upon ourselves and others.

Conscience. — *Milton.*

HE that has light within his own clear Breast,
May sit i' th' centre, and enjoy bright day:
But he that hides a dark Soul, and foul Thoughts,
Benighted walks under the mid-day sun:
Himself is his own dungeon.

Conscience. — *Young.*

CONSCIENCE, what art thou? thou tremendous power!
Who dost inhabit us without our leave;
And art within ourselves, another self,
A master-self, that loves to domineer,
And treat the monarch frankly as the slave:
How dost thou light a torch to distant deeds?
Make the past, present, and the future frown?
How, ever and anon, awake the soul,
As with a peal of thunder, to strange horrors,
In this long restless dream, which idiots hug,
Nay, wise men flatter with the name of life.

Conscience. — *Shakspeare.*

THOU turn'st mine eyes into my very Soul;
And there I see such black and grained spots,
As will not leave their tinct.

Conscience. — *Shakspeare.*

BETTER be with the dead,
Whom we, to gain our place, have sent to peace,
Than on the Torture of the Mind to lie
In restless ecstasy.

Conscience. — *Crabbe.*

OH! Conscience! Conscience! Man's most faithful friend,
Him canst thou comfort, ease, relieve, defend:
But if he will thy friendly checks forego,
Thou art, oh! wo for me, his deadliest foe!

Conscience. — *Byron.*

HORROR and doubt distract
His troubled Thoughts, and from the bottom stir
The Hell within him; for within him Hell
He brings, and round about him, nor from Hell
One step no more than from himself can fly
By change of place.

Conscience. — *Byron.*

YET still there whispers the Small Voice within,
Heard through Gain's silence, and o'er Glory's din:
Whatever creed be taught or land be trod,
Man's Conscience is the oracle of God!

Conscience. — *Byron.*

THE Mind, that broods o'er guilty woes,
Is like the scorpion girt by fire,
In circle narrowing as it glows,
The flames around their captive close,
Till inly search'd by thousand throes,
And maddening in her ire,
One and sole relief she knows:
The sting she nourish'd for her foes,
Whose venom never yet was vain,
Gives but one pang, and cures all pain,
And darts into her desperate brain.
So do the dark in Soul expire,
Or live like scorpion girt by fire;
So writhes the Mind Remorse hath riven,
Unfit for earth, undoom'd for Heaven,
Darkness above, despair beneath,
Around it flame, within it death!

Conscience. — *Shakspeare.*

I FEEL within me
A peace above all earthly dignities,
A still and quiet Conscience.

Conscience. — *Shakspeare.*

MY Conscience hath a thousand several tongues,
And every tongue brings in a several tale,
And every tale condemns me for a Villain.

Conscience. — *Byron.*

THERE is no future pang
Can deal that justice on the self-condemn'd
He deals on his own soul.

Consciousness. — *Bruyere.*

TO feel the want of reason is next to having it; an idiot is not capable of this sensation. The best thing next to wit is a Consciousness that it is not in us; without wit, a man might then know how to behave himself, so as not to appear to be a fool or a coxcomb.

Consequences. — *Colton.*

AS the dimensions of the tree are not always regulated by the size of the seed, so the Consequences of things are not always proportionate to the apparent magnitude of those events that have produced them. Thus, the American Revolution, from which little was expected, produced much; but the French Revolution, from which much was expected, produced little.

Consolation. — *Rousseau.*

CONSOLATION indiscreetly pressed upon us, when we are suffering under affliction, only serves to increase our pain, and to render our grief more poignant.

Conspiracy. — *Shakspeare.*

O CONSPIRACY!
Sham'st thou to show thy dangerous brow by night,
When evils are most free? O, then, by day,
Where wilt thou find a cavern dark enough
To mask thy monstrous visage? Seek none, Conspiracy;
Hide it in smiles and affability.

Contemplation. — *Burnet.*

THERE is no lasting pleasure but Contemplation; all others grow flat and insipid upon frequent use; and when a man hath run through a set of vanities, in the declension of his age, he knows not what to do with himself, if he cannot think: he saunters about from one dull business to another, to wear out time; and hath no reason to value Life but because he is afraid of Death.

Contempt. — *Shakspeare.*

MAJESTY might never yet endure
The moody frontier of a servant brow.

Contempt. — *Byron.*

PARDON is for men,
And not for reptiles—we have none for Steno,
And no resentment; things like him must sting,
And higher beings suffer: 'tis the charter
Of life. The man who dies by the adder's fang
May have the crawler crush'd, but feels no anger:
'Twas the worm's nature; and some men are worms
In soul more than the living things of tombs.

Contempt. — *Shakspeare.*

WHAT valour were it, when a cur doth grin,
For one to thrust his hand between his teeth,
When he might spurn him with his foot away?

Contempt. — *Chesterfield.*

IT is very often more necessary to conceal Contempt than Resentment, the former being never forgiven, but the latter sometimes forgot.

Contempt. — *Massinger.*

THE Prince that pardons
The first affront offer'd to Majesty,
Invites a second, rendering that power,
Subjects should tremble at, contemptible.
Ingratitude is a monster,
To be strangled in the birth.

Content. — *Spenser.*

IT is the Mynd that maketh good or ill,
That maketh wretch or happie, rich or poore;
For some, that hath abundance at his will,
Hath not enough, but wants in greatest store;
And other, that hath little, asks no more,
But in that little is both rich and wise;
For Wisdome is most riches; Fooles therefore
They are which Fortune's doe by vowes devize,
Sith each unto himself his life may fortunize.

Content. — *Shakspeare.*

BEST State, contentless
Hath a distracted and most wretched being,
Worse than the worse, Content.

Content. — *Shakspeare.*

HE that commends me to mine own Content,
Commends me to the thing I cannot get.

Content. — *Shakspeare.*

MY Crown is in my Heart, not on my Head;
Not deck'd with diamonds and Indian stones,
Nor to be seen: my Crown is called Content;
A Crown it is that seldom Kings enjoy.

Content. — *Shakspeare.*

POOR, and Content, is rich and rich enough;
But riches, fineless, is as poor as winter,
To him that ever fears he shall be poor.

Content. — *Mrs. Sigourney.*

THINK'ST thou the man whose mansions hold
The worldling's pomp and miser's gold,
Obtains a richer prize
Than he who, in his cot at rest,
Finds heavenly peace a willing guest,
And bears the promise in his breast
Of treasure in the skies?

Contentment. — *Tucker.*

THE Point of Aim for our Vigilance to hold in view, is to dwell upon the brightest parts in every prospect, to call off the Thoughts when running upon disagreeable Objects, and strive to be pleased with the present circumstances surrounding us.

Contentment. — *Colton.*

THERE can be no doubt that the seat of perfect Contentment is in the Head; for every individual is thoroughly satisfied with his own proportion of Brains. Socrates was so well aware of this, that he would not start as a Teacher of Truth, but as an Inquirer after it. As a teacher, he would have had many disputers, but no disciples: he therefore adopted the humbler mode of investigation, and instilled his knowledge into others, under the mask of seeking information from them.

Contentment. — *Greville.*

WITHOUT Content, we shall find it almost as difficult to please others as ourselves.

Contiguity. — *Greville.*

MEN and Statues that are admired in an elevated Situation, have a very different effect upon us when we approach them: the first appear less than we imagined them, the last bigger.

Contiguity. — *Colton.*

SPEAKING generally, no man appears great to his Contemporaries, for the same reason that no man is great to his Servants —both know too much of him.

Self Control. — *Cato.*

I THINK the first Virtue is to restrain the Tongue: he approaches nearest to the Gods, who knows how to be silent, even though he is in the right.

Self Control. — *Shakspeare.*

BETTER conquest never can'st thou make,
Than arm thy constant and thy nobler Parts
Against giddy, loose Suggestions.

Controversy. — *Butler.*

HE could raise Scruples dark and nice,
And after solve 'em in a trice;
As if Divinity had catch'd
The itch on purpose to be scratch'd.

Controversy. — *Colton.*

WE are more inclined to hate one another for Points on which we differ, than to love one another for Points on which we agree. The reason perhaps is this; when we find others that agree with us, we seldom trouble ourselves to confirm that Agreement; but when we chance on those that differ with us, we are zealous both to convince, and to convert them. Our Pride is hurt by the Failure, and disappointed Pride engenders Hatred.

Controversy. — *Dryden.*

I TELL thee, Mufti, if the world were wise,
They would not wag one finger in thy quarrels:
Your Heav'n you promise, but our Earth you covet,
The Phaëtons of mankind, who fire that worl
Which you were sent by preaching but to warm.

Religious Controversy. — *Dryden.*

IS not the Care of Souls a load sufficient?
Are not your holy stipends paid for this?
Were you not bred apart from worldly noise,
To study Souls, their Cures and their Diseases?
The province of the Soul is large enough
To fill up every cranny of your time,
And leave you much to answer, if one wretch
Be damn'd by your neglect.

Conversation. — *Addison.*

ONE would think that the larger the Company is in which we are engaged, the greater variety of Thoughts and Subjects would be started into discourse; but instead of this, we find that Conversation is never so much straitened and confined as in numerous assemblies.

Conversation. — *Colton.*

WHEN we are in the Company of sensible men, we ought to be doubly cautious of talking too much, lest we lose two good things, their good opinion, and our own improvement; for what we have to say we know, but what they have to say we know not.

Conversation. — *Addison.*

IN private Conversation between intimate Friends, the wisest men very often talk like the weakest; for indeed the talking with a Friend is nothing else but thinking aloud.

Conversation. — *La Bruyere.*

THERE is speaking well, speaking easily, speaking justly, and speaking seasonably: It is offending against the last, to speak of entertainments before the indigent; of sound limbs and health before the infirm; of houses and lands before one who has not so much as a dwelling; in a word, to speak of your prosperity before the miserable; this Conversation is cruel, and the comparison which naturally arises in them betwixt their condition and yours is excruciating.

Conversation. — *La Bruyere.*

AMONGST such as out of Cunning hear all and talk little, be sure to talk less; or if you must talk, say little.

Conversation. — *Burke.*

THE Perfection of Conversation is not to play a regular sonata, but, like the Æolian harp, to await the Inspiration of the passing breeze.

Conversation. — *Johnson.*

HE only will please long, who by tempering the acidity of Satire with the sugar of Civility, and allaying the heat of Wit with the frigidity of Humble Chat, can make the true Punch of Conversation; and as that punch can be drunk in the greatest quantity which has the largest proportion of water, so that Companion will be oftenest welcome, whose Talk flows out with unoffensive copiousness, and unenvied insipidity.

Conversation. — *Steele.*

IT is a Secret known but to few, yet of no small use in the conduct of Life, that when you fall into a man's Conversation, the first thing you should consider is, whether he has a greater inclination to hear you, or that you should hear him.

Conversation. — *Sir William Temple.*

IN Conversation, Humour is more than Wit, Easiness more than Knowledge; few desire to learn, or to think they need it; all desire to be pleased, or, if not, to be easy.

Conversation. — *Colton.*

SOME men are very entertaining for a first Interview, but after that they are exhausted, and run out; on a second Meeting we shall find them very flat and monotonous: like hand-organs, we have heard all their tunes.

Conversation. — *Lavater.*

HE who sedulously attends, pointedly asks, calmly speaks, coolly answers, and ceases when he has no more to say, is in possession of some of the best requisites of Man.

Conversation. — *Colton.*

SOME Praters are so full of their own Gabble, and so fond of their own Discord, that they would not suspend their eternal Monotonies, to hear the Wit of Sheridan, or the Point of Swift; one might as well attempt to stop the saw of a task-working stone-cutter, by the melodies of an Æolian harp. Others again there are, who hide that Ignorance in silent Gravity that these expose by silly Talk; but they are so coldly correct, and so methodically dull, that any attempt to raise the slumbering sparks of Genius by means of such instruments, would be to stir up a languishing fire with a poker of ice. There is a third class, forming a great majority, being a heavy compound of the two former, and possessing many of the properties peculiar to each; thus they have just Ignorance enough to talk amongst Fools, and just Sense enough to be silent amongst Wits. But they have no Vivacity in themselves, nor relish for it in another: to attempt to keep up the ball of Conversation with such partners would be to play a game of Fives against a bed of feathers.

Conversation. — *Addison.*

THAT part of life which we ordinarily understand by the word Conversation, is an indulgence to the sociable part of our make; and should incline us to bring our proportion of good-will or good-humour among the Friends we meet with, and not to trouble them with relations which must of necessity oblige them to a real or feigned affliction. Cares, distresses, diseases, uneasinesses, and dislikes of our own, are by no means to be obtruded upon our Friends. If we would consider how little of this vicissitude of motion and rest, which we call life, is spent with satisfaction, we should be more tender of our friends, than to bring them little sorrows which do not belong to them. There is no real life but cheerful life; therefore valetudinarians should be sworn, before they enter into Company, not to say a word of themselves until the meeting breaks up.

Conversation. — *From the French.*

SPEAK little and well if you wish to be considered as possessing merit.

Conversation. — *Fuller.*

NEVER contend with one that is foolish, proud, positive, testy; or with a superior, or a clown, in matter of Argument.

Conversation. — *Steele.*

BEAUTY is never so lovely as when adorned with the Smile, and Conversation never sits easier upon us than when we now and then discharge ourselves in a symphony of Laughter, which may not improperly be called the Chorus of Conversation.

Conversation. — *Swift.*

NOTHING is more generally exploded than the folly of talking too much; yet I rarely remember to have seen five people together, where some one among them has not been predominant in that kind, to the great constraint and disgust of all the rest. But among such as deal in Multitudes of Words, none are comparable to the sober deliberate Talker, who proceeds with much thought and caution, makes his preface, branches out into several digressions, finds a hint that puts him in mind of another Story, which he promises to tell you when this is done; comes back regularly to his subject, cannot readily call to mind some person's name, holding his head, complains of his memory: the whole Company all this while is in suspense; at length, he says it is no matter, and so goes on. And, to crown the business, it perhaps proves at last a Story the Company has heard fifty times before.

Conversation. — *Sir William Temple.*

THE first ingredient in Conversation is Truth, the next Good Sense, the third Good Humour, and the fourth Wit.

Conversation. —*La Rochefoucauld.*

THE extreme pleasure we take in talking of ourselves should make us fear that we give very little to those who listen to us.

Conversation. — *Swift.*

ONE of the best Rules in Conversation is, never to say a thing which any of the Company can reasonably wish we had rather left unsaid: nor can there any thing be well more contrary to the ends for which people meet together, than to part unsatisfied with each other or themselves.

Conversation. — *Voltaire.*

THE secret of tiring is to say every thing that can be said on the subject.

Conversation. — *La Rochefoucauld.*

ONE thing which makes us find so few people who appear reasonable and agreeable in Conversation is, that there is scarcely any one who does not think more of what he is about to say than of answering precisely what is said to him. The cleverest and most complaisant people content themselves with merely showing an attentive Countenance, while we can see in their eyes and mind a wandering from what is said to them, and an impatience to return to what they wish to say; instead of reflecting that it is a bad method of pleasing or persuading others, to be so studious of pleasing oneself; and that listening well and answering well is one of the greatest Perfections that can be attained in Conversation.

Conversation. — *Colton.*

WHEN I meet with any that write obscurely, or converse confusedly, I am apt to suspect two things; first, that such persons do not understand themselves; and, secondly, that they are not worthy of being understood by others.

Conversion. — *Colton.*

THE most zealous Converters are always the most rancorous, when they fail of producing Conviction; but when they succeed, they love their new Disciples far better than those whose establishment in the Faith neither excited their zeal to the combat, nor rewarded their prowess with victory.

Conversion. — *Goethe.*

AS to the value of Conversions, God alone can judge. God alone can know how wide are the steps which the soul has to take before it can approach to a Community with him, to the dwelling of the Perfect, or to the Intercourse and Friendship of higher natures.

Convibiality. — *Armstrong.*

WHAT dext'rous thousands just within the goal
Of wild Debauch direct their nightly course!
Perhaps no sickly qualms bedim their days,
No morning admonitions shock the head.
But ah! what woes remain? life rolls apace,
And that incurable disease, old age,
In youthful bodies more severely felt,
More sternly active, shakes their blasted prime.

Convibiality. — *Charles Johnson.*

O WHEN we swallow down
Intoxicating Wine, we drink Damnation;
Naked we stand the sport of mocking fiends,
Who grin to see our noble nature vanquish'd,
Subdued to beasts.

The Coquette. — *Joanna Baillie.*

SHE who only finds her Self-esteem
In others' Admiration, begs an alms;
Depends on others for her daily food,
And is the very servant of her slaves;
Tho' oftentimes, in a fantastic hour,
O'er men she may a childish pow'r exert,
Which not ennobles, but degrades her state.

Corrupted Talent. — *Shakspeare.*

THE gentleman is learn'd, and a most rare Speaker,
To nature none more bound; his Training such,

That he may furnish and instruct great teachers,
And never seek for aid out of himself.
Yet see,
When these so noble benefits shall prove
Not well disposed, the mind growing once corrupt,
They turn to vicious forms, ten times more ugly
Than ever they were fair.

Corruption. — *Burke.*

THE age unquestionably produces, (whether in a greater or less number than in former times, I know not,) daring Profligates and insidious Hypocrites. What then? Am I not to avail myself of whatever good is to be found in the world, because of the mixture of evil that will always be in it? The smallness of the quantity in currency only heightens the value.

Corruption. — *Shakspeare.*

O THAT estates, degrees and offices
Were not derived corruptly! and that clear Honour
Were purchased by the Merit of the wearer!
How many then should cover, that stand bare!
How many be commanded, that command!
How much low peasantry would then be glean'd
From the true seed of honour! And how much Honour
Pick'd from the chaff and ruin of the times,
To be new garnish'd!

Corruption. — *Colton.*

MEN, by associating in large masses, as in camps, and in cities, improve their Talents, but impair their Virtues, and strengthen their Minds, but weaken their Morals; thus a retrocession in the one, is too often the price they pay for a refinement in the other.

Corruption. — *Shakspeare.*

THEY that have power to hurt and will do none,
That do not do the thing they most do show,
Who, moving others, are themselves of stone,
Unmoved, cold, and to temptation slow;
They rightly do inherit Heav'n's graces,
And husband Nature's riches from expense;
They are the lords and owners of their faces,
Others but stewards of their excellence.
The summer's flower is to the summer sweet,
Though to itself it only live and die;
But if that flower with base Infection meet,
The basest weed outbraves his dignity;
For sweetest things turn sourest by their deeds;
Lilies that fester smell far worse than weeds.

Corruption. — *Shakspeare.*

IF that the Heavens do not their visible spirits
Send quickly down to tame these vile Offences,
'Twill come,
Humanity must perforce prey on itself,
Like monsters of the deep.

Counsel. — *Fuller.*

GOOD Counsels observed are chains to grace.

Counsel. — *Seneca.*

CONSULT your Friend on all things, especially on those which respect yourself. His Counsel may then be useful, where your own self-love might impair your Judgment.

Council. — *Shakspeare.*

LET our Alliance be combined,
Our best Friends made, and our best Means stretch'd out;
And let us presently go sit in Council,
How covert matters may be best disclosed,
And open perils surest answer'd.

Country. — *Halleck.*

THEY love their land because it is their own,
And scorn to give aught other reason why.

The Country. — *Milton.*

A WILDERNESS of sweets; for Nature here
Wanton'd as in her prime, and play'd at will
Her virgin fancies, pouring forth more sweet,
Wild above rule or art, enormous bliss.

Country Life. — *Milton.*

WISDOM'S self
Oft seeks so sweet retired Solitude;
Where, with her best nurse, Contemplation,
She plumes her feathers, and lets grow her wings,
That in the various bustle of Resort
Were all too ruffled, and sometimes impair'd.

Country Life. — *Cowper.*

HOW various his employments, whom the world
Calls idle, and who justly in return
Esteems that busy world an idler too!
Friends, books, a Garden, and perhaps his pen,
Delightful industry enjoyed at home,
And Nature in her cultivated trim,
Dress'd to his taste, inviting him abroad.

Country Life. — *Thomson.*

Now from the town
Buried in smoke, and sleep, and noisome damps,
Oft let me wander o'er the dewy Fields,
Where freshness breathes, and dash the trembling drops
From the bent Bush, as through the verdant Maze
Of Sweet-brier Hedges I pursue my walk.

Country Life. — *Cowper.*

'TIS pleasant through the loop-holes of Retreat,
To peep at such a world.
To see the stir of the great Babel, and not feel the crowd.
To hear the roar she sends through all her gates,
At a safe distance, where the dying sound
Falls a soft murmur on th' uninjur'd ear.

Country Life. — *Cowper.*

THEY love the Country, and none else, who seek
For their own sake its Silence and its Shade:
Delights which who would leave that has a heart
Susceptible of pity, or a mind
Cultured and capable of sober thought.

Country Life. — *Cowper.*

GOD made the Country, and man made the Town.
What wonder, then, that health and virtue, gifts
That can alone make sweet the bitter draught
That life holds out to all, should most abound
And least be threatened in the Fields and Groves.

Country Life. — *Cowper.*

OH for a Lodge in some vast Wilderness,
Some boundless Contiguity of Shade,
Where rumour of oppression and deceit,
Of unsuccessful and successful war
Might never reach me more! My ear is pain'd,
My soul is sick with every day's report
Of wrong and outrage with which earth is fill'd.

Country Life. — *Cowper.*

THE spleen is seldom felt where Flora reigns;
The low'ring eye, the petulance, the frown,
And sullen sadness that o'ershade, distort,
And mar the face of beauty, when no cause
For such immeasurable wo appears,
These Flora banishes, and gives the fair
Sweet smiles and bloom less transient than her own.

Country Life. — *Thomson.*

THRICE happy he! who on the sunless side
Of a romantic Mountain, Forest crown'd,
Beneath the whole collected Shade reclines;
Or in the gelid Caverns, Wood-bine wrought,
And fresh bedew'd with ever-spouting Streams,
Sits coolly calm; while all the world without,
Unsatisfy'd, and sick, tosses at noon.
Emblem instructive of the virtuous man,
Who keeps his temper'd mind serene, and pure,
And every passion aptly harmoniz'd,
Amid a jarring world with vice inflam'd.

Country Life. — *Peter Pindar.*

THERE Health, so wild and gay, with bosom bare,
And rosy cheek, keen eye, and flowing hair,
Trips with a smile the breezy Scene along,
And pours the spirit of Content in song.

Country Life. — *Thomson.*

HERE too dwells simple Truth; plain Innocence;
Unsullied Beauty; sound unbroken Youth,
Patient of labour, with a little pleas'd;
Health ever blooming; unambitious Toil:
Calm Contemplation, and poetic Ease.

Country Life. — *Thomson.*

OH knew he but his happiness, of men
The happiest he! who far from public rage,
Deep in the Vale, with a choice few retired,
Drinks the pure pleasures of the Rural Life.

Country Life. — *Thomson.*

PERHAPS thy loved Lucinda shares thy Walk,
With soul to thine attuned. Then Nature all
Wears to the lover's eye a look of love;
And all the tumult of a guilty world,
Toss'd by ungenerous passions, sinks away.

Courage. — *Shakspeare.*

I DO not think a Braver Gentleman,
More active valiant, or more valiant-young,
More daring, or more bold, is now alive,
To grace this latter age with noble deeds.

Courage. — *Byron.*

A REAL Spirit
Should neither court neglect, nor dread to bear it.

Courage. — *Ben Jonson.*

A VALIANT Man
Ought not to undergo or tempt a danger,
But worthily, and by selected ways,
He undertakes by reason, not by chance.
His Valour is the salt t' his other virtues,
They're all unseason'd without it.

Courage. — *Joanna Baillie.*

THE Brave Man is not he who feels no fear,
For that were stupid and irrational;
But he, whose noble Soul its Fear subdues,
And bravely dares the Danger nature shrinks from.
As for your youth, whom blood and blows delight,
Away with them! there is not in their crew
One valiant Spirit.

Courage. — *Shakspeare.*

COME all to ruin;
Let thy mother rather feel thy Pride, than fear
Thy dangerous Stoutness; for I mock at death,
With a big Heart as thou. Do as thou list.
Thy Valiantness was mine, thou suck'dst it from me;
But owe thy Pride thyself.

Courage. — *Colton.*

PHYSICAL Courage, which despises all danger, will make a man brave in one way; and Moral Courage, which despises all opinion, will make a man brave in another. The former would seem most necessary for the camp, the latter for council; but to constitute a great man, both are necessary.

Courage. — *Shaftesbury.*

TRUE Courage is cool and calm. The bravest of men have the least of a brutal bullying insolence; and in the very time of danger are found the most serene and free. Rage, we know, can make a coward forget himself and fight. But what is done in fury or anger can never be placed to the account of Courage.

Courage. — *Dryden.*

AN intrepid Courage is at best but a holiday-kind of virtue, to be seldom exercised, and never but in cases of necessity: affability, mildness, tenderness, and a word which I would fain bring back to its original signification of virtue, I mean good-nature, are of daily use; they are the bread of mankind, and staff of life.

Courage. — *Greville.*

MOST men have more Courage than even they themselves think they have.

Courage. — *Shakspeare.*

He bore him in the thickest troop,
As doth a Lion in a herd of Neat:
Or as a Bear, encompass'd round with Dogs;
Who having pinch'd a few and made them cry,
The rest stand all aloof, and bark at him.

Courage. — *Shakspeare.*

He stopp'd the fliers;
And, by his rare example, made the coward
Turn Terror into Sport; as waves before
A vessel under sail, so men obey'd,
And fell below his stem.

The Court. — *La Bruyere.*

THE Court does not render a man contented, but it prevents his being so elsewhere.

The Court. — *Burke.*

IT is of great importance (provided the thing is not over done) to contrive such an establishment as must, almost whether a Prince will or not, bring into daily and hourly offices about his person, a great number of his first Nobility; and it is rather an useful prejudice that gives them pride in such a servitude. Though they are not much the better for a Court, a Court will be much the better for them.

Court Jealousy. — *Shakspeare.*

No simple man that sees
This jarring Discord of Nobility,
This should'ring of each other in the Court,
This factious bandying of their Favourites,
But that it doth presage some ill event.
'Tis much, when sceptres are in children's hands;
But more, when envy breeds unkind division;
There comes the ruin, there begins confusion.

Courtesy. — *Shakspeare.*

O,
Dissembling Courtesy! how fine this tyrant
Can tickle where she wounds!

The Courtier. — *Dryden.*

See how he sets his Countenance for Deceit,
And promises a Lie before he speaks.

Courtship. — *Shakspeare.*

Win her with Gifts, if she respect not Words;
Dumb Jewels often, in their silent kind,
More quick than Words, do move a Woman's Mind.

Courtship. — *Shakspeare.*

THOU hast by moon-light at her window sung,
With feigning voice, verses of feigning Love;
And stol'n the impression of her fantasy
With bracelets of thy hair, rings, gauds, conceits,
Knacks, trifles, nosegays, sweet-meats; messengers
Of strong prevailment in unharden'd youth.

Courtship. — *Shakspeare.*

SAY, that she rail; Why, then I'll tell her plain,
She sings as sweetly as a nightingale:
Say, that she frown: I'll say, she looks as clear
As morning roses newly wash'd with dew:
Say, she be mute, and will not speak a word;
Then I'll commend her volubility,
And say—she uttereth piercing eloquence.
If she do frown 'tis not in hate of you,
But rather to beget more love in you:
If she do chide, 'tis not to have you gone;
For why, the fools are mad if left alone.
Take no repulse, whatever she doth say;
For, *get you gone*, she doth not mean, *away.*

Courtship. — *Blair.*

OH, then the longest summer's day
Seem'd too, too much in haste: still the full Heart
Had not imparted half: 'twas Happiness
Too exquisite to last. Of joys departed,
Not to return, how painful the remembrance!

Courtship. — *Hill.*

WITH Women worth the being won,
The softest Lover ever best succeeds.

Courtship. — *Thomson.*

COME then, ye virgins and ye youths, whose Hearts
Have felt the raptures of refining Love;
And thou, Amanda, come, pride of my song!
Form'd by the Graces, Loveliness itself!
Come with those downcast eyes, sedate and sweet,
Those looks demure, that deeply pierce the soul,
Where with the light of thoughtful reason mix'd,
Shines lively fancy and the feeling heart:
Oh come! and while the rosy-footed May
Steals blushing on, together let us tread
The morning dews and gather in their prime
Fresh-blooming flowers, to grace thy braided hair,
And thy lov'd bosom that improves their sweets.

Courtship. — *Shakspeare.*

SAY, that upon the altar of her Beauty
 You sacrifice your Tears, your Sighs, your Heart:
Write, till your ink be dry; and with your tears
Moist it again; and frame some feeling line,
That may discover such integrity.

Courtship. — *Shakspeare.*

 WOMEN are angels wooing:
Things won are done, joy's soul lies in the doing:
That she belov'd knows nought, that knows not this,—
Men prize the thing ungain'd more than it is.

Courtship. — *Shakspeare.*

WHY should you think that I should woo in scorn?
 Scorn and derision never come in tears?
Look, when I vow, I weep; and vows so born,
 In their nativity all truth appears.

Covetousness. — *South.*

THE Covetous Person lives as if the world were made altogether for him, and not he for the world; to take in every thing, and part with nothing.

Covetousness. — *Colton.*

AFTER Hypocrites, the greatest dupes the Devil has are those who exhaust an anxious existence in the Disappointments and Vexations of Business, and live miserably and meanly only to die magnificently and rich. For, like the Hypocrites, the only *disinterested* action these men can accuse themselves of is, that of serving the Devil, without receiving his wages: he that stands every day of his life behind a counter, until he drops from it into the grave, may negotiate many very profitable bargains; but he has made a single bad one, so bad indeed, that it counterbalances all the rest; for the empty foolery of dying rich, he has paid down his health, his happiness, and his integrity.

Covetousness. — *Burton.*

COVETOUS men are fools, miserable wretches, buzzards, madmen, who live by themselves, in perpetual slavery, fear, suspicion, sorrow, discontent, with more of gall than honey in their enjoyments; who are rather possessed by their Money than Possessors of it; *mancipati pecuniis*, bound 'prentices to their property; and, *servi divitiarum*, mean slaves and drudges to their Substance.

Covetousness. — *F. Osborn.*

COVETOUSNESS, like a candle ill made, smothers the splendour of a happy fortune in its own grease.

Covetousness. — *Shakspeare.*

MASTER, I marvel how the fishes live in the sea.

1st Fisherman:

Why as men do a-land: the great ones eat up the little ones. I can compare our rich Misers to nothing so fitly as to a whale; 'a plays and tumbles, driving the poor fry before him and at last devours them all at a mouthful. Such whales have I heard on the land, who never leave gaping, till they've swallowed the whole parish, church, steeple, bells, and all.

Covetousness. — *Shakspeare.*

WHEN workmen strive to do better than well,
They do confound their skill in Covetousness.

Cowardice. — *Shakspeare.*

YOU are the hare of whom the proverb goes,
Whose valour plucks dead lions by the beard.

The Coxcomb. — *Shakspeare.*

BUT, I remember, when the fight was done,
When I was dry with rage, and extreme toil,
Breathless, and faint, leaning upon my sword,
Came there a certain Lord, neat, trimly dress'd:
Fresh as a Bridegroom, and his chin, new reap'd,
Show'd like a stubble land at harvest home.
He was perfumed like a Milliner;
And 'twixt his finger and his thumb, he held
A pouncet box, which ever and anon
He gave his nose: and still he smiled and talk'd;
And as the soldiers bore dead bodies by,
He call'd them—untaught knaves, unmannerly,
To bring a slovenly unhandsome corpse
Betwixt the wind and his Nobility.

Creed. — *Colton.*

HE that will believe only what he can fully comprehend, must have a very long head, or a very short Creed.

Creed. — *Colton.*

IN Politics, as in Religion, it so happens that we have less charity for those who believe the half of our Creed, than for those that deny the whole of it, since if Servetus had been a Mohammedan, he would not have been burnt by Calvin.

Credulity. — *Colton.*

THE Testimony of those who doubt the least, is, not unusually, that very Testimony that ought most to be doubted.

Credulity. — *Sir Philip Sidney.*

THE only disadvantage of an honest heart is Credulity.

Credulity. — *Colton.*

IT is a curious paradox, that precisely in proportion to our own intellectual weakness, will be our Credulity as to those mysterious powers assumed by others; and in those regions of darkness and ignorance where man cannot effect even those things that are within the power of man, there we shall ever find that a blind belief in feats that are far beyond those powers, has taken the deepest root in the minds of the deceived, and produced the richest harvest to the knavery of the deceiver. An impostor that would starve in Edinburgh, might luxuriate in his Gynæceum at Constantinople. But the more we know as to those things that can be done, the more skeptical do we become as to all things that cannot.

Credulity. — *From the French.*

THE common people are to be caught by the ears as one catches a pot by the handle.

Crime. —*La Rochefoucauld.*

FOR the credit of Virtue it must be admitted that the greatest evils which befall mankind are caused by their Crimes.

Criticism. — *Washington Irving.*

THERE is a certain meddlesome spirit, which, in the garb of learned research, goes prying about the traces of history, casting down its monuments, and marring and mutilating its fairest trophies. Care should be taken to vindicate great names from such pernicious erudition.

Critics. —*Aiken.*

HE whose first emotion, on the view of an excellent production, is to undervalue it, will never have one of his own to show.

Critics. — *Washington Irving.*

CRITICS are a kind of Freebooters in the republic of Letters— who, like deer, goats, and divers other graminivorous animals, gain subsistence by gorging upon buds and leaves of the young shrubs of the forest, thereby robbing them of their verdure, and retarding their progress to maturity.

Critics. — *Longfellow.*

CRITICS are sentinels in the grand army of letters, stationed at the corners of newspapers and reviews, to challenge every new author.

Crown. — *Halleck.*

EMPIRES to-day are upside down,
The castle kneels before the town,
The monarch fears a printer's frown,
A brickbat's range;
Give me, in preference to a crown,
Five shillings change.

Cunning. — *Bruyere.*

CUNNING is none of the best nor worst qualities: it floats between Virtue and Vice: there is scarce any exigence where it may not, and perhaps ought not to be supplied by Prudence.

Cunning. — *Lord Greville.*

THE common Contrivances of Cunning put me in mind of the preservative instinct I have sometimes observed in Beasts, which lay a plot that is extremely artful and well concealed in many parts, but at the same time left so open in some one that it is perfectly easy for superior intelligence to see and understand the whole complication of the contrivance.

Cunning. — *Plato.*

KNOWLEDGE without Justice ought to be called Cunning rather than Wisdom.

Cunning. — *La Bruyere.*

CUNNING leads to Knavery; it is but a step from one to the other, and that very slippery; Lying only makes the difference: add that to Cunning, and it is Knavery.

Cunning. — *Colton.*

TAKING things not as they ought to be, but as they are, I fear it must be allowed that Machiavelli will always have more disciples than Jesus. Out of the millions who have studied and even admired the precepts of the Nazarite, how few are there that have reduced them to practice. But there are numbers numberless who throughout the whole of their lives have been practising the principles of the Italian, without having even heard of his name; who cordially believe with him that the tongue was given us to *discover* the thoughts of others, and to conceal our own.

Cunning. — *Goldsmith.*

THE bounds of a man's knowledge are easily concealed, if he has but prudence.

Cunning. — *La Rochefoucauld.*

THE most sure method of subjecting yourself to be deceived, is to consider yourself more Cunning than others.

Cunning. — *Lord Greville.*

WE should do by our Cunning as we do by our Courage,—always have it ready to defend ourselves, never to offend others.

Cunning. — *Lord Bacon.*

WE take Cunning for a sinister or crooked wisdom, and certainly there is a great difference between a Cunning Man and a wise man, not only in point of honesty but in point of ability.

Cunning. — *Colton.*

HURRY and Cunning are the two apprentices of Dispatch and of Skill; but neither of them ever learn their masters' trade.

Cunning. — *Addison.*

CUNNING has only private selfish aims, and sticks at nothing which may make them succeed. Discretion has large and extended views, and, like a well-formed eye, commands a whole horizon; Cunning is a kind of short-sightedness, that discovers the minutest objects which are near at hand, but is not able to discern things at a distance. Discretion, the more it is discovered, gives a greater authority to the person who possesses it. Discretion is the perfection of Reason, and a guide to us in all the duties of life: Cunning is a kind of Instinct, that only looks out after our immediate interest and welfare. Discretion is only found in men of strong sense and good understandings: Cunning is often to be met with in brutes themselves, and in persons who are but the fewest removes from them. In short, Cunning is only the mimic of Discretion, and may pass upon weak men, in the same manner as Vivacity is often mistaken for Wit, and Gravity for Wisdom.

Cunning. — *Sterne.*

THE paths of Virtue are plain and straight, so that the blind, persons of the meanest capacity, shall not err. Dishonesty requires skill to conduct it, and as great art to conceal—what 'tis every one's interest to detect. And I think I need not remind you how often it happens in attempts of this kind—where worldly men, in haste to be rich, have overrun the only means to it,—and for want of laying their contrivances with proper Cunning, or managing them with proper Secrecy and Advantage, have lost for ever what they might have certainly secured with Honesty and Plain-dealing.

Curses. — *Shakspeare.*

FEED not thy sovereign's foe, my gentle earth,
Nor with thy sweets comfort his rav'nous sense:
But let thy spiders, that suck up thy venom,
And heavy gaited toads, lie in their way.

Custom. — *Hill.*

CUSTOM forms us all;
Our thoughts, our morals, our most fix'd belief,
Are consequences of our place of birth.

Custom. — *Rabelais.*

CAN there be any greater dotage in the world, than for one tc guide and direct his Courses by the sound of a bell, and not by his own judgment and discretion.

Custom. — *Cowper.*

To follow foolish Precedents, and wink
With both our eyes, is easier than to think.

Custom. — *Colton.*

WHEN all moves equally (says Pascal) nothing seems to move, as in a vessel under sail; and when all run by common consent into vice, none appear to do so. He that stops first, views as from a fixed point the horrible extravagance that transports the rest.

Custom. — *Shakspeare.*

NEW Customs,
Though they be never so ridiculous,
Nay let them be unmanly, yet are follow'd.

Death. — *Steele.*

ALL that nature has prescribed must be good; and as Death is natural to us, it is absurdity to fear it. Fear loses its purpose when we are sure it cannot preserve us, and we should draw resolution to meet it, from the impossibility to escape it.

Death. — *La Rochefoucauld.*

NEITHER the sun nor Death can be looked at steadily.

Death. — *Colton.*

THE hand that unnerved Belshazzar derived its most horrifying influence from the want of *a body;* and Death itself is not formidable in what we do know of it, but in what we do *not.*

Death. — *Martial.*

YOU should not fear, nor yet should you wish for your Last Day.

Death. — *Pascal.*

DEATH itself is less painful when it comes upon us unawares, than the bare contemplation of it, even when danger is far distant.

Death. — *Shakspeare.*

THE tongues of dying Men
Enforce attention like deep harmony;
Where words are scarce, they are seldom spent in vain,
For they breathe truth, that breathe their words in pain.
He, that no more must say, is listened more
Than they, whom youth and ease have taught to glose;
More are men's ends mark'd, than their lives before:
The setting sun, and music at the close,
As the last taste of sweets, is sweetest last;
Writ in remembrance, more than things long past.

Death. — *Shakspeare.*

DEATH is a fearful thing,
And shamed life a hateful.
To die, and go we know not where;
To lie in cold obstruction, and to rot;
This sensible warm motion to become
A kneaded Clod; and the delighted Spirit
To bathe in fiery floods, or to reside
In thrilling regions of thick-ribb'd ice;
To be imprison'd in the viewless winds,
And blown with restless violence round about
The pendant world, or to be worse than worst
Of those, that lawless and uncertain thoughts
Imagine howling!—'tis too horrible!
The weariest and most loathed worldly life,
That age, ache, penury, and imprisonment,
Can lay on Nature, is a paradise
To what we fear of Death.

Death. — *Shakspeare.*

NOTHING can we call our own, but Death;
And that small model of the barren earth,
Which serves as paste and cover to our bones.

Death. — *Metastasio.*

IT is by no means a fact, that Death is the worst of all evils; when it comes, it is an alleviation to mortals who are worn out with sufferings.

Death. — *Shakspeare.*

TO what base uses we may return! Why may not imagination trace the noble dust of Alexander, till it find it stopping a bung-hole? As thus, Alexander died, Alexander was buried, Alexander returneth to dust; the dust is earth: of earth we make loam: And why of that loam, whereto he was converted, might they not stop a beer barrel?

Death. — *Colton.*

DEATH is the Liberator of him whom freedom cannot release, the Physician of him whom medicine cannot cure, and the Comforter of him whom time cannot console.

Death. — *Shakspeare.*

FOR within the hollow crown,
That rounds the mortal temples of a king,
Keeps Death his court; and there the Antick sits
Scoffing his state, and grinning at his pomp;
Allowing him a breath, a little scene
To monarchize, be feared, and kill with looks;
Infusing him with self and vain conceit,
As if this flesh, which walls about our life,
Were brass impregnable: and, humour'd thus,
Comes at the last, and with a little pin
Bores through his castle-walls, and farewell King!

Death. — *Shakspeare.*

OH my love, my wife!
Death, that hath suckt the honey of thy breath,
Hath had no power yet upon thy beauty:
Thou art not conquer'd; beauty's ensign yet
Is crimson in thy lips, and in thy cheeks,
And Death's pale flag is not advanced there.
Why art thou yet so fair? shall I believe,
That unsubstantial Death is amorous,
And that the lean abhorr'd Monster keeps
Thee here in dark, to be his paramour?

Death. — *Shakspeare.*

DEATH lies on her, like an untimely frost
Upon the sweetest flow'r of all the field.

Death. — *Shakspeare.*

OH, now doth Death line his dead chaps with steel;
The swords of soldiers are his teeth, his fangs;
And now he feasts, mouthing the flesh of men,
In undetermined differences of kings.

Death. — *Shakspeare.*

NOW boast thee, Death, in thy possession lies
A lass unparallel'd.——Downy windows close;
And golden Phœbus never be beheld
Of eyes again so royal!

Death. — *Shakspeare.*

MOUNT, mount, my Soul! thy seat is up on high;
Whilst my gross Flesh sinks downward here to die.

Death. — *Shakspeare.*

FULL of repentance,
Continual meditations, tears and sorrows,
He gave his honours to the world again,
His blessed part to Heaven, and slept in peace.

Death. — *Shakspeare.*

HAVE I not hideous Death within my view?
Retaining but a quantity of life,
Which bleeds away, ev'n as a form of wax
Resolveth from its figure 'gainst the fire?
What in the world should make me now deceive,
Since I must lose the use of all deceit?
Why should I then be false, since it is true,
That I must die here, and live hence by truth?

Death. — *Shakspeare.*

NOTHING in his life
Became him like the leaving it. He died,
As one that had been studied in his Death,
To throw away the dearest thing he ow'd,
As 'twere a careless trifle.

Death. — *Shakspeare.*

IT is too late; the life of all his blood
Is touch'd corruptibly; and his pure brain,
(Which some suppose, the soul's frail dwelling-house,)
Doth, by the idle comments that it makes,
Foretell the ending of Mortality.

Death. — *Shakspeare.*

OH, AMIABLE lovely Death!
Thou odoriferous stench! sound rottenness!
Arise forth from the couch of lasting night,
Thou hate and terror to prosperity,
And I will kiss thy detestable bones;
And ring these fingers with thy household worms;
And stop this gap of breath with fulsome dust,
And be a carrion Monster like thyself:
Come, grin on me; and I will think thou smil'st,
And buss thee as thy wife! Mercy's love,
Oh come to me!

Death. — *Shakspeare.*

IF thou and nature can so gently part,
The stroke of Death is as a lover's pinch,
Which hurts, and is desir'd.

Death. — *Shakspeare.*

Death,——
Being an ugly Monster,
'Tis strange, he hides him in fresh cups, soft beds,
Sweet words: or hath more ministers than we
That draw his knives i' the war.

Death. — *Shakspeare.*

To die,—to sleep,—
No more;—and, by a sleep, to say we end
The heart-ache, and the thousand natural shocks
That flesh is heir to,—'tis a consummation
Devoutly to be wish'd.

Death. — *Shakspeare.*

Do not, for ever, with thy veiled lids
Seek for thy noble father in the dust:
Thou know'st, 'tis common; all, that live, must die,
Passing through Nature to Eternity.

Death. — *Shakspeare.*

For who would bear the whips and scorns of time,
The oppressor's wrong, the proud man's contumely,
The pangs of despised love, the law's delay,
The insolence of office, and the spurns
That patient merit of the unworthy takes,
When he himself might his quietus make
With a bare bodkin? who would fardels bear,
To grunt and sweat under a weary life;
But that the dread of something after Death,—
The undiscover'd country, from whose bourn
No traveller returns, puzzles the will;
And makes us rather bear those ills we have,
Than fly to others that we know not of?

Death. — *Shakspeare.*

I am a tainted wether of the flock,
Meetest for Death: the weakest kind of fruit
Drops earliest to the ground, and so let me.

Death. — *Shakspeare.*

O mighty Cæsar! dost thou lie so low?
Are all thy conquests, glories, triumphs, spoils,
Shrunk to this little measure?
But yesterday the word of Cæsar might
Have stood against the world: now lies he there,
And none so poor to do him reverence.

Death. — *Shakspeare.*

LAY her i' the earth;—
And from her fair and unpolluted flesh
May violets spring! I tell thee, churlish priest,
A ministering angel shall my sister be,
When thou liest howling.

Death. — *Young.*

WHEN down thy vale unlock'd by midnight thought
That loves to wander in thy sunless realms,
O Death! I stretch my view; what visions rise!
What triumphs! toils imperial! arts divine!
In wither'd laurels glide before my sight!
What lengths of far-famed ages, billow'd high
With human agitation, roll along
In unsubstantial images of air!
The melancholy ghosts of dead renown,
Whispering faint echoes of the world's applause
With penitential aspect, as they pass,
All point at earth, and hiss at human pride,
The wisdom of the wise, and prancings of the great.

Death. — *Shakspeare.*

THE sense of Death is most in apprehension;
And the poor beetle, that we tread upon,
In corporal sufferance finds a pang as great
As when a giant dies.

Death. — *Shakspeare.*

HERE lurks no treason, here no envy swells,
Here grow no damned grudges; here are no storms,
No noise, but Silence and Eternal Sleep.

Death. — *Shakspeare.*

COWARDS die many times before their Deaths;
The valiant never taste of Death but once.
Of all the wonders that I yet have heard,
It seems to me most strange that men should fear;
Seeing that Death, a necessary end,
Will come, when it will come.

Death. — *Blair.*

O GREAT Man-eater!
Whose every day is Carnival, not sated yet!
Unheard of Epicure! without a fellow!
The veriest gluttons do not always cram;
Some intervals of abstinence are sought
To edge the appetite; thou seekest none.

Death. — *Shakspeare.*

THAT life is better Life, past fearing Death,
Than that which lives to fear.

Death. — *Southey.*

DEATH! to the happy thou art terrible,
But how the wretched love to think of thee!
O thou true comforter, the friend of all
Who have no friend beside.

Death. — *Young.*

EARLY, bright, transient,
Chaste as morning dew,
She sparkled, was exhaled,
And went to Heaven.

Death. — *Dryden.*

I FEEL Death rising higher still and higher
Within my bosom; every breath I fetch
Shuts up my life within a shorter compass:
And, like the vanishing sound of bells, grows less
And less each pulse, till it be lost in air.

Death. — *Byron.*

DEATH, so called, is a thing that makes men weep,
And yet a third of life is pass'd in sleep.

Death. — *Blair.*

HOW shocking must thy summons be, O Death!
To him that is at ease in his possessions;
Who, counting on long years of pleasure here,
Is quite unfurnish'd for that world to come!
In that dread moment, how the frantic soul
Raves round the walls of her clay tenement,
Runs to each avenue, and shrieks for help,
But shrieks in vain!

Death. — *Young.*

DEATH is the crown of life:
Were Death denied, poor men would live in vain;
Were Death denied, to live would not be life;
Were Death denied, even fools would wish to die.

Death. — *Byron.*

CAN this be Death? there's bloom upon her cheek;
But now I see it is no living hue,
But a strange hectic—like the unnatural red
Which Autumn plants upon the perish'd leaf.
It is the same! Oh, God! that I should dread
To look upon the same.

Death. — *Young.*

WHY start at Death? Where is he? Death arrived,
Is past; not come, or gone, he's never here.
Ere hope, sensation fails; black-boding man
Receives, not suffers, Death's tremendous blow.
The knell, the shroud, the mattock, and the grave;
The deep damp vault, the darkness, and the worm;
These are the bugbears of a winter's eve,
The terrors of the living, not the dead.
Imagination's fool, and error's wretch,
Man makes a Death which Nature never made;
Then on the point of his own fancy falls;
And feels a thousand Deaths in fearing one.

Death. — *Young.*

EACH friend by Fate snatch'd from us, is a plume
Pluckt from the wing of human vanity,
Which makes us stoop from our aërial heights,
And, dampt with omen of our own disease,
On drooping pinions of ambition lower'd,
Just skim earth's surface, ere we break it up,
O'er putrid earth to scratch a little dust,
And save the world a nuisance.

Death. — *Mrs. Tighe.*

O THOU most terrible, most dreaded Power,
In whatsoever form thou meetest the eye!
Whether thou biddest thy sudden arrow fly
In the dread silence of the midnight hour;
Or whether, hovering o'er the lingering wretch,
Thy sad cold javelin hangs suspended long,
While round the couch the weeping Kindred throng,
With Hope and Fear alternately on stretch;
Oh say, for me what horrors are prepared?
Am I now doom'd to meet thy fatal arm?
Or wilt thou first from life steal every charm,
And bear away each good my soul would guard?
That thus, deprived of all it loved, my heart
From life itself contentedly may part.

Death. — *Campbell.*

SOON may this fluttering spark of vital flame
Forsake its languid melancholy frame!
Soon may these eyes their trembling lustre close,
Welcome the dreamless night of long Repose!
Soon may this wo-worn spirit seek the bourn
Where, lull'd to slumber, Grief forgets to mourn!

Death.—*Byron.*

A SLEEP without dreams, after a rough day
Of toil, is what we covet most; and yet
How clay shrinks back from more quiescent clay.

Death.—*Byron.*

"WHOM the gods love die young" was said of yore,
And many Deaths do they escape by this:
The Death of Friends, and that which slays even more,
The Death of Friendship, Love, Youth, all that is,
Except mere breath; and since the silent Shore
Awaits at last even those whom longest miss
The old Archer's shafts, perhaps the early Grave
Which men weep over may be meant to save.

Death.—*Johnson.*

IN Life's last Scene what prodigies surprise,
Fears of the brave, and follies of the wise?
From Marlb'rough's eyes the streams of dotage flow,
And Swift expires a driv'ler and a show.

Death.—*Dryden.*

OH! that I less could fear to lose this being!
Which, like a snow-ball in my coward hand,
The more 'tis grasp'd, the faster melts away.

Death.—*Webster.*

ONE may live as a conqueror, a king, or a magistrate; but he must die as a man. The bed of death brings every human being to his pure individuality; to the intense contemplation of that deepest and most solemn of all relations, the relation between the creature and his Creator. Here it is that fame and renown cannot assist us; that all external things must fail to aid us; that even friends, affection, and human love and devotedness, cannot succour us.

Death in the Country.—*Paulding.*

THERE is to my mind and to my early recollections, something exquisitely touching in the tolling of a church-bell amid the silence of the country. It communicates for miles around the message of mortality. The ploughman stops his horse to listen to the solemn tidings; the housewife remits her domestic occupations, and sits with the needle idle in her fingers, to ponder who it is that is going to the long home; and even the little, thoughtless children, playing and laughing their way from school, are arrested for a moment in their evening gambols by these sounds of melancholy import, and cover their heads when they go to rest.

Death of Tyrants. — *Fisher Ames.*

IT is not by destroying tyrants that we are to extinguish tyranny; nature is not thus to be exhausted of her power to produce them. The soil of a republic sprouts with the rankest fertility; it has been sown with dragon's teeth. To lessen the hopes of usurping demagogues, we must enlighten, animate, and combine the spirit of freemen; we must fortify and guard the constitutional ramparts about liberty. When its friends become indolent or disheartened, it is no longer of any importance how long-lived are its enemies: they will prove immortal.

Death. — *Bryant.*

SO live, that, when thy summons comes to join
The innumerable caravan, that moves
To that mysterious realm, where each shall take
His chamber in the silent halls of death,
Thou go not, like the quarry-slave at night,
Scourged to his dungeon; but sustain'd and sooth'd
By an unfaltering trust, approach thy grave,
Like one that draws the drapery of his couch
About him, and lies down to pleasant dreams.

Debt. — *Franklin.*

CREDITORS have better memories than Debtors; and Creditors are a superstitious sect, great observers of set days and times.

Debt. — *Sir M. Hale.*

RUN not into Debt, either for wares sold, or money borrowed; be content to want things that are not of absolute necessity, rather than to run up the score.

Debt. — *Chesterfield.*

A MAN who owes a little can clear it off in a very little time, and, if he is a prudent man, he will: whereas a man, who, by long negligence, owes a great deal, despairs of ever being able to pay, and therefore never looks into his accounts at all.

Debt. — *Franklin.*

THINK—think what you do when you run in debt; you give to another power over your liberty. If you cannot pay at the time, you will be ashamed to see your creditor; you will be in fear when you speak to him; you will make poor, pitiful, sneaking excuses, and by degrees come to lose your veracity, and sink into base, downright lying; for the second vice is lying, the first is running in debt, as Poor Richard says; and again, to the same purpose, Lying rides upon Debt's back; whereas a freeborn Englishman ought not to be ashamed nor afraid to see or speak to any man living. But poverty often deprives a man of all spirit and virtue. It is hard for an empty bag to stand upright.

Debt. — *Franklin.*

WHAT would you think of that prince, or of that government, who should issue an edict forbidding you to dress like a gentleman or gentlewoman, on pain of imprisonment or servitude? Would you not say that you were free, have a right to dress as you please, and that such an edict would be a breach of your privileges, and such a government tyrannical? And yet you are about to put yourself under such tyranny, when you run in debt for such dress! Your creditor has authority, at his pleasure, to deprive you of your liberty, by confining you in jail till you shall be able to pay him. When you have got your bargain, you may, perhaps, think little of payment, but as Poor Richard says, Creditors have better memories than debtors; creditors are a superstitious sect, great observers of set days and times. The day comes round before you are aware, and the demand is made before you are prepared to satisfy it; or, if you bear your debt in mind, the term, which at first seemed so long, will, as it lessens, appear extremely short. Time will seem to have added wings to his heels as well as his shoulders. Those have a short Lent who owe money to be paid at Easter.

Debts. — *Fuller.*

LOSE not thy own for want of asking for it; 'twill get thee no thanks.

Deceit. — *Shakspeare.*

LOOK to her, Moor; have a quick eye to see:
She has deceived her Father, and may thee.

Defence. — *Shakspeare.*

IN causes of Defence, 'tis best to weigh
The enemy more mighty than he seems;
So the proportions of Defence are fill'd;
Which of a weak and niggardly projection
Doth, like a miser, spoil his coat with scanting
A little cloth.

Deference. — *Shenstone.*

DEFERENCE is the most complicate, the most indirect, and the most elegant of all Compliments.

Deference. — *Shenstone.*

DEFERENCE often shrinks and withers as much upon the approach of Intimacy, as the sensitive plant does upon the touch of one's finger.

The Deity. — *Milton.*

AND thou, O Spirit, that dost prefer,
Before all temples, the upright heart and pure,
Instruct me, for thou know'st.

The Deity.—*Prior.*

REPINE not, nor reply:
View not what Heaven ordains with Reason's eye,
Too bright the object is; the distance is too high.
The man, who would resolve the work of Fate,
May limit number, and make crooked straight:
Stop thy inquiry then, and curb thy sense,
Nor let dust argue with Omnipotence.

The Deity.—*Prior.*

FROM Nature's constant or eccentric laws,
The thoughtful soul this general inference draws,
That an Effect must presuppose a Cause:
And, while she does her upward flight sustain,
Touching each link of the continued chain,
At length she is obliged and forced to see
A First, a Source, a Life, a Deity;
What has for ever been, and must for ever be.

The Deity.—*Thomson.*

AND yet was every faltering tongue of man,
Almighty Father! silent in thy praise!
Thy works themselves would raise a general voice,
Even in the depth of solitary woods
By human foot untrod, proclaim thy power,
And to the quire celestial Thee resound,
The eternal Cause, Support, and End of all!

The Deity.—*Thomson.*

HAIL, Source of Being! Universal Soul
Of Heaven and Earth! Essential Presence, hail!
To Thee I bend the knee; to Thee my thoughts
Continual climb; who, with a Master hand,
Hast the great whole into perfection touch'd.

The Deity.—*Thomson.*

WITH what an awful world-revolving power
Were first the unwieldy planets launch'd along
The illimitable void! Thus to remain,
Amid the flux of many thousand years,
That oft has swept the toiling race of men
And all their labour'd monuments away,
Firm, unremitting, matchless in their course;
To the kind-temper'd change of Night and Day,
And of the Seasons ever stealing round,
Minutely faithful: Such the all-perfect Hand!
That poised, impels, and rules the steady whole.

The Deity. — *Cowper.*

IN the vast, and the minute, we see
The unambiguous footsteps of the God,
Who gives its lustre to an insect's wing,
And wheels his throne upon the rolling worlds.

Delay. — *Shakspeare.*

O THAT comfort comes too late;
'Tis like a pardon after execution:
That gentle physic, given in time, had cured me;
But now I am past all comfort here, but prayers.

Delicacy. — *Greville.*

WEAK men often, from the very principle of their weakness, derive a certain Susceptibility, Delicacy, and Taste, which render them, in those particulars, much superior to men of stronger and more consistent minds, who laugh at them.

Delicacy. — *Novalis.*

SHAME is a feeling of profanation. Friendship, Love, and Piety ought to be handled with a sort of mysterious secrecy; they ought to be spoken of only in the rare moments of perfect confidence—to be mutually understood in silence. Many things are too delicate to be thought; many more, to be spoken.

The Deluge. — *Byron.*

THE Heavens and Earth are mingling—God! O God!
What have we done? yet spare!
Hark! even the forest beasts howl forth their pray'r!
The dragon crawls from out his den,
To herd in terror innocent with men;
And the birds scream their agony through air.

Delusion. — *La Rochefoucauld.*

WHEN our vices quit us, we flatter ourselves with the belief that it is we who quit them.

Delusion. — *Colton.*

WE strive as hard to hide our hearts from ourselves as from others, and always with more success; for in deciding upon our own case, we are both judge, jury, and executioner; and where Sophistry cannot overcome the first, or Flattery the second, Self-love is always ready to defeat the sentence by bribing the third; a bribe that in this case is never refused, because she always comes up to the price.

Delusion. — *Sir Philip Sidney.*

IT many times falls out, that we deem ourselves much deceived in others, because we first deceived ourselves.

Delusion. — *Shakspeare.*

O, WHO can hold a fire in his hand,
By thinking on the frosty Caucasus?
Or cloy the hungry edge of appetite,
By bare Imagination of a feast?
Or wallow naked in December snow,
By thinking on fantastic Summer's heat?
O no! the apprehension of the good
Gives but the greater feeling to the worse:
Fell Sorrow's tooth doth never rankle more,
Than when it bites, but lanceth not the sore.

Delusion. — *Shakspeare.*

THIS is the excellent Foppery of the World! that, when we are sick in fortune, (often the surfeit of our own behaviour,) we make guilty of our disasters, the sun, the moon, and the stars: as if we were villains by necessity; fools, by heavenly compulsion; knaves, thieves, and treachers, by spherical predominance; drunkards, liars, and adulterers, by an enforced obedience of planetary influence; and all that we are evil in by a divine thrusting on.

Delusion. — *Shakspeare.*

DANGEROUS Conceits are, in their natures, poisons,
Which, at the first, are scarce found to distaste;
But with a little act upon the blood,
Burn like the mines of sulphur.

Delusion. — *Shakspeare.*

O THOUGHTS of men accurst!
Past, and to come, seem best; things present, worst.

Delusion. — *Froude.*

HOW oft that Virtue, which some Women boast,
And pride themselves in, is but an Empty Name,
No real good: in thought alone possess'd.
Safe in the want of charms, the homely Dame,
Secure from the seducing arts of man,
Deceives herself, and thinks she's passing chaste;
Wonders how others e'er could fall, yet when
She talks most loud about the noisy nothing,
Look on her Face, and there you read her Virtue.

Delusion. — *Shakspeare.*

FOR love of Grace,
Lay not that flattering unction to your soul;
It will but skin and film the ulcerous place;
Whiles rank Corruption, mining all within,
Infects unseen.

The Demagogue. — *Sir A. Hunt.*

I DO despise these Demagogues, that fret
The angry Multitude: they are but as
The froth upon the mountain-wave—the bird
That shrieks upon the sullen tempest's wing.

Democracy. — *Fisher Ames.*

INTELLECTUAL superiority is so far from conciliating confidence, that it is the very spirit of a democracy, as in France, to proscribe the aristocracy of talents. To be the favourite of an ignorant multitude, a man must descend to their level; he must desire what they desire, and detest all they do not approve: he must yield to their prejudices, and substitute them for principles. Instead of enlightening their errors, he must adopt them; he must furnish the sophistry that will propagate and defend them.

American Democracy. — *Jefferson.*

EQUAL and exact justice to all men, of whatever state or persuasion, religious or political; peace, commerce, and honest friendship with all nations, entangling alliances with none; the support of the state governments in all their rights, as the most competent administrations for our domestic concerns, and the surest bulwarks against anti-republican tendencies; the preservation of the general government in its whole constitutional vigour, as the sheet-anchor of our peace at home, and safety abroad; a jealous care of the right of election by the people; a mild and safe corrective of abuses, which are lopped by the sword of revolution where peaceable remedies are unprovided; absolute acquiescence in the decisions of the majority, the vital principle of republics, from which there is no appeal but to force, the vital principle and immediate parent of despotism; a well disciplined militia, our best reliance in peace, and for the first moments of war, till regulars may relieve them; the supremacy of the civil over the military authority; economy in the public expense, that labour may be lightly burdened; the honest payment of our debts, and sacred preservation of the public faith; encouragement of agriculture, and of commerce, as its handmaid; the diffusion of information, and arraignment of all abuses at the bar of the public reason; freedom of religion; freedom of the press; and freedom of person, under the protection of the *habeas corpus*; and trial by juries impartially selected.

Deputy. — *Shakspeare.*

A SUBSTITUTE shines brightly as a King,
Until a King be by; and then his state
Empties itself, as doth an inland brook
Into the main of waters.

Desire. — *Shakspeare.*

All impediments in Fancy's course
Are motives of more Fancy.

Desolation. — *Byron.*

My mother Earth!
And thou, fresh breaking Day, and you, ye Mountains,
Why are ye beautiful? I cannot love ye.
And thou, the bright eye of the Universe,
That openest over all, and unto all
Art a delight—thou shin'st not on my heart.

Desolation. — *Maturin.*

The fountain of my heart dried up within me;
With naught that loved me, and with naught to love,
I stood upon the desert earth alone.
And in that deep and utter Agony,
Though then than ever most unfit to die,
I fell upon my knees, and pray'd for Death.

Desolation. — *Thomson.*

Unhappy he! who from the first of joys
Society, cut off, is left alone
Amid this world of Death. Day after day,
Sad on the jutting eminence he sits,
And views the main that ever toils below;
Still fondly forming in the farthest verge,
Where the round ether mixes with the wave,
Ships, dim-discover'd, dropping from the clouds;
At evening, to the setting sun he turns
A mournful eye, and down his dying heart
Sinks helpless.

Despair. — *Milton.*

All Hope is lost
Of my reception into grace; what worse?
For where no Hope is left, is left no Fear.

Despair. — *Joanna Baillie.*

Be it what it may, or bliss, or torment,
Annihilation, dark and endless rest,
Or some dread thing, man's wildest range of thought
Hath never yet conceived, that change I'll dare
Which makes me any thing but what I am.

Despair. — *Thomson.*

'Tis late before
The brave Despair.

Despair. — *Milton.*

Me miserable! which way shall I fly
Infinite wrath, and infinite Despair?
Which way I fly is Hell; myself am Hell?
And in the lowest deep a lower deep
Still threat'ning to devour me opens wide,
To which the Hell I suffer seems a Heaven.

Despair. — *Shakspeare.*

I am one,
Whom the vile blows and buffets of the world
Have so incensed, that I am reckless what
I do to spite the world.
And I another,
So weary with disasters, tugg'd with Fortune,
That I would set my life on any chance,
To mend it or be rid on't.
So cowards fight, when they can fly no farther;
So doves do peck the falcon's piercing talons;
So desperate thieves, all hopeless of their lives,
Breathe out invectives 'gainst the officers.

Despair. — *Beattie.*

Dreadful is their doom, whom doubt has driven
To censure Fate, and pious Hope forego:
Like yonder blasted boughs by lightning riven,
Perfection, Beauty, Life, they never know,
But frown on all that pass, a Monument of Wo.

Despair. — *Collier.*

Despair makes a despicable figure, and descends from a mean original. 'Tis the offspring of Fear, of Laziness, and Impatience; it argues a defect of spirit and resolution, and oftentimes of honesty too. I would not despair, unless I saw misfortune recorded in the Book of Fate, and signed and sealed by necessity.

Despair. — *Greville.*

Despair gives the shocking ease to the Mind, that a mortifi cation gives to the Body.

The Despised. — *La Rochefoucauld.*

It is only those who are despicable who fear being despised.

Spiritual Despotism.—*Milton.*

THEN shall they seek to avail themselves of names,
Places, and titles, and with these to join
Secular pow'r, though feigning still to act
By spiritual, to themselves appropriating
The Spirit of God, promised alike and given
To all believers; and from that pretence,
Spiritual Laws by Carnal Power shall force
On every conscience; laws which none shall find
Left them enroll'd, or what the spirit within
Shall on the heart engrave.

Spiritual Despotism.—*Milton.*

WOLVES shall succeed for teachers, grievous wolves,
Who all the sacred mysteries of Heaven
To their own vile advantages shall turn
Of lucre and ambition, and the Truth
With superstitions and traditions taint.

Destiny.—*Robert Hall.*

THE wheels of Nature are not made to roll backward: every thing presses on toward Eternity: from the birth of Time an impetuous current has set in, which bears all the sons of men towards that interminable ocean. Meanwhile Heaven is attracting to itself whatever is congenial to its nature, is enriching itself by the spoils of Earth, and collecting within its capacious bosom whatever is pure, permanent, and divine.

Destiny.—*Colton.*

OUR minds are as different as our faces; we are all travelling to one Destination—Happiness; but few are going by the same road.

Destiny.—*Cumberland.*

I DO not mean to expose my ideas to ingenious ridicule by maintaining that every thing happens to every man for the best; but I will contend, that he who makes the best use of it, fulfils the part of a wise and good man.

Diet.—*Franklin.*

IN general, mankind, since the improvement of cookery, eat about twice as much as nature requires.

Diet.—*Sir W. Temple.*

ALL courageous animals are carnivorous, and greater courage is to be expected in a people, such as the English, whose Food is strong and hearty, than in the half-starved commonalty of other countries.

Diet. — *Burton.*

FOOD improperly taken, not only produces original diseases, but affords those that are already engendered both matter and sustenance; so that, let the father of disease be what it may, Intemperance is certainly its mother.

Diet. — *Pliny.*

SIMPLE Diet is best;—for many Dishes bring many diseases; and rich Sauces are worse than even heaping several Meats upon each other.

Diet. — *Horace.*

THE chief pleasure (in Eating) does not consist in costly Seasoning, or exquisite Flavour, but in yourself. Do you seek for Sauce by sweating.

Diet. — *Shakspeare.*

THE veins unfill'd, our blood is cold, and then
We pout upon the morning, are unapt
To give or to forgive; but when we have stuff'd
These pipes, and these conveyances of our blood,
With Wine and Feeding, we have suppler souls
Than in our priest-like fasts.

Diligence. — *Franklin.*

WHAT though you have found no treasure, nor has any rich relation left you a legacy. Diligence is the mother of good luck, and God gives all things to industry. Then plough deep while sluggards sleep, and you shall have corn to sell and to keep. Work while it is called to-day, for you know not how much you may be hindered to-morrow. One to-day is worth two to-morrows, as Poor Richard says; and further, never leave that till to-morrow which you can do to-day.

Dining. — *Johnson.*

BEFORE Dinner, men meet with great inequality of understanding; and those who are conscious of their inferiority have the modesty not to talk: when they have drunk Wine, every man feels himself happy, and loses that modesty, and grows impudent and vociferous; but he is not improved; he is only not sensible of his defects.

Discernment. — *Greville.*

DISCERNMENT is a power of the understanding in which few excel. Is not that owing to its connection with Impartiality and Truth? for are not Prejudice and Partiality blind?

Discipline. — *Seneca.*

NO evil propensity of the human heart is so powerful that it may not be subdued by Discipline.

Discipline. — *Anon.*

DISCIPLINE, like the bridle in the hand of a good rider, should exercise its influence without appearing to do so; should be ever active, both as a support and as a restraint, yet seem to lie easily in hand. It must always be ready to check or to pull up, as occasion may require; and only when the horse is a runaway, should the action of the curb be perceptible.

Discipline. — *Shakspeare.*

Now, as fond fathers,
Having bound up the threat'ning twigs of birch,
Only to stick it in their children's sight,
For terror, not to use; in time the rod
Becomes more mock'd than fear'd: so our decrees,
Dead to infliction, to themselves are dead;
And Liberty plucks Justice by the nose;
The baby beats the nurse, and quite athwart
Goes all Decorum.

Discipline. — *Shakspeare.*

HAD doting Priam check'd his son's desire,
Troy had been bright with fame, and not with fire.

Discontent. — *Bishop Hall.*

THE Malecontent is neither well, full nor fasting; and though he abound with complaints, yet nothing dislikes him but the present; for what he condemns while it was, once passed, he magnifies and strives to recall it out of the jaws of time. What he hath he seeth not, his eyes are so taken up with what he wants; and what he sees he careth not for, because he cares so much for that which is not.

Discord. — *Peter Pindar.*

DISCORD, a sleepless hag, who never dies,
With snipe-like nose, and ferret-glowing eyes;
Lean, sallow cheeks, long chin, with beard supplied,
Poor crackling joints, and wither'd parchment hide,
As if old drums, worn out with martial din,
Had clubb'd their yellow heads to form her skin.

Discord. — *Shakspeare.*

THIS late Dissension, grown betwixt the peers,
Burns under feign'd ashes of forged love,
And will at last break out into a flame,
As fester'd members rot but by degrees,
Till bones, and flesh, and sinews, fall away,
So will this base and envious Discord breed.

Discordance. — *Shakspeare.*

How sour sweet Music is,
When Time is broke, and no Proportion kept!
So is it in the Music of Men's Lives.

Discovery. — *Colton.*

IT has been asked, which are the greatest minds, and to which do we owe the greatest reverence? To those who by the powerful deductions of their Reason, and the well-grounded suggestions of Analogy, have made profound discoveries in the sciences, as it were *à priori;* or to those, who, by the patient road of Experiment, and the subsequent improvement of instruments, have brought these discoveries to perfection, as it were *à posteriori?* Who have rendered that certain which before was only conjectural, practical which was problematical, safe which was dangerous, and subservient which was unmanageable? It would seem that the first class demand our admiration, and the second our gratitude. Seneca predicted another hemisphere, but Columbus presented us with it.

Discoveries. — *Colton.*

IT is a mortifying truth, and ought to teach the wisest of us humility, that many of the most valuable Discoveries have been the result of chance, rather than of contemplation, and of accident rather than of design.

Discretion. — *Sir Walter Raleigh.*

JEST not openly at those that are simple, but remember how much thou art bound to God, who hath made thee wiser. Defame not any woman publicly, though thou know her to be evil; for those that are faulty cannot endure to be taxed, but will seek to be avenged of thee; and those that are not guilty, cannot endure unjust reproach. As there is nothing more shameful and dishonest than to do wrong, so truth itself cutteth his throat that carrieth her publicly in every place. Remember the divine saying, *he that keepeth his mouth, keepeth his life.*

Discretion. — *Hume.*

THE greatest parts without Discretion may be fatal to their owner; as Polyphemus, deprived of his eye, was only the more exposed on account of his enormous strength and stature.

Discretion. — *Zimmerman.*

OPEN your mouth and purse cautiously; and your stock of wealth and reputation shall, at least in repute, be great.

Discretion. — *Colton.*

IF a cause be good, the most violent attack of its enemies will not injure it so much as an injudicious defence of it by its friends. Theodoret and others, who gravely defend the monkish miracles, and the luminous cross of Constantine, by their zeal without knowledge, and devotion without Discretion, have hurt the cause of Christianity more by such friendship than the apostate Julian by his hostility, notwithstanding all the wit and vigour with which it was conducted.

Discretion. —*Addison.*

THERE are many more shining qualities in the mind of man, but there is none so useful as Discretion; it is this indeed which gives a value to all the rest, which sets them at work in their proper times and places, and turns them to the advantage of the person who is possessed of them. Without it, Learning is Pedantry and Wit Impertinence; Virtue itself looks like Weakness; the best parts only qualify a man to be more sprightly in errors, and active to his own prejudice.

Discussion.—*Bishop Watson.*

WHOSOEVER is afraid of submitting any Question, civil or religious, to the test of free Discussion, is more in love with his own opinion than with Truth.

Diseases. — *Shakspeare.*

DISEASES, desperate grown,
By desperate appliances are relieved,
Or not at all.

Disinterestedness. — *Anon.*

MEN of the world hold that it is impossible to do a Disinterested Action, except from an Interested Motive; for the sake of admiration, if for no grosser, more tangible gain. Doubtless they are also convinced, that, when the sun is showering light from the sky, he is only standing there to be stared at.

Disputation. — *Socrates.*

IF thou continuest to take delight in idle Argumentation, thou mayst be qualified to combat with the Sophists, but wilt never know how to live with men.

Family Dissension. — *From the Latin.*

FROM what stranger can you expect attachment, if you are at variance with your own Relations?

Dissimulation. — *La Bruyere.*

DISSIMULATION, even the most innocent in its nature, is ever productive of embarrassment; whether the design is evil or not, artifice is always dangerous and almost inevitably disgraceful. The best and the most safe policy is, never to have recourse to Deception, to avail yourself of Quirks, or to practise low Cunning, and to prove yourself in every circumstance of your life equally upright and sincere. This system is naturally that which noble minds will adopt, and the dictates of an enlightened and superior understanding would be sufficient to insure its adoption.

Dissimulation. — *Lord Bacon.*

DISSIMULATION is but a faint kind of policy or wisdom; for it asketh a strong wit and a strong heart to know when to tell truth, and to do it: therefore it is the weaker sort of politicians that are the greatest Dissemblers.

Docility. — *Manlius.*

A Docile Disposition will, with application, surmount every difficulty.

Dogmatism. — *Hume.*

WHERE men are the most sure and arrogant, they are commonly the most mistaken, and have there given reins to passion, without that proper deliberation and suspense, which can alone secure them from the grossest absurdities.

Drams. — *Cowper.*

TEN thousand Casks,
For ever dribbling out their base contents,
Touch'd by the Midas finger of the state,
Bleed gold for Ministers to sport away.
Drink and be mad then. 'Tis your Country bids.
Gloriously drunk, obey th' important call,
Her cause demands th' assistance of your Throats:
Ye all can swallow, and she asks no more.

Dreaming. — *Novalis.*

WE are near waking, when we dream that we dream.

Dreams. — *Shakspeare.*

IF I may trust the flattering truth of Sleep,
My dreams presage some joyful news at hand:
My bosom's lord sits lightly on his throne,
And, all this day, an unaccustom'd spirit
Lifts me above the ground with cheerful thoughts.
I dreamt, my lady came and found me dead,
(Strange Dream! that gives a dead man leave to think,)
And breath'd such life with kisses in my lips,
That I revived, and was an emperor.
Ah me! how sweet is love itself possest,
When but love's shadows are so rich in joy?

Dreams. — *Colton.*

METAPHYSICIANS have been learning their lesson for the last four thousand years, and it is high time that they should now begin to teach us something. Can any of the tribe inform us why all the operations of the mind are carried on with undiminished strength and activity in Dreams, except the Judgment, which alone is suspended, and dormant. This faculty of the mind is in a state of total inefficiency during Dreams. Let any man carefully examine his own experience on this subject, and he will find that the most glaring incongruities of time, the most palpable contradictions of place, and the grossest absurdities of circumstance, are most glibly swallowed down by the Dreamer, without the slightest dissent or demurrage of the Judgment. The moment we are wide awake the Judgment reassumes her functions, and shocks us with surprise at a credulity that even in sleep could reconcile such a tissue of inconsistencies.

Dreams. — *Shakspeare.*

THY spirit within thee hath been so at war,
And thus hath so bestirr'd thee in thy Sleep
That beads of sweat have stood upon thy brow,
Like bubbles in a late-disturbed stream;
And in thy face strange motions have appear'd,
Such as we see when men restrain their breath
On some great sudden haste.

Dreams.—*Dryden.*

DREAMS are but interludes which Fancy makes.
When monarch Reason sleeps, this mimic wakes:
Compounds a medly of disjointed things,
A mob of cobblers, and a court of kings:
Light fumes are merry, grosser fumes are sad
Both are the reasonable soul run mad:
And many monstrous forms in Sleep we see,
That neither were, nor are, nor e'er can be.
Sometimes forgotten things, long cast behind,
Rush forward in the brain, and come to mind.

Dress. — *Shakspeare.*

WHAT, is the Jay more precious than the Lark
Because his feathers are more beautiful?
Or is the Adder better than the Eel,
Because his painted skin contents the eye?
Oh no, good Kate; neither art thou the worse
For this poor Furniture, and mean Array.

Dreams. — *Shakspeare.*

DREAMS are the children of an idle brain,
Begot of nothing but vain Fantasy;
Which is as thin of substance as the air;
And more inconstant than the wind.

Dress. — *Sir Jonah Barrington.*

DRESS has a moral effect upon the conduct of mankind. Let any gentleman find himself with dirty Boots, old Surtout, soiled Neckcloth, and a general negligence of Dress, he will, in all probability, find a corresponding disposition by negligence of *address.*

Dress. — *Cowper.*

WE sacrifice to Dress, till household joys
And comforts cease. Dress drains our cellar dry,
And keeps our larder lean. Puts out our fires,
And introduces Hunger, Frost, and Wo,
Where Peace and Hospitality might reign.

Dress. — *Goldsmith.*

PROCESSIONS, Cavalcades, and all that fund of gay Frippery, furnished out by tailors, barbers, and tire-women, mechanically influence the mind into veneration: an emperor in his night-cap would not meet with half the respect of an emperor with a crown.

Drowning. — *Shakspeare.*

O LORD! methought what pain it was to drown!
What dreadful noise of Water in my ears!
What sights of ugly death within mine eyes!
Methought I saw a thousand fearful wrecks,
A thousand men, that fishes gnaw'd upon.

Drudgery. — *Longfellow.*

THE every-day cares and duties, which men call drudgery, are the weights and counterpoises of the clock of time, giving its pendulum a true vibration, and its hands a regular motion; and when they cease to hang upon the wheels, the pendulum no longer swings, the hands no longer move, the clock stands still.

Drunkenness. — *Shenstone.*

PEOPLE say, "Do not regard what he says, now he is in liquor." Perhaps it is the only time he ought to be regarded: *Aperit præcordia liber.*

Drunkenness. — *Colton.*

DRUNKENNESS is the vice of a good Constitution, or of a bad Memory; of a Constitution so treacherously good, that it never bends until it breaks; or of a Memory that recollects the pleasures of getting drunk, or forgets the pains of getting sober.

Drunkenness. — *Shakspeare.*

O THOU invisible spirit of Wine, if thou hast no name to be known by, let us call thee—Devil! * * * O, that men should put an enemy to their mouths, to steal away their brains! that we should, with joy, revel, pleasure, and applause, transform ourselves into beasts!

Drunkenness. — *Sir Walter Raleigh.*

IT were better for a man to be subject to any vice, than to Drunkenness: for all other vanities and sins are recovered, but a Drunkard will never shake off the delight of Beastliness; for the longer it possesseth a man, the more he will delight in it, and the elder he groweth the more he shall be subject to it; for it dulleth the spirits, and destroyeth the body as ivy doth the old tree; or as the worm that engendereth in the kernel of the nut.

Drunkenness. — *Shakspeare.*

WHAT'S a Drunken Man like? Like a drown'd man, a fool, and a madman: one draught above heat makes him a fool; the second mads him; and a third drowns him.

Dull Men. — *Bishop Earle.*

GREAT brains (like brightest glass) crack straight, while those
Of stone or wood hold out, and fear no blows;
And we their ancient hoary heads can see
Whose Wit was never their Mortality.

Dull Men. — *Saville.*

A DULL Man is so near a dead man, that he is hardly to be ranked in the list of the living; and as he is not to be buried whilst he is half alive, so he is as little to be employed whilst he is half dead.

Duping. — *Bulwer Lytton.*

THE surest way of making a Dupe is to let your Victim suppose that you are his.

Duplicity. — *Shakspeare.*

O WHAT may man within him hide,
Though angel on the outward side!
How many Likeness, made in crimes,
Making practice on the times,
Draw with idle spiders' strings
Most pond'rous and substantial things!

Social Duties. — *Kant.*

BOTH Love of Mankind, and Respect for their Rights, are Duties; the former, however, are only a conditional, the latter an unconditional, purely imperative Duty, which he must be perfectly certain not to have transgressed, who would give himself up to the secret emotions arising from Beneficence.

Duty. — *Anon.*

DUTY is above all consequences, and often, at a crisis of difficulty, commands us to throw them overboard. *Fiat Justitia, pereat mundus.* It commands us to look neither to the right, nor to the left, but straight onward. Hence every signal act of Duty is altogether an act of Faith. It is performed in the assurance that God will take care of the consequences, and will so order the course of the world, that, whatever the immediate results may be, His word shall not return to Him empty.

Early Rising. — *Thomson.*

Is there aught in Sleep can charm the wise
To lie in dead oblivion, losing half
The fleeting moments of too short a life;
Total extinction of the enlighten'd soul!
Or else to feverish vanity alive,
Wilder'd, and tossing thro' distemper'd Dreams?
Who would in such a gloomy state remain
Longer than nature craves; when ev'ry muse
And every blooming pleasure wait without,
To bless the wildly devious Morning walk?

Early Rising. — *Colton.*

OLD men, it would seem, were to be found among those who had travelled, and those who had never been out of their own parish. Excess could produce her veterans, no less than Temperance, since some had kept off the grim tyrant by libations of wine, as successfully as others by potations of water; and some by copious applications of brandy and of gin seem to have kept off their summons to the Land of Spirits. In short it appeared that many who agreed in scarcely any thing else, agreed in having attained longevity. But there were only two questions, in which they all agreed, and these two questions, when put, were always answered in the affirmative by the oldest of those Greenwich and Chelsea pensioners to whom they were proposed. The questions were these: Were you descended from parents of good stamina? and have you been in the habit of Early Rising? Early Rising, therefore, not only gives to us more life in the same number of our years, but adds likewise to their number; and not only enables us to enjoy more of existence in the same measure of time, but increases also the measure.

Early Rising.—*Colton.*

NO man can promise himself even fifty years of life, but any man may, if he please, live in the proportion of fifty years in forty;—let him rise early, that he may have the day before him, and let him make the most of the day, by determining to expend it on two sorts of acquaintance only,—those by whom something may be got, and those from whom something may be learnt.

Earnestness.—*Anon.*

THE reason why Delivery is of such force, is that, unless a man appears by his outward Look and Gesture to be himself animated by the truths he is uttering, he will not animate his hearers. It is the live coal that kindles others, not the dead. Nay, the same principle applies to all oratory; and what made Demosthenes the greatest of orators, was that he appeared the most entirely possest by the feelings he wished to inspire. The main use of his ὑπόκρισις was, that it enabled him to remove the natural hinderances which checked and clogged the stream of those feelings, and to pour them forth with a free and mighty torrent that swept his audience along. The effect produced by Charles Fox, who by the exaggeration of party-spirit was often compared to Demosthenes, seems to have arisen wholly from this earnestness, which made up for the want of almost every grace, both of manner and style.

Earthquake.—*Shakspeare.*

DISEASED Nature oftentimes breaks forth
In strange eruptions; and the teeming Earth
Is with a kind of cholic pinch'd and vext,
By the imprisoning of unruly wind
Within her womb; which, for enlargement striving,
Shakes the old beldam Earth, and topples down
Steeples, and moss-grown towers.

Earthy.—*Shakspeare.*

'TIS but a base ignoble Mind,
That mounts no higher than a Bird can soar.

Easy Temper—*Greville.*

IT is an unhappy, and yet I fear a true reflection, that they who have uncommon Easiness and Softness of Temper, have seldom very noble and nice sensations of soul.

Economy.—*Hawkesworth.*

ECONOMY is the parent of Integrity, of Liberty, and of Ease; and the beauteous sister of Temperance, of Cheerfulness, and Health: and Profuseness is a cruel and crafty demon, that gradually involves her followers in dependence and debts; that is, fetters them with "irons that enter into their souls."

Education. — *Colton.*

IT is adverse to talent, to be consorted and trained up with inferior minds, or inferior companions, *however high they may rank.* The foal of the racer neither finds out his speed, nor calls out his powers, if pastured out with the common herd, that are destined for the collar and the yoke.

Education. — *Horace.*

UNLESS your cask is perfectly clean, whatever you pour into it turns sour.

Education. — *Greville.*

THE more perfect the nature, the more weak, the more wrong, the more absurd, may be the something in a character: to explain the paradox, if a mind is delicate and susceptible, false impressions in Education will have a bad effect in proportion to that susceptibility, and consequently may produce an evil which a stupid and insensible nature might have avoided.

Education. — *Shakspeare.*

Now 'tis the spring, and weeds are shallow rooted;
Suffer them now, and they'll o'ergrow the garden,
And choke the herbs for want of husbandry.

Education. — *Webster.*

KNOWLEDGE does not comprise all which is contained in the large term of *education.* The feelings are to be disciplined, the passions are to be restrained; true and worthy motives are to be inspired; a profound religious feeling is to be instilled, and pure morality inculcated under all circumstances. All this is comprised in education.

Popular Education. — *Washington.*

PROMOTE, as an object of primary importance, institutions for the general diffusion of knowledge. In proportion as the structure of a government gives force to public opinion, it should be enlightened.

Egotism. — *Lavater.*

THE more any one speaks of himself, the less he likes to hear another talked of.

Egotism. — *La Rochefoucauld.*

HE who thinks he can find in himself the means of doing without others is much mistaken; but he who thinks that others cannot do without him is still more mistaken.

Eloquence. — *Dryden.*

YOUR Words are like the notes of dying swans,
Too sweet to last!

Eloquence. — *Byron.*

SINCERE he was—at least you could not doubt it,
In listening merely to his Voice's Tone.
The Devil hath not in all his quiver's choice,
An arrow for the heart like a Sweet Voice.

Eloquence. — *Milton.*

His Tongue
Dropt manna, and could make the worse appear
The better reason, to perplex and dash
Maturest counsels

Eloquence. — *Havard.*

O ELOQUENCE! thou violated fair,
How art thou woo'd, and won to either bed
Of Right or Wrong! Oh! when Injustice folds thee,
Dost thou not curse thy charms for pleasing him,
And blush at conquest?

Eloquence. — *Rowe.*

Oh! I know
Thou hast a tongue to charm the wildest tempers;
Herds would forget to graze, and savage beasts
Stand still, and lose their fierceness, but to hear thee,
As if they had reflection: and by reason,
Forsook a less enjoyment for a greater.

Eloquence. — *Dryden.*

When he spoke, what tender Words he used!
So softly, that like flakes of feather'd snow,
They melted as they fell.

Eloquence. — *Colton.*

EXTEMPORANEOUS and oral harangues will always have this advantage over those that are read from a manuscript; every burst of Eloquence or spark of genius they may contain, however studied they may have been beforehand, will appear to the audience to be the effect of the sudden inspiration of talent. Whereas similar efforts, when written, although they may not cost the writer half the time in his closet, will never be appreciated as any thing more than the slow efforts of long study and laborious application; *olebunt oleum, esti non oleant!* and this circumstance it is that gives such peculiar success to a pointed reply, since the hearers are certain that in this case all study is out of the question, that the Eloquence arises *ex re nata*, and that the brilliancy has been elicited from the collision of another mind, as rapidly as the spark from the steel.

Eloquence. — *La Rochefoucauld.*

THERE is as much Eloquence in the Tone of Voice, in the eyes, and in the air of a Speaker, as in his choice of Words.

Eloquence. — *La Rochefoucauld.*

TRUE eloquence consists in saying all that is necessary, and nothing but what is necessary.

Eloquence. — *Hare.*

MANY are ambitious of saying grand things, that is, of being grandiloquent. Eloquence is speaking out . . . a quality few esteem, and fewer aim at.

Eloquence. — *Sterne.*

GREAT is the power of Eloquence; but never is it so great as when it pleads along with nature, and the culprit is a child strayed from his duty, and returned to it again with tears.

Eloquence. — *Webster.*

TRUE eloquence, indeed, does not consist in speech. It cannot be brought from far. Labour and learning may toil for it, but they will toil in vain. Words and phrases may be marshalled in every way, but they cannot compass it. It must exist in the man, in the subject, and in the occasion. Affected passion, intense expression, the pomp of declamation, all may aspire after it—they cannot reach it. It comes, if it come at all, like the outbreaking of a fountain from the earth, or the bursting forth of volcanic fires with spontaneous, original, native force. The graces taught in the schools, the costly ornaments and studied contrivances of speech, shock and disgust men, when their own lives, and the fate of their wives, their children, and their country hang on the decision of the hour. Then, words have lost their power, rhetoric is vain, and all elaborate oratory contemptible. Even genius itself then feels rebuked and subdued, as in the presence of higher qualities. Then, patriotism is eloquent; then, self-devotion is eloquent. The clear conception outrunning the deduction of logic, the high purpose, the firm resolve, the dauntless spirit, speaking on the tongue, beaming from the eye, informing every feature, and urging the whole man onward, right onward to his object—this, this is eloquence; or rather it is something greater and higher than all eloquence—it is action, noble, sublime, godlike action.

Eminence. — *Addison.*

IT is a folly for an Eminent Man to think of escaping censure, and a weakness to be affected with it. All the illustrious persons of Antiquity, and indeed of every age in the world, have passed through this fiery persecution.

Employment. — *Young.*

LIFE'S cares are comforts; such by Heaven design'd;
He that has none, must make them, or be wretched.
Cares are Employments; and without Employ
The soul is on a rack; the rack of rest,
To souls most adverse; Action all their joy.

Employment. — *Burton.*

EMPLOYMENT, which Galen calls "nature's physician," is so essential to human happiness, that Indolence is justly considered as the mother of Misery.

Employment. — *La Bruyere.*

LAZINESS begat wearisomeness, and this put men in quest of diversions, play and company, on which however it is a constant attendant; he who works hard, has enough to do with himself otherwise.

Energy. — *Shakspeare.*

OUR remedies oft in ourselves do lie,
Which we ascribe to Heaven: the fated sky
Gives us free scope; only, doth backward pull
Our slow designs, when we ourselves are dull.

Energy. — *Rowe.*

THE wise and active conquer difficulties,
By daring to attempt them: sloth and folly
Shiver and shrink at sight of toil and hazard,
And make the impossibility they fear.

England. — *Shakspeare.*

Is not their climate foggy, raw and dull?
On whom, as in despite, the sun looks pale,
Killing their fruit with frowns?

Enjoyment. — *St. Evremond.*

IMPERFECT Enjoyment is attended with regret; a surfeit of pleasure with disgust. There is a certain nick of time, a certain medium to be observed, with which few people are acquainted.

Enjoyment. — *Horace.*

BUSY yourself not in looking forward to the events of to-morrow; but whatever may be those of the days Providence may yet assign you, neglect not to turn them to advantage.

Enthusiasm. — *S. T. Coleridge.*

ENLIST the interests of stern Morality and religious Enthusiasm in the cause of Political Liberty, as in the time of the old Puritans, and it will be irresistible.

Enthusiasm. — *Kant.*

ENTHUSIASM is always connected with the Senses, whatever be the object that excites it. The true strength of Virtue is *serenity of mind*, combined with a deliberate and steadfast Determination to execute her laws. That is the healthful condition of the Moral Life; on the other hand, Enthusiasm, even when excited by representations of goodness, is a brilliant but feverish glow, which leaves only exhaustion and languor behind.

Enthusiasm. — *Colton.*

THE Romans laid down their liberties at the feet of Nero, who would not even lend them to Cæsar; and we have lately seen the whole French Nation rush as one man from the very extremes of Loyalty, to behead the mildest Monarch that ever ruled them, and conclude a sanguinary career of plunder, by pardoning and rewarding a Tyrant, to whom their blood was but water, and their groans but wind; thus they sacrificed one that died a martyr to his clemency, and they rewarded another, who lived to boast of his murders.

Enthusiasm. — *Fitzosborne.*

I LOOK upon Enthusiasm, in all other points but that of Religion, to be a very necessary turn of mind; as indeed it is a vein which nature seems to have marked with more or less strength, in the tempers of most men. No matter what the object is, whether Business, Pleasures, or the Fine Arts; whoever pursues them to any purpose, must do so *con amore.*

Enthusiasm. — *Shakspeare.*

I HAVE seen
The dumb men throng to see him, and the blind
To hear him speak: The matrons flung their gloves,
Ladies and maids their scarfs and handkerchiefs,
Upon him as he pass'd: the nobles bended,
As to Jove's statue; and the commons made
A shower and thunder, with their caps and shouts;
I never saw the like.

Ennui. — *Byron.*

FOR *Ennui* is a growth of English-root,
Though nameless in our language:—we retort
The fact for words, and let the French translate
That awful Yawn which Sleep cannot abate.

Envy. — *Ovid.*

ENVY feeds upon the living; after death it ceases; then every man's well-earned Honours defend him against Calumny.

Envy. — *Spenser.*

AND if she hapt of any good to heare,
That had to any happily betid,
Then would she inly fret, and grieve, and teare
Her flesh for felnesse, which she inward hid:
But if she heard of ill that any did,
Or harme that any had, then would she make
Great cheare, like one unto a banquet bid;
And in another's losse great pleasure take,
As she had got thereby, and gayned a great stake.

Envy. — *Pope.*

THERE is some good in Public Envy, whereas in Private there is none; for Public Envy is as an ostracism that eclipseth men when they grow too great; and therefore it is a bridle also to great ones to keep within bounds.

Envy. — *Shenstone.*

THERE is nothing more universally commended than a fine day; the reason is, that people can commend it without Envy.

Envy. — *Spenser.*

HER hands were foule and durtie, never washt
In all her life, with long nayles over raught,
Like puttock's clawes, with th' one of which she scratcht
Her cursed head, although it itched naught;
The other held a snake with venime fraught,
On which she fed and gnawed hungrily,
As if that long she had not eaten aught;
That round about her jawes one might descry
The bloudie gore and poyson dropping loathsomely.

Envy. — *Lord Clarendon.*

IF Envy, like Anger, did not burn itself in its own fire, and consume and destroy those persons it possesses, before it can destroy those it wishes worst to, it would set the whole world on fire, and leave the most excellent persons the most miserable.

Envy. — *Colton.*

THE benevolent have the advantage of the Envious, even in this present life; for the Envious is tormented not only by all the ill that befalls himself, but by all the good that happens to another; whereas the benevolent man is the better prepared to bear his own calamities unruffled, from the complacency and serenity he has secured, from contemplating the prosperity of all around him.

Envy. — *Colton.*

THE Hate which we all bear with the most Christian Patience, is the Hate of those who Envy us.

Envy. — *S. T. Coleridge.*

GENIUS may co-exist with Wildness, Idleness, Folly, even with Crime; but not long, believe me, with Selfishness and the indulgence of an Envious Disposition. Envy is κάκιστος καὶ δικαιότατος ϑεός, as I once saw it expressed somewhere in a page of Stobæus: it dwarfs and withers its worshippers.

Envy. — *La Rochefoucauld.*

THE truest mark of being born with great qualities is being born without Envy.

Envy. — *Clarendon.*

ENVY is a Weed that grows in all soils and climates, and is no less luxuriant in the Country than in the Court; is not confined to any rank of men or extent of fortune, but rages in the breasts of all degrees. Alexander was not prouder than Diogenes; and it may be, if we would endeavour to surprise it in its most gaudy dress and attire, and in the exercise of its full empire and tyranny, we should find it in Schoolmasters and Scholars, or in some Country Lady, or the Knight her Husband; all which ranks of people more despise their neighbours, than all the degrees of honour in which courts abound: and it rages as much in a sordid affected dress, as in all the silks and embroideries which the excess of the age and the folly of youth delight to be adorned with. Since then, it keeps all sorts of Company, and wriggles itself into the liking of the most contrary natures and dispositions, and yet carries so much poison and venom with it, that it alienates the affections from Heaven, and raises rebellion against God himself, it is worth our utmost care to watch it in all its disguises and approaches, that we may discover it in its first entrance, and dislodge it before it procures a shelter or retiring place to lodge and conceal itself.

Envy. — *Colton.*

ENVY ought, in strict truth, to have no place whatever allowed it in the heart of man; for the goods of this present world are so vile and low, that they are beneath it; and those of the future world are so vast and exalted, that they are above it.

Envy. — *Colton.*

TO diminish Envy, let us consider not what others possess, but what they enjoy: mere Riches may be the gift of lucky accident or blind chance, but Happiness must be the result of prudent preference and rational design; the highest Happiness then can have no other foundation than the deepest Wisdom; and the happiest fool is only as happy as he knows how to be.

Envy. — *Colton.*

EMULATION looks out for merits, that she may exalt herself by a victory; Envy spies out blemishes, that she may lower another by a defeat.

Envy. — *Spenser.*

AND next to him malicious Envy rode
Upon a ravenous wolfe, and still did chaw
Between his cankred teeth a venemous tode,
That all the poison ran about his jaw;
But inwardly he chawed his owne maw
At neighbour's welth that made him ever sad;
For death it was when any good he saw;
And wept, that cause of weeping none he had;
And when he heard of harme he wexed wondrous glad.

Equality. — *Langstaff.*

EQUALITY is one of the most consummate scoundrels that ever crept from the brain of a political juggler—a fellow who thrusts his hand into the pocket of honest Industry or enterprising Talent, and squanders their hard-earned profits on profligate Idleness or indolent Stupidity.

Equality. — *Shakspeare.*

TAKE but Degree away, untune that string,
And, hark, what discord follows! each thing meets
In mere oppugnancy: The bounded waters
Should lift their bosoms higher than the shores,
And make a sop of all this solid globe:
Strength should be lord of Imbecility,
And the rude son should strike his father dead:
Force should be Right.

Equality. — *Shakspeare.*

ARE we not Brothers?
So man and man should be;
But clay and clay differs in dignity,
Whose dust is both alike.

Equality. — *Shakspeare.*

THE King is but a Man, as I am: the violet smells to him as it doth to me; the element shows to him as it doth to me; all his senses have but human conditions: his ceremonies laid by, in his nakedness he appears but a Man; and though his affections are higher mounted than ours, yet, when they stoop, they stoop with the like wing.

Equality. — *From the Latin.*

IF all men were on an Equality, the consequence would be that all must perish; for who would till the ground? who would sow it? who would plant? who would press wine?

Equality. — *Johnson.*

SO far is it from being true that men are naturally equal, that no two people can be half an hour together but one shall acquire an evident Superiority over the other.

Equivocation. — *Shakspeare.*

But yet,—
I do not like but yet, it does allay
The good precedence; fye upon but yet:
But yet is as a gaoler to bring forth
Some monstrous malefactor.

Error. — *Shakspeare.*

O HATEFUL Error, Melancholy's child!
Why dost thou show to the apt thoughts of men
The things that are not? O Error, soon conceived,
Thou never com'st unto a happy birth,
But kill'st the mother that engender'd thee.

Esteem. — *From the French.*

MANY people are Esteemed merely because they are not known.

Eternity. — *Addison.*

ETERNITY, thou pleasing dreadful Thought!
Thro' what variety of untried beings,
Thro' what new scenes and changes must we pass?
The wide, the unbounded Prospect lies before me;
But shadows, clouds, and darkness rest upon it.

Eternity. — *Dowe.*

ETERNITY, thou awful Gulph of Time,
This wide creation on thy surface floats.
Of life—of death—what is, or what shall be,
I nothing know. The world is all a dream,
The consciousness of something that exists,
Yet is not what it seems. Then what am I?
Death must unfold the mystery!

Eternity. — *Colton.*

HE that will often put Eternity and the World before him, and who will dare to look steadfastly at both of them, will find that the more often he contemplates them, the former will grow greater and the latter less.

Eternity. — *Colton.*

ALAS! what is Man? whether he be deprived of that light which is from on high, or whether he discard it; a frail and trembling creature, standing on Time, that bleak and narrow isthmus between two Eternities, he sees nothing but impenetrable Darkness on the one hand, and Doubt, Distrust, and Conjecture still more perplexing on the other. Most gladly would he take an observation, as to whence he has come, or whither he is going. Alas, he has not the means; his telescope is too dim, his compass too wavering, his plummet too short. Nor is that little spot, his present state, one whit more intelligible, since it may prove a quicksand that may sink in a moment from his feet; it can afford him no certain reckoning, as to that immeasurable ocean that he may have traversed, or that still more formidable one that he must.

Eternity. — *Burnet.*

WHAT is this Life but a circulation of little mean actions? We lie down and rise again, dress and undress, feed and wax hungry, work or play, and are weary, and then we lie down again, and the circle returns. We spend the day in trifles, and when the night comes we throw ourselves into the bed of folly, among dreams, and broken thoughts, and wild imaginations. Our reason lies asleep by us, and we are for the time as arrant brutes as those that sleep in the stalls, or in the field. Are not the capacities of man higher than these? And ought not his ambition and expectations to be greater? Let us be adventurers for another world. It is at least a fair and noble chance; and there is nothing in this worth our thoughts or our passions. If we should be disappointed, we are still no worse than the rest of our fellow-mortals; and if we succeed in our expectations, we are eternally happy.

Etiquette. — *Shakspeare.*

UNBIDDEN Guests
Are often welcomest when they are gone.

Evasion. — *Lavater.*

EVASIONS are the common shelter of the hard-hearted, the false, and impotent, when called upon to assist; the real great alone plan instantaneous help, even when their looks or words presage difficulties.

Evening. — *Byron.*

IT is the Hour when from the boughs
The Nightingale's high note is heard;
It is the Hour when lover's vows
Seem sweet in every whisper'd word;
And gentle winds, and waters near,
Make music to the lonely ear.

Evening. — *Byron.*

AVE-MARIA! blessed be the Hour!
The time, the clime, the spot, where I so oft
Have felt that moment in its fullest power
Sink o'er the earth so beautiful and soft,
While swung the deep bell in the distant tower,
Or the faint dying day-hymn stole aloft,
And not a breath crept through the rosy air,
And yet the forest leaves seem'd stirr'd with prayer.
Soft Hour! which wakes the wish and melts the heart
Of those who sail the seas, on the first day
When they from their sweet friends are torn apart;
Or fills with love the pilgrim on his way
As the far bell of Vesper makes him start,
Seeming to weep the dying day's decay;
Is this a fancy which our reason scorns?
Ah! surely nothing dies but something mourns!

Evening. — *Montgomery.*

I LOVE thee, Twilight! for thy gleams impart
Their dear, their dying influence to my heart,
When o'er the harp of thought thy passing wind
Awakens all the music of the mind,
And joy and sorrow, as the spirit burns,
And hope and memory sweep the chords by turns.

Evening Dews. — *Chesterfield.*

THE Dews of the Evening most carefully shun;
Those tears of the sky for the loss of the sun.

Evil. — *Colton.*

I ADMIT the existence of Evil to its full extent, and I also admit my own Ignorance, which is not the least part of the Evil I deplore. I also find in the midst of all this Evil, a tolerably fair proportion of Good. I can discover that I did not make myself, and also that the Being that did make me, has shown a degree of power and of wisdom far beyond my powers of comprehension. I can also see so much Good proceeding from his system even here, that I am inclined to love him; but I can see so much Evil, that I am inclined also to fear him. I find myself a compound being, made up of Body and Mind, and the union is so intimate, that the one appears to perish at the dissolution of the other. In attempting to reconcile this last Evil, Death, and the many more that lead to it, with the wisdom, power, and goodness that I see displayed on many other occasions, I find that I have strong aspirings after a state that *may* survive this apparent dissolution, and I find that I have this feeling in common with all the rest of my species; I find also, on looking within, that I have a mind capable of much higher delight than matter or earth can afford. On looking still more closely into myself, I find every reason to believe that this is the first state of existence I ever enjoyed; I can recollect no other, I am conscious of no other. Here then I stand as upon a point acknowledged, that this world is the first stage of existence to that compound animal Man, and that it is to him at least the first link in that order of things in which Mind is united to Matter.

Evil. — *Horace.*

Better one thorn pluck'd out than all remain.

Evil. — *Chalmers.*

By the very constitution of our nature, Moral Evil is its own curse.

Evil. — *South.*

He who will fight the Devil at his own weapon, must not wonder if he finds him an overmatch.

Evil. — *Anon.*

As there is a law of continuity, whereby in ascending we can only mount step by step, so is there a law of continuity, whereby they who descend must sink, and that too with an ever increasing velocity. No propagation or multiplication is more rapid than that of Evil, unless it be checked; no growth more certain. He who is in for a Penny, to take another expression belonging to the same family, if he does not resolutely fly, will find he is in for a Pound.

Evil. — *Horace.*

Fire, for a short time neglected, acquires irresistible force.

Evil. — *Menander.*

All animals are more happy than Man. Look, for instance, on yonder ass: all allow him to be miserable: his Evils, however, are not brought on by himself and his own fault; he feels only those which Nature has inflicted. We, on the contrary, besides our necessary Ills, draw upon ourselves a multitude of others. We are melancholy if any person happen to sneeze; we are angry if any speak reproachfully of us; one man is affrighted with an unlucky dream, another at the hooting of an owl. Our Contentions, our Anxieties, our Opinions, our Ambition, our Laws, are all Evils, which we ourselves have superadded to Nature.

Evil. — *Shakspeare.*

Ill deeds are doubled with an evil word.

Evil. — *Colton.*

There is this of good in real Evils,—they deliver us, while they last, from the petty despotism of all that were imaginary.

Evil. — *Colton.*

EVILS in the journey of life are like the hills which alarm travellers upon their road; they both appear great at a distance, but when we approach them we find that they are far less insurmountable than we had conceived.

Evil. — *La Rochefoucauld.*

THERE are no circumstances, however unfortunate, that clever people do not extract some advantage from.

Example. — *Proctor.*

I KNOW not how it is;
But a foreboding presses on my heart,
At times, until I sicken.—I have heard,
And from men learned, that before the touch
(The common, coarser touch) of Good, or Ill,—
That oftentimes a subtler sense informs
Some spirits of the approach of "things to be."

Example. — *Cicero.*

BE a Pattern to others, and then all will go well; for as a whole city is infected by the licentious passions and vices of great men, so it is likewise reformed by their moderation.

Example. — *Juvenal.*

EXAMPLES of vicious courses, practised in a domestic circle, corrupt more readily and more deeply, when we behold them in persons in authority.

Example. — *Goldsmith.*

PEOPLE seldom improve, when they have no other Model but themselves to copy after.

Excelling. — *Colton.*

IF you want Enemies, excel others; if you want Friends, let others excel you.

Excelling. —*La Bruyere.*

HE who excels in his art so as to carry it to the utmost height of perfection of which it is capable, may be said in some measure to go beyond it; his transcendent productions admit of no appellations.

Excess. — *Horace.*

THE Body oppressed by Excesses, bears down the Mind, and depresses to the earth any portion of the divine Spirit we had been endowed with.

Excess. — *Tacitus.*

VITELLIUS possessed all that Pliability and Liberality, which, when not restrained within due Bounds, must ever turn to the ruin of their possessor.

Excess. — *Shakspeare.*

VIOLENT fires soon burn out themselves.
Small showers last long, but sudden storms are short;
He tires betimes, that spurs too fast betimes;
With eager feeding, food doth choke the feeder;
Light Vanity, insatiate Cormorant,
Consuming means, soon preys upon itself.

Excess. — *Knox.*

THE misfortune is, that when man has found honey, he enters upon the feast with an appetite so voracious, that he usuallv destroys his own delight by Excess and Satiety.

Excess. — *Shakspeare.*

EVERY Inordinate Cup is unblessed, and the ingredient is a devil.

Excess. — *Colton.*

THE Excesses of our youth are drafts upon our old age, payable with interest, about thirty years after date.

Excitement. — *Goldsmith.*

BUT me, not destined such delights to share,
My prime of life in wandering spent and care:
Impell'd, with steps unceasing, to pursue
Some fleeting good, that mocks me with the view;
That, like the circle bounding earth and skies,
Allures from far, yet, as I follow, flies;
My fortune leads to traverse realms alone,
And find no spot of all the world my own.

Mental Excitement. — *Montaigne.*

THE beasts show us plainly how much our diseases are owing to the Perturbations of our Minds. We are told that the inhabitants of Brazil die merely of old age, owing to the serenity and tranquillity of the air in which they live; but I ascribe it rather to the Serenity and Tranquillity of their Souls, which are free from all Passion, Thought, or laborious and unpleasant Employment. As great enmities spring from great friendships, and mortal distempers from vigorous health, so do the most surprising and the wildest phrensies from the high and lively Agitations of our Souls.

Exercise. — *Cowper.*

THE Sedentary stretch their lazy length
When custom bids, but no refreshment find,—
For none they need: the languid eye, the cheek
Deserted of its bloom, the flaccid, shrunk,
And wither'd muscle, and the vapid soul,
Reproach their owner with that Love of Rest
To which he forfeits e'en the Rest he loves.

Expectation. — *Shakspeare.*

How slow,
This old moon wanes: she lingers my desires,
Like to a stêp-dame, or a dowager,
Long withering out a young man's revenue.

Expectation. — *Mrs. Tighe.*

OH! how Impatience gains upon the soul
When the long-promised hour of joy draws near!
How slow the tardy moments seem to roll!
What spectres rise of inconsistent fear!
To the fond doubting heart its hopes appear
Too brightly fair, too sweet to realize:
All seem but day-dreams of delight too dear!
Strange hopes and fears in painful contest rise,
While the scarce-trusted bliss seems but to cheat the eyes.

Expectation. — *Shakspeare.*

OFT Expectation fails, and most oft there
Where most it promises: and oft it hits
Where Hope is coldest, and Despair most sits.

Expectations. — *Martial.*

YOU give me nothing during your life, but you promise to provide for me at your death. If you are not a fool, you know what I wish for.

Expectation. — *Shakspeare.*

So tedious is this day,
As is the night before some festival
To an impatient child, that hath new robes,
And may not wear them.

Expense. — *Franklin.*

WHAT maintains one vice would bring up two children. You may think, perhaps, that a little tea, or a little punch now and then, diet a little more costly, clothes a little finer, and a little entertainment now and then, can be no great matter; but remember, Many a little makes a mickle. Beware of little expenses. A small leak will sink a great ship, as Poor Richard says; and again, Who dainties love, shall beggars prove; and moreover, Fools make feasts, and wise men eat them.

Experience. — *Sir P. Sidney.*

All is but lip-wisdom which wants Experience.

Experience. — *Shakspeare.*

He cannot be a perfect man,
Not being tried, and tutor'd in the world:
Experience is by Industry achieved,
And perfected by the swift course of Time.

Experience. — *Shakspeare.*

Our own precedent passions do instruct us
What levity's in youth.

Experience. — *Terence.*

No man was ever endowed with a judgment so correct and judicious, in regulating his life, but that Circumstances, Time, and Experience, would teach him something new, and apprize him that of those things with which he thought himself the best acquainted, he knew nothing; and that those ideas, which in theory appeared the most advantageous, were found, when brought into practice, to be altogether inapplicable.

Experience. — *Coleridge.*

To most men Experience is like the stern-lights of a ship, which illumine only the track it has passed.

Experience. — *Shakspeare.*

To wilful men,
The injuries that they themselves procure,
Must be their schoolmasters.

Experience. — *Green.*

Experience join'd with Common Sense,
To mortals is a Providence.

Experience. — *Byron.*

Adversity is the first path to Truth.
He who hath proved war, storm, or woman's rage,
Whether his winters be eighteen or eighty,
Hath won the Experience which is deem'd so weighty.

Externals. — *Johnson.*

In civilized society, External Advantages make us more respected. A man with a good coat upon his back meets with a better reception than he who has a bad one. You may analyze this and say, what is there in it? But that will avail you nothing, for it is a part of a general system. Pound St. Paul's church into atoms, and consider any single atom; it is, to be sure, good for nothing: but put all these atoms together, and you have St. Paul's church. So it is with human felicity, which is made up of many ingredients, each of which may be shown to be very insignificant.

Extravagance. — *Pope.*

FOR what has Virro painted, built, and planted?
Only to show how many tastes he wanted.
What brought Sir Visto's ill-got wealth to waste?
Some demon whisper'd, Visto has a taste!

Extravagance. — *Young.*

THE man who builds, and wants wherewith to pay,
Provides a home from which to run away.

The Eye. — *Addison.*

A BEAUTIFUL Eye makes Silence eloquent, a kind Eye makes Contradiction an assent, an enraged Eye makes Beauty deformed. This little Member gives life to every other part about us; and I believe the story of Argus implies no more, than that the Eye is in every part; that is to say, every other part would be mutilated were not its force represented more by the Eye than even by itself.

The Eye. — *Moore.*

THOSE Eyes, whose light seem'd rather given
To be adored than to adore—
Such Eyes, as may have look'd from Heaven,
But ne'er were raised to it before!

Faith. — *Anon.*

ENTIRENESS, illimitableness is indispensable to Faith. What we believe, we must believe wholly and without reserve; wherefore the only perfect and satisfying object of Faith is God. A Faith that sets bounds to itself, that will believe so much and no more, that will trust thus far and no farther, is none.

Faith. — *Anon.*

THE power of Faith will often shine forth the most, where the character is naturally weak. There is less to intercept and interfere with its workings.

Faith. — *Addison.*

THE natural homage which such a creature as Man bears to an infinitely wise and good God, is a firm Reliance on him for the blessings and conveniences of life, and an habitual Trust in him for deliverance out of all such dangers and difficulties as may befall us. The man who always lives in this disposition of mind, when he reflects upon his own weakness and imperfection, comforts himself with the contemplation of those Divine attributes which are employed for his safety and welfare. He finds his want of foresight made up by the omniscience of him who is his support. He is now sensible of his own want of strength when he knows that his Helper is Almighty. In short, the person who has a firm Trust on the Supreme Being, is powerful in his power, wise by his wisdom, happy by his happiness.

Loss of Faith. — *Shakspeare.*

PRAY can I not,
Though inclination be as sharp as will;
My stronger guilt defeats my strong intent;
And, like a man to double business bound,
I stand in pause where I shall first begin,
And both neglect.

Faith and Works. — *Colton.*

WE should act with as much energy, as those who expect every thing from themselves; and we should pray with as much earnestness as those who expect every thing from God.

Friends Falling off. — *Shakspeare.*

THEY answer, in a joint and corporate voice,
That now they are at Fall, want treasure, cannot
Do what they would; are sorry—you are honourable,—
But yet they could have wish'd—they know not—but
Something hath been amiss'd—a noble nature
May catch a wrench—would all were well—'tis pity—
And so, intending other serious matters,
After distasteful looks, and these hard fractions,
With certain half-caps, and cold-moving nods,
They froze me into silence.

Falsehood. — *Colton.*

FALSEHOOD is never so successful as when she baits her hook with Truth, and that no opinions so fatally mislead us, as those that are not wholly wrong, as no watches so effectually deceive the wearer, as those that are sometimes right.

False Security. — *Shakspeare.*

WE hear this fearful tempest sing,
Yet seek no shelter to avoid the storm;
We see the wind sit sore upon our sails,
And yet we strike not, but securely perish.

Fame. — *Mallet.*

I COURTED Fame but as a spur to brave
And honest deeds; and who despises Fame,
Will soon renounce the virtues that deserve it.

Fame. — *Colton.*

OF present Fame think little and of future less; the Praises that we receive after we are buried, like the posies that are strewed over our grave, may be gratifying to the living, but they are nothing to the dead; the dead are gone, either to a place where they hear them not, or where, if they do, they will despise them.

Fame. — *Sterne.*

THE way to Fame is like the way to Heaven—through much Tribulation.

Fame. — *Shakspeare.*

GLORY grows guilty of detested crimes;
When, for Fame's sake, for Praise, an outward part,
We bend to that the working of the heart.

Fame. — *Shakspeare.*

IF a man do not erect in this age his own tomb ere he dies, he shall live no longer in monument than the bell rings, and the widow weeps.

Fame. — *Shakspeare.*

DEATH makes no conquest of this conqueror;
For now he lives in Fame, though not in life.

Fame. — *Shakspeare.*

THE Evil, that men do, lives after them;
The Good is oft interred with their bones.

Fame. — *Byron.*

THY fanes, thy temple, to the surface bow,
Commingling slowly with heroic earth,
Broke by the share of every rustic plough:
So perish Monuments of mortal Birth,
To perish all in turn, save well-recorded Worth.

Fame. — *Byron.*

WHAT of them is left, to tell
Where they lie, and how they fell?
Not a stone on their turf, nor a bone in their graves;
But they live in the Verse that immortally saves.

Fame. — *Moore.*

WHO, that surveys this span of earth we press,
This speck of life in time's great wilderness,
This narrow isthmus 'twixt two boundless seas,
The past, the future, two eternities!—
Would sully the bright spot or leave it bare,
When he might build him a proud Temple there,
A Name, that long shall hallow all its space,
And be each purer soul's high resting-place!

Fame. — *Shakspeare.*

MEN'S Evil Manners live in brass: their Virtues
We write in water.

Fame. — *Shenstone.*

AH me! full sorely is my heart forlorn
To think how modest Worth neglected lies,
While partial Fame doth with her blasts adorn
Such deeds alone, as Pride and Pomp disguise,
Deeds of ill sort, and mischievous emprise.

Fame. — *Byron.*

'TIS as a snowball which derives assistance
From every flake, and yet rolls on the same,
Even till an iceberg it may chance to grow;
But after all 'tis nothing but cold snow.

Fame. — *Young.*

OF boasting more than of a bomb afraid,
A soldier should be modest as a maid:
Fame is a bubble the reserved enjoy;
Who strive to grasp it, as they touch, destroy;
'Tis the world's debt to deeds of high degree;
But if you pay yourself, the world is free.

Fame. — *Young.*

FAME is a public mistress, none enjoys,
But, more or less, his rival's peace destroys.

Fame. — *Pope.*

WHAT'S Fame? a fancied life in others' breath,
A thing beyond us, even before our death.
Just what you hear, you have; and what's unknown,
The same, my lord, if Tully's, or your own.
All that we feel of it begins and ends
In the small circle of our foes or friends;
To all beside as much an empty shade
An Eugene living, as a Cæsar dead.

Fame. — *Milton.*

FAME is the spur that the clear sp'rit doth raise
(That last infirmity of noble mind)
To scorn delights, and live laborious days;
But the fair guerdon when we hope to find,
And think to burst out into sudden blaze,
Comes the blind Fury with th' abhorr'd shears,
And slits the thin-spun life.

Literary Fame. — *Voltaire.*

THE path to Literary Fame is more difficult than that which leads to Fortune. If you are so unfortunate as not to soar above mediocrity, remorse is your portion; if you succeed in your object, a host of enemies spring up around you: thus you find yourself on the brink of an abyss between Contempt and Hatred.

Worldly Fame. — *John Quincy Adams.*

FAME, that common crier, whose existence is only known by the assemblage of multitudes; that pander of wealth and greatness, so eager to haunt the palaces of fortune, and so fastidious to the houseless dignity of virtue; that parasite of pride, ever scornful to meekness, and ever obsequious to insolent power; that heedless trumpeter, whose ears are deaf to modest merit, and whose eyes are blind to bloodless, distant excellence.

Fancy. — *Shakspeare.*

ALL impediments in Fancy's course
Are motives of more Fancy.

Farewell and Welcome. — *Shakspeare.*

TIME is like a fashionable host,
That slightly shakes his parting guest by the hand;
And with his arms out-stretch'd, as he would fly,
Grasps in the comer; Welcome ever smiles,
And Farewell goes out sighing.

Followers of Fashion. — *Musæ Anglic.*

AN empty, thoughtless tribe.

Fashion. — *Greville.*

WE laugh heartily to see a whole flock of sheep jump because one did so: might not one imagine that superior beings do the same by us, and for exactly the same reason.

Fashion. — *Byron.*

IN the Great World—which being interpreted
Meaneth the West end of a city,
And about twice two thousand people bred
By no means to be very wise or witty,
But to sit up while others lie in bed,
And look down on the Universe with pity.

Fashion. — *Byron.*

THE Company is "mixed," (the phrase I quote is
As much as saying, they're below your notice.)

Fashion. — *Churchill.*

FASHION, a word which knaves and fools may use
Their knavery and folly to excuse.

Fashion. — *Shakspeare.*

WHERE doth the World thrust forth a Vanity,
(So it be knew, there's no respect how vile,)
That is not quickly buzz'd into the ears?

Fate. — *Horace.*

WITH equal foot, rich friend, impartial Fate,
Knocks at the cottage and the palace gate:
Life's span forbids thee to extend thy cares,
And stretch thy hopes, beyond thy destined years:
Night soon will seize, and you must quickly go
To storied ghosts, and Pluto's house below.

Faults. — *Shakspeare.*

IF little Faults, proceeding on Distemper,
Shall not be wink'd at, how shall we stretch our eye,
When Capital Crimes, chew'd, swallow'd, and digested,
Appear before us?

Favour. — *La Bruyere.*

FAVOUR exalts a man above his equals, but his dismissal from that Favour places him below them.

Favours. — *Publius Syrus.*

IT is conferring a kindness, to deny at once a Favour which you intend to refuse.

Fate of Favourites. — *Shakspeare.*

GREAT Princes' Favourites their fair leaves spread,
But as the marigold, at the sun's eye;
And in themselves their pride lies buried,
For at a frown they in their glory die.
The painful warrior famoused for fight,
After a thousand victories once foil'd,
Is from the Book of Honour razed quite,
And all the rest forgot for which he toil'd.

Fear. — *Shaftesbury.*

THE passion of Fear (as a modern philosopher informs me) determines the spirits to the muscles of the knees, which are instantly ready to perform their motion, by taking up the legs with incomparable celerity, in order to remove the body out of harm's way.

Fear. — *Montaigne.*

THE thing in the world I am most afraid of is Fear; and with good reason, that Passion alone, in the trouble of it, exceeding all other accidents.

Fear. — *Shakspeare.*

I FIND the people strangely fantasied;
Possess'd with Rumours, full of idle Dreams;
Not knowing what they fear, but full of Fear.

Fear. — *Shakspeare.*

But that I am forbid
To tell the secrets of my prison-house,
I could a tale unfold, whose lightest word
Would harrow up thy soul; freeze thy young blood;
Make thy two eyes, like stars, start from their spheres;
Thy knotted and combined locks to part,
And each particular hair to stand on end,
Like quills upon the fretful porcupine.

Fear. — *Shakspeare.*

THIS man's brow, like to a title-leaf,
Foretells the nature of a tragic volume:
So looks the strond, whereon the imperious flood
Hath left a witness'd usurpation.
Thou tremblest; and the Whiteness in thy Cheek
Is apter than thy tongue to tell thy errand.
Even such a man, so faint, so spiritless,
So dull, so dead in look, so wo-begone,
Drew Priam's curtain in the dead of night,
And would have told him, half his Troy was burn'd.

Ghostly Fear. — *Shakspeare.*

What man dare, I dare:
Approach thou like the rugged Russian bear,
The arm'd Rhinoceros, or the Hyrcan tiger,
Take any shape but that, and my firm nerves
Shall never tremble: or, be alive again,
And dare me to the desert with thy sword;
If trembling I inhibit thee, protest me
The baby of a girl. Hence, horrible shadow!
Unreal Mockery, hence!

Unmanly Fear. — *Milton.*

Be not over exquisite
To cast the fashion of uncertain evils:
For grant they be so, while they rest unknown,
What need a man forestall his date of grief,
And run to meet what he would most avoid?

Feasting. — *Peter Pindar.*

The turnpike road to people's hearts, I find,
Lies through their Mouths, or I mistake mankind

Feasting. — *Clarendon.*

IT is not the quantity of the Meat, but the cheerfulness of the guests, which makes the Feast; at the Feast of the Centaurs, they ate with one hand, and had their drawn swords in the other; where there is no peace, there can be no Feast.

Feasting. — *Peter Pindar.*

VEN'SON'S a Cæsar in the fiercest fray;
Turtle! an Alexander in its way:
And then, in quarrels of a slighter nature,
Mutton's a most successful mediator!
So much superior is the stomach's smart
To all the vaunted horrors of the heart.
E'en Love, who often triumphs in his grief,
Hath ceased to feed on sighs, to pant on beef.

Feasting. — *Peter Pindar.*

I OWN that nothing like Good Cheer succeeds—
A man's a God whose hogshead freely bleeds:
Champagne can consecrate the damned'st evil;
A hungry Parasite adores a Devil.

Feasting. — *Byron.*

BUT 'twas a public Feast, and public day—
Quite full, right dull, guests hot, and Dishes cold,
Great plenty, much formality, small Cheer,
And everybody out of their own sphere.

Feasting. — *Byron.*

Of all appeals,—although
I grant the power of pathos, and of gold,
Of beauty, flattery, threats, a shilling,—no
Method's more sure at moments to take hold
Of the best feelings of mankind, which grow
More tender, as we every day behold,
Than that all-softening, overpow'ring knell,
The tocsin of the soul—the Dinner Bell.

Feeling. — *Richter.*

THE last, best fruit which comes to late perfection, even in the kindliest soul, is, Tenderness toward the hard, Forbearance toward the unforbearing, Warmth of Heart toward the cold, Philanthropy toward the misanthropic.

Feeling. — *Sterne.*

A WORD—a Look, which at one time would make no impression —at another time wounds the Heart; and like a shaft flying with the wind, pierces deep, which, with its own natural force, would scarce have reached the object aimed at.

Feeling. — *Colton.*

IT is far more easy not to feel, than always to feel rightly, and not to act, than always to act well. For he that is determined to admire only that which is beautiful, imposes a much harder task upon himself, than he that being determined not to see that which is the contrary, effects it by simply shutting his eyes.

Feeling. — *Shakspeare.*

O HERO! what a Hero had'st thou been,
If half thy outward graces had been placed
About thy thoughts, and counsels of thy Heart.

Feeling. — *La Rochefoucauld.*

WHEN the Heart is still agitated by the remains of a Passion, we are more ready to receive a new one than when we are entirely cured.

Feeling. — *Byron.*

I WISH'D but for a single Tear,
As something welcome, new, and dear;
I wish'd it then, I wish it still,
Despair is stronger than my will.

Feeling. — *Byron.*

IN a gushing stream
The Tears rush'd forth from her unclouded Brain
Like mountain mists, at length dissolved in rain.

Feeling. — *Shakspeare.*

WHY does my Blood thus muster to my Heart,
Making both that unable for itself,
And dispossessing all my other parts
Of necessary fitness?
So play the foolish throngs with one that swoons;
Come all to help him, and so stop the air
By which he should revive.

Feeling. — *Shakspeare.*

How sometimes Nature will betray its Folly,
Its Tenderness, and make itself a pastime
To harder bosoms!

Feeling and Reason. — *Ziegler.*

THE Heart of Man is older than his Head. The first-born is sensitive, but blind—his younger brother has a cold, but all-comprehensive glance. The blind must consent to be led by the clear-sighted, if he would avoid falling.

Want of Feeling. — *Juvenal.*

WHO can all sense of others' ills escape,
Is but a brute, at best, in human shape.

Feeling and Reason. — *Anon.*

SOME people carry their Hearts in their Heads; very many carry their Heads in their Hearts. The difficulty is to keep them apart, and yet both actively working together.

Fickleness. — *Shakspeare.*

WOULD I, being but a moonish youth, grieve, be effeminate, changeable, longing, and liking; proud, fantastical, apish, shallow, inconstant, full of tears, full of smiles; for every passion something, and for no passion truly any thing, as boys and women are for the most part cattle of this colour; would now like him, now loath him; then entertain him, then forswear him; now weep for him, then spit at him.

Fidelity. — *Shakspeare.*

He that can endure
To follow with Allegiance a fallen lord,
Does conquer him that did his master conquer,
And earns a place i' the story.

Fidelity. — *Shakspeare.*

I'll yet follow
The wounded chance of Antony, though my reason
Sits in the wind against me.

Fidelity. — *Shakspeare.*

But now 'tis odds beyond arithmetic;
And Manhood is called Foolery, when it stands
Against a falling fabric.

Fidelity. — *Shakspeare.*

HIS Words are bonds, his Oaths are Oracles;
His Love sincere, his Thoughts immaculate;
His Tears, pure messengers sent from his Heart;
His Heart as far from Fraud as heaven from earth.

Fidelity. — *Shakspeare.*

THOUGH all the world should crack their Duty
And throw it from their soul; though perils did
Abound, as thick as thought could make them, and
Appear in forms more horrid; yet my duty,
As doth a rock against the chiding flood,
Should the approach of the wild river break,
And stand unshaken yours

Fidelity. — *Shakspeare.*

I am constant as the Northern Star,
Of whose true-fix'd, and resting Quality,
There is no fellow in the firmament.

Fidelity. — *Shakspeare.*

I DURST, my lord, to wager she is honest,
Lay down my soul at stake: if you think other,
Remove your thought; it doth abuse your bosom.
If any wretch hath put this in your head,
Let Heaven requite it with the serpent's curse!
For, if she be not honest, chaste, and true,
There's no man happy: the purest of their wives
Is foul as slander.

Fidelity. — *Shakspeare.*

O HEAVEN! were Man
But constant, he were perfect: that one Error
Fills him with faults.

Fidelity. —*Shakspeare.*

HE which hath no stomach to this fight,
Let him depart, his passport shall be made,
And crowns for convoy put into his purse:
We would not die in that man's company,
That fears his fellowship to die with us.
I speak not this, as doubting any here:
For, did I but suspect a fearful man,
He should have leave to go away betimes;
Lest, in our need, he might infect another,
And make him of like spirit to himself.
If any such be here, as God forbid!
Let him depart, before we need his help.

Fidelity. — *Shakspeare.*

IF to preserve this vessel for my lord,
From any other foul unlawful touch,
Be—not to be a strumpet, I am none.
False to his bed! What is it to be false?
To lie in watch there, and to think on him?
To weep 'twixt clock and clock? if sleep charge nature,
To break it with a fearful dream of him,
And cry myself awake? that's false to his bed,
Is it?
Unkindness may do much;
And his unkindness may defeat my life,
But never taint my love.

Fidelity. — *Moore.*

COME rest in this bosom, my own stricken deer!
Tho' the herd hath fled from thee, thy home is still here;
Here still is the smile that no cloud can o'ercast,
And the Heart and the Hand all thy own to the Last!

Fidelity.—*Shakspeare.*

CHAIN me with roaring bears;
Or shut me nightly in a charnel-house,
O'er-cover'd quite with dead men's rattling bones,
With reeky shanks, and yellow chapless skulls;
Or bid me go into a new-made grave,
And hide me with a dead man in his shroud;
Things that, to hear them told, have made me tremble;
And I will do it without Fear or Doubt,
To live an unstain'd Wife of my sweet Love.

Fidelity.—*Byron.*

THOUGH human, thou didst not deceive me,
Though woman, thou didst not forsake,
Though loved, thou foreborest to grieve me,
Though slander'd, thou never couldst shake,—
Though trusted, thou didst not disclaim me,
Though parted, it was not to fly,
Though watchful, 'twas not to defame me,
Nor, mute, that the World might belie.

Finery.—*Shakspeare.*

ALL that glisters is not Gold,
Gilded Tombs do Worms infold.

First Impressions.—*Horace.*

WHAT season'd first the Vessel, keeps the Taste.

Flattery.—*Anon.*

WHEN Flatterers meet, the Devil goes to Dinner.

Flattery.—*Greville.*

WE do not always like people the better, for paying us *all* the Court which we ourselves think our due.

Flattery.—*Colton.*

FLATTERY is often a traffic of mutual Meanness, where, although both parties intend Deception, neither are deceived.

Flattery.—*Jean Paul.*

MEN find it more easy to Flatter than to Praise.

Flattery.—*Shakspeare.*

HE loves to hear,
That Unicorns may be betray'd with trees,
And Bears with glasses, Elephants with holes,
Lions with toils, and Men with Flatterers:
But, when I tell him, he hates Flatterers,
He says, he does; being then most Flatter'd.

Flattery.—*Shakspeare.*

HE that loves to be Flattered is worthy o' the Flatterer.

Flattery. — *Shakspeare.*

Be not fond,
To think that Cæsar bears such rebel blood,
That will be thaw'd from the true quality
With that which melteth Fools: I mean, Sweet Words,
Low-crook'd Curt'sies, and base Spaniel Fawning.

Flattery. — *Shakspeare.*

You play the Spaniel,
And think with wagging of your Tongue to win me.

Flattery. — *Shakspeare.*

Why these looks of Care?
Thy Flatterers yet wear silk, drink wine, lie soft;
Hug their diseased perfumes, and have forgot
That ever Timon was. Shame not these words,
By putting on the cunning of a Carper.
Be thou a Flatterer now, and seek to thrive
By that which has undone thee: hinge thy Knee,
And let his very breath, whom thou'lt observe,
Blow off thy cap; praise his most vicious strain,
And call it excellent.

Flattery. — *Shakspeare.*

AH! when the means are gone, that buy this Praise,
The Breath is gone whereof this Praise is made:
Feast-one, fast-lost; one cloud of winter showers,
These flies are couch'd.

Flattery. — *Shakspeare.*

Why, what a deal of candied Courtesy,
This fawning Greyhound then did proffer me!
The Devil take such Cozeners!—God forgive me!

Flattery. — *Shakspeare.*

No visor does become black Villany
So well as soft and tender Flattery.

Flattery. — *Otway.*

NO Flatt'ry, boy! an honest man can't live by't:
It is a little sneaking art, which knaves
Use to cajole and soften fools withal.
If thou hast Flatt'ry in thy nature, out with't;
Or send it to a court, for there 'twill thrive.

Flattery. — *Hannah More.*

Hold!
No Adulation: 'tis the death of Virtue!
Who flatters is of all mankind the lowest,
Save he who courts the Flattery.

Flattery. — *Shakspeare.*

My beauty, though but mean,
Needs not the painted flourish of your Praise.
Beauty is bought by judgment of the eye,
Not utter'd by base sale of chapmen's tongues.

Kingly Flattery. — *Shakspeare.*

THEY do abuse the King that flatter him:
For Flattery is the bellows blows up sin;
The thing the which is flatter'd, but a spark,
To which that breath gives heat and stronger glowing;
Whereas reproof, obedient and in order,
Fits Kings, as they are Men, for they may err.

The Fool. — *Goethe.*

OF all thieves Fools are the worst: they rob you of time and temper.

The Fool. — *La Bruyere.*

A Fool cannot look, nor stand, nor walk like a man of sense.

The Fool. — *Anon.*

HE must be a thorough Fool who can learn nothing from his own Folly.

Follies. — *La Rochefoucauld.*

There are Follies as catching as contagious disorders.

Folly. — *Hare.*

None but a Fool is always right.

Folly. — *Horace.*

When free from Folly, we to Wisdom rise.

Folly. — *Colton.*

A FOOL is often as dangerous to deal with as a Knave, and always more incorrigible.

Folly. — *Shakspeare.*

NONE are so surely caught, when they are catch'd,
As Wit turn'd Fool: Folly, in Wisdom hatch'd,
Hath Wisdom's warrant, and the help of school;
And Wit's own grace, to grace a learned Fool.
The blood of youth burns not with such excess,
As Gravity's revolt to wantonness.
Folly in Fools bears not so strong a note,
As Foolery in the wise, when Wit doth dote;
Since all the power thereof it doth apply,
To prove, by Wit, worth in Simplicity.

Foppery.—*Johnson.*

FOPPERY is never cured; it is the bad stamina of the mind, which, like those of the body, are never rectified; once a Coxcomb, and always a Coxcomb.

Forbearance.—*Epictetus.*

EVERY thing hath two handles: the one soft and manageable, the other such as will not endure to be touched. If then your brother do you an injury, do not take it by the hot and hard handle, by representing to yourself all the aggravating circumstances of the fact; but look rather on the soft side, and extenuate it as much as is possible, by considering the nearness of the relation, and the long friendship and familiarity between you—obligations to kindness which a single provocation ought not to dissolve. And thus you will take the accident by its manageable handle.

Forbearance.—*Shakspeare.*

USE every man after his desert, and who shall 'scape whipping?

Foreign Influence.—*Washington.*

AGAINST the insidious wiles of foreign influence, the jealousy of a free people ought to be constantly awake; since history and experience prove, that foreign influence is one of the most baneful foes of republican government.

Foresight.—*Colton.*

ACCUSTOM yourself to submit on all and every occasion, and on the most minute, no less than on the most important circumstances of life, to a small Present Evil, to obtain a greater Distant Good. This will give decision, tone, and energy to the Mind, which, thus disciplined, will often reap victory from defeat, and honour from repulse.

Foresight.—*Shakspeare.*

To fear the worst, oft cures the worst.

Forgiveness.—*Shakspeare.*

KNEEL not to me:
The power that I have on you, is to spare you;
The malice towards you, to forgive you: live,
And deal with others better.

Forgiveness.—*Shakspeare.*

THOUGH with their high wrongs I am struck to the quick,
Yet, with my nobler Reason, against my Fury
Do I take part: the rarer action is
In Virtue than in Vengeance.

Forms. — *Hare.*

OF what use are Forms, seeing that at times they are empty?
Of the same use as barrels, which at times are empty too.

Fortitude. — *Shakspeare.*

Bid that welcome
Which comes to punish us, and we punish it,
Seeming to bear it lightly.

Fortitude. — *Shakspeare.*

WISE men ne'er sit and wail their loss,
But cheerly seek how to redress their harms.
What though the mast be now blown overboard,
The cable broke, the holding anchor lost,
And half our sailors swallow'd in the flood?
Yet lives our Pilot still: Is it meet, that he
Should leave the helm, and, like a fearful lad,
With tearful eyes add water to the sea,
And give more strength to that which hath too much;
Whiles, in his moan, the ship splits on a rock,
Which industry and courage might have saved?

Fortitude. — *Shakspeare.*

THE Mind I sway by, and the Heart I bear,
Shall never sagg with doubt, nor shake with Fear.

Fortitude. — *Byron.*

EXISTENCE may be borne, and the deep root
Of life and Sufferance make its firm abode
In bare and desolated bosoms: mute
The camel labours with the heaviest load,
And the wolf dies in silence,—not bestow'd
In vain should such example be; if they,
Things of ignoble or of savage mood,
Endure and shrink not, we of nobler clay
May temper it to bear,—it is but for a day.

Fortitude. — *Shakspeare.*

THOUGH Fortune's malice overthrow my state,
My Mind exceeds the compass of her wheel.

Fortitude. — *Channing.*

THE greatest man is he who chooses the right with invincible Resolution; who resists the sorest temptations from within and without; who bears the heaviest burdens cheerfully; who is the calmest in storms, and whose reliance on Truth, on Virtue, on God, is the most unfaltering.

Fortitude. —*Byron.*

HAVE I not had my brain sear'd, my heart riven,
Hopes sapp'd, name blighted, life's life lied away?
And only not to Desperation driven,
Because not altogether of such clay,
As rots into the souls of those whom I survey.

Fortunate Men. — *Cicero.*

THE man who is always Fortunate cannot easily have a great reverence for Virtue.

Fortune. — *Shakspeare.*

WILL Fortune never come with both hands full,
But write her fair words still in foulest letters?
She either gives a stomach, and no food,—
Such are the poor in health; or else a feast,
And takes away the stomach,—such the rich,
That have abundance, and enjoy it not.

Fortune. — *Thomson.*

OFT, what seems
A trifle, a mere nothing, by itself,
In some nice situations, turns the scale
Of Fate, and rules the most important actions.

Fortune. — *Shakspeare.*

OF Nature's Gifts thou may'st with lilies boast,
And with the half-blown rose: but Fortune, Oh!
She is corrupted, changed, and won from thee.

Fortune. — *Shakspeare.*

FORTUNE is merry,
And in this mood will give us any thing.

Fortune. — *Shakspeare.*

WHEN Fortune means to men most good,
She looks upon them with a threat'ning eye.

Fortune. — *Colton.*

THERE are some men who are Fortune's Favourites, and who, like cats, light for ever upon their legs.

Fortune. — *From the French.*

GOOD Fortune and Bad are equally necessary to Man, to fit him to meet the contingencies of this life.

Fortune. — *Goldsmith.*

WHAT real Good does an addition to a fortune already sufficient, procure? Not any. Could the great man, by having his Fortune increased, increase also his appetites, then precedence might be attended with real amusement.

Fortune. — *Greville.*

SURELY no man can reflect, without wonder, upon the Vicissitudes of Human Life arising from causes in the highest degree accidental and trifling. If you trace the necessary concatenation of Human Events, a very little way back, you may perhaps discover that a person's very going in or out of a door has been the means of colouring with misery or happiness the remaining current of his life.

Fortune. — *Montaigne.*

FORTUNE does us neither good nor hurt; she only presents us the matter and the seed, which our soul, more powerful than she, turns and applies as she best pleases, being the sole cause and sovereign mistress of her own happy or unhappy condition. All external accessions receive taste and colour from the internal constitution, as clothes warm us not with their heat, but our own, which they are adapted to cover and keep in.

Fortune. — *Rousseau.*

WE do not know what is really Good or Bad Fortune.

Fortune. — *La Rochefoucauld.*

GOOD or Bad Fortune generally pursue those who have the greatest share of either. The prosperous man seems as a magnet to attract Prosperity.

Fortune. — *La Rochefoucauld.*

THE Good or the Bad Fortune of Men depend not less upon their own dispositions than upon Fortune.

Fortune. — *Tacitus.*

THERE are many Men who appear to be struggling against Adversity, and yet are happy; but yet more, who, although abounding in Wealth, are miserable.

Fortune. — *La Rochefoucauld.*

WE should manage our Fortune as we do our health—enjoy it when good, be patient when it is bad, and never apply violent remedies except in an extreme necessity.

Fortune. — *La Rochefoucauld.*

THE moderation of Fortunate People comes from the calm which Good Fortune gives to their tempers.

Fortune. — *Shenstone.*

THE worst inconvenience of a Small Fortune is that it will not admit of inadvertency.

Playing with Fortune. — *Shakspeare.*

HAPPINESS courts thee in her best array;
But, like a misbehaved and sullen wench,
Thou pout'st upon thy Fortune and thy Love.
Take heed, take heed, for such die miserable.

Fortune. — *La Rochefoucauld.*

It requires greater virtues to support Good than Bad Fortune.

Frailty. — *Shakspeare.*

Where's that palace, whereinto foul things
Sometimes intrude not? who has a Breast so pure,
But some uncleanly apprehensions
Keep leets, and law-days, and in session sit
With meditations lawful?

Freedom. — *Rahel.*

To have Freedom, is only to have that which is absolutely necessary to enable us to be what we ought to be, and to possess what we ought to possess.

Freedom. — *Channing.*

The only freedom worth possessing is that which gives enlargement to a people's energy, intellect, and virtues. The savage makes his boast of freedom. But what is its worth? Free as he is, he continues for ages in the same ignorance, leads the same comfortless life, sees the same untamed wilderness spread around him. He is, indeed, free from what he calls the yoke of civil institutions. But other and worse chains bind him. The very privation of civil government is in effect a chain; for, by withholding protection from property, it virtually shackles the arm of industry, and forbids exertion for the melioration of his lot. Progress, the growth of power, is the end and boon of liberty; and, without this, a people may have the name, but want the substance and spirit of freedom

The truly Free. — *Horace.*

Who then is Free?—The Wise, who well maintains
An empire o'er himself; whom neither Chains,
Nor Want, nor Death, with slavish Fear inspire;
Who boldly answers to his warm desire;
Who can Ambition's vainest gifts despise;
Firm in himself, who on himself relies;
Polish'd and round, who runs his proper course,
And breaks misfortune with superior force.

Friendship. — *Joanna Baillie.*

Friendship is no plant of hasty growth.
Though planted in esteem's deep-fix'd soil,
The gradual culture of kind Intercourse
Must bring it to perfection.

Friendship. — *Burton.*

The Attachments of mere Mirth are but the shadows of that true Friendship, of which the sincere Affections of the Heart are the substance.

Friendship. — *Shakspeare.*

THOU art e'en as just a Man,
As e'er my conversation coped withal.
Nay, do not think I flatter:
For what advancement may I hope from thee,
That no revenue hast, but thy good spirits,
To feed and clothe thee? Should the poor be flatter'd?
No, let the candied tongue lick absurd Pomp,
And crook the pregnant hinges of the knee,
Where thrift may follow fawning. Dost thou hear?
Since my dear Soul was mistress of her choice,
And could of men distinguish, her election
Hath seal'd thee for herself. For thou hast been
As one, in suffering all, that suffers nothing:
A Man, that Fortune's buffets and rewards
Hast ta'en with equal thanks. And blest are those,
Whose blood and judgment are so well commingled,
That they are not a pipe for Fortune's finger
To sound what stop she please. Give me that Man
That is not Passion's slave, and I will wear him
In my Heart's core: ay, in my Heart of Hearts,
As I do thee.

Friendship. — *Shakspeare.*

O WORLD, thy slippery turns! Friends now fast sworn,
Whose double Bosoms seem to wear one Heart,
Whose hours, whose bed, whose meal and exercise,
Are still together, who twin, as 'twere in Love
Unseparable, shall within this hour,
On a dissension of a doit, break out
To bitterest Enmity.

Friendship. — *Lavater.*

THE qualities of your Friends will be those of your Enemies: cold Friends, cold Enemies; half Friends, half Enemies; fervid Enemies, warm Friends.

Friendship. — *Fitzosborne.*

THOUGH judgment must collect the materials of the goodly structure of Friendship, it is Affection that gives the cement; and Passion as well as Reason should concur in forming a firm and lasting coalition. Hence, perhaps, it is, that not only the most powerful, but the most lasting Friendships are usually the produce of the early season of our lives, when we are most susceptible of the warm and affectionate impressions. The connections into which we enter in any after period, decrease in strength as our passions abate in heat

Friendship. — *Shakspeare.*

THE Amity that Wisdom knits not, Folly may easily untie.

Friendship. — *Cicero.*

FRIENDSHIP is the only thing in the world concerning the usefulness of which all mankind are agreed.

Friendship. — *Horace.*

WISE were the Kings who never chose a Friend
Till with full cups they had unmask'd his Soul,
And seen the bottom of his deepest thoughts.

Friendship. — *Shakspeare.*

OH, lest the World should task you to recite
What merit lived in me, that you should love
After my death,—dear love, forget me quite,
For you in me can nothing worthy prove;
Unless you would devise some virtuous lie,
To do more for me than mine own desert,
And hang more praise upon deceased I,
Than niggard truth would willingly impart;
Oh, lest your true love may seem false in this,
That you for love speak well of me untrue,
My name be buried where my body is,
And live no more to shame nor me nor you.
For I am shamed by that which I bring forth,
And so should you, to love things nothing worth.

Friendship. — *Greville.*

TO say, with La Rochefoucauld, that "in the adversity of our best Friends there is something that does not displease us;" and to say, that in the prosperity of our best Friends there is something that does not please us, seems to be the same thing; yet I believe the first is false, and the latter true.

Friendship. — *Colton.*

THOSE who have resources within themselves, who can dare to live alone, want Friends the least, but, at the same time, best know how to prize them the most. But no company is far preferable to bad, because we are more apt to catch the vices of others than their virtues, as disease is far more contagious than health.

Friendship. — *Shakspeare.*

FRIENDS condemn'd
Embrace, and kiss, and take ten thousand leaves,
Loather a hundred times to part than die.

Friendship. — *Shakspeare.*

Now do I play the touch,
To try if thou be current gold, indeed.

Friendship.—*Sallust.*

TO be influenced by a passion for the same pursuits, and to have similar dislikes, is the rational groundwork of lasting Friendship.

Friendship.—*Socrates.*

GET not your Friends by bare compliments, but by giving them sensible tokens of your love. It is well worth while to learn how to win the heart of a man the right way. Force is of no use to make or preserve a Friend, who is an animal that is never caught nor tamed but by kindness and pleasure. Excite them by your civilities, and show them that you desire nothing more than their satisfaction; oblige with all your soul that Friend who has made you a present of his own.

Friendship.—*Shakspeare.*

IS all the Counsel that we two have shared,
The Sisters' Vows, the hours that we have spent,
When we have chid the hasty-footed time
For parting us,—Oh, and is all forgot?
All school-days' Friendship, Childhood Innocence?
We, Hermia, like two artificial gods,
Have with our neelds created both one flower,
Both on one sampler, sitting on one cushion,
Both warbling of one song, both in one key;
As if our hands, our sides, voices, and minds,
Had been incorporate. So we grew together,
Like a double cherry, seeming parted;
But yet a union in partition,
Two lovely berries moulded on one stem:
So, with two seeming bodies, but one Heart;
Two of the first, like coats in heraldry,
Due but to one, and crown'd with one crest.
And will you rend our ancient Love asunder?

Friendship.—*Southern.*

FRIENDSHIP is power and riches all to me;
Friendship's another element of life:
Water and fire not of more general use,
To the support and comfort of the world,
Than Friendship to the being of my joy:
I would do every thing to serve a Friend.

Friendship.—*Shakspeare.*

I COUNT myself in nothing else so happy,
As in a soul rememb'ring my good Friends;
And, as my fortune ripens with thy love,
It shall be still thy true love's recompense.

Friendship. — *Colton.*

AN act, by which we make one Friend and one Enemy, is a losing game; because Revenge is a much stronger principle than Gratitude.

Friendship. — *Sir Walter Raleigh.*

THOU mayst be sure that he that will in private tell thee of thy faults, is thy Friend, for he adventures thy dislike, and doth hazard thy hatred; for there are few men that can endure it, every man for the most part delighting in self-praise, which is one of the most universal follies that bewitcheth Mankind.

Friendship. — *Young.*

CELESTIAL Happiness! Whene'er she stoops
To visit earth, one shrine the Goddess finds,
And one alone, to make her sweet amends
For absent heaven,—the bosom of a Friend,
Where Heart meets Heart,
Each other's pillow to repose divine.

Friendship. — *Sir Walter Raleigh.*

THERE is nothing more becoming any wise man, than to make choice of Friends, for by them thou shalt be judged what thou art: let them therefore be wise and virtuous, and none of those that follow thee for gain; but make election rather of thy betters, than thy inferiors, shunning always such as are needy; for if thou givest twenty gifts, and refuse to do the like but once, all that thou hast done will be lost, and such men will become thy mortal enemies.

Friendship. — *Sir Philip Sidney.*

THE lightsome countenance of a Friend giveth such an inward decking to the house where it lodgeth, as proudest palaces have cause to envy the gilding.

Friendship. — *Shakspeare.*

BY Heaven, I cannot flatter: I defy
The tongues of soothers; but a braver place
In my Heart's Love hath no man than yourself;
Nay, task me to my word; approve me.

Friendship. — *Fuller.*

LET Friendship creep gently to a height; if it rush to it, it may soon run itself out of breath.

Friendship. — *Johnson.*

IF a man does not make new Acquaintance as he advances through life, he will soon find himself left alone. A man should keep his Friendship in constant repair.

Friendship. — *Goldsmith.*

THERE are few subjects which have been more written upon, and less understood, than that of friendship. To follow the dictates of some, this virtue, instead of being the assuager of pain, becomes the source of every inconvenience. Such speculatists, by expecting too much from Friendship, dissolve the connection, and by drawing the bands too closely, at length break them.

Friendship. — *Sir William Temple.*

SOMETHING like home that is not home, like alone that is not alone, is to be wished, and only found in a Friend, or in his house.

Friendship. — *Shakspeare.*

In Companions
That do converse and waste the time together,
Whose Souls do bear an equal Yoke of Love,
There must be needs a like proportion
Of lineaments, of manners, and of spirit.

Friendship. — *Chesterfield.*

REAL Friendship is a slow grower; and never thrives, unless engrafted upon a stock of known and reciprocal Merit.

Friendship. — *La Rochefoucauld.*

Rare as is true Love, true Friendship is still rarer.

Friendship. — *Hawkesworth.*

FEW men are calculated for that close connection which we distinguish by the appellation of Friendship: the Acquaintance is in a post of progression; and after having passed through a course of proper experience, and given sufficient evidence of his merit, takes a new title.

Friendship. — *Shakspeare.*

Give thy thoughts no tongue,
Nor any unproportion'd thought his act.
Be thou familiar, but by no means vulgar.
The Friends thou hast, and their adoption tried,
Grapple them to thy soul with hooks of steel;
But do not dull thy palm with entertainment
Of each new-hatch'd, unfledged comrade.

Friendship. — *Chesterfield.*

THOSE who in the common course of the world will call themselves your Friends; or whom, according to the common notions of Friendship, you may probably think such, will never tell you of your faults, still less of your weaknesses. But on the contrary, more desirous to make you their Friend than to prove themselves yours, they will flatter both, and, in truth, not be sorry for either.

Friendship. — *Catherine Phillips.*

ESSENTIAL honour must be in a friend,
Not such as every breath fans to and fro;
But born within, is its own judge and end,
And dares not sin, though sure that none should know.
Where Friendship's spoke, Honesty's understood;
For none can be a Friend that is not good.

Friendship. — *Shakspeare.*

NO longer mourn for me when I am deaa
Than you shall hear the surly sullen bell
Give warning to the world that I am fled
From this vile world, with vilest worms to dwell:
Nay, if you read this line, remember not
The Hand that writ it; for I love you so,
That I in your sweet Thoughts would be forgot,
If thinking on me then should make you wo.
Oh if (I say) you look upon this verse,
When I perhaps compounded am with clay,
Do not so much as my poor name rehearse;
But let your Love even with my life decay:
Lest the wise world should look into your moan,
And mock you with me after I am gone.

Friendship. — *La Fontaine.*

NOTHING more dangerous than a Friend without discretion; even a prudent Enemy is preferable.

Friendship. — *From the Latin.*

OF no worldly good can the enjoyment be perfect, unless it is shared by a Friend.

Friendship. — *Hazlitt.*

THE youth of Friendship is better than its old age.

Friendship. — *Fuller.*

MAKE not thy Friends too cheap to thee, nor thyself to thy Friend.

Friendship. — *Shakspeare.*

BRUTUS hath rived my heart:
A Friend should bear his Friend's infirmities,
But Brutus makes mine greater than they are

Friendship. — *Havard.*

I HAVE too deeply read Mankind
To be amused with Friendship; 'tis a name
Invented merely to betray credulity:
'Tis intercourse of Interest—not of Souls.

Friendship. — *Clarendon.*

FRIENDSHIP is compounded of all those soft ingredients which can insinuate themselves and slide insensibly into the nature and temper of men of the most different constitutions, as well as of those strong and active spirits which can make their way into perverse and obstinate dispositions; and because Discretion is always predominant in it, it works and prevails least upon Fools. Wicked men are often reformed by it, weak men seldom.

Friendship. — *Fuller.*

PURCHASE not Friends by gifts; when thou ceasest to give, such will cease to love.

Friendship. — *Savage.*

YOU'LL find the Friendship of the World a show!
Mere outward show! 'Tis like the harlot's tears,
The statesman's promise, or false patriot's zeal,
Full of fair seeming, but delusion all.

Friendship. — *Addison.*

THE Friendships of the World are oft
Confed'racies in vice, or leagues of pleasure.

Friendship. — *Trap.*

FRIENDSHIP must be accompanied with Virtue,
And always lodged in great and gen'rous Minds.

Friendship. — *Blair.*

FRIENDSHIP! mysterious cement of the Soul!
Sweet'ner of Life and solder of Society!
I owe thee much. Thou hast deserved of me
Far, far beyond what I can ever pay.
Oft have I proved the labours of thy Love,
And the warm efforts of the gentle Heart
Anxious to please.

Friendship. — *Spenser.*

NE, certes can that Friendship long endure,
However gay and goodly be the style,
That doth ill cause or evill end enure,
For Vertue is the band that bindeth Harts most sure

Friendship. — *Lee.*

IN their nonage, a sympathy
Unusual join'd their Loves:
They pair'd like Turtles; still together drank,
Together eat, nor quarrell'd for the choice.
Like twining Streams both from one Fountain fell,
And as they ran still mingled smiles and tears.

Friendship. — *Addison.*

Great Souls by instinct to each other turn,
Demand Alliance, and in Friendship burn.

Friendship. — *Dryden.*

I can forgive
A Foe, but not a Mistress, and a Friend:
Treason is there in its most horrid shape,
Where trust is greatest! and the Soul resign'd
Is stabb'd by her own guards.

Friendship. — *Fuller.*

MAKE not a Bosom Friend of a melancholy soul: he'll be sure to aggravate thy adversity, and lessen thy prosperity. He goes always heavy loaded; and thou must bear half. He's never in a good humour; and may easily get into a bad one, and fall out with thee.

Frugality. — *Burke.*

FRUGALITY is founded on the principle, that all riches have limits.

Frugality. — *Johnson.*

FRUGALITY may be termed the Daughter of Prudence, the Sister of Temperance, and the Parent of Liberty. He that is extravagant will quickly become Poor, and Poverty will enforce dependence, and invite corruption.

Frugality. — *Cicero.*

The World has not yet learned the Riches of Frugality.

The Future. — *Seneca.*

THE state of that Man's Mind who feels too intense an interest as to Future Events, must be most deplorable.

Future State. — *Addison.*

WHY will any man be so impertinently officious as to tell me all prospect of a Future State is only fancy and delusion? Is there any merit in being the messenger of ill news? If it is a dream, let me enjoy it, since it makes me both the happier and better man.

Future State. — *Cicero.*

THERE is, I know not how, in the minds of men, a certain presage, as it were, of a Future Existence, and this takes the deepest root, and is most discoverable, in the greatest geniuses and most exalted souls.

Future State. — *Colton.*

HEAVEN may have happiness as utterly unknown to us, as the gift of perfect vision would be to a man born blind. If we consider the inlets of pleasure from five senses only, we may be sure that the same Being who created us, could have given us five hundred, if he had pleased. Mutual love, pure and exalted, founded on charms both mental and corporeal, as it constitutes the highest happiness on earth, may, for any thing we know to the contrary, also form the lowest happiness of Heaven. And it would appear consonant with the administration of Providence in other matters, that there should be such a link between Earth and Heaven; for, in all cases, a Chasm seems to be *purposely* avoided "*prudente Deo.*" Thus, the Material World has its links, by which it is made to shake hands, as it were, with the Vegetable,—the vegetable with the Animal,—the animal with the Intellectual,—and the intellectual with what we may be allowed to hope of the Angelic.

A Future State. — *Dryden.*

SURE there is none but fears a Future State;
And when the most obdurate swear they do not,
Their trembling hearts belie their boasting tongues.

A Future State. — *Dryden.*

DIVINES but peep on undiscover'd worlds,
And draw the distant landscape as they please;
But who has e'er return'd from those bright regions,
To tell their manners, and relate their laws.

Futurity. — *Shakspeare.*

O Heaven! that one might read the Book of Fate,
And see the revolution of the times
Make mountains level, and the continent,
Weary of solid firmness, melt itself
Into the sea.
Oh, if this were seen,
The happiest youth,—viewing his progress through,
What perils past, what crosses to ensue,—
Would shut the book, and sit him down and die.

Futurity. — *Pope.*

SEE dying vegetables life sustain,
See life dissolving, vegetate again:
All forms that perish other forms supply,
(By turns we catch the vital breath and die,)
Like bubbles on the sea of matter borne,
They rise, they break, and to that sea return.

Nothing is foreign; parts relate to whole;
One all-extending, all-preserving soul
Connects each being, greatest with the least;
Made beast in aid of man, and man of beast;
All served, all serving: nothing stands alone;
The chain holds on, and where it ends unknown.

Gambling. — *Lavater.*

IT is possible that a wise and good man may be prevailed on to game; but it is impossible that a professed Gamester should be a wise and good man.

Gambling. — *Tom Brown.*

GAMING finds man a cully, and leaves him a knave.

Gambling. — *Steele.*

THERE is nothing that wears out a fine face like the vigils of the Card-table, and those cutting passions which naturally attend them. Hollow eyes, haggard looks, and pale complexions are the natural indications of a female Gamester. Her morning sleeps are not able to repay her midnight watchings.

Gambling. — *La Bruyere.*

AN assembly of the states, a court of justice, shows nothing so serious and grave as a Table of Gamesters playing very high; a melancholy solicitude clouds their looks; envy and rancour agitate their minds while the meeting lasts, without regard to friendship, alliances, birth, or distinctions.

Games and Sports. — *Fuller.*

TAKE heed to avoid all those Games and Sports that are apt to take up much of thy time, or engage thy affections. He that spends all his life in Sports, is like one who wears nothing but fringes, and eats nothing but sauces.

The Garden in Town. — *Cowper.*

EV'N in the stifling bosom of the Town,
A Garden in which nothing thrives has charms
That soothe the rich possessor; much consoled
That here and there some sprigs of mournful mint,
Of nightshade or valerian, grace the wall
He cultivates.

The Gay. — *Cowper.*

WHOM call we gay? That honour has been long
The boast of mere pretenders to the name.
The innocent are gay—the Lark is gay,
That dries his feathers saturate with Dew
Beneath the rosy cloud, while yet the beams
Of Day-spring overshot his humble nest.

Generosity. — *Greville.*

ONE great reason why men practise Generosity so little in the world is, their finding so little there: Generosity is catching; and if so many men escape it, it is in a great degree from the same reason that countrymen escape the Small-pox,—because they meet with no one to give it them.

Generosity. — *Lucan.*

UNLIKE the ribald, whose licentious jest
Pollutes his banquet, and insults his guest;
From wealth and grandeur easy to descend,
Thou joy'st to lose the Master in the Friend:
We round thy Board the cheerful menials see,
Gay with the smile of bland Equality;
No social care the gracious lord disdains;
Love prompts to Love, and Reverence Reverence gains.

Generosity. — *Shakspeare.*

OH! the World is but a word;
Were it all yours, to give it in a breath,
How quickly were it gone!

Generosity. — *Shakspeare.*

POOR honest lord, brought low by his own Heart;
Undone by Goodness! Strange, unusual Blood,
When Man's worst sin is, he does too much Good!

Genius. — *Plautus.*

How oft we see the greatest Genius buried in obscurity.

Genius. — *Anon.*

IT is a lesson which Genius and Wisdom of every kind must learn, that its kingdom is not of this world. It must learn to know this, and to be content that this should be so, to be content with the thought of a Kingdom in a higher, less transitory region. Then peradventure may the saying be fulfilled with regard to it, that he who is ready to lose his life shall save it. The Wisdom which aims at something nobler and more lasting than the Kingdom of this World, may now and then find that the Kingdom of this World will also fall into its lap.

Genius. — *Anon.*

FEW Minds are sun-like, sources of light in themselves and to others. Many more are Moons, that shine with a derivative and reflected light. Among the tests to distinguish them is this: the former are always full, the latter only now and then, when their Suns are shining full upon them.

Genius. — *Seneca.*

THERE is no great Genius free from some tincture of Madness.

Genius. — *Swift.*

WHEN a true Genius appears in the world, you may know him by this sign, that the Dunces are all in confederacy against him.

Genius. — *Sir J. Reynolds.*

GENIUS is supposed to be a power of producing excellences which are out of the reach of the rules of Art: a power which no precepts can teach, and which no industry can acquire.

Genius. — *Aristotle.*

THERE is no distinguished Genius altogether exempt from some infusion of Madness.

Genius. — *Cicero.*

TO be endowed with Strength by Nature, to be actuated by the powers of the Mind, and to have a certain Spirit almost Divine infused into you.

Genius. — *Anon.*

SECONDARY men, men of talents, may be mixed up, like an apothecary's prescription, of so many grains of one quality, and so many of another. But Genius is one, individual, indivisible: like a star, it dwells alone. That which is essential in a Man of Genius, his central spirit, shows itself once, and passes away never to return: and in few men is this more conspicuous than in Milton, in whom there is nothing Homeric, and hardly any thing Virgilian. In sooth, one might as accurately describe the elephant, as being made up of the force of the lion and the strength of the tiger.

Genius. — *Colton.*

THE greatest Genius is never so great, as when it is chastised and subdued by the highest Reason.

Genius. — *Horace.*

HE alone can claim this name, who writes
With Fancy high, and bold and daring Flights.

Genius. — *Horace.*

YOUR friend is passionate; perhaps unfit
For the brisk petulance of modern wit:
His hair ill cut, his robe that awkward flows,
Or his large shoes, to raillery expose
The man————
But underneath this rough, uncouth disguise
A Genius of extensive Knowledge lies.

Genius. —*S. T. Coleridge.*

TALENT, lying in the Understanding, is often inherited; Genius, being the action of Reason and Imagination, rarely or never

Genius. — *Cicero.*

All Great Men are in some degree Inspired.

Genius. — *Colton.*

THE drafts which true Genius draws upon posterity, although they may not always be honoured so soon as they are due, are sure to be paid with compound interest in the end. Milton's expressions on his right to this remuneration, constitute some of the finest efforts of his mind.

Genius. — *Lavater.*

THE proportion of Genius to the vulgar is like one to a million; but Genius without Tyranny, without Pretension, that judges the weak with Equity, the superior with Humanity, and equals with Justice, is like one to ten millions.

Genius. — *Crabbe.*

GENIUS! thou Gift of Heaven! thou Light divine!
Amid what dangers art thou doom'd to shine!
Oft will the body's weakness check thy force,
Oft damp thy Vigour, and impede thy course;
And trembling nerves compel thee to restrain
Thy noble efforts, to contend with pain;
Or Want (sad guest!) will in thy presence come,
And breathe around her melancholy gloom;
To life's low cares will thy proud thought confine,
And make her sufferings, her impatience, thine.

Genius. — *Longfellow.*

MEN of genius are often dull and inert in society; as the blazing meteor, when it descends to earth, is only a stone.

The Gentleman. — *Shaftesbury.*

THE taste of Beauty, and the relish of what is decent, just and amiable, perfects the character of the Gentleman and the Philosopher. And the study of such a taste or relish will, as we suppose, be ever the great employment and concern of him who covets as well to be wise and good, as agreeable and polite.

The Gentleman. — *Hare.*

A CHRISTIAN is God Almighty's Gentleman: a Gentleman in the vulgar, superficial way of understanding the word, is the Devil's Christian. But to throw aside these polished and too current counterfeits for something valuable and sterling, the Real Gentleman should be gentle in every thing, at least in every thing that depends on himself,—in carriage, temper, constructions, aims, desires. He ought therefore to be mild, calm, quiet, even, temperate,—not hasty in judgment, not exorbitant in ambition, not overbearing, not proud, not rapacious, not oppressive; for these things are con trary to Gentleness. Many such Gentlemen are to be found, I trust; and many more would be were the true meaning of the name borne in mind and duly inculcated.

The Gentleman. — *Steele.*

IT is no very uncommon thing in the World to meet with Men of Probity; there are likewise a great many Men of Honour to be found. Men of Courage, Men of Sense, and Men of Letters, are frequent; but a True Gentleman is what one seldom sees. He is properly a compound of the various good qualities that embellish mankind. As the great poet animates all the different parts of learning by the force of his genius, and irradiates all the compass of his knowledge by the lustre and brightness of his imagination; so all the great and solid perfections of life appear in the Finished Gentleman, with a beautiful gloss and varnish; every thing he says or does is accompanied with a manner, or rather a charm, that draws the admiration and good-will of every beholder.

The Gentleman. — *Colton.*

HE that can enjoy the intimacy of the Great, and on no occasion disgust them by familiarity, or disgrace himself by servility, proves that he is as perfect a Gentleman by Nature, as his companions are by Rank.

Gifts. — *Shakspeare.*

AND, with them, words of so sweet breath composed
As made the things more rich: their perfume lost,
Take these again; for to the noble mind
Rich Gifts wax poor, when Givers prove unkind.

Gifts. — *Fuller.*

GIVE freely to him that deserveth well, and asketh nothing: and that is a way of giving to thyself.

Gifts. — *Seneca.*

THERE is no grace in a Benefit that sticks to the fingers.

Gifts. — *Lavater.*

A GIFT—its kind, its value and appearance; the silence or the pomp that attends it; the style in which it reaches you, may decide the dignity or vulgarity of the Giver.

Gifts. — *Ovid.*

PRESENTS which our love for the Donor has rendered precious are ever the most acceptable.

Gifts. — *Cato.*

TENDER not twice to any man the Favours you may have it in your power to confer, and be not too loquacious, while you wish to be esteemed for your kindness.

Glory. — *Byron.*

THERE shall they rot—ambition's honour'd fools.
Yes, Honour decks the turf that wraps their clay.
Vain sophistry! in these behold the tools,
The broken tools, that tyrants cast away
By myriads, when they dare to pave their way
With human hearts—to what?—a dream alone.

Glory. — *Byron.*

MEDALS, Ranks, Ribbands, Lace, Embroidery, Scarlet,
Are things immortal to a mortal man,
As purple to the Babylonian harlot:
An Uniform to boys is like a fan
To women; there is scarce a crimson varlet
But deems himself the first in Glory's van.
But Glory's Glory; and if you would find
What that is—ask the pig who sees the wind!

Glory. — *Dryden.*

THE brave abroad fight for the wise at home:
You are but camp chameleons, fed with air;
Thin Fame is all the bravest hero's share.

Glory. — *Byron.*

THE Groan, the Roll in Dust, the all-white Eye
Turn'd back within its socket,—these reward
Your rank and file by thousands, while the rest
May win perhaps a Ribbon at the breast.

Glory. — *Cowper.*

LET eternal infamy pursue
The wretch to naught but his Ambition true,
Who for the sake of filling with one blast
The post-horns of all Europe, lays her waste.

Glory. — *Byron.*

WHAT boots the oft-repeated tale of strife,
The feast of vultures, and the waste of life?
The varying fortune of each separate field,
The fierce that vanquish, and the faint that yield?
The smoking ruin and the crumbled wall?
In this the struggle was the same with all.

Glory. — *Young.*

ONE to destroy is murder by the law,
And gibbets keep the lifted hand in awe:
To murder thousands takes a specious name,
War's Glorious art, and gives immortal Fame.

Glory (sacking a City.) — *Byron.*

ALL that the mind would shrink from of excesses;
All that the body perpetrates of bad;
All that we read, hear, dream of man's distresses;
All that the Devil would do if run stark mad;
All that defies the worst which pen expresses;
All by which Hell is peopled, or as sad
As Hell—mere mortals who their power abuse,—
Was here (as heretofore and since) let loose.

Glory. — *Porteus.*

WHOLE kingdoms fell
To sate the Lust of Power: more horrid still,
The foulest stain and scandal of our nature
Became its boast. One murder made a villain;
Millions a Hero.
Numbers sanctified the crime.

Glory. — *Byron.*

ENOUGH of battle's minions! let them play
Their game of lives, and barter breath for Fame;
Fame that will scarce reanimate their clay,
Though thousands fall to deck some single name.
In sooth 'twere sad to thwart their noble aim,
Who strike, blest hirelings! for their country's good,
And die, that living might have proved her shame.

Glory. — *Cicero.*

TRUE Glory takes root, and even spreads: all false pretences, like flowers, fall to the ground; nor can any counterfeit last long.

Glory. — *Wayland.*

THE aged crone, or the smooth-tongued beadle, as now he hurries you through aisles and chapel, utters, with measured cadence and unmeaning tone, for the thousandth time, the name and lineage of the once honoured dead; and then gladly dismisses you, to repeat again his well-conned lesson to another group of idle passers-by. Such, in its most august form, is all the immortality that matter can confer..... It is by what we ourselves have done, and not by what others have done for us, that we shall be remembered by after ages. It is by thought that has aroused my intellect from its slumbers, which has "given lustre to virtue, and dignity to truth," or by those examples which have inflamed my soul with the love of goodness, and not by means of sculptured marble, that I hold communion with Shakspeare and Milton, with Johnson and Burke, with Howard and Wilberforce.

The Glutton. — *Shakspeare.*

FAT Paunches have lean Pates; and dainty Bits
Make rich the ribs, but bank'rout quite the Wits.

The Glutton. — *Joanna Baillie.*

SOME men are born to feast, and not to fight;
Whose sluggish Minds, e'en in fair Honour's field,
Still on their Dinner turn.

The Glutton. — *Milton.*

SWINISH Gluttony
Ne'er looks to Heaven amidst his gorgeous Feast,
But with besotted, base ingratitude
Crams, and blasphemes his feeder.

The Glutton. — *Juvenal.*

SUCH, whose sole bliss is eating, who can give
But that one brutal reason why they live.

The Glutton. — *South.*

HE that prolongs his Meals, and sacrifices his time, as well as his other conveniences, to his Luxury, how quickly does he outset his pleasure! And then, how is all the following time bestowed upon Ceremony and Surfeit! until at length, after a long fatigue of eating, and drinking, and babbling, he concludes the great work of dining genteelly, and so makes a shift to rise from table, that he may lie down upon his bed; where, after he has slept himself into some use of himself, by much ado he staggers to his table again, and there acts over the same brutish scene: so that he passes his whole life in a dozed condition, between sleeping and waking, with a kind of drowsiness and confusion upon his senses, which what pleasure it can be, is hard to conceive. All that is of it, dwells upon the tip of his tongue, and within the compass of his palate. A worthy prize for a man to purchase with the loss of his time, his reason, and himself.

God. — *Horace.*

WHO guides below, and rules above,
The great Disposer, and the mighty King;
Than He none greater, next Him none,
That can be, is, or was:
Supreme He singly fills the Throne.

God. — *Boethius.*

GIVE me, O Father, to thy throne access,
Unshaken seat of endless happiness!
Give me, unvail'd, the Source of Good to see!
Give me Thy light, and fix mine eyes on Thee!

God. — *Jacobi.*

WHAT is there in Man so worthy of honour and reverence as this,—that he is capable of contemplating something higher than his own reason, more sublime than the whole universe; that Spirit which alone is self-subsistent, from which all truth proceeds, without which is no truth?

Ingratitude to God. — *Seneca.*

WE can be thankful to a friend for a few acres, or a little money; and yet for the freedom and command of the whole earth, and for the great benefits of our Being, our Life, Health, and Reason, we look upon ourselves as under no obligation.

God's Beneficence. — *Burke.*

THOSE things that are not practicable, are not desirable. There is nothing in the world really beneficial, that does not lie within the reach of an informed understanding and a well-directed pursuit. There is nothing that God has judged good for us, that He has not given us the means to accomplish, both in the natural and the moral world.

Mocking God. — *Casaubon.*

IT is a common frenzy of the ignorant multitude, to be always engaging Heaven on their side; and indeed it is a successful stratagem of any general to gain authority among his soldiers, if he can persuade them he is the man by Fate appointed for such or such an action, though most impracticable.

God's Procedure. — *Shakspeare.*

YOU snatch some hence for little faults; that's love,
To have them fall no more: you some permit
To second ills with ills, each elder worse;
And make them dread it to the doer's thrift.

Seeing God. — *Schleiermacher.*

LET the majestic serenity with which you estimate the great and the small, prove that you refer every thing to the Immutable,—that you perceive the Godhead alike in every thing; let the bright cheerfulness with which you encounter every proof of our transitory nature, reveal to all men that you live above time and above the world; let your easy and graceful self-denial prove how many of the bonds of egotism you have already broken; and let the ever quick and open spirit from which neither what is rarest nor most ordinary escapes, show with what unwearied ardour you seek for every trace of the Godhead, with what eagerness you watch for its slightest manifestation. If your whole life, and every movement of your outward and inward being, is thus guided by religion, perhaps the hearts of many will be touched by this mute language, and will open to the reception of that spirit which dwells within you.

Gold. — *Shakspeare.*

Foul-cankering rust the hidden Treasure frets;
But Gold, that's put to use, more Gold begets.

Gold. — *Shakspeare.*

Oh, what a world of vile ill-favour'd faults
Looks handsome in Three Hundred Pounds a year.

Gold. — *Shakspeare.*

Why this
Will lug your priests and servants from your sides;
Pluck stout men's pillows from below their heads:
This Yellow Slave
Will knit and break religions; bless the accursed;
Make the hoar leprosy adored; place thieves,
And give them title, knee, and approbation,
With senators on the bench.
This is it,
That makes the wappen'd widow wed again:
She, whom the spital-house and ulcerous sores
Would cast the gorge at, this embalms and spices
To the April day again.
For this, the foolish over-careful fathers
Have broke their sleep with thoughts, their brains with care,
Their bones with industry.

Gold. — *Shakspeare.*

There is thy Gold; worse Poison to men's souls,
Doing more murders in this loathsome world,
Than these poor compounds that thou may'st not sell:
I sell thee Poison, thou hast sold me none.

Gold. — *Shakspeare.*

O thou sweet King-killer, and dear Divorce
'Twixt natural son and sire! thou bright Defiler
Of Hymen's purest bed! thou valiant Mars!
Thou ever young, fresh, loved, and delicate Wooer,
Whose blush doth thaw the consecrated snow
That lies on Dian's lap! thou visible God,
That solder'st close impossibilities,
And makest them kiss! that speak'st with every tongue,
To every purpose! O thou Touch of Hearts!
Think, thy slave Man rebels; and by thy virtue
Set them into confounding odds, that beasts
May have the world in empire!

Gold. — *Shakspeare.*

How quickly nature
Falls to revolt, when Gold becomes her object!

Gold. — *Addison.*

A MAN who is furnished with arguments from the Mint, will convince his antagonist much sooner than one who draws them from Reason and Philosophy. Gold is a wonderful clearer of the understanding; it dissipates every doubt and scruple in an instant; accommodates itself to the meanest capacities; silences the loud and clamorous, and brings over the most obstinate and inflexible. Philip of Macedon was a man of most invincible reason this way. He refuted by it all the wisdom of Athens, confounded their statesmen, struck their orators dumb, and at length argued them out of all their liberties.

Gold. — *Shakspeare.*

GIVE him Gold enough, and marry him to a puppet, or an aglet-baby; or an old trot with ne'er a tooth in her head, though she have as many diseases as two and fifty horses; why, nothing comes amiss, so money comes withal.

Gold. — *Dekker.*

HE that upon his back Rich Garments wears,
Is wise, though on his head grow Midas' ears:
Gold is the strength, the sinews of the world;
The health, the soul, the beauty most divine;
A mask of Gold hides all deformities;
Gold is Heaven's Physic, Life's Restorative.

Gold. — *Massinger.*

HERE's music
In this Bag shall wake her, though she had drunk opium,
Or eaten mandrakes.

*　　*　　*　　*　　*

The Picklock
That never fails.

Gold. — *Johnson.*

THE lust of Gold succeeds the lust of conquests;
The lust of Gold, unfeeling and remorseless,
The last corruption of degenerate Man.

Gold. — *Shakspeare.*

THAT Broker, that still breaks the pate of Faith;
That daily Break-vow; he that wins of all,
Of kings, of beggars, old men, young men, maids—
Who having no external thing to lose
But the word Maid,—cheats the poor maid of that.

Gold. — *Shakspeare.*

'Tis Gold
Which buys admittance, (oft it doth,) yea, makes
Diana's rangers, false themselves, yield up
Their deer to th' stand o' th' stealer: and 'tis Gold
Which makes the true man kill'd, and saves the thief;
Nay, sometimes, hangs both thief and true man: what
Can it not do, and undo?

Gold. — *Horace.*

Stronger than Thunder's winged force,
All-powerful Gold can spread its course,
Through watchful guards its passage make
And loves through solid walls to break:
From Gold the overwhelming woes
That crush'd the Grecian augur rose:
Philip with Gold through Cities broke,
And rival Monarchs felt his yoke.

Gold. — *Anon.*

Epicharmus, indeed, calls the Winds, the Water, the Earth, the Sun, the Fire, and the Stars, Gods. But I am of opinion, that Gold and Silver are our only powerful and propitious Deities. For when once you have introduced these into your house, wish for what you will, you shall quickly obtain it; an Estate, a Habitation, Servants, Plate, Friends, Judges, Witnesses.

Gold. — *Colton*

There are two Metals, one of which is omnipotent in the Cabinet, and the other in the Camp,—Gold and Iron. He that knows how to apply them both, may indeed attain the highest station, but he must know something *more* to keep it.

Good from Fear. — *Goldsmith.*

Fear guides more to their duty than Gratitude; for one Man who is virtuous from the Love of Virtue, from the obligation which he thinks he lies under to the Giver of all, there are ten thousand who are good only from their Apprehensions of Punishment.

Doing Good. — *Seneca.*

He that does Good to another man, does also Good to himself; not only in the consequence, but in the very act of doing it; for the Conscience of well-doing is an ample reward.

Doing Good. — *Shaftesbury.*

Never did any soul do Good, but it came readier to do the same again, with more enjoyment. Never was Love, or Gratitude, or Bounty practised but with increasing Joy, which made the practiser still more in love with the fair act.

Doing Good. — *Cicero.*

IN nothing do men approach so nearly to the Gods, as in giving health to men.

Doing Good. — *La Bruyere.*

HE is Good that does Good to others. If he suffers for the Good he does, he is better still; and if he suffers from them to whom he did Good, he is arrived to that height of Goodness, that nothing but an increase of his sufferings can add to it: if it proves his death, his Virtue is at its summit; it is Heroism complete.

Good and Ill Fortune. — *Anon.*

WE often live under a Cloud; and it is well for us that we should do so. Uninterrupted Sunshine would parch our hearts: we want Shade and Rain to cool and refresh them. Only it behooves us to take care, that, whatever Cloud may be spread over us, it should be a Cloud of Witnesses. And every Cloud may be such, if we can only look through to the Sunshine that broods behind it.

Good Humour. — *Greville.*

GOOD Humour will sometimes conquer Ill Humour, but Ill Humour will conquer it oftener; and for this plain reason, Good Humour must operate on Generosity; Ill Humour on Meanness.

Extreme Good Nature. — *Terence.*

WHAT shall we call it? Folly, or Good Nature?
So soft, so simple, and so kind a creature!
Where Charity so blindly plays its part,
It only shows the weakness of her heart.

Goodness. — *Anon.*

TRUE Goodness is like the glowworm in this, that it shines most when no eyes, except those of Heaven, are upon it.

Goodness. — *Bishop Hall.*

A GOOD Man is kinder to his Enemy than Bad Men are to their Friends.

Good and Evil. — *La Rochefoucauld.*

SOME Bad People would be less dangerous if they had not some Goodness.

Good and Evil. — *La Rochefoucauld.*

NO man deserves to be praised for his Goodness unless he has strength of character to be wicked.

Good and Evil. — *Shakspeare.*

IN Nature, there's no blemish, but the Mind;
None can be call'd deform'd, but the unkind;
Virtue is beauty; but the beauteous evil
Are empty trunks, o'erflourish'd by the Devil.

Good and Evil. — *Lord Bacon.*

THE Rabbins note a principle of nature, that putrefaction is more dangerous before maturity than after, and another noteth a position in moral philosophy, that men abandoned to Vice do not so much corrupt manners as those that are half Good and half Evil.

Good and Evil. — *Anon.*

THE difference between those whom the World esteems as Good, and those whom it condemns as Bad, is in many cases little else than that the former have been better sheltered from temptation.

Good and Evil. — *Anon.*

OPEN Evil at all events does this Good: it keeps Good on the alert. When there is no likelihood of an enemy's approaching, the garrison slumber on their post.

Good and Evil. — *Shakspeare.*

VIRTUE, as it never will be moved,
Though Lewdness court it in a shape of Heaven;
So Lust, though to a radiant angel link'd,
Will sate itself in a celestial bed,
And prey on garbage.

Good and Evil. — *Shakspeare.*

THERE is some Soul of Goodness in things Evil,
Would men observingly distil it out.

Good and Evil. — *Colton.*

NATURAL Good is so intimately connected with Moral Good, and Natural Evil with Moral Evil, that I am as certain as if I heard a voice from Heaven proclaim it, that God is on the side of Virtue. He has learnt much, and has not lived in vain, who has practically discovered that most strict and necessary connection, that does, and will ever exist, between Vice and Misery, and Virtue and Happiness.

Good and Evil. — *S. T. Coleridge.*

AS there is much Beast and some Devil in Man, so is there some Angel and some God in him. The Beast and the Devil may be conquered, but in this life never destroyed.

Good and Evil. — *Hare.*

IT is a proof of our natural bias to Evil, that gain is slower and harder than loss, in all things Good: but in all things bad, getting is quicker and easier than getting rid of.

Good and Evil. — *S. T. Coleridge.*

THE history of all the World tells us, that Immoral Means will ever intercept Good Ends.

Good and Evil. — *Anon.*

HE who has observed how throughout History, while Man is continually misusing Good, and turning it into Evil, the overruling sway of God's Providence out of Evil is ever bringing forth Good, will never be cast down, or led to despond, or to slacken his efforts, however untoward the immediate aspect of things may appear. For he will know that, whenever he is labouring in the cause of Heaven, the powers of Heaven are working with him; that, though the Good he is aiming at may not be attainable in the very form he has in view, the ultimate result will assuredly be Good; that, were man diligent in fulfilling his part, this result would be immediate; and that no one who is thus diligent shall lose his precious reward, of seeing that every Good Deed is a part of the life of the world.

Good and Evil. — *S. T. Coleridge.*

GOOD and Bad Men are each less so than they seem.

Good and Evil. — *Sterne.*

WE are born to Trouble; and we may depend upon it whilst we live in this world we shall have it, though with intermissions: that is, in whatever state we are, we shall find a mixture of Good and Evil; and therefore the true way to Contentment is to know how to receive these certain vicissitudes of life,—the returns of Good and Evil, so as neither to be exalted by the one, or overthrown by the other, but to bear ourselves toward every thing which happens with such ease and indifference of mind, as tc hazard as little as may be.

Good and Evil. — *Milton.*

GOOD and Evil, we know, in the field of this world grow up together almost inseparably: and the Knowledge of Good is so involved and interwoven with the Knowledge of Evil, and in so many cunning resemblances hardly to be discerned, that those confused seeds which were imposed upon Psyche as an incessant labour to cull out and sort asunder, were not more intermixed. It was from out the rind of one Apple tasted, that the Knowledge of Good and Evil, as two Twins cleaving together, leaped forth into the world.

Good for Evil. — *Shakspeare.*

THE strawberry grows underneath the nettle,
And wholesome berries thrive, and ripen best,
Neighbour'd by fruit of baser quality:
And so the Prince obscured his contemplation
Under the vail of wildness; which, no doubt,
Grew like the summer grass, fastest by night,
Unseen, yet crescive in his faculty.

Good for Evil. — *Tillotson.*

A MORE glorious victory cannot be gained over another man than this, that when the Injury began on his part, the Kindness should begin on ours.

Good-will. — *Seneca.*

THE Good-will of the benefactor is the fountain of all Benefits; nay, it is the Benefit itself; or, at least, the stamp that makes it valuable and current.

The Gossip. — *Zimmerman.*

NEWS-HUNTERS have great Leisure, with little Thought; much petty Ambition to be thought intelligent, without any other pretension than being able to communicate what they have just learnt.

Governing. — *Selden.*

THEY that govern most make least noise.

Governing. — *Steele.*

IF the Commission of the Peace finds out the true Gentleman, he faithfully dischargeth it. I say finds him out; for a public office is a Guest, which receives the best usage from them who never invited it.

Government. — *Livy.*

WHEN Tarquin the Proud was asked what was the best mode of governing a conquered City, he replied only by beating down with his Staff all the tallest Poppies in his Garden.

Government. — *Shakspeare.*

THIS might have been prevented, and made whole,
With very easy Arguments of Love:
Which now the Manage of two kingdoms must
With fearful bloody Issue arbitrate.

Government. — *Hare.*

A STATESMAN, we are told, should follow Public Opinion. Doubtless . . . as a Coachman follows his horses; having firm hold on the Reins, and guiding them.

Government. — *Cowper.*

SOME seek Diversion in the tented field,
And make the sorrows of mankind their Sport.
But War's a Game, which, were their subjects wise,
Kings should not play at. Nations would do well
T' extort their truncheons from the puny hands
Of Heroes, whose infirm and baby minds
Are gratified with mischief, and who spoil
Because men suffer it, their toy the World.

Government. — *Colton.*

OUR Constitution is the proudest political Monument of the combined and progressive wisdom of Man; throughout the whole civilized World its preservation ought to be prayed for, as a choice and peerless Model, uniting all the beauties of proportion with all the solidity of strength. But nothing human is perfect, and experience has shown that this proud Monument of human Wisdom wants that which its earlier designers had conceived that it possessed; a self-preserving power. Those, therefore, are its truest friends who are most vigilant and unremitting in their efforts to keep it from Corruption, and to guard it from Decay; whose veneration, as it regards what it has been, and whose affection, as it relates to what it may be, is exceeded only by their fears for its safety, when they reflect what it is.

Government. — *Montaigne.*

THERE is little less trouble in forming a private Family than a whole Kingdom: wherever the mind is perplexed, it is an entire disorder, and domestic Employments are not less troublesome for being less important.

Government. — *Shakspeare.*

WITH common men
There needs too oft the Show of War to keep
The Substance of sweet Peace; and for a King,
'Tis sometimes better to be fear'd than loved.

Government. — *Shakspeare.*

THE Providence, that's in a watchful State,
Knows almost every grain of Pluto's Gold;
Finds bottom in th' uncomprehensive Deep;
Keeps place with thought; and almost, like the Gods,
Does even our thoughts unveil in their dumb cradles:
There is a Mystery (with which relation
Durst never meddle) in the Soul of State;
Which hath an operation more divine,
Than breath, or pen, can give expressure to.

Government. — *Anon.*

THE true Reformer is he who creates new Institutions, and gives them life and energy, and trusts to them for throwing off such evil humours as may be lying in the Body Politic. The true Reformer is the seminal Reformer, not the radical. And this is the way the Sower, who went forth to sow His seed, did really reform the World, without making any open assault to uproot what was already existing.

Government. — *Seneca.*

He who too much fears Hatred, is unfit to reign.

Government. — *Shakspeare.*

THE still and mental Parts,
That do contrive how many hands shall strike,
When Fitness call them on, and know by measure
Of their observant toil, the enemies' weight;
Why, this hath not a finger's dignity;
They call this bed-work Mapp'ry, closet War;
So that the Ram, that batters down the wall,
For the great swing and rudeness of his poise,
They place before his Hand that made the Engine:
Or those that with the Fineness of their Souls
By reason guide his Execution.

Government. — *Pope.*

A KING may be a tool, a thing of straw; but if he serves to frighten our enemies, and secure our property, it is well enough: a Scarecrow is a thing of straw, but it protects the Corn.

Government. — *Anon.*

IT is a dangerous thing to try new Experiments in a Government: Men do not foresee the ill consequences that must happen, when they go about to alter the essential parts of it upon which the whole Frame depends: for all Governments are artificial things, and every part of them has a dependence one upon another.

Government. — *Shakspeare.*

If we cannot defend our own door from the Dog,
Let us be worried; and our nation lose
The name of Hardiness and Policy.

Government. — *Colton.*

IN all Governments, there must of necessity be both the Law and the Sword: Laws without Arms would give us not Liberty, but Licentiousness; and Arms without Laws, would produce not Subjection, but Slavery.

Government. — *Montesquieu.*

CHANCE, or as it is here termed, Fortune, does not govern the world. The truth of this position might be referred to the Romans, who enjoyed a continued course of Prosperity while their Government was conducted on a certain plan, and an uninterrupted series of Reverses when they adopted a different one. There always exist certain general causes, either moral or physical, which act upon the affairs of every Monarchy, raise it to grandeur, support it in its prosperity, or precipitate it to its decadence or dissolution.

Government. — *Colton.*

IT is an easy work to govern wise men, but to govern Fools or madmen, a continual Slavery. It is from the blind zeal and stupidity cleaving to Superstition, it is from the ignorance, rashness, and rage attending Faction, that so many mad and so sanguinary Evils have destroyed men, dissolved the best Governments, and thinned the greatest Nations. As a people well instructed will certainly esteem the blessings they enjoy, and study public Peace for their own sake, there is a great merit in instructing the people and cultivating their understandings. They are certainly less credulous in proportion as they are more knowing, and consequently less liable to be the dupes of Demagogues and the property of Ambition. They are not then to be surprised with false cries, nor animated by imaginary danger. And wherever the understanding is well principled and informed, the passions will be tame, and the heart well disposed. They, therefore, who communicate true Knowledge to their species, are true Friends to the World, Benefactors to Society, and deserve all encouragement from those who preside over Society, with the applause and good wishes of all good and honest men.

Government. — *La Rochefoucauld.*

THE display of Clemency by Princes is, not unfrequently, a political Manœuvre to gain the affections of the People.

Government. — *Shakspeare.*

IT is most meet we arm us 'gainst the foe:
For Peace itself should not so dull a Kingdom,
(Though war, nor no known quarrel, were in question,)
But that Defences, musters, preparations,
Should be maintain'd, assembled, and collected,
As were a War in expectation.

Government. — *Cornelius Nepos.*

THE Power is detested, and miserable is the life, of him who wishes rather to be feared than to be loved.

Government.— *Shakspeare.*

IT is a purposed thing, and grows by plot,
To curb the Will of the Nobility:
Suffer it, and live with such as cannot rule,
Nor ever will be ruled.

Government. — *Sir Walter Raleigh.*

A MAN must first govern himself, ere he be fit to govern a Family; and his Family, ere he be fit to bear the Government in the Commonwealth.

Government. — *Hare.*

IN times of public Dissatisfaction add readily, to gratify men's wishes. So the change be made without trepidation, there is no contingent danger in the changing. But it is difficult to diminish safely, except in times of perfect quiet. The first is giving; the last is giving up.

Government. — *Shakspeare.*

NOW call we our high court of Parliament;
And let us choose such limbs of noble Counsel,
That the great body of our State may go
In equal rank with the best-govern'd Nation.

Government. — *Rousseau.*

THE science of Government is merely a science of combinations, of applications, and of exceptions, according to time, place, and circumstances.

Government. — *Shakspeare.*

THUS we debase
The nature of our Seats, and make the rabble
Call our Cares, fears; which will in time break ope
The locks o' the Senate, and bring in the Crows
To peck the Eagles.

Government. — *Burke.*

REFINED Policy ever has been the parent of Confusion; and ever will be so, as long as the world endures. Plain Good Intention, which is as easily discovered at the first view, as Fraud is surely detected at last, is of no mean force in the Government of Mankind. Genuine simplicity of heart is a healing and cementing Principle.

Government. — *Cicero.*

IT is necessary for a Senator to be thoroughly acquainted with the Constitution; and this is a knowledge of the most extensive nature; a matter of science, of diligence, of reflection, without which no Senator can possibly be fit for his office.

Government. — *Tacitus.*

THE repose of Nations cannot be secure without Arms, Armies cannot be maintained without Pay, nor can the Pay be produced except by Taxes.

Government. — *Lord Bacon.*

THE surest way to prevent Seditions (if the times do bear it) is to take away the matter of them; for if there be Fuel prepared, it is hard to tell whence the Spark shall come that shall set it on fire.

Government. — *De Moy.*

GOOD is never more effectually performed than when it is produced by slow degrees.

Government. — *Tom Brown.*

THOUGH a soldier, in time of peace, is like a Chimney in Summer, yet what wise man would pluck down his Chimney because his almanac tells him 'tis the middle of June.

Government. — *Antigonus.*

HE who forms the mind of a Prince, and implants in him good Principles, may see the precepts he had inculcated extend through a large portion of his Subjects.

Government. — *Goldsmith.*

POLITICS resemble Religion: attempting to divest either of Ceremony is the most certain method of bringing either into contempt. The weak must have their inducements to admiration as well as the wise; and it is the business of a sensible Government to impress all ranks with a sense of subordination, whether this be effected by a diamond or a virtuous edict, a sumptuary law or a glass necklace.

Government. — *Seneca.*

POWER exercised with Violence has seldom been of long duration, but Temper and Moderation generally produce permanence in all things.

Government. — *Rousseau.*

A CONTRACT made with its subjects by any Government, is so far dissolved by the exercise of Despotism, that the Despot is only able to enforce it while he continues the strongest; but as soon as it is practicable to expel him, he has no good grounds on which to found a protest against the proceeding.

Governing Favourites. — *Fuller.*

WHEN a Favourite grows insolent, it is wisdom to raise another into favour, who may give check to the other's Presumption.

Kingly Graces. — *Shakspeare.*

KING-BECOMING Graces
Are Justice, Verity, Temperance, Stableness,
Bounty, Perseverance, Mercy, Lowliness,
Devotion, Patience, Courage, Fortitude.

Gratitude. — *La Rochefoucauld.*

WHAT causes such a miscalculation in the amount of Gratitude which men expect for the favours they have done, is, that the Pride of the giver and that of the receiver can never agree as to the value of the Benefit.

Gratitude. — *La Rochefoucauld.*

ALMOST every one takes a Pleasure in requiting trifling Obligations; many people are grateful for moderate ones; but there is scarcely any one who does not show Ingratitude for great ones.

Gratitude. — *La Rochefoucauld.*

WHILE we retain the power of rendering Service, and conferring Favours, we seldom experience Ingratitude.

Gratitude. — *Charron.*

HE who receives a Good Turn, should never forget it: he who does one, should never remember it.

Gratitude. — *Pope.*

WHEREVER I find a great deal of Gratitude in a poor man, I take it for granted there would be as much Generosity if he were a rich man.

Gratitude. — *La Rochefoucauld.*

THERE is a certain lively Gratitude which not only acquits us of the Obligations we have received, but, by paying what we owe them, makes our Friends indebted to us.

Gratitude. — *Shakspeare.*

I HAVE five hundred crowns,
The thrifty hire I saved under your Father,
Which I did store, to be my foster nurse,
When service should in my old limbs lie lame,
And unregarded age in corners thrown.
Take that: and He that doth the ravens feed,
Yea, providently caters for the sparrow,
Be comfort to my age!

Gratitude. — *Shakspeare.*

THE hedge-sparrow fed the cuckoo so long,
That it had its head bit off by its young.

Gratitude. — *Shakspeare.*

I CAN no other answer make, but, Thanks,
And Thanks, and ever Thanks: Often Good Turns
Are shuffled off with such uncurrent pay:
But, were my worth, as is my conscience, firm,
You should find better dealing.

Gratitude. — *Congreve.*

O CALL not to my mind what you have done!
It sets a Debt of that account before me,
Which shows me poor and bankrupt even in hopes!

Gratitude. — *Queen Christina.*

IT is a species of agreeable servitude, to be under an Obligation to those we esteem.

The Grave. — *Blair.*

HERE are the Prude severe, and gay Coquette,
The sober Widow, and the young green Virgin,
Cropp'd like a rose before 'tis fully blown,
Or half its worth disclosed. Strange medley here!
Here garrulous Old Age winds up his tale;
And Jovial Youth, of lightsome, vacant heart,
Whose every day was made of melody,
Hears not the voice of mirth: the shrill-tongued Shrew,
Meek as the turtle-dove, forgets her chiding.
Here are the Wise, the Generous, and the Brave;
The Just, the Good, the Worthless, the Profane,
The downright Clown, and perfectly Well-bred;
The Fool, the Churl, the Scoundrel, and the Mean.

The Grave. — *Blair.*

HERE all the mighty Troublers of the Earth,
Who swam to sovereign rule through seas of blood;
The oppressive, sturdy, man-destroying Villains,
Who ravaged kingdoms, and laid empires waste,
And in a cruel wantonness of power
Thinn'd states of half their people, and gave up
To want the rest; now, like a storm that's spent,
Lie hush'd, and meanly sneak behind thy Covert.
Vain thought! to hide them from the general scorn
That haunts and dogs them like an injured ghost
Implacable.

Gravity. — *La Rochefoucauld.*

GRAVITY is a mystery of the Body, invented to conceal the defects of the Mind.

Gravity. — *Saville.*

THERE is a false Gravity that is a very ill symptom; and it may be said, that as rivers, which run very slowly, have always the most Mud at the bottom; so a solid Stiffness in the constant course of a man's life, is a sign of a thick bed of Mud at the bottom of his Brain.

Gravity. — *Pliny.*

AS in a man's life, so in his studies, I think it is the most beautiful and humane thing in the world, so to mingle Gravity with Pleasure, that the one may not sink into Melancholy, nor the other rise up into Wantonness.

Gravity. — *Young.*

WHAT'S the bent brow, or neck in Thought reclined?
The body's Wisdom to conceal the mind.
A man of sense can Artifice disdain;
As men of wealth may venture to go plain;
And be this Truth eternal ne'er forgot,—
Solemnity's a cover for a sot.

Gravity. — *Lord Shaftesbury.*

GRAVITY is of the very essence of Imposture; it does not only make us mistake other things, but is apt perpetually almost to mistake itself.

Gravity. — *Lavater.*

Too much Gravity argues a shallow mind.

Gravity. — *Sterne.*

YORICK sometimes in his wild way of talking would say, that Gravity was an arrant Scoundrel, and, he would add, of the most dangerous kind too, because a sly one: and that he verily believed more honest well-meaning people were bubbled out of their goods and money by it in one twelvemonth than by pocket-picking and shop-lifting in seven. In the naked temper which a merry heart discovered, he would say, there was no danger but to itself; whereas the very essence of Gravity was Design, and consequently Deceit; it was a taught trick to gain Credit of the world for more sense and knowledge than a man was worth, and that, with all its pretensions, it was no better, but often worse, than what a French wit had long ago defined it, viz. "a mysterious carriage of the Body to cover the defects of the Mind;" which definition of Gravity Yorick, with great imprudence, would say deserved to be wrote in letters of gold.

Great Men. — *Colton.*

GREAT Men often obtain their ends by means beyond the Grasp of vulgar intellect, and even by Methods diametrically opposite to those which the multitude would pursue. But, to effect this, bespeaks as profound a knowledge of Mind, as that philosopher evinced of Matter, who first produced ice by the agency of heat.

Great Men. — *Colton.*

I THINK it is Warburton who draws a very just distinction between a man of true Greatness and a Mediocrist. "If," says he, "you want to recommend yourself to the former, take care that he quits your Society with a good opinion of you; if your object is to please the latter, take care that he leaves you with a good opinion of himself."

Great Men.—*Anon.*

MOUNTAINS never shake hands. Their roots may touch: they may keep together some way up: but at length they part company, and rise into individual, insulated peaks. So is it with Great Men. As mountains mostly run in chains and clusters, crossing the plain at wider or narrower intervals, in like manner are there epochs in History when Great Men appear in clusters also. At first too they grow up together, seeming to be animated by the same Spirit, to have the same desires and antipathies, the same purposes and ends. But after a while the Genius of each begins to know itself, and to follow its own bent; they separate and diverge more and more: and those who, when young, were working in consort, stand alone in their old age. But if mountains do not shake hands, neither do they kick each other. Their human counterparts unfortunately are more pugnacious. Although they break out of the throng, and strive to soar in solitary Eminence, they cannot bear that their neighbours should do the same, but complain that they impede the View, and often try to overthrow them, especially if they are higher.

Great Men.—*La Rochefoucauld.*

O be a Great Man one must know how to profit by the whole of one's Fortune.

Great Men.—*Colton.*

IN life, we shall find many men that are great, and some men that are good, but very few Men that are both great and good.

Great Men.—*Colton.*

THE reason why Great men Meet with so little pity or attachment in Adversity, would seem to be this. The Friends of a Great Man were made by his Fortunes, his Enemies by himself, and Revenge is a much more punctual paymaster than Gratitude.

Great Men.—*Colton.*

SUBTRACT from a Great Man all that he owes to Opportunity, and all that he owes to Chance, all that he has gained by the wisdom of his friends, and by the folly of his enemies, and our Brobdinag will often become a Lilliputian. I think it is Voltaire who observes, that it was very fortunate for Cromwell that he appeared upon the stage at the precise moment when the people were tired of Kings; and as unfortunate for his son Richard, that he had to make good his pretensions at a moment when the people were equally tired of Protectors.

Great Men.—*Fisher Ames.*

THE most substantial glory of a country is in its virtuous great men: its prosperity will depend on its docility to learn from their example. That nation is fated to ignominy and servitude, for which such men have lived in vain. Power may be seized by a nation that is yet barbarous; and wealth may be enjoyed by one that it finds or renders sordid: the one is the gift and sport of accident, and the other is the sport of power. Both are mutable, and have passed away without leaving behind them any other memorial than ruins that offend taste, and traditions that baffle conjecture. But the glory of Greece is imperishable, or will last as long as learning itself, which is its monument: it strikes an everlasting root, and leaves perennial blossoms on its grave.

Greatness of Washington. — *Sparks.*

IF the title of great man ought to be reserved for him who cannot be charged with an indiscretion or a vice, who spent his life in establishing the independence, the glory, and durable prosperity of his country; who succeeded in all that he undertook, and whose successes were never won at the expense of honour, justice, integrity, or by the sacrifice of a single principle—this title will not be denied to Washington.

Greatness. — *Seneca.*

A GREAT, a Good, and a Right Mind is a kind of Divinity lodged in flesh, and may be the blessing of a slave as well as of a prince: it came from Heaven, and to Heaven it must return; and it is a kind of heavenly felicity, which a pure and virtuous Mind enjoys, in some degree, even upon earth.

Greatness. — *Shakspeare.*

THE mightier man, the mightier is the thing
  That makes him honor'd, or begets him Hate:
For greatest Scandal waits on greatest state.
The Moon being clouded presently is miss'd,
But little Stars may hide them when they list.
  The crow may bathe his coal-black wings in mire,
And unperceived fly with the filth away;
  But if the like the snow-white swan desire,
The stain upon his silver down will stay.
Poor grooms are sightless night, Kings glorious day.
Gnats are unnoted wheresoe'er they fly,
But Eagles gazed upon with every eye.

Greatness. — *La Bruyere.*

GREATNESS and Discernment are two different things, and a love of Virtue and of Virtuous Men is a third thing.

Greatness. — *La Rochefoucauld.*

HOWEVER brilliant an Action may be, it ought not to pass for great when it is not the result of a great design.

Greatness. — *Shakspeare.*

THEY that stand high, have many blasts to shake them;
And, if they fall, they dash themselves to piece.

Greatness. — *Colton.*

THE truly Great consider first, how they may gain the approbation of God; and secondly, that of their own Conscience; having done this, they would then willingly conciliate the good Opinion of their fellow-men.

Greatness. — *Colton.*

THE Wealthy and the Noble, when they expend large sums in decorating their houses with the rare and costly efforts of Genius, with busts from the chisel of a Canova, and with cartoons from the pencil of a Raphael, are to be commended, if they do not stand still here, but go on to bestow some pains and cost, that the Master himself be not inferior to the Mansion, and that the Owner be not the only thing that is little, amidst every thing else that is great.

Greatness. — *La Rochefoucauld.*

GREAT Souls are not those which have less Passion and more Virtue than common souls, but only those which have greater Designs.

Greatness. — *Colton.*

A GREAT Mind may change its objects, but it cannot relinquish them; it must have something to pursue; Variety is its relaxation, and Amusement its repose.

Greatness. — *Sir Philip Sidney.*

THE Hero passes through the multitude, as a man that neither disdains a People, nor yet is any thing tickled with their Vanity.

Greatness. — *Shakspeare.*

O PLACE and Greatness, millions of false eyes
Are stuck upon thee! volumes of report
Run with these false and most contrarious quests
Upon thy doings! thousand 'scapes of wit
Make thee the father of their idle dream,
And rack thee in their fancies.

Greatness. — *From the Latin.*

THAT which is great or splendid is not always laudable, but what ever is laudable must be great.

Greatness. — *Shakspeare.*

GREAT men may jest with Saints: 'tis wit in them;
But, in the less, foul profanation.
That in the Captain's but a choleric word,
Which in the soldier is flat blasphemy.

Greatness.—*From the Latin.*

NEVER less alone than when alone.

Greatness.—*Shakspeare.*

THESE signs have mark'd me extraordinary;
And all the Courses of my life do show
I am not in the roll of common men.

Greatness.—*La Bruyere.*

A GREAT Mind is above doing an unjust act, above giving way to Grief, above descending to Buffoonery; and it would be invulnerable, if Compassion did not prey upon its sensibility.

Greatness.—*Shakspeare.*

WHY, man, he doth bestride the narrow world,
Like a Colossus; and we petty men
Walk under his huge legs, and peep about
To find ourselves dishonourable Graves.

Greatness.—*Anon.*

THE greatest Truths are the simplest: so are the greatest Men.

Greatness.—*Shakspeare.*

I HAVE touch'd the highest point of all my Greatness;
And from that full Meridian of my glory,
I haste now to my setting: I shall fall
Like a bright exhalation in the Evening,
And no man see me more.

Greatness.—*Sir Philip Sidney.*

THE Great, in affliction, bear a countenance more Princely than they are wont; for it is the temper of the highest Hearts, like the Palm-tree, to strive most upward when it is most burdened.

Greatness.—*Shakspeare.*

THOUGH Fortune's malice overthrow my State,
My Mind exceeds the compass of her wheel.

Greatness.—*Cicero.*

THERE never was a Great Man, unless through Divine Inspiration.

Greatness.—*Shakspeare.*

HIS Greatness was no guard
To bar Heaven's shaft, but Sin had his reward.

Greatness.—*Hall.*

EARTHLY Greatness is a nice thing, and requires so much chariness in the managing, as the Contentment of it cannot requite.

Greatness.—*Young.*

IF we did but know how little some enjoy of the great things that they possess, there would not be much Envy in the world.

Greatness. — *Shakspeare.*

RIGHTLY to be great,
Is, not to stir without great Argument;
But greatly to find quarrel in a straw,
When Honour's at the stake.

Greatness. — *Shakspeare.*

O PLACE! O Form!
How often dost thou with thy case, thy habit,
Wrench awe from Fools, and tie the wiser souls
To thy false seeming.

Greatness. — *Lavater.*

HE only is Great who has the Habits of Greatness; who, after performing what none in ten thousand could accomplish, passes on like Samson, and "tells neither father nor mother of it."

Greatness. — *Shakspeare.*

OH, be sick, great Greatness
And bid thy Ceremony give thee cure!
Think'st thou, the fiery fever will go out
With titles blown from Adulation?
Will it give place to flexure and low bending?
Can'st thou, when thou command'st the Beggar's knee,
Command the Health of it?

Greatness. — *Shakspeare.*

OH, hard condition! and twin-born with Greatness,
Subjected to the breath of every fool,
Whose Sense no more can feel but his own wringing!
What infinite heart's ease must Kings neglect
That private men enjoy! and what have Kings
That privates have not too, save Ceremony?

Greatness. — *Shakspeare.*

OH, it is excellent
To have a Giant's strength; but it is tyrannous
To use it like a Giant.

Greatness. — *Horne.*

THE truly Generous is the truly wise;
And he who loves not others, lives unblest.

Greatness. — *Thomson.*

THE generous pride of Virtue
Disdains to weigh too nicely the returns
Her Bounty meets with. Like the liberal Gods,
From her own gracious nature she bestows,
Nor stoops to ask reward.

Greatness. — *Seneca.*

THERE is as much Greatness of Mind in the owning of a good turn as in the doing of it; and we must no more force a Requital out of season, than be wanting in it.

Greatness. — *Byron.*

UNEQUAL fortune
Made him my debtor for some courtesies,
Which bind the good more firmly.

Greatness. — *La Rochefoucauld.*

THERE is a kind of Elevation which does not depend on fortune. It is a certain air which distinguishes us, and seems to destine us for great things; it is a Price which we imperceptibly set on ourselves. By this quality we usurp the Deference of other men; and it puts us, in general, more above them than Birth, Dignity, or even Merit itself.

Greatness. — *Shakspeare.*

BE great in act, as you have been in thought;
Be stirring as the time; be Fire with fire;
Threaten the Threat'ner, and outface the brow
Of bragging Horror: so shall inferior eyes,
That borrow their behaviours from the great,
Grow great by your Example, and put on
The dauntless spirit of Resolution.

Greatness. — *Addison.*

TRUE Fortitude is seen in great exploits
That Justice warrants, and that Wisdom guides:
All else is tow'ring Phrensy and Distraction.

Greatness. — *Thomson.*

BUT to the generous still improving Mind,
That gives the hopeless heart to sing for joy,
Diffusing kind Beneficence around,
Boastless, as now descends the silent dew;
To him the long review of order'd life
Is inward rapture, only to be felt.

Greatness. — *Shakspeare.*

I LOVE the People,
But do not like to stage me to their eyes:
Though it do well, I do not relish well
Their loud Applause, and *aves* vehement:
Nor do I think the man of safe Discretion,
That does affect it.

Greatness. — *Shakspeare.*

SOME are born Great, some achieve Greatness,
And some have Greatness thrust upon them.

Greatness. — *Shakspeare.*

LET me not live,
After my Flame lacks oil, to be the snuff
Of younger spirits, whose apprehensive senses
All but new things disdain; whose Judgments are
Mere fathers of their Garments; whose constancies
Expire before their Fashions.

Greatness. — *Shakspeare.*

'TIS certain, Greatness, once fallen out with Fortune,
Must fall out with men too: what the declined is,
He shall as soon read in the eyes of others,
As feel in his own fall; for men, like Butterflies,
Show not their mealy wings but to the Summer.

Greatness. — *Young.*

'TIS great, 'tis manly, to disdain disguise;
It shows our Spirit, or it proves our strength.

Greatness. — *Shakspeare.*

I HAVE ventured,
Like little wanton boys that swim on bladders,
This many summers in a sea of Glory;
But far beyond my depth: my high-blown Pride
At length broke under me; and now has left me,
Weary, and old with service, to the mercy
Of a rude stream, that must for ever hide me.
Vain Pomp, and Glory of this world, I hate ye:
I feel my heart new open'd.
I know myself now; and I feel within me
A Peace above all earthly dignities,
A still and quiet Conscience.

Greatness. — *Pope.*

IN parts superior what advantage lies?
Tell (for you can) what is it to be wise?
'Tis but to know how little can be known;
To see all others' faults, and feel our own:
Condemn'd in Business or in arts to drudge,
Without a second, or without a Judge:
Truths would you teach, or save a sinking Land?
All fear, none aid you, and few understand.
Painful Pre-eminence! yourself to view
Above life's weakness, and its comforts too.

Greatness. — *Rowe.*

GREAT Minds, like Heaven, are pleased in doing Good,
Though the ungrateful subjects of their favours
Are barren in return.

Greatness. — *Young.*

HIGH Stations tumult, but not bliss, create:
None think the Great unhappy, but the Great.

Greatness. — *Pope.*

BRING then these Blessings to a strict account;
Make fair deductions; see to what they 'mount:
How much of other each is sure to cost;
How much for other oft is wholly lost;
How inconsistent greater goods with these;
How sometimes Life is risk'd, and always Ease;
Think, and if still the things thy envy call,
Say, would'st thou be the man to whom they fall?
To sigh for ribbons, if thou art silly,
Mark how they grace Lord Umbra, or Sir Billy.
Is yellow dirt the passion of thy life?
Look but on Gripus, or on Gripus' wife.
If parts allure thee, think how Bacon shined,
The wisest, brightest, meanest of Mankind.

Greatness. — *Byron.*

FROM my youth upward
My Spirit walk'd not with the Souls of men,
Nor look'd upon the earth with human eyes;
The thirst of their Ambition was not mine,
The aim of their Existence was not mine;
My joys, my griefs, my passions, and my powers,
Made me a Stranger.

Greatness. — *Thomson.*

'Tis hardship, toil;
'Tis sleepless nights, and never-resting days;
'Tis pain, 'tis danger, 'tis affronted Death;
'Tis equal fate for all, and changing Fortune;
That rear the mind to Glory, that inspire
The noblest Virtues, and the gentlest Manners.

Greatness. — *Joanna Baillie.*

HE died that Death which best becomes a man,
Who is with keenest sense of conscious ill
And deep Remorse assail'd, a wounded Spirit.
A death that kills the Noble and the Brave,
And only them. He had no other wound.

Greatness. — *Thomson.*

REAL Glory
Springs from the silent conquest of ourselves;
And without that the Conqueror is naught
But the first slave.

Grief. — *Shakspeare.*

THE violence of either Grief or Joy
Their own enactures with themselves destroy:
Where Joy most revels, Grief doth most lament;
Grief joys, Joy grieves, on slender accident.

Grief. — *Greville.*

WHAT an argument in favour of social connections is the observation that by communicating our Grief we have less, and by communicating our Pleasure we have more.

Grief. — *Shakspeare.*

GIVE me no help in Lamentation,
I am not barren to bring forth laments:
All springs reduce their currents to mine Eyes,
That I, being govern'd by the watery moon,
May send forth plenteous Tears to drown the world!

Grief. — *Dryden.*

MINE is a Grief of fury, not Despair!
And if a manly drop or two fall down,
It scalds along my cheeks, like the green wood,
That sputtering in the flames, works outward into Tears.

Grief. — *Shakspeare.*

GRIEF softens the Mind,
And makes it fearful and degenerate.

Grief. — *Metastasio.*

IF the internal Griefs of every man could be read, written on his forehead, how many who now excite Envy, would appear to be objects of Pity?

Grief. — *Shakspeare.*

WEEP I cannot,
But my heart bleeds.

Grief. — *Shakspeare.*

OH how her eyes and tears did lend and borrow!
Her eyes seen in the Tears, tears in her eye;
Both crystals, where they view'd each other's Sorrow;
Sorrow, that friendly Sighs sought still to dry;
But like a stormy day, now wind, now rain,
Sighs dry her cheeks, Tears make them wet again.

Grief. — *Joanna Baillie.*

I'll do whate'er thou wilt, I will be silent;
But oh! a reined Tongue, and bursting Heart,
Are hard at once to bear.

Grief. — *Shakspeare.*

Oh, what a noble Combat hast thou fought,
Between compulsion and a brave respect!
Let me wipe off this honourable Dew,
That silverly doth progress on thy cheeks.
My Heart hath melted at a lady's tears,
Being an ordinary inundation:
But this effusion of such manly drops,
This shower, blown up by Tempest of the Soul,
Startles mine eyes, and makes me more amazed,
Than had I seen the vaulty top of Heaven
Figured quite o'er with burning meteors.
Lift up thy brow,
And with a great heart heave away this storm.
Commend these waters to those baby-eyes,
That never saw the giant World enraged;
Nor met with Fortune, other than at feasts,
Full-warm of blood, of mirth, of gossiping.

Grief. — *Thomson.*

Sweet Source of every virtue,
O Sacred Sorrow! he who knows not thee,
Knows not the best emotions of the Heart,
Those tender Tears that humanize the Soul,
The Sigh that charms, the Pang that gives delight.

Grief. — *Joanna Baillie.*

I felt a sudden tightness grasp my throat
As it would strangle me: such as I felt,
I knew it well, some twenty years ago,
When my good father shed his Blessing on me:
I hate to weep, and so I came away.

Grief. — *Shakspeare.*

She shook
The holy water from her heavenly eyes,
And clamour moisten'd: then away she started
To deal with Grief alone.

Grief. — *Shakspeare.*

Oh! Grief hath changed me, since you saw me last
And careful hours with Time's deformed hand
Have written strange defeatures in my Face.

Grief. — *Shakspeare.*

WHY tell you me of moderation;
The Grief is fine, full, perfect, that I taste,
And violenteth in a sense as strong
As that which causeth it: How can I moderate it?
If I could temporize with my Affection,
Or brew it to a weak and colder palate,
The like allayment could I give my Grief;
My Love admits no qualifying dross:
No more my Grief, in such a precious loss.

Grief. — *Shakspeare.*

WHEN the Sun sets, the air doth drizzle Dew.
What, still in tears?
Evermore showering? In one little body
Thou counterfeit'st a Bark, a Sea, a Wind:
For still thy eyes, which I may call the Sea,
Do ebb and flow with Tears; the Bark thy body is,
Sailing in this salt Flood; the Winds, thy Sighs;
Who,—raging with thy Tears, and they with them,—
Without a sudden Calm, will overset
Thy tempest-toss'd body.

Grief. — *Byron.*

YET disappointed joys are Woes as deep
As any man's clay mixture undergoes.
Our least of Sorrows are such as we weep;
'Tis the vile daily drop on drop that wears
The Soul out (like the stone) with petty Cares.

Grief. — *Byron.*

UPON her face there was the tint of Grief,
The settled Shadow of an inward Strife,
And an unquiet drooping of the Eye,
As if its lid were charged with unshed tears.

Grief. — *Shakspeare.*

I AM not prone to Weeping, as our sex
Commonly are; the want of which vain dew,
Perchance, shall dry your Pities; but I have
That honourable Grief lodged here, which burns
Worse than Tears drown.

Grief. — *Young.*

WHO fails to grieve, when just occasion calls,
Or grieves too much, deserves not to be blest;
Inhuman, or effeminate, his Heart.

Grief. — *Spenser.*

LONG thus he chew'd the cud of inward Griefe,
And did consume his Gall with Anguish sore;
Still when he mused on his late mischiefe,
Then still the smart thereof increased more,
And seem'd more grievous than it was before.

Grief. — *Spenser.*

THUS is my Summer worn away and wasted,
Thus is my Harvest hasten'd all to rathe;
The ear that budded fair is burnt and blasted;
And all my hoped gain is turn'd to scathe.
Of all the seed that in my youth was sown,
Was none but Brakes and Brambles to be mown.

Grief. — *Shakspeare.*

GRIEF fills the room up of my absent Child;
Lies in his bed, walks up and down with me;
Puts on his pretty looks, repeats his words,
Remembers me of all his gracious parts;
Stuffs out his vacant garments with his form:
Then have I reason to be fond of Grief.

Grief. —*Spenser.*

WHICH when she heard, as in despightfull wise
She wilfully her sorrow did augment,
And offer'd hope of comfort did despise:
Her golden lockes most cruelly she rent,
And scratcht her face with ghastly Dreriment;
Ne would she speake, ne see, ne yet be seene,
But hid her Visage, and her Head downe bent,
Either for grievous Shame, or for great Teene,
As if her Heart with Sorrow had transfixed beene.

Grief. — *Byron.*

THROUGH many a clime 'tis mine to go,
With many a retrospection curst,
And all my Solace is to know,
Whate'er betides, I've known the worst.
What is that worst? Nay, do not ask,
In pity from the search forbear:
Smile on—nor venture to unmask
Man's heart, and view the Hell that's there.

Grief. — *Shakspeare.*

EVERY one can master a Grief, but he that has it.

Grief. — *Shakspeare.*

HONEST plain words best pierce the ear of Grief.

Grief. — *Spenser.*

WHAT equall torment to the Griefe of Mind,
And pyning Anguish hid in gentle hart,
That inly feeds itselfe with thoughts unkind,
And nourisheth her owne consuming Smart?
What medicine can any leach's art
Yeeld such a sore, that doth her Grievance hide,
And will to none her Maladie impart?

Grief. — *Spenser.*

WHICH whenas Scudamour did heare, his heart
Was thril'd with inward Griefe, as when in chace
The Parthian strikes a stag with shivering dart,
The beast astonisht stands in middest of his Smart.

Grief. — *Shakspeare.*

I PRAY thee, cease thy counsel,
Which falls into mine ears as profitless
As water in a sieve: give not me counsel;
Nor let no comforter delight mine ear,
But such a one, whose wrongs do suit with mine.
Bring me a Father, that so loved his Child,
Whose joy of her is overwhelm'd like mine,
And bid him speak of Patience;
Measure his woe the length and breadth of mine,
And let it answer every strain for strain;
As thus for thus, and such a grief for such,
In every lineament, branch, shape, and form:
If such a one will smile, and stroke his beard;
Cry—Sorrow, wag! and hem, when he should groan;
Patch Grief with proverbs; make Misfortune drunk
With candle-wasters; bring him yet to me,
And I of him will gather Patience.
But there is no such man.

Grief. — *Shakspeare.*

AH, my tender Babes!
My unblown flowers, new-appearing sweets!
If yet your gentle Souls fly in the air—
Hover about me with your airy wings,
And hear your mother's Lamentation.

Grief. — *Dryden.*

ALAS! I have not words to tell my Grief;
To vent my Sorrow would be some relief;
Light Sufferings give us leisure to complain;
We groan, we cannot speak, in greater Pain.

Grief. — *Shakspeare.*

THE shadow of my Sorrow? Ha! let's see:—
'Tis very true, my Grief lies all within;
And these external manners of Lament
Are merely shadows to the unseen Grief,
That swells with silence in the tortured Soul;
There lies the Substance.

Grief. — *Moore.*

THE world had just begun to steal,
Each hope, that led me lightly on;
I felt not as I used to feel,
And life grew dark, and Love was gone!
No eye to mingle Sorrow's tear,
No lip to mingle Pleasure's breath,
No tongue to call me kind and dear—
'Twas gloomy, and I wish'd for Death!

Grief. — *Shakspeare.*

OH that this too too solid Flesh would melt,
Thaw, and resolve itself into a dew!
Or that the Everlasting had not fix'd
His Canon 'gainst Self-slaughter! O God! O God!
How weary, stale, flat, and unprofitable
Seem to me all the uses of this world!
Fie on't! O fie! 'tis an unweeded Garden,
That grows to Seed; things rank, and gross in nature,
Possess it merely.

Grief. — *Campbell.*

I ALONE am left on earth!
To whom nor Relative nor Blood remains;
No!—not a kindred drop that runs in human veins.

Grief. — *Shakspeare.*

THE robb'd that smiles, steals something from the thief;
He robs himself, that spends a bootless Grief.

Grief. — *Byron.*

WHAT is the worst of woes that wait on Age?
What stamps the wrinkle deeper on the brow?
To view each loved one blotted from life's page,
And be alone on Earth, as I am now.

Grief. — *Moore.*

ALAS! the Breast that inly bleeds
Hath nought to dread from outward blow:
Who falls from all he knows of Bliss
Cares little into what abyss.

Grief. — *Shakspeare.*

To mourn a Mischief that is past and gone,
Is the next way to draw new Mischief on.

Grief. — *Shakspeare.*

EACH substance of a Grief hath twenty shadows,
Which show like Grief itself, but are not so:
For Sorrow's eye, glazed with blinding Tears,
Divides one thing entire, to many objects.

Grief. — *Spenser.*

SO all the world, and all in it I hate,
Because it changeth ever to and fro,
And never standeth in one certain state,
But still unsteadfast, round about doth go
Like a mill-wheel, in midst of Misery,
Driven with streams of wretchedness and woe,
That dying lives, and living still does die.

Grief. — *Shakspeare.*

SOME Grief shows much of Love;
But much of Grief shows still some want of Wit.

Grief. — *Byron.*

THE wither'd frame, the ruin'd mind,
The wrack by passion left behind,
A shrivell'd scroll, a scatter'd leaf,
Sear'd by the autumn-blast of Grief!

Grief. — *Dryden.*

HE withers at his Heart, and looks as wan
As the pale spectre of a murder'd man.

Grief. — *Shakspeare.*

HAD he the motive and the cue for Passion,
That I have, he would drown the stage with Tears,
And cleave the general ear with horrid speech;
Make mad the Guilty, and appal the Free,
Confound the ignorant; and amaze, indeed,
The very faculties of eyes and ears.

Grief. — *Shakspeare.*

HE raised a Sigh so piteous and profound,
As it did seem to shatter all his bulk,
And end his being.

Grief. — *Shakspeare.*

WHAT, man! ne'er pull your hat upon your brows;
Give Sorrow words: the Grief, that does not speak,
Whispers the o'er-fraught Heart, and bids it break.

Grief. — *Spenser.*

NEXT him went Griefe and Fury, matcht yfere;
Griefe all in sable sorrowfully clad,
Downe hanging his dull head with heavy chere,
Yet inly being more than seeming sad;
A paire of pincers in his hand he had,
With which he pinched many people to the Hart,
That from thenceforth a wretched life they ladd
In wilfull languor and consuming smart,
Dying each day with inward wounds of Dolour's dart.

Grief. — *Shakspeare.*

MOST subject is the fattest soil to weeds;
And he, the noble Image of my youth,
Is overspread with them: therefore my Grief
Stretches itself beyond the hour of death.

Grief. — *Joanna Baillie.*

LIKE a pent-up flood, swoln to the height,
He pour'd his Griefs into my breast with Tears,
Such as the manliest men in their cross'd lives
Are sometimes forced to shed.

Grief. — *Shakspeare.*

My Grief lies all within,
And these external manners of laments
Are merely shadows to the unseen Grief,
That swells with silence in the tortured Sou

Grief. — *Spenser.*

WITH that adowne, out of her christall eyne,
Few trickling Teares she softly forth let fall,
That like two orient perles did purely shyne
Upon her snowy Cheeke; and therewithall
She sighed soft, that none so bestiall
Nor salvage hart, but ruth of her sad plight
Would make to melt, or pitteously appall.

Grief. — *Shakspeare.*

OH, break, my Heart!—poor bankrupt, break at once!
To prison, eyes! ne'er look on liberty!
Vile earth, to earth resign; end motion here;
And thou, and Romeo, press one heavy Bier.

Grief. — *Shakspeare.*

No, I'll not weep:—
I have full cause of weeping; but this Heart
Shall break into a hundred thousand flaws,
Ere I'll weep:—O Fool, I shall go mad!

Grief. — *La Rochefoucauld.*

THERE are divers sorts of hypocrisy in Grief. In one, under pretext of lamenting the loss of a person who is dear to us, we lament ourselves, we lament the diminution of our Advantages, of our Pleasures, of our Consideration. We regret the good opinion that was entertained of us. Thus the Dead get the credit of tears which are only shed for the Living. I call this a species of hypocrisy, because in this sort of Grief we deceive ourselves. There is yet another species of Tears which have very petty sources, which flow easily, and as easily are dried: we weep to acquire the reputation of a tender Heart; we weep to be pitied; we weep to be wept over; in fine, we weep to avoid the shame of not weeping.

Grief. — *Martial.*

SHE grieves sincerely who grieves when alone.

Grief. — *Shakspeare.*

LIKE the Lily,
That once was mistress of the field, and flourished,
I'll hang my Head, and perish.

Grief. — *Pliny.*

HOWEVER, I by no means wish to become less susceptible of Tenderness. I know these kind of misfortunes would be estimated by other persons only as common losses, and from such Sensations they would conceive themselves great and wise men. I shall not determine either their Greatness or their Wisdom; but I am certain they have no Humanity. It is the part of a man to be affected with Grief, to feel Sorrow, at the same time that he is to resist it, and to admit of Comfort.

Grief. — *Shakspeare.*

AH, cut my lace asunder!
That my pent Heart may have some scope to beat,
Or else I swoon with this dead-killing news.

Grief. — *Shakspeare.*

SPIRITS of Peace, where are ye? Are ye all gone?
And leave me here in Wretchedness behind ye?

Grief. — *Shakspeare.*

WHEN remedies are past, the Griefs are ended,
By seeing the worst, which late on hopes depended.
To mourn a Mischief that is past and gone,
Is the next way to draw new Mischief on.
What cannot be preserved when Fortune takes,
Patience her injury a mockery makes.
The robb'd, that smiles, steals something from the Thief;
He robs himself, that spends a bootless Grief.

Grief. — *Byron.*

HIDE thy Tears—
I do not bid thee not to shed them—'twere
Easier to stop Euphrates at its source
Than one tear of a true and tender Heart—
But let me not behold them; they unman me.

Grief. — *Shakspeare.*

'TIS double Death to drown in ken of shore:
He ten times pines, that pines beholding food:
To see the salve, doth make the Wound ache more;
Great Grief grieves most at that would do it good:
Deep Woes roll forward like a gentle flood,
Who, being stopp'd, the bounding banks o'erflows;
Grief dallied with, nor law nor limits knows.

Grief. — *Shakspeare.*

MEN
Can counsel, and speak comfort to that Grief,
Which they themselves not feel; but tasting it,
Their counsel turns to Passion, which before
Would give preceptial medicine to Rage,
Fetter strong Madness in a silken thread,
Charm Ache with air, and Agony with words:
No, no: 'tis all men's office to speak Patience
To those that wring under the load of Sorrow;
But no man's virtue, nor Sufficiency,
To be so moral, when he shall endure
The like himself.

Grovellers. — *Persius.*

O SOULS, in whom no heavenly Fire is found,
Fat Minds, and ever grovelling on the ground!

Grumbling. — *Graves.*

EVERY one must see daily instances of people who complain from a mere Habit of Complaining.

Grumbling. — *Greville.*

THERE is an unfortunate disposition in a man to attend much more to the Faults of his companions which offend him, than to their Perfections which please him.

Guilt. — *Milton.*

EARTH felt the wound, and Nature from her seat
Sighing through all her works gave signs of Wo.

Habit. — *Colton.*

IT is almost as difficult to make a man unlearn his Errors as his Knowledge.

Habit. — *Seneca.*

TO things which you bear with Impatience you should accustom yourself, and, by Habit, you will bear them well.

Habit. — *Tucker.*

THERE are Habits contracted by bad example, or bad management, before we have Judgment to discern their approaches, or because the eye of Reason is laid asleep, or has not compass of view sufficient to look around on every quarter.

Habit. — *Shakspeare.*

KEEP a Gamester from the dice, and a good Student from his book, and it is wonderful.

Habit. — *Horace.*

A NEW Cask will long preserve the Tincture of the liquor with which it is first impregnated.

Habit. — *Shakspeare.*

THAT monster, Custom, who all sense doth eat
Of Habit's devil, is angel yet in this;
That to the use of Actions fair and good
He likewise gives a frock, or livery,
That aptly is put on; Refrain to-night:
And that shall lend a kind of easiness
To the next Abstinence: the next more easy:
For Use almost can change the stamp of nature,
And either curb the Devil, or throw him out
With wondrous potency.

Happiness. — *From the French.*

THE Happiness of the human race in this world does not consist in our being devoid of Passions, but in our learning to command them.

Happiness. — *Addison.*

TRUE Happiness is of a retired nature, and an enemy to pomp and noise; it arises, in the first place, from the enjoyment of one's self: and in the next, from the Friendship and Conversation of a few select Companions: false Happiness loves to be in a crowd, and to draw the eyes of the world upon her. She does not receive any Satisfaction from the applauses which she gives herself, but from the admiration which she raises in others.

Happiness. — *Shakspeare.*

THEY are as sick that surfeit with too much, as they that starve with nothing: It is no mean Happiness, therefore, to be seated in the mean: Superfluity comes sooner by white hairs, but Competency lives longer.

Happiness. — *Goldsmith.*

EVERY mind seems capable of entertaining a certain quantity of Happiness, which no institutions can increase, no circumstances alter, and entirely independent on Fortune. Let any man compare his present Fortune with the past, and he will probably find himself, upon the whole, neither better nor worse than formerly.

Happiness. — *Steele.*

INDOLENCE of body and mind, when we aim at no more, is very frequently enjoyed; but the very inquiry after Happiness has something restless in it, which a man who lives in a series of temperate meals, friendly conversations, and easy slumbers, gives himself no trouble about it. While men of Refinement are talking of Tranquillity, he possesses it.

Happiness. — *Thomson.*

EVEN not all these, in one rich lot combined,
Can make the happy man, without the mind;
Where Judgment sits clear-sighted, and surveys
The Chain of Reason with unerring gaze;
Where Fancy lives, and to the brightening eyes,
His fairer scenes, and bolder figures rise;
Where social Love exerts her soft command,
And plays the Passions with a tender hand,
Whence every Virtue flows, in rival strife,
And all the moral Harmony of life.

Happiness. — *Shakspeare.*

THE bitter past, more welcome is the Sweet.

Happiness. — *Pope.*

ORDER is heaven's first law; and this confest,
Some are, and must be, greater than the rest,
More rich, more wise; but who infers from hence
That such are happier, shocks all common sense.
Heaven to mankind impartial we confess,
If all are equal in their Happiness:
But mutual wants this Happiness increase
All Nature's difference keeps all Nature's peace.
Condition, circumstance, is not the thing;
Bliss is the same in subject or in King,
In who obtain defence, or who defend,
In him who is, or him who finds a friend:
Heaven breathes through every member of the whole,
One common blessing, as one common Soul.

Happiness.—*La Rochefoucauld.*

IT is a kind of Happiness to know to what extent we may be unhappy.

Happiness.—*Mrs. Tighe.*

OH happy you! who, blest with present Bliss,
See not with fatal prescience future tears,
Nor the dear moment of Enjoyment miss
Through gloomy Discontent, or sullen Fears
Foreboding many a storm for coming years;
Change is the lot of all. Ourselves with scorn
Perhaps shall view what now so fair appears;
And wonder whence the fancied Charm was born,
Which now with vain Despair from our fond grasp is torn!

Happiness.—*Shakspeare.*

HIS overthrow heap'd Happiness upon him;
For then, and not till then, he felt himself,
And found the Blessedness of being little:
And, to add greater Honours to his age
Than man could give him, he died, fearing God.

Happiness.—*Greville.*

HARDLY a man, whatever his circumstances and situation, but if you get his Confidence, will tell you that he is not happy. It is however certain all men are not unhappy in the same degree, though by these accounts we might almost be tempted to think so. Is not this to be accounted for, by supposing that all men measure the Happiness they possess by the Happiness they desire, or think they deserve.

Happiness.—*Horace.*

"WHAT you demand is here, or at Ulubræ." You traverse the world in search of Happiness, which is within the reach of every man; a contented Mind confers it on all.

Happiness.—*Shakspeare.*

WHAT! we have many goodly days to see:
The liquid drops of Tears that you have shed,
Shall come again, transform'd to orient Pearl;
Advantaging their loan, with interest
Often-times-double gain of Happiness.

Happiness.—*Colton.*

HAPPINESS is that single and glorious thing, which is the very Light and Sun of the whole animated universe, and where she is not, it were better that nothing should be. Without her, Wisdom is but a shadow, and Virtue a name; she is their sovereign mistress.

Happiness. — *Pope.*

OH, Happiness! our being's end and aim;
Good, Pleasure, Ease, Content,—whate'er thy name:
That something still which prompts th' eternal sigh,
For which we bear to live, or dare to die,
Which still so near us, yet beyond us lies,
O'erlook'd, seen double, by the Fool and Wise:
Plant of celestial seed! if dropp'd below,
Say in what mortal Soil thou deign'st to grow?

Happiness. — *Mrs. Tighe.*

VAIN schemer, think not to prolong thy Joy!
But cherish while it lasts the heavenly boon!
Expand thy sails! thy little bark shall fly
With the full tide of Pleasure! though it soon
May feel the influence of the changeful Moon,
It yet is thine! then let not doubts obscure
With cloudy vapours vail thy brilliant Noon,
Nor let Suspicion's tainted breath impure
Poison the favouring gale which speeds thy course secure!

Happiness. — *Colton.*

IN the constitution both of our mind and of our body, every thing must go on right, and harmonize well together to make us happy: but should one thing go wrong, that is quite enough to make us miserable; and, although the Joys of this world are vain and short, yet its Sorrows are real and lasting; for I will show you a ton of perfect Pain with greater ease than one ounce of perfect Pleasure; and he knows little of himself, or of the world, who does not think it sufficient Happiness to be free from Sorrow; therefore, give a wise man Health, and he will give himself every other thing.

Happiness. — *Cowper.*

THE heart is hard in nature, and unfit
For human fellowship, as being void
Of Sympathy, and therefore dead alike
To Love and Friendship both, that is not pleased
With sight of animals enjoying life,
Nor feels their Happiness augment his own.

Happiness. — *Colton.*

HAPPINESS is much more equally divided than some of us imagine. One man shall possess most of the Materials, but little of the Thing; another may possess much of the Thing, but very few of the Materials.

Happiness. — *Shakspeare.*

I EARN that I eat, get that I wear; owe no man Hate, envy no man's Happiness; glad of other men's good, content with my harm.

Happiness. — *Pope.*

KNOW, all the good that individuals find,
Or God and Nature meant to mere mankind,
Reason's whole pleasure, all the joys of sense,
Lie in three words, Health, Peace, and Competence
But Health consists with temperance alone;
And Peace, O Virtue! Peace is all thy own.
The good or bad the gifts of Fortune gain;
But these less taste them, as they worse obtain.

Happiness. — *Beaumont and Fletcher.*

THERE is no man but may make his Paradise,
And it is nothing but his Love and Dotage
Upon the World's foul joys, that keeps him out on't;
For he that lives retired in mind and spirit,
Is still in Paradise.

Happiness. — *Burns.*

THINK ye, that sic as you and I,
Wha drudge and drive thro' wet and dry,
Wi' never-ceasing toil;
Think ye, are we less blest than they,
Wha scarcely tent us in their way,
As hardly worth their while?

Happiness. — *Dryden.*

THEY live too long, who Happiness out-live:
For life and death are things indifferent;
Each to be chose, as either brings Content.

Happiness. — *Shakspeare.*

OH, how bitter a thing it is to look into Happiness through another man's eyes!

Happiness. — *Shakspeare.*

SILENCE is the perfectest herald of Joy: I were but little Happy, if I could say how much.

Happiness. — *Burns.*

ITS no' in Books, its no' in lear,
To make us truly blest:
If Happiness has not her seat
And centre in the Breast,
We may be wise, or rich or great,
But never can be blest.

Happiness. — *Joanna Baillie.*

THE Bliss e'en of a moment, still is Bliss.
Thou wouldst not of her dew-drops spoil the thorn
Because her Glory will not last till noon;
Nor still the lightsome gambols of the Colt,
Whose neck to-morrow's yoke will gall.

Happiness. — *Young.*

WHAT makes Man wretched? Happiness denied?
No: 'tis Happiness disdain'd.
She comes too meanly drest to win our smile;
And calls herself Content, a homely name!
Our flame is Transport, and Content our scorn.
Ambition turns, and shuts the door against her,
And weds a Toil, a Tempest, in her stead.

Happiness. — *Greville.*

I KNOW not whether the truest and best state of Nature be not a state of more Prejudice and Ignorance than we are aware of.

Happiness. — *Duchesse de Praslin.*

OUR Happiness in this world depends on the affections we are enabled to inspire.

Happiness. — *Prudentius.*

WE thro' this maze of Life one Lord obey,
Whose Light and Grace unerring lead the way.
By Hope and Faith secure of future bliss,
Gladly the joys of present Life we miss;
For baffled mortals still attempt in vain,
Present and future Bliss at once to gain.

Happiness. — *Shenstone.*

IT is one species of Despair to have no room to hope for any addition to one's Happiness. His following wish must then be to wish he had some fresh object for his wishes; a strong Argument that our minds and bodies were both meant to be for ever active.

Happiness. — *Sterne.*

ALAS! if the principles of Contentment are not within us,—the height of Station and worldly Grandeur will as soon add a cubit to a man's stature as to his Happiness.

Happiness. — *Johnson.*

THE fountain of Content must spring up in the Mind; and he, who has so little knowledge of human nature, as to seek Happiness by changing any thing but his own Dispositions, will waste his life in fruitless efforts, and multiply the Griefs which he purposes to remove.

Happiness. — *Landor.*

GOODNESS does not more certainly make men happy, than Happiness makes them good. We must distinguish between Felicity and Prosperity, for Prosperity leads often to Ambition, and Ambition to Disappointment; the course is then over, the wheel turns round but once, while the reaction of Goodness and Happiness is perpetual.

Happiness. — *Paley.*

HAPPINESS consists in the constitution of the Habits.

Happiness. — *Anon.*

IF Happiness were an attainment of the Mind, to be acquired as a science or an art is learnt from the master, the teacher might justly be considered as the Vicegerent of God, and no place could contain the numbers that would flock to his School; but in this, the Almighty has delegated his power to every person only respecting himself.

Happiness. — *Seneca.*

THE great Blessings of mankind are within us, and within our reach, but we shut our Eyes, and, like people in the dark, we fall foul upon the very thing we search for, without finding it.

Happiness. — *Addison.*

CONTENTMENT produces, in some measure, all those effects which the Alchemist usually ascribes to what he calls the Philosopher's Stone; and if it does not bring Riches, it does the same thing by banishing the desire of them.

Happiness. — *Mackenzie.*

I HAVE observed one ingredient somewhat necessary in a man's composition toward Happiness, which people of feeling would do well to acquire—a certain respect for the follies of mankind: for there are so many Fools whom the world entitles to regard, whom accident has placed in heights of which they are unworthy, that he who cannot restrain his Contempt or Indignation at the sight, will be too often quarrelling with the disposal of things to relish that share which is allotted to himself.

Happiness. — *Burton.*

AS the Ivy twines around the Oak, so does Misery and Misfortune encompass the Happiness of man. Felicity, pure and unalloyed Felicity, is not a plant of earthly growth; her gardens are the Skies.

Happiness. — *Longfellow.*

THE rays of Happiness, like those of light, are colourless when unbroken.

Happiness. — *Seneca.*

HE must be Miserable who does not consider himself Happy, although he could command the Universe; no man can be Happy who does not think himself so, for it signifies not how exalted soever your Station may be, if it appears to you bad.

Happiness. — *Budgell.*

AS nothing is more natural than for every one to desire to be happy, it is not to be wondered at that the wisest men in all ages have spent so much time to discover what Happiness is, and wherein it chiefly consists. An eminent writer, named Varro, reckons up no less than two hundred and eighty-eight different Opinions upon this subject; and another, called Lucian, after having given us a long catalogue of the notions of several philosophers, endeavours to show the Absurdity of all of them, without establishing any thing of his own.

Hardness. — *Shakspeare.*

YET famine,
Ere clean it o'erthrow Nature, makes it valiant.
Plenty, and peace, breeds Cowards; Hardness ever
Of Hardness is mother.

Hardness. — *Shakspeare.*

I HAVE almost forgot the taste of Fears:
The time has been, my senses would have cool'd
To hear a night-shriek; and my fell of hair
Would at a dismal treatise rouse, and stir
As life were in't: I have supp'd full of Horrors;
Direness, familiar to my slaughterous Thoughts,
Cannot once start me.

The Harlot. — *Shakspeare.*

'TIS the Strumpet's plague,
To beguile many, and be beguiled by one.

Hatred. — *Plutarch.*

IF you hate your Enemies, you will contract such a vicious habit of mind, as by degrees will break out upon those who are your Friends, or those who are indifferent to you.

Hatred. — *La Bruyere.*

THE passion of Hatred is so durable, and so inveterate, that the surest prognostic of Death in a sick man is a wish for Reconciliation.

Hatred. — *Tacitus.*

IT is the nature of the human disposition to Hate him whom you have injured.

Hatred.—*La Rochefoucauld.*

WHEN our Hatred is too keen, it places us beneath those we hate.

Hatred.—*La Bruyere.*

TO be deprived of the person we love, is a Happiness in comparison of living with one we hate.

Hatred.—*Byron.*

WARP'D by the world in Disappointment's school,
In words too wise, in conduct there a fool;
Too firm to yield, and far too proud to stoop,
Doom'd by his very virtues for a dupe,
He cursed those Virtues as the cause of ill,
And not the traitors who betray'd him still;
Nor deem'd that gifts bestow'd on better men,
Had left him joy, and means to give again.
Fear'd, shunn'd, belied, ere Youth had lost her force,
He hated man too much to feel Remorse,
And thought the voice of Wrath a sacred call,
To pay the Injuries of some on all.

Health.—*Sir W. Temple.*

THE only way for a rich man to be healthy is, by Exercise and Abstinence, to live as if he was poor.

Health.—*Shakspeare.*

INFIRMITY doth still neglect all office
Whereto our Health is bound; we are not ourselves
When Nature, being oppress'd, commands the mind
To suffer with the body.

Health.—*Johnson.*

HEALTH is certainly more valuable than Money, because it is by Health that Money is procured; but thousands and millions are of small avail to alleviate the protracted tortures of the Gout, to repair the broken organs of sense, or resuscitate the powers of Digestion. Poverty is, indeed, an evil from which we naturally fly; but let us not run from one enemy to another, nor take shelter in the arms of Sickness.

Health.—*Sterne.*

O BLESSED Health! thou art above all Gold and Treasure; 'tis thou who enlargest the Soul, and openest all its powers to receive instruction, and to relish Virtue.—He that has thee has little more to wish for! and he that is so wretched as to want thee, wants every thing with thee.

Health.—*Churchill.*

THE surest road to Health, say what they will,
Is never to suppose we shall be ill.

Health. — *Lucan.*

THOU chiefest Good!
Bestow'd by Heaven, but seldom understood.

Health. — *Sir W. Temple.*

HEALTH is the soul that animates all enjoyments of life, which fade, and are tasteless, if not dead, without it: a man starves at the best and the greatest Tables, makes faces at the noblest and most delicate Wines, is old and impotent in Seraglios of the most sparkling beauties, poor and wretched in the midst of the greatest treasures and fortunes; with common diseases Strength grows decrepit, Youth loses all vigour, and Beauty all charms; Music grows harsh, and Conversation disagreeable; Palaces are prisons, or of equal confinement; Riches are useless, Honour and Attendance are cumbersome, and crowns themselves are a burden: but if Diseases are painful and violent, they equal all conditions of life, make no difference between a Prince and a Beggar; and a fit of the stone or the colic puts a King to the rack, and makes him as miserable as he can do the meanest, the worst, and most criminal of his subjects.

Health. — *Martial.*

FOR Life is not to live, but to be Well.

Health. — *Claudian.*

HAIL, greatest Good Dardanian fields bestow,
At whose command Pæonian waters flow;
Unpurchased Health! that dost thy aid impart
Both to the Patient and the Doctor's art!

Health. — *Colton.*

THERE is this difference between those two temporal blessings, Health and Money: Money is the most envied, but the least enjoyed; Health is the most enjoyed, but the least envied: and this superiority of the latter is still more obvious when we reflect, that the poorest man would not part with Health for Money, but that the richest would gladly part with all their Money for Health.

Health. — *Colton.*

ANGUISH of Mind has driven thousands to suicide; Anguish of Body, none. This proves that the Health of the Mind is of far more consequence to our Happiness than the Health of the Body, although both are deserving of much more attention than either of them receives.

Health. — *Sterne.*

PEOPLE who are always taking care of their Health are like misers, who are hoarding up a treasure which they have never spirit enough to enjoy.

Health. — *La Rochefoucauld.*

PRESERVING the Health by too strict a regimen is a wearisome Malady.

Health. — *Sir Philip Sidney.*

GREAT Temp'rance, open air,
Easy labour, little Care.

The Heart. — *Shakspeare.*

ALL offences come from the Heart.

Great Hearts. — *Byron.*

LOOK on me! there is an order
Of mortals on the earth, who do become
Old in their youth, and die ere middle age,
Without the violence of warlike Death;
Some perishing of Pleasure—some of Study—
Some worn with Toil—some of mere weariness—
Some of Disease—and some of Insanity—
And some of wither'd, or of broken Hearts;
For this last is a malady which slays
More than are number'd in the lists of Fate,
Taking all shapes, and bearing many names.

Heaven. — *Lavater.*

THE Generous who is always Just, and the Just who is always Generous, may, unannounced, approach the throne of Heaven.

Heavenly Love. — *Edwards.*

EVERY saint in Heaven is as a flower in the garden of God, and holy love is the fragrance and sweet odour that they all send forth, and with which they fill the bowers of that paradise above. Every soul there is as a note in some concert of delightful music, that sweetly harmonizes with every other note, and all together blend in the most rapturous strains in praising God and the Lamb for ever.

The Heavens. — *Young.*

ONE Sun by day, by night ten thousand shine;
And light us deep into the Deity;
How boundless in Magnificence and Might!
Oh what a confluence of ethereal Fires,
From urns unnumber'd, down the steep of Heaven,
Streams to a point, and centers in my sight!
Nor tarries there; I feel it at my Heart;
My Heart, at once, it humbles and exalts;
Lays it in dust, and calls it to the Skies.

The Heavens. — *Byron.*

YE Stars! which are the poetry of Heaven,
 If in your bright leaves we would read the Fate
Of men and empires,—'tis to be forgiven,
 That in our Aspirations to be great,
 Our destinies o'erleap their mortal state,
And claim a kindred with you; for ye are
 A Beauty and a Mystery, and create
In us such love and reverence from afar,
That Fortune, Fame, Power, Life, have named themselves a star.

The Heavens. — *Pope.*

NATURE, and Nature's laws, lay hid in night;
God said, let Newton be; and all was Light.

The Heavens. — *Young.*

WHAT involution! what extent! what swarms
 Of worlds, that laugh at Earth! immensely great!
Immensely distant from each other's spheres;
What then the wond'rous Space through which they roll?
At once it quite engulfs all human thought;
'Tis comprehension's absolute Defeat.

The Heavens. — *Young.*

THIS Prospect vast, what is it?—weigh'd aright,
 'Tis Nature's system of Divinity,
And every student of the Night inspires.
'Tis elder Scripture, writ by God's own hand:
Scripture authentic! uncorrupt by man.

The Heavens. — *Byron.*

Oh, thou beautiful
And unimaginable Ether! and
Ye multiplying masses of increased
And still-increasing Lights! what are ye? what
Is this blue wilderness of interminable
Air, where ye roll along, as I have seen
The leaves along the limpid streams of Eden?
Is your course measured for ye? Or do ye
Sweep on in your unbounded Revelry
Through an aërial universe of endless
Expansion, at which my soul aches to think,
Intoxicated with Eternity?
O God! O Gods! or whatsoe'er ye are!
How beautiful ye are! how beautiful
Your works, or accident, or whatsoe'er
They may be! Let me die, as atoms die,

(If that they die,) or know ye in your Might
And Knowledge! My thoughts are not in this hour
Unworthy what I see, though my dust is;
Spirit! let me expire, or see them nearer.

The Hero. — *Byron.*

ALL these he wielded to command assent:
But where he wish'd to win, so well unbent,
That kindness cancell'd Fear in those who heard,
And others' gifts show'd mean beside his word,
When echoed to the Heart as from his own,
His deep yet tender melody of tone:
But such was foreign to his wonted mood,
He cared not what he soften'd, but subdued;
The evil passions of his youth had made
Him value less who loved—than what obey'd.

The Hero. — *Churchill.*

THINGS of the noblest kind his Genius drew,
And look'd through Nature at a single view:
A loose he gave to his unbounded Soul,
And taught new lands to rise, new seas to roll;
Call'd into being scenes unknown before,
And, passing Nature's bounds, was something more.

The Hero. — *Byron.*

WELL had he learn'd to curb the crowd,
By arts that vail, and oft preserve the proud;
His was the lofty Port, the distant Mien,
That seems to shun the sight—and awes if seen:
The solemn Aspect, and the high-born Eye,
That checks low mirth, but lacks not Courtesy.

The Hero. — *Scott.*

PROUD was his Tone, but calm; his Eye
Had that compelling Dignity,
His Mien that bearing haught and high,
Which common spirits fear.

The Hero. — *Byron.*

'TIS thus the spirit of a single mind
Makes that of multitudes take one direction,
As roll the waters to the breathing wind,
Or roams the herd beneath the bull's protection;
Or as a little dog will lead the blind,
Or a bell-wether form the flock's connection,
By tinkling sounds, when they go forth to victual;—
Such is the sway of your Great Men o'er little.

The Hero. — *Byron.*

THEY crouch'd to him, for he had Skill
To warp and wield the vulgar will.

The Hero. — *Byron.*

THAT Man of loneliness and mystery,
Scarce seen to smile, and seldom heard to sigh;
Whose name appals the fiercest of his crew,
And tints each swarthy cheek with sallower hue;
Still sways their Souls with that commanding art
That dazzles, leads, yet chills the vulgar heart.
What is that Spell, that thus his lawless train
Confess and envy, yet oppose in vain?
What should it be that thus their faith can bind?
The power of Thought—the magic of the Mind!
Link'd with success, assumed and kept with skill,
That moulds another's weakness to its will;
Wields with their hands, but, still to these unknown,
Makes even their mightiest deeds appear his own.
Such hath it been—shall be—beneath the sun
The many still must labour for the one!
'Tis Nature's doom—but let the wretch who toils
Accuse not, hate not him who wears the spoils;
Oh! if he knew the Weight of splendid chains,
How light the Balance of his humbler pains!

Heroism. — *Shakspeare.*

I HAVE, thou gallant Trojan, seen thee oft,
Labouring for destiny, make cruel way
Through ranks of Greekish youth: and I have seen thee,
As hot as Perseus, spur thy Phrygian steed,
Despising many forfeits and subduements,
When thou hast hung thy advanced sword i' the air,
Nor letting it decline on the declined;
That I have said to some my standers-by,
Lo, Jupiter is yonder, dealing life!
And I have seen thee pause, and take thy breath,
When that a ring of Greeks have hemm'd thee in,
Like an Olympian wrestling.

Heroism. — *Colton.*

WE cannot think too highly of our Nature, nor too humbly of ourselves. When we see the Martyr to Virtue, subject as he is to the infirmities of a man, yet suffering the tortures of a demon, and bearing them with the magnanimity of a God, do we not behold a Heroism that angels may indeed surpass, but which they cannot imitate, and must admire.

Personal History. — *La Bruyere.*

AN old Courtier, with veracity, good sense, and a faithful memory, is an inestimable treasure: he is full of transactions and maxims; in him one may find the History of the Age, enriched with a great many curious circumstances, which we never meet with in books.

Use of History. — *Tacitus.*

THIS I hold to be the chief office of History, to rescue virtuous actions from the oblivion to which a want of Records would consign them, and that men should feel a dread of being considered infamous in the opinions of Posterity, from their depraved expressions and base actions.

Hollowness. — *Shakspeare.*

THERE are no tricks in plain and simple Faith:
But hollow men, like Horses hot at hand,
Make gallant show and promise of their mettle:
But when they should endure the bloody spur,
They fall their crests, and, like deceitful Jades,
Sink in the Trial.

Holy War. — *Shakspeare.*

THEN if you fight against God's enemy,
God will in justice ward you as his soldiers.
If you do swear to put a Tyrant down,
You sleep in peace, the tyrant being slain.
If you do fight against your Country's foes,
Your Country's Fat shall pay your pains the Hire.
If you do fight in safeguard of your Wives,
Your wives shall welcome home the conquerors.
If you do free your Children from the sword,
Your children's children quit it in your Age.

Home. — *Burns.*

AT length his lonely Cot appears in view,
Beneath the shelter of an aged tree;
Th' expectant wee things, todlin, stacher through
To meet their Dad, wi' flichterin noise and glee.
His wee-bit ingle blinkin bonnilie,
His clean hearth-stane, his thrifty Wifie's smile,
The lisping infant prattling on his knee,
Does a' his weary kiaugh and care beguile,
And makes him quite forget his labour and his toil.

Home. — *Shenstone.*

THE proper means of increasing the love we bear our Native Country, is to reside some time in a foreign one.

Home. — *Byron.*

HE enter'd in his house—his Home no more,
For without Hearts there is no Home;—and felt
The solitude of passing his own door
Without a Welcome.

Home. — *Moore.*

O Nature! though blessed and bright are thy rays,
O'er the brow of Creation enchantingly thrown,
Yet faint are they all to the lustre, that plays
In a smile from the Heart that is dearly our own!

Home. — *Goldsmith.*

IN all my wanderings round this world of care,
In all my Griefs—and God has given my share—
I still had hopes my latest hours to crown,
Amidst these humble Bowers to lay me down;
To husband out life's taper at the close,
And keep the flame from wasting, by repose:
I still had hopes, for pride attends us still,
Amidst the swains to show my book-learn'd skill,
Around my fire an evening group to draw,
And tell of all I felt, and all I saw;
And as a hare, whom hounds and horns pursue,
Pants to the place from whence at first she flew,
I still had hopes, my long vexations past,
Here to return—and die at Home at last.

Home. — *Hannah More.*

THE angry word suppress'd, the taunting thought;
Subduing and subdued, the petty strife,
Which clouds the colour of domestic Life;
The sober comfort, all the peace which springs
From the large aggregate of little things;
On these small cares of daughter, wife, or friend,
The almost sacred joys of Home depend.

Home. — *Mrs. Opie.*

HENCE far from me, ye senseless joys,
That fade before ye reach the Heart,—
The crowded dome's distracted noise,
Where all is pomp and useless art!
Give me my Home, to quiet dear,
Where hours untold and peaceful move;
So fate ordain I sometimes there
May hear the Voice of him I love.

Home. — *Thomson.*

THE touch of kindred too and love he feels;
The modest eye, whose beams on his alone
Ecstatic shine: the little strong embrace
Of prattling children, twined around his neck,
And emulous to please him, calling forth
The fond paternal soul. Nor purpose gay,
Amusement, dance, or song, he sternly scorns;
For Happiness and true Philosophy
Are of the social, still, and smiling kind.
This is the Life which those who fret in guilt,
And guilty cities, never know; the life,
Led by primeval ages, uncorrupt,
When angels dwelt, and God himself, with man!

Home. — *Young.*

THE first sure symptom of a mind in Health,
Is rest of heart, and pleasure felt at Home.

Home. — *Southey.*

FAREWELL my Home, my Home no longer now,
Witness of many a calm and happy day;
And thou, fair eminence, upon whose brow
Dwells the last sunshine of the evening ray.
Farewell! Mine eyes no longer shall pursue
The westering sun beyond the utmost height,
When slowly he forsakes the fields of light.
No more the freshness of the falling dew,
Cool and delightful here shall bathe my head,
As from this western window dear, I lean
Listening the while I watch the placid scene,—
The martins twittering underneath the shed.
Farewell my Home, where many a day has past
In joys whose loved Remembrance long shall last.

Honesty. — *Shakspeare.*

THERE is no terror in your threats;
For I am arm'd so strong in Honesty,
That they pass by me as the idle wind,
Which I respect not.

Honesty. — *Rowe.*

THE brave do never shun the Light;
Just are their thoughts, and open are their tempers;
Freely without Disguise they love or hate:
Still are they found in the fair face of day,
And Heaven and Men are Judges of their actions.

Honesty. — *Colton.*

NOTHING more completely baffles one who is full of trick and Duplicity himself, than straightforward and simple Integrity in another. A knave would rather quarrel with a brother-knave, than with a Fool, but he would rather avoid a quarrel with one Honest Man, than with both. He can combat a Fool by management and address, and he can conquer a Knave by temptations. But the Honest Man is neither to be bamboozled nor bribed.

Honesty. — *Cowley.*

THE best kind of Glory is that which is reflected from Honesty, such as was the glory of Cato and Aristides; but it was harmful to them both, and is seldom beneficial to any man while he lives.

Honesty. — *Socrates.*

THE shortest and surest way to live with Honour in the world, is to be in reality what we would appear to be; and if we observe, we shall find, that all human Virtues increase and strengthen themselves by the practice and Experience of them.

Honesty. — *Shakspeare.*

WHILE others fish with craft for great opinion,
I with great Truth catch mere Simplicity;
Whilst some with Cunning gild their copper crowns,
With Truth and Plainness I do wear mine bare.
Fear not my Truth; the moral of my Wit
Is—plain, and true,—there's all the reach of it.

Honesty. — *Cicero.*

WHAT is becoming is Honest, and whatever is Honest must always be becoming.

Honesty. — *Shakspeare.*

BECAUSE I cannot flatter, and speak fair,
Smile in men's faces, smooth, deceive, and cog,
Duck with French nods and apish Courtesy,
I must be held a rancorous enemy.
Cannot a plain man live, and think no Harm,
But thus his simple Truth must be abused
By silken, sly, insinuating Jacks?

Honesty. — *Shakspeare.*

AN Honest Man is able to speak for himself, when a Knave is not.

Honesty. — *Montaigne.*

ALL other Knowledge is hurtful to him who has not Honesty and good-nature.

Honesty. — *Shakspeare.*

TO be Honest, as this World goes, is to be one man picked out of ten thousand.

Honesty. — *Lavater.*

HE who freely praises what he means to purchase, and he who enumerates the Faults of what he means to sell, may set up a partnership with Honesty.

Honesty. — *Shakspeare.*

HIS nature is too noble for the World:
He would not flatter Neptune for his trident,
Or Jove for his power to thunder. His Heart's his mouth:
What his Breast forges, that his tongue must vent;
And being angry, does forget that ever
He heard the name of Death.

Honesty. — *Shakspeare.*

NEVER any thing can be amiss,
When Simpleness and Duty tender it.

Honesty. — *Colton.*

IT is much easier to ruin a man of principle, than a man of none, for he may be ruined through his Scruples. Knavery is supple, and can bend, but Honesty is firm and upright, and yields not.

Honesty. — *Shaftesbury.*

A RIGHT mind and generous affection hath more Beauty and charms than all other symmetries in the world besides; and a grain of Honesty and native Worth is of more value than all the adventitious ornaments, estates, or preferments; for the sake of which some of the better sort so oft turn Knaves.

Honesty. — *Shenstone.*

IT should seem that Indolence itself would incline a person to be Honest, as it requires infinitely greater pains and contrivance to be a Knave.

Honesty. — *Franklin.*

LET Honesty be as the breath of thy soul, and never forget to have a penny, when all thy expenses are enumerated and paid: then shalt thou reach the point of Happiness, and independence shall be thy shield and buckler, thy helmet and crown; then shall thy Soul walk upright, nor stoop to the silken wretch because he hath riches, nor pocket an Abuse because the hand which offers it wears a ring set with Diamonds.

Honour. — *Dryden.*

WOMAN'S Honour,
Is nice as Ermine, will not bear a soil.

Honour. — *Shakspeare.*

MINE Honour is my Life; both grow in one;
Take Honour from me, and my Life is done.

Honour. — *Byron.*

WHERE is Honour,
Innate and precept-strengthen'd, 'tis the rock
Of Faith connubial: where it is not—where
Light thoughts are lurking, or the vanities
Of worldly pleasure rankle in the heart,
Or sensual throbs convulse it, well I know
'Twere hopeless for Humanity to dream
Of Honesty in such infected blood,
Although 'twere wed to him it covets most.

Honour. — *Shakspeare.*

BY Jove I am not covetous of Gold,
Nor care I, who doth feed upon my cost;
It yearns me not if men my garments wear;
Such outward things dwell not in my desires:
But, if it be a sin to covet Honour,
I am the most offending soul alive.

Honour. — *Colton.*

HONOUR is unstable, and seldom the same; for she feeds upon Opinion, and is as fickle as her food. She builds a lofty structure on the sandy foundation of the esteem of those who are of all beings the most subject to change. But Virtue is uniform and fixed, because she looks for approbation only from Him who is the same yesterday, to-day, and for ever.

Honour. — *Shakspeare.*

IF well-respected Honour bid me on,
I hold as little counsel with weak fear,
As you.

Honour. — *Shakspeare.*

THE mere word's a slave,
Debauch'd on every Tomb; on every grave,
A lying Trophy; and as oft is dumb,
Where dust, and damn'd oblivion, is the Tomb
Of honour'd bones indeed.

Honour. — *Phædrus.*

THE Athenians erected a large statue to Æsop, and placed him, though a Slave, on a lasting pedestal; to show that the way to Honour lies open indifferently to all.

Honour. — *Shakspeare.*

WHAT I did, I did in Honour,
Led by th' impartial conduct of my soul;
And never shall you see, that I will beg
A ragged and forestall'd remission.

Honours. — *La Bruyere.*

THERE is what is called the highway to Posts and Honours, and there is a cross and by-way, which is much the shortest.

Hope. — *Von Knebel.*

TRUE Hope is based on energy of character. A strong mind always hopes, and has always cause to hope, because it knows the Mutability of human affairs, and how slight a circumstance may change the whole course of events. Such a spirit too rests upon itself; it is not confined to partial views, or to one particular object. And if at last all should be lost, it has saved itself—its own integrity and worth. Hope awakens Courage, while Despondency is the last of all evils; it is the abandonment of good,—the giving up of the battle of life with dead nothingness. He who can implant Courage in the human soul is the best physician.

Hope. — *From the French.*

HOPE is the Dream of a waking man.

Hope. — *Cowley.*

HOPE! Fortune's cheating lottery!
Where for one prize a hundred blanks there be;
Fond archer, Hope! who takest thy aim so far,
That still or short or wide thine Arrows are!

Hope. — *Spenser.*

HOPE in rancke, a handsome mayd,
Of cheareful looke and lovely to behold;
In silken samite she was light arayd,
And her fayre locks were woven up in Gold.
She always smyld, and in her hand did hold
An holy-water sprinckle, dipt in deowe,
With which she sprinkled Favours manifold
On whom she list, and did great liking sheowe,
Great liking unto many, but true love to feowe.

Hope. — *Leighton.*

A LIVING Hope, living in Death itself. The world dares say no more for its device than *dum spiro spero,* (whilst I breathe I hope;) but the children of God can add, by virtue of this living Hope, *dum expiro spero,* (whilst I expire I hope.)

Hope. — *S. T. Coleridge.*

IN the treatment of nervous cases, he is the best Physician who is the most ingenious inspirer of Hope.

Hope. — *Hume.*

A PROPENSITY to Hope and Joy is real riches; one to Fear and Sorrow, real poverty.

Hope. — *Collins.*

BUT thou, O Hope, with eyes so fair,
What was thy delighted measure?
Still it whisper'd promised pleasure,
And bade the lovely scenes at distance hail!
Still would her touch the strain prolong,
And from the rocks, the woods, the vale,
She call'd on Echo still through all her song;
And where her sweetest theme she chose,
A soft responsive voice was heard at every close,
And Hope enchanted smiled, and waved her golden hair.

Hope. — *Prior.*

THUS, through what path soe'er of life we rove,
Rage companies our hate, and Grief our love.
Vex'd with the present moment's heavy gloom,
Why seek we brightness from the years to come?
Disturb'd and broken like a sick man's sleep,
Our troubled thoughts to distant prospects leap,
Desirous still what flies us to o'ertake,
For Hope is but the dream of those that wake.

Hope. — *Shakspeare.*

HOPE is a lover's Staff; walk hence with that,
And manage it against despairing Thoughts.

Hope. — *Campbell.*

AUSPICIOUS Hope! in thy sweet garden grow
Wreaths for each toil, a charm for every wo:
Won by their sweets, in Nature's languid hour,
The way-worn Pilgrim seeks thy summer bower;
There, as the wild bee murmurs on the wing,
What peaceful dreams thy handmaid spirits bring!
What viewless forms th' Æolian organ play,
And sweep the furrow'd lines of anxious Thought away!

Hope. — *Shakspeare.*

THE Miserable hath no other Medicine,
But only Hope.

Hope. — *Byron.*

WHITE as a white sail on a dusky sea,
When half the Horizon's clouded and half free,
Fluttering between the dun wave and the sky,
Is Hope's last gleam in man's extremity.

Hope. — *Shakspeare.*

TRUE Hope is swift, and flies with swallow's wings,
Kings it makes Gods, and meaner creatures Kings.

Hope. — *Shakspeare.*

THE ample proposition, that Hope makes
In all designs begun on earth below,
Fails in the promised largeness.

Hope. — *Pope.*

HOPE humbly then; with trembling pinions soar,
Wait the great teacher, Death, and God adore:
What future bliss, He gives not thee to know,
But gives that Hope to be thy blessing now.
Hope springs eternal in the human breast:
Man never Is, but always To be blest;
The soul, uneasy, and confined from Home,
Rests and expatiates in a life to come.

Hope. — *Proctor.*

WHAT'S i' the air?—
Some subtle spirit runs through all my veins.
Hope seems to ride this morning on the Wind,
And Joy outshines the sun.

Hope. — *Young.*

HOPE, of all passions, most befriends us here;
Passions of prouder name befriend us less.
Joy has her tears; and transport has her Death:
Hope, like a cordial, innocent though strong,
Man's heart at once inspirits, and serenes;
Nor makes him pay his wisdom for his joys;
'Tis all our present state can safely bear,
Health to the frame, and vigour to the mind!
A joy attemper'd! a chastised delight!
Like the fair summer evening, mild and sweet!
'Tis man's full cup: his Paradise below!

Hope. — *Shakspeare.*

HE hath persecuted Time with Hope; and finds no other advantage in the process but only the losing of Hope by Time.

Hope. — *Shakspeare.*

EVEN through the hollow eyes of Death,
I spy life peering; but I dare not say
How near the tidings of our Comfort is.

Hope. — *Cowley.*

HOPE! of all ills that men endure,
The only cheap and universal cure!
Thou captive's Freedom, and thou sick man's Health!
Thou lover's Victory, and thou beggar's Wealth!

Hope. — *Cowley.*

BROTHER of Fear, more gayly clad!
The merrier fool o' th' two, yet quite as mad:
Sire of Repentance! child of fond Desire!
That blow'st the chymics' and the lovers' fire,
Leading them still insensibly on
By the strange witchcraft of "anon!"
By thee the one does changing Nature, through
Her endless labyrinths, pursue;
And th' other chases Woman, while she goes
More ways and turns than hunted Nature knows.

Hope. — *Moore.*

HER precious pearl, in Sorrow's cup,
Unmelted at the bottom lay,
To shine again, when, all drunk up,
The bitterness should pass away.

Hospitality. — *Goldsmith.*

BLEST be that Spot, where cheerful Guests retire
To pause from Toil, and trim their evening fire;
Blest that Abode, where want and pain repair,
And every Stranger finds a ready chair:
Blest be those Feasts with simple plenty crown'd,
Where all the ruddy family around
Laugh at the jest or pranks, that never fail,
Or sigh with pity at some mournful tale,
Or press the bashful Stranger to his food,
And learn the luxury of doing Good.

Human Nature. — *Shakspeare.*

HATH not a Jew eyes? hath not a Jew hands, organs, dimension, senses, affections, passions? fed with the same Food, hurt with the same Weapons, subject to the same Diseases, healed by the same means, warmed and cooled by the same Winter and Summer, as a Christian is? if you prick us, do we not bleed? if you tickle us, do we not laugh? if you poison us, do we not die?

Human Nature. — *Anon.*

IT is only when blinded by Self-love, that we can think proudly of our Nature. Take away that blind; and in our judgments of others we are quicksighted enough to see there is very little in that Nature to rely on.

Human Nature. — *From the Latin.*

To escape Hatred is to gain a Triumph.

Human Perfectibility. — *Anon.*

THE strange inconsistency is, that, the very persons who have indulged in the most splendid visions about the Perfectibility of Mankind, have mostly rejected the only principle of Perfectibility which has ever found place in man, the only principle by which man's natural corruptibility has ever been checked, the only principle by which nations or individuals have ever been regenerated. The natural Life of Nations, as well as of individuals, has its fixed course and term. It springs forth, grows up, reaches its maturity, decays, perishes. Only through Christianity has a nation ever risen again: and it is solely on the operation of Christianity that we can ground any thing like a reasonable hope of the Perfectibility of Mankind; a hope that what has often been wrought in individuals, may also in the fulness of time be wrought by the same power in the Race.

Human Perfectibility. — *Anon.*

IT may be regarded as one of those instances of irony so frequent in History, that the moment chosen by Man to assert his Perfectibility should have been the very moment when all the powers of Evil were about to be let loose, and to run riot over the Earth. Happiness was the idol; and lo! the idol burst; and the spectral form of Misery rose out of it, and stretched out its gaunt hand over the heads of the Nations; and millions of hearts shrank and were frozen by its touch. Liberty was the watchword, Liberty and Equality: and an iron despotism strode from north to south, and from east to west; and all men cowered at its approach, and crouched beneath its feet, and were trampled on, and found the Equality they coveted in universal Prostration. Peace was the promise; and the fulfilment was more than twenty years of fierce, desolating War.

Human Progress. — *Colton.*

ANALOGY, although it is not infallible, is yet that telescope of the mind by which it is marvellously assisted in the discovery of both physical and moral Truth. Analogy has much in store for Men; but Babes require milk, and there may be intellectual food which the present state of society is not fit to partake of; to lay such before it, would be as absurd as to give a quadrant to an Indian, or a loom to a Hottentot.

Humanity. — *From the French.*

FEW men are raised in our estimation by being too closely examined.

Humanity. — *Steele.*

A WEALTHY Doctor who can help a poor man, and will not without a fee, has less sense of Humanity than a poor Ruffian, who kills a rich man to supply his necessities.

Humility. — *St. Augustin.*

THE sufficiency of my Merit is to know that my Merit is not sufficient.

Humility. — *Fuller.*

SEARCH others for their Virtues, and thyself for thy Vices.

Humility. — *Moore.*

HUMILITY, that low, sweet root
From which all heavenly Virtues shoot.

Humility. — *Shakspeare.*

HE that commends me to my own Content,
Commends me to the thing I cannot get.
I to the world am like a drop of water,
That in the Ocean seeks another drop;
Who failing there to find his fellow forth,
Unseen, inquisitive, confounds himself.

Humility. — *Selden.*

HUMILITY is a virtue all preach, none practise, and yet every body is content to hear. The Master thinks it good doctrine for his Servant, the Laity for the Clergy, and the Clergy for the Laity.

Humility. — *Shakspeare.*

OFTEN to our comfort, shall we find
The sharded Beetle in a safer hold
Than is the full-wing'd Eagle.

Humour. — *Anon.*

LET your Humour always be Good Humour, in both senses. If it comes of a Bad Humour, it is pretty sure not to belie its Parentage.

Humour. — *La Rochefoucauld.*

THERE are more faults in the Humour than in the Mind.

Humour. — *La Rochefoucauld.*

THE Humours of the body have a stated and regular course, which impels and imperceptibly guides our Will. They co-operate with each other, and exercise successively a secret Empire within us; so that they have a considerable part in all our Actions without our being able to know it.

Good Humour. — *Sterne.*

I LIVE in a constant endeavour to fence against the infirmities of ill-health, and other evils of Life, by Mirth. I am persuaded that every time a man smiles—but much more so when he laughs—it adds something to this Fragment of life.

Humour. — *La Rochefoucauld.*

IT may be said of men's Humours as of many buildings, that they have divers Aspects,—some agreeable, others disagreeable.

Good Humour. — *Steele.*

THE portable quality of Good Humour seasons all the parts and occurrences we meet with, in such a manner that there are no moments lost: but they all pass with so much Satisfaction, that the heaviest of loads, (when it is a load,) that of Time, is never felt by us.

Good Humour. — *Johnson.*

GAYETY is to Good Humour as animal perfumes to vegetable fragrance. The one overpowers weak spirits, the other recreates and revives them. Gayety seldom fails to give some pain; Good Humour boasts no faculties which every one does not believe in his own Power, and pleases principally by not offending.

Hunger. — *Byron.*

THAT famish'd people must be slowly nurst,
And fed by Spoonfuls, else they always burst.

Hunger. — *Persius.*

THE Belly is a master of arts and a bestower of Genius. Necessity often draws forth Talent which had before lain dormant, and unknown even to its possessor.

Hurry. — *Colton.*

NO two things differ more than Hurry and Despatch. Hurry is the mark of a weak mind, Despatch of a strong one. A weak man in office, like a squirrel in a cage, is labouring eternally, but to no purpose, and in constant motion without getting on a jot; like a Turnstile, he is in everybody's way, but stops nobody; he talks a great deal, but says very little; looks into every thing, but sees into nothing; and has a hundred Irons in the fire, but very few of them are hot, and with those few that are he only burns his Fingers.

The Hypochondriac. — *Seneca.*

O SAVE, ye Gods omnipotent and kind,
From such abhorr'd Chimeras save the mind!

Hypocrisy. — *Fuller.*

TRUST not in him that seems a Saint.

Hypocrisy. — *Shakspeare.*

HAST thou that holy feeling in thy Soul,
To counsel me to make my peace with God,
And art thou yet to thy own Soul so blind,
That thou wilt war with God?

Hypocrisy. — *Young.*

THE world's all Title-page: there's no Contents;
The world's all Face; the man who shows his Heart
Is whooted for his nudities, and scorn'd.

Hypocrisy. — *Lavater.*

EVERY thing may be mimicked by Hypocrisy, but Humility and Love united. The more rare the more radiant when they meet.

Hypocrisy. — *Shakspeare.*

OH! cunning enemy, that, to catch a Saint,
With Saints dost bait thy hook! Most dangerous
Is that Temptation, that doth goad us on
To sin in loving Virtue.

Hypocrisy. — *Colton.*

IF the Devil ever laughs, it must be at Hypocrites: they are the greatest dupes he has; they serve him better than any others, and receive no wages; nay, what is still more extraordinary, they submit to greater Mortifications to go to Hell, than the sincerest Christian to go to Heaven.

Hypocrisy. — *Milton.*

HYPOCRISY, the only evil that walks
Invisible, except to God alone,
By his permissive will, through Heaven and Earth.
And oft though Wisdom wakes, Suspicion sleeps
At Wisdom's gate, and to Simplicity
Resigns her charge, while Goodness thinks no ill
Where no ill seems.

Hypocrisy. — *Colton.*

THERE is only one circumstance in which the upright man will imitate the Hypocrite: I mean in his attempts to conciliate the good opinion of his fellow-men. But here the similarity must cease, for their respective motives are wider than the poles asunder; the former will attempt this to increase his power of doing good, the latter to augment his means of doing harm.

Hypocrisy. — *Shakspeare.*

To beguile the Time,
Look like the Time; bear welcome in your eyes,
Your hand, your tongue: look like the innocent flower;
But be the Serpent under it.

Hypocrisy. — *Addison.*

'TIS not my talent to conceal my thoughts,
Or carry Smiles and Sunshine in my face,
When Discontent sits heavy at my heart.

Hypocrisy. — *Spenser.*

THERETO when needed, she could weep and pray,
And when her listed she could fawne and flatter;
Now smyling smoothly, like to Sommer's day,
Now glooming sadly, so to cloke her matter:
Yet were her Words but wynd, and all her Tears but water.

Hypocrisy. — *Peter Pindar.*

TO wear long faces, just as if our Maker,
The God of Goodness, was an undertaker,
Well pleased to wrap the Soul's unlucky mien
In sorrow's dismal crape or bombasin.

Hypocrisy. — *Shakspeare.*

THE Devil can cite Scripture for his purpose.
An evil soul, producing holy witness,
Is like a villain with a smiling cheek;
A goodly Apple rotten at the Heart:
Oh, what a goodly outside Falsehood hath!

Hypocrisy. — *Joanna Baillie.*

THINK'ST thou there are no Serpents in the world
But those who slide along the grassy sod,
And sting the luckless foot that presses them?
There are who in the path of social life
Do bask their spotted skins in Fortune's sun,
And sting the Soul—Ay, till its healthful frame
Is changed to secret, festering, sore Disease,
So deadly is the Wound.

Hypocrisy. — *Shakspeare.*

BUT then I sigh, and, with a piece of Scripture,
Tell them—that God bids us do good for evil:
And thus I clothe my naked villany
With old odd ends, stolen forth of Holy Writ;
And seem a Saint, when most I play the Devil.
Why, I can smile, and murder while I smile:
And cry, Content, to that which grieves my heart;
And wet my cheeks with artificial Tears,
And frame my Face to all occasions.

Hypocrisy. — *Shakspeare.*

BE not you spoke with, but by mighty suit:
And look you get a Prayer-Book in your hand,
And stand between two churchmen, good my Lord;
For on that ground I'll make a holy descant:
And be not easily won to our Requests;
Play the maid's part,—still answer Nay, and take it.

Hypocrisy. — *Shakspeare.*

O NATURE! what hadst thou to do in Hell,
When thou did'st bower the spirit of a Fiend
In mortal paradise of such sweet flesh?—
Was ever Book, containing such vile matter,
So fairly bound? Oh, that Deceit should dwell
In such a gorgeous palace!
O serpent heart! hid with a flowering face!
Did ever Dragon keep so fair a cave?
Beautiful tyrant! Fiend angelical!
Dove-feather'd raven! Wolvish-ravening lamb!
Despised substance of divinest show!
Just opposite to what thou justly seem'st!

Hypocrisy. — *Milton.*

I, UNDER fair pretence of friendly ends,
And well-placed words of glossy Courtesy,
Baited with reason not unplausible,
Wind me into the easy-hearted man,
And hug him into Snares.

Hypocrisy. — *Shakspeare.*

He was a Man
Of an unbounded Stomach, ever ranking
Himself with Princes; one that, by Suggestion,
Tied all the Kingdom: Simony was fair Play;
His own Opinion was his Law: I' the Presence,
He would say Untruths; and be ever double,
Both in his Words and Meaning. He was never,
But where he meant to ruin, pitiful;
His Promises were, as he then was, mighty;
But his Performance, as he is now, nothing.

Hypocrisy. — *Shakspeare.*

To the common people,
How did he seem to dive into their hearts
With humble and familiar Courtesy;
What reverence he did throw away on slaves;
Wooing poor craftsmen with the craft of Smiles,
And patient under-bearing of his fortune,
As 'twere to banish their Affects with him.
Off goes his bonnet to an oyster-wench;
A brace of dray-men bid, God speed him well!
And had the tribute of his supple Knee;
With,—Thanks, my countrymen, my loving friends.

Hypocrisy. — *Shakspeare.*

THOUGH I do hate him as I do Hell pains,
Yet, for necessity of present lift,
I must show out a flag and sign of Love,
Which is indeed but Sign.

One Idea. — *Swift.*

COMMON speakers have only one set of Ideas, and one set of words to clothe them in; and these are always ready at the Mouth: so people come faster out of a Church when it is almost empty, than when a crowd is at the Door.

One Idea. — *Swift.*

THERE is a Brain that will endure but one scumming: let the owner gather it with Discretion, and manage his little stock with Husbandry; but of all things let him beware of bringing it under the lash of his betters.

One Idea. — *Shakspeare.*

HE doth nothing but talk of his Horse; and he makes it a great appropriation to his own good parts, that he can shoe him himself.

Idleness. — *Cowper.*

ABSENCE of Occupation is not rest,
A mind quite vacant is a mind distress'd.

Idleness. — *Spenser.*

FROM worldly Cares himself he did esloyne,
And greatly shunned manly exercise;
From everie worke he chalenged essoyne,
For Contemplation sake: yet otherwise,
His life he led in lawlesse riotise,
By which he grew to grievous malady;
For in his lustesse limbs through evil guise,
A shaking fever raign'd continually:
Such one was Idlenesse, first of this company.

Idleness. — *Young.*

LEISURE is pain; takes off our chariot wheels;
How heavily we drag the load of Life!
Blest Leisure is our curse; like that of Cain,
It makes us wander; wander earth around
To fly that tyrant Thought. As Atlas groan'd
The World beneath, we groan beneath an Hour.

Idleness. — *From the Latin.*

EVIL thoughts intrude in an unemployed Mind, as naturally as Worms are generated in a stagnant pool.

Idleness. — *Burton.*

IDLENESS is the badge of Gentry, the bane of body and mind, the nurse of Naughtiness, the step-mother of Discipline, the chief author of all Mischief, one of the seven deadly sins, the cushion upon which the Devil chiefly reposes, and a great cause not only of Melancholy, but of many other diseases: for the mind is naturally active; and if it be not occupied about some honest business, it rushes into Mischief, or sinks into Melancholy.

Idleness. — *Franklin.*

IT would be thought a hard government that should tax its people one-tenth part of their time, to be employed in its service; but Idleness taxes many of us much more; sloth, by bringing on diseases, absolutely shortens life. Sloth, like rust, consumes faster than labour wears; while the used key is always bright. Dost thou love life, then do not squander time, for that is the stuff life is made of. How much more than is necessary do we spend in sleep, forgetting that the sleeping fox catches no poultry, and there will be sleeping enough in the grave!

Ignorance. — *Colton.*

IT is with Nations as with individuals, those who know the least of others think the highest of themselves; for the whole family of Pride and Ignorance are incestuous, and mutually beget each other.

Ignorance. — *Seneca.*

SOME men, like Pictures, are fitter for a Corner than a full light.

Illness. — *Shakspeare.*

MAY be he is not well:
Infirmity doth still neglect all office,
Whereto our Health is bound; we're not ourselves,
When Nature, being oppress'd, commands the Mind
To suffer with the Body.

Illness. — *Colton.*

SOME persons will tell you, with an air of the miraculous, that they recovered although they were given over; whereas they might with more Reason have said, they recovered because they were given over.

Illusion. — *Shakspeare.*

SOME there be, that Shadows kiss;
Such have but a shadow's bliss.

The Image of his Father. — *Shakspeare.*

BEHOLD, my Lords,
Although the print be little, the whole matter
And Copy of the Father: Eye, Nose, Lip,
The trick of his Frown, his Forehead; nay, the valley,
The pretty dimples of his Chin, and Cheek; his Smiles!
The very mould and frame of Hand, Nail, Finger.

Imagination. — *Burton.*

A CONTENTED citizen of Milan, who had never passed beyond its walls during the course of sixty years, being ordered by the Governor not to stir beyond its gates, became immediately miserable, and felt so powerful an inclination to do that which he had so long contentedly neglected, that, on his application for a release from this restraint being refused, he became quite melancholy, and at last died of Grief. The pains of imprisonment also, like those of servitude, are more in conception than in reality. We are all prisoners. What is Life, but the prison of the Soul?

Imagination. — *Shakspeare.*

THE lunatic, the lover, and the poet,
Are of Imagination all compact:
One sees more devils than vast Hell can hold;
The madman. While the lover, all as frantic,
Sees Helen's beauty in a brow of Egypt.
The poet's eye, in a fine frenzy rolling,
Doth glance from Heaven to Earth, from Earth to Heaven;
And as Imagination bodies forth
The forms of things unknown, the poet's pen
Turns them to shape, and gives to airy nothing
A local habitation and a name.
Such tricks hath strong Imagination,
That if he would but apprehend some joy,
It comprehends some bringer of that joy;
Or in the night imagining some fear,
How easy is a Bush supposed a Bear?

Imagination. — *Shakspeare.*

DANGEROUS Conceits are, in their natures, poisons,
Which, at the first, are scarce found to distaste;
But, with a little act upon the Blood,
Burn like the mines of sulphur.

Imagination. — *Rogers.*

DO what he will, he cannot realize
Half he conceives—the glorious Vision flies.
Go where he may, he cannot hope to find
The Truth, the Beauty pictured in his mind.

Imitation. — *Colton.*

IMITATION is the sincerest of Flattery.

Imitation. — *Colton.*

THE secret of some men's Attractions might be safely told to all the world, for under any other management but that of the possessor, they would cease to attract. Those who attempted to imitate them, would find that they had got the Fiddle, but not the Fiddle-stick.

Imitation. — *Shakspeare.*

IT is certain that either wise bearing, or ignorant carriage, is caught, as men take Diseases, one of another: therefore, let men take heed of their Company.

Imitation. — *Lavater.*

HE who is always in want of something cannot be very rich. 'Tis a poor wit who lives by borrowing the Words, decisions, mien, inventions, and Actions of others.

Imitation. — *Greville.*

I HARDLY know so true a mark of a little Mind, as the servile Imitation of others.

Immortality. — *Young.*

STILL seems it strange that thou shouldst live for ever?
Is it less strange that thou shouldst live at all?
This is a Miracle; and that no more.

Immortality. — *Young.*

CAN it be?
Matter immortal? and shall Spirit die?
Above the nobler, shall less noble rise?
Shall Man alone, for whom all else revives,
No Resurrection know? shall Man alone,
Imperial Man! be sown in barren ground,
Less privileged than grain, on which he feeds?

Impertinence. — *Lavater.*

RECEIVE no satisfaction for premeditated Impertinence; forget it, forgive it, but keep him inexorably at a distance who offered it.

Begging Impostors. — *Ben Jonson.*

THERE is no bounty to be show'd to such
As have no real Goodness: Bounty is
A spice of Virtue: and what virtuous act
Can take effect on them that have no power
Of equal habitude to apprehend it?

Improvement. — *Colton.*

WHERE we cannot invent, we may at least improve; we may give somewhat of Novelty to that which was old, Condensation to that which was diffuse, Perspicuity to that which was obscure, and Currency to that which was recondite.

Impulse. — *Hare.*

SINCE the generality of persons act from Impulse much more than from Principle, men are neither so good nor so bad as we are apt to think them.

Impulses. — *Cooper.*

A TRUE history of human events would show that a far larger proportion of our acts are the results of sudden Impulses and accident, than of that reason of which we so much boast.

Inconsistency. — *Anon.*

AMONG the numberless Contradictions in our nature, hardly any is more glaring than this, between our sensitiveness to the slightest Disgrace which we fancy cast upon us from without, and our callousness to the Filth within ourselves. In truth, they who are the most sensitive to the one are often the most callous to the other.

Independence. — *Smollett.*

THY spirit, Independence, let me share!
Lord of the lion heart and eagle eye,
Thy steps I follow with my bosom bare,
Nor heed the storm that howls along the sky.
Deep in the frozen regions of the north,
A goddess violated brought thee forth,
Immortal Liberty, whose look sublime,
Hath bleach'd the Tyrant's cheek in every varying clime.

Independence. — *Heinzelmain.*

BE and continue poor, young man, while others around you grow rich by fraud and disloyalty; be without place or Power, while others beg their way upward; bear the pain of disappointed Hopes, while others gain the accomplishment of theirs by flattery; forego the gracious pressure of the hand for which others cringe and crawl. Wrap yourself in your own Virtue, and seek a Friend and your daily bread. If you have in such a course grown gray with unblenched Honour, bless God, and die.

Independence. — *Anon.*

THE King is the least independent man in his dominions,—the Beggar the most so.

Independence. — *Cowper.*

I PRAISE you much, ye meek and patient pair
For ye are worthy; choosing rather for
A dry but independent Crust, hard-earn'd
And eaten with a sigh, than to endure
The rugged frowns and insolent rebuffs
Of Knaves in office.

Indian Character. — *Cooper.*

FEW men exhibit greater diversity, or, if we may so express it, greater antithesis of character, than the native warrior of North America. In war, he is daring, boastful, cunning, ruthless, self-denying, and self-devoted; in peace, just, generous, hospitable, revengeful, superstitious, modest, and commonly chaste. These are qualities, it is true, which do not distinguish all alike; but they are so far the predominating traits of these remarkable people as to be characteristic.

Indiscretion. — *La Bruyere.*

THE generality of men expend the early part of their lives in contributing to render the latter part miserable.

The Indiscreet. — *Addison.*

AN Indiscreet Man is more hurtful than an ill-natured one; for as the latter will only attack his Enemies, and those he wishes ill to; the other injures indifferently both Friends and Foes.

Individuality. — *S. T. Coleridge.*

IN the very lowest link in the vast and mysterious chain of Being, there is an effort, although scarcely apparent, at Individualization; but it is almost lost in the mere Nature. A little higher up, the Individual is apparent and separate, but subordinate to any thing in Man. At length, the animal rises to be on a par with the lowest power of the human nature. There are some of our natural desires which only remain in our most perfect state on Earth as means of the higher powers acting.

Industry. — *Franklin.*

THE way to Wealth is as plain as the way to Market. It depends chiefly on two words, Industry and Frugality: that is, waste neither Time nor Money, but make the best use of both. Without Industry and Frugality nothing will do, and with them every thing.

Industry. — *Franklin.*

SLOTH makes all things difficult, but Industry all easy; and he that riseth late must trot all day, and shall scarce overtake his business at night: while Laziness travels so slowly, that Poverty soon overtakes him.

Industry. — *Colton.*

HE that from small beginnings has deservedly raised himself to the highest Stations, may not always find that full satisfaction in the possession of his object, that he anticipated in the pursuit of it. But although the individual may be disappointed, the Community are benefited, first by his exertions, and secondly, by his example; for, it has been well observed, that the Public are served not by what the Lord Mayor feels who rides in his coach, but by what the Apprentice Boy feels who looks at him.

Industry. — *Franklin.*

INDUSTRY need not wish, and he that lives upon hopes will die fasting. There are no gains without pains; then help, hands, for I have no lands; or, if I have, they are smartly taxed. He that hath a trade hath an estate, and he that hath a calling, hath an office of profit and honour; but then the trade must be worked at, and the calling followed, or neither the estate nor the office will enable us to pay our taxes. If we are industrious, we shall never starve; for, at the working-man's house hunger looks in, but dares not enter. Nor will the bailiff or the constable enter, for Industry pays debts, while despair increaseth them.

Inebriety. — *Prior.*

I DRANK; I liked it not, 'twas rage, 'twas noise,
An airy scene of transitory joys.
In vain I trusted that the flowing bowl
Would banish Sorrow, and enlarge the Soul.
To the late revel, and protracted feast,
Wild Dreams succeeded, and disorder'd rest.

Inexperience. — *Shakspeare.*

THE untainted Virtue of your years
Hath not yet dived into the World's deceit:
Nor more can you distinguish of a man
Than of his outward show, which, God he knows,
Seldom or never jumpeth with the Heart.

Inexperience. — *Anon.*

THOUSANDS of the brave, the gifted and the beautiful, have waked from dreams of juvenile Idolatry, amid the cold realities of every-day life, and loathed the long remnant of a scarce budding existence, for the rash vows of its opening dawn. The world is peopled with such mourners, and if in time the cloak of Indifference, or the mantle of Resignation, or the pall of Despair, shroud it from the world's unfeeling gaze, the broken heart is not the less surely there.

Infection. — *Shakspeare.*

How oft the sight of Means to do ill Deeds,
Makes Deeds ill done!

Infidelity. — *Shakspeare.*

She's gone; I am abused; and my relief
Must be—to loathe her.

Infidelity. — *Shakspeare.*

Such an act,
That blurs the grace and blush of Modesty:
Calls Virtue, Hypocrite: takes off the rose
From the fair forehead of an innocent love,
And sets a blister there: makes marriage vows
As false as dicers' oaths; Oh, such a deed,
As from the body of Contraction plucks
The very soul; and sweet Religion, makes
A rhapsody of words.

Infidelity. — *Moore.*

Oh! colder than the Wind that freezes
Founts that but now in sunshine play'd,
Is that congealing Pang which seizes
The trusting bosom when betray'd.

Infidelity. — *Shakspeare.*

Oh, she is fallen
Into a pit of Ink! that the wide Sea
Hath drops too few to wash her clean again;
And Salt too little, which may season give
To her foul tainted flesh!

Infidelity. — *Shakspeare.*

O thou Weed,
Who art so lovely fair, and smell'st so sweet,
That the sense aches at thee,—Would, thou had'st ne'er been born!

Infidelity. — *Shakspeare.*

This was your Husband.—Look you now, what follows:
Here is your Husband; like a mildew'd ear,
Blasting his wholesome Brother. Have you eyes?
Could you on this fair mountain leave to feed,
And batten on this moor? Ha! have you eyes?
You cannot call it, Love: for, at your age,
The hey-day in the blood is tame, it's humble,
And waits upon the Judgment; And what judgment
Would step from this, to this?

Infidelity. — *Shakspeare.*

I SHOULD make very forges of my cheeks,
That would to cinders burn up Modesty,
Did I but speak thy Deeds.

Noble Infirmity. — *Young.*

SOME, when they die, die all: their mould'ring clay
Is but an Emblem of their Memories;
The space quite closes up thro' which they pass'd:
That I have lived, I leave a mark behind,
Shall pluck the shining age from vulgar time,
And give it whole to late Posterity.

Ingratitude. — *Shakspeare.*

THEN burst his mighty Heart:
And, in his mantle muffling up his face,
Even at the base of Pompey's statue,
Which all the while ran blood, great Cæsar fell.

Ingratitude. — *Shakspeare.*

SHE hath tied
Sharp-tooth'd Unkindness, like a vulture.

Ingratitude. — *Shakspeare.*

INGRATITUDE is monstrous; and for the Multitude to be ingrateful, were to make a Monster of the Multitude.

Ingratitude. — *Shakspeare.*

TIME hath a wallet at his back
Wherein he puts alms for Oblivion,
A great-sized monster of Ingratitudes;
Those scraps are good deeds past; which are devour'd
As fast as they are made, forgot as soon
As done.

Ingratitude. — *Shakspeare.*

BLOW, blow, thou Winter Wind,
Thou art not so unkind
As man's Ingratitude;
Thy tooth is not so keen,
Because thou art not seen,
Although thy breath be rude.

Ingratitude. — *Anon.*

THOUGH Ingratitude is too frequent in the most of those who are obliged, yet Encouragement will work on generous minds; and if the experiment be lost on thousands, yet it never fails on all; and one virtuous man in a whole nation is worth the buying, as one Diamond is worth the search in a heap of rubbish.

Ingratitude. — *Shakspeare.*

I HATE Ingratitude more in a man,
Than lying, vainness, babbling, drunkenness,
Or any taint of Vice, whose strong corruption
Inhabits our frail Blood.

Ingratitude. — *Butler.*

THAT he alone is ungrateful, who makes returns of Obligations, because he does it merely to free himself from owing so much as Thanks.

Ingratitude. — *From the Italian.*

THE animal with long ears, after having drunk, gives a kick to the bucket.

Ingratitude. — *Ausonius.*

NOTHING more detestable does the Earth produce than an Ungrateful Man.

Ingratitude. — *La Rochefoucauld.*

WE seldom find people ungrateful as long as we are in a condition to render them Services.

Ingratitude. — *Shakspeare.*

'TIS a common proof,
That lowliness is young Ambition's ladder,
Whereto the climber upward turns his face;
But when he once attains the upmost round,
He then unto the Ladder turns his back,
Looks in the clouds, scorning the base degrees
By which he did ascend.

Ingratitude. — *Shakspeare.*

INGRATITUDE! thou marble-hearted Fiend,
More hideous, when thou show'st thee in a child,
Than the Sea Monster.

Ingratitude. — *From the Latin.*

IF you say he is Ungrateful, you can impute to him no more detestable act.

Ingratitude. — *Publius Syrius.*

ONE Ungrateful Man does an Injury to all who stand in need of aid.

Injuries. — *Diogenes.*

No man is hurt but by himself.

Injuries. — *Fuller.*

SLIGHT small Injuries, and they'll become none at all.

Injuries. — *La Rochefoucauld.*

MEN are not only prone to lose the Remembrance of Benefits and of Injuries; they even hate those who have obliged them, and cease to hate those who have grievously injured them. The constant study to recompense Good and avenge Evil appears to them a slavery, to which they feel it difficult to submit.

Self-Injury. — *Johnson.*

A MAN should be careful never to tell tales of himself to his own Disadvantage: people may be amused, and laugh at the time, but they will be remembered, and brought up against him upon some subsequent occasion.

Self-Injury. — *Shakspeare.*

WHAT Things are we!
Merely our own Traitors. And as in the common course of all treasons, we still see them reveal themselves, till they attain to their abhorred ends; so he, that contrives against his own Nobility, in his proper Stream o'erflows himself.

Innocence. — *From the French.*

INNOCENCE and Mysteriousness never dwell long together.

Innocence. — *Novalis.*

INNOCENCE and Ignorance are sisters. But there are noble and vulgar sisters. Vulgar Innocence and Ignorance are mortal, they have pretty faces, but wholly without expression, and of a transient Beauty; the noble sisters are immortal, their lofty forms are unchangeable, and their countenances are still radiant with the light of Paradise. They dwell in Heaven, and visit only the noblest and most severely tried of Mankind.

Innocence. — *Horace.*

TRUE, conscious Honour, is to feel no sin;
He's arm'd without that's innocent within:
Be this thy screen, and this thy wall of brass.

Innocence. — *Shakspeare.*

THOU shalt not see me blush,
Nor change my Countenance for this arrest;
A Heart unspotted is not easily daunted.
The purest spring is not so free from mud,
As I am clear from Treason.

Innocence. — *Milton.*

SO dear to Heaven is saintly Chastity,
That when a soul is found sincerely so,
A thousand liveried angels lacquey her,
Driving far off each thing of Sin and Guilt.

Innocence. — *Shakspeare.*

FOR unstain'd thoughts do seldom dream on Evil;
Birds never limed no secret Bushes fear.

Insanity. — *Shakspeare.*

THERE is a willow grows ascaunt the brook,
That shows his hoar leaves in the glassy stream;
Therewith fantastic Garlands did she make
Of crow-flowers, nettles, daisies, and long purples,
That liberal Shepherds give a grosser name,
But our cold maids do dead men's fingers call them:
There on the pendant boughs her coronet weeds
Clambering to hang, an envious sliver broke;
When down her weedy trophies, and herself,
Fell in the weeping Brook. Her clothes spread wide;
And, Mermaid-like, a while they bore her up:
Which time, she chanted snatches of old tunes;
As one incapable of her own Distress,
Or like a creature native and indued
Unto that element: but long it could not be,
Till that her garments, heavy with their drink,
Pulled the poor Wretch from her melodious lay
To muddy Death.

Insanity. — *Shakspeare.*

OH, what a noble Mind is here o'erthrown!
The Courtier's, Soldier's, Scholar's, eye, tongue, sword!
Th' expectancy and rose of the fair State,
The glass of fashion, and the mould of form,
Th' observed of all observers, quite, quite down!
I am of ladies most deject and wretched,
That suck'd the honey of his music vows:
Now see that noble and most sovereign reason,
Like sweet bells jangled out of tune, and harsh;
That unmatch'd form, and feature of blown youth,
Blasted with ecstasy.

Insanity. — *Shakspeare.*

HE was met even now
As mad as the vex'd Sea: singing aloud!
Crown'd with rank fumiter, and furrow weeds,
With harlocks, hemlock, nettles, cuckoo-flowers,
Darnel, and all the idle weeds, that grow
In our sustaining Corn.

Self-Inspection. — *Shakspeare.*

THY Glass will show thee how thy beauties wear,
  Thy Dial how thy precious minutes waste;
The vacant Leaves thy mind's imprint will bear,
  And of this Book this learning may'st thou taste.
The wrinkles which thy Glass will truly show,
  Of mouthed graves will give thee memory;
Thou by thy Dial's shady stealth may'st know
  Time's thievish progress to Eternity.
Look, what thy memory cannot contain,
  Commit to these waste Blanks, and thou shalt find
Those children nursed, deliver'd from thy brain,
  To take a new acquaintance of thy mind.
These offices, so oft as thou wilt look,
Shall profit thee, and much enrich thy Book.

Inspiration. — *Shakspeare.*

OUR poesy is as a Gum, which oozes
  From whence 'tis nourish'd: The fire i' the flint
Shows not till it be struck; our gentle Flame
Provokes itself, and, like the current, flies
Each bound it chafes.

Inspiration. — *Greville.*

A LIVELY and agreeable man has not only the merit of Liveliness and Agreeableness himself, but that also of awakening them in others.

Insults. — *Colton.*

INJURIES accompanied with Insults are never forgiven: all men, on these occasions, are good haters, and lay out their Revenge at compound interest.

Intellect. — *La Bruyere.*

IT is a proof of Mediocrity of Intellect to be addicted to relating stories.

Intellect. — *Colton.*

TIMES of general Calamity and Confusion have ever been productive of the greatest Minds. The purest ore is produced from the hottest Furnace, and the brightest thunderbolt is elicited from the darkest Storm.

Jealousy. — *Byron.*

HER maids were old, and if she took a new one,
  You might be sure she was a perfect fright:
She did this during even her Husband's life—
I recommend as much to every Wife.

Jealousy. — *Hannah More.*

O Jealousy,
Thou ugliest Fiend of Hell! thy deadly venom
Preys on my vitals, turns the healthful hue
Of my fresh cheek to haggard sallowness,
And drinks my Spirit up!

Jealousy. — *Shakspeare.*

Oh, beware of Jealousy;
It is the green-eyed Monster, which doth mock
The meat it feeds on.

Jealousy. — *Shakspeare.*

These are the forgeries of Jealousy:
And never, since the middle summer's spring,
Met we on hill, in dales, forest, or mead,
By paved fountain, or by rushy brook,
Or on the beached margent of the Sea,
To dance our ringlets to the whistling wind,
But with thy Brawls thou hast disturb'd our sport.

Jealousy. — *Mrs. Tighe.*

That anxious torture may I never feel,
Which doubtful, watches o'er a wandering heart.
Oh! who that bitter Torment can reveal,
Or tell the pining anguish of that Smart!
In those affections may I ne'er have part,
Which easily transferr'd can learn to rove:
No, dearest Cupid! when I feel thy dart,
For thy sweet Psyche's sake may no false Love,
The tenderness I prize lightly from me remove!

Jealousy. — *Shakspeare.*

Oh, how hast thou with Jealousy infected
The Sweetness of affiance!

Jealousy. — *Thomson.*

But through the heart
Should Jealousy its venom once diffuse,
'Tis then delightful Misery no more,
But Agony unmix'd, incessant gall,
Corroding every thought, and blasting all
Love's Paradise. Ye fairy prospects then,
Ye beds of roses, and ye bowers of joy,
Farewell! ye gleamings of departed peace,
Shine out your last! the yellow tinging Plague
Internal vision taints, and in a night
Of vivid gloom Imagination wraps.

Jealousy. — *Shakspeare.*

I NEVER gave him cause.
But jealous souls will not be answer'd so;
They are not ever jealous for the Cause,
But jealous, for they are jealous: 'tis a Monster,
Begot upon itself, born on itself.

Jealousy. — *Spenser.*

NE ever is he wont on ought to feed
But todes and frogs (his pasture poysonous)
Which in his cold Complexion doe breed
A filthy blood, or humor rancorous,
Matter of Doubt and dread suspitious,
That doth with cureless care consume the Hart,
Corrupts the stomacke with gall vitious,
Cross-cuts the liver with eternall Smart,
And doth transfixe the soule with Death's eternall dart.

Jealousy. — *Shakspeare.*

TRIFLES, light as air,
Are, to the Jealous, Confirmations strong
As proofs of Holy Writ.

Jealousy. — *Tacitus.*

HE who is next heir to supreme Power, is always suspected and hated by him who actually wields it.

Jealousy. — *Spenser.*

YET is there one more cursed than they all,
That Canker-worm, that Monster, Jealousie,
Which eats the heart and feeds upon the gall,
Turning all Love's delight to misery,
Through fear of losing his felicity.
Ah, Gods! that ever ye that Monster placed
In gentle love, that all his joys defaced!

Jealousy. — *Sir Thomas Overbury.*

A JEALOUS Man sleeps dog sleep.

Jealousy. — *Spenser.*

FOWLE Jealousie! that turnest love divine
To joyless dread, and mak'st the loving Hart
With hatefull thoughts to languish and to pine,
And feed itselfe with selfe-consuming Smart:
Of all the Passions in the mind thou vilest art.

The Jester. — *Horace.*

YONDER he drives—avoid that furious beast:
If he may have his Jest, he never cares
At whose expense; nor Friend nor patron spares.

Jesting. — *Fuller.*

TAKE heed of Jesting: many have been ruined by it. It's hard to Jest, and not sometimes jeer too; which oftentimes sinks deeper than was intended, or expected.

Jesting. — *Sheridan.*

TO smile at the Jest which plants a Thorn in another's breast, is to become a principal in the Mischief.

Joking. — *La Bruyere.*

NEVER risk a Joke, even the least offensive in its nature and the most common, with a person who is not well bred, and possessed of sense to comprehend it.

Joy. — *Shakspeare.*

JOY had the like conception in our eyes,
And, at that instant, like a Babe sprung up.

Joy. — *Shakspeare.*

THE night of Sorrow now is turn'd to day:
Her two blue windows faintly she up-heaveth,
Like the fair Sun, when in his fresh array
He cheers the morn, and all the world relieveth:
And as the bright Sun glorifies the sky,
So is her face illumined with her Eye.

Joy. — *Shakspeare.*

YOU have bereft me of all words,
Only my Blood speaks to you in my veins;
And there is such confusion in my powers,
As, after some oration fairly spoke
By a beloved Prince, there doth appear
Among the buzzing pleased Multitude;
Where every something, being blent together,
Turns to a wild of nothing, save of Joy
Exprest, and not exprest.

Joy. —*Dryden.*

MY heart's so full of Joy,
That I shall do some wild extravagance
Of Love in public; and the foolish world,
Which knows not Tenderness, will think me mad.

Joy. — *Shakspeare.*

GIVE me a gash, put me to present Pain;
Lest this great sea of Joys rushing upon me,
O'erbear the shores of my Mortality,
And drown me with their Sweetness.

Joy. — *Shakspeare.*

I HAVE felt so many quirks of Joy, and Grief,
That the first face of neither, on the start,
Can woman me unto 't.

Joy. — *Young.*

NATURE, in zeal for human amity,
Denies, or damps, an undivided Joy.
Joy is an import; Joy is an exchange;
Joy flies monopolists: it calls for two;
Rich Fruit! Heaven planted! never pluck'd by one.

The Judge. — *Peter Pindar.*

WHEN Judges a campaigning go,
And on their benches look so big,
What gives them consequence, I trow,
Is nothing but a Bushel Wig.

Judging Others. — *Greville.*

HE that sees ever so accurately, ever so finely into the motives of other people's Acting, may possibly be entirely ignorant as to his own: it is by the mental as the corporeal Eye, the object may be placed too near the Sight to be seen truly, as well as so far off; nay, too near to be seen at all.

Judgment. — *Shakspeare.*

WHAT we oft do best
By sick Interpreters, once weak ones, is
Not ours, or not allow'd; what worst, as oft,
Hitting a grosser quality, is cried up
For our best Act.

Judgment. — *La Rochefoucauld.*

WE are mistaken in supposing that Intellect and Judgment are two different things. Judgment is merely the Greatness of the Light of the Mind; this Light penetrates into the recesses of things; it observes there every thing remarkable, and perceives what appears to be imperceptible. Thus it must be allowed that it is the Greatness of the Light of the Mind which produces all the effects attributed to Judgment.

Judgment. — *Swift.*

INVENTION is the talent of youth, and Judgment of age: so that our Judgment grows harder to please, when we have fewer things to offer it: this goes through the whole commerce of Life. When we are old, our friends find it difficult to please us, and are less concerned whether we be pleased or not.

Judgment. — *Shakspeare.*

MEN'S Judgments are
A parcel of their Fortunes; and things outward
Do draw the inward Quality after them,
To suffer all alike.

Judgment. — *Steele.*

THE most necessary talent in a man of Conversation, which is what we ordinarily intend by a Gentleman, is a good Judgment. He that has this in perfection is master of his Companion, without letting him see it; and has the same advantage over men of any other qualifications whatsoever, as one that can see would have over a blind man of ten times his strength.

Jurisprudence. — *Webster.*

JUSTICE is the great interest of man on earth. It is the ligament which holds civilized beings and civilized nations together. Wherever her temple stands, and so long as it is duly honoured, there is a foundation for social security, general happiness, and the improvement and progress of our race. And whoever labours on this edifice with usefulness and distinction, whoever clears its foundations, strengthens its pillars, adorns its entablatures, or contributes to raise its august dome still higher in the skies, connects himself, in name, and fame, and character, with that which is and must be as durable as the frame of human society.

Justice. — *Colton.*

IF strict Justice be not the rudder of all our other Virtues, the faster we sail, the farther we shall find ourselves from "that Haven where we would be."

Justice. — *La Rochefoucauld.*

JUSTICE is in general only a lively apprehension of being deprived of what belongs to us; hence arise our great consideration and respect for all the interests of our Neighbour, and our scrupulous care to avoid doing him an injury. This fear retains men within the limits of those advantages which Birth or Fortune has given them; and, without it, they would be making continual Inroads upon others.

Justice. — *Colton.*

CARNEADES, whom Cicero so much dreaded, maintained that there was no such thing as Justice! and he supported his theory by such Sophisms as these: that the condition of men is such that if they have a mind to be just, they must act imprudently; and that if they have a mind to act prudently, they must be unjust; and that, it follows, there can be no such thing as Justice, because a Virtue inseparable from a Folly cannot be just.

Lactantius is correct when he affirms that the heathens could not answer this Sophism, and that Cicero dared not undertake it. The error was this, the restricting of the value of Justice to temporal things: for to those who disbelieve a future state, or even have doubts about it, "Honesty is not always the best policy;" and it is reserved for Christians, who take into their consideration the whole existence of man, to argue clearly and consequentially on the sterling value of Justice. It is well known that Hume himself was never so much puzzled as when peremptorily asked, by a lady at Bath, to declare, upon his Honour as a Gentleman, whether he would choose his own confidential domestics from such as held his own principles, or from those who conscientiously believed the eternal truths of Revelation. He frankly decided in favour of the latter!

Justice. — *Shakspeare.*

Poise the cause in Justice' equal scales,
Whose Beam stands sure, whose rightful cause prevails.

Justice and Decency. — *Cicero.*

JUSTICE consists in doing no injury to men; Decency, in giving them no offence.

Kindness. — *Shakspeare.*

You are liberal in offers:
You taught me first to beg; and now, methinks,
You teach me how a Beggar should be answer'd.

Kindness. — *Joanna Baillie.*

A willing Heart adds feather to the heel,
And makes the clown a winged Mercury.

The King. — *Shakspeare.*

There is such divinity doth hedge a King,
That Treason can but peep to what it would,
Acts little of his will.

The King. — *Shakspeare.*

O Majesty!
When thou dost pinch thy bearer, thou dost sit
Like a rich Armour worn in heat of day,
That scalds with Safety.

Knowledge of the World. — *Colton.*

HE that knows a little of the World, will admire it enough to fall down and worship it: but he that knows it most, will most despise it.

Superficial Knowledge. — *Fuller.*

He that sips of many Arts, drinks of none.

Spiritual Knowledge. — *Bishop Sprat.*

'TIS the property of all true Knowledge, especially spiritual, to enlarge the Soul by filling it; to enlarge it without swelling it; to make it more capable, and more earnest to know, the more it knows.

Self-Knowledge. — *Colton.*

MAN, if he compare himself with all that he can see, is at the Zenith of Power; but if he compare himself with all that he can conceive, he is at the Nadir of Weakness.

Subtle Knowledge. — *Joanna Baillie.*

DEEP subtle wits,
In truth, are master-spirits in the world.
The brave man's Courage, and the student's Lore,
Are but as tools his secret ends to work,
Who hath the Skill to use them.

Knowledge. — *Colton.*

THAT is indeed a twofold Knowledge, which profits alike by the Folly of the foolish, and the Wisdom of the wise. It is both a shield and a sword; it borrows its Security from the darkness, and its confidence from the light.

Knowledge. — *Cowper.*

KNOWLEDGE and Wisdom, far from being one,
Have ofttimes no connexion. Knowledge dwells
In heads replete with Thoughts of other men,
Wisdom in minds attentive to their own.

Knowledge. — *Lavater.*

THREE days of uninterrupted Company in a vehicle will make you better acquainted with another, than one hour's Conversation with him every day for three years.

Knowledge. — *Byron.*

KNOWLEDGE is not Happiness, and Science
But an exchange of Ignorance for that
Which is another kind of Ignorance.

Knowledge. — *Colton.*

THE profoundly wise do not declaim against superficial Knowledge in others, so much as the profoundly ignorant; on the contrary, they would rather assist it with their Advice than overwhelm it with their Contempt; for they know that there was a period when even a Bacon or a Newton were superficial, and that he who has a little Knowledge is far more likely to get more than he that has none.

Knowledge. — *Milton.*

Not to know at large of things remote
From use, obscure and subtle, but to know
That which before us lies in daily life,
Is the prime Wisdom; what is more, is fume,
Or Emptiness, or fond Impertinence,
And renders us in things that most concern
Unpractised, unprepared, and still to seek.

Knowledge. — *Shakspeare.*

MEN'S faults do seldom to themselves appear,
Their own Transgressions partially they smother:
Oh! how are they wrapt in with infamies,
That from their own Misdeeds askance their eyes!

Knowledge. — *Colton.*

TO despise our species, is the price we must too often pay for our Knowledge of it.

Knowledge. — *Prior.*

REMEMBER that the cursed desire to know,
Offspring of Adam! was thy source of Wo.
Why wilt thou then renew the vain pursuit,
And rashly catch at the forbidden Fruit;
With empty labour and eluded strife
Seeking, by Knowledge, to attain to life;
For ever from that fatal tree debarr'd,
Which flaming Swords and angry cherubs guard?

Knowledge. — *Spenser.*

Base minded they that want Intelligence;
For God himself for Wisdom most is praised,
And men to God thereby are nighest raised.

Knowledge. — *Moore.*

THE wish to know—that endless Thirst,
Which even by quenching is awaked,
And which becomes or blest or curst,
As is the Fount whereat 'tis slaked—
Still urged me onward, with Desire
Insatiate, to explore, inquire.

Knowledge. — *Colton.*

EVEN human Knowledge is permitted to approximate in some degree, and on certain occasions, to that of the Deity, its pure and primary source; and this assimilation is never more conspicuous than when it converts evil into the means of producing its opposite good.

Knowledge. — *Butler.*

He knew what's what, and that's as high
As metaphysic Wit can fly.

Knowledge. — *Shakspeare.*

Ignorance is the curse of God,
Knowledge the wing wherewith we fly to Heaven.

Knowledge. — *Milton.*

Knowledge is as food, and needs no less
Her temp'rance over appetite, to know
In measure what the mind may well contain;
Oppresses else with surfeit, and soon turns
Wisdom to Folly.

Labour. — *La Rochefoucauld.*

BODILY Labour alleviates the pains of the Mind; and hence arises the Happiness of the poor.

Labour. — *Cowper.*

COME hither, ye that press your beds of down,
And sleep not: see him sweating o'er his bread
Before he eats it.—'Tis the primal curse,
But soften'd into Mercy; made the pledge
Of cheerful Days, and Nights without a groan.

Labour. — *Anon.*

THE pernicious, debilitating tendencies of bodily Pleasure need to be counteracted by the invigorating exercises of bodily Labour; whereas bodily Labour without bodily Pleasure converts the body into a mere machine, and brutifies the Soul.

Language. — *P. G. Niebuhr.*

THE writer, or even the student, of History, ought, if possible, to know all nations in their own Tongue. Languages have one inscrutable origin—as have all national peculiarities—and he has but an imperfect knowledge of a people who does not know their Language.

Language. — *W. B. Clulow.*

THE study of Languages has given a character to modern minds, by the habits of discrimination and analysis which it requires, and has partly contributed to the present advancement of Science and reasoning. To represent it as nothing but a criticism of words, or an exercise of memory, is utterly erroneous. It demands no trifling Perspicacity and Judgment; admits the operations even of Fancy, picturing things of which words are but the symbols; and tends to promote quickness and depth of Apprehension. A good Linguist is always a man of considerable acuteness, and often of pre-eminent taste.

Language. — *Coleridge.*

SUBLIMITY is Hebrew by birth.

Language. — *Anon.*

ESCHEW fine Words, as you would rouge: love simple ones, as you would native Roses on your cheeks. Act as you might be disposed to do on your estate: employ such Words as have the largest families, keep clear of Foundlings, and of those of which nobody can tell whence they come, unless he happens to be a scholar.

The Lark. — *Thomson.*

UP springs the Lark,
Shrill voiced and loud, the messenger of Morn;
Ere yet the shadows fly, he mounted sings,
Amid the dawning clouds, and from their haunts
Calls up the tuneful Nations.

The Lark. — *Southey.*

LOUD sung the Lark, the awaken'd maid
Beheld him twinkling in the morning light,
And wish'd for Wings and Liberty like his.

Laughter. — *Greville.*

MAN is the only creature endowed with the power of Laughter; is he not also the only one that deserves to be laughed at?

Laughter. — *Sir Philip Sidney.*

OUR comedians think there is no Delight without Laughter, which is very wrong; for though Laughter may come with Delight, yet cometh it not of Delight, as though Delight should be the cause of Laughter; but well may one thing breed two together.

Law and Physic. — *Colton.*

PETTIFOGGERS in Law, and Empirics in Medicine, whether their patents lose or save their property, or their lives, take care to be, in either case, equally remunerated; they profit by both horns of the Dilemma, and press defeat no less than success into their service. They hold, from time immemorial, the fee simple of a vast estate, subject to no alienation, diminution, revolution, nor tax; the Folly and Ignorance of Mankind.

Law and Physic. — *Fuller.*

COMMONLY, Physicians, like beer, are best when they are old; and Lawyers, like bread, when they are young and new.

Law of Development. — *Colton.*

THE light of other minds is as necessary to the play and the Development of Genius, as the light of other bodies is to the play and radiation of the Diamond. A Diamond, incarcerated in its subterraneous prison, rough and unpolished, differs not from a common stone; and a Newton or a Shakspeare, deprived of kindred minds, and born amongst savages—Savages had died.

Law Learning. — *Wirt.*

THERE is a great deal of Law Learning that is dry, dark, cold, revolting—but it is an old feudal castle, in perfect preservation, which the legal architect, who aspires to the first honours of his profession, will delight to explore, and learn all the uses to which its various parts used to be put: and he will the better understand, enjoy and relish the progressive improvements of the science in modern times.

Law. — *Colton.*

THE science of Legislation is like that of Medicine in one respect: that it is far more easy to point out what will do harm, than what will do good.

Law. — *Shakspeare.*

WE must not make a scarecrow of the Law,
Setting it up to fear the Birds of Prey,
And let it keep one shape, till Custom make it
Their perch, and not their terror.

Learning. — *Chesterfield.*

A MAN of the best parts and greatest Learning, if he does not know the world by his own experience and observation, will be very absurd, and consequently very unwelcome in Company. He may say very good things; but they will be probably so ill-timed, misplaced, or improperly addressed, that he had much better hold his tongue.

Learning. — *Steele.*

HE that wants Good Sense is unhappy in having Learning, for he has thereby only more ways of exposing himself; and he that has Sense, knows that Learning is not Knowledge, but rather the art of using it.

Learning. — *Sir William Temple.*

WHO can tell whether Learning may not even weaken Invention, in a man that has great advantages from nature and birth; whether the weight and number of so many men's thoughts and notions may not suppress his own, or hinder the motion and agitation of them, from which all Invention arises; as heaping on wood, or too many sticks, or too close together, suppresses, and sometimes quite extinguishes a little Spark, that would otherwise have grown up to a noble Flame.

Learning. — *Bishop Taylor.*

To be proud of Learning, is the greatest Ignorance.

Learning. — *Young.*

YOUR Learning, like the lunar beam, affords
Light, but not heat; it leaves you undevout,
Frozen at heart, while Speculation shines.

Learning. — *Milton.*

THE end of Learning is to know God, and out of that knowledge to love him, and to imitate him, as we may the nearest, by possessing our souls of true Virtue.

Learning. — *Bishop Earle.*

A PRETENDER to Learning is one that would make all others more fools than himself, for though he know nothing, he would not have the world know so much. He conceits nothing in Learning but the opinion, which he seeks to purchase without it, though he might with less labour cure his ignorance than hide it. His business and retirement is his Study, and he protests no delight to it comparable. He is a great Nomenclator of Authors, which he has read in general in the catalogue, and in particular in the Title, and goes seldom so far as the Dedication. He never talks of any thing but Learning, and learns all from talking. Three encounters with the same men pump him. He has taken pains to be an Ass, though not to be a Scholar, and is at length discovered and laughed at.

Learning. — *Selden.*

NO man is the wiser for his Learning: it may administer matter to work in, or objects to work upon; but Wit and Wisdom are born with a man.

Learning. — *Young.*

VORACIOUS Learning, often over-fed,
Digests not into Sense her motley meal.
This Bookcase, with dark booty almost burst,
This forager on others' Wisdom, leaves
Her native farm, her reason, quite untill'd.

Learning. — *Powell.*

HE who has no Inclination to learn more, will be very apt to think that he knows enough.

Leisure. — *Franklin.*

EMPLOY thy time well, if thou meanest to gain leisure; and since thou art not sure of a minute, throw not away an hour. Leisure is time for doing something useful; this leisure the diligent man will obtain, but the lazy man never; for a life of leisure and a life of laziness are two things.

Leisure. — *Johnson.*

YOU cannot give an instance of any man who is permitted to lay out his own Time, contriving not to have tedious Hours.

Lenity. — *Goethe.*

IT is only necessary to grow old to become more indulgent. I see no Fault committed that I have not committed myself.

Lenity. — *Shakspeare.*

WHEN Lenity and Cruelty play for a kingdom, the gentler gamester is the soonest winner.

Levity. — *Seneca.*

LEVITY of Behaviour is the bane of all that is good and virtuous.

The Liar. — *Shakspeare.*

PAST all shame, so past all Truth.

Liberality. — *La Bruyere.*

LIBERALITY consists less in giving profusely, than in giving judiciously.

Liberty. — *Addison.*

O LIBERTY, thou goddess, heavenly bright,
Profuse of bliss, and pregnant with delight!
Eternal Pleasures in thy presence reign,
And smiling Plenty leads thy wanton train;
Eased of her load Subjection grows more light,
And poverty looks cheerful in thy sight;
Thou mak'st the gloomy face of Nature gay,
Givest Beauty to the sun, and Pleasure to the day.

Liberty. — *Dryden.*

THE love of Liberty with life is given,
And life itself th' inferior gift of Heaven.

Liberty. — *Byron.*

So let them ease their Hearts with prate
Of equal rights, which man ne'er knew.

Liberty. — *Byron.*

ETERNAL Spirit of the chainless mind!
Brightest in dungeons, Liberty! thou art,
For there thy habitation is the Heart—
The Heart which love of thee alone can bind:
And when thy sons to fetters are consign'd—
To fetters and the damp vault's dayless gloom,
Their country conquers with their Martyrdom,
And Freedom's fame finds wings on every wind.

Liberty. — *Byron.*

'TIS vain—my tongue cannot impart
My almost drunkenness of Heart,
When first this liberated eye
Survey'd Earth, Ocean, Sun, and Sky,
As if my spirit pierced them through
And all their inmost wonders knew!
One word alone can paint to thee
That more than feeling—I was Free!
E'en for thy presence ceased to pine:
The World—nay—Heaven itself was mine!

Liberty. — *Byron.*

MOTION was in their days, Rest in their slumbers,
And Cheerfulness the handmaid of their toil;
Nor yet too many nor too few their numbers;
Corruption could not make their hearts her soil;
The lust which stings, the Splendour which encumbers;
With the free foresters divide no spoil;
Serene not sullen, were the Solitudes
Of this unsighing people of the woods.

Liberty. —*Byron.*

The Wish—which ages have not yet subdued
In Man—to have no master save his mood.

Life. — *Addison.*

AS it is the chief concern of wise men to retrench the evils of Life by the reasonings of Philosophy, it is the employment of fools to multiply them by the Sentiments of Superstition.

Life. — *La Bruyere.*

THERE is a time, which precedes Reason, when, like other animals, we live by instinct alone; of which the Memory retains no vestiges. There is a second term, when Reason discovers itself, when it is formed, and might act, if it were not hoodwinked, as it were, and manacled by vices of the Constitutiom, and a chain of Passions, which succeed one another, till the third and last age: Reason then being in its full force, naturally should assert its dignity, and control the appetites; but it is impaired and benumbed by years, sickness, and pains, and shattered by the disorder of the declining Machine; yet these years, with their several imperfections, constitute the Life of Man.

Life.— *Colton.*

IF you would be known, and not know, vegetate in a Village; if you would know, and not be known, live in a City.

Life. — *Shakspeare.*

ALL the world's a Stage,
And all the men and women merely Players;
They have their Exits and their Entrances,
And one man in his time plays many parts:
His acts being seven ages. At first the Infant,
Mewling and puking in the nurse's arms:
And then the whining School-boy, with his satchel,
And shining morning face, creeping like snail
Unwillingly to school. And then the lover;
Sighing like Furnace, with a woful ballad
Made to his mistress' eye-brow. Then a Soldier;
Full of strange oaths, and bearded like the pard,
Jealous in Honour, sudden and quick in quarrel;
Seeking the bubble Reputation
Even in the cannon's mouth. And then the Justice
In fair round belly, with good capon lined,
With eyes severe, and beard of formal cut,
Full of wise saws and modern instances,
And so he plays his Part. The sixth age shifts
Into the lean and slipper'd Pantaloon,
With spectacles on nose, and pouch on side:
His youthful hose well saved, a world too wide
For his shrunk Shank; and his big manly voice,
Turning again toward childish treble, pipes,
And whistles in his sound. Last Scene of all,
That ends this strange eventful History,
Is second Childishness, and mere oblivion,
Sans teeth, sans eyes, sans taste, sans every thing.

Life. — *South.*

SELDOM shall we see in Cities, Courts, and rich families where men live plentifully, and eat and drink freely, that perfect Health, that athletic soundness and vigour of Constitution, which is commonly seen in the country, in poor houses and cottages, where Nature is their cook, and Necessity their caterer, and where they have no other doctor but the Sun and fresh air, and that such a one as never sends them to the Apothecary.

Life. —*Byron.*

THERE still are many Rainbows in your sky,
But mine have vanish'd. All, when Life is new,
Commence with feelings warm, and prospects high;
But Time strips our Illusions of their hue,
And one by one in turn, some grand mistake,
Casts off its bright skin yearly like the Snake.

Life. — *Pope.*

THE vanity of Human Life is like a River, constantly passing away, and yet constantly coming on.

Life. — *Shakspeare.*

REASON thus with Life: A breath thou art,
(Servile to all the skiey influences,)
That dost this Habitation, where thou keep'st,
Hourly afflict: merely, thou art Death's fool;
For him thou labour'st by thy flight to shun,
And yet run'st toward him still: Thou art not noble;
For all the accommodations that thou bear'st
Are nursed by Baseness: Thou art by no means valiant;
For thou dost fear the soft and tender fork
Of a poor worm: Thy best of rest is sleep,
And that thou oft provokest.
Thou art not thyself;
For thou exist'st on many a thousand grains
That issue out of Dust: Happy thou art not:
For what thou hast not, still thou strivest to get;
And what thou hast, forget'st: Thou art not certain;
For thy complexion shifts to strange effects,
After the Moon: If thou art rich, thou art poor;
For, like an ass, whose back with ingots bows,
Thou bear'st thy heavy riches but a Journey,
And Death unloads thee: Friends hast thou none;
For thine own bowels, which do call thee sire,
The mere effusion of thy proper loins,
Do curse the Gout, serpigo, and the rheum,
For ending thee no sooner: Thou hast nor youth nor age;
But, as it were, an after-dinner's sleep,
Dreaming on both: for all thy blessed Youth
Becomes as aged, and doth beg the alms
Of palsied eld; and when thou art old, and rich,
Thou hast neither Heart, affection, limb, nor beauty,
To make thy riches pleasant. Yet in this life
Lie hid more thousand deaths: yet Death we fear.

Life. — *Shakspeare.*

THIS is the state of Man; to-day he puts forth
The tender leaves of Hope, to-morrow blossoms,
And bears his blushing Honours thick upon him:
The third day, comes a Frost, a killing Frost;
And,—when he thinks, good easy man, full surely
His Greatness is a ripening,—nips his Fruit,
And then he falls.

Life. — *Sir Walter Raleigh.*

BESTOW thy Youth so that thou mayst have comfort to remember it, when it hath forsaken thee, and not sigh and grieve at the account thereof. Whilst thou art young thou wilt think it will never have an end: but behold, the longest day hath his evening, and that thou shalt enjoy it but once, that it never turns again; use it therefore as the Spring-time, which soon departeth, and wherein thou oughtest to plant and sow all provisions for a long and happy Life.

Life. — *Prior.*

A FLOWER that does with opening morn arise,
And, flourishing the day, at evening dies;
A winged Eastern Blast, just skimming o'er
The ocean's brow, and sinking on the shore;
A Fire, whose flames through crackling stubble fly,
A Meteor shooting from the summer sky;
A Bowl adown the bending Mountain roll'd;
A Bubble breaking, and a Fable told;
A Noontide Shadow, and a Midnight Dream;
Are emblems which, with semblance apt, proclaim
Our Earthly Course.

Life. — *La Bruyere.*

A MAN is thirty years old before he has any settled thoughts of his Fortune: it is not completed before fifty; he falls a building in his old age, and dies by that time his House is in a condition to be painted and glazed.

Life. — *Addison.*

THE ready way to the right enjoyment of Life is, by a prospect toward another, to have but a very mean opinion of it.

Life. — *Byron.*

WHEN we have made our love, and gamed our gaming,
Dress'd, voted, shone, and, may be, something more;
With dandies dined; heard senators declaiming;
Seen beauties brought to market by the score ·
Sad rakes to sadder husbands chastely taming;
There's little left but to be bored or bore.
Witness those "ci devant jeunes hommes," who stem
The stream, nor leave the world that leaveth them.

Life. — *Scott.*

AND there the fisherman his sail unfurl'd,
The goat-herd drove his kids to steep Ben-Ghoil,
Before the hut the dame her spindle turn'd,
Courting the sunbeam as she plied her toil;
For, wake where'er he may, man wakes to Care and toil.

Life. — *Moore.*

FOR Time will come with all its blights,
The ruin'd Hope—the friend unkind—
The love, that leaves, where'er it lights,
A chill'd or burning Heart behind!

Life. — *La Bruyere.*

IF you suppress the exorbitant love of Pleasure and Money, idle Curiosity, iniquitous pursuits and wanton Mirth, what a stillness would there be in the greatest Cities! the necessaries of life do not occasion, at most, a third part of the Hurry.

Life. — *Byron.*

AMBITION was my idol, which was broken
Before the shrines of Sorrow and of Pleasure;
And the two last have left me many a token
O'er which reflection may be made at leisure.

Life. — *La Bruyere.*

IF this Life is unhappy, it is a burden to us which it is difficult to bear; if it is in every respect happy, it is dreadful to be deprived of it; so that in either case the result is the same, for we must exist in Anxiety and Apprehension.

Life. — *Prior.*

WHO breathes, must suffer; and who thinks, must mourn,
And he alone is bless'd, who ne'er was born.

Life. — *Byron.*

BETWEEN two worlds Life hovers like a star,
'Twixt night and morn, upon the horizon's verge.
How little do we know that which we are!
How less what we may be! The eternal surge
Of Time and Tide rolls on, and bears afar
Our bubbles; as the old burst, new emerge,
Lash'd from the foam of ages; while the Graves
Of Empires heave but like some passing waves.

Life. — *Steele.*

THERE is nothing which must end, to be valued for its continuance. If hours, days, months, and years pass away, it is no matter what hour, what day, what month, or what year we die. The applause of a good Actor is due to him at whatever scene of the play he makes his exit. It is thus in the Life of a man of sense; a short life is sufficient to manifest himself a man of Honour and Virtue; when he ceases to be such, he has lived too long; and while he is such, it is of no consequence to him how long he shall be so, provided he is so to his life's end.

Life. — *Cowley.*

THERE is no fooling with Life, when it is once turned beyond forty; the seeking of a Fortune then is but a desperate after-game: it is a hundred to one if a man fling two sixes, and recover all: especially if his hand be no luckier than mine.

Life. — *Beattie.*

AH! who can tell how hard it is to climb
The steep where Fame's proud temple shines afar;
Ah! who can tell how many a Soul sublime
Has felt the influence of malignant star,
And waged with Fortune an eternal War;
Check'd by the scoff of Pride, by Envy's frown,
And Poverty's unconquerable bar,
In Life's low vale remote has pined alone,
Then dropt into the grave, unpitied and unknown!

Life. — *Shakspeare.*

So we'll live,
And pray, and sing, and tell old tales, and laugh
At gilded butterflies; and hear poor rogues
Talk of Court-news, and we'll talk with them too;
Who loses and who wins; who's in, who's out;
And take upon us the mystery of things,
As if we were God's spies: And we'll wear out,
In a wall'd prison, packs and sets of great ones,
That ebb and flow by th' Moon.

Life. — *Steele.*

IT is not perhaps much thought of, but it is certainly a very important lesson, to learn how to enjoy ordinary Life, and to be able to relish your being without the transport of some Passion, or gratification of some Appetite. For want of this capacity, the world is filled with whetters, tipplers, cutters, sippers, and all the numerous train of those who, for want of thinking, are forced to be ever exercising their feeling or tasting.

Life. — *Colton.*

LIFE is the jailer of the soul in this filthy prison, and its only deliverer is Death: what we call Life is a journey to Death, and what we call Death is a passport to Life. True wisdom thanks Death for what he takes, and still more for what he brings. Let us then, like sentinels, be ready because we are uncertain, and calm because we are prepared. There is nothing formidable about Death but the consequences of it, and these we ourselves can regulate and control. The shortest Life is long enough if it lead to a better, and the longest Life is too short if it do not.

Life.—*Byron.*

ALAS! such is our Nature! all but aim
At the same end by pathways not the same;
Our means, our Birth, our nation, and our name,
Our fortune, temper, even our outward frame,
Are far more potent o'er our yielding clay
Than aught we know beyond our little day.

Life.—*Sir W. Temple.*

WHEN all is done, Human Life is, at the greatest and best, but like a froward child, that must be played with, and humoured a little to keep it quiet, till it falls asleep, and then the Care is over.

Life.—*Byron.*

LOVE'S the first net which spreads its deadly mesh;
Ambition, Avarice, Vengeance, Glory, glue
The glittering lime-twigs of our latter days,
Where still we flutter on for peace or Praise.

Life.—*Sir Philip Sidney.*

YOUTH will never live to Age, without they keep themselves in breath with exercise, and in heart with joyfulness. Too much thinking doth consume the spirits: and oft it falls out, that while one thinks too much of doing, he leaves to do the effect of his thinking.

Life.—*Sir W. Temple.*

WE bring into the world with us a poor, needy, uncertain Life, short at the longest, and unquiet at the best: all the imaginations of the witty and the wise have been perpetually busied to find out the ways how to revive it with Pleasures, or relieve it with Diversions; how to compose it with Ease, and settle it with Safety. To some of these ends have been employed the institutions of Lawgivers, the reasonings of Philosophers, the inventions of Poets, the pains of labouring, and the extravagances of voluptuous men. All the world is perpetually at work about nothing else, but only that our poor mortal Lives should pass the easier and happier for that little time we possess them, or else end the better when we lose them.

Life.—*Dryden.*

SINCE every man who lives is born to die,
And none can boast sincere Felicity,
With equal mind what happens let us bear,
Nor joy nor grieve too much for things beyond our care.
Like pilgrims to the appointed place we tend;
The World's an inn, and Death the journey's end.

Life. — *Young.*

THE present moment, like a wife, we shun,
And ne'er enjoy, because it is our own.

Life. — *Campbell.*

COUNT o'er the Joys thine hours have seen,
Count o'er thy days from Anguish free,
And know, whatever thou hast been,
'Tis something better not to be.

Life. — *Prior.*

WE Happiness pursue; we fly from pain;
Yet the pursuit, and yet the flight is vain:
And, while poor Nature labours to be blest,
By day with Pleasure, and by night with rest,
Some stronger power eludes our sickly will,
Dashing our rising Hopes with certain ill;
And makes us, with reflective trouble, see
That all destined, which we fancy free.

Life. — *Dryden.*

BUT ah! how insincere are all our Joys!
Which, sent from Heaven, like lightning make no stay;
Their palling taste the Journey's length destroys,
Or Grief sent post o'ertakes them on the way.

Life. — *Pope.*

Is that a Birth-day? 'tis, alas; too clear,
'Tis but the fun'ral of the former year.

Life. — *La Rochefoucauld.*

THERE happen sometimes accidents in Life from which it requires a degree of madness to extricate ourselves well.

Life. — *Spenser.*

BUT what on earth can long abide in state?
Or who can him assure of happy day?
Sith morning fair may bring foul evening late,
And least mishap the most bless alter may?
For thousand perils lie in close await
About us daily, to work our decay,
That none, except a god, or God him guide,
May them avoid, or Remedy provide.

Life. — *Steele.*

THE date of human Life is too short to recompense the cares which attend the most private condition: therefore it is that our Souls are made, as it were, too big for it; and extend themselves in the prospect of a longer Existence.

Life. — *Colton.*

SOCIETY is a sphere that demands all our Energies, and deserves all that it demands. He therefore that retires to cells and to caverns, to Stripes and to Famine, to court a more arduous conflict, and to win a richer Crown, is doubly deceived; the conflict is less, the reward is nothing. He may indeed win a race, if he can be admitted to have done so who had no Competitors, because he chose to run alone; but he will be entitled to no Prize, because he ran out of the course.

Life. — *Spenser.*

WHEN I beheld this fickle, trustless state
Of vain world's glory, flitting to and fro,
And mortal men toss'd by troublous Fate,
In restless seas of Wretchedness and Woe,
I wish I might this weary Life forego,
And shortly turn unto my happy rest,
Where my free Spirit might not any more
Be vex'd with sights that do her peace molest.

Life. — *Young.*

LIKE some fair hum'rists, Life is most enjoy'd,
When courted least; most worth, when disesteem'd.

Life. — *Pope.*

LOVE, Hope, and Joy, fair Pleasure's smiling train;
Hate, Fear, and Grief, the family of Pain;
These, mixt with Art, and to due bounds confined,
Make and maintain the balance of the Mind;
The lights and shades, whose well-accorded strife
Gives all the strength and colour of our Life.

Life. — *Byron.*

O LOVE! O Glory! what are ye? who fly
Around us ever, rarely to alight:
There's not a Meteor in the polar Sky
Of such transcendent and more fleeting flight.
Chill, and chain'd to cold earth, we lift on high
Our eyes in search of either lovely light;
A thousand and a thousand colours they
Assume, then leave us on our freezing way

Life. — *Shakspeare.*

THE time of Life is short;
To spend that shortness basely, were too long,
If Life did ride upon a dial's point,
Still ending at the arrival of an hour.

Life. — *Shakspeare.*

YOUR worm is your only Emperor for diet; we fat all creatures else, to fat us; and we fat ourselves for Maggots; your fat King, and your lean Beggar, is but variable service; two dishes, but to one table; that's the end. A man may fish with the worm that hath eat of a King: and eat of the fish that hath fed of that Worm.

Life. — *Byron.*

WE wither from our youth, we gasp away—
Sick—sick; unfound the boon—unslaked the thirst,
Though to the last, in verge of our decay,
Some Phantom lures, such as we thought at first—
But all too late,—so we are doubly curst.
Love, Fame, Ambition, Avarice—'tis the same,
Each idle—and all ill—and none the worst—
For all are meteors with a different name,
And Death the sable smoke where vanishes the Flame.

Life. — *Byron.*

WELL—well, the world must turn upon its axis,
And all mankind turn with it, heads or tails,
And live and die, make love and pay our taxes,
And as the veering wind shifts, shift our sails;
The King commands us, and the Doctor quacks us,
The Priest instructs, and so our life exhales;
A little Breath, Love, Wine, Ambition, Fame,
Fighting, Devotion, Dust,—perhaps a Name.

Life. — *Prior.*

THUS we act; and thus we are,
Or toss'd by Hope, or sunk by Care.
With endless pain this man pursues
What, if he gained, he could not use:
And t'other fondly hopes to see
What never was, nor e'er shall be.
We err by use, go wrong by rules,
In gesture grave, in action fools:
We join Hypocrisy to Pride,
Doubling the faults we strive to hide.

Life. — *Milton.*

BETTER end here unborn. Why is Life given
To be thus wrested from us? rather why
Obtruded on us thus? who if we knew
What we receive, would either not accept
Life offer'd, or soon beg to lay it down,
Glad to be so dismiss'd in Peace.

Life. — *Spenser.*

AND ye, fond men! on Fortune's wheel that ride,
Or in aught under Heaven repose assurance,
Be it Riches, Beauty, or Honour's pride,
Be sure that they shall have no long endurance,
But ere ye be aware will flit away;
For naught of them is yours, but only th' usance
Of a small time, which none ascertain may.

Life. — *Shakspeare.*

THAT time of year thou may'st in me behold,
When yellow leaves, or none, or few, do hang
Upon those boughs which shake against the cold,
Bare ruin'd choirs, where late the sweet birds sang.
In me thou seest the twilight of such day
As after sunset fadeth in the west;
Which by and by black Night doth take away,
Death's second self, that seals up all in rest.
In me thou seest the glowing of such fire,
That on the ashes of his Youth doth lie;
As the death-bed whereon it must expire,
Consumed with that which it was nourish'd by.

Life. — *Young.*

WHY all this toil for triumphs of an hour?
What tho' we wade in Wealth, or soar in Fame?
Earth's highest station ends in "Here he lies:"
And "Dust to dust" concludes her noblest song.

Life. — *Milton.*

NOR love thy Life, nor hate; but whilst thou livest
Live well; how long, how short, permit to Heaven.

Life. — *Young.*

THERE'S not a day, but, to the Man of Thought,
Betrays some secret, that throws new reproach
On Life, and makes him sick of seeing more.

Life. — *Young.*

ERE man has measured half his weary Stage,
His luxuries have left him no reserve,
No maiden relishes, no unbroach'd delights;
On cold-served repetitions he subsists,
And in the tasteless present chews the past;
Disgusted chews, and scarce can swallow down.
Like lavish ancestors, his earlier years
Have disinherited his future Hours,
Which starve on orts, and glean their former field.

Life. — *Dryden.*

WHEN I consider Life, 'tis all a cheat;
Yet, fool'd with Hope men favour the deceit;
Trust on, and think to-morrow will repay;
To-morrow's falser than the former day;
Lies worse, and, while it says, we shall be blest,
With some new Joys, cuts off what we possest.
Strange cozenage! None would live past years again,
Yet all hope Pleasure in what yet remain;
And, from the dregs of life, think to receive,
What the first sprightly running could not give.
I'm tired with waiting for this chemic Gold,
Which fools us young, and beggars us when old.

Life. — *Byron.*

GRIEF should be the instructor of the wise;
Sorrow is Knowledge: they who know the most
Must mourn the deepest o'er the fatal Truth,
The Tree of Knowledge is not that of Life.

Life. — *Burns.*

O LIFE! how pleasant is thy morning,
Young Fancy's rays the hills adorning!
Cold-pausing Caution's lesson scorning,
We frisk away,
Like school-boys, at th' expected warning,
To joy and play.

We wander there, we wander here,
We eye the Rose upon the brier,
Unmindful that the Thorn is near,
Among the leaves;
And though the puny wound appear,
Short while it grieves.

Life. — *Shakspeare.*

THERE'S nothing in this World can make me joy:
Life is as tedious as a twice-told Tale
Vexing the dull ear of a drowsy man.

Life. — *Young.*

LIFE'S little stage is a small eminence,
Inch-high the grave above: that home of man,
Where dwells the multitude: we gaze around;
We read their Monuments; we sigh; and while
We sigh, we sink; and are what we deplored;
Lamenting, or lamented, all our lot!

Life. — *Thomson.*

EVEN so luxurious men, unheeding, pass
An idle Summer-life in Fortune's shine,
A season's glitter! Thus they flutter on
From toy to toy, from Vanity to Vice;
Till, blown away by Death, Oblivion comes
Behind, and strikes them from the Book of Life.

Life. — *Young.*

HOW must a spirit, late escaped from Earth,
The truth of things new-blazing in his eye,
Look back, astonish'd, on the ways of Men,
Whose Lives' whole drift is to forget their graves!

Life. — *Spenser.*

OH, vain world's glory, and unsteadfast state,
Of all that lives on face of sinful Earth!
Which from their first until their utmost date
Taste no one hour of Happiness or Mirth,
But like as at the ingate of their birth,
They crying creep out of their mother's womb,
So wailing back go to their woeful Tomb.

Life. — *Byron.*

WE are fools of Time and Terror: days
Steal on us and steal from us; yet we live,
Loathing our Life, and dreading still to die.
In all the days of this detested yoke—
This vital weight upon the struggling Heart,
Which sinks with sorrow, or beats quick with pain,
Or joy that ends in Agony or faintness—
In all the days of past and future, for
In Life there is no present, we can number
How few, how less than few—wherein the soul
Forbears to pant for Death, and yet draws back
As from a stream in winter, though the chill
Be but a moment's.

Life. — *Spenser.*

OH, why doe wretched men so much desire
To draw their Dayes unto the utmost date,
And doe not rather wish them soone expire,
Knowing the Miserie of their estate,
And thousand perills which them still awate,
Tossing them like a boate amid the mayne,
That every houre they knocke at Deathe's gate?
And he that happie seemes and leaste in payne,
Yet is as nigh his End as he that most doth playne.

Life. — *Shakspeare.*

TO-MORROW, and to-morrow, and to-morrow,
Creeps in this petty pace from day to day,
To the last syllable of recorded Time:
And all our yesterdays have lighted fools
The way to dusty Death. Out, out, brief candle!
Life's but a walking shadow; a poor player,
That struts and frets his hour upon the stage,
And then is heard no more: it is a Tale
Told by an idiot, full of sound and fury,
Signifying nothing.

Life. — *Spenser.*

AFTER long storms and tempests overblowne,
The Sunne at length his joyous face doth cleare:
So when as Fortune all her spight hath showne,
Some blissful hours at last must needes appeare;
Else should afflicted wights ofttimes despeire.

Life. — *Shakspeare.*

LOVE all, trust a few,
Do wrong to none; be able for thine Enemy
Rather in power, than use; and keep thy Friend
Under thy own life's key; be check'd for Silence,
But never tax'd for Speech.

Life. — *Young.*

THE world's infectious; few bring back at eve
Immaculate, the Manners of the morn.
Something we thought, is blotted; we resolved,
Is shaken; we renounced, returns again.

Life. — *Thomson.*

THE human race are sons of Sorrow born;
And each must have his portion. Vulgar minds
Refuse, or crouch beneath their load; the Brave
Bear theirs without repining.

Life. — *Spenser.*

SUCH is the weaknesse of all mortall Hope;
So fickle is the state of earthly things;
That ere they come unto their aymed scope,
They fall too short of our fraile reckonings,
And bring us bale and bitter sorrowings,
Instead of Comfort which we should embrace:
This is the state of Keasars and of Kings!
Let none, therefore, that is in meaner place,
Too greatly grieve at his unlucky case!

Life. — *Cowper.*

ASK what is Human Life—the Sage replies,
With disappointment low'ring in his eyes,
A painful Passage o'er a restless flood,
A vain Pursuit of fugitive false good,
A sense of fancied Bliss and heartfelt care,
Closing at last in Darkness and despair.

Life. — *Keats.*

FOUR seasons fill the measure of the year:
There are four seasons in the Mind of man:
He has his lusty Spring, when fancy clear
Takes in all beauty with an easy span:
He has his Summer, when luxuriously
Spring's honey'd cud of youthful thought he loves
To ruminate, and by such dreaming high
Is nearest unto Heaven: quiet coves
His soul hath in its Autumn, when his wings
He furleth close; contented so to look
On mists in Idleness—to let fair things
Pass by unheeded as a threshold brook.
He has his Winter too of pale misfeature,
Or else he would forego his mortal nature.

The King's Life. — *Shakspeare.*

THE single and peculiar Life is bound,
With all the strength and armour of the Mind,
To keep itself from 'noyance; but much more
That Spirit, upon whose weal depend and rest
The lives of many. The cease of Majesty
Dies not alone; but, like a gulf, doth draw
What's near it, with it: it is a massy wheel,
Fix'd on the summit of the highest mount,
To whose huge spokes ten thousand lesser things
Are mortised and adjoin'd; which, when it falls,
Each small annexment, petty consequence,
Attends the boist'rous ruin. Never alone
Did the King sigh, but with a general Groan

Light. — *Milton.*

HAIL holy Light, offspring of Heaven first born,
Or of the eternal co-eternal beam,
May I express thee unblamed? since God is light,
And never but in unapproached light,
Dwelt from Eternity, dwell then in thee,
Bright effluence of bright essence increate.

Light. — *Milton.*

Before the Sun,
Before the Heavens thou wert, and at the voice
Of God, as with a mantle didst invest
The rising world of Waters dark and deep
Won from the void and formless Infinite.

Celestial Light.— *Shakspeare.*

Angels are bright still, though the brightest fell:
Though all things foul would wear the brows of Grace,
Yet Grace must still look so.

Listening. — *Colton.*

WERE we as eloquent as Angels, yet should we please some Men, some Women, and some Children much more by listening than by talking.

Literature. — *Anon.*

LITERARY Dissipation is no less destructive of sympathy with the living world, than sensual Dissipation. Mere Intellect is as hard-hearted and as heart-hardening as mere Sense; and the union of the two, when uncontrolled by the Conscience, and without the softening, purifying influences of the moral affections, is all that is requisite to produce the diabolical ideal of our Nature. Nor is there any repugnance in either to coalesce with the other: witness Iago, Tiberius, Borgia.

Literature. — *Prescott.*

THE triumphs of the warrior are bounded by the narrow theatre of his own age; but those of a Scott or a Shakspeare will be renewed with greater and greater lustre in ages yet unborn, when the victorious chieftain shall be forgotten, or shall live only in the song of the minstrel and the page of the chronicler.

Living. — *Addison.*

THE man who will live above his present circumstances, is in great danger of living in a little time much beneath them.

Living well. — *Fuller.*

HE lives long that lives well; and Time misspent, is not lived, but lost. Besides, God is better than his promise if he takes from him a long lease, and gives him a Freehold of a better value.

Living well. — *Seneca.*

IT is the bounty of Nature that we live, but of Philosophy that we live well; which is, in truth, a greater benefit than Life itself.

London.—*Johnson.*

HERE Malice, Rapine, Accident, conspire,
And now a Rabble rages, and now a Fire;
Their ambush here relentless ruffians lay,
And here the fell Attorney prowls for prey;
Here falling houses thunder on your head,
And here a female Atheist talks you dead.

London.—*Byron.*

A MIGHTY Mass of Brick, and smoke, and shipping,
Dirty and dusky, but as wide as eye
Could reach, with here and there a sail just skipping
In sight, then lost amidst the forestry
Of masts; a wilderness of Steeples peeping
On tiptoe through their sea-coal canopy,
A huge dun Cupola, like a foolscap crown
On a fool's head—and there is London Town!

London.—*Johnson.*

LONDON! the needy Villain's gen'ral home,
The common sewer of Paris and of Rome;
With eager Thirst, by folly or by fate,
Sucks in the dregs of each corrupted State.

Longevity.—*Colton.*

WERE the Life of man prolonged, he would become such a proficient in villany, that it would be necessary again to drown or to burn the World. Earth would become a Hell: for future rewards, when put off to a great distance, would cease to encourage, and future punishments to alarm.

Looking upward.—*Colton.*

"OUR thoughts," says an eloquent divine, "like the waters of the sea, when exhaled toward Heaven, will lose all their bitterness and saltness, and sweeten into an amiable Humanity, until they descend in gentle showers of love and kindness upon our fellow-men."

Loquacity.—*Fuller.*

LEARN to hold thy Tongue. Five Words cost Zacharias forty Weeks' Silence.

Loquacity.—*Fuller.*

THOU may'st esteem a Man of many Words and many Lies much alike.

Love.—*Shakspeare.*

SHE is so conjunctive to my life and Soul,
That, as the Star moves not but in his Sphere,
I could not but by her.

Love. — *Shakspeare.*

OR, that persuasion could but thus convince me,
That my Integrity and Truth to you
Might be affronted with the match and weight
Of such a winnow'd purity in Love:
How were I then up-lifted! but alas,
I am as true as Truth's simplicity,
And simpler than the infancy of Truth.

Love. — *Shakspeare.*

THIS bud of Love, by summer's ripening breath,
May prove a beauteous Flower, when next we meet.

Love. — *Campbell.*

IN joyous Youth, what soul hath never known
Thought, feeling, taste, harmonious to its own?
Who hath not paused while Beauty's pensive eye
Ask'd from his Heart the homage of a sigh?
Who hath not own'd, with rapture-smitten frame,
The power of Grace, the magic of a Name?

Love. — *Shakspeare.*

O BRAWLING Love! O loving Hate!
O anything, of nothing first create!
O heavy lightness! serious Vanity!
Mis-shapen Chaos of well-seeming forms!
Feather of Lead, bright smoke, cold fire, sick Health!
Still-waking Sleep, that is not what it is!

Love. — *Moore.*

LOVE was to his impassion'd soul
Not, as with others, a mere part
Of its existence, but the whole—
The very Life Breath of his Heart!

Love. — *Byron.*

INSTEAD of poppies, Willows
Waved o'er his couch; he meditated, fond
Of those sweet bitter thoughts which banish sleep,
And make the Worldling sneer, the Youngling weep.

Love. — *Spenser.*

So Love does raine
In stoutest minds, and maketh monstrous Warre:
He maketh warre: he maketh Peace againe,
And yett his Peace is but continuall Jarre:
Oh miserable men that to him subject arre!

Love. — *Mrs. Tighe.*

OH! never may Suspicion's gloomy sky
   Chill the sweet glow of fondly trusting Love!
Nor ever may he feel the scowling eye
   Of dark Distrust his Confidence reprove!
   In pleasing error may I rather rove,
With blind reliance on the hand so dear,
   Than let cold Prudence from my eyes remove
Those sweet delusions, where no doubt nor fear,
Nor foul Disloyalty, nor cruel Change appear.

Love. — *Shakspeare.*

SHE loved me for the Dangers I had pass'd;
And I loved her, that she did pity them.

Love. — *Shakspeare.*

A LOVER'S pinch,
Which hurts, and is desired.

Love. — *Byron.*

OH! I envy those
Whose Hearts on Hearts as faithful can repose,
Who never feel the void—the wandering thought
That sighs o'er visions—such as mine hath wrought.

Love. — *Shakspeare.*

IF ever thou shalt love,
In the sweet pangs of it remember me:
For, such as I am, all true Lovers are;
Unstaid and skittish in all motions else,
Save, in the constant Image of the creature
That is beloved.

Love. — *Shakspeare.*

I TELL thee, I am mad
In Cressid's love. Thou answer'st, she is fair;
Pour'st in the open ulcer of my Heart
Her eyes, her hair, her cheek, her gait, her voice;
Handlest in thy discourse—O that! her hand!
(In whose comparison, all whites are Ink
Writing their own reproach) to whose soft seizure
The Cygnet's down is harsh, and spirit of Sense
Hard as the palm of Ploughman.

Love. — *Shakspeare.*

IF he be not one that truly loves you,
That errs in Ignorance, and not in cunning,
I have no judgment in an Honest face.

Love. — *Mrs. Tighe.*

OH! who the exquisite delight can tell,
The joy which mutual Confidence imparts?
Or who can paint the charm unspeakable
Which links in tender bands two faithful Hearts?
In vain assail'd by Fortune's envious darts,
Their mitigated woes are sweetly shared,
And doubled Joy reluctantly departs:
Let but the sympathizing heart be spared,
What Sorrow seems not light, what Peril is not dared?

Love. — *Shakspeare.*

BOLDNESS comes to me now, and brings me Heart:
Prince Troilus, I have loved you night and day,
For many weary months.
Why was my Cressid then so hard to win?
Hard to seem won: but I was won, my lord,
With the first glance that ever—pardon me—
If I confess much, you will play the Tyrant:
I love you now; but not till now, so much
But I might master it—in faith, I lie—
My thoughts were, like unbridled children, grown
Too headstrong for their Mother; see, we fools!
Why have I blabb'd? who shall be true to us,
When we are so unsecret to ourselves?
But though I loved you well, I woo'd you not;
And yet, good faith, I wish'd myself a Man:
Or that We women had men's privilege,
Of speaking first. Sweet, bid me hold my tongue;
For in this rapture I shall surely speak
The thing I shall repent; see, see, your silence
(Cunning in dumbness) from my Weakness draws
My very Soul of Counsel.

Love. —*Dryden.*

THE power of Love,
In Earth, and Seas, and Air, and Heaven above,
Rules, unresisted, with an awful nod;
By daily miracles declared a god:
He blinds the Wise, gives eyesight to the blind;
And moulds and stamps anew the Lover's mind.

Love. — *Sir Samuel E. Brydges.*

O Love! requited Love, how fine thy thrills,
That shake the trembling flame with ecstasy;
Even every vein celestial pleasure fills,
And inexpressive Bliss is in each sigh.

Love. — *Shakspeare.*

To be
In love, where Scorn is bought with Groans; coy Looks,
With heart-sore Sighs; one fading moment's Mirth,
With twenty watchful, weary, tedious nights:
If haply won, perhaps, a hapless gain;
If lost, why then a grievous labour won;
However, but a Folly bought with Wit,
Or else a Wit by Folly vanquished.

Love. — *Shakspeare.*

Why, what would you?
Make me a Willow cabin at your gate,
And call upon my Soul within the house;
Write loyal cantos of contemned Love,
And sing them loud even in the dead of night;
Holla your name to the reverberate Hills,
And make the babbling gossip of the air
Cry out, Olivia! Oh, you should not rest
Between the elements of Air and Earth,
But you should pity me.

Love. — *Shakspeare.*

But Love, first learned in a lady's Eyes,
Lives not alone immured in the Brain;
But with the motion of all elements,
Courses as swift as Thought in every power;
And gives to every power a double power,
Above their functions and their offices.
It adds a precious seeing to the Eye:
A Lover's Eyes will gaze an Eagle blind!
A Lover's Ear will hear the lowest sound,
When the suspicious head of thrift is stopt.
Love's Feeling is more soft and sensible,
Than are the tender horns of cockled snails.
Love's Tongue proves dainty Bacchus gross in Taste;
For Savour, is not Love a Hercules?
Still climbing trees in the Hesperides.
Subtle as Sphinx; as sweet and musical
As bright Apollo's lute, strung with his hair:
And when Love speaks the voice of all the Gods,
Mark, Heaven drowsie with the harmony!
Never durst Poet touch a pen to write,
Until his ink were temper'd with Love's sighs;
Oh, then his lines would ravish savage ears,
And plant in Tyrants mild humility.

Love. — *Shakspeare.*

ALAS, that Love, whose view is muffled still,
Should, without eyes, see pathways to his Will!

Love. — *Sir A. Hunt.*

WHAT is Love? 'tis not the kiss
Of a harlot lip—the Bliss
That doth perish
Even while we cherish
The fleeting Charm: and what so fleet as this?
He is bless'd in Love alone,
Who loves for years, and loves but one.

Love. — *Shakspeare.*

How wayward is this foolish Love,
That, like a testy babe, will scratch the nurse,
And presently, all humbled, kiss the Rod?

Love. — *Shakspeare.*

OUR separation so abides, and flies,
That thou, residing here, go'st yet with me,
And I, hence fleeting, here remain with thee.

Love. — *Campbell.*

O LOVE! in such a wilderness as this,
Where Transport and Security entwine,
Here is the empire of thy perfect Bliss,
And here thou art a God indeed divine;
Here shall no forms abridge, no hours confine
The views, the walks, that boundless Joy inspire!
Roll on, ye days of raptured influence, shine!
Nor blind with Ecstasy's celestial fire,
Shall Love behold the spark of earth-born Time expire.

Love. — *Shakspeare.*

OH, for a Falconer's voice,
To lure this tassel-gentle back again!
Bondage is hoarse, and may not speak aloud;
Else would I tear the cave where Echo lies,
And make her airy Tongue more hoarse than mine
With repetition of my Romeo's name.

Love. — *Shakspeare.*

WHAT! keep a Week away? seven Days and Nights?
Eightscore Eight Hours? and Lovers' absent Hours,
More tedious than the dial, eightscore times?
Oh weary Reck'ning!

Love. — *Shakspeare.*

So holy and so perfect is my Love,
And I in such a poverty of Grace,
That I shall think it a most plenteous crop
To glean the broken ears after the man
That the main Harvest reaps: loose now and then
A scatter'd Smile, and that I'll live upon.

Love. — *Byron.*

ALAS! the Love of Women! it is known
To be a lovely and a fearful thing;
For all of theirs upon that Die is thrown:
And if 'tis lost, Life has no more to bring
To them but mockeries of the past alone.

Love. — *Shakspeare.*

I DID not take my leave of him, but had
Most pretty things to say: ere I could tell him,
How I would think on him, at certain Hours,
Such Thoughts, and such;
Or have charged him
At the sixth hour of Morn, at Noon, at Midnight,
To encounter me with Orisons, for then
I am in Heaven for him; or ere I could
Give him that parting Kiss, which I had set
Betwixt two charming words, comes in my Father,
And, like the tyrannous breathing of the north,
Shakes all our Buds from growing.

Love. — *Shakspeare.*

WHILE injury of chance
Puts back Leave-taking, justles roughly by
All time of pause, rudely beguiles our Lips
Of all rejoyndure, forcibly prevents
Our lock'd Embraces, strangles our dear Vows,
Even in the birth of our own labouring Breath.
We two, that with so many thousand Sighs
Each other bought, must poorly sell ourselves
With the rude Brevity and Discharge of one.
Injurious Time now, with a robber's haste,
Crams his rich thiev'ry up, he knows not how.
As many Farewells as be stars in Heaven,
With distinct breath and consign'd Kisses to them,
He fumbles up all in one loose Adieu;
And scants us with a single famish'd Kiss,
Distasted with the salt of broken Tears.

Love. — *Spenser.*

For Lovers' Eyes more sharply sighted be
Than other men's, and in dear Love's delight
See more than any other Eyes can see.

Love. — *Moore.*

OH! who, that has ever had Rapture complete,
Would ask how we feel it, or why it is sweet;
How rays are confused, or how particles fly,
Through the medium refined of a Glance or a Sigh!
Is there one, who but once would not rather have known it?
Than written. with Harvey, whole Volumes upon it?

Love. — *Shakspeare.*

A loss of her,
That, like a Jewel, has hung twenty years,
About his neck, yet never lost her Lustre.

Love. — *Shakspeare.*

YOU are a Lover; borrow Cupid's wings,
And soar with them above a common bound. . . .
I am too sore empierced with his Shaft,
To soar with his light feathers; and so bound,
I cannot bound a pitch above dull Wo:
Under Love's heavy burden do I sink.

Love. — *Shakspeare.*

Love goes toward Love, as school-boys from their books;
But Love from Love, toward school with heavy looks.

Love. — *Spenser.*

No lesse was she in secret Hart affected,
But that she masked it with Modestie
For feare she should of Lightnesse be detected.

Love. — *Shakspeare.*

I would have thee gone;
And yet no farther than a wanton's Bird,
That lets it hop a little from her hand,
Like a poor Prisoner in his twisted gyves,
And with a silk thread plucks it back again,
So loving-jealous of his Liberty.

Love. — *Shakspeare.*

I will wind thee in my arms;
So doth the Woodbine, the sweet Honey-suckle,
Gently entwist the Maple; Ivy so
Enrings the barky fingers of the Elm.

Love. — *Shakspeare.*

LOVERS and Madmen have such seething brains,
Such shaping fantasies, that apprehend
More than cool Reason ever comprehends.

Love. — *Spenser.*

SHEE greatly gan enamoured to wex,
And with vain thoughts her falsed fancy vex:
Her fickle Hart conceived hasty Fyre,
Like sparkes of Fire that fall in sclender flex,
That shortly brent into extreme Desyre,
And ransackt all her veines with Passion entyre.

Love. — *Moore.*

SHE loves—but knows not whom she loves,
Nor what his race, nor whence he came;—
Like one who meets, in Indian groves,
Some beauteous Bird without a name,
Brought by the last ambrosial Breeze,
From isles in th' undiscover'd seas,
To show his Plumage for a day
To wondering eyes, and wing away!

Love. — *Shakspeare.*

Now by the jealous queen of Heaven, that Kiss
I carried from thee, dear; my true Lip
Hath virgin'd it e'er since.

Love. — *Spenser.*

SAD, solemne, sowre, and full of Fancies fraile
She woxe, yet wist she nether how nor why;
She wist not (silly mayd) what she did aile,
Yet wist she was not well at ease perdy,
Yet thought it was not Love but some Melancholy.

Love. — *Shakspeare.*

OH, what damn'd Minutes tells he o'er,
Who dotes, yet doubts; suspects, yet strongly loves!

Love. — *Byron.*

IT was such pleasure to behold him, such
Enlargement of Existence to partake
Nature with him, to thrill beneath his touch,
To watch him slumbering, and to see him wake:
To live with him for ever were so much;
But then the thought of parting made her quake:
He was her own, her Ocean-treasure, cast
Like a rich Wreck—her First love, and her Last.

Love. — *Mrs. Tighe.*

UNHAPPY Psyche! soon the latent wound
The fading Roses of her Cheek confess,
Her Eyes' bright Beams, in swimming sorrows drown'd,
Sparkle no more with Life and Happiness,
Her parent's fond Heart to bless;
She shuns adoring crowds, and seeks to hide
The pining sorrows which her Soul oppress,
Till to her mother's tears no more denied,
The secret Grief she owns, for which she lingering sigh'd.

Love. — *Shakspeare.*

ALL thy vexations
Were but my trials of thy Love, and thou
Hast strangely stood the Test.

Love. — *Spenser.*

THE rolling Wheel, that runneth often round,
The hardest Steel in tract of Time doth tear;
And drizzling Drops, that often do redound,
Firmest Flint doth in continuance wear:
Yet cannot I, with many a dropping tear,
And long entreaty, soften her hard Heart,
That she will once vouchsafe my plaint to hear,
Or look with pity on my painful Smart:
But when I plead, she bids me play my part;
And when I weep, she says Tears are but water;
And when I sigh, she says I know the art;
And when I wail, she turns herself to Laughter:
So do I weep and wail, and plead in vain,
Whiles she as Steel and Flint doth still remain.

Love. — *Shakspeare.*

TAKE, oh, take those Lips away,
That so sweetly were forsworn;
And those Eyes, the break of day,
Lights that do mislead the Morn;
But my Kisses bring again,
Seals of Love, but seal'd in vain.

Love. — *Shakspeare.*

MINE Eyes
Were not in fault, for she was beautiful;
Mine Ears, that heard her flattery; nor my Heart,
That thought her like her Seeming: it had been vicious,
To have mistrusted her.

Love. — *Shakspeare.*

How all the other passions fleet to air,
As doubtful Thoughts, and rash-embraced Despair,
And shudd'ring Fear, and green-eyed Jealousie.
O Love, be moderate, allay thy ecstacie;
In measure rein thy joy, scant this excess;
I feel too much thy blessing, make it less,
For fear I surfeit.

Love. — *Byron.*

HOW beautiful she look'd! her conscious Heart
Glow'd in her Cheek, and yet she felt no wrong.
O Love, how perfect is thy mystic Art,
Strengthening the Weak, and trampling on the Strong!
How self-deceitful is the sagest part
Of mortals whom thy Lure hath led along!

Love. — *Shakspeare.*

THAT which I show, Heaven knows, is merely Love
Duty and zeal to your unmatch'd mind,
Care of your food and living: and, believe it,
For any benefit that points to me,
Either in Hope, or present, I'd exchange
For this one wish, that you had Power and Wealth,
To requite me, by making rich yourself.

Love. — *Byron.*

THE World was not for them, nor the World's art
For beings passionate as Sappho's song;
Love was born with them, in them, so intense,
It was their very Spirit—not a sense.

Love. — *Moore.*

THE world!—ah, Fanny! Love must shun
The path where many rove;
One Bosom to recline upon,
One Heart to be his only-one,
Are quite enough for Love!

Love. — *Shakspeare.*

I GROW to you, and our Parting is a tortured body.

Love. — *La Bruyere.*

LOVE seizes on us suddenly, without giving warning, and our Disposition or our Weakness favours the Surprise; one Look, one Glance from the fair, fixes and determines us. Friendship, on the contrary, is a long time in forming; it is of slow growth, through many trials and months of Familiarity.

Love. — *Shakspeare.*

SHOULD we be taking Leave
As long a term as yet we have to live,
The Loathness to depart would grow.

Love. — *Shakspeare.*

WHAT shall I do to win my Lord again?
Good friend, go to him; for, by this light of Heaven,
I know not how I lost him. Here I kneel:
If e'er my will did trespass 'gainst his Love,
Either in discourse of thought, or actual deed;
Or that mine Eyes, mine Ears, or any sense,
Delighted them in any other form;
Or that I do not yet, and ever did,
And ever will,—though he do shake me off
To beggarly Divorcement,—love him dearly,
Comfort forswear me; Unkindness may do much;
And his Unkindness may defeat my Life,
But never taint my Love.

Love. — *Byron.*

THEY should have lived together deep in Woods,
Unseen as sings the Nightingale; they were
Unfit to mix in these thick Solitudes
Call'd social, where all vice and hatred are;
How lonely every freeborn creature broods!
The sweetest Song-birds nestle in a pair;
The Eagle soars alone: the Gull and Crow
Flock o'er their Carrion, just as mortals do.

Love. — *Shakspeare.*

FRIENDSHIP is constant in all other things,
Save in the office and affairs of Love:
Therefore, all hearts in Love use their own Tongues;
Let every Eye negotiate for itself,
And trust no agent: for Beauty is a witch,
Against whose charms Faith melteth into Blood.

Love. — *Shakspeare.*

LOVE is not Love,
When it is mingled with Respects, that stand
Aloof from the entire point.

Love. — *Byron.*

OH beautiful! and rare as beautiful!
But theirs was Love in which the mind delights
To lose itself, when the old world grows dull,
And we are sick of its hack Sounds and Sights.

Love. — *Shakspeare.*

A MURD'ROUS guilt shows not itself more soon,
Thans Love that would seem hid; Love's night is Noon.

Love. — *Shakspeare.*

SWEET Love, changing his property,
Turn to the sourest and most deadly Hate.

Love. — *Moore.*

'TWAS his own Voice. She could not err,
Throughout the breathing world's extent
There was but one such Voice for her,
So kind, so soft, so eloquent;
Oh! sooner shall the Rose of May
Mistake her own sweet Nightingale,
And to some meaner minstrel's lay
Open her bosom's glowing vail,
Than Love shall ever doubt a tone,
A breath of the beloved One!

Love. — *Shakspeare.*

NATURE is fine in Love; and, where 'tis fine,
It sends some precious instance of itself
After the thing it loves.

Love. — *Shakspeare.*

THERE lives within the very flame of Love
A kind of Wick, or Snuff, that will abate it;
And nothing is at a like goodness still:
For goodness, growing to a Pleurisy,
Dies in his own too-much.

Love. — *Byron.*

AH, happy she! to 'scape from him whose Kiss
Had been pollution unto aught so chaste;
Who soon had left her charms for vulgar Bliss,
And spoil'd her goodly Lands to gild his waste,
Nor calm domestic Peace had ever deign'd to taste.

Love. — *Shakspeare.*

WHERE Love is great, the littlest doubts are fear;
Where little Fears grow great, great Love grows there

Love. — *Shakspeare.*

LOOKS kill Love, and Love by looks reviveth:
A Smile recures the wounding of a Frown,
But blessed bankrupt, that by Love so thriveth.

Love.—*Byron.*

The river
Damm'd from its Fountain—the Child from the Knee
And Breast maternal wean'd at once for ever,
Would wither less than these two torn apart!
Alas! there is no instinct like the Heart!

Love.—*Byron.*

AND he was mourn'd by one whose quiet Grief
Less loud, outlasts a people's for their chief.
Vain was all question ask'd her of the past,
And vain e'en menace—silent to the last;
She told nor whence nor why she left behind
Her all for one who seem'd but little kind.
Why did she love him? Curious fool!—be still—
Is human Love the growth of human will?
To her he might be Gentleness; the stern
Have deeper thoughts than your dull eyes discern,
And when they love, your smilers guess not how
Beats the strong Heart, though less the Lips avow.

Love.—*Shakspeare.*

She never told her Love,
But let Concealment, like a worm i' the bud,
Feed on her damask Cheek; she pined in thought;
And, with a green and yellow Melancholy
She sat (like patience on a monument)
Smiling at Grief.

Love.—*Byron.*

BUT there was something wanting on the whole—
I don't know what, and therefore cannot tell—
Which, pretty women—the sweet souls!—call Soul:
Certes is was not Body; he was well
Proportion'd as a poplar or a pole—
A handsome man, that human miracle;
And in each circumstance of Love or War
Had still preserved his Perpendicular.

Love.—*Shakspeare.*

If I prove her haggard,
Tho' that her jesses were my dear heart-strings,
I'd whistle her off, and let her down the wind
To prey at Fortune.
I had rather be a Toad,
And live upon the vapour of a dungeon,
Than keep a Corner in the thing I love,
For others' use.

Love. — *Shakspeare.*

O SHE, that hath a Heart of that fine frame,
 To pay this debt of Love but to a Brother,
How will she love, when the rich golden shaft
Hath kill'd the flock of all Affections else
That live in her? when Liver, Brain, and Heart,
These sov'reign Thrones, are all supplied and filled,
Her sweet perfections, with one self-same King!

Love. — *Shakspeare.*

HER passions are made of nothing but the finest part of pure Love: we cannot call her winds and waters, sighs and tears; they are greater storms and tempests than almanacs can report: this cannot be Cunning in her; if it be, she makes a Shower of Rain as well as Jove.

Love. — *Byron.*

WITH thee all toils are sweet, each clime hath charms;
Earth—Sea alike—our World within our arms!

Love. — *Byron.*

O Love! no habitant of earth thou art—
 An unseen Seraph, we believe in thee;
A faith whose martyrs are the broken Heart:
 But never yet hath seen, nor e'er shall see,
 The naked eye, thy form, as it should be;
The mind hath made thee, as it peopled Heaven,
 Even with its own desiring phantasy,
And to a thought such shape and image given,
As haunts the unquench'd Soul—parched—wearied—wrung—and riven.

Love. — *Shakspeare.*

WHEN Love begins to sicken and decay,
It useth an enforced Ceremony.

Love. — *Shakspeare.*

WHEN the Blood burns, how prodigal the soul
 Lends the Tongue vows. These blazes, Daughter,
Giving more light than heat, extinct in both,
Even in their promise as it is a making,
You must not take for Fire.
Be somewhat scanter of your maiden presence,
Set your Intreatments at a higher rate,
Than a command to parley.

Love. — *Shakspeare.*

BASE men, being in Love, have then a Nobility in their natures more than is native to them.

Love. — *Shakspeare.*

As in the sweetest Bud
The eating Canker dwells, so eating Love
Inhabits in the finest wits of all.
As the most forward Bud
Is eaten by the Canker ere it blow,
Even so by Love the young and tender Wit
Is turn'd to Folly; blasting in the bud,
Losing his verdure even in the prime,
And all the fair effects of future Hopes.

Love. — *Milton.*

FORSAKE me not thus, witness Heaven
What Love sincere, and Reverence in my heart
I bear thee, and unweeting have offended,
Unhappily deceived! Thy suppliant,
I beg and clasp thy Knees; bereave me not,
Whereon I live, thy gentle looks, thy aid,
Thy counsel in this uttermost Distress,
My only strength and stay: forlorn of thee,
Whither shall I betake me, where subsist?

Love. — *Shakspeare.*

MY Love is strengthen'd, though more weak in seeming;
I love not less, though less the Show appear:
That Love is merchandised, whose rich esteeming
The owner's Tongue doth publish everywhere.
Our Love was new, and then but in the spring,
When I was wont to greet it with my Lays;
As Philomel in Summer's front doth sing,
And stops his pipe in growth of riper days;
Not that the Summer is less pleasant now
Than when her mournful Hymns did hush the night,
But that wild Music burdens every bough,
And sweets grown common lose their dear delight.

Love. — *Scott.*

THE Rose is fairest when 'tis budding new,
And Hope is brightest when it dawns from fears;
The Rose is sweetest wash'd with morning Dew,
And Love is loveliest when embalm'd in Tears.

Love. — *Byron.*

LOVE'S a capricious power: I've known it hold
Out through a Fever caused by its own heat;
But be much puzzled by a Cough and Cold,
And find a Quinsy very hard to treat.

Love. — *Spenser.*

BUT who can tell what cause had that fair Maid
 To use him so, that loved her so well?
Or who with blame can justly her upbraid,
 For loving not—for who can Love compel?
And sooth to say, it is fool-hardy thing
 Rashly to witen creatures so divine!
For demigods they be, and first did spring
 From Heaven, though graft in Frailness Feminine.

Love. — *Byron.*

MAN's love is of man's life a thing, a Part:
'Tis Woman's whole Existence.

Love. — *Shakspeare.*

HEAVEN witness,
I've been to you a true and humble Wife,
At all times to your Will conformable:
Ever in fear to kindle your Dislike,
Yea, subject to your count'nance; glad or sorry,
As I saw it inclined: when was the hour,
I ever contradicted your Desire?
Or made it not mine too? which of your Friends
Have I not strove to love, although I knew
He were mine Enemy? what friend of mine,
That had to him derived your Anger, did I
Continue in my liking? nay, gave notice
He was from thence discharged. Sir, call to mind,
That I have been your Wife, in this obedience,
Upward of twenty years; and have been blest
With many Children by you. If in the course
And process of this time you can report,
And prove it too, against mine Honour aught,
My bond of Wedlock, or my Love and Duty
Against your sacred person, in God's name,
Turn me away; and let the foul'st contempt
Shut door upon me, and so give me up
To th' sharpest kind of Justice.

Love. — *Shakspeare.*

LOVE is full of unbefitting strains;
 All wanton as a Child, skipping, and vain;
Form'd by the eye, and, therefore, like the Eye,
Full of strange shapes, of habits and of forms,
Varying in subjects as the Eye doth roll
To every varied object in his Glance.

Love. — *Shakspeare.*

HAVE I lived thus long (let me speak myself,
Since Virtue finds no friends) a Wife, a true one?
A woman (I dare say, without Vain Glory;)
Never yet branded with suspicion?
Have I, with all my full Affections,
Loved him next Heaven, obey'd him?
Been, out of fondness, superstitious to him;
Almost forgot my Prayers to content him·
And am I thus rewarded? 'tis not well.
Bring me a constant Woman to her husband,
One, that ne'er dream'd a joy beyond his Pleasure:
And to that woman, when she has done most,
Yet will I add an Honour; a great Patience.

Love. — *Mrs. Tighe.*

WHEN Pleasure sparkles in the cup of youth,
And the gay hours on downy wing advance,
Oh! then 'tis sweet to hear the lip of Truth
Breathe the soft vows of Love, sweet to entrance
The raptured soul by intermingling glance
Of mutual Bliss; sweet amid roseate bowers,
Led by the hand of Love, to weave the dance,
Or unmolested crop Life's fairy flowers,
Or bask in Joy's bright sun through calm unclouded hours

Love. — *Shakspeare.*

LOVE is blind, and Lovers cannot see
The pretty follies that themselves commit.

Love. — *Dryden.*

LOVE never fails to master what he finds,
But works a different way in different minds:
The Fool enlightens, and the Wise he blinds.

Love. — *Shakspeare.*

OH, thou didst then ne'er love so heartily:
If thou remember'st not the slightest Folly
That ever Love did make thee run into,
Thou hast not loved:
Or if thou hast not sat, as I do now,
Wearying thy hearer in thy Mistress' praise,
Thou hast not loved:
Or if thou hast not broke from company,
Abruptly, as my Passion now makes me,
Thou hast not loved.

Love.—*Milton.*

With thee
Certain my resolution is to die;
How can I live without thee, how forego
Thy sweet converse and Love so dearly join'd,
To live again in these wild woods forlorn?
Should God create another Eve, and I
Another rib afford, yet loss of thee
Would never from my Heart: no, no, I feel
The link of nature draw me: flesh of flesh,
Bone of my bone thou art, and from thy state
Mine never shall be parted, Bliss or Woe.

Love.—*Mrs. Tighe.*

AND thou, sweet sprite, whose power doth far extend,
Smile on the mean historian of thy fame!
My heart in each distress and fear befriend,
Nor ever let it feel a fiercer Flame
Than Innocence may cherish free from blame,
And Hope may nurse, and Sympathy may own:
For, as thy rights I never would disclaim,
But true Allegiance offer'd to thy throne,
So may I love but one, by one beloved alone.

Love.—*Byron.*

IF changing cheek, and scorching Vein,
Lips taught to writhe, but not complain,
If bursting Heart, and madd'ning brain,
And daring deed, and vengeful Steel,
And all that I have felt, and feel,
Betoken Love—that love was mine.

Love.—*Shakspeare.*

THEN let me go, and hinder not my course:
I'll be as patient as a gentle stream,
And make a Pastime of each weary step,
Till the last step has brought me to my Love
And there I'll rest, as, after much turmoil,
A blessed Soul doth in Elysium.

Love.—*Shakspeare.*

What Passion hangs these weights upon my Tongue?
I cannot speak to her; yet she urged Conference.

Love.—*Shakspeare.*

Her virtues, graced with external Gifts,
Do breed Love's settled passions in my heart.

Love. — *Byron.*

THUS Passion's fire and Woman's art
Can turn and tame the Sterner Heart;
From these its form and tone are ta'en,
And what they make it, must remain,
But break—before it bend again.

Love. — *Byron.*

I DEEM'D that time, I deem'd that Pride,
Had quench'd at length my boyish Flame
Nor knew, till seated by thy side,
My Heart in all, save Hope, the same.

Love. — *Shakspeare.*

WE, that are true Lovers, run into strange capers; but as all is mortal in Nature, so is all Nature in love mortal in Folly.

Love. — *Byron.*

EARTH holds no other like to thee,
Or if it doth, in vain for me.

Love. — *South.*

"LOVE covers a multitude of sins." When a Scar cannot be taken away, the next kind office is to hide it.—Love is never so blind as when it is to spy Faults.

Love. — *Shakspeare.*

THEY love least, that let men know their Love.

Love. — *Shakspeare.*

I LOVE your son:
My friends were poor, but honest; so's my Love.
Be not offended; for it hurts not him,
That he is loved of me: I follow him not
By any token of presumptuous suit:
Nor would I have him, till I do deserve him;
Yet never know how that Desert should be.
I know I love in vain, strive against Hope.
Yet, in this captious and intenible sieve,
I still pour in the waters of my Love,
And lack not to lose still.

Love. — *Milton.*

CONFIRM'D then I resolve,
Adam shall share with me in Bliss or Wo:
So dear I love him, that with him all deaths
I could endure, without him live no Life.

— **Love.** — *Ovid.*

THAT you may be beloved, be amiable.

Love. — *La Rochefoucauld.*

INFIDELITIES ought to extinguish Love, and we should not be jealous, even when we have reason to be so; it is only persons who avoid causing Jealousy who are worth being jealous of.

Love. — *Shakspeare.*

O GIVE Pity
To her, whose state is such, that cannot choose
But lend and give, where she is sure to lose;
That seeks not to find that her Search implies,
But, riddle-like, lives sweetly where she dies.

Love. — *Shakspeare.*

HE says, he loves my Daughter;
I think so too; for never gazed the Moon
Upon the water, as he'll stand and read
As 'twere my daughter's Eyes: and, to be plain,
I think, there is not half a Kiss to choose
Who loves another best.

Love. — *La Rochefoucauld.*

ENVY is destroyed by true Friendship, and Coquetry by true Love.

Love. — *Shakspeare.*

SWEET, rouse yourself; and the weak wanton Cupid
Shall from your neck unloose his amorous fold,
And, like a Dewdrop from the Lion's mane,
Be shook to air.

Love. — *Addison.*

THE intelligence of Affection is carried on by the Eye only, good-breeding has made the Tongue falsify the heart, and act a part of continued restraint, while nature has preserved the Eyes to herself, that she may not be disguised or misrepresented.

Love. — *Shakspeare.*

LOVE is a smoke raised with the fume of Sighs:
Being purged, a Fire sparkling in lovers' eyes;
Being vext, a Sea nourish'd with lovers' tears;
What is it else? a Madness most discreet,
A choking Gall, and a preserving Sweet.

Love. — *Greville.*

AS Love will often make a Wise man act like a Fool, so will Interest often make a Fool act like a Wise man.

Love. — *Bulwer.*

THERE is so little to redeem the dry mass of Follies and Errors from which the materials of this Life are composed, that any thing to love or to reverence becomes, as it were, the Sabbath for the mind.

Love. — *Tucker.*

LOVE, peculiarly so called, must always centre in a single object, because that thorough coincidence of interests and participation of pleasures necessary to render it perfect, cannot obtain between more than two persons. Friendship may take in a little larger compass, but can extend only to a few chosen objects; the friendships recorded in history have always run in pairs, as between Theseus and Pirithous, Orestes and Pylades, Scipio and Lelius, Cicero and Atticus.

Love. — *Shakspeare.*

OH, 'tis the curse in Love, and still approved,
When Women cannot love where they're beloved

Love. — *Shakspeare.*

Too light winning
Makes the Prize light.

Love. —*Byron.*

THE cold in Clime are cold in Blood,
And love as scarce deserves the name;
But mine is like the Lava flood
That burns in Etna's breast of Flame.

Love. — *Terence.*

IF indeed you can keep to your Resolution, you will act a noble and a manly part: but if, when you have set about it, your Courage fails you, and you make a voluntary Submission, acknowledging the violence of your Passion, and your inability to hold out any longer, all is over with you; you are undone, and may go hang yourself; she will insult over you, when she finds you her Slave.

Love. — *Greville.*

THE poets judged like Philosophers, when they feigned Love to be Blind; how often do we see in a Woman what our judgment and taste approve, and yet feel nothing toward her; how often what they both condemn, and yet feel a great deal!

Love. — *Shakspeare.*

SHE stripp'd it from her arm; I see her yet;
Her pretty Action did outsell her gift,
And yet enrich'd it too.

Love. — *Shakspeare.*

KIND is my Love to-day, to-morrow kind,
Still constant in a wondrous Excellence;
Fair, Kind, and True, have often lived alone,
Which three, till now, never kept seat in one.

Love. — *Shakspeare.*

MEN'S vows are women's Traitors!

Love. — *Shakspeare.*

THERE'S beggary in the Love that can be reckon'd.

Love. — *Greville.*

CASUAL disagreements have been considered as springs that give new force to Love; and I believe they are so; yet as a spring too frequently or too forcibly used, remains at the place to which it is drawn back instead of flying forward; so Lovers will find, that disagreements, if they are too frequent, will at length lose their Elasticity and impel to Love no more.

Love. — *Shakspeare.*

I WILL be gone:
My being here it is, that keeps thee hence:
Shall I stay here? No, no, although
The air of Paradise did fan the house,
And Angels officed all.

Love. — *Shakspeare.*

LOVERS break not hours,
Unless it be to come before their time;
So much they spur their Expedition.

Love. — *Terence.*

IT is possible that a man can be so changed by Love, that one could not recognise him to be the same person.

Love. — *Shakspeare.*

ADMIRED Miranda!
Indeed, the top of Admiration; worth
What's dearest to the world! full many a Lady
I've eyed with best regard, and many a time
Th' harmony of their tongues hath into bondage
Brought my too diligent Ear; for several virtues
Have I liked sev'ral Women, never any
With so full soul, but some defect in her
Did quarrel with the noblest grace she owed,
And put it to the foil. But you, O you,
So perfect, and so peerless, are created
Of every Creature's best.

Love. — *Colton.*

THE plainest man that can convince a Woman that he is really in Love with her, has done more to make her in Love with him than the handsomest man, if he can produce no such conviction. For the Love of Woman is a shoot, not a seed, and flourishes most vigorously only when ingrafted on that Love which is rooted in the breast of another.

Love. — *Shakspeare.*

To be wise, and Love,
Exceeds Man's might.

Love. — *Hume.*

WHEN a person is once heartily in Love, the little faults and caprices of his Mistress, the jealousies and quarrels to which that Commerce is so subject, however unpleasant they be, and rather connected with Anger and Hatred, are yet to be found, in many instances, to give additional force to the prevailing Passion.

Love. — *Middleton.*

THE treasures of the deep are not so precious
As are the conceal'd Comforts of a man
Lock'd up in Woman's Love.

Love. — *Shakspeare.*

WISH chastely, and love dearly.

Love. — *Laberius.*

TO be in Love, and at the same time to act wisely, is scarcely within the Power of a god.

Love. — *Shakspeare.*

DIDST thou but know the inly touch of Love,
Thou would'st as soon go kindle fire with snow,
As seek to quench the fire of Love with words.
I do not seek to quench your Love's hot fire,
But qualify the Fire's extreme rage,
Lest it should burn above the bounds of reason.
The more thou dam'st it up, the more it burns;
The current that with gentle murmur glides,
Thou know'st, being stopp'd, impatiently doth rage;
But, when his fair course is not hinder'd,
He makes sweet Music with the enamell'd stones,
Giving a gentle Kiss to every sedge
He overtaketh in his pilgrimage;
And so by many winding nooks he strays,
With willing sport, to the wild Ocean.

Love. — *Erasmus.*

LOVE, that has nothing but Beauty to keep it in good health, is short-lived.

Love. — *Burton.*

NO Cord or Cable can draw so forcibly, or bind so fast, as Love can do with only a single Thread.

Love. — *Shakspeare.*

THE expedition of my violent Love
Out-ran the pauser Reason.

Love. — *La Fontaine.*

O LOVE, when thou gettest Dominion over us, we may bid good-by to Prudence.

Love. — *Milton.*

SMILES from reason flow, to Brutes denied,
And are of Love the food.

Love. — *Shakspeare.*

BASHFUL sincerity, and comely Love.

Love. — *Goldsmith.*

LOVE, when founded in the Heart, will show itself in a thousand unpremeditated sallies of Fondness; but every cool deliberate exhibition of the Passions only argues little understanding or great Insincerity.

Love. — *Fuller.*

AFFECTIONS, like the Conscience, are rather to be led than drawn; and 'tis to be feared, they that marry where they do not love, will love where they do not marry.

Love. — *Shakspeare.*

O SPIRIT of Love, how quick and fresh art thou!
That, notwithstanding thy capacity,
Receiveth as the Sea, naught enters there,
Of what validity and pitch soe'er,
But falls into abatement and low price,
Even in a minute! so full of Shapes is Fancy
That it alone is high-fantastical.

Love. — *Dryden.*

LET Grace and Goodness be the principal loadstone of thy Affections. For Love which hath ends, will have an end; whereas that which is founded on true Virtue, will always continue.

Love. — *Shakspeare.*

LET me but bear your Love, I'll bear your Cares

Love.—*Saville.*

IT is as false to play with Fire as to dally with Gallantry. Love is a passion that hath friends in the garrison, and for that reason must by a Woman be kept at such a distance, that she may not be within the danger of doing the most usual thing in the world, which is conspiring against herself: else the humble Gallant, who is only admitted as a trophy, very often becometh the conqueror; he putteth on the style of Victory, and from an admirer groweth into a Master, for so he may be called from the moment he is in possession.

Love.—*Shakspeare.*

DOUBT thou, the stars are Fire;
Doubt, that the Sun doth move:
Doubt Truth to be a Liar;
But never doubt, I love.

Love.—*Valerius Maximus.*

WHERE there exists the most ardent and true Love, it is often better to be united in Death than separated in Life.

Love.—*Mrs. Cowley.*

THE woman that has not touched the Heart of a man, before he leads her to the Altar, has scarcely a chance to charm it, when Possession and Security turn their powerful arms against her.

Love.—*Colton.*

CORPOREAL charms may indeed gain admirers, but there must be mental ones to retain them; and Horace had a delicate feeling of this, when he refused to restrict the Pleasures of the Lover merely to his eyes, but added also those of the Ear.

Qui sedens identidem, te
Spectat et audit!

Love.—*Plautus.*

WHERE Love has once obtained influence, any Seasoning, I believe, will please.

Love.—*Shakspeare.*

My Love is thaw'd;
Which, like a waxen image 'gainst a Fire,
Bears no impression of the thing it was.

Love.—*Shenstone.*

LOVE can be founded upon Nature only, or the appearance of it, for this reason; however a peruke may tend to soften the human features, it can very seldom make amends for the mixture of Artifice which it discovers.

Love. — *Shakspeare.*

Dost thou love Pictures? we will fetch thee strait
Adonis, painted by a running brook;
And Citherea all in sedges hid;
Which seem to move, and wanton with her Breath,
Ev'n as the waving Sedges play with wind.

Love. — *Lavater.*

LOVE sees what no eye sees; Love hears what no ear hears; and what never rose in the heart of man Love prepares for its object.

Love. — *Shakspeare.*

She bids you,
All on the wanton Rushes lay you down,
And rest your gentle Head upon her lap,
And she will sing the song that pleaseth you,
And on your eyelids crown the God of sleep,
Charming your Blood with pleasing heaviness;
Making such difference betwixt wake and sleep,
As is the difference betwixt day and night,
The hour before the heavenly-harness'd team
Begins his Golden progress in the east.

Love. — *La Bruyere.*

WE never love heartily but once, and that is the first time we love. Succeeding inclinations are less involuntary.

Love. — *Colton.*

IT is a dangerous experiment to call in Gratitude as an ally to Love. Love is a debt, which inclination always pays, obligation never; and the moment it becomes luke-warm and evanescent, reminiscences on the score of Gratitude serve only to smother the flame.

Love. — *Shakspeare.*

It were all one
That I should love a bright particular Star,
And think to wed it; he is so above me:
In his bright Radiance and collateral light
Must I be comforted, not in his sphere.
Th' ambition in my Love thus plagues itself;
The hind, that would be mated by the Lion,
Must die for Love.

Love. — *Colton.*

LOVE is an alliance of Friendship and of Lust; if the former predominate, it is a Passion exalted and refined, but if the latter, gross and sensual.

Love. — *Addison.*

RIDICULE, perhaps, is a better expedient against Love, than sober advice; and I am of opinion, that Hudibras and Don Quixote may be as effectual to cure the extravagancies of this Passion, as any one of the old philosophers.

Love. — *Shakspeare.*

IF music be the food of Love, play on;
Give me excess of it; that, surfeiting,
The appetite may sicken, and so die.——
That strain again; it had a dying fall:
Oh, it came o'er my Ear like the sweet south
That breathes upon a bank of violets,
Stealing and giving Odour.

Love. — *Shakspeare.*

TELL this youth what 'tis to Love.—
It is to be all made of Sighs and Tears;
It is to be all made of Faith and Service :—
It is to be all made of Fantasy,
All made of Passion, and all made of wishes;
All Adoration, Duty, and Observance,
All Humbleness, all Patience, and Impatience,
All Purity, all Trial, all Observance.

Love. — *Addison.*

THE pleasantest part of a man's life is generally that which passes in Courtship, provided his Passion be sincere, and the party beloved kind with Discretion. Love, Desire, Hope, all the pleasing motions of the Soul, rise in the pursuit.

Love. — *Hawkesworth.*

AS Love without Esteem is volatile and capricious; Esteem without Love is languid and cold.

Love. — *Shakspeare.*

LOVE is like a Child,
That longs for every thing that he can come by.

Love. — *Shakspeare.*

LEAVE you your power to draw,
And I shall have no Power to follow you.

Love. — *Shakspeare.*

IF ever (as that ever may be near)
You meet in some fresh cheek the power of Fancy,
Then shall you know the Wounds invisible
That Love's keen Arrows make.

Love. — *Sir Philip Sidney.*

TRUE Love can no more be diminished by showers of evil than Flowers are marred by timely Rains.

Love. — *Euripides.*

THAT Love alone, which Virtue's laws control,
Deserves reception in the human Soul.

Love. — *Terence.*

ALL these inconveniences are incidents to Love: Reproaches, Jealousies, Quarrels, Reconcilements, War, and then Peace.

Love. — *Colton.*

LOVE may exist without Jealousy, although this is rare; but Jealousy may exist without Love, and this is common.

Love. — *Shakspeare.*

O YOU leaden messengers,
That ride upon the violent speed of Fire,
Fly with false aim: move the still-piercing air,
That sings with piercing, do not touch my Lord!

Love. — *La Rochefoucauld.*

WE always dread the sight of the person we Love when we have been coquetting elsewhere.

Love. — *Shakspeare.*

TIME, Force, and Death,
Do to this body what extremes you can:
But the strong base and building of my Love
Is as the very centre of the Earth,
Drawing all things to it.

Love. — *Shakspeare.*

I LEAVE myself, my friends, and all for Love.
Thou, thou hast metamorphosed me;
Made me neglect my Studies, lose my time,
War with good Counsel, set the world at naught;
Made wit with musing weak; Heart sick with thought.

Love. — *La Rochefoucauld.*

A MAN of sense may Love like a Madman, but never like a Fool.

Love. — *Shakspeare.*

How silver-sweet sound Lovers' tongues by night,
Like softest music to attending ears!

Love. — *Shakspeare.*

I HAVE done penance for contemning Love;
Whose high imperious thoughts have punish'd me
With bitter fasts, with penitential groans;
With nightly tears, and daily heart-sore sighs.
For, in revenge of my contempt of Love,
Love hath chased Sleep from my enthralled Eyes,
And made them watchers of mine own Heart's Sorrow.
O gentle Protheus, Love's a mighty lord;
And hath so humbled me, as I confess,
There is no wo to his correction;
Nor to his service, no such Joy on earth.
Now no discourse, except it be of Love;
Now can I break my fast, dine, sup, and sleep
Upon the very naked name of Love.

Love. — *La Reine de Navarre.*

IT is said that Jealousy is Love, but I deny it; for though Jealousy be produced by Love, as Ashes are by Fire, yet Jealousy extinguishes Love as Ashes smother the Flame.

Love. — *La Rochefoucauld.*

IN Jealousy there is more self-love than Love.

Love. — *Sterne.*

IT is sweet to feel by what fine-spun threads our Affections are drawn together.

Love. — *Shakspeare.*

THE gifts, she looks from me, are pack'd and lock'd
Up in my Heart; which I have given already,
But not deliver'd.

Love. — *Shakspeare.*

WE cannot fight for Love, as men may do;
We should be woo'd, and were not made to woo.

Love. — *La Rochefoucauld.*

ALL the Passions make us commit faults, but Love makes us commit the most ridiculous ones.

Love. — *Goethe.*

HATE makes us vehement partisans, but Love still more so.

Love. — *Shakspeare.*

LOVE
Will creep in Service where it cannot go.

Love. — *La Rochefoucauld.*

WE forgive so long as we love.

Love. — *Shakspeare.*

O HARD-BELIEVING Love! how strange it seems
Not to believe, and yet too credulous!
Thy weal and woe are both of them extremes.
Despair and Hope make thee Ridiculous!
The one doth flatter thee, in thoughts unlikely,
With likely Thoughts, the other kills thee quickly.

Love. — *La Rochefoucauld.*

THE pleasure of Love is in loving. We are happier in the Passion we feel than in that we excite.

Love. — *Shakspeare.*

If the measure of thy Joy
Be heap'd like mine, and that thy skill be more
To blazon it, then sweeten with thy Breath
This neighbour air, and let rich music's tongue
Unfold the imagined Happiness, that both
Receive in either by this dear encounter.

Love. — *Shakspeare.*

Oh my soul's joy!
If after every Tempest come such calms,
May the wind blow till they have waken'd Death!
And let the labouring bark climb hills of seas,
Olympus-high; and duck again as low
As Hell's from Heaven! If it were now to die,
'Twere now to be most happy; for, I fear,
My soul hath her content so absolute,
That not another Comfort like to this
Succeeds in unknown fate.

Love. — *Hazlitt.*

IT makes us proud when our love of a mistress is returned; it ought to make us prouder still when we can love her for herself alone, without the aid of any such selfish reflection. This is the Religion of Love.

Love. — *Shakspeare.*

IF thou dost love, pronounce it faithfully:
Or if you think I am too quickly won,
I'll frown and be perverse, and say thee nay,
So thou wilt woo: but, else, not for the World.

Love. — *La Rochefoucauld.*

IT is difficult to define Love. All that we can say of it is, that in the Soul it is a passion for reigning; in Minds it is a sympathy; and in the Body it is nothing but a latent and delicate Desire to possess the loved object.

Love. — *La Rochefoucauld.*

LOVE, like Fire, cannot subsist without continual movement; as soon as it ceases to hope and fear, it ceases to exist.

Love. — *Hazlitt.*

IT is better to desire than to enjoy, to love than to be loved.

Love. — *Shakspeare.*

THE course of true Love never did run smooth;
  But, either, it was different in Blood—
Or else misgraffed, in respect of Years—
Or else it stood upon the choice of Friends—
Or if there were a sympathy in choice,
War, Death, or Sickness did lay siege to it;
Making it momentary as a sound,
Swift as a Shadow, short as any Dream,
Brief as the lightning in the collied night,
That (in a spleen) unfolds both Heav'n and Earth;
And ere a man hath power to say, Behold!
The jaws of Darkness do devour it up;
So quick bright things come to confusion.

Love. — *La Rochefoucauld.*

THERE is no Disguise which can long conceal Love where it does, or feign where it does not, exist.

Love. — *Jean Paul.*

FRIENDSHIP requires Actions: Love requires not so much proofs, as Expressions of Love. Love demands little else than the power to feel and to requite Love.

Love. — *Shakspeare.*

LOVE is not Love,
Which alters when it alteration finds;
  Or bends, with the remover to remove:
Oh no! it is an ever-fixed mark,
  That looks on tempests, and is never shaken;
It is the Star to every wandering bark,
  Whose worth's unknown, although his height be taken.
Love's not Time's fool, though rosy Lips and Cheeks
  Within his bending sickle's compass come:
Love alters not with his brief Hours and Weeks,
  But bears it out even to the edge of Doom.

Love. — *La Rochefoucauld.*

IT is with true Love as with Apparitions. Every one talks of it, but few have ever seen it.

Love. — *Anon.*

ALL tatlers delight in getting hold of any thing akin to a Love Story; not merely from a fondness for scandal, but because the most powerful and pleasurable of human Feelings is in some measure awakened and excited thereby.

Love. — *Shakspeare.*

BIND up those tresses; Oh, what Love I note
In the fair multitude of those her hairs;
Where but by chance a silver drop hath fall'n,
Even to that drop ten thousand wiery Friends
Do glew themselves in sociable Grief;
Like true, inseparable, faithful Loves,
Sticking together in Calamity.

Love. — *Shakspeare.*

I SWEAR to thee by Cupid's strongest bow;
By his best Arrow with the golden head,
By the simplicity of Venus' doves,
By that, which knitteth Souls, and prospers Loves;
And by that fire which burn'd the Carthage Queen,
When the false Trojan under sail was seen;
By all the Vows that ever men have broke,
In number more than ever Women spoke;
In that same place thou hast appointed me,
To-morrow truly will I meet with thee.

Love. — *Shakspeare.*

OH, how this spring of Love resembleth
The uncertain glory of an April day;
Which now shows all the beauty of the Sun,
And by and by a Cloud takes all away.

Love. — *La Rochefoucauld.*

MEN are almost equally difficult to satisfy, when they have very much Love, and when they have scarcely any left.

Love. —*Byron.*

IN her first passion woman loves her Lover,
In all the others what she loves, is Love.

Love. — *Shakspeare.*

FAREWELL; one Eye yet looks on thee,
But with my heart the other Eye doth see.——
Ah, poor our sex! this fault in us I find,
The error of our Eye directs our mind.
What error leads, must err; Oh then conclude,
Minds sway'd by Eyes are full of turpitude.

Love. — *Shakspeare.*

Love's heralds should be thoughts,
Which ten times faster glide than the Sun's beams,
Driving back Shadows over low'ring hills:
Therefore do nimble-pinion'd Doves draw Love,
And therefore hath the wind-swift Cupid wings.

Love. — *Ovid.*

Let him who does not choose to be considered a lazy Fellow fall in Love.

Love. — *La Rochefoucauld.*

Women often fancy themselves in Love even when they are not. The occupation of an Intrigue, the emotion of mind which Gallantry produces, the natural leaning to the pleasure of being loved, and the pain of refusing, persuade them that they feel the passion of Love, when in reality they feel nothing but Coquetry.

Love. — *Shakspeare.*

Love like a Shadow flies, when substance Love pursues;
Pursuing that that flies, and flying what pursues.

Love. — *Shakspeare.*

Things base and vile, holding no quantity,
Love can transpose to form and Dignity.
Love looks not with the Eyes, but with the mind;
And therefore is winged Cupid painted blind;
Nor hath Love's mind of any Judgment taste;
Wings, and no eyes, figure unheedy Haste:
And therefore is Love said to be a child,
Because in choice he is so oft beguiled.
As waggish boys in game themselves forswear,
So the boy Love is perjured everywhere.

Love. — *La Rochefoucauld.*

It is impossible to love a second time what we have once really ceased to love.

Love. — *Colton.*

Friendship often ends in Love; but Love, in Friendship—never.

Love. — *Shakspeare.*

Tell me, where is Fancy bred,
Or in the Heart, or in the Head?
How begot, how nourished?
It is engender'd in the eyes,
With gazing fed; and Fancy dies
In the Cradle where it lies.

Love. — *Shakspeare.*

THEY do not love, that do not show their Love.

Love. — *Colton.*

AGE and Love associate not: if they are ever allied, the firmer the Friendship, the more fatal is its termination; and an old man, like a Spider, can never make Love, without beating his own death-watch.

Love. — *Colton.*

LOVE is an alchymist that can transmute Poison into food—and a Spaniel, that prefers even Punishment from one hand, to caresses from another. But it is in Love, as in War, we are often more indebted for our success to the weakness of the defence, than to the energy of the attack; for mere Idleness has ruined more women than Passion, Vanity more than Idleness, and Credulity more than either.

Love. — *Shakspeare.*

O MOST potential Love! vow, bond, nor space,
In thee hath neither sting, knot, nor confine,
For thou art all, and all things else are thine.
When thou impressest, what are Precepts worth
Of stale example? When thou wilt inflame,
How coldly those impediments stand forth
Of Wealth, of filial Fear, Law, Kindred, Fame?
Love's arms are Peace, 'gainst rule, 'gainst sense, 'gainst shame;
And sweetens, in the suffering pangs it bears,
The Aloes of all forces, shocks, and fears.

Love. — *Byron.*

OURS too the Glance none saw beside;
The Smile none else might understand;
The whisper'd Thought of hearts allied,
The pressure of the thrilling hand.

Love. — *Moore.*

THE time I've lost in wooing,
In watching and pursuing
The Light, that lies
In woman's Eyes,
Has been my Heart's undoing.
Tho' Wisdom oft has sought me,
I scorn'd the Love she brought me,
My only books
Were woman's looks,
And Folly's all they've taught me.

Love. — *Moore.*

I COULD have loved you—oh so well;—
The dream, that wishing boyhood knows,
Is but a bright, beguiling Spell,
Which only lives, while Passion glows:
But, when this early flush declines,
When the Heart's vivid morning fleets,
You know not then how close it twines
Round the first kindred soul it meets!
Yes, yes, I could have loved, as one
Who, while his youth's enchantments fall,
Finds something dear to rest upon,
Which pays him for the Loss of all!

Love. — *Shakspeare.*

LOVE's counsellors should fill the bores of hearing,
To the smothering of the Sense.

Love. — *Shakspeare.*

VIOLENT delights have violent ends,
And in their Triumph die; like fire and powder,
Which, as they kiss, consume: the sweetest Honey
Is loathsome in his own Deliciousness,
And in the taste confounds the appetite:
Therefore, love moderately; long Love doth so,
Too swift arrives as tardy as too slow.

Love. — *Byron.*

THEN there were Sighs the deeper for suppression,
And stolen Glances, sweeter for the theft,
And burning Blushes, though for no transgression,
Trembling, when met, and restlessness when left.

Love. — *Moore.*

ALAS—how light a cause may move
Dissension between Hearts that love!
Hearts that the world in vain had tried,
And sorrow but more closely tied;
That stood the Storm, when waves were rough,
Yet in a sunny hour fall off,
Like ships that have gone down at sea,
When Heaven was all tranquillity.

Love. — *Prior.*

LOVE, well thou know'st no partnership allows:
Cupid averse rejects divided Vows.

Love. —*Byron.*

To me she gave her Heart, that all
Which Tyranny can ne'er enthrall.

Love. — *Byron.*

NOR was all Love shut from him, though his days
Of passion had consumed themselves to dust.
It is in vain that we would coldly gaze
On such that smile upon us; the Heart must
Leap kindly back to kindness, though disgust
Hath wean'd it from all worldlings: thus he felt;
For there was soft Remembrance, and sweet trust,
In one fond Breast, to which his own would melt,
And in its tenderer hour on that his Bosom dwelt.

Love. — *Byron.*

NONE are all evil—quickening round his heart,
One softer feeling would not yet depart;
Oft could he sneer at others as beguiled
By Passions worthy of a fool or child;
Yet 'gainst that passion vainly still he strove.
And even in him it asks the name of Love!
Yes, it was Love—unchangeable—unchanged,
Felt but for one from whom he never ranged;
Though fairest captives daily met his eye,
He shunn'd, not sought, but coldly pass'd them by;
Though many a Beauty droop'd in prison'd bower,
None ever sooth'd his most unguarded hour.
Yes—it was Love—if thoughts of tenderness,
Tried in temptation strengthened by distress,
Unmoved by Absence, firm in every clime,
And yet—Oh more than all! untired by time;
Which nor defeated hope, nor baffled wile,
Could render sullen were she near to smile;
Nor rage could fire, nor sickness fret to vent
On her one murmur of his discontent;
Which still would meet with joy, with calmness part,
Lest that his look of grief should reach her heart;
Which naught removed, nor menaced to remove—
If there be Love in mortals—this was Love!

Love. — *Higgons.*

LOVE is that passion which refines the Soul;
First made men Heroes, and those heroes Gods;
Its genial fires inform the sluggish mass;
The rugged soften, and the tim'rous warm;
Gives wit to Fools, and manners to the Clown:
The rest of life is an ignoble calm;
The soul unmoved by Love's inspiring breath,
Like lazy waters stagnates and corrupts.

Love. — *Dryden.*

I FIND she loves him much because she hides it.
Love teaches cunning even to Innocence;
And where he gets possession, his first work
Is to dig deep within a Heart, and there
Lie hid, and like a Miser in the dark,
To feast alone.

Love. — *Dryden.*

THERE is no satiety of Love in thee;
Enjoy'd, thou still art new: Perpetual spring
Is in thy arms; the ripen'd Fruit but falls,
And blossoms rise to fill its empty place,
And I grow rich by giving.

Love. — *Otway.*

I HAD so fix'd my Heart upon her,
That wheresoe'er I framed a scheme of life
For time to come, she was my only joy,
With which I used to sweeten future cares:
I fancied Pleasures, none but one who loves
And doats as I did, can imagine like them.

Love. — *Dryden.*

LOVE gives Esteem, and then he gives Desert;
He either finds equality, or makes it:
Like Death, he knows no difference in degrees,
But planes and levels all.

Love. — *Addison.*

LOVE is not to be reason'd down, or lost
In high Ambition, or a thirst of Greatness:
'Tis second life, it grows into the soul.
Warms every vein, and beats in every pulse:
I feel it here: my Resolution melts.

Love. — *Addison.*

WHEN Love's well-timed, 'tis not a fault to love:
The Strong, the Brave, the Virtuous, and the Wise,
Sink in the soft captivity together.

Love. — *Milton.*

IN loving thou dost well, in passion not,
Wherein true Love consists not; Love refines
The thoughts, and Heart enlarges, hath its seat
In Reason, and is judicious, is the scale
By which to Heavenly love thou may'st ascend,
Not sunk in carnal Pleasure, for which cause
Among the beasts no mate for thee was found.

Love.—*Byron.*

ALL the stars of Heaven,
The deep blue noon of night, lit by an orb
Which looks a spirit, or a spirit's world—
The hues of Twilight—the sun's gorgeous coming—
His setting indescribable, which fills
My eyes with pleasant tears as I behold
Him sink, and feel my heart float softly with him
Along the western paradise of clouds—
The forest shade—the green bough—the bird's voice,
The vesper bird's, which seems to sing of love,
And mingles with the song of Cherubim,
As the day closes over Eden's walls;—
All these are nothing, to my eyes and Heart
Like ——'s face: I turn from Earth to Heaven
To gaze on it.

Love.—*Young.*

OH the soft commerce! Oh the tender ties,
Close-twisted with the fibres of the heart!
Which, broken, break them; and drain off the Soul
Of human Joy; and make it pain to live—
And is it then to live? when such Friends part,
'Tis the survivor dies.

Love.—*Mrs. Tighe.*

OH, who art thou who darest of Love complain?
He is a gentle Spirit and injures none!
His foes are ours; from them the bitter Pain,
The keen deep Anguish, the heart-rending Groan,
Which in his milder reign are never known.
His Fears are softer than the April showers,
White-handed Innocence supports his throne;
His Sighs are sweet as breath of earliest Flowers,
Affection guides his steps, and Peace protects his bowers.

Love.—*Spenser.*

WONDER it is to see in diverse mindes
How diversely Love doth his pageaunts play,
And shewes his Powre in variable kindes:
The baser wit, whose ydle thoughts alway
Are wont to cleave unto the lowly clay,
It stirreth up to sensuall Desire
And in lewd slouth to waste his carelesse day;
But in brave sprite it kindles goodly fire,
That to all high Desert and Honour doth aspire.

Love. — *Lord Lyttelton.*

None without Hope e'er loved the brightest fair;
But Love can hope where Reason would despair.

Love. — *Byron.*

YES, Love indeed is light from Heaven,
A spark of that immortal fire
With Angels shared, by Alla given,
To lift from Earth our low desire.
Devotion wafts the mind above,
But Heaven itself descends in Love;
A feeling from the Godhead caught,
To wean from self each sordid thought;
A ray of Him who form'd the whole;
A glory circling round the Soul!

Love. — *Spenser.*

NAUGHT under heaven so strongly doth allure
The sence of man and all his minde possesse,
As Beautie's lovely baite, that doth procure
Great Warriours oft their rigour to represse,
And mighty hands to forget their Manlinesse,
Drawne with the powre of an heart-robbing eye,
And wrapt in fetters of a golden Tresse,
That can with melting pleasaunce mollifye
Their harden'd Hearts enured to bloud and cruelty.

Love. — *Young.*

Art thou not dearer to my eyes than light?
Dost thou not circulate thro' all my veins,
Mingle with Life, and form my very Soul?

Love. — *Byron.*

O LOVE! what is it in this world of ours
Which makes it fatal to be loved? Ah, why
With cypress branches hast thou wreathed thy bowers,
And made thy best interpreter a sigh?

Love. — *Spenser.*

GREAT enimy to it, and to all the rest
That in the Gardin of Adonis springs,
Is wicked Time, who with his scyth addrest,
Does mow the flowring herbes and goodly things,
And all their glory to the ground downe flings,
Where they do wither, and are fowly mard:
He flyes about, and with his flaggy wings
Beates downe both Leaves and Buds without regard,
Ne ever pitty may relent his Malice hard.

Love. — *Young.*

WHO never Loved ne'er suffered; he feels nothing,
Who nothing feels but for himself alone;
And when we feel for others, Reason reels
O'erloaded, from her path, and Man runs mad.

Love. — *Spenser.*

TRUE he it said, whatever man it sayd,
That Love with Gall and Hony doth abound;
But if the one be with the other wayd,
For every dram of Hony therein found
A pound of Gall doth over it redound.

Love. — *Spenser.*

THE joyes of Love, if they should ever last
Without affliction or Disquietnesse,
That worldly chances do among them cast,
Would be on Earth too great a blessednesse
Liker to Heaven than mortal wretchednesse;
Therefore the winged God, to let men weet
That here on Earth is no sure happinesse,
A thousand sowres hath tempted with one sweet,
To make it seem more deare and dainty, as is meet.

Love. — *Butler.*

FOR what can earth produce, but Love
To represent the joys above?
Or who but lovers can converse,
Like Angels, by the eye discourse?
Address and compliment by vision;
Make Love and court by Intuition.

Love. — *Prior.*

O MIGHTY Love! from thy unbounded power
How shall the human bosom rest secure?
How shall our thought avoid the various snare?
Or wisdom to our caution'd Soul declare
The different shapes thou pleasest to employ,
When bent to hurt, and certain to destroy?

Love. — *Young.*

NOT all the pride of Beauty;
Those eyes, that tell us what the Sun is made of;
Those lips, whose touch is to be bought with Life;
Those hills of driven snow, which seen are felt:
All these possest are naught, but as they are
The proof, the substance of an inward passion,
And the rich plunder of a taken Heart.

Love. — *Young.*

IF Love were endless, Men were Gods; 'tis that
Does counterbalance travail, danger, pain,—
'Tis Heaven's expedient to make mortals bear
The light, and cheat them of the peaceful Grave.

Love. — *Shakspeare.*

THE more thou dam'st it up, the more it burns;
The current, that with gentle murmur glides,
Thou know'st, being stopp'd, impatiently doth rage;
But, when his fair course is not hinder'd,
He makes sweet Music with the enamell'd stones,
Giving a gentle kiss to every sedge
He overtaketh in his Pilgrimage.

Love. — *Shakspeare.*

OH how this spring of Love resembleth
The uncertain Glory of an April day;
Which now shows all the beauty of the Sun,
And by and by a Cloud takes all away!

Love. — *Moore.*

OH magic of Love! unembellish'd by you,
Has the garden a blush or the herbage a hue?
Or blooms there a prospect in Nature or Art,
Like the vista that shines through the eye to the Heart?

Love. — *Scott.*

IN peace, Love tunes the shepherd's reed;
In War, he mounts the warrior's steed;
In halls, in gay attire is seen;
In hamlets, dances on the green.
Love rules the Court, the Camp, the Grove,
And Men below, and Saints above;
For Love is Heaven, and Heaven is Love.

Love. — *Scott.*

TRUE Love's the gift which God hath given
To man alone beneath the Heaven!
It is not Fantasy's hot fire,
Whose wishes, soon as granted, fly;
It liveth not in fierce Desire,
With dead Desire it doth not die;
It is the secret Sympathy,
The Silver link, the Silken tie,
Which Heart to Heart, and Mind to Mind,
In Body and in Soul can bind.

Love. — *Burns.*

OH happy Love! where Love like this is found!
Oh heartfelt raptures! Bliss beyond compare!
I've paced much this weary mortal round,
And sage Experience bids me this declare—
"If Heaven a draught of heavenly Pleasure spare,
One cordial in this melancholy vale,
'Tis when a youthful, loving, modest pair,
In other's arms breathe out the tender tale,
Beneath the milk-white Thorn that scents the evening gale."

Love. — *Prior.*

OH impotent estate of human life!
Where Hope and Fear maintain eternal strife;
Where fleeting Joy does lasting Doubt inspire;
And most we question what we most desire!
Among thy various gifts, great Heaven, bestow
Our cup of Love unmix'd; forbear to throw
Bitter ingredients in; nor pall the draught
With nauseous grief: for our ill-judging thought
Hardly enjoys the pleasurable taste;
Or deem'd it not sincere; or fears it cannot last.

Love. —*Byron.*

LOVE bears within its breast the very germ
Of change; and how should this be otherwise?
That violent things more quickly find a term
Is shown through Nature's whole analogies:
And how should the most fierce of all be firm?
Would you have endless Lightning in the skies?
Methinks Love's very title says enough:
How should "the *tender* passion" e'er be *tough?*

Love. — *Spenser.*

FOR Love is a celestial Harmony
Of likely hearts composed of stars' consent,
Which join together in sweet Sympathy,
To worke each other's joy and true consent,
Which they have harbour'd since their first descent
Out of their heavenly bowres, where they did see
And know each other here beloved to be.

Love. —*Joanna Baillie.*

FAIN would I speak the thoughts I bear to thee,
But they do choke and flutter in my throat,
And make me like a Child.

Love. — *Butler.*

LOVE is a fire, that burns and sparkles
In men as nat'rally as in charcoals,
Which sooty Chemists stop in holes
When out of wood they extract coals:
So Lovers should their passion choke,
That though they burn, they may not smoke.

Love. — *Spenser.*

LOVE is life's End; an end but never ending;
All joys, all sweets, all happiness, awarding;
Love is life's Wealth (ne'er spent, but ever spending)
More rich by giving, taking by discarding,
Love's Life's Reward, rewarded in rewarding:
Then from thy wretched heart fond Care remove:
Ah! shouldst thou live but once Love's sweets to prove,
Thou wilt not love to live, unless thou live to love.

Love. — *Thomson.*

THOSE fond sensations, those enchanting dreams,
Which cheat a toiling World from day to day,
And form the whole of Happiness they know.

Love. — *Thomson.*

BUT sure, my friend,
There is a time for Love; or life were vile,
A tedious circle of unjoyous days
With senseless hurry fill'd, distasteful, wretched,
Till Love comes smiling in, and brings his sweets,
His healing sweets, soft cares, transporting joys,
That make the poor account of Life complete,
And justify the Gods.

Love. — *Joanna Baillie.*

OFT in the watchful post, or weary march,
Oft in the nightly silence of my tent,
My fixed mind shall gaze upon it still;
But it will pass before my Fancy's eye,
Like some delightful vision of the Soul,
To soothe, not trouble it.

Love. — *Milton.*

BUT now lead on;
In me is no delay; with thee to go
Is to stay here; with thee here to stay,
Is to go hence unwilling; thou to me
Art all things under Heaven, all places thou.

Love. — *Thomson.*

WHY should we kill the best of passions, Love?
It aids the Hero, bids Ambition rise
To nobler heights, inspires Immortal deeds,
Even softens brutes, and adds a Grace to Virtue.

Love. — *Shakspeare.*

BUT Love, first learned in a lady's eyes,
Lives not alone immured in the Brain:
But with the motion of all elements,
Courses as swift as Thought in every power;
And gives to every power a double power,
Above their functions and their offices.

Love. — *Swift.*

LOVE why do we one Passion call,
When 'tis a compound of them all?
Where hot and cold, where sharp and sweet,
In all their equipages meet;
Where Pleasures mix'd with Pains appear,
Sorrow with Joy, and Hope with Fear.

Love. — *Byron.*

THE war of elements no fears impart
To Love, whose deadliest bane is Human art:
There lie the only Rocks our course can check.

Love. — *Prior.*

FANTASTIC Tyrant of the amorous heart,
How hard thy Yoke! how cruel is thy dart!
Those 'scape thy Anger who refuse thy sway,
And those are punished most who most obey.

Love. — *Spenser.*

SUCH is the powre of that sweet Passion,
That it all sordid baseness doth expel,
And the refined mind doth newly fashion
Unto a fairer form, which now doth dwell
In his high Thought, that would itself excel,
Which he beholding still with constant Sight,
Admires the Mirrour of so heavenly light.

Love. — *Moore.*

WHY, the World are all thinking about it,
And as for myself, I can swear,
If I fancied that Heaven were without it,
I'd scarce feel a wish to go there.

Love. — *Shakspeare.*

The blood of youth burns not with such excess,
As Gravity's revolt to Wantonness.

Love. — *Prior.*

SOFT Love, spontaneous tree, its parted root
Must from two Hearts with equal vigour shoot:
Whilst each delighted and delighting gives
The pleasing ecstasy which each receives;
Cherish'd with Hope, and fed with Joy it grows;
Its cheerful buds their opening bloom disclose,
And round the happy soil diffusive odour flows.
If angry Fate that mutual care denies,
The fading plant bewails its due supplies;
Wild with Despair, or sick with Grief, it dies.

Love. — *Mrs. Tighe.*

OH! most adored! Oh! most regretted Love!
Oh! joys that never must again be mine,
And thou, lost hope, farewell—vainly I rove,
For never shall I reach that land divine.
Nor ever shall thy Beams celestial shine
Again upon my sad unheeded way!
Oh! let me here with Life my woes resign,
Or in this glomy den for ever stay,
And shun the scornful World, nor see detested day.

Love. — *Scott.*

IT was but with that dawning Morn
That Roderick Dhu had proudly sworn
To drown his Love in war's wild roar,
Nor think of Ellen Douglas more;
But he who stems a Stream with Sand,
And fetters Flame with flaxen band,
Has yet a harder task to prove—
By firm Resolve to conquer Love!

Love. — *Byron.*

Love will find its way
Through paths where Wolves would fear to prey,
And if it dares enough, 'twere hard
If passion met not some reward.

Love. — *Shakspeare.*

Methinks, I feel this Youth's perfections,
With an invisible and subtle stealth,
To creep in at mine Eyes. Well, let it be.

Love. — *Spenser.*

THE gnawing Envy, the heart-fretting Fear,
The vain surmises, the distrustful shows,
The false reports that flying tales do bear,
The Doubts, the dangers, the delays, the Woes,
The feigned Friends, the unassured foes,
With thousands more than any tongue can tell,
Do make a Lover's life a wretch's Hell.

Love. — *Aaron Hill.*

THERE are, in Love, the extremes of touch'd Desire;
The noblest brightness! or the coarsest Fire:
In vulgar bosoms vulgar wishes move;
Nature guides choice, and as men think they love.
In the loose Passion men profane the name,
Mistake the purpose, and pollute the Flame:
In nobler bosoms Friendship's form it takes,
And sex alone the lovely difference makes.

Love. — *Peter Pindar.*

ECONOMY in Love is peace to nature,
Much like Economy in worldly matter:
We should be prudent, never live too fast;
Profusion will not, cannot always last.

Love. — *Shakspeare.*

EVEN in so short a space, my woman's heart
Grossly grew captive to his Honey Words,
And proved the subject of mine own soul's Curse.

Love. — *Goldsmith.*

AND Love is still an emptier sound,
The modern fair one's jest:
On Earth unseen, or only found
To warm the Turtle's nest.

Love. — *Shakspeare.*

I NEVER sued to Friend nor enemy;
My tongue could never learn sweet soothing word;
But now thy beauty is proposed my fee,
My proud Heart sues, and prompts my Tongue to speak

Love. — *Cowley.*

A MIGHTY Pain to Love it is,
And 'tis a Pain that Pain to miss;
But of all Pains, the greatest Pain
It is to Love, and Love in vain.

Love. — *Thomson.*

WHERE lives the man (if such a man there be)
In idle Wilderness, or Desert drear,
To Beauty's sacred power an enemy?
Let foul fiends harrow him; I'll drop no tear.
I deem that carl by Beauty's power unmoved
Hated of Heaven, of none but Hell approved;
Oh may he never Love, Oh never be beloved!

Love. — *Dryden.*

FOOL, not to know, that Love endures no tie,
And Jove but laughs at lovers' perjury.

Love. — *Johnson.*

TIRED with vain Joys, and false alarms,
With mental and corporeal Strife,
Snatch me, my Stella, to thy arms,
And screen me from the ills of Life.

Love. — *Shenstone.*

AH! Love every Hope can inspire;
It banishes Wisdom the while:
And the lip of the nymph we admire
Seems for ever adorn'd with a Smile.

Love. — *Spenser.*

NE may Love be compeld to maistery;
Fo soone as maistery comes, sweet Love anone
Taketh his nimble Winges, and soone away is gone.

Love. — *Shakspeare.*

LOVE is full of unbefitting strains;
All wanton as a Child, skipping, and vain;
Form'd by the eye, and therefore like the Eye,
Full of strange shapes, of Habits, and of forms.

Love. — *Johnson.*

LET us now, in whisper'd Joy
Evening's silent hours employ:
Silence best, and conscious Shades,
Please the Hearts that Love invades;
Other pleasures give them pain,
Lovers all but Love disdain.

Love. — *Moore.*

LOVE will never bear enslaving;
Summer garments suit him best;
Bliss itself is not worth having,
If we're by Compulsion blest.

Love. — *Pope.*

OH happy state! when Souls each other draw,
When Love is liberty, and Nature law:
All then is full, possessing and possess'd,
No craving void left aching in the breast:
Even thought meets thought, ere from the lips it part,
And each warm wish springs mutual from the Heart.

Love. — *Spenser.*

HUMBLED with feare and awfull reverence,
Before the footstoole of his Majestie
Throwe thyselfe downe, with trembling innocence,
Ne dare looke up with corruptible eye
On the dread face of that great Deity,
For feare, lest if he chance to look on thee,
Thou turne to nought, and quite confounded be.

Love. — *Dryden.*

O LOVE! thou sternly dost thy power maintain,
And wilt not bear a Rival in thy reign,
Tyrants and thee all fellowship disdain.

Love. — *Mrs. Tighe.*

WHEN vex'd by cares and harass'd by distress,
The storms of Fortune chill thy soul with dread,
Let Love, consoling Love! still sweetly bless,
And his assuasive balm benignly shed:
His downy plumage o'er thy pillow spread,
Shall lull thy weeping Sorrows to repose;
To Love the tender heart hath ever fled,
As on its mother's breast the infant throws
Its sobbing face, and there in Sleep forgets its woes.

Love. — *Southey.*

LOVE'S holy flame for ever burneth;
From Heaven it came, to Heaven returneth:
Too oft on earth a troubled guest,
At times deceived, at times opprest,
It here is tried and purified,
Then hath in Heaven its perfect rest:
It soweth here with toil and care,
But the harvest-time of Love is there.

Love. — *Moore.*

THAT happy minglement of Hearts,
Where, changed as chemic compounds are,
Each with its own Existence parts,
To find a new one, happier far!

Love. — *Mrs. Tighe.*

OH, you for whom I write! whose hearts can melt
At the soft thrilling Voice whose power you prove,
You know what charm unutterably felt
Attends the unexpected voice of Love;
Above the Lyre, the lute's soft notes above,
With sweet enchantment to the soul it steals,
And bears it to Elysium's happy grove;
You best can tell the rapture Psyche feels
When Love's Ambrosial Lip the vows of Hymen seals.

Love. — *Scott.*

OH why should man's success remove
The very charms that wake his Love!

Love. — *Moore.*

TO see thee every day that came,
And find thee every day the same;
In Pleasure's smile or Sorrow's tear
The same benign, consoling Dear!
To meet thee early, leave thee late,
Has been so long my bliss, my fate,
That Life, without this cheering ray,
Which came, like Sunshine, every day,
And all my pain, my sorrow chased,
Is now a lone and loveless waste.

Love. — *Shakspeare.*

HIS soul is so enfetter'd to her Love,
That she may make, unmake, do what she list,
Even as her appetite shall play the God
With his weak function.

Love. — *Byron.*

HE who hath loved not, here would learn to Love,
And make his Heart a spirit; he who knows
That tender mystery, will love the more,
For this is Love's recess, where vain men's woes
And the world's waste, hath driven him far from those,
For 'tis his nature to advance or die;
He stands not still, but or decays, or grows
Into a boundless blessing, which may vie
With the Immortal lights, in its Eternity!

Love. — *Lamb.*

MAN, while he Loves, is never quite depraved,
And Woman's triumph is a Lover saved.

Love. — *Moore.*

OH what, while I could hear and see
Such words and looks, was Heaven to me?
Though gross the air on Earth I drew,
'Twas blessed, while she breathed it too;
Though dark the flowers, though dim the sky,
Love lent them Light, while she was nigh.

Love. — *Burns.*

IT warms me, it charms me,
To mention but her Name:
It heats me, it beets me,
And sets me a' on flame!

Love. —*Mrs. Tighe.*

OH! have you never known the silent charm
That undisturb'd Retirement yields the soul,
Where no intruder might your peace alarm,
And Tenderness have wept without control,
While melting Fondness o'er the bosom stole?
Did Fancy never, in some lonely grove,
Abridge the hours which must in absence roll?
Those pensive Pleasures did you never prove,
Oh, you have never Loved! you know not what is Love!

Love. — *Addison.*

WHY dost thou frown upon me?
My Blood runs cold, my Heart forgets to heave,
And Life itself goes out at thy displeasure!

Love. — *Moore.*

'TWAS but for a moment—and yet in that time
She crowded th' impressions of many an hour:
Her eye had a glow, like the Sun of her clime,
Which waked every feeling at once into Flower!

Love. — *Milton.*

SO cheer'd he his fair spouse, and she was cheer'd,
But silently a gentle Tear let fall
From either eye, and wiped them with her hair;
Two other precious drops that ready stood,
Each in their crystal sluice, he ere they fell
Kiss'd, as the gracious signs of sweet Remorse
And pious awe, that fear'd to have offended.

Love. — *Dryden.*

LOVE is a child that talks in broken Language,
Yet then he speaks most plain.

Love. — *Milton.*

LOVE, like odorous Zephyr's grateful breath,
Repays the Flower that sweetness which it borrow'd;
Uninjuring, uninjured, Lovers move
In their own sphere of happiness confest,
By mutual Truth avoiding mutual blame.

Love. — *Pope.*

SHOULD at my feet the world's great master fall,
Himself, his throne, his World, I'd scorn them all:
Not Cæsar's Empress would I deign to prove;
No, make me Mistress to the man I love.

Disappointed Love. — *Washington Irving.*

THE Love of a delicate female is always shy and silent. Even when fortunate, she scarcely breathes it to herself; but when otherwise, she buries it in the recesses of her bosom, and there lets it cower and brood among the ruins of her peace. She is like some tender tree, the pride and beauty of the grove; graceful in its form, bright in its foliage, but with the worm preying at its heart. We find it suddenly withering when it should be most fresh and luxuriant. We see it drooping its branches to the earth and shedding leaf by leaf; until, wasted and perished away, it falls even in the stillness of the forest; and as we muse over the beautiful ruin, we strive in vain to recollect the blast or thunderbolt that could have smitten it with decay.

Love of Plants. — *Claudian.*

THE very leaves live but to Love, and throughout the lofty grove the happy trees have their amours: the Palm nodding to the Palm, ratifies their leagues; the Poplar sighs for the Poplar's embrace; and the Platanus hisses its love to the Platanus; the Alder to the Alder.

Love of the World. — *Clarendon.*

THEY take very unprofitable pains who endeavour to persuade men that they are obliged wholly to despise this World and all that is in it, even whilst they themselves live here: God hath not taken all that pains in forming and framing and furnishing and adorning this World, that they who were made by him to live in it should despise it; it will be well enough if they do not love it so immoderately, to prefer it before him who made it.

Elderly Love. — *Shakspeare.*

I, AN old Turtle,
Will wing me to some wither'd bough, and there
My Mate, that's never to be found again,
Lament till I am lost.

Love of Country. — *Shakspeare.*

THIS royal Throne of Kings, this scepter'd Isle,
This Earth of Majesty, this seat of Mars,
This other Eden, demi-paradise;
This Fortress, built by Nature for herself,
Against infection, and the hand of war;
This Happy breed of men, this little world;
This precious Stone set in the Silver Sea,
Which serves it in the office of a wall,
Or as a moat defensive to a house,
Against the envy of less happier lands;
This blessed plot, this Earth, this Realm, this England,
Dear for her Reputation through the world.

Self-Love. — *Shakspeare.*

SIN of Self-love possesseth all mine eye,
And all my Soul, and all my every part;
And for this sin there is no remedy,
It is so grounded inward in my Heart.
Methinks no face so gracious is as mine,
No shape so true, no Truth of such account;
And for myself mine own worth do define,
As I all other in all worths surmount.
But when my glass shows me myself indeed,
Beated and chopp'd with tann'd Antiquity,
Mine own Self-love quite contrary I read,
Self so Self-loving were Iniquity.

Woman's Love. — *Washington Irving.*

MAN is the creature of interest and ambition. His nature leads him forth into the struggle and bustle of the world. Love is but the establishment of his early life, or a song piped in the intervals of the acts. He seeks for fame, for fortune, for space in the world's thought, and dominion over his fellow-men. But a woman's whole life is a history of the affections. The heart is her world: it is there her ambition strives for empire; it is there her avarice seeks for hidden treasures. She sends forth her sympathies on adventure; she embarks her whole soul in the traffic of affection; and if shipwrecked, her case is hopeless—for it is a bankruptcy of the heart.

Loyalty. — *Cowper.*

WE too are friends to Loyalty. We love
The King who loves the Law; respects his bounds,
And reigns content within them. Him we serve

Freely and with delight, who leaves us free.
But recollecting still that he is Man,
We trust him not too far.

Lust. — *Milton.*

CAPRICIOUS, wanton, bold, and brutal Lust,
Is meanly selfish; when resisted, cruel;
And, like the blast of Pestilential Winds,
Taints the sweet bloom of Nature's fairest forms.

Lust. — *Spenser.*

AS pale and wan as ashes was his looke,
His body leane and meagre as a Rake,
And skin all wither'd like a dryed rooke;
Thereto as cold and drery as a Snake,
That seem'd to tremble evermore and quake.

Lust. — *Milton.*

But when Lust,
By unchaste looks, loose Gestures, and foul talk,
But most by lewd and lavish acts of Sin,
Lets in defilement to the inward parts,
The Soul grows clotted by contagion,
Imbodies, and imbrutes, till she quite lose
The divine Property of her first being.

Lust. — *Shakspeare.*

THE expense of spirit in a waste of Shame
Is Lust in action; and till action, Lust
Is perjured, murderous, bloody, full of blame,
Savage, extreme, rude, cruel, not to trust;
Enjoy'd no sooner, but despised straight;
Past Reason hunted; and, no sooner had,
Past Reason hated, as a swallow'd bait,
On purpose laid to make the taker mad:
Mad in pursuit, and in possession so;
Had, having, and in quest to have, extreme;
A bliss in proof,—and proved, a very wo;
Before, a Joy proposed; behind, a dream:
All this the world well knows; yet none knows well
To shun the Heaven that leads men to this Hell.

Lust. — *Shakspeare.*

The flesh being proud, Desire doth fight with Grace,
For there it revels, and when that decays,
The guilty Rebel for remission prays.

Luxury. — *Shakspeare.*

Weariness
Can snore upon the Flint, when restive Sloth
Finds the Down pillow hard.

Luxury. — *Johnson.*

SUCH is the Diligence with which, in countries completely civilized, one part of mankind labour for another, that wants are supplied faster than they can be formed, and the Idle and luxurious find Life stagnate for want of some desire to keep it in motion. This species of Distress furnishes a new set of occupations; and multitudes are busied from day to day in finding the Rich and the Fortunate something to do.

Lying. — *Montaigne.*

AFTER a tongue has once got the knack of Lying, 'tis not to be imagined how impossible almost it is to reclaim it. Whence it comes to pass that we see some men, who are otherwise very honest, so subject to this vice.

Lying. — *Addison.*

Falsehood and Fraud grow up in every soil,
The product of all climes.

Lying. — *From the Latin.*

THE first step toward useful Knowledge, is to be able to detect Falsehood.

Lying. — *Montaigne.*

LYING is a hateful and accursed Vice. We are not men, nor have other tie upon one another, but our word. If we did but discover the Horror and consequences of it, we should pursue it with Fire and Sword, and more justly than other Crimes.

Madness. — *Byron.*

SHE look'd on many a face with vacant Eye,
On many a token without knowing what;
She saw them watch her without asking why,
And reck'd not who around her pillow sate;
Not speechless though she spoke not; not a sigh
Relieved her thoughts; dull silence and quick chat
Were tried in vain by those who served; she gave
No sign, save breath, of having left the Grave.

Madness. — *Moore.*

This wretched brain gave way,
And I became a Wreck, at random driven
Without one glimpse of Reason or of Heaven.

Madness. — *Byron.*

EVERY sense
Had been o'erstrung by pangs intense,
And each frail fibre of her brain
(As bow-strings, when relax'd by rain,
The erring Arrow launch aside)
Sent forth her Thoughts all wild and wide.

The Magnet. — *Darwin.*

THE obedient Steel with living instinct moves,
And veers for ever to the Pole it loves.

The Magnet. — *Byron.*

THAT trembling vassal of the Pole,
The feeling Compass, Navigation's soul.

Man. — *Colton.*

MAN is that compound Being, created to fill that wide hiatus, that must otherwise have remained unoccupied, between the Natural world and the Spiritual; and he sympathizes with the one in his death, and will be associated with the other by his resurrection. Without another state, it would be utterly impossible for him to explain the difficulties of this: possessing Earth, but destined for Heaven, he forms the link between two orders of Being, and partakes much of the grossness of the one, and somewhat of the refinement of the other. Reason, like the magnetic influence imparted to iron, gives to matter properties and powers which it possessed not before, but without extending its bulk, augmenting its weight, or altering its Organization; like that to which I have compared it, it is visible only by its effects, and perceptible only by its operations. Reason, superadded to Man, gives him peculiar and characteristic views, Responsibilities, and destinations, exalting him above all existences that are visible, but which perish, and associating him with those that are invisible, but which remain. Reason is that Homeric and golden chain descending from the throne of God even unto Man, uniting Heaven with Earth, and Earth with Heaven. For all is connected, and without a chasm; from an Angel to an atom, all is proportion, harmony and strength.

Man. — *Colton.*

MAN, though individually confined to a narrow spot of this Globe, and limited, in his existence, to a few courses of the Sun, has nevertheless an Imagination which no despotism can control, and which, unceasingly, seeks for the Author of his destiny, through the immensity of space, and the ever-rolling current of Ages.

Man. — *Pascal.*

WHAT a chimera is Man! what a confused Chaos! what a subject of contradiction! a professed judge of all things, and yet a feeble worm of the Earth! the great depositary and guardian of Truth, and yet a mere huddle of uncertainty! the glory and the scandal of the Universe.

Man. — *Byron.*

ADMIRE, exult,—despise,—laugh, weep,—for here
There is such matter for all feeling;—Man!
Thou pendulum betwixt a smile and tear.

Man. — *Tucker.*

THERE are limits to the progress of Man's Animal Frame: it is stationary, it declines, and is dissolved; but to this progress of Intelligence, in ascending the scale of Knowledge and of Wisdom, there are not any physical limits short of the Universe itself, which the happy mind aspires to know, and to the order of which he would conform his will. The animals are qualified, by their organization and their instincts, for the particular Element and the circumstances in which they are placed, and they are not fit for any other; but Man, by his intelligent powers, is qualified for any scene of which the circumstances may be observed and in which the proprieties of conduct may be understood.

Man. — *Shakspeare.*

DARE do all that may become a man:
Who dares do more is none, is none.

Man. — *Shakspeare.*

HIS nature is too noble for the World:
He would not flatter Neptune for his trident,
Or Jove for his power to thunder. His Heart's his mouth:
What his breast forges, that his Tongue must vent.

Man. — *Peter Pindar.*

THE mind of Man is vastly like a hive;
His thoughts so busy ever—all alive!
But here the simile will go no further;
For Bees are making Honey, one and all;
Man's thoughts are busy in producing Gall,
Committing, as it were, Self-murther.

Man. — *Crabbe.*

IN that rock are shapes of shells, and forms
Of creatures in old Worlds, of nameless worms,
Whose generations lived and died ere Man,
A worm of other class, to crawl began.

Man. — *Prior.*

BUT do these worlds display their beams, or guide
Their orbs, to serve thy use, to please thy pride?
Thyself but dust, thy stature but a span,
A moment thy duration, foolish Man!
As well may the minutest emmet say,
That Caucasus was raised to pave his way;
The snail, that Lebanon's extended wood
Was destined only for his walk and food;
The vilest Cockle, gaping on the coast
That rounds the ample seas, as well may boast,
The craggy rock projects above the sky,
That he in safety at its foot may lie;
And the whole Ocean's confluent waters swell,
Only to quench his thirst, or move and blanch his shell.

Man. — *Young.*

HOW poor, how rich, how abject, how august,
How complicate, how wonderful, is Man!
How passing wonder He, who made him such!
Who centred in our make such strange extremes
From different natures marvellously mixt,
Connexion exquisite of distant Worlds!
Distinguish'd link in Being's endless chain!
Midway from nothing to the Deity!
A beam ethereal, sullied, and absorped!
Though sullied and dishonour'd, still divine!
Dim miniature of greatness absolute!
An heir of Glory! a frail child of dust!
Helpless Immortal! Insect infinite!
A Worm! a God!

Man. — *Prior.*

CEASE, Man of woman born, to hope relief
From daily Trouble and continued Grief;
Thy hope of Joy deliver to the wind,
Suppress thy passions, and prepare thy mind;
Free and familiar with Misfortune grow,
Be used to Sorrow, and inured to Woe;
By weakening toil and hoary age o'ercome,
See thy decrease, and hasten to thy Tomb.

Man. — *Pope.*

NOT always actions show the Man: we find
Who does a kindness, is not therefore kind;
Perhaps Prosperity becalm'd his breast,
Perhaps the wind just shifted from the east:

Not therefore humble he who seeks retreat,
Pride guides his steps, and bids him shun the great:
Who combats bravely is not therefore brave,
He dreads a Death-bed like the meanest slave:
Who reasons wisely is not therefore wise,
His pride in reasoning, not in acting, lies.

Man. — *Bacon.*

READING maketh a full Man; Conference a ready Man; and Writing an exact Man.

Man. — *Prior.*

CONDEMN'D to sacrifice his childish years
To babbling Ignorance, and to empty fears;
To pass the riper period of his age,
Acting his part upon a crowded stage;
To lasting toils exposed and endless Cares,
To open dangers, and to secret snares;
To malice, which the vengeful Foe intends,
And the more dangerous Love of seeming Friends.

Man. — *Pope.*

BEHOLD the child, by Nature's kindly law
Pleased with a rattle, tickled with a straw;
Some livelier plaything gives his Youth delight,
A little louder, but as empty quite;
Scarfs, Garters, Gold amuse his riper stage;
And beads and prayer-books are the toys of age;
Pleased with this Bauble still, as that before;
Till tired he sleeps, and Life's poor play is o'er.

Man. — *Pope.*

SEE him from Nature rising slow to art!
To copy instinct then was reason's part:
Thus then to man the voice of Nature spake—
Go, from the creatures thy instructions take:
Learn from the Birds what food the thickets yield;
Learn from the Beasts the physics of the field;
Thy arts of building from the Bee receive;
Learn of the Mole to plough, the Worm to weave:
Learn of the little Nautilus to sail,
Spread the thin oar, and catch the driving Gale.

Man. — *Shakspeare.*

HOWEVER we do praise ourselves,
Our Fancies are more giddy and infirm,
More longing, wavering, sooner lost and won,
Than Women's are.

Man. — *Young.*

FATHER of Mercies! why from silent earth
Did'st thou awake, and curse me into birth?
Tear me from quiet, ravish me from night,
And make a thankless present of thy Light?
Push into being a reverse of thee,
And animate a Clod with Misery?

Man. — *Spenser.*

SO greatest and most glorious thing on ground
May often need the helpe of weaker hand;
So feeble is Man's state, and Life unsound,
That in assurance it may never stand,
Till it dissolved be from earthly Band.

Man. — *Steele.*

A MAN that is Temperate, Generous, Valiant, Chaste, Faithful, and Honest, may, at the same time, have Wit, Humour, Mirth, Good-breeding, and Gallantry. While he exerts these latter qualities, twenty occasions might be invented to show he is master of the other noble Virtues.

Man. — *Parnell.*

LET business vex him, Avarice blind,
Let doubt and Knowledge rack his mind,
Let Errour act, Opinion speak,
And Want afflict, and Sickness break,
And Anger burn, Dejection chill,
And Joy distract, and Sorrow kill,
Till arm'd by Care, and taught to mow,
Time draws the long destructive blow.

Manhood. — *Shakspeare.*

HE is but the counterfeit of a Man, who hath not the life of a Man.

Manhood. — *Scott.*

HE turn'd away—his Heart throbb'd high,
The tear was bursting from his eye.

Manhood. — *Scott.*

WITH haughty Laugh his head he turn'd,
And dash'd away the Tear he scorn'd.

Manhood. — *Shakspeare.*

I'LL never
Be such a gostling to obey instinct; but stand,
As if a Man were Author of himself,
And knew no other kin.

Manners. — *Addison.*

COMPLAISANCE renders a Superior amiable, an Equal agreeable, and an Inferior acceptable. It smooths distinction, sweetens conversation, and makes every one in the company pleased with himself. It produces Good Nature and mutual benevolence, encourages the timorous, soothes the turbulent, humanizes the fierce, and distinguishes a society of civilized persons from a confusion of savages.

Manners. — *La Bruyere.*

A MAN'S worth is estimated in this world according to his Conduct.

Manners. — *Steele.*

I TAKE it for a rule, that the natural, and not the acquired man, is the companion. Learning, wit, gallantry, and Good-breeding are all but subordinate qualities in society, and are of no value, but as they are subservient to Benevolence, and tend to a certain manner of being or appearing equal to the rest of the Company.

Manners. — *Addison.*

THE true art of being agreeable is to appear well pleased with all the Company, and rather to seem well entertained with them, than to bring entertainment to them. A man thus disposed, perhaps, may have not much Learning, nor any Wit; but if he has Common Sense and something friendly in his behaviour, it conciliates men's minds more than the brightest parts without this disposition: it is true indeed that we should not dissemble and flatter in company; but a man may be very agreeable, strictly consistent with Truth and Sincerity, by a prudent silence where he cannot concur, and a pleasing assent where he can. Now and then you meet with a person so exactly formed to please, that he will gain upon every one that hears or beholds him; this disposition is not merely the gift of Nature, but frequently the effect of much Knowledge of the world, and a command over the Passions.

Manners. — *Shakspeare.*

THOSE that are Good Manners at the Court are as ridiculous in the Country, as the Behaviour of the Country is most mockable at the Court.

Manners. — *Swift.*

IF a man makes me keep my Distance, the comfort is, he keeps his at the same time.

Manners. — *Chesterfield.*

GOOD-BREEDING is the result of much Good Sense, some Good Nature, and a little Self-denial for the sake of others, and with a view to obtain the same indulgence from them.

Manners. — *Greville.*

YOU will, I believe, in general ingratiate yourself with others, still less by paying them too much Court than too little.

Manners. — *Chesterfield.*

A MAN'S own Good-breeding is the best security against other people's Ill-manners.

Manners. — *Addison.*

ONE may now know a man that never conversed in the world, by his excess of Good-breeding. A polite country Esquire shall make you as many bows in half an hour, as would serve a Courtier for a week. There is infinitely more to do about place and precedancy in a meeting of Justices' wives, than in an assembly of Duchesses.

Manners. — *Cumberland.*

THE happy gift of being agreeable seems to consist not in one, but in an assemblage of Talents tending to communicate delight; and how many are there, who, by easy Manners, sweetness of Temper, and a variety of other undefinable qualities, possess the power of pleasing without any visible effort, without the aids of Wit, Wisdom, or Learning, nay, as it should seem, in their defiance; and this without appearing even to know that they possess it.

Manners. — *Addison.*

THERE is no society or conversation to be kept up in the world without Good-nature, or something which must bear its appearance, and supply its place. For this reason mankind have been forced to invent a kind of artificial humanity, which is what we express by the word Good-breeding.

Manners. — *Addison.*

GOOD-BREEDING shows itself most, where to an ordinary Eye it appears the least.

Manners. — *Fuller.*

IN conversation use some, but not too much Ceremony: it teaches others to be courteous too. Demeanours are commonly paid back in their own Coin.

Manners. — *South.*

I HAVE known men, grossly injured in their affairs, depart pleased, at least silent, only because they were injured in good Language, ruined in Caresses, and kissed while they were struck under the fifth Rib.

Manners. — *Chesterfield.*

AN able man shows his spirit by gentle Words and resolute Actions: he is neither hot nor timid.

Manners. — *Fuller.*

LET thy Carriage be friendly, but not foolishly free: An unwary Openness causeth Contempt, but a little Reservedness, Respect; and handsome Courtesy, Kindness.

Manners. — *Swift.*

GOOD Manners is the art of making those people easy with whom we converse. Whoever makes the fewest persons uneasy, is the best bred in the Company.

Manners. — *Hume.*

AMONG well-bred people, a mutual Deference is affected; Contempt of others disguised; Authority concealed; attention given to each in his turn; and an easy stream of conversation maintained, without vehemence, without interruption, without eagerness for Victory, and without any airs of superiority.

Manners. — *Goldsmith.*

CEREMONIES are different in every country; but true Politeness is everywhere the same. Ceremonies, which take up so much of our attention, are only artificial helps which Ignorance assumes in order to imitate Politeness, which is the result of Good Sense and Good Nature. A person possessed of those qualities, though he had never seen a Court, is truly agreeable; and if without them, would continue a Clown, though he had been all his life a gentleman usher.

Manners. — *Chesterfield.*

GOOD-BREEDING carries along with it a Dignity that is respected by the most petulant. Ill-breeding invites and authorizes the Familiarity of the most timid.

Manners. — *Sterne.*

HAIL! ye small sweet Courtesies of life, for smooth do ye make the road of it, like Grace and Beauty which beget inclinations to love at first sight; 'tis ye who open the door and let the stranger in.

Manners. — *Zimmerman.*

DO not think that your Learning and Genius, your Wit or Sprightliness, are welcome everywhere. I was once told that my Company was disagreeable because I appeared so uncommonly happy.

Manners. — *Swift.*

PRIDE, Ill-nature, and want of Sense, are the three great sources of Ill-manners; without some one of these defects, no man will behave himself ill for want of Experience, or what, in the language of fools, is called knowing the World.

Manners. — *Pope.*

ALL Manners take a tincture from our own,
Or come discolour'd thro' our Passions shown;
Or Fancy's beam enlarges, multiplies,
Contracts, invests, and gives ten thousand dyes.

Manners. — *Swift.*

ONE principal point of Good-breeding is to suit our behaviour to the three several degrees of men; our Superiors, our Equals, and those below us.

Manners. — *Shakspeare.*

THE sauce to meat is Ceremony
(Meeting were bare without it.)

Manners. — *Shakspeare.*

HE could not
Carry his Honours even; whether pride,
(Which out of daily fortune ever taints
The happy man;) whether defect of Judgment
(To fail in the disposing of those chances,
Whereof he was the Lord;) or whether Nature,
(Not to be other than one thing; not moving
From th' cask to th' cushion; but commanding Peace
Even with the same austerity and garb
As he controll'd the War.)

Manners. — *Steele.*

WE see a world of pains taken, and the best years of Life spent in collecting a set of Thoughts in a college for the conduct of Life, and, after all, the man so qualified shall hesitate in his speech to a good suit of clothes, and want common sense before an agreeable Woman. Hence it is, that Wisdom, Valour, Justice, and Learning cannot keep a man in countenance that is possessed with these excellences, if he wants that inferior art of life and behaviour called Good-Breeding.

Manners. — *La Bruyere.*

ALTHOUGH a man may possess Virtue, Talent, and Good Conduct, he may nevertheless be disagreeable. There is a certain fashion in Manners, which is too often neglected as of no consequence, but which frequently becomes the basis on which the World will form a favourable or an unfavourable opinion of you; and a little attention to render them engaging and polished, will prevent others from entertaining prepossessions respecting you, which in their consequences may operate greatly to your disadvantage.

Manners. — *La Rochefoucauld.*

GRACE is to the Body what Good Sense is to the Mind.

Manners. — *Fuller.*

AS the Sword of the best tempered metall is most flexible; so the truly generous are most pliant and courteous in their Behaviour to their inferiors.

Manners. — *Bishop Middleton.*

VIRTUE itself offends, when coupled with forbidding Manners.

Manners. — *Colton.*

ALWAYS suspect a man who affects great Softness of Manner, an unruffled Evenness of Temper, and an Enunciation studied, slow, and deliberate. These things are all unnatural, and bespeak a degree of mental discipline into which he that has no purpose of Craft or Design to answer, cannot submit to drill himself. The most successful Knaves are usually of this description, as smooth as Razors dipped in oil, and as sharp. They affect the innocence of the Dove, which they have not, in order to hide the cunning of the Serpent, which they have.

Manners. — *Chesterfield.*

PREPARE yourselves for the World, as the athletæ used to do for their exercises; oil your Mind and your Manners, to give them the necessary suppleness and flexibility; Strength alone will not do.

Manners. — *La Rochefoucauld.*

THERE are some persons on whom their Faults sit well, and others who are made ungraceful by their Good Qualities.

Manners. — *La Rochefoucauld.*

NOTHING so much prevents our being natural as the desire of appearing so.

Manners. — *Greville.*

UNBECOMING forwardness oftener proceeds from Ignorance than Impudence.

Manners. — *Shakspeare.*

AGE cannot wither her, nor Custom stale
Her infinite variety: Other Women cloy
The appetites they feed; but she makes hungry,
Where most she satisfies.

Marriage. — *Shakspeare.*

THE instances that second Marriage move
Are base respects of Thrift, but none of Love.

Marriage. — *Thomson.*

WHERE Friendship full exerts her softest power,
Perfect Esteem enliven'd by Desire
Ineffable, and Sympathy of Soul;
Thought meeting thought, and will preventing will,
With boundless confidence: for naught but Love
Can answer Love, and render bliss secure.

Marriage. — *Fuller.*

TAKE the Daughter of a good Mother.

Marriage. — *Milton.*

HERE Love his golden shafts employs, here lights
His constant lamp, and waves his purple wings,
Reigns here and revels; not in the bought smile
Of Harlots, loveless, joyless, unendear'd,
Casual fruition; nor in Court Amours,
Mix'd dance, or wanton mask, or midnight ball,
Or serenade, which the starved Lover sings
To his proud Fair, best quitted with disdain.

Marriage. — *Johnson.*

MARRIAGE is the strictest tie of perpetual Friendship, and there can be no Friendship without Confidence, and no Confidence without Integrity; and he must expect to be wretched, who pays to Beauty, Riches, or Politeness that regard which only Virtue and Piety can claim.

Marriage. — *Lord Rochester.*

MOTHERS who force their Daughters into interested Marriage, are worse than the Ammonites who sacrificed their children to Moloch—the latter undergoing a speedy death, the former suffering years of Torture, but too frequently leading to the same result

Marriage. — *Cowper.*

THOU art the nurse of Virtue. In thine arms
She smiles, appearing as in truth she is,
Heaven-born and destined to the skies again.
Thou art not known where Pleasure is adored,
That reeling goddess with the zoneless waist
And wand'ring eye, still leaning on the arm
Of novelty, her fickle, frail support;
For thou art meek and constant, hating change,
And finding in the calm of Truth-tied Love
Joy that her stormy Raptures never yield.

Marriage. — *William Penn.*

NEVER marry but for Love, but see that thou lovest what is lovely

Marriage. — *Sir Walter Raleigh.*

REMEMBER, that if thou marry for Beauty, thou bindest thyself all thy Life for that which perchance will neither last nor please thee one year; and when thou hast it, it will be to thee of no price at all; for the Desire dieth when it is attained, and the Affection perisheth when it is satisfied.

Marriage. — *Byron.*

FEW—none—find what they love or could have loved,
Though accident, blind contact, and the strong
Necessity of loving, have removed
Antipathies—but to recur, ere long,
Envenom'd with irrevocable wrong.

Marriage. — *Shakspeare.*

'TIS not to make me jealous
To say—my Wife is fair, feeds well, loves company,
Is free of speech, sings, plays, and dances well;
Where Virtue is, these are more virtuous:
Nor from mine own weak merits will I draw
The smallest fear or doubt of her revolt;
For she had Eyes, and chose me: No,
I'll see, before I doubt; when I doubt, prove;
And, on the proof, there is no more but this,—
Away at once with Love, or Jealousy.

Marriage. — *Cowper.*

OH friendly to the best pursuits of man,
Friendly to Thought, to Virtue, and to Peace,
Domestic Life in rural leisure pass'd!
Few know thy value, and few taste thy sweets.

Marriage. — *Sir Thomas Overbury.*

AS good and wise; so she be fit for me,
That is, to will, and not to will the same;
My wife is my adopted self, and she
As me, to what I love, must frame.
And when by Marriage both in one concur,
Woman converts to Man, not Man to her.

Marriage. — *Butler.*

FOR Wedlock without Love, some say,
Is but a lock without a Key;
It is a kind of rape to marry
One that neglects, or cares not for ye;
For what does make it ravishment,
But being against the Mind's consent?

Marriage. — *Addison.*

AN Idol may be undeified by many accidental causes. Marriage in particular is a kind of counter-apotheosis, or a Deification inverted. When a man becomes familiar with his Goddess, she quickly sinks into a Woman.

Marriage. — *Colton.*

MATRIMONY is an engagement which must last the life of one of the parties, and there is no retracting, *vestigia nulla retrorsum;* therefore, to avoid all the horror of a Repentance that comes too late, men should thoroughly know the real causes that induce them to take so important a step, before they venture upon it: do they stand in need of a Wife, an Heiress, or a Nurse; is it their Passions, their Wants, or their Infirmities, that solicit them to wed? Are they candidates for that happy state, *propter opus, opes* or *opem?* according to the epigram. These are questions much more proper to be proposed before men go to the altar, than after it; they are points which, well ascertained, would prevent many Disappointments, often deplorable, often ridiculous, always remediless.

Marriage. — *Justus Moser.*

I TRY to make myself and all around me agreeable. It will not do to leave a Man to himself till he comes to you, to take no pains to attract him, or to appear before him with a long face. It is not so difficult as you think, dear child, to behave to a Husband so that he shall remain for ever in some measure a Husband. I am an old Woman, but you can still do what you like; a word from you at the right time will not fail of its effect; what need have you to play the suffering Virtue? The tear of a loving Girl, says an old Book, is like a Dewdrop on the Rose; but that on the cheek of a Wife is a drop of Poison to her Husband. Try to appear cheerful and contented, and your husband will be so; and when you have made him happy you will become so, not in appearance, but reality. The skill required is not so great. Nothing flatters a man so much as the happiness of his Wife; he is always proud of himself as the source of it. As soon as you are cheerful, you will be lively and alert, and every moment will afford you an opportunity of letting fall an agreeable word. Your Education, which gives you an immense advantage, will greatly assist you; and your sensibility will become the noblest gift that Nature has bestowed on you, when it shows itself in affectionate assiduity, and stamps on every action a soft, kind, and tender Character, instead of wasting itself in secret repinings.

Marriage. — *Ovid.*

IF you wish to marry suitably, marry your Equal.

Marriage. — *Shakspeare.*

LET still the woman take
An elder than herself; so wears she to him,
So sways she level in her Husband's heart.

Marriage. — *Shakspeare.*

As for my Wife,
I would you had her Spirit in such another:
The third o' the world is yours: which with a snaffle
You may pace easy, but not such a Wife.

Marriage. — *Fuller.*

IN Marriage, he best bowls at the mark of his own Contentment, who, besides the aim of his own eye, is directed by his Father, who is to give him the ground.

Marriage. — *Colton.*

MARRIAGE is a feast where the Grace is sometimes better than the Dinner.

Marriage. — *Rogers.*

ACROSS the threshold led,
And every Tear kiss'd off as soon as shed,
His house she enters, there to be a Light
Shining within when all without is night;
A guardian-Angel o'er his life presiding,
Doubling his Pleasure, and his Cares dividing!

Marriage. — *Fuller.*

JARRES concealed are half reconciled; which if generally known, 'tis a double task, to stop the breach at home and men's mouths abroad. To this end, a good Husband never publicly reproves his Wife. An open reproof puts her to do penance before all that are present; after which, many study rather Revenge than Reformation.

Marriage. — *Thomson.*

WHAT is the World to them,
Its pomp, its pleasure, and its nonsense all?
Who in each other clasp whatever fair
High Fancy forms, and lavish Hearts can wish;
Or on the mind, or mind-illumined face;
Truth, Goodness, Honour, Harmony, and Love,
The richest bounty of indulgent Heaven.

Marriage. — *Milton.*

LET us no more contend, nor blame
Each other, blamed enough elsewhere, but strive
In offices of Love, how we may lighten
Each other's burden, in our share of Woe.

Marriage. —*Jean Paul.*

"DON'T put on your left stocking to-morrow morning; I must first mend a hole in it." "The author of this history hereby asserts that he has often gone nearly out of his Mind in consequence of such like feminine Interludes. It is in truth to be wished that the said author, in case he enter into the estate of Matrimony, may find a woman to whom he can read the most essential principles and dictata of Metaphysics and Astronomy, and who will not, in his most towering flights, cast up his Stockings at him. He will however be satisfied if one fall to his lot who has humbler merits, but who is capable of soaring with him to a certain height:—one on whose opened eyes and heart the flowery Earth and beaming Heavens strike not in infinitesimals, but in large and towering masses; for whom the great whole is something more than a Nursery or a Ball-room; one who, with a feeling at once tender and discriminating, and with a Heart at once pious and large, for ever improves the Man whom she has wedded. This it is, and no more, to which the Author of this history limits his wishes."

Marriage. — *Steele.*

THE good Husband keeps his Wife in the wholesome ignorance of unnecessary Secrets. They will not be starved with the ignorance, who perchance may surfeit with the knowledge of weighty Counsels, too heavy for the weaker sex to bear. He knows little who will tell his Wife all he knows.

Marriage. —*Lord Lyttelton.*

EVEN in the happiest choice, where fav'ring Heaven
Has equal Love and easy Fortune given,—
Think not, the Husband gain'd, that all is done;
The prize of Happiness must still be won:
And, oft, the careless find it to their cost,
The Lover in the Husband may be lost;
The Graces might, alone, his heart allure;
They and the Virtues, meeting, must secure.

Marriage. — *Shakspeare.*

I AM ashamed, that Women are so simple
To offer War where they should kneel for Peace;
Or seek for Rule, Supremacy, and Sway,
When they are bound to serve, love, and obey.

Marriage. —*From the Italian.*

THE admiral of Castile said, that he who marries a Wife and he who goes to War must necessarily submit to every thing that may happen.

Marriage. — *Anon.*

BE sure you like the Parents of the Girl you are about to wed; it is almost as essential to your future Happiness as to truly love the object of your wishes.

Marriage. — *Colton.*

THAT alliance may be said to have a double tie, where the Minds are united as well as the Body, and the union will have all its strength, when both the links are in perfection together.

Marriage. — *Ben Jonson.*

HE that would have fine Guests, let him have a fine Wife.

Marriage. — *Prior.*

AND now your matrimonial Cupid,
Lash'd on by Time, grows tired and stupid.
For story and experience tell us
That Man grows old, and woman jealous.
Both would their little ends secure:
He sighs for Freedom, she for Power:
His wishes tend abroad to roam,
And her's to domineer at home.

Marriage. — *Fuller.*

THE good Wife commandeth her Husband, in any equal matter, by constantly obeying him. It was always observed, that what the English gained of the French in battle by valour, the French regained of the English in cunning by treaties. So if the Husband should chance by his power in his passion to prejudice his Wife's right, she wisely knoweth, by compounding and complying, to recover and rectify it again.

Marriage. — *Steele.*

IT is common to hear both sexes repine at their change, relate the Happiness of their earlier years, blame the Folly and Rashness of their own choice, and warn those whom they see coming into the world against the same precipitance and infatuation. But it is to be remembered that the days which they so much wish to call back, are the days not only of Celibacy but of Youth, the days of novelty and improvement, of ardour and of Hope, of health and vigour of body, of Gayety and Lightness of Heart. It is not easy to surround life with any circumstances in which Youth will not be delightful; and I am afraid that whether married or unmarried, we shall find the vesture of terrestrial Existence more heavy and cumbrous the longer it is worn.

Marriage. — *Spenser.*

FROM that day forth, in Peace and joyous Bliss
They lived together long without debate;
Ne private Jarre, ne spite of Enemies,
Could shake the safe assurance of their state.

Marriage. — *Terence.*

IT does not appear essential that, in forming Matrimonial Alliances, there should be on each side a parity of Wealth; but that, in Disposition and Manners, they should be alike. Chastity and Modesty form the best dowry a parent can bestow.

Marriage. — *Moore.*

SOMETHING, light as air—a look,
A word unkind or wrongly taken—
Oh! Love, that tempests never shook,
A breath, a touch like this hath shaken.
And ruder words will soon rush in
To spread the breach that words begin;
And Eyes forget the gentle ray
They wore in Courtship's smiling day;
And Voices lose the tone that shed
A tenderness round all they said;
Till fast declining, one by one,
The sweetnesses of Love are gone,
And Hearts, so lately mingled, seem
Like broken clouds,—or like the stream,
That smiling left the Mountain's brow,
As though its waters ne'er could sever,
Yet, ere it reach the plain below,
Breaks into Floods, that part for ever.

Marriage. — *Johnson.*

MARRIAGE is the best state for Man in general; and every Man is a worse Man in proportion as he is unfit for the Married State.

Marriage. — *Beattie.*

NO Jealousy their dawn of Love o'ercast,
Nor blasted were their wedded days with Strife;
Each season look'd delightful as it past,
To the fond Husband and the faithful Wife.
Beyond the lowly vale of shepherd life
They never roam'd! secure beneath the storm
Which in Ambition's lofty land is rife,
Where Peace and Love are canker'd by the worm
Of Pride, each bud of Joy industrious to deform.

Marriage.—*Shakspeare.*

A Father
Is, at the nuptial of his Son, a guest
That best becomes the table.

Marriage.—*Plutarch.*

MEN that marry Women very much superior to themselves, are not so truly Husbands to their Wives, as they are unawares made Slaves to their Portions.

Marriage.—*Martial.*

PERPETUAL Harmony their bed attend,
And Venus still the well-match'd pair befriend!
May she, when Time has sunk him into years,
Love her old man, and cherish his white hairs;
Nor he perceive her Charms thro' age decay,
But think each happy sun his Bridal day!

Marriage.—*Milton.*

IT is a less breach of Wedlock to part, with wise and quiet consent, betimes, than still to foil and profane that Mystery of Joy and Union with a polluting sadness and perpetual distemper.

Marriage.—*Shakspeare.*

THY Husband is thy Lord, thy life, thy keeper,
Thy head, thy Sovereign: one that cares for thee,
And for thy maintenance: commits his body
To painful labour, both by sea and land;
To watch the night in storms, the day in cold,
While thou liest warm at home, secure and safe,
And craves no other Tribute at thy hands,
But Love, fair Looks, and true Obedience;
Too little Payment for so great a Debt.

Marriage.—*Swift.*

THE reason who so few Marriages are happy, is because young Ladies spend their time in making Nets, not in making Cages.

Marriage.—*Shakspeare.*

HAPPY in this, she is not yet so old,
But she may learn; and happier than this,
She is not bred so dull but she can learn;
Happiest of all, is, that her gentle Spirit
Commits itself to yours, to be directed.

Marriage.—*Simonides.*

Of earthly goods the best, is a good Wife;
A bad, the bitterest Curse of human life.

Marriage. — *Shakspeare.*

GOD the best maker of all Marriages.

Marriage. — *Selden.*

MARRIAGE is a desperate thing: the Frogs in Æsop were extremely wise; they had a great mind to some Water, but they would not leap into the Well, because they could not get out again.

Marriage.— *Massillon.*

EVERY effort is made in forming Matrimonial Alliances to reconcile matters relating to Fortune, but very little is paid to the Congeniality of Dispositions, or to the Accordance of Hearts.

Marriage. — *Milton.*

HAIL Wedded Love, mysterious law, true source
Of human offspring, sole propriety
In Paradise of all things common else.
By thee adult'rous Lust was driven from men
Among the bestial herds to range; by thee
Founded in Reason, loyal, just and pure,
Relations dear, and all the Charities
Of Father, Son, and Brother first were known.

Marriage. — *Shakspeare.*

MARRIAGE is a matter of more worth
Than to be dealt in by attorneyship.
For what is Wedlock forced, but a Hell,
An age of discord and continual Strife?
Whereas the contrary bringeth forth Bliss,
And is a pattern of Celestial Peace.

Marriage. — *Osborne.*

I PITY from my heart the unhappy Man who has a bad Wife. She is Shackles on his feet, a Palsy to his hands, a Burden on his shoulder, Smoke to his eyes, Vinegar to his teeth, a Thorn to his side, a Dagger to his heart.

Marriage. — *Shakspeare.*

WITHIN a month;
Ere yet the salt of most unrighteous Tears
Had left the flushing of her galled Eyes,
She married:—O most wicked speed.

Marriage. — *Vanbrugh.*

IF Idleness be the root of all Evil, then Matrimony's good for something, for it sets many a poor Woman to work.

Marriage. — *Shakspeare.*

HASTY Marriage seldom proveth well.

Marriage. — *Shakspeare.*

SHOULD all despair,
That have revolted Wives, the tenth of Mankind
Would hang themselves.

Marriage. — *Fuller.*

THE good Wife is none of our dainty dames, who love to appear in a variety of suits every day new; as if a good gown, like a stratagem in War, were to be used but once. But our good Wife sets up a sail according to the keel of her husband's estate; and if of high Parentage, she doth not so remember what she was by birth, that she forgets what she is by match.

Marriage. — *Shakspeare.*

REASON, my son
Should choose himself a Wife; but as good reason,
The Father (all whose joy is nothing else
But fair Posterity) should hold some counsel
In such a business.

Marriage. — *Shakspeare.*

SHE is mine own;
And I as rich in having such a Jewel,
As twenty seas, if all their sand were pearl,
The water Nectar, and the rocks pure Gold.
I will be master of what is mine own:
She is my Goods, my chattels; she is my house,
My Household-stuff, my field, my barn,
My horse, my ox, my ass, my any thing;
And here she stands, touch her whoever dare;
I'll bring mine Action on the proudest he
That stops my way in Padua.

Marriage. — *Shakspeare.*

SUCH duty as the Subject owes the Prince,
Even such a Woman oweth to her Husband:
And, when she's froward, peevish, sullen, sour,
And, not obedient to his honest will,
What is she but a foul contending Rebel,
And graceless Traitor to her loving lord?

Marriage. — *Fuller.*

FIRST get an absolute Conquest over thyself, and then thou wilt easily govern thy Wife.

Marriage.—*Shakspeare.*

A LIGHT Wife doth make a heavy Husband.

Marriage.—*Parnell.*

YET here and there we grant a gentle Bride,
Whose temper betters by the father's side;
Unlike the rest that double human care,
Fond to relieve, or resolute to share:
Happy the Man whom thus his stars advance!
The Curse is general, but the Blessing chance.

Marriage.—*Sir Walter Raleigh.*

THE best time for Marriage, will be toward thirty, for as the younger times are unfit, either to choose or to govern a Wife and family, so, if thou stay long, thou shalt hardly see the education of thy children, who, being left to strangers, are in effect lost; and better were it to be unborn than ill-bred: for thereby thy Posterity shall either perish, or remain a shame to thy Name.

Marriage.—*Shakspeare.*

WITHIN the bond of Marriage, tell me, Brutus
Is it excepted, I should know no secrets
That appertain to you? Am I yourself
But, as it were, on sort, or limitation;
To keep with you at Meals, comfort your bed,
And talk to you sometimes? Dwell I but in the suburbs
Of your good Pleasure? If it be no more,
Portia is Brutus' Harlot, not his Wife.

Martyrdom.—*Colton.*

HE that dies a Martyr, proves that he was not a Knave, but by no means that he was not a Fool.

Martyrdom.—*Colton.*

TWO things are necessary to a modern Martyr,—some to pity, and some to persecute; some to regret, and some to roast him.

The Master.—*Steele.*

IT is not only paying wages, and giving commands, that constitutes a Master of a Family; but Prudence, equal behaviour, with a readiness to protect and cherish them, is what entitle a man to that character in their very Hearts and Sentiments.

Masters and Servants.—*Fuller.*

IF thou art a Master, be sometimes Blind; if a Servant, sometimes Deaf.

Matter *vs.* Manner. — *Wirt.*

IN composing, think much more of your Matter than your Manner. To be sure, spirit, grace, and dignity of manner are of great importance both to the speaker and writer; but of infinitely more importance is the weight and worth of matter. The fashion of the times is much changed since Thomson wrote his Seasons, and Hervey his Meditations. It will no longer do to fill the ear only with pleasant sounds, or the fancy with fine images. The mind, the understanding, must be filled with solid thought. The age of ornament is over, that of utility has succeeded. The "pugnæ quam pompæ aptius" is the order of the day, and men fight now with clenched fist, not with open hand—with logic, and not with rhetoric.

Means and Conceptions. — *Colton.*

SOME men possess Means that are great, but fritter them away in the execution of Conceptions that are little; and there are others who can form great Conceptions, but who attempt to carry them into Execution with little Means. These two descriptions of men might succeed if united, but as they are usually kept asunder by Jealousy, both fail. It is a rare thing to find a combination of great Means and of great Conceptions in one Mind.

Mediocrity. — *La Rochefoucauld.*

MINDS of moderate Calibre ordinarily condemn every thing which is beyond their range.

Mediocrity. — *La Bruyere.*

WE meet with few utterly dull and stupid Souls: the Sublime and Transcendent are still fewer; the generality of Mankind stand between these two extremes: the interval is filled with multitudes of ordinary Geniuses, but all very useful, and the ornaments and supports of the Commonwealth.

Mediocrity. — *Colton.*

THERE are circumstances of peculiar Difficulty and Danger, where a Mediocrity of Talent is the most fatal quantum that a man can possibly possess. Had Charles the First, and Louis the Sixteenth, been more Wise or more Weak, more Firm or more Yielding, in either case they had both of them saved their heads.

Melancholy. — *Shakspeare.*

O MELANCHOLY!
Who ever yet could sound thy bottom? find
The ooze, to show what coast thy sluggish Carrack
Might eas'liest harbour in?

Melancholy. — *Shakspeare.*

I HAVE of late (but wherefore I know not,) lost all my Mirth, foregone all custom of Exercises: and, indeed, it goes so heavily with my disposition, that this goodly frame, the Earth, seems to me a sterile promontory; this most excellent canopy, the Air, look you, this brave o'erhanging Firmament, this majestical Roof fretted with golden Fire, why it appears no other thing to me, than a foul and pestilent congregation of Vapours.

Memory. — *Byron.*

BUT ever and anon of griefs subdued,
There comes a token like a Scorpion's sting,
Scarce seen but with fresh bitterness imbued;
And slight withal may be the things which bring
Back on the Heart the weight which it would fling
Aside for ever: it may be a sound—
A tone of music—summer's eve—or spring,
A flower—the wind—the Ocean—which shall wound,
Striking the electric chain wherewith we're darkly bound;
And how and why we know not, nor can trace
Home to its cloud this Lightning of the Mind,
But feel the shock renew'd, nor can efface
The blight and blackening which it leaves behind,
Which out of things familiar, undesign'd,
When least we deem of such, calls up to view
The Spectres whom no exorcism can bind,
The cold—the changed—perchance the dead—anew,
The mourn'd, the loved, the lost—too many! yet how few!

Memory. — *Goldsmith.*

THOU, like the World, th' opprest oppressing,
Thy smiles increase the wretch's Woe!
And he who wants each other blessing,
In thee must ever find a Foe.

Memory. — *Goldsmith.*

REMEMBRANCE wakes with all her busy train,
Swells at my Breast, and turns the Past to pain.

Memory. — *Byron.*

BUT in that instant, o'er his Soul
Winters of Memory seem'd to roll,
And gather in that drop of time
A life of Pain, an age of Crime:
O'er him who loves, or hates, or fears,
Such moment pours the Grief of years.

Mental Anguish. —*Byron.*

FOR Pleasures past I do not grieve,
Nor Perils gathering near;
My greatest Grief is that I leave
No thing that claims a Tear.

Mental Anguish. — *Shakspeare.*

ALAS, how is't with you?
That you do bend your eye on Vacancy,
And with the incorporal air do hold discourse?
Forth at your eyes your Spirits wildly peep;
And, as sleeping Soldiers in the alarm,
Your bedded hair, like Life in excrements,
Starts up, and stands on end.

Mental Anguish. — *Shakspeare.*

HIS flaw'd Heart,
(Alack, too weak the conflict to support!)
'Twixt two extremes of passion, Joy and Grief,
Burst smilingly.

Mental Anguish. — *Shakspeare.*

WHEN I would pray and think, I think and pray
To several subjects: Heaven in my mouth,
As if I did but only chew His name;
And in my Heart, the strong and swelling evil
Of my Conception.

Mental Anguish. —*Byron.*

I FLY, like a Bird of the air,
In search of a home and a rest;
A balm for the sickness of Care:
A Bliss for a bosom unblest.

Mental Anguish. —*Milton.*

RETIRING from the popular noise, I seek
This unfrequented place to find some ease,
Ease to the body some, none to the mind
From restless thoughts, that like a deadly swarm
Of Hornets arm'd, no sooner found alone,
But rush upon me thronging, and present
Time past, what once I was, and what am now.

Mental Anguish. — *Shakspeare.*

WHAT is in thy Mind,
That makes thee stare thus? Wherefore breaks that sigh
From the inward of thee? One, but painted thus,
Would be interpreted a thing perplex'd
Beyond self-explication.

Mental Anguish. — *Shakspeare.*

TELL me, what is't that takes from thee
Thy stomach, Pleasure, and thy golden Sleep;
Why dost thou bend thine eyes upon the Earth;
And start so often, when thou sitt'st alone?
Why hast thou lost the fresh blood in thy cheeks;
And given my treasures, and my rights of thee,
To thick-eyed Musing, and cursed Melancholy?
In thy faint slumbers I by thee have watch'd,
And heard thee murmur tales of iron Wars,
And all the currents of a heady Fight.
Thy Spirit within thee hath been so at war,
And thus hath so bestirr'd thee in thy sleep,
That beads of Sweat have stood upon thy brow,
Like bubbles in a late disturbed stream:
And in thy face strange motions have appear'd,
Such as we see, when men restrain their Breath
On some great sudden haste. Oh what Portents are these?

Mental Anguish. — *Milton.*

OH might I here
In solitude live Savage, in some glade
Obscured, where highest woods impenetrable
To star or sun-light, spread their umbrage broad
And brown as evening: cover me ye Pines,
Ye Cedars, with innumerable boughs
Hide me, where I may never see them more.

Mental Anguish. — *Shakspeare.*

GRIEVED I, I had but one?
Chid I for That at frugal Nature's frame?
I've one too much by thee. Why had I one?
Why ever wast thou lovely in my eyes?
Why had I not, with charitable hand,
Took up a Beggar's issue at my gates?
Who smeer'd thus, and mired with infamy,
I might have said, no part of it is mine;
This Shame derives itself from unknown loins:
But mine, and mine I loved, and mine I praised,
And mine that I was proud on, mine so much,
That I myself was to myself not mine,
Valuing of her; why, she,—Oh, she is fall'n
Into a pit of Ink, that the wide Sea
Hath drops too few to wash her clean again;
And Salt too little which may season give
To her foul tainted Flesh!

Mental Anguish. — *Shakspeare.*

BETWEEN the acting of a dreadful thing,
And the first motion, all the interim is
Like a Phantasma, or a hideous dream:
The Genius, and the mortal instruments,
Are then in council; and the state of a man,
Like to a little Kingdom, suffers then
The nature of an insurrection.

Mental Anguish. — *Shakspeare.*

MY Mind is troubled like a Fountain stirr'd;
And I myself see not the bottom of it.

Mental Anguish. — *Byron.*

To be thus—
Gray-hair'd with anguish, like these blasted pines,
Wrecks of a single Winter, barkless, branchless,
A blighted trunk upon a cursed root,
Which but supplies a feeling to decay—
And to be thus, eternally but thus,
Having been otherwise! Now furrow'd o'er
With wrinkles, plough'd by moments, not by Years;
And hours—all tortured into ages—hours
Which I outlive! Ye toppling crags of Ice!
Ye Avalanches, whom a breath draws down
In mountainous o'erwhelming, come and crush me!
I hear ye momently above, beneath,
Crash with a frequent Conflict; but ye pass,
And only fall on things that still would live.

Mental Anguish. — *Joanna Baillie.*

OH that I were upon some desert coast!
Where howling Tempests and the Lashing Tide
Would stun me into deep and senseless Quiet!
Come Madness! come unto me, senseless Death!
I cannot suffer this! Here, rocky wall,
Scatter these Brains, or dull them!

Mental Anguish. — *Shakspeare.*

YET could I bear that too; well, very well:
But there, where I have garner'd up my Heart;
Where either I must live, or bear no Life;
The fountain from the which my current runs,
Or else dries up; to be discarded thence!
Or keep it as a cistern, for foul toads
To knot and gender in! turn thy Complexion there!
Patience, thou young and rose-lipp'd Cherubin;
Ay, there, look grim as Hell!

Mental Anguish. — *Shakspeare.*

HAD it pleased Heaven
To try me with Affliction; had he rain'd
All kinds of sores, and shames, on my bare Head;
Steep'd me in Poverty to the very lips;
Given to Captivity me and my utmost hopes;
I should have found in some part of my Soul
A drop of Patience: but (alas!) to make me
A fixed figure, for the type of Scorn
To point his low, unmoving finger at,—
Oh! Oh!

Mental Anguish. — *Shakspeare.*

PR'YTHEE, lead me in:
There take an inventory of all I have,
To the last penny; 'tis the King's; my robe,
And my integrity to Heaven, is all
I dare now call my own. O Cromwell, Cromwell,
Had I but served my God with half the zeal
I served my King, he would not in mine age
Have left me naked to mine Enemies.

Mental Anguish. — *Shakspeare.*

WE'LL no more meet, no more see one another:
But yet thou art my flesh, my blood, my Daughter,
Or, rather, a Disease that's in my flesh,
Which I must needs call mine; thou art a boil,
A plague-sore, or imboss'd Carbuncle,
In my corrupted Blood: But I'll not chide thee.

Mental Anguish. — *Byron.*

LOOK on me in my Sleep,
Or watch my watchings—Come and sit by me!
My Solitude is Solitude no more,
But peopled with the Furies:—I have gnash'd
My teeth in darkness till returning morn,
Then cursed myself till sunset;—I have pray'd
For Madness as a blessing—'tis denied me.

Mental Anguish. — *Shakspeare.*

CANST thou not minister to a Mind diseased;
Pluck from the Memory a rooted Sorrow;
Raze out the written troubles of the Brain;
And, with some sweet oblivious Antidote,
Cleanse the foul bosom of that perilous stuff,
Which weighs upon the Heart?

Mental Anguish. — *Shakspeare.*

SOME strange commotion
Is in his Brain: he bites his Lip, and starts:
Stops on a sudden, looks upon the ground,
Then lays his finger on his Temple; straight,
Springs out into fast gait; then, stops again,
Strikes his Breast hard; and anon, he casts
His eye against the Moon; in most strange postures
We have seen him set himself.

Mental Anguish. — *Shakspeare.*

O VANITY of Sickness! fierce extremes,
In their continuance, will not feel themselves.
Death, having prey'd upon the outward parts,
Leaves them insensible; and his Siege is now
Against the Mind, the which he pricks and wounds
With many Legions of strange fantasies,
Which, in their throng and press to that last hold,
Confound themselves.

Mercy. — *Spenser.*

SOME clarkes doe doubt in their devicefull art
Whether this Heavenly thing whereof I treat,
To weeten Mercie, be of Justice part,
Or drawne forth from her by divine entreate;
This well I wote, that sure she is as great,
And meriteth to have as high a place,
Sith in the Almightie's everlasting seat,
She first was bred, and born of heavenly race,
From thence pour'd down on men by influence of Grace.

Mercy. — *Moore.*

OF God she sung, and of the mild
Attendant Mercy, that beside
His awful throne for ever smiled,
Ready, with her white hand, to guide
His bolts of vengeance to their prey—
That she might quench them on their way!

Mercy. — *Shakspeare.*

How would you be,
If He, which is the top of Judgment, should
But judge you as you are? Oh, think on that,
And Mercy then will breathe within your lips,
Like man new made.

Mercy. — *Shakspeare.*

THE quality of Mercy is not strain'd :
It droppeth, as the gentle rain from Heaven
Upon the place beneath : it is twice bless'd;
It blesseth him that gives, and him that takes :
'Tis mightiest in the mightiest : it becomes
The throned Monarch better than his Crown :
His Sceptre shows the force of temporal power,
The attribute to awe and majesty,
Wherein doth sit the dread and fear of kings;
But Mercy is above this scepter'd sway,
It is an attribute to God himself;
And earthly power doth then show likest God's,
When Mercy seasons Justice.
Consider this,—
That, in the course of Justice, none of us
Should see Salvation : we do pray for Mercy;
And that same prayer doth teach us all to render
The deeds of Mercy.

Mercy. — *Shakspeare.*

WILT thou draw near the nature of the Gods?
Draw near them then in being merciful :
Sweet Mercy is Nobility's true badge.

Merit. — *La Rochefoucauld.*

ELEVATION is to Merit what Dress is to a handsome person.

Merit. — *La Rochefoucauld.*

THERE is Merit without Elevation, but there is no Elevation without some Merit.

Merit. — *La Rochefoucauld.*

THE mark of extraordinary Merit is to see those most envious of it constrained to praise.

Merit. — *La Bruyere.*

I AM told so many ill things of a man, and I see so few in him, that I begin to suspect he has a real but troublesome Merit, as being likely to eclipse that of others.

Merit. — *La Rochefoucauld.*

THE art of being able to make a good use of moderate abilities wins Esteem, and often confers more Reputation than real Merit.

Merit. — *La Rochefoucauld.*

NATURE creates Merit, and Fortune brings it into play.

Merit. — *Queen Christina.*

MERIT is boin with Men; happy those with whom it dies.

Mind. — *Goldsmith.*

THE Little Mind who loves itself, will write and think with the vulgar; but the Great Mind will be bravely eccentric, and scorn the beaten road, from universal Benevolence.

Mind. — *Swift.*

A WISE Man is never less alone, than when he is alone.

Mind. — *Gallus.*

WE in vain summon the Mind to intense application, when the Body is in a languid state.

Mind. — *Colton.*

IF the most skilful Musician in the world were placed before an unstrung or broken instrument, he could not produce the Harmony which he was accustomed to do when that instrument was perfect, nay, on the contrary, the sounds would be discordant; and yet it would be manifestly most illogical to conclude, from such an effect, that the powers of the Musician were impaired, since they merely appeared to be so from the imperfection of the instrument. Now what the Instrument is to the Musician, the Brain may be to the Mind, for aught we know to the contrary; and to pursue the figure, as the musician has an existence distinct from that of the instrument, so the Mind may have an existence distinct from that of the Brain; for in truth we have no proof whatever of Mind being a property dependent upon any arrangement of Matter. We perceive, indeed, the properties of Matter wonderfully modified in the various things of the Universe, which strike our senses with the force of their Sublimity or Beauty; but in all these we recognise certain radical and common properties, that bear no conceivable relation to those mysterious capacities of Thought and of Feeling, referable to that something which, to designate and distinguish from Matter, we term Mind. In this way, I conceive, the Common Sense of Mankind has made the distinction which everywhere obtains between Mind and Matter; for it is natural to conclude, that the essence of Mind may be distinct from the essence of Matter, as the operations of the one are so distinct from the properties of the other. But when we say that Mind is immaterial, we only mean that it has not the properties of Matter; for the consciousness which informs us of the operations, does not reveal the abstract nature of Mind, neither do the properties reveal the essence of Matter.

Mind. — *Fuller.*

HARD, rugged, and dull natures of youth acquit themselves afterward the Jewels of the Countrey, and therefore their dulnesse at first is to be borne with, if they be diligent. That schoolmaster deserves to be beaten himself who beats Nature in a boy for a fault. And I question whether all the whipping in the world can make their parts, which are naturally sluggish, rise one minute before the houre Nature hath appointed.

Mind. — *Novalis.*

A CERTAIN degree of Solitude seems necessary to the full growth and spread of the highest Mind; and therefore must a very extensive Intercourse with Men stifle many a holy germ, and scare away the gods, who shun the restless tumult of noisy Companies and the discussion of petty Interests.

Mind. — *Colton.*

WE may also doubt about the existence of Matter as learnedly and as long as we please, as some have done before us, and yet we shall not establish the existence of Matter by any such dubitations; but the moment we begin to doubt about the existence of Mind, the very act of doubting proves it.

Mind. — *La Rochefoucauld.*

INTREPIDITY is an extraordinary strength of Mind, which raises it above the troubles, the disorders, and the emotions, which the sight of great perils is calculated to excite; it is by this strength that Heroes maintain themselves in a tranquil state of Mind, and preserve the free use of their Reason under the most surprising and terrible circumstances.

Mind. — *Terence.*

NO man was ever so completely skilled in the conduct of Life, as not to receive new information from Age and Experience; insomuch that we find ourselves really ignorant of what we thought we understood, and see cause to reject what we fancied our truest Interest.

Mind. — *Anon.*

THE blessing of an active Mind, when it is in a good condition, is, that it not only employs itself, but is almost sure to be the means of giving wholesome Employment to others.

Mind. — *La Bruyere.*

THE Mind, like all other things, will become impaired; the Sciences are its food; they nourish, but at the same they consume it.

Mind. — *Babo.*

AS it is in himself alone that Man can find true and enduring Happiness, so in himself alone can he find true and efficient Consolation in Misfortune.

Mind. — *Seneca.*

AS the Soil, however rich it may be, cannot be productive without Culture, so the Mind without Cultivation can never produce good Fruit.

Mind. — *Lord Chesterfield.*

FRIVOLOUS Curiosity about trifles, and laborious attention to little objects, which neither require nor deserve a moment's thought, lower a Man, who from thence is thought (and not unjustly) incapable of greater Matters. Cardinal de Retz very sagaciously marked out Cardinal Chigi for a little mind, from the moment he told him that he had wrote three years with the same Pen, and that it was an excellent good one still.

Mind. — *Seneca.*

TO see a man fearless in Dangers, untainted with Lusts, happy in Adversity, composed in a tumult, and laughing at all those things which are generally either coveted or feared, all men must acknowledge that this can be nothing else but a beam of Divinity that influences a mortal body.

Mind. — *La Rochefoucauld.*

WE find means to cure Folly, but none to reclaim a distorted Mind.

Mind. — *Pope.*

I BELIEVE it is no wrong observation, that persons of Genius, and those who are most capable of Art, are always most fond of Nature: as such are chiefly sensible, that all Art consists in the imitation and study of Nature. On the contrary, people of the common level of understanding are principally delighted with the little niceties and fantastical operations of Art, and constantly think that finest which is least natural.

Mind. — *Fuller.*

IF thou desirest Ease, in the first place take care of the Ease of thy Mind; for that will make all other sufferings easy: But nothing can support a Man whose Mind is wounded.

Mind. — *Shakspeare.*

FOR Nature, crescent, does not grow alone
In Thews and Bulk; but as this Temple waxes,
The inward service of the Mind and Soul
Grows wide withal.

Mind. — *Shakspeare.*

'Tis the Mind that makes the Body rich;
And as the Sun breaks through the darkest clouds,
So Honour peereth in the meanest habit.
What, is the Jay more precious than the Lark,
Because his Feathers are more beautiful?
Or is the Adder better than the Eel,
Because his painted skin contents the eye?

Mind. — *Goldsmith.*

A MIND too vigorous and active serves only to consume the Body to which it is joined, as the richest Jewels are soonest found to wear their Settings.

Mind. — *Colton.*

HE that has no resources of Mind, is more to be pitied than he who is in want of necessaries for the Body; and to be obliged to beg our daily Happiness from others, bespeaks a more lamentable Poverty than that of him who begs his daily bread.

Mind. — *Goldsmith.*

FOR just Experience tells, in ev'ry soil,
That those who think must govern those that toil;
And all that Freedom's highest aims can reach
Is but to lay proportion'd loads on each.

Mind. — *Young.*

Our outward act, indeed, admits restraint,
'Tis not in things o'er Thought to domineer;
Guard well thy Thoughts: our Thoughts are heard in Heaven

Mind. — *Shakspeare.*

This man so complete,
Who was enroll'd 'mongst wonders, and when we,
Almost with list'ning ravish'd, could not find
His hour of speech, a minute; he, my Lady,
Hath into monstrous Habits put the Graces
That once were his; and is become as black,
As if besmear'd in Hell.

Mind. — *Brown.*

THERE is a Rabble amongst the Gentry, as well as the Commonalty, a sort of plebeian heads, whose fancy moves with the same wheel as these men—in the same level with mechanics; though their Fortunes do somewhat gild their infirmities, and their Purses compound for their Follies.

The Mind. — *Young.*

A Soul without Reflection, like a Pile
Without Inhabitant, to ruin runs.

The Mind. — *Anon.*

A WEAK Mind sinks under Prosperity, as well as under Adversity. A strong and deep Mind has two highest tides,—when the Moon is at the full, and when there is no Moon.

Mind Uncultivated. — *Shakspeare.*

'Tis an unweeded Garden,
That grows to Seed; things rank, and gross in nature,
Possess it merely.

Mirth. — *Peter Pindar.*

Care to our Coffin adds a nail, no doubt;
And ev'ry Grin so merry draws one out.

Miseries. — *Colton.*

SMALL Miseries, like small Debts, hit us in so many places, and meet us at so many turns and corners, that what they want in weight, they make up in number, and render it less hazardous to stand the fire of one Cannon Ball, than a Volley composed of such a shower of Bullets.

Miseries. — *Greville.*

IT is often better to have a great deal of Harm to happen to one than a little: a great deal may rouse you to remove what a little will only accustom you to endure.

Miseries. — *Shakspeare.*

MEN'S natures wrangle with inferior things,
Though great ones are their object. 'Tis even so;
For let our Finger ache, and it indues
Our other healthful members ev'n to that sense
Of Pain.

Miseries. — *Plutarch.*

AS small letters hurt the Sight, so do small matters him that is too much intent upon them: they vex and stir up Anger, which begets an evil habit in him in reference to greater Affairs.

Misery. — *Shakspeare.*

Famine is in thy cheeks,
Need and Oppression starveth in thy eyes,
Upon thy back hangs ragged Misery,
The world is not thy Friend, nor the world's law.

Misfortunes. — *Joanna Baillie.*

Those who bear Misfortunes over meekly
Do but persuade mankind that they and Want
Are all too fitly match'd to be disjoin'd,
And so to it they leave them.

Misfortune. — *Addison.*

A Soul exasperated in ills, falls out
With every thing, its Friend, itself.

Misfortune. — *Shakspeare.*

THO' now this grained face of mine be hid
In sap-consuming Winter's drizzled snow,
And all the conduits of my Blood froze up;
Yet hath my night of life some memory;
My wasting lamp some fading Glimmer left,
My dull, deaf ears a little use to hear.

Misfortune. — *Shakspeare.*

TIME hath not yet so dried this Blood of mine,
Nor Age so eat up my invention,
Nor Fortune made such havock of my Means,
Nor my bad life reft me so much of Friends
But they shall find awaked, in such a kind,
Both strength of limb, and policy of Mind,
Ability in Means, and choice of Friends
To quit me of them thoroughly.

Misfortune. — *Shakspeare.*

ALL things, that we ordained Festival,
Turn from their office to black Funeral:
Our instruments to melancholy bells;
Our Wedding cheer to a sad burial feast;
Our solemn Hymns to sullen Dirges change;
Our bridal flowers serve for a buried corse,
And all things change them to the contrary.

Misfortune. — *La Rochefoucauld.*

WE have all of us sufficient Fortitude to bear the Misfortunes of others.

Misfortune. — *Shakspeare.*

THOU were better in thy Grave than to answer with thy uncovered body this extremity of the Skies.—Is man no more than this? Consider him well: Thou owest the Worm no silk, the Beast no hide, the Sheep no wool, the Cat no perfume: unaccommodated Man is no more but such a poor, bare, forked animal as thou art.

Misfortune. — *Shakspeare.*

Sick in the World's regard, wretched and low.

Misfortune. — *Mallet.*

Who hath not known Ill-fortune, never knew
Himself, or his own Virtue.

Misfortune. — *Shakspeare.*

My May of life
Is fall'n into the sear, the yellow leaf:
And that which should accompany old Age,
As Honour, Love, Obedience, troops of Friends,
I must not look to have; but, in their stead,
Curses, not loud, but deep, Mouth-honour, breath,
Which the poor heart would fain deny, but dare not.

Misfortune. — *Shakspeare.*

MY blood, my want of strength, my sick heart, shows
That I must yield my body to the Earth,
And, by my fall, the conquest to my foe.
Thus yields the Cedar to the axe's edge,
Whose arms gave shelter to the princely Eagle,
Under whose shade the ramping Lion slept;
Whose top-branch overpeer'd Jove's spreading tree
And kept low shrubs from Winter's powerful wind.

Misfortune. — *Shakspeare.*

A most poor man, made tame by Fortune's blows;
Who, by the art of known and feeling Sorrows,
Am pregnant to good Pity.

Misfortune. — *Shakspeare.*

Myself,
Who had the world as my Confectionary,
The mouths, the tongues, the eyes, and hearts of men
At duty, more than I could frame employment;
That numberless upon me stuck, as leaves
Do on the Oak, have with one Winter's brush
Fell from their boughs, and left me open, bare
For every Storm that blows.

Misfortune. — *Shakspeare.*

This world to me is like a lasting Storm,
Whirring me from my Friends.

Misfortune. — *Shakspeare.*

Good stars, that were my former guides,
Have empty left their Orbs, and shot their fires
Into the abysm of Hell.

Misfortune. — *Shakspeare.*

WHAT, are my doors opposed against my passage?
Have I been ever free, and must my house
Be my retentive Enemy, my Gaol?
The place, which I have feasted, does it now,
Like all Mankind, show me an iron Heart?

Misfortune.— *Shakspeare.*

'TIS certain, Greatness, once fallen out with Fortune,
Must fall out with men too: What the declined is,
He shall as soon read in the eyes of others,
As feel in his own fall: for men, like Butterflies,
Show not their mealy wings, but to the summer;
And not a man, for being simply Man,
Hath any Honour; but honour for those Honours
That are without him, as Place, Riches, Favour,
Prizes of accident as oft as Merit:
Which when they fall, as being slippery standers,
The Love that lean'd on them as slippery too,
Do one pluck down another, and together
Die in the fall.

Misfortune. — *Shakspeare.*

To some kind of men,
Their graces serve them but as enemies.—
Oh, what a World is this, when what is comely
Envenoms him that bears it!

Misfortune. — *Shakspeare.*

Oh, sick to Death:
My legs, like loaden branches, bow to the earth,
Willing to leave their Burden.

Misfortune. — *From the French.*

MISFORTUNES are, in Morals, what bitters are in medicine: each is at first disagreeable; but as the bitters act as corroborants to the stomach, so Adversity chastens and ameliorates the disposition.

Misfortune. — *From the French.*

IT is much better to endeavour to forget one's Misfortunes, than to speak often of them.

Misuse. — *Shakspeare.*

Oh, who shall believe
But you misuse the Reverence of your place;
Employ the countenance and Grace of Heaven,
As a false favourite doth his Prince's name,
In deeds dishonourable?

The Mob. — *Thomson.*

Inconstant, blind,
Deserting Friends at need, and duped by Foes;
Loud and seditious, when a Chief inspired
Their headlong fury, but, of him deprived,
Already Slaves that lick'd the scourging hand.

The Mob. — *Dryden.*

THE Scum
That rises upmost, when the Nation boils.

The Mob. — *Joanna Baillie.*

'TIS ever thus: Indulgence spoils the base;
Raising up Pride, and lawless Turbulence,
Like noxious vapours from the fulsome Marsh
When Morning shines upon it.

The Mob. — *Mackenzie.*

MANKIND in the gross is a Gaping Monster, that loves to be deceived, and has seldom been disappointed.

The Mob. — *Otway.*

THESE wide-mouth'd brutes, that bellow thus for Freedom;
Oh! how they run before the hand of Pow'r,
Flying for shelter into every Brake!

Moderation. — *Shakspeare.*

THEY are as sick that surfeit with too much, as they that starve with nothing. It is no mean Happiness, therefore, to be seated in the mean: Superfluity comes sooner by white hairs, but Competency lives longer.

Moderation. — *La Rochefoucauld.*

MODERATION is a fear of falling into envy, and into the Contempt which those deserve who become intoxicated with their Good Fortune; it is a vain ostentation of the strength of our mind; in short, the Moderation of men in their highest elevation is a desire of appearing greater than their Fortune.

Moderation. — *La Rochefoucauld.*

MODERATION is like Temperance: we should wish to eat more, but are afraid of injuring our health.

Modesty. — *Steele.*

A MODEST person seldom fails to gain the Goodwill of those he converses with, because nobody envies a man who does not appear to be pleased with himself.

Modesty. — *Young*

THAT modest Grace subdued my soul;
That chastity of look, which seems to hang
A veil of purest light o'er all her Beauties.

Modesty. — *Shakspeare.*

I ASK, that I might waken Reverence,
And bid the cheek be ready with a blush,
Modest as Morning when she coldly eyes
The youthful Phœbus.

Modesty. — *Shakspeare.*

THE chariest maid is prodigal enough,
If she unmask her beauty to the Moon:
Virtue itself 'scapes not calumnious strokes:
The canker galls the infants of the Spring,
Too oft before their buttons be disclosed;
And in the morn and liquid dew of Youth,
Contagious blastments are most imminent.
Be wary then: best Safety lies in Fear.

Modesty. — *La Bruyere.*

MODESTY is to Merit as Shades to Figures in a Picture; giving it Strength and Beauty.

Modesty. — *Addison.*

A JUST and reasonable Modesty does not only recommend Eloquence, but sets off every great talent which a man can be possessed of: it heightens all the Virtues which it accompanies; like the Shades in Paintings, it raises and rounds every Figure, and makes the colours more beautiful, though not so glaring as they would be without.

Modesty. — *Hughes.*

MERE Bashfulness without Merit is awkward: and Merit without Modesty is insolent. But Modest Merit has a double claim to acceptance.

Modesty. — *Baxter.*

YOU little know what you have done, when you have first broke the bounds of Modesty; you have set open the door of your fancy to the Devil, so that he can, almost at his pleasure ever after, represent the same sinful pleasure to you anew: he hath now access to your fancy to stir up lustful Thoughts and Desires, so that when you should think of your calling, or of your God, or of your soul, your thoughts will be worse than swinish, upon the filth that is not fit to be named. If the Devil here get in a foot, he will not easily be got out.

Money. — *Franklin.*

REMEMBER that Money is of a prolific, generating nature. Money can beget Money, and its offspring can beget more, and so on. Five shillings turned is six: turned again it is seven and threepence; and so on till it becomes a Hundred Pounds. The more there is of it, the more it produces every turning, so that the profits rise quicker and quicker. He that kills a breeding Sow, destroys all her Offspring to the thousandth generation. He that murders a Crown, destroys all that it might have produced, even Scores of Pounds.

Money. — *Colton.*

TO cure us of our immoderate Love of Gain, we should seriously consider how many goods there are that Money will not purchase, and these the best; and how many Evils there are that Money will not remedy, and these the worst.

Money and Time. — *Johnson.*

MONEY and Time are the heaviest burdens of Life, and the unhappiest of all mortals are those who have more of either than they know how to use.

Money. — *Bouhours.*

MONEY is a good Servant, but a dangerous Master.

The Moon. — *Byron.*

THE Devil's in the Moon for mischief; they
Who call'd her *chaste*, methinks, began too soon
Their nomenclature: there is not a day,
The longest, not the twenty-first of June,
Sees half the business in a wicked way
On which three single hours of Moonshine smile—
And then she looks so modest all the while.

Morality. — *Longfellow.*

MORALITY without Religion is only a kind of dead-reckoning—an endeavour to find our place on a cloudy sea by measuring the distance we have to run, but without any observation of the heavenly bodies.

Morals. — *Colton.*

THERE are two principles of established acceptance in Morals; first, that Self-interest is the main spring of all our actions, and, secondly, that Utility is the test of their value. Now there are some cases where these maxims are not tenable, because they are not true; for some of the noblest energies of Gratitude, of Affection, of Courage, and of Benevolence, are not resolvable into the first. If it be said indeed that these estimable qualities may after all be traced to Self-interest, because all the duties that flow from them are a source of the highest Gratification to those that perform them; this I presume savours rather too much of an identical proposition, and is only a round-about mode of informing us that virtuous men will act virtuously. Take care of Number One, says the worldling, and the Christian says so too; for he has taken the best care of Number One, who takes care that Number One shall go to Heaven: that blessed place is full of those same selfish beings who by having constantly done good to others, have as constantly gratified themselves. I humbly conceive, therefore, that it is much nearer the Truth to say that all men have an Interest in being good, than that all men are good from Interest. As to the standard of Utility, this is a mode of examining human actions that looks too much to the event; for there are occasions where a man may effect the greatest General Good by the smallest Individual Sacrifice, and there are others where he may make the greatest Individual Sacrifice, and yet produce but little General Good. If indeed the Moral Philosopher is determined to do all his work with the smallest possible quantity of tools, and would wish to cope with the Natural Philosopher, who has explained such wonders from the two simple causes of Impulse and of Gravity, in this case he must look out for maxims as universal as those occasions to which he would apply them. Perhaps he might begin by affirming with me that—Men are the same; and this will naturally lead him to another conclusion, that if men are the same, they can have but one common principle of action, the Attainment of apparent Good; those two simple truisms contain the whole of my Philosophy, and as they have not been worn out in the performance of one undertaking, I trust they will not fail me in the execution of another.

Morning. — *Shakspeare.*

HOW bloodily the Sun begins to peer
  Above yon busky hill! the day looks pale
At his distemperature.
        The southern Wind
Doth play the Trumpet to his purposes;
And, by his hollow whistling in the leaves
Foretells a Tempest, and a blustering day.

Morning. — *Milton.*

NOW the bright Morning-star, Day's harbinger,
  Comes dancing from the east, and leads with her
The flow'ry May, who from her green lap throws
The yellow Cowslip, and the pale Primrose.

Morning. — *Beattie.*

BUT who the melodies of Morn can tell?
  The wild Brook babbling down the mountain's side;
The lowing Herd; the sheepfold's simple Bell;
  The Pipe of early Shepherd dim descried
  In the lone valley; echoing far and wide
The clamorous Horn along the cliffs above;
  The hollow murmur of the Ocean tide;
The hum of Bees, the linnet's lay of Love,
And the full Choir that wakes the universal Grove.

Morning.—*Byron.*

BUT mighty Nature bounds as from her birth:
The sun is in the Heavens, and life on Earth;
Flowers in the Valley, splendour in the Beam,
Health on the Gale, and freshness in the Stream.

Morning.—*Scott.*

WHAT various scenes, and, oh! what scenes of Wo,
Are witness'd by that red and struggling beam!
The fever'd Patient, from his pallet low,
Through crowded hospitals beholds it stream;
The ruin'd Maiden trembles at its gleam,
The Debtor wakes to thought of gyve and jail,
The Love-lorn wretch starts from tormenting dream;
The wakeful mother, by the glimmering pale,
Trims her sick Infant's couch, and soothes his feeble wail.

Morning.—*Byron.*

THE Morn is up again, the dewy Morn,
With breath all incense, and with cheek all bloom,
Laughing the clouds away with playful Scorn,
And living as if Earth contain'd no tomb,—
And glowing into Day.

Morning.—*Dryden.*

THE Morning Lark, the messenger of Day,
Saluted in her song the Morning gray,
And soon the Sun arose with beams so bright
That all th' horizon laugh'd to see the joyous sight;
He with his tepid rays the Rose renews,
And licks the drooping leaves, and dries the Dews.

Morning.—*Webster.*

THE Morning itself, few people, inhabitants of cities, know any thing about. Among all our good people, not one in a thousand sees the sun rise once in a year. They know nothing of the morning. Their idea of it is that it is that part of the day which comes along after a cup of coffee and a beef-steak or a piece of toast. With them, morning is not a new issuing of light, a new bursting forth of the sun, a new waking-up of all that has life from a sort of temporary death, to behold again the works of God, the heavens and the earth: it is only a part of the domestic day, belonging to reading newspapers, answering notes, sending the children to school, and giving orders for dinner. The first streak of light, the earliest purpling of the east, which the lark springs up to greet, and the deeper and deeper colouring into orange and red, till at length the "glorious sun is seen, regent of the day"—this they never enjoy, for they never see it. I never thought that Adam had much the advantage of us from having seen the world while it was new. The manifestations of the power of God, like his mercies, are "new every morning" and fresh every moment. We see as fine risings of the sun as ever Adam saw; and its risings are as much a miracle now as they were in his day—and, I think, a good deal more, because it is now a part of the miracle, that for thousands and thousands of years he has come to his appointed time, without the variation of a millionth part of a second. Adam could not tell how this might be. I know the morning—I am acquainted with it, and I love it. I love it fresh and sweet as it is—a daily new creation, breaking forth and calling all that have life and breath and being to new adoration, new enjoyments, and new gratitude.

Morning. — *Milton.*

AWAKE
My fairest, my espoused, my latest found,
Heaven's last Gift, my ever new delight,
Awake; the Morning shines, and the fresh field
Calls us; we lose the prime, to mark how spring
Our tender plants, how blows the citron grove,
What drops the Myrrh, and what the balmy reed,
How Nature paints her colours, how the Bee
Sits on the bloom.

Moroseness. — *Bacon.*

MEN possessing minds which are morose, solemn, and inflexible, enjoy, in general, a greater share of Dignity than of Happiness.

Motives. — *La Rochefoucauld.*

WE should often have reason to be ashamed of our most brilliant Actions, if the world could see the Motives from which they spring.

The Mountain Air. — *Byron.*

OH! there is sweetness in the Mountain Air,
And Life, that bloated Ease can never hope to share.

Murder. — *Shakspeare.*

BEYOND the infinite and boundless reach
Of mercy, if thou didst this deed of Death,
Art thou damn'd.

Murmuring. — *Colton.*

MURMUR at nothing; if our ills are reparable, it is ungrateful; if remediless, it is vain.

Music. — *Collins.*

MUSIC, sphere-descended maid,
Friend of Pleasure, Wisdom's aid!

Music. — *Shakspeare.*

DO but note a wild and wanton herd,
  Or race of youthful and unhandled colts,
Fetching mad bounds, bellowing and neighing loud,
Which is the hot condition of their Blood;
If they but hear perchance a Trumpet sound,
Or any air of Music touch their ears,
You shall perceive them make a mutual stand,
Their savage eyes turn'd to a modest gaze,
By the sweet power of Music: Therefore, the poet
Did feign, that Orpheus drew Trees, stones, and floods;
Since naught so stockish, hard, and full of rage,
But Music for the time doth change his nature.
The man that hath no Music in himself,
Nor is not moved with Concord of sweet Sounds,
Is fit for Treasons, stratagems, and spoils;
The motions of his Spirit are dull as night,
And his affections dark as Erebus:
Let no such man be trusted.

Music. — *Greville.*

A GOOD *ear* for music, and a *taste* for Music are two very different things which are often confounded: and so is *comprehending* and *enjoying* every object of Sense and Sentiment.

Music. — *Shakspeare.*

WHEN griping Grief the Heart doth wound,
  And doleful dumps the Mind oppress,
Then Music, with her silver sound,
  With speedy help doth lend redress.

Music. — *Moore.*

MUSIC!—oh! how faint, how weak,
  Language fades before thy spell!
Why should Feeling ever speak,
  When thou can'st breathe her Soul so well?
Friendship's balmy words may feign,
  Love's are ev'n more false than they;
Oh! 'tis only Music's strain
  Can sweetly soothe, and not betray!

Music. — *Montgomery.*

THROUGH every pulse the Music stole,
And held sublime communion with the Soul;
Wrung from the coyest Breast the imprison'd sigh,
And kindled rapture in the coldest Eye.

Music. — *Pope.*

BY Music, minds an equal temper know,
Nor swell too high, nor sink too low:
If in the Breast tumultuous joys arise,
Music her soft assuasive voice applies;
Or, when the Soul is press'd with cares,
Exalts her in enliv'ning airs.
Warriors she fires with animated sounds,
Pours balm into the bleeding Lover's wounds:
Melancholy lifts her head,
Morpheus rouses from his bed,
Sloth unfolds her arms and wakes,
List'ning Envy drops her snakes;
Intestine War no more our passions wage,
And giddy Factions hear away their rage.

Music. — *Beattie.*

IS there a Heart that Music cannot melt?
Alas! how is that rugged heart forlorn;
Is there, who ne'er those mystic transports felt
Of Solitude and Melancholy born!
He needs not woo the Muse; he is her scorn.
The sophist's rope of cobweb he shall twine;
Mope o'er the schoolman's peevish page; or mourn,
And delve for life in Mammon's dirty mine;
Sneak with the scoundrel Fox, or grunt with glutton Swine.

Music. — *Moore.*

FOR mine is the Lay that lightly floats,
And mine are the murmuring dying notes,
That fall as soft as Snow on the sea,
And melt in the Heart as instantly!
And the passionate strain that, deeply going,
Refines the Bosom it trembles through,
As the musk-wind, over the water blowing,
Ruffles the wave, but sweetens it too!

Music. — *Shakspeare.*

PREPOSTEROUS ass! that never read so far
To know the cause why Music was ordain'd!
Was it not to refresh the mind of man,
After his studies, or his usual Pain?

Music. — *Shakspeare.*

THIS Music crept by me upon the waters;
Allaying both their Fury, and my Passion,
With its sweet Air.

Mystery. — *Chesterfield.*

A PROPER Secrecy is the only mystery of able Men; Mystery is the only Secrecy of weak and cunning ones.

Mystery. — *Colton.*

MYSTERY magnifies Danger, as a fog the Sun.

Mystery. — *Tom Brown.*

CONSIDER that the trade of a vintner is a perfect Mystery, (for that is the term the law bestows on it;) now, as all Mysteries in the world are wholly supported by hard and unintelligible terms, so you must take care to christen your Wines by some hard names, the farther fetched so much the better; and this policy will serve to recommend the most execrable stuff in all your cellar. A plausible name to an indifferent Wine is what a gaudy title is to a Fop, or fine clothes to a Woman: it helps to conceal the defects it has, and bespeaks the world in its favour. Men naturally love to be cheated, and provided the imposition is not too barefaced, will meet you half-way with all their Hearts.

Power of Names. — *Zimmerman.*

WITH the vulgar, and the learned, Names have great weight; the wise use a writ of inquiry into their legitimacy when they are advanced as authorities.

Narrow Mind. — *Addison.*

A MAN who has been brought up among Books, and is able to talk of nothing else, is a very indifferent companion, and what we call a Pedant. But we should enlarge the title, and give it to every one that does not know how to think out of his Profession and particular way of Life.

Narrow Mind. — *La Bruyere.*

SHORT-SIGHTED people,—I mean such who have but narrow Conceptions, never extended beyond their own little sphere,—cannot comprehend that universality of Talents which is sometimes observable in one person. They allow no solidity in whatever is agreeable: or when they see in any one the graces of the Body, activity, suppleness, and dexterity, they conclude he wants the endowments of the Mind, Judgment, Prudence, and Perspicacity Let History say what it will, they will not believe that Socrates ever danced.

Fall of Nations. — *Bacon.*

IN the Youth of a state, Arms do flourish: in the Middle Age of a state, Learning; and then both of them together for a time; in the Declining Age of a state, Mechanical Arts and Merchandise.

Fall of Nations. — *Byron.*

THERE is the moral of all human tales;
'Tis but the same rehearsal of the past,
First Freedom, and then Glory—when that fails,
Wealth, Vice, Corruption—Barbarism at last.
And History, with all her volumes vast,
Hath but one page.

National Character. — *Clay.*

A NATION'S Character is the sum of its splendid deeds; they constitute one common patrimony, the nation's inheritance. They awe foreign powers, they arouse and animate our own people.

Nature. — *Young.*

LOOK Nature through, 'tis revolution all;
All change; no Death. Day follows Night; and Night
The dying Day; Stars rise, and set, and rise;
Earth takes th' example. See, the Summer gay,
With her green chaplet, and ambrosial flowers,
Droops into pallid Autumn: Winter gray,
Horrid with frost, and turbulent with storm,
Blows Autumn, and his golden fruits, away:
Then melts into the Spring: soft Spring, with breath
Favonian, from warm chambers of the south,
Recalls the first. All, to re-flourish, fades;
As in a wheel, all sinks, to reascend.
Emblems of Man, who passes, not expires.

Nature. — *Shakspeare.*

HATH not old custom made this life more sweet
Than that of painted Pomp? Are not these woods
More free from peril than the envious Court?
Here feel we but the penalty of Adam,
The Season's difference; as, the icy fang,
And churlish chiding of the Winter's wind;
Which, when it bites and blows upon my body,
Even till I shrink with cold, I smile, and say,—
This is no flattery; these are Counsellors
That feelingly persuade me what I am.
And this our Life, exempt from public haunt,
Finds tongues in Trees, books in the running Brooks,
Sermons in Stones, and good in every thing.

Nature. — *Milton.*

IN contemplation of created things
By steps we may ascend to God.

Nature. — *Shakspeare.*

All love the womb that their first beings bred.

Nature. — *Young.*

Who lives to Nature, rarely can be poor;
Who lives to Fancy, never can be rich.

Nature. — *Thomson.*

Who can paint
Like Nature? Can Imagination boast,
Amid its gay creation, hues like hers?
Or can it mix them with that matchless skill,
And lose them in each other, as appears
In every Bud that blows?

Nature. — *Byron.*

Not vainly did the early Persian make
His Altar the high places and the peak
Of earth—o'er gazing mountains, and thus take
A fit and unwall'd Temple, there to seek
The Spirit, in whose honour shrines are weak,
Uprear'd of Human Hands. Come, and compare
Columns and idol-dwellings, Goth, or Greek,
With Nature's realms of worship, Earth and Air,
Nor fix on fond abodes to circumscribe thy prayer!

Nature. — *Thomson.*

Nature! Great Parent! whose unceasing hand
Rolls round the seasons of the changeful year,
How mighty, how majestic, are thy works!
With what a pleasing Dread they swell the soul!
That sees astonish'd! and astonish'd sings!

Nature. — *Byron.*

Live not the Stars and Mountains? Are the waves
Without a Spirit? Are the dropping caves
Without a feeling in their silent Tears?
No, No;—they woo and clasp us to their spheres,
Dissolve this clog and clod of clay before
Its hour, and merge our Soul in the great shore.

Nature. — *Shakspeare.*

The Earth, that's Nature's mother, is her tomb;
What is her burying Grave, that is her womb:
And from her womb, children of divers kind,
We sucking on her natural Bosom find;
Many for many virtues excellent,
None but for some, and yet all different.

Nature. — *Byron.*

THERE'S Music in the sighing of a reed;
There's Music in the gushing of a rill;
There's Music in all things, if men had ears;
Their Earth is but an echo of the spheres.

Nature. — *Byron.*

WHERE rose the Mountains, there to him were friends;
Where roll'd the Ocean, thereon was his home;
Where a blue sky, and glowing clime extends,
He had the Passion and the power to roam:
The Desert, Forest, Cavern, Breaker's foam,
Were unto him companionship; they spake
A mutual language, clearer than the tone
Of his land's Tongue, which he would oft forsake
For Nature's pages glass'd by sunbeams on the lake.

Nature. — *Beattie.*

O NATURE, how in every charm supreme!
Whose votaries feast on raptures ever new!
Oh for the voice and fire of Seraphim,
To sing thy Glories with devotion due!
Blest be the day I 'scaped the wrangling crew,
From Pyrrho's maze, and Epicurus' sty;
And held high converse with the godlike few,
Who to th' enraptured Heart, and ear, and eye,
Teach Beauty, Virtue, Truth, and Love, and Melody

Nature. — *Dryden.*

BY viewing Nature, Nature's handmaid, Art,
Makes mighty things from small beginnings grow:
Thus Fishes first to Shipping did impart,
Their tail the Rudder, and their head the Prow.

Nature. — *Pope.*

SEE, through this Air, this Ocean, and this Earth,
All matter quick, and bursting into birth.
Above, how high progressive life may go!
Around, how wide! how deep extend below!
Vast chain of Being! which from God began,
Nature's ethereal, human, angel, man;
Beast, Bird, Fish, Insect—what no eye can see,
No glass can reach, from infinite to Thee,
From Thee to nothing.

Nature. — *Juvenal.*

NATURE never says that which Wisdom will contradict.

Nature. — *Cowper.*

SCENES must be beautiful which daily view'd
Please daily, and whose novelty survives
Long Knowledge and the scrutiny of Years.

Nature. — *Shakspeare.*

OH, mickle is the powerful grace that lies
In Herbs, Plants, Stones, and their true qualities:
For naught so vile, that on the earth doth live,
But to the Earth some special good doth give;
Nor aught so good, but, strain'd from that fair use,
Revolts from true birth, stumbling on abuse;
Virtue itself turns Vice, being misapplied;
And Vice sometime's by action dignified.

Nature. — *Anon.*

ANY thing may become Nature to Man: the rare thing is to find a Nature that is truly natural.

Nature. — *Anon.*

NATURE is mighty. Art is mighty. Artifice is weak. For Nature is the work of a mightier power than Man. Art is the work of Man under the guidance and inspiration of a mightier power. Artifice is the work of mere Man in the imbecility of his mimic understanding.

Nature. — *Longfellow.*

NATURE alone is permanent. Fantastic idols may be worshipped for awhile; but at length they are overturned by the continual and silent progress of Truth, as the grim statues of Copan have been pushed from their pedestals by the growth of forest-trees, whose seeds were sown by the wind in the ruined walls.

Good Nature. — *Dryden.*

GOOD Sense and Good Nature are never separated, though the ignorant world has thought otherwise. Good Nature, by which I mean Beneficence and Candour, is the product of Right Reason

The Negative. — *Greville.*

THERE is in some men a dispassionate Neutrality of Mind, which, though it generally passes for Good Temper, can neither gratify nor warm us: it must indeed be granted that these men can only negatively offend; but then it should also be remembered that they cannot positively please.

The Negative. — *Lavater.*

HE that has no Friend and no Enemy is one of the vulgar; and without Talents, Powers, or Energy.

The Negative. — *Shenstone.*

WHAT numbers live to the age of fifty or sixty years! yet, if estimated by their Merit, are not worth the price of a Chick the moment it is hatched.

The Newspaper. — *Bishop Horne.*

THE follies, vices, and consequent miseries of multitudes, displayed in a Newspaper, are so many admonitions and warnings, so many Beacons, continually burning, to turn others from the Rocks on which they have been shipwrecked.

Newspaper Marvels. — *Fisher Ames.*

IT seems really as if our Newspapers were busy to spread superstition. Omens, and dreams, and prodigies are recorded, as if they were worth minding. The increasing fashion for printing wonderful tales of crimes and accidents is worse than ridiculous, as it corrupts both the public taste and morals. It multiplies fables, prodigious monsters, and crimes, and thus makes shocking things familiar; while it withdraws all popular attention from familiar truth, because it is not shocking. Surely, extraordinary events have not the best title to our studious attention. To study nature or man, we ought to know things that are in the ordinary course, not the unaccountable things that happen out of it.

Night. — *Shakspeare.*

HOW sweet the Moonlight sleeps upon this bank!
Here will we sit, and let the sounds of Music
Creep in our ears; soft Stillness, and the Night
Become the touches of sweet Harmony.
Look, how the floor of Heav'n
Is thick inlaid with patines of bright gold;
There's not the smallest Orb, which thou behold'st,
But in his motion like an Angel sings,
Still quiring to the young-eyed Cherubins;
Such harmony is in immortal sounds!
But whilst this muddy vesture of decay
Doth grossly close us in, we cannot hear it.

Night. — *Spenser.*

UNDER thy mantle black ther hidden lye
Light-shonning Thefte, and traiterous Intent,
Abhorr'd Bloodshed, and vile Felony,
Shameful Deceipt and Daunger imminent,
Fowle Horror, and eke Hellish Dreriment.

Night. — *Byron.*

THE Night
Shows Stars and Women in a better light.

Night. — *Byron.*

'TIS Midnight: on the Mountain's brown
The cold, round Moon shines deeply down:
Blue roll the waters, blue the sky
Spreads like an Ocean hung on high,
Bespangled with those isles of light,
So wildly, spiritually bright;
Who ever gazed upon them shining,
And turn'd to Earth without repining,
Nor wish'd for Wings to flee away,
And mix with their eternal ray.

Night. — *Young.*

THE Sun went down in clouds, and seem'd to mourn
The sad necessity of his return;
The hollow wind, and melancholy rain,
Or did, or was imagined, to complain:
The tapers cast an inauspicious light;
Stars there were none, and doubly dark the Night.

Night. — *Spenser.*

NOW gan the golden Phœbus for to steepe
His fierie face in billowes of the west,
And his faint Steedes watred in Ocean deepe.
Whiles from their journall labours they did rest.

Night. — *Spenser.*

WHERE griesly Night, with visage deadly sad,
That Phœbus' chearefull face dust never vew,
And in a foule blacke pitchy Mantle clad,
She findes forth coming from her darksome mew,
Where she all day did hide her hated hew;
Before the dore her yron Charet stood
Already harnessed for a journey new;
And coleblacke steeds yborne of Hellish brood,
That on their rusty bits did champ as they were wood.

The Night. — *Milton.*

WHY sleep'st thou, Eve? now is the pleasant time,
The cool, the silent, save where Silence yields
To the Night-warbling Bird, that now awake,
Tunes sweetest his love-labour'd song; now reigns
Full-orb'd the Moon, and with more pleasing light
Shadowy sets-off the face of things; in vain,
If none regard.

The Night. — *Byron.*

In her starry shade
Of dim and solitary Loveliness,
I learn the language of another World.

The Night. — *Byron.*

All is gentle: naught
Stirs rudely; but congenial with the Night,
Whatever walks is gliding like a Spirit.

The Night. — *Byron.*

HOW sweet and soothing is this hour of Calm!
I thank thee, Night! for thou hast chased away
These horrid bodements which, amidst the throng,
I could not dissipate: and with the Blessing
Of thy benign and quiet influence
Now will I to my couch, although to rest
Is almost wronging such a Night as this.

Night. — *Southey.*

How beautiful is Night!
A dewy freshness fills the silent air,
No mist obscures, nor cloud, nor speck, nor stain,
Breaks the serene of Heaven:
In full-orb'd Glory yonder Moon divine
Rolls through the dark blue depths.
Beneath her steady ray
The desert circle spreads
Like the round Ocean, girdled with the sky.

Night. — *Young.*

DARKNESS has divinity for me;
It strikes thought inward; it drives back the Soul
To settle on herself, our point supreme!
There lies our Theatre; there sits our judge.
Darkness the curtain drops o'er Life's dull scene;
'Tis the kind hand of Providence stretch'd out
'Twixt Man and Vanity: 'tis Reason's reign,
And Virtue's too; these tutelary shades
Are Man's asylum from the tainted throng.
Night is the good man's friend, and guardian too;
It no less rescues Virtue, than inspires.

Night. — *Shakspeare.*

DARK Night, that from the Eye his function takes,
The Ear more quick of Apprehension makes;
Wherein it doth impair the seeing sense,
It pays the hearing double recompense.

The Night.—*Young.*

NIGHT, sable Goddess! from her ebon throne,
In rayless Majesty, now stretches forth
Her leaden sceptre o'er a slumb'ring world.
Silence, how dead! and Darkness, how profound!
Nor eye, nor list'ning ear, an object finds;
Creation sleeps. 'Tis as the general pulse
Of Life stood still, and Nature made a pause;
An awful pause! prophetic of her end.

The Night.—*Young.*

THIS sacred Shade, and Solitude, what is it?
'Tis the felt presence of the Deity.
Few are the faults we flatter when alone.
Vice sinks in her allurements, is ungilt,
And looks, like other objects, black by Night.
By Night an Atheist half-believes a God.

The Night.—*Young.*

HOW is Night's sable mantle labour'd o'er,
How richly wrought with attributes divine!
What Wisdom shines! what Love! This Midnight pomp,
This gorgeous Arch, with golden worlds inlaid!
Built with divine Ambition.

The Nightingale.—*Shakspeare.*

THE Nightingale, if she should sing by day,
When every Goose is cackling, would be thought
No better a Musician than the wren.
How many things by season season'd are
To their right praise and true Perfection!

The Nightingale.—*Milton.*

O NIGHTINGALE, that on yon bloomy spray
Warblest at eve, when all the woods are still;
Thou with fresh hope the Lover's heart doth fill,
While the jolly hours lead on propitious May.
Thy liquid notes that close the eye of Day,
First heard before the shallow Cuckoo's bill,
Portend success in Love; Oh, if Jove's will
Have link'd that amorous power to thy soft lay,
Now timely sing, ere the rude Bird of hate
Foretell my hopeless doom in some grove nigh;
As thou from year to year hast sung too late
For my relief, yet had'st no reason why:
Whether the Muse or Love call thee his mate,
Both them I serve, and of their train am I.

The Nightingale. — *Milton.*

SWEET Bird that shunn'st the noise of folly,
Most musical, most Melancholy!

The Nightingale. — *Southern.*

THUS perch'd all Night alone in shady groves,
Tunes her soft voice to sad complaints of Love,
Making her life one great harmonious wo.

Nobility. — *Spenser.*

VAIN-GLORIOUS Man, when fluttering wind does blow
In his light winges, is lifted up to skye;
The scorne of Knighthood and trew Chevalrye,
To thinke, without desert of gentle deed,
And noble worth, to be advanced hye,
Such Praise is shame; but Honour, Vertue's meed,
Doth bear the fayrest flowre in honourable seed.

Nobility. — *Joanna Baillie.*

EVEN to the dullest Peasant standing by,
Who fasten'd still on him a wondering Eye,
He seem'd the master spirit of the Land.

Novelty. — *Shakspeare.*

NEW Customs,
Though they be never so ridiculous,
Nay, let them be unmanly, yet are follow'd.

Oaths. — *Shakspeare.*

THE gods are deaf to hot and peevish Vows;
They are polluted Offerings, more abhorr'd
Than spotted livers in the Sacrifice.

Oaths. — *Shakspeare.*

Do not give Dalliance
Too much the rein; the strongest Oaths are straw
To the fire i' the Blood; be more abstemious,
Or else!

Oaths. — *Butler.*

OATHS were not purposed, more than Law,
To keep the good and just in awe,
But to confine the bad and sinful,
Like moral Cattle, in a pinfold.

Obedience. — *Shakspeare.*

LET them obey that know how to rule.

Obedience. — *Goldsmith.*

FILIAL Obedience is the first and greatest requisite of a State; by this we become good subjects to our Emperors, capable of behaving with just subordination to our superiors, and grateful dependants on Heaven; by this we become fonder of Marriage, in order to be capable of exacting Obedience from others in our turn: by this we become good Magistrates; for early Submission is the truest lesson to those who would learn to rule. By this the whole State may be said to resemble one Family.

Obligation. — *La Rochefoucauld.*

WE are always much better pleased to see those whom we have obliged, than those who have obliged us.

Observation. — *Lavater.*

HE alone is an acute Observer, who can observe minutely without being observed.

Observation. — *Wirt.*

PERHAPS there is no property in which men are more strikingly distinguished from each other, than in the various degrees in which they possess this faculty of Observation. The great herd of mankind, the "fruges consumere nati," pass their lives in listless inattention and indifference as to what is going on around them, being perfectly content to satisfy the mere cravings of nature, while those who are destined to distinction have a lynx-eyed vigilance that nothing can escape. You see nothing of the Paul Pry in them; yet they know all that is passing, and keep a perfect reckoning, not only of every interesting passage, but of all the characters of the age who have any concern in them.

Vulgar Obstinacy. — *Swift.*

THERE are few, very few, that will own themselves in a Mistake.

Small Offences. — *Greville.*

A VERY Small Offence may be a just cause for great Resentment; it is often much less the particular instance which is obnoxious to us, than the proof it carries with it of the general tenor and disposition of the Mind from whence it sprung.

Occupation. — *Sir Philip Sidney.*

EVERY base Occupation makes one sharp in its practice, and dull in every other.

Office. — *Shakspeare.*

THOU hast seen a Farmer's dog bark at a beggar?
And the Creature run from the Cur?
There thou might'st behold the great image of Authority: a Dog's obeyed in Office.

Office. — *Shakspeare.*

COULD great men thunder
As Jove himself does, Jove would ne'er be quiet,

For every pelting, petty Officer
Would use his Heaven for thunder: nothing but thunder.—
Merciful Heaven!
Thou rather, with thy sharp and sulphurous bolt,
Split'st the unwedgeable and gnarled Oak,
Than the soft Myrtle!—Oh! but Man, proud Man,
Drest in a little brief Authority—
Most ignorant of what he's most assured,
His glassy essence,—like an angry Ape,
Plays such fantastic tricks before high Heaven,
As make the Angels weep.

Omission.—*Shakspeare.*

OMISSION to do what is necessary
Seals a commission to a blank of Danger;
And Danger, like an ague, subtly taints
Even then when we sit idly in the sun.

Opinion.—*Swift.*

THAT was excellently observed, say I, when I read a passage in an Author, where his Opinion agrees with mine.

Opinion.—*Colton.*

IT will be possible to have one set of Opinions for the high, and another for the low, only when they cease to see by the same Sun, to respire by the same Air, and to feel by the same Sensorium. For Opinions, like showers, are generated in high places, but they invariably descend into low ones, and ultimately flow down to the People, as the rains unto the Sea.

Opinion.—*Cicero.*

NO liberal man would impute a charge of Unsteadiness to another for having changed his opinion.

Opportunity.—*Shakspeare.*

TAKE the instant way;
For Honour travels in a strait so narrow,
Where one but goes abreast: keep then the path:
For Emulation hath a thousand sons,
That one by one pursue: If you give way,
Or hedge aside from the direct forthright,
Like to an enter'd Tide, they all rush by,
And leave you hindmost;—
Or, like a gallant Horse fallen in first rank,
Lie there for pavement to the abject rear,
O'er-run and trampled on.

Opportunity. — *Shakspeare.*

UNRULY blasts wait on the tender spring;
Unwholesome weeds take root with precious flowers;
The Adder hisses where the sweet birds sing;
What Virtue breeds, Iniquity devours:
We have no good that we can say is ours:
But ill annexed Opportunity
Or kills his life, or else his quality.
O Opportunity! thy Guilt is great:
'Tis thou that execut'st the traitor's Treason;
Thou set'st the Wolf where he the Lamb may get;
Whoever plots the Sin, thou 'point'st the Season;
'Tis thou that spurn'st at right, at law, at reason;
And in thy shady cell, where none may spy him,
Sits Sin, to seize the Souls that wander by him.
Thou mak'st the Vestal violate her oath:
Thou blow'st the fire when Temperance is thaw'd;
Thou smother'st Honesty, thou murder'st Troth;
Thou foul abettor! thou notorious bawd!
Thou plantest Scandal and displacest laud:
Thou ravisher, thou Traitor, thou false thief,
Thy Honey turns to gall, thy joy to grief!
Thy secret pleasure turns to open shame,
Thy private feasting to a public fast;
Thy smoothing titles to a ragged name;
Thy sugar'd tongue to bitter Wormwood taste:
Thy violent Vanities can never last.
How comes it then, vile Opportunity,
Being so bad, such numbers seek for thee?
When wilt thou be the humble suppliant's friend,
And bring him where his suit may be obtain'd?
When wilt thou sort an hour great strifes to end?
Or free that soul which Wretchedness hath chain'd?
Give Physic to the sick, Ease to the pain'd?
The poor, lame, blind, halt, creep, cry out for thee;
But they ne'er meet with Opportunity.
The Patient dies while the Physician sleeps;
The Orphan pines while the Oppressor feeds;
Justice is feasting while the Widow weeps;
Advice is sporting while Infection breeds;
Thou grant'st no time for charitable deeds;
Wrath, Envy, Treason, Rape, and Murder's rages,
Thy heinous hours wait on them as their pages.
When Truth and Virtue have to do with Thee,
A thousand crosses keep them from thy aid;

They buy thy help: but Sin ne'er gives a fee,
He gratis comes; and thou art well appay'd,
As well to hear as grant what he hath said.
Guilty thou art of Murder and of Theft;
Guilty of Perjury and Subornation;
Guilty of Treason, Forgery, and Shift;
Guilty of Incest, that abomination:
An accessary by thine inclination
To all sins past, and all that are to come,
From the Creation to the General Doom.

Opportunity. — *Shakspeare.*

THERE is a Tide in the affairs of men,
Which, taken at the flood, leads on to Fortune;
Omitted, all the voyage of their Life
Is bound in shallows, and in miseries:
And we must take the Current when it serves,
Or lose our ventures.

Opportunity. — *Shakspeare.*

He had not dined:
The veins unfill'd, our Blood is cold, and then
We pout upon the morning, are unapt
To give or to forgive: but when we have stuff'd
These Pipes and these conveyances of our Blood
With wine and feeding, we have suppler Souls.

Opportunity. — *Shakspeare.*

A little Fire is quickly trodden out;
Which, being suffer'd, rivers cannot quench.

Opportunity. — *Pliny.*

NO man possesses a genius so commanding that he can attain Eminence, unless a subject suited to his talents should present itself, and an Opportunity occur for their development.

Opportunity. — *Greville.*

THERE sometimes wants only a stroke of Fortune to discover numberless latent good or bad qualities, which would otherwise have been eternally concealed; as words written with a certain liquor appear only when applied to the Fire.

Opportunity. — *From the Latin.*

OPPORTUNITY has Hair in front, behind she is bald; if you seize her by the forelock, you may hold her, but, if suffered to escape, not Jupiter himself can catch her again.

Oppression. — *Shakspeare.*

The smallest Worm will turn, being trodden on;
And Doves will peck, in safeguard of their brood.

Oppression. — *Shakspeare.*

You must not think,
That we are made of stuff so flat and dull,
That we can let our Beard be shook with Danger,
And think it Pastime.

Oppression. — *Tacitus.*

A DESIRE to resist Oppression is implanted in the nature of Man.

The Orator. — *Prior.*

AND 'tis remarkable, that they
Talk most that have the least to say.
Your dainty Speakers have the curse,
To plead their causes down to worse:
As Dames, who native Beauty want,
Still uglier look the more they paint.

The Orator. — *Spenser.*

THEREFORE the vulgar did about him flocke,
And cluster thicke unto his leasings vaine,
(Like foolish Flies about an Hony-crocke,)
In hope by him great benefite to gaine,
And uncontrolled Freedome to obtaine.

Order and Obedience. — *Shakspeare.*

WHILE that the armed Hand doth fight abroad,
The advised Head defends itself at home:
For Government, though high, and low, and lower,
Put into parts, doth keep in one consent;
Congruing in a full and natural close,
Like Music. . . . .
Therefore doth Heaven divide
The state of Man in divers functions,
Setting endeavour in continual motion;
To which is fixed, as an aim or butt,
Obedience: for so work the Honey-bees;
Creatures, that, by a rule in nature, teach
The act of order to a peopled Kingdom.
They have a King, and Officers of sorts:
Where some, like Magistrates, correct at home;
Others, like Merchants, venture trade abroad;
Others, like Soldiers, armed in their stings,
Make boot upon the summer's velvet buds;
Which pillage they with merry march bring home
To the tent-royal of their Emperor:
Who, busied in his Majesty, surveys

The singing Masons, building roofs of gold;
The civil Citizens kneading up the honey;
The poor mechanic porters crowding in
Their heavy burdens at his narrow gate;
The sad-eyed Justice, with his surly hum,
Delivering o'er to executors pale,
The lazy yawning Drone. I this infer,—
That many things, having full reference
To one consent, may work contrariously:
As many Arrows, loosed several ways,
Fly to one mark;
As many several ways meet in one Town;
As many fresh streams run in one self Sea·
As many lines close in the Dial's centre;
So may a thousand actions, once afoot,
End in one purpose, and be all well borne
Without defeat.

Originality. — *Colton.*

MEN of strong minds, and who think for themselves, should not be discouraged on finding occasionally that some of their best Ideas have been anticipated by former writers; they will neither anathematize others with a *pereant qui ante nos nostra dixerint,* nor despair themselves. They will rather go on in Science, like John Hunter in Physics, discovering things before discovered, until, like him, they are rewarded with a *terra* hitherto *incognita* in the Sciences, an Empire indisputably their own, both by right of conquest and of Discovery.

Originality. — *Anon.*

THEY who have Light in themselves, will not revolve as Satellites.

Ornament. — *Shakspeare.*

BEING season'd with a gracious voice,
Obscures the show of evil. In Religion,
What damned error, but some sober brow
Will bless it, and approve it with a text,
Hiding the grossness with fair Ornament?

Paradise. — *Milton.*

UNDER a tuft of shade that on the green
Stood whisp'ring soft, by a fresh Fountain side
They sat them down; and after no more toil
Of their sweet gard'ning labour than sufficed
To recommend cool Zephyr, and made Ease
More easy, wholesome Thirst and Appetite
More grateful, to their supper fruits they fell.

Parliaments. — *Franklin.*

WE assemble Parliaments and Councils, to have the benefit of their collected Wisdom; but we necessarily have, at the same time, the inconveniences of their collected passions, prejudices, and private interests. By the help of these, artful men overpower their Wisdom, and dupe its possessors.

Parting. — *Shakspeare.*

WHAT! gone without a word?
Ay, so true Love should do: it cannot speak;
For Truth hath better deeds, than words, to grace it.

Party Spirit. — *Washington.*

THERE is an opinion that Parties in free countries are useful checks upon the administration of the government, and serve to keep alive the spirit of liberty. This, within certain limits, is probably true; and, in governments of a monarchical cast, patriotism may look with indulgence, if not with favour, upon the spirit of party. But in those of the popular character, in governments purely elective, it is a spirit not to be encouraged. From their natural tendency, it is certain there will always be enough of that spirit for every salutary purpose. And there being constant danger of excess, the effort ought to be, by force of public opinion, to mitigate and assuage it. A fire not to be quenched, it demands a uniform vigilance to prevent it bursting into a flame, lest, instead of warming, it should consume.

The Passions. — *Spenser.*

WHAT Warre so cruel, or what siege so sore
As that which strong affections doe apply
Against the forte of Reason evermore,
To bring the Soul into captivity?
Their force is fiercer through infirmity
Of the fraile Flesh, relenting to their rage,
And exercise most bitter tyranny
Upon the partes, brought into their bondage:
No wretchedness is like to sinful villenage.

The Passions. — *Byron.*

ALAS! our young Affections run to waste,
Or water but the desert; whence arise
But weeds of dark Luxuriance, Tares of haste,
Rank at the core, though tempting to the eyes,
Flowers whose wild odours breathe but agonies,
And trees whose gums are poison; such the plants
Which spring beneath her steps as Passion flies
O'er the World's wilderness, and vainly pants
For some celestial fruit, forbidden to our wants.

The Passions. — *Lillo.*

EXALTED souls,
Have Passions in proportion violent,
Resistless, and tormenting: they're a tax
Imposed by Nature on pre-eminence,
And Fortitude, and Wisdom must support them.

The Passions. — *Moore.*

ALAS! too well, too well they know,
The pain, the penitence, the Wo,
That Passion brings down on the best,
The wisest and the loveliest.

The Passions. — *Crabbe.*

OH how the Passions, insolent and strong,
Bear our weak minds their rapid course along;
Make us the madness of their will obey;
Then die, and leave us to our griefs a Prey!

The Passions. — *Byron.*

SHE stopt, and raised her head to speak, but paused
And then moved on again with rapid pace;
Then slacken'd it, which is the march most caused
By deep Emotion: you may sometimes trace
A feeling in each footstep, as disclosed
By Sallust in his Catiline, who, chased
By all the demons of all Passions, show'd
Their work even by the way in which he trode.

The Passions. — *Burke.*

IN doing good, we are generally cold, and languid, and sluggish; and of all things afraid of being too much in the right. But the works of Malice and Injustice are quite in another style. They are finished with a bold masterly hand; touched as they are with the Spirit of those vehement Passions that call forth all our Energies, whenever we oppress and persecute.

The Passions. — *Scott.*

HIS soul, like bark with rudder lost,
On Passion's changeful tide was tost;
Nor Vice nor Virtue had the power
Beyond the impression of the hour;
And oh, when Passion rules, how rare
The hours that fall to Virtue's share.

The Passions. — *Fuller.*

HOLD not Conference, debate, or Reasoning with any Lust; tis but a preparatory for thy Admission of it. The way is at the very first flatly to deny it.

The Passions. — *Shaftesbury.*

A MAN is by nothing so much himself, as by his Temper and the character of his Passions and Affections. If he loses what is manly and worthy in these, he is as much lost to himself, as when he loses his Memory and Understanding.

The Passions. — *Cumberland.*

THE Passions may be humoured till they become our master, as a Horse may be pampered till he gets the better of his rider; but early discipline will prevent Mutiny, and keep the helm in the hands of Reason.

The Passions. — *Tillotson.*

NO man's body is as strong as his appetites, but Heaven has corrected the boundlessness of his voluptuous desires by stinting his strength and contracting his capacities.

The Passions. — *Byron.*

THE Nightingale that sings with the deep thorn,
Which Fable places in her breast of wail,
Is lighter far of Heart and voice than those
Whose headlong Passions form their proper Woes.

The Passions. — *Claudian.*

WHAT profits us, that we from Heaven derive
A Soul immortal, and with looks erect
Survey the stars, if, like the brutal kind,
We follow where our Passions lead the way?

The Passions. — *La Rochefoucauld.*

THE Passions are the only orators that always persuade: they are, as it were, a natural Art, the rules of which are infallible; and the simplest man, with Passion, is more persuasive than the most eloquent without it.

The Passions. — *From the French.*

THE Passions act as Winds to propel our vessel, our Reason is the Pilot that steers her; without the Winds she would not move, without the Pilot she would be lost.

The Passions. — *Sprat.*

PASSION is the great mover and spring of the Soul; when men's Passions are strongest, they may have great and noble Effects; but they are then also apt to fall into the greatest miscarriages.

The Passions. — *Lavater.*

HE submits to be seen through a microscope, who suffers himself to be caught in a fit of Passion.

Passion. — *Johnson.*

THE round of a passionate man's life is in contracting debts in his Passion, which his Virtue obliges him to pay. He spends his time in Outrage and acknowledgment, injury and Reparation.

Passions. — *Colton.*

PRINCES rule the People; and their own Passions rule Princes; but Providence can overrule the whole, and draw the instruments of his inscrutable purpose from the Vices, no less than from the Virtues of Kings.

Passions. — *Longfellow.*

OUR passions never wholly die; but in the last cantos of life's romantic epos, they rise up again and do battle, like some of Ariosto's heroes, who have already been quietly interred, and ought to be turned to dust.

The Good Pastor. — *Byron.*

FATHER! thy days have pass'd in peace,
'Mid counted beads, and countless Prayer;
To bid the sins of others cease,
Thyself without a crime or care,
Save transient ills that all must bear,
Has been thy lot, from Youth to Age.

Patience. — *Fuller.*

IF the Wicked flourish, and thou suffer, be not discouraged. They are fatted for Destruction: thou are dieted for Health.

Patience. — *Shakspeare.*

How poor are they that have not Patience!
What wound did ever heal, but by degrees?

Patience. — *Shakspeare.*

PATIENCE—
Of whose soft grace, I have her sovereign aid,
And rest myself content.

Patience. — *Shakspeare.*

I DO note,
That Grief and Patience, rooted in him both,
Mingle their spurs together.
Grow, Patience!
And let the stinking elder, Grief, untwine
His perishing root, with the increasing Vine!

Patriotism. — *Shakspeare.*

HAD I a dozen sons,—each in my love alike,—I had rather had eleven die nobly for their country, than one voluptuously surfeit out of Action.

Patriotism. — *Sir W. Jones.*

WHAT constitutes a State?
Not high-raised Battlement or labour'd mound,
Thick wall or moated Gate;
Not cities proud with spires and turrets crown'd;
Not bays and broad-arm'd ports,
Where, laughing at the storm, rich Navies ride;
Not starr'd and spangled courts,
Where low-brow'd baseness wafts perfume to Pride.
No:—MEN, high-minded MEN,
With Powers as far above dull brutes endued,
In forest, brake, or den,
As beasts excel cold rocks and brambles rude;
Men, who their Duties know,
But know their Rights, and knowing, dare maintain,
Prevent the long-aim'd blow,
And crush the Tyrant, while they rend the chain:
These constitute a State.

Patriotism. — *Pope.*

STATESMAN, yet friend to Truth! of soul sincere,
In action faithful, and in Honour clear!
Who broke no promise, served no private end,
Who gain'd no title, and who lost no friend;
Ennobled by himself, by all approved,
Praised, wept, and honour'd by the Muse he loved.

Peace. — *Shakspeare.*

'TIS death to me, to be at Enmity;
I hate it, and desire all good men's Love.

Peace. —*Petrarch.*

FIVE great enemies to Peace inhabit with us, viz. Avarice, Ambition, Envy, Anger, and Pride, and that if those enemies were to be banished, we should infallibly enjoy perpetual Peace.

Peace. — *Shakspeare.*

I DO not know that Englishman alive,
With whom my Soul is any jot at odds,
More than the infant that is born to-night.

Peasant Life. — *Goldsmith.*

THEIR level life is but a mould'ring fire,
Unquench'd by Want, unfann'd by strong Desire:
Unfit for raptures, or, if raptures cheer
On some high festival of once a year,
In wild Excess the vulgar breast takes fire,
Till, buried in debauch, the bliss expire.

Peasant Life.—*Fletcher.*

HIS bed of wool yields safe and quiet sleeps,
While by his side his faithful spouse hath place;
His little Son into his bosom creeps,
The lively picture of his father's face:
Never his humble house nor state torment him;
Less he could like, if less his God had sent him!
And when he dies, green turfs, with grassy tomb, content him.

Penetration.—*La Rochefoucauld.*

WE like to divine others, but we do not like to be divined ourselves.

Penetration.—*Greville.*

PENETRATION seems a kind of inspiration; it gives me an idea of Prophecy.

Penetration.—*La Rochefoucauld.*

PENETRATION has an air of divination, which flatters our Vanity more than all the other qualities of the Mind.

Penetration.—*La Rochefoucauld.*

THE greatest fault in Penetration is not the not reaching the mark, but overshooting it.

Noisy Persons.—*Pope.*

IT is with narrow-souled people as with narrow-necked Bottles; the less they have in them, the more noise they make in pouring it out.

Retired Persons.—*Goldsmith.*

IT has been said that he who retires to solitude is either a Beast or an Angel. The censure is too severe, and the praise un merited. The discontented being who retires from society is generally some good-natured man, who has begun his Life without Experience, and knew not how to gain it in his intercourse with mankind.

Perfection.—*Voltaire.*

PERFECTION is attained by slow degrees; she requires the hand of Time.

Perfection.—*Shakspeare.*

In speech, in gait,
In diet, in affections of delight,
In Military rules, humours of blood,
He was the Mark and glass, copy and Book,
That fashion'd others.

Perfection. — *Chesterfield.*

AIM at Perfection in every thing, though in most things it is unattainable. However, they who aim at it, and persevere, will come much nearer to it than those whose Laziness and Despondency make them give it up as unattainable.

Perfection. — *Shakspeare.*

TO gild refined Gold, to paint the Lily,
To throw a perfume on the Violet,
To smooth the Ice, or add another hue
Unto the Rainbow, or with taper-light
To seek the beauteous eye of Heaven to garnish,
Is wasteful, and ridiculous.

Perseverance. — *Lucretius.*

A FALLING Drop at last will cave a Stone.

Perseverance. — *From the Latin.*

HE will never enjoy the sweets of the spring, nor will he obtain the Honeycombs of Mount Hybla, if he dreads his face being stung, or is annoyed by Briers. The Rose is guarded by its Thorn, the Honey is defended by the Bee.

Perversity. — *Greville.*

SOME men put me in mind of Half-bred Horses, which often grow worse in proportion as you feed and exercise them for Improvement.

Perversity. — *From the Latin.*

WE have all a propensity to grasp at Forbidden Fruit.

Philanthropy. — *Cumberland.*

IT is an old saying, that Charity begins at home; but this is no reason it should not go abroad: a man should live with the world as a Citizen of the World; he may have a preference for the particular quarter or square, or even alley in which he lives, but he should have a generous feeling for the welfare of the whole.

Philosophers. — *Shakspeare.*

THERE was never yet Philosopher
That could endure the Toothache patiently,
However they have writ the style of Gods,
And made a push at chance and sufferance.

Philosophy. — *Shakspeare.*

ADVERSITY'S sweet milk—Philosophy.

Philosophy. — *Voltaire.*

THE discovery of what is true, and the practice of that which is good, are the two most important objects of Philosophy.

Philosophy. — *Colton.*

THE Philosopher will draw his estimate of Human Nature, by varying as much as possible his own situation, to multiply the points of view under which he observes her. Uncircumscribed by lines of latitude or of longitude, he will examine her "buttoned up and laced in the forms and ceremonies of Civilization, and at her ease, and unrestrained in the light and feathered Costume of the Savage." He will also associate with the highest, without servility, and with the lowest, without vulgarity.

Philosophy. — *Epictetus.*

IT is the peculiar quality and character of an undisciplined man, and a Man of the World, to expect no advantage, and to apprehend no mischief from himself, but all from objects without him. Whereas the Philosopher, quite contrary, looks only inward, and apprehends no good or evil can happen to him, but from himself alone.

Philosophy. — *Seneca.*

PHILOSOPHY is the art and law of Life, and it teaches us what to do in all cases, and, like good Marksmen, to hit the white at any distance.

Philosophy. — *Cowley.*

TO be a Husbandman, is but a retreat from the city; to be a Philosopher, from the world, as it is Man's; into the world, as it is God's.

Philosophy. — *Seneca.*

PHILOSOPHY does not regard pedigree: she did not receive Plato as a noble, but she made him so.

Philosophy. — *Selden.*

WHEN men comfort themselves with Philosophy, 'tis not because they have got two or three sentences, but because they have digested those sentences, and made them their own: so upon the matter, Philosophy is nothing but Discretion.

Philosophy. — *Shaftesbury.*

TO philosophize in a just signification, is but to carry Good Breeding a step higher. For the accomplishment of breeding is, to learn what is decent in company, or beautiful in arts; and the sum of Philosophy is, to learn what is just in society, and beautiful in Nature and the order of the world.

Philosophy. — *Tillotson.*

PHILOSOPHY hath given us several plausible rules for attaining Peace and Tranquillity of Mind, but they fall very much short of bringing men to it.

Philosophy. — *La Rochefoucauld.*

PHILOSOPHY triumphs easily over past, and over future Evils, but present Evils triumph over Philosophy.

Philosophy. — *Thomson.*

PHILOSOPHY consists not
In airy schemes, or idle speculations;
The rule and conduct of all social life
Is her great Province. Not in lonely cells
Obscure she lurks, but holds her heavenly light
To Senates and to Kings, to guide their councils,
And teach them to reform and bless mankind.

Philosophy. — *Pope.*

IN lazy Apathy let Stoics boast
Their Virtue fix'd; 'tis fix'd as in a frost;
Contracted all, retiring to the breast;
But strength of mind is exercise, not rest:
The rising Tempest puts in act the soul;
Parts it may ravage, but preserves the whole.

Philosophy. — *Moore.*

SUCH was the rigid Zeno's plan
To form his philosophic man;
Such were the modes he taught mankind
To weed the Garden of the mind:
They tore away some Weeds, 'tis true,
But all the Flowers were ravish'd too.

Philosophy. — *Shakspeare.*

A MAN, whose blood
Is very Snow-broth; one who never feels
The wanton stings and motions of the sense;
But doth rebate and blunt his natural edge
With profits of the mind, Study and Fast.

Philosophy. — *Moore.*

THEN far be all the Wisdom hence,
And all the lore, whose tame control
Would wither joy with chill delays!
Alas! the fertile fount of sense,
At which the young, the panting Soul
Drinks Life and Love, too soon decays!

Philosophy. — *Goldsmith.*

THIS same Philosophy is a good Horse in a stable, but an arrant Jade on a journey.

Philosophy. — *Shaftesbury.*

'TIS not wit merely, but a temper, which must form the well-bred man. In the same manner 'tis not a Head merely, but a Heart and Resolution, which complete the real Philosopher.

Physiognomy. — *Shakspeare.*

THE devil damn thee black, thou Cream-faced Loon!
Where got'st thou that Goose Look?

Physiognomy. — *Addison.*

WHEN I see a man with a sour, rivell'd face, I cannot forbear pitying his Wife: and when I meet with an open, ingenuous countenance, think on the happiness of his Friends, his Family, and Relations.

Physiognomy. — *Virgil.*

TRUST not too much to an enchanting face.

Physic. — *Bacon.*

PHYSIC is of little use to a temperate person, for a man's own observation on what he finds does him good, and what hurts him, is the best physic to preserve Health.

Physic. — *Addison.*

PHYSIC, for the most part, is nothing else but the substitute of Exercise or Temperance.

Pictures. — *Horace.*

A PICTURE is a Poem without words.

Every one in his Place. — *Greville.*

THE neglecting to put yourself above those that ought to be Inferior to you, will often be as disgustful to those very people, as the not putting yourself under those who ought to be Superior to you, will be disgustful to them.

Plagiarism. — *S. T. Coleridge.*

PLAGIARISTS are always suspicious of being stolen from.

Pleading. — *Percival.*

THERE is too much reason to apprehend, that the custom of pleading for any Client, without discrimination of right or wrong, must lessen the regard due to those important distinctions, and deaden the Moral Sensibility of the Heart.

Pleasure. — *Shakspeare.*

FLOWERS are like the Pleasures of the world.

Pleasure. — *Seneca.*

LET not the enjoyment of Pleasures now within your grasp, be carried to such Excess, as to incapacitate you from future repetition.

Pleasure. — *Moore.*

PLEASURE'S the only noble end
To which all Human powers should tend;
And Virtue gives her heavenly lore,
But to make Pleasure please us more!
Wisdom and she were both design'd
To make the senses more refined,
That man might revel free from cloying,
Then most a sage, when most enjoying!

Pleasure. — *Byron.*

THOUGH sages may pour out their Wisdom's treasure,
There is no sterner Moralist than Pleasure.

Pleasure. — *Moore.*

O SAGES! think on joy like this,
And where's your boast of Apathy.

Pleasure. — *Shakspeare.*

WHY, all Delights are vain; but that most vain,
Which, with Pain purchased, doth inherit Pain.

Pleasure. — *Spenser.*

HIS sports were fair, his Joyance innocent,
Sweet without soure, and Honey without gall;
And he himself seem'd made for Merriment,
Merrily masking both in Bower and Hall.

Pleasure. — *Fuller.*

CHOOSE such Pleasures as recreate much, and cost little.

Pleasure. — *Shakspeare.*

WHO riseth from a feast,
With that keen Appetite that he sits down?
Where is the Horse that doth untread again
His tedious measures with the unbated fire
That he did pace them first? All things that are,
Are with more spirit chased than enjoy'd.
How like a younker, or a Prodigal,
The scarf'd bark puts from her native bay,
Hugg'd and embraced by the strumpet Wind!
How like the Prodigal doth she return,
With over-weather'd ribs, and ragged sails,
Lean, rent, and beggar'd.

Pleasure. — *Pope.*

PLEASURE, or wrong or rightly understood,
Our greatest Evil, or our greatest Good.

Pleasure. — *Shakspeare.*

IF all the year were playing Holidays,
To sport would be as tedious as to work;
But when they seldom come, they wish'd-for come,
And nothing pleaseth but rare Accidents.

Pleasure. — *Colton.*

THE seeds of Repentance are sown in youth by Pleasure, but the Harvest is reaped in age by Pain.

Pleasure. — *Colton.*

PAIN may be said to follow Pleasure as its shadow.

Pleasure. — *Chesterfield.*

PLEASURE is a necessary Reciprocal: no one feels, who does not at the same time give it. To be pleased, one must please. What pleases you in others, will in general please them in you.

Pleasure. — *Goldsmith.*

NONE has more frequent conversations with disagreeable self than the man of Pleasure; his Enthusiasms are but few and transient; his Appetites, like angry creditors, continually making fruitless demands for what he is unable to pay; and the greater his former Pleasures, the more strong his regret, the more impatient his expectations.

Pleasure. — *Colton.*

MENTAL Pleasures never cloy; unlike those of the body, they are increased by Repetition, approved of by Reflection, and strengthened by Enjoyment.

Poetry. — *S. T. Coleridge.*

POETRY has been to me its own exceeding great reward: it has given me the habit of wishing to discover the Good and Beautiful in all that meets and surrounds me.

Poetry. — *Anon.*

SO entirely do great Poets soar beyond the reach, and almost beyond the ken of their own Age, that we have only lately begun to have a right understanding of Shakspeare, or of the masters of the Greek drama,—to discern the principles which actuated them, the purposes they had in view, the laws they acknowledged, and the ideas they wished to impersonate.

Poetry. — *Shakspeare.*

THE truest Poetry is the most feigning; and Lovers are given to Poetry; and what they swear in Poetry, may be said, as lovers they do feign.

Poetry. — *Goldsmith.*

AND thou, sweet Poetry, thou loveliest maid,
Still first to fly where sensual joys invade!
Unfit, in these degenerate times of Shame,
To catch the heart, or strike for honest fame,
Dear charming Nymph, neglected and decried,
My shame in crowds, my solitary Pride;
Thou source of all my bliss, and all my woe,
That found'st me poor at first, and keep'st me so;
Thou Guide, by which the nobler arts excel,
Thou nurse of every Virtue.

Poetry. — *Mrs. Tighe.*

TO charm the languid hours of solitude
He oft invites her to the Muse's lore,
For none have vainly e'er the Muse pursued,
And those whom she delights, regret no more
The social, joyous hours, while rapt they soar
To worlds unknown, and live in Fancy's dream:
O Muse divine! thee only I implore,
Shed on my Soul thy sweet inspiring beams,
And Pleasure's gayest scene insipid Folly seems

Poetry. — *Jean Paul.*

THERE are so many tender and holy Emotions flying about in our inward world, which, like angels, can never assume the body of an outward act; so many rich and lovely Flowers spring up which bear no seed, that it is a happiness Poetry was invented, which receives into its limbus all these incorporeal Spirits, and the Perfume of all these Flowers.

Poetry. — *Sir William Temple.*

THE mind of man is like the Sea, which is neither agreeable to the beholder nor the voyager, in a calm or in a storm; but is so to both, when a little agitated by gentle gales; and so the Mind, when moved by soft and easy Passions and Affections. I know very well, that many, who pretend to be wise by the forms of being grave, are apt to despise both Poetry and Music, as toys and trifles too light for the use or entertainment of serious men: but whoever find themselves wholly insensible to these charms, would, I think, do well to keep their own Council, for fear of reproaching their own temper, and bringing the goodness of their natures, if not of their Understandings, into question: it may be thought at least an ill sign, if not an ill constitution; since some of the Fathers went so far as to esteem the love of music a sign of predestination; as a thing divine, and reserved for the felicities of Heaven itself.

Poetry. — *Pope.*

SAGES and chiefs long since had birth,
Ere Cæsar was, or Newton named;
These raised new empires o'er the earth;
And those, new Heavens and systems framed:
Vain was the chiefs', the sages' pride!
They had no Poet, and they died.
In vain they schemed, in vain they bled!
They had no Poet, and are dead.

The Poet. — *Spenser.*

HEAPS of huge words uphoorded hideously,
With horrid sound, though having little sense,
They think to be chief praise of Poetry,
And thereby wanting due intelligence,
Have marr'd the face of goodly Poesie,
And made a Monster of their fantasie.

The Poet. — *Catullus.*

SUFFENUS has no more wit than a mere Clown when he attempts to write verses; and yet he is never happier than when he is scribbling, so much does he admire himself and his Compositions; and, indeed, this is the foible of every one of us; for there is no man living who is not a Suffenus in one thing or other.

The Poet. — *Swift.*

THEN, rising with Aurora's light,
The Muse invoked, sit down to write;
Blot out, correct, insert, refine,
Enlarge, diminish, interline;
Be mindful, when Invention fails,
To scratch you head, and bite your nails.

The Poet. — *Sir W. Temple.*

NONE ever was a great Poet that applied himself much to any thing else.

Policy. — *Greville.*

I HAVE heard some of the first judges of Whist say, that it was not those who played best by the true laws of the game that would win most, but those who played best to the false play of others; and I am sure it is true of the great Game of the World

Policy. — *Shakspeare.*

SUCH is the infection of the time,
That, for the Health and Physic of our Right
We cannot deal but with the very hand
Of stern Injustice and confused Wrong.

Politeness. — *Greville.*

AS Charity covers a multitude of sins before God, so does Politeness before men.

Politeness. — *Colton.*

THAT Politeness which we put on, in order to keep the assuming and the presumptuous at a proper distance, will generally succeed. But it sometimes happens, that these obtrusive characters are on such excellent terms with themselves, that they put down this very Politeness to the score of their own great Merits and high pretensions, meeting the coldness of our Reserve with a ridiculous condescension of Familiarity, in order to set us at ease with ourselves.

Politeness. — *Shaftesbury.*

ALL Politeness is owing to Liberty. We polish one another, and rub off our corners and rough sides by a sort of amicable collision. To restrain this is inevitably to bring a rust upon men's Understandings.

Politeness. — *Cumberland.*

POLITENESS is nothing more than an elegant and concealed species of Flattery, tending to put the person to whom it is addressed in Good-humour and Respect with himself: but if there is a parade and display affected in the exertion of it, if a man seems to say—Look how condescending and gracious I am!—whilst he has only the common offices of civility to perform, such Politeness seems founded in mistake, and this mistake I have observed frequently to occur in French manners.

Politeness. — *Monro.*

TO the acquisition of the rare quality of Politeness, so much of the enlightened Understanding is necessary that I cannot but consider every Book in every science, which tends to make us wiser, and of course better men, as a treatise on a more enlarged system of Politeness, not excluding the Experiments of Archimedes, or the Elements of Euclid.

The Populace. — *Shakspeare.*

THERE have been many Great Men that have flattered the People, who never loved them; and there be many that they have loved, they know not wherefore: so that, if they love they know not why, they hate upon no better ground.

The Populace. — *Shakspeare.*

YOU common cry of Curs! whose breath I hate
As reek o' the rotten fens, whose loves I prize
As the dead Carcasses of unburied men
That do corrupt the Air.

The Populace. — *Cowper.*

SOME shout him, and some hang upon his car
To gaze in 's eyes and bless him. Maidens wave
Their 'kerchiefs, and old Women weep for joy.
While others not so satisfied unhorse
The gilded Equipage, and turning loose
His Steeds, usurp a place they well deserve.

The Populace. — *Colton.*

THE Mob is a monster with the hands of Briareus, but the head of Polyphemus—strong to execute, but blind to perceive.

The Populace. — *Shakspeare.*

FOR the mutable, rank-scented Many, let them
Regard me as I do not flatter, and
Therein behold themselves: I say again
In soothing them, we nourish 'gainst our Senate
The cockle of Rebellion, insolence, sedition,
Which we ourselves have plough'd for, sow'd and scatter'd,
By mingling them with us, the honour'd number;
Who lack not Virtue, no, nor power, but that
Which they have given to Beggars.

The Populace. — *Milton.*

WHAT is the People but a Herd confused,
A miscellaneous Rabble, who extol
Things vulgar, and well weigh'd, scarce worth the praise?
They praise, and they admire they know not what,
And know not whom, but as one leads the other;
And what delight to be by such extoll'd,
To live upon their Tongues, and be their talk,
Of whom to be dispraised were no small Praise?

The Populace. — *Shakspeare.*

I WILL not choose what many men desire,
Because I will not jump with common spirits,
And rank me with the barbarous Multitude.

The Populace. — *Shakspeare.*

OUR slippery People,
Whose love is never link'd to the Deserver,
Till his deserts are passed.

The Populace. — *Colton.*

IT is an easy and a vulgar thing to please the Mob, and not a very arduous task to astonish them; but essentially to benefit and to improve them, is a work fraught with Difficulty, and teeming with Danger.

The Populace. — *Shakspeare.*

The fool Multitude, that choose by show,
Not learning more than the fond eye doth teach;
Which pries not to th' interior, but, like the Martlet,
Builds in the Weather on the outward wall,
Even in the force and road of Casualty.

The Populace. — *Cowper.*

O POPULAR Applause! what heart of man
Is proof against thy sweet seducing charms?
The wisest and the best feel urgent need
Of all their Caution in thy gentlest gales;
But swell'd into a gust—who then, alas!
With all his Canvas set, and inexpert
And therefore heedless, can withstand thy Power?

The Populace. — *Dryden.*

THE Rabble gather round the Man of News,
And listen with their mouths wide open; some
Tell, some hear, some judge of News, some make it,
And he that lies most loud, is most believed.

The Populace. — *Cicero.*

They condemn what they do not understand.

The Populace. — *Shakspeare.*

THEY'LL sit by th' fire, and presume to know
What's done i' the Capitol: who's like to rise,
Who thrives, and who declines: side Factions, and give out
Conjectural Marriages; making parties strong,
And feebling such as stand not in their liking,
Below their cobbled shoes.

The Populace. — *Shakspeare.*

Your affections are
A sick man's appetite, who desires most that
Which would increase his Evil. He that depends
Upon your favours, swims with fins of Lead,
And hews down Oaks with Rushes. Hang ye! Trust ye?
With every minute you do change a mind;
And call him noble, that was now your hate—
Him vile, that was your Garland.

The Populace. — *Shakspeare.*

You have many Enemies, that know not
Why they are so, but, like to village Curs,
Bark when their fellows do.

The Populace. — *Shakspeare.*

WHAT would you have, you Curs,
That like nor Peace, nor War? the one affrights you,
The other makes you proud. He that trusts you,
Where he should find you Lions, finds you Hares;
Where Foxes, Geese: you are no surer, no,
Than is the coal of fire upon the Ice,
Or hailstone in the Sun.

The Populace. — *Shakspeare.*

LOOK, as I blow this Feather from my face,
And as the air blows it to me again,
Obeying with my Wind when I do blow,
And yielding to another when it blows,
Commanded always by the greater Gust;
Such is the likeness of you Common Men.

Popularity. — *Shakspeare.*

AN habitation giddy and unsure
Hath he that buildeth on the Vulgar Heart.
Oh thou fond Many! with what loud applause
Did'st thou beat Heaven with blessing Bolingbroke,
Before he was what thou would'st have him be!
And now, being trimm'd up in thine own desires,
Thou, beastly Feeder, art so full of him,
That thou provokest thyself to cast him up.

Popularity. — *Spenser.*

AND after all the Raskall Many ran,
Heap'd together in rude Rablement,
To see the face of that victorious man,
Whom all admired as from Heaven sent,
And gazed upon with gaping Wonderment.

Popularity. — *Scott.*

THEIR'S was the glee of martial breast,
And laughter their's at little jest;
And oft Lord Marmion deign'd to aid,
And mingle in the mirth they made:
For though, with men of High degree,
The proudest of the Proud was he,
Yet, train'd in camps, he knew the art
To win the Soldier's hardy Heart.

Possession. — *Young.*

POSSESSION, why, more tasteless than pursuit?
Why is a wish far dearer than a Crown?
That wish accomplish'd, why, the grave of Bliss?

Because, in the great future buried deep,
Beyond our plans of Empire and Renown,
Lies all that man with ardour should pursue;
And He who made him, bent him to the right.

Possession. — *Shakspeare.*

It so falls out,
That what we have we prize not to the worth,
Whiles we enjoy it; but being lack'd and lost,
Why, then we rack the Value; then we find
The Virtue, that Possession would not show us
Whiles it was ours.

Posterity. — *Colton.*

WITH respect to the authority of great names, it should be remembered, that he alone deserves to have any weight or influence with Posterity, who has shown himself superior to the particular and predominant Error of his own times.

Poverty. — *St. Evremond.*

WHEN it is not despicable to be poor, we want fewer things to live in Poverty with satisfaction, than to live magnificently with Riches

Poverty. — *Dryden.*

WANT is a bitter and a hateful good,
Because its Virtues are not understood;
Yet many things, impossible to thought,
Have been by need to full perfection brought.
The daring of the Soul proceeds from thence,
Sharpness of Wit, and active Diligence;
Prudence at once, and Fortitude it gives;
And, if in patience taken, mends our lives.

Poverty. — *Juvenal.*

Rarely they rise by Virtue's aid, who lie
Plunged in the depth of helpless Poverty.

Poverty. — *Turkish Spy.*

POVERTY eclipses the brightest Virtues, and is the very Sepulchre of brave designs, depriving a man of the means to accomplish what Nature has fitted him for, and stifling the noblest thoughts in their embryo. Many illustrious Souls may be said to have been dead among the living, or buried alive in the obscurity of their condition, whose perfections have rendered them the darlings of Providence, and companions of angels.

Poverty and Riches. — *Shakspeare.*

TWINN'D brothers of one womb,—
Whose procreation, residence, and birth,
Scarce is dividant,—touch them with several Fortunes;
The greater scorns the lesser: Not Nature,
To whom all lay siege, can bear great fortune,
But by contempt of Nature.
Raise me this Beggar, and denude that Lord;
The Senator shall bear contempt hereditary;
The Beggar native honour.
It is the pasture lards the browser's sides,
The want that makes him lean.

Poverty and Wisdom. — *Dekker.*

A WISE man poor,
Is like a Sacred Book that's never read;
To himself he lives, and to all else seems dead.

Power. — *Colton.*

POWER will intoxicate the best hearts, as Wine the strongest heads. No man is wise enough, nor good enough to be trusted with unlimited Power; for, whatever qualifications he may have evinced to entitle him to the possession of so dangerous a privilege, yet, when possessed, others can no longer answer for him, because he can no longer answer for himself.

Power. — *Colton.*

LORD BACON has compared those who move in higher spheres to those heavenly bodies in the Firmament, which have much admiration, but little rest. And it is not necessary to invest a wise man with Power, to convince him that it is a garment bedizened with gold, which dazzles the beholder by its Splendour, but oppresses the wearer by its Weight.

Dormant Power. — *Swift.*

ALTHOUGH men are accused for not knowing their own Weakness, yet perhaps as few know their own Strength. It is in men as in soils, where sometimes there is a vein of Gold, which the owner knows not of.

Power and Liberty. — *Saville.*

POWER and Liberty are like Heat and Moisture; where they are well mixt, every thing prospers; where they are single, they are destructive.

Praise. — *Fuller.*

THOU may'st be more prodigal of Praise when thou writest a letter than when thou speakest in presence.

Praise. — *Young.*

THE love of Praise, howe'er conceal'd by art,
Reigns, more or less, and glows in every Heart:
The proud, to gain it, toils on toils endure,
The modest shun it but to make it sure.

Praise. —*Spenser.*

OR who would ever care to do brave deed,
Or strive in Virtue others to excel,
If none should yield him his deserved meed,
Due Praise, that is the spur of doing well?
For if Good were not praised more than ill,
None would chuse Goodness of his own free will.

Praise. — *Steele.*

ALLOW no man to be so free with you as to praise you to your Face. Your Vanity by this means will want its food. At the same time your passion for esteem will be more fully gratified; men will praise you in their actions: where you now receive one Compliment, you will then receive twenty Civilities.

Praise. — *Fuller.*

PRAISE not people to their faces, to the end that they may pay thee in the same Coin. This is so thin a Cobweb, that it may with little difficulty be seen through; 'tis rarely strong enough to catch flies of any considerable magnitude.

Praise. — *From the Latin.*

IT is the greatest possible Praise to be praised by a man who is himself deserving of Praise.

Praise. — *Shakspeare.*

THE worthiness of Praise distains his worth,
If that the praised himself bring the Praise forth:
But what the repining enemy commends,
That breath Fame follows; that Praise, sole pure, transcends.

Praise. — *Greville.*

THOSE men who are commended by everybody, must be very extraordinary men; or, which is more probable, very inconsiderable men.

Prayer. — *H. More.*

FOUNTAIN of Mercy! whose pervading eye
Can look within and read what passes there,
Accept my thoughts for thanks: I have no words.
My soul, o'erfraught with Gratitude, rejects
The aid of Language—Lord! behold my Heart.

Prayer. — *Fuller.*

LEAVE not off praying to God: for either praying will make thee leave off sinning; or continuing in Sin will make thee desist from praying.

Prayer. — *Archibald Alexander.*

IT is as natural and reasonable for a dependent creature to apply to its Creator for what it needs, as for a child thus to solicit the aid of a parent who is believed to have the disposition and ability to bestow what it needs.

Prayer. — *Thomson.*

FATHER of Light and Life! thou Good Supreme!
Oh teach me what is good! teach me thyself!
Save me from Folly, Vanity, and Vice,
From every low pursuit! and feed my Soul
With Knowledge, conscious Peace, and Virtue pure;
Sacred, substantial, never-fading Bliss!

Prayer. — *Shakspeare.*

FOR holy offices I have a time; a time
To think upon the part of business, which
I bear i' the State; and Nature does require
Her times of preservation, which perforce,
I, her frail son, amongst my brethren mortal,
Must give my tendance to.

Prayer. — *Shakspeare.*

LEND me a Heart replete with thankfulness!
For thou hast given me in this beauteous face,
A world of earthly blessings to my Soul,
If sympathy of Love unite our thoughts.

Prayer. — *Shakspeare.*

O ENGLAND!—model to thy inward greatness,
Like little body with a mighty Heart,—
What might'st thou do, that Honour would thee do
Were all thy children kind and natural!

Precept. — *Shakspeare.*

DO not, as some ungracious Pastors do,
Show me the steep and thorny way to Heaven;
Whilst, like a puff'd and reckless libertine,
Himself the primrose path of Dalliance treads,
And recks not his own read.

Precept. — *Anon.*

ONE of the saddest things about Human Nature is, that a man may guide others in the path of Life, without walking in it himself; that he may he a Pilot, and yet a castaway.

Precept. — *Colton.*

IT was observed of the Jesuits, that they constantly inculcated a thorough contempt of worldly things in their Doctrines, but eagerly grasped at them in their Lives. They were "wise in their generation," for they cried down Worldly things, because they wanted to obtain them, and cried up Spiritual things, because they wanted to dispose of them.

Precept and Example. — *Johnson.*

NOTHING is more unjust, however common, than to charge with Hypocrisy him that expresses zeal for those Virtues which he neglects to practise; since he may be sincerely convinced of the advantages of conquering his Passions, without having yet obtained the Victory; as a man may be confident of the advantages of a voyage or a journey, without having Courage or Industry to undertake it, and may honestly recommend to others those attempts which he neglects himself.

Precept and Example. — *Shakspeare.*

IF to do were as easy as to know what were good to do, Chapels had been Churches, and poor men's cottages princes' palaces. It is a good Divine that follows his own instructions; I can easier teach twenty what were good to be done, than be one of the twenty to follow mine own teaching.

The Precipice. — *Shakspeare.*

THE very place puts toys of Desperation,
Without more motive, into every brain,
That looks so many fathoms to the Sea,
And hears it roar beneath.

Precipitancy. — *Shakspeare.*

HEAT not a Furnace for your foe so hot,
That it do singe yourself. We may out-run
By violent swiftness, that which we run at;
And lose by over-running: know you not,
The Fire that mounts the Liquor 'till't run o'er,
Seeming t' augment it, wastes it?

Prejudice. — *Greville.*

SOME Prejudices are to the mind what the Atmosphere is to the body; we cannot feel without the one, nor breathe without the other.

Prejudice. — *Greville.*

REMOVING Prejudices, is, alas! too often removing the boundary of a delightful near prospect, in order to let in a shocking extensive one.

Prejudice. — *Tucker.*

THERE are habits of Misapprehension and misjudging, common among all degrees of men; Fretfulness, industrious to seek or even feign and chew upon matter that may nourish it; Captiousness, ingenious in perverting the meaning of words; Partiality, warping every thing to its own purpose; Censoriousness, unable to discern a bright part in characters; Self-conceit, averse to discern the real motives of acting; Melancholy, augurating always for the worst; besides many more, some of which I am afraid every man may find lurking in his own breast, if he will but look narrowly enough.

Prejudice. — *Terence.*

HUMAN nature is so constituted, that all see, and judge better, in the Affairs of other men, than in their own.

Prejudice. —*La Rochefoucauld.*

WE seldom find persons whom we acknowledge to be possessed of Good Sense, except those who agree with us in opinion.

Prejudice. — *Greville.*

TO divest one's self of some Prejudices, would be like taking off the skin to feel the better.

The Present. — *Horace.*

ABRIDGE your Hopes in proportion to the shortness of the span of Human Life; for while we converse, the hours, as if envious of our Pleasure, fly away: enjoy therefore the present time, and trust not too much to what to-morrow may produce.

The Present. — *Horace.*

IN the midst of Hopes and Cares, of Apprehensions and of Disquietude, regard every day that dawns upon you as if it was to be your last; and superadded hours, to the enjoyment of which you had not looked forward, will prove an acceptable boon.

The Present. — *Fuller.*

TRY to be happy in this very present Moment; and put not off being so to a Time to come: as though that Time should be of another make from this, which is already come, and is ours.

The Present. — *Colton.*

MEN spend their lives in Anticipations, in determining to be vastly happy at some period or other, when they have time. But the present time has one advantage over every other—it is our own. Past opportunities are gone, future are not come. We may lay in a stock of Pleasures, as we would lay in a stock of Wine; but if we defer the tasting of them too long, we shall find that both are soured by age.

The Present.— *Armstrong.*

WHAT avails it that indulgent Heaven
From mortal Eyes has wrapt the woes to come,
If we, ingenious to torment ourselves,
Grow pale at hideous Fictions of our own?
Enjoy the Present; nor with needless cares
Of what may spring from blind Misfortune's womb,
Appal the surest hour that life bestows.
Serene, and master of yourself, prepare
For what may come; and leave the rest to Heaven.

The Present and the Eternal. — *Colton.*

IF indeed that marvellous microcosm, Man, with all the costly cargo of his faculties and powers, were indeed a rich Argosy, fitted out and freighted only for Shipwreck and Destruction, who amongst us that tolerate the Present only from the Hope of the Future, who that have any aspirings of a high and intellectual Nature about them, could be brought to submit to the disgusting Mortifications of the voyage? As to the common and the sensual herd, who would be glad, perhaps, under *any* terms, to sweat and groan beneath the load of Life, they would find that the creed of the Materialist would only give a fuller swing to the suicidal energies of a Selfism as unprincipled as unrelenting; a Selfism that would not only make that giftless Gift of Life a boon the most difficult to preserve, but would at the same time render it wholly unworthy of the task and the trouble of its preservation. Knowledge herself, that fairest daughter of Heaven, would be immediately transformed into a changeling of Hell; the brightest Reason would be the blackest Curse, and Weakness more salutary than Strength; for the Villany of man would increase with the Depravity of his will, and the depravity of his will with every augmentation of his Power. The force of Intellect imparted to that which was corrupt, would be like the destructive energies communicated by an Earthquake to that which is inert; where even things inanimate, as rocks and mountains, seem endowed with a momentary impulse of motion and Life, only to overwhelm, to destroy, and to be destroyed.

Making Presents. — *Fuller.*

WHEN thou makest Presents, let them be of such things as will last long; to the end they may be in some sort immortal, and may frequently refresh the Memory of the Receiver.

The Pretender. — *Shakspeare.*

THIS is some fellow,
Who, having been praised for Bluntness, doth affect
A saucy Roughness; and constrains the garb,

Quite from his Nature: He cannot flatter, he!—
An honest mind and plain,—he must speak Truth:
An they will take it, so; if not, he's plain.
These kind of Knaves I know, which in this plainness
Harbour more craft and more corrupter ends,
Than twenty silly ducking Observants,
That stretch their duties nicely.

Pretension. — *Lavater.*

HE who gives himself airs of Importance, exhibits the credentials of Impotence.

Pretension. — *Johnson.*

IT is the care of a very great part of Mankind to conceal their indigence from the rest. They support themselves by temporary Expedients, and every day is lost in contriving for to-morrow.

Pretension. — *La Rochefoucauld.*

THE desire of appearing Clever often prevents our becoming so.

Pretension. — *Cicero.*

TRUE Glory strikes root, and even extends itself; all false Pretensions fall as do Flowers, nor can any thing feigned be lasting.

Pretension. — *Plutarch.*

IT is no Disgrace not to be able to do every thing; but to undertake, or pretend to do, what you are not made for, is not only Shameful, but extremely Troublesome and Vexatious.

Pretension. — *Lavater.*

WHERE there is much Pretension, much has been borrowed: Nature never pretends.

Pride. — *Anon.*

TO no kind of begging are people so averse, as to begging Pardon; that is, when there is any serious ground for doing so. When there is none, this phrase is as soon taken in vain, as other momentous words are upon light Occasions.

Pride. — *Shakspeare.*

HE that is proud, eats up himself: Pride is his own Glass, his own Trumpet, his own Chronicle; and whatever praises itself but in the deed, devours the deed in the Praise.

Pride. — *Clarendon.*

WITHOUT the sovereign influence of God's extraordinary and immediate Grace, men do very rarely put off all the trappings of their Pride, till they who are about them put on their winding-sheet.

Pride. — *Colton.*

PRIDE is a paradoxical Proteus, eternally diverse yet ever the same; for Plato adopted a most magnificent mode of displaying his Contempt for Magnificence, while Neglect would have restored Diogenes to common sense and clean linen, since he would have had no Tub, from the moment he had no Spectators. "Thus I trample," said Diogenes, "on the pride of Plato." "But," rejoined Plato, "with *greater pride, O Diogenes.*"

Pride. — *Greville.*

A PROUD man never shows his Pride so much as when he is civil.

Pride. — *Shakspeare.*

Pride hath no other Glass
To show itself, but Pride; for supple knees
Feed Arrogance, and are the Proud Man's fees.

Pride. — *Shenstone.*

MEN are sometimes accused of Pride merely because their accusers would be proud themselves if they were in their places.

Pride. — *Colton.*

THERE is this paradox in Pride,—it makes some men ridiculous, but prevents others from becoming so.

Pride. — *Selden.*

PRIDE may be allowed to this or that degree, else a man cannot keep up his Dignity. In Gluttony there must be eating, in Drunkenness there must be drinking; 'tis not the eating, nor 'tis not the drinking that must be blamed, but the Excess. So in Pride.

Pride. — *Greville.*

PRIDE is a Virtue—let not the moralist be scandalized—Pride is also a Vice. Pride, like Ambition, is sometimes virtuous and sometimes vicious, according to the character in which it is found, and the object to which it is directed. As a Principle, it is the Parent of almost every Virtue, and every Vice,—every thing that pleases and displeases in mankind; and as the effects are so very different, nothing is more easy than to discover, even to ourselves, whether the Pride that produces them is virtuous or vicious: the first object of virtuous Pride is Rectitude, and the next Independence.

Pride. — *Colton.*

Pride requires very costly food—its keeper's Happiness.

Pride. — *Colton.*

TO quell the Pride, even of the greatest, we should reflect how much we owe to others, and how little to ourselves. Philip having made himself master of Potidœa, received three Messengers in one day: the first brought him an account of a great Victory, gained over the Illyrians, by his General Parmenio; the second told him, that he was proclaimed Victor at the Olympic games; and the third informed him of the birth of Alexander. But there was nothing in all these events that ought to have fed the Vanity, or that would have justified the Pride, of Philip, since, as an elegant writer remarks, "for the first he was indebted to his General; for the second, to his Horse; and his Wife is shrewdly suspected of having helped him to the third."

Pride. — *Shakspeare.*

I WILL from henceforth rather be myself,
Mighty, and to be fear'd, than my condition;
Which hath been smooth as Oil, soft as young Down,
And therefore lost that title of Respect,
Which the proud Soul ne'er pays, but to the Proud.

Procrastination. — *Young.*

Be wise to-day; 'tis Madness to defer;
Next day the fatal precedent will plead;
Thus on, till Wisdom is push'd out of Life.

Procrastination. — *Tillotson.*

TO be always intending to live a new Life, but never to find time to set about it: this is as if a man should put off Eating, and Drinking, and Sleeping, from one day and night to another, till he is starved and destroyed.

Procrastination. — *Persius.*

Corn. Unhappy he, who does his work adjourn,
And to To-morrow would the Search delay:
His lazy morrow will be like to-day.
Pers. But is one day of Ease too much to borrow?
Corn. Yes, sure; for Yesterday was once To-morrow.
That Yesterday is gone, and nothing gain'd;
And all thy fruitless days will thus be drain'd:
For thou hast more To-morrows yet to ask,
And wilt be ever to begin thy Task;
Who, like the hindmost Chariot Wheels, art curst,
Still to be near, but ne'er to reach, the first.

Procrastination. — *Hesiod.*

It will not always be Summer.

Procrastination. — *Shakspeare.*

THAT we would do,
We should do when we would; for this *would* changes,
And hath abatements and Delays as many,
As there are Tongues, are hands, are accidents;
And then this *should* is like a spendthrift Sigh,
That hurts by easing.

Procrastination. — *Horace.*

WHATEVER things injure your Eye, you are anxious to remove: but things which affect your Mind you defer

Prodigies. — *Shakspeare.*

WHEN Beggars die, there are no Comets seen.

Profligacy. — *Colton.*

HE that has never suffered extreme Adversity, knows not the full extent of his own Depravation; and he that has never enjoyed the summit of Prosperity, is equally ignorant how far the Iniquity of others can go. For our Adversity will excite temptations in ourselves, our Prosperity in others. Sir Robert Walpole observed, it was fortunate that few men could be Prime Ministers, because it was fortunate that few men could know the abandoned Profligacy of the Human Mind.

Prognostication. — *Shakspeare.*

WHEN Clouds are seen, wise men put on their cloaks;
When great leaves fall, then Winter is at hand;
When the Sun sets, who doth not look for Night·
Untimely Storms make men expect a Dearth.

Progress. — *Colton.*

THE wisest Man may be wiser to-day than he was yesterday, and to-morrow than he is to-day. Total freedom from Change would imply total freedom from Error; but this is the Prerogative of Omniscience alone.

Progress. — *Colton.*

WHO for the most part are they, that would have all Mankind look backward instead of forward, and regulate their Conduct by things that have been done? those who are the most ignorant as to all things that are doing. Lord Bacon said, time is the greatest of Innovators; he might also have said the greatest of Improvers; and I like Madame de Stael's observation on this subject, quite as well as Lord Bacon's: it is this, "that Past which is so presumptuously brought forward as a precedent for the Present, was itself founded on an alteration of some Past that went before it."

Progress. — *Genz.*

TWO principles govern the moral and intellectual World. One is perpetual Progress, the other the necessary limitations to that Progress. If the former alone prevailed, there would be nothing steadfast and durable on Earth, and the whole of social Life would be the sport of Winds and Waves. If the latter had exclusive sway, or even if it obtained a mischievous preponderancy, every thing would petrify or rot. The best ages of the World are always those in which these two principles are the most equally balanced. In such ages every enlightened man ought to adopt both principles into his whole Mind and Conduct, and with one hand develop what he *can*, with the other restrain and uphold what he *ought.*

Progress. — *Burke.*

BY the disposition of a stupendous Wisdom, moulding together the great mysterious incorporation of the Human Race, the whole, at one time, is never old, or middle-aged, or young; but, in a condition of unchangeable Constancy, moves on through the varied tenour of perpetual Decay, Fall, Renovation, and Progression.

Progress. — *Colton.*

WE ought not to be over anxious to encourage Innovation, in cases of *doubtful* Improvement, for an old system must ever have two advantages over a new one; it is established and it is understood.

Promises. — *Fuller.*

THOU oughtest to be nice, even to Superstition, in keeping thy Promises; and therefore thou shouldst be equally cautious in making them.

Promises. — *Rousseau.*

HE who is most slow in making a Promise is the most faithful in the Performance of it.

Promptitude. — *Wirt.*

SEIZE the moment of excited curiosity on any subject, to solve your doubts; for if you let it pass, the desire may never return, and you may remain in ignorance.

Prophecy. — *Shakspeare.*

THERE is a History in all men's lives.
Figuring the Nature of the times deceased;
The which observed, a man may prophesy,
With a near aim, of the main Chance of things
As yet not come to Life, which in their seeds,
And weak beginnings, lie intreasured.

Prosperity. — *Shakspeare.*

Prosperity is the very bond of Love;
Whose fresh complexion and whose Heart together
Affliction alters.

Prosperity. — *Zimmerman.*

TAKE care to be an economist in Prosperity: there is no fear of your being one in Adversity.

Providence. — *Shakspeare.*

THAT high All-seer which I dallied with,
Hath turn'd my feigned Prayer on my head,
And given in earnest what I begg'd in jest.
Thus doth He force the Swords of wicked men
To turn their own points on their masters' bosoms.

Providence. — *Hannah More.*

YES, Thou art ever present, Power Supreme!
Not circumscribed by Time, nor fixt to Space,
Confined to altars, nor to temples bound.
In Wealth, in Want, in Freedom or in Chains,
In Dungeons or on Thrones, the faithful find thee!

Providence. — *Thomson.*

THIS is thy work, Almighty Providence!
Whose Power, beyond the stretch of human thought,
Revolves the orbs of Empire; bids them sink
Deep in the dead'ning Night of thy displeasure,
Or rise majestic o'er a wondering world.

Providence. — *Shakspeare.*

OUR Indiscretion sometimes serves us well;
When our deep plots do pall: and that should teach us,
There's a Divinity that shapes our ends,
Rough-hew them how we will.

Providence. — *Racine.*

HE who ruleth the raging of the Sea, knows also how to check the designs of the Ungodly.—I submit myself with reverence to his Holy Will. O Abner, I fear my God, and I fear none but him.

Providence. — *Cowper.*

GO, mark the matchless working of the Power
That shuts within the seed the future Flower;
Bids these in elegance of form excel,
In colour these, and those delight the smell;
Sends Nature forth, the Daughter of the skies,
To dance on Earth, and charm all human Eyes

Providence. — *Spenser.*

AND is there care in Heaven? and is there love
In heavenly Spirits to the creatures base,
That may compassion of their evills move?
There is; else much more wretched were the case
Of men than beasts. But oh! th' exceeding Grace
Of highest God that loves his creatures so,
And all his works with Mercy doth embrace,
That blessed angels he sends to and fro
To serve to wicked man, to serve his wicked foe!
How oft do they their silver bowres leave
To come to succour us that succour want?
How oft do they with golden pinions cleave
The flitting skyes, like flying Pursuivant,
Against fowle feendes to ayd us militant?
They for us fight, they watch and dewly ward,
And their bright Squadrons round about us plant;
And all for Love, and nothing for reward:
Oh why should heavenly God to men have such regard!

Prudence. — *Shakspeare.*

WHO buys a minute's mirth, to wail a week?
Or sells Eternity to get a toy?
For one sweet grape, who will the Vine destroy?
Or what fond beggar, but to touch the Crown,
Would with the Sceptre straight be strucken down?

Prudence. — *Colton.*

MEN are born with two Eyes, but with one Tongue, in order that they should see twice as much as they say.

Prudence. — *Colton.*

THOSE characters, who, like Ventidius, spring from the very dregs of society, and going through every gradation of Life, continue, like him, to rise with every change, and who never quit a single step in the ladder, except it be to gain a higher one, these men are superior to Fortune, and know how to enjoy her Caresses without being the slaves of her Caprice.

Prudence. — *Shakspeare.*

'Tis better using France, than trusting.
Let us be back'd with God, and with the Seas,
Which he hath given for Fence impregnable,
And with their helps alone defend ourselves:
In them, and in ourselves, our Safety lies.

Prudence. — *Juvenal.*

NO other Protection is wanting, provided you are under the guidance of Prudence.

Punishment. — *Wilkes.*

THE very worst use to which you can put a Man is to hang him.

Punishment. — *From the Latin.*

THE slightest corporal Punishment falls more heavily than the most weighty pecuniary Penalty.

Puritanism. — *Bancroft.*

CHIVALRY delighted in outward show, favoured pleasure, multiplied amusement, and degraded the human race by an exclusive respect for the privileged classes; Puritanism bridled the passions, commended the virtues of self-denial, and rescued the name of man from dishonour. The former valued courtesy; the latter justice. The former adorned society by graceful refinements; the latter founded national grandeur on universal education. The institutions of chivalry were subverted by the gradually increasing weight, and knowledge, and opulence of the industrious classes. The Puritans, rallying upon those classes, planted in their hearts the undying principles of democratic liberty.

Purity. — *Shakspeare.*

HER smoothness,
Her very Silence, and her Patience,
Speak to the people, and they pity her.

Purity. — *Buckingham.*

MAKE my breast
Transparent as pure Crystal, that the world,
Jealous of me, may see the foulest thought,
My Heart does hold.

Purity. — *Shakspeare.*

A MAIDEN never bold;
Of spirit so still and quiet, that her motion
Blush'd at herself.

Purity. — *Shakspeare.*

THERE'S nothing ill can dwell in such a Temple.
If the Ill spirit have so fair a house,
Good things will strive to dwell with't.

Purity. — *Hare.*

PURITY is the feminine, Truth the masculine, of Honour.

Purity. — *Hare.*

BY the ancients, Courage was regarded as practically the main part of Virtue: by us, though I hope we are not less brave, Purity is so regarded now. The former is evidently the animal excellence, a thing not to be left out when we are balancing the one against the other. Still the following considerations weigh more with me. Courage, when not an instinct, is the creation of society, depending for occasions of Action (which is essential to it) on outward circumstances, and deriving much both of its character and its motives from popular Opinion and Esteem. But Purity is inward, secret, self-sufficing, harmless, and, to crown all, thoroughly and intimately personal. It is indeed a Nature, rather than a Virtue; and, like other natures, when most perfect, is least conscious of itself and its perfection. In a word, Courage, however kindled, is fanned by the breath of man: Purity lives and derives its life solely from the Spirit of God.

Pursuits. — *Terence.*

I TAKE it to be a principal rule of Life, not to be too much addicted to any one thing

Quarrels. — *Tacitus.*

THE Hatred of those who are the most nearly connected, is the most inveterate.

Quarrels. — *Shakspeare.*

ACCURSED and unquiet wrangling days!
How many of you have mine Eyes beheld.

Quarrels. — *Colton.*

IF you cannot avoid a quarrel with a Blackguard, let your Lawyer manage it, rather than yourself. No man sweeps his own chimney, but employs a chimney-sweeper, who has no objection to dirty work, because it is his trade.

Quarrels. — *Shakspeare.*

CONTENTION, like a Horse,
Full of high feeding, madly hath broke loose,
And bears down all before him.

Quarrels. — *Shakspeare.*

BEWARE
Of entrance to a Quarrel: but, being in,
Bear it that the Opposer may beware of thee.

Rank. — *Juvenal.*

EVERY Error of the mind is the more conspicuous, and culpable, in proportion to the Rank of the person who commits it.

Rank. — *Goldsmith.*

QUALITY and Title have such allurements, that hundreds are ready to give up all their own importance, to cringe, to flatter, to look little, and to pall every pleasure in constraint, merely to be among the Great, though without the least hopes of improving their Understanding or sharing their Generosity: they might be happy among their equals, but those are despised for company where they are despised in turn.

Ranks and Degrees. — *Shakspeare.*

WHEN that the General is not like the hive,
To whom the foragers shall all repair,
What Honey is expected? Degree being vizarded
Th' unworthiest shows as fairly in the mask.
The Heavens themselves, the Planets, and this Centre
Observe Degree, Priority, and Place,
Insisture, Course, Proportion, Season, Form,
Office and Custom, in all line of Order:
And therefore is the glorious planet Sol
In noble eminence enthroned and sphered
Amidst the rest, whose med'cinable eye
Corrects the ill aspects of Planets evil,
And posts like the commandment of a King,
Sans check, to good and bad. But when the Planets
In evil mixture to Disorder wander,
What plagues, and what portents, what mutiny?
What raging of the Sea? shaking of Earth?
Commotion in the Winds? frights, changes, horrors,
Divert and crack, rend, and deracinate
The unity and married calm of States
Quite from their fixure? Oh, when Degree is shaken,
(Which is the ladder to all high designs)
The enterprise is sick. How could communities,
Degrees in schools, and Brotherhoods in cities,
Peaceful commerce from dividable shores,
The primogeniture, and due of birth,
Prerogative of age, crowns, sceptres, laurels,
(But by Degree) stand in authentic place?
Take but Degree away, untune that string,
And hark what Discord follows; each thing meets
In mere oppugnancy. The bounded waters
Would lift their bosoms higher than the shores,
And make a sop of all this solid Globe:
Strength would be lord of Imbecility,
And the rude son would strike his father dead:

Force would be Right; or rather, Right and Wrong
(Between whose endless jar Justice resides)
Would lose their names, and so would Justice too.
Then every thing includes itself in power,
Power into Will, Will into Appetite;
And Appetite, an universal Wolf,
So doubly seconded with Will and Power,
Must make perforce an universal prey,
And, last, eat up himself.—
This chaos, when Degree is suffocate,
Follows the choking.
And this neglection of Degree it is,
That by a pace goes backward, with a purpose
It hath to climb. The General's disdain'd
By him one step below; he, by the next;
That next, by him beneath; so every step,
Exampled by the first pace, that is sick
Of his superior, grows to an envious fever
Of pale and bloodless Emulation.

Rationality. — *Greville.*

MAN is said to be a Rational Creature; but should it not rather be said, that Man is a Creature *capable* of being Rational, as we say a Parrot is a Creature *capable* of Speech?

Rashness. — *Shakspeare.*

THAT'S a valiant Flea, that dare eat his breakfast on the lip of a Lion.

Reading. — *Pliny.*

HE picked something out of every thing he read.

Reading. — *Johnson.*

WHAT we read with inclination makes a stronger impression. If we read without inclination, half the mind is employed in fixing the Attention, so there is but half to be employed on what we read. If a man begins to read in the middle of a Book, and feels an inclination to go on, let him not quit it to go to the beginning. He may perhaps not feel again the inclination.

Reading. — *Bacon.*

READ not to contradict and confute, nor to believe and take for granted, nor to find Talk and Discourse, but to weigh and consider.

Reason. — *Sir Philip Sidney.*

REASON cannot show itself more reasonable, than to leave reasoning on things above Reason.

Reason. — *Burke.*

WE are afraid to put men to live and trade each on his own private stock of Reason; because we suspect that this stock in each man is small, and that the individuals would do better to avail themselves of the general Bank and Capital of Nations and of Ages.

Reason. — *Sir W. Drummond.*

HE that will not Reason is a Bigot, he that cannot Reason is a Fool, and he that dares not Reason is a Slave.

Reason. — *La Rochefoucauld.*

HE is not a reasonable Man who by chance stumbles upon Reason, but he who derives it from Knowledge, from Discernment, and from Taste.

Reason. — *Anon.*

ONE can never repeat too often, that Reason, as it exists in man, is only our intellectual eye, and that, like the eye, to see, it needs Light,—to see clearly and far, it needs the Light of Heaven.

Rebellion. — *Shakspeare.*

WHAT rein can hold licentious Wickedness,
When down the hill he holds his fierce career?
We may as bootless spend our vain command,
Upon th' enraged Soldiers in their spoil,
Or send precepts to th' Leviathan.

Rebuking. — *Shakspeare.*

WHAT though the mast be now blown overboard,
The cable broke, the holding Anchor lost,
And half our sailors swallow'd in the flood?
Yet lives our Pilot still: Is't meet, that he
Should leave the helm, and, like a fearful lad,
With tearful eyes add water to the Sea,
And give more strength to that which hath too much,
Whiles, in his moan, the Ship splits on the rock,
Which Industry and Courage might have saved?
Ah, what a shame! ah, what a fault were this!

Rebuking. — *Fuller.*

IN all Reprehensions, observe to express rather thy Love than thy Anger; and strive rather to convince than exasperate: but if the Matter do require any special Indignation, let it appear to be the zeal of a displeased Friend, rather than the passion of a provoked Enemy.

Recreation. — *Saville.*

DIVERSIONS are the most properly applied, to ease and relieve those who are oppressed, by being too much employed. Those that are idle have no need of them, and yet they, above all others, give themselves up to them. To unbend our Thoughts, when they are too much stretched by our Cares, is not more natural than it is necessary; but to turn our whole Life into a holyday, is not only ridiculous, but destroyeth Pleasure instead of promoting it.

Refinement. — *Greville.*

TRUE Delicacy, as true Generosity, is more wounded by an offence *from* itself, if I may be allowed the expression, than *to* itself.

Refinement. — *La Bruyere.*

THE most delicate, the most sensible of all Pleasures, consists in promoting the Pleasures of others.

Refinement. — *Greville.*

THERE seems to be something satisfactory resulting from every defect in Human Nature! and it is in that satisfaction, methinks, that all the endearing refinements of Society consist; there are a thousand little and undefinable Delicacies in our conversation, our looks, and even Gestures, arising from these defects, which mutually require to be understood and returned; nay, there are little indulgences due to these Defects, which the well-disposed and well-conceiving Mind feels a want to bestow as well as to receive, and will be uneasy and dissatisfied till an opportunity offers to do it; and hence that first of Concerts, the play and harmony of according Minds!

Refinement. — *Hume.*

IF refined sense, and exalted sense, be not so useful as Common Sense, their rarity, their novelty, and the nobleness of their objects, make some compensation, and render them the admiration of Mankind.

Reform. — *Lavater.*

HE who reforms himself, has done more toward reforming the Public, than a crowd of noisy, impotent Patriots.

Reforms. — *Colton.*

CHARLES FOX said that Restorations were the most bloody of all Revolutions; and, he might have added, that Reformations are the best mode of preventing the necessity of either.

Regret. — *Shakspeare.*

WHAT! old Acquaintance! could not all this flesh
Keep in a little life? Poor Jack, farewell!
I could have better spared a better man.

Religion. — *Burke.*

WE know, and what is better, we feel inwardly, that Religion is the basis of civil Society, and the source of all good and of all comfort. In England we are so convinced of this, that there is no rust of Superstition with which the accumulated absurdity of the human mind might have crusted it over in the course of ages, that ninety-nine in a hundred of the People of England would not prefer to Impiety.

Religion. — *Hare.*

WORDSWORTH has told us the law of his own mind, the fulfilment of which has enabled him to reveal a new world of poetry: "Wisdom is oft-times nearer when we stoop than when we soar." That it is so likewise in Religion, we are assured by those most comfortable words, "Except ye become as little children, ye shall not enter into the Kingdom of Heaven."

Religion. — *Colton.*

CHARLES the Fourth, after his abdication, amused himself in his retirement at St. Juste, by attempting to make a number of watches go exactly together. Being constantly foiled in this attempt, he exclaimed, "What a fool have I been to neglect my own concerns, and to waste my whole Life in a vain attempt to make all men think alike on matters of Religion, when I cannot even make a few Watches keep time together."

Religion. — *S. T. Coleridge.*

UNLESS Christianity be viewed and felt in a high and comprehensive way, how large a portion of our intellectual and moral Nature does it leave without Object and Action!

Religion. — *South.*

TRUTH, like a stately dame, will not be seen, nor show herself at the first visit, nor match with the Understanding upon an ordinary Courtship or address. Long and tedious attendances must be given, and the hardest fatigues endured and digested: nor did ever the most pregnant Wit in the world bring forth any thing great, lasting, and considerable, without some Pain and Travail, some pangs and Throes before the delivery. Now all this that I have said is to show the force of diligence in the investigation of Truth, and particularly of the noblest of all Truths, which is that of Religion.

Religion. — *Fuller.*

PLACE not thy amendment only in increasing thy Devotion, but in bettering thy Life. This is the damning Hypocrisy of this age; that it slights all good Morality, and spends its zeal in matters of Ceremony, and a form of Godliness without the Power of it.

Religion. — *Colton.*

RELIGION, like its votaries, while it exists on Earth, must have a body as well as a soul. A Religion purely spiritual might suit a being as pure, but Men are compound animals; and the body too often lords it over the Mind.

Religion. — *S. T. Coleridge.*

YOU may depend upon it, Religion is, in its essence, the most gentlemanly thing in the World. It will *alone* gentilize, if unmixed with cant; and I know nothing else that will, *alone.* Certainly not the Army, which is thought to be the grand embellisher of Manners.

Religion. — *Lavater.*

THE more Honesty a man has, the less he affects the air of a Saint.

Religion. — *Hare.*

MANY people make their own God; and he is much what the French may mean, when they talk of *Le bon Dieu,*—very indulgent, rather weak, near at hand when we want any thing, but far away out of sight when we have a mind to do wrong. Such a God is as much an Idol as if he were an Image of stone.

Religion. — *Colton.*

PHILOSOPHY is a bully that talks very loud, when the danger is at a distance; but the moment she is hard pressed by the Enemy, she is not to be found at her post, but leaves the brunt of the Battle to be borne by her humbler but steadier comrade, Religion.

Religion. — *Anon.*

RELIGION is the whole Bible: Sects pick out a part of it. But what whole? The Living whole, to be sure—not the Dead whole: THE SPIRIT! not the letter.

Religion. — *Selden.*

THEY that cry down Moral Honesty, cry down that which is a great part of my Religion—my Duty toward God, and my Duty toward Man. What care I to see a man run after a sermon, if he cozens and cheats as soon as he comes home. On the other side, Morality must not be without Religion; for if so, it may change, as I see convenience. Religion must govern it.

Religion.—*S. T. Coleridge.*

IF a man is not rising upward to be an Angel, depend upon it, he is sinking downward to be a Devil. He cannot stop at the Beast. The most savage of men are not Beasts; they are worse, a great deal worse.

Religion.—*South.*

HE that is a Good Man, is three-quarters of his way toward the being a Good Christian, wheresoever he lives, or whatsoever he is called.

Religion.—*S. T. Coleridge.*

IF you bring up your children in a way which puts them out of sympathy with the Religious feelings of the Nation in which they live, the chances are, that they will ultimately turn out Ruffians or Fanatics, and one as likely as the other.

Religion.—*Pascal.*

LET it not be imagined that the Life of a good Christian must necessarily be a Life of Melancholy and Gloominess; for he only resigns some Pleasures, to enjoy others infinitely greater.

Religion.—*Melmoth.*

I CANNOT but take notice of the wonderful love of God to mankind, who, in order to encourage obedience to his Laws, has annexed a present, as well as future reward to a Good Life; and has so interwoven our Duty and Happiness together, that while we are discharging our obligations to the one, we are, at the same time, making the best provision for the other.

Religion.—*Anon.*

LIKE every other Power, Religion too, in widening her empire, may impair her sway. It has been seen too often, both in Philosophy and elsewhere, that, when people have fancied that the world was becoming Christian, Christianity was in fact becoming worldly.

Religion.—*Anon.*

WHEN a man is told that the whole of Religion and Morality is summed up in the two Commandments, to love God, and to love our neighbour, he is ready to cry, like Charoba in Gebir, at the first sight of the Sea, "Is this the mighty Ocean? Is this all?" Yes! all: but how small a part of it do your eyes survey! only trust yourself to it; launch out upon it; sail abroad over it: you will find it has no end: it will carry you round the World.

Religion.—*Fuller.*

MEASURE not Men by Sundays, without regarding what they do all the Week after.

Religion.—*Colton.*

ALL who have been great and good without Christianity, would have been much greater and better with it. If there be, among the Sons of men, a single exception to this maxim, the divine Socrates may be allowed to put in the strongest claim. It was his high Ambition to deserve, by Deeds, not by creeds, an *unrevealed* Heaven, and by works, not by faith, to enter an *unpromised* land.

Religion.—*Anon.*

WHO are the most godlike of men? The question might be a puzzling one, unless our language answered it for us: the Godliest.

Religion.—*Colton.*

THAT country where the Clergy have the most influence, and use it with the most Moderation, is England.

Religion.—*Pope.*

FOR Virtue's self may too much zeal be had;
The worst of madmen is a Saint run mad.

Religion.—*Colton.*

WHEN the Methodists first decide on the doctrine they approve, and then choose such Pastors as they know beforehand will preach no other, they act as wisely as a Patient, who should send for a Physician, and then prescribe to him what Medicines he ought to advise.

Religion.—*Colton.*

THERE can be no Christianity where there is no Charity, but the censorious cultivate the forms of Religion, that they may more freely indulge in the only pleasure of their lives—that of calumniating those who to their other feelings add not the Sin of Hypocrisy.

Religion.—*Colton.*

PHILOSOPHY is a goddess, whose head indeed is in Heaven, but whose feet are upon Earth; she attempts more than she accomplishes, and promises more than she performs; she can teach us to *hear* of the calamities of others with Magnanimity; but it is Religion only that can teach us to bear our own with Resignation.

Religion.—*Addison.*

HYPOCRISY itself does great Honour, or rather Justice, to Religion, and tacitly acknowledges it to be an ornament to human nature. The Hypocrite would not be at so much pains to put on the appearance of Virtue, if he did not know it was the most proper and effectual means to gain the Love and Esteem of mankind.

Religion. — *Colton.*

MEN will wrangle for Religion; write for it; fight for it; die for it; any thing but—*live* for it.

Religion. — *Pope.*

THERE is nothing wanting to make all rational and disinterested people in the world of one Religion, but that they should talk together every day.

Religion. — *Colton.*

AS all who frequent any place of Public Worship, however they may differ from the doctrines there delivered, are expected to comport themselves with Seriousness and Gravity, so in religious Controversies, Ridicule ought never to be resorted to on either side.

Religion. — *Moore.*

THOUGH thus, my Friend, so long employ'd,
And so much midnight Oil destroy'd,
I must confess, my Searches past,
I only learn'd to doubt at last.

Religion. — *Sprat.*

THE Head truly enlightened will presently have a wonderful influence in purifying the Heart; and the Heart really affected with Goodness, will much conduce to the directing of the Head.

Religion. — *Colton.*

IT has been said that men carry on a kind of coasting trade with Religion. In the voyage of life, they profess to be in search of Heaven, but take care not to venture so far in their approximations to it, as entirely to lose sight of the Earth; and should their frail vessel be in danger of Shipwreck, they will gladly throw their darling Vices overboard, as other Mariners their treasures, only to fish them up again when the Storm is over.

Religion. — *Baxter.*

IT is one thing to take God and Heaven for your portion, as believers do, and another thing to be desirous of it, as a reserve when you can keep the World no longer. It is one thing to submit to Heaven, as a lesser evil than Hell: and another thing to desire it as a greater good than Earth. It is one thing to lay up treasures and hopes in Heaven, and seek it first; and another thing to be contented with it in our necessity, and to seek the world before it, and give God that the flesh can spare. Thus differeth the Religion of serious Christians, and of carnal, worldly Hypocrites.

Religion. — *Pope.*

AN Atheist is but a mad, ridiculous derider of Piety; but a Hypocrite makes a sober jest of God and Religion; he finds it easier to be upon his knee than to rise to a good action.

Religion.—*Baxter.*

IF it were only the exercise of the body, the moving of the Lips, the bending of the Knee, men would as commonly step to Heaven as they go to visit a friend: but to separate our thoughts and affections from the world, to draw forth all our Graces, and increase each in its proper object, and to hold them to it till the Work prospers in our hands,—this, this is the difficulty.

Religion.—*Shakspeare.*

LOVE thyself last; cherish those Hearts that hate thee;
Corruption wins not more than Honesty.
Still in thy right hand carry gentle Peace,
To silence envious tongues. Be just, and fear not.
Let all the ends thou aim'st at be
Thy God's, and Truth's; then, when thou fall'st,
Thou fall'st a blessed Martyr.

Religion.—*South.*

THE Pleasure of the Religious Man is an easy and portable Pleasure, such an one as he carries about in his Bosom, without alarming either the Eye or the Envy of the world.—A man putting all his Pleasures into this one, is like a traveller's putting all his goods into one Jewel; the value is the same, and the convenience greater.

Religion.—*Anon.*

THE Religious are often charged with judging uncharitably of others; and perhaps the charge may at times be deserved. With our narrow, partial views, it is very difficult to feel the evil of an Error strongly, and yet to think kindly of him in whom we see it.

Religion.—*Colton.*

THERE are three modes of bearing the Ills of Life; by Indifference, which is the most common; by Philosophy, which is the most ostentatious; and by Religion, which is the most effectual.

Religion.—*Shaftesbury.*

IF we are told a man is religious, we still ask, what are his Morals? But if we hear at first that he has honest Morals, and is a man of natural Justice and Good Temper, we seldom think of the other question, whether he be religious and devout?

Religion.—*Hare.*

THE Imagination and the Feelings have each their Truths, as well as the Reason. The absorption of the three, so as to concentrate them in the same point, is one of the universalities requisite in a true Religion.

Religion.—*Young.*

KNOW,
Without Star, or Angel, for their Guide,
Who worship God, shall find him. Humble Love,
And not proud Reason, keeps the door of Heaven;
Love finds admission, where proud Science fails.

Religion.—*Dryden.*

BUT whither went his Soul, let such relate
Who search the secrets of a future state:
Divines can say but what themselves believe;
Strong proofs they have, but not demonstrative:
For, were all plain, then all sides must agree,
And Faith itself be lost in certainty.
To live uprightly then is sure the best:
To save ourselves, and not to damn the rest.

Religion.—*Colton.*

IN all places, and in all times, those Religionists who have believed too much, have been more inclined to Violence and Persecution, than those who have believed too little.

Religion.—*Shakspeare.*

IT is an Heretic that makes the Fire,
Not he which burns in't.

Religion.—*From the Latin.*

A MAN devoid of Religion, is like a Horse without a bridle.

Religion.—*Shakspeare.*

IT is Religion that doth make vows kept.

Religion.—*Byron.*

MY altars are the Mountains and the Ocean,
Earth, Air, Stars,—all that springs from the great Whole,
Who hath produced, and will receive the Soul.

Religion.—*Pope.*

SLAVE to no sect, who takes no private road,
But looks through Nature up to Nature's God.

Religion.—*Cowper.*

I VENERATE the man, whose Heart is warm,
Whose hands are pure; whose doctrine and whose Life
Coincident, exhibit lucid proof
That he is honest in the Sacred Cause.

Personal Religion. — *Webster.*

POLITICAL eminence and professional fame fade away and die with all things earthly. Nothing of character is really permanent but virtue and personal worth. These remain. Whatever of excellence is wrought into the soul itself belongs to both worlds. Real goodness does not attach itself merely to this life; it points to another world. Political or professional reputation cannot last forever; but a conscience void of offence before God and man is an inheritance for eternity. Religion, therefore, is a necessary and indispensable element in any great human character. There is no living without it. Religion is the tie that connects man with his Creator, and holds him to his throne. If that tie be all sundered, all broken, he floats away, a worthless atom in the universe; its proper attractions all gone, its destiny thwarted, and its whole future nothing but darkness, desolation, and death. A man with no sense of religious duty is he whom the Scriptures describe, in such terse but terrific language, as living "without God in the world." Such a man is out of his proper being, out of the circle of all his duties, out of the circle of all his happiness, and away, far, far away, from the purposes of his creation.

Religion and Morality. — *Washington.*

OF all the dispositions and habits which lead to political prosperity, Religion and Morality are indispensable supports. In vain would that man claim the tribute of patriotism, who should labour to subvert these great pillars of human happiness, these firmest props of the duties of men and citizens. And let us with caution indulge the supposition that morality can be maintained without religion. Whatever may be conceded to the influence of refined education on minds of peculiar structure, reason and experience both forbid us to expect that national morality can prevail in exclusion of religious principle.

Reason in Religion. — *Archibald Alexander.*

THAT it is the right and the duty of all men to exercise their Reason in inquiries concerning Religion, is a truth so manifest, that it may be presumed there are none who will be disposed to call it in question. Without reason, there can be no religion; for in every step we take in examining the evidences of revelation, in interpreting its meaning, or in assenting to its doctrines, the exercise of this faculty is indispensable. When the evidences of Christianity are exhibited, an appeal is made to the reason of men for its truth; but all evidence and all argument would be perfectly futile, if reason were not permitted to judge of their force. This noble faculty was certainly given to man to be a guide in religion as well as in other things. He possesses no other means by which he can form a judgment on any subject or assent to any truth; and it would be no more absurd to talk of seeing without eyes, than of knowing any thing without reason.

Remembrance. — *Shakspeare.*

REMEMBER thee?
Yea, from the table of my Memory
I'll wipe away all trivial fond records,
All saws of Books, all forms, all pressures past,
That Youth and Observation copied there;
And thy commandment all alone shall live
Within the Book and volume of my Brain,
Unmix'd with baser matter.

Remembrance. — *Shakspeare.*

DISPUTE it like a Man.
I shall do so:
But I must also feel it as a Man.
I cannot but remember such things were,
That were most precious to me.

Remorse. — *Scott.*

HIGH minds, of native Pride and force,
Most deeply feel thy pangs, Remorse!
Fear for their scourge mean Villains have;
Thou art the torturer of the Brave.

Repentance. — *Shakspeare.*

THEY say, best Men are moulded out of faults:
And, for the most, become much more the better
For being a little bad.

Repentance. — *Colton.*

SOME well-meaning Christians tremble for their Salvation, because they have never gone through that valley of Tears and of Sorrow, which they have been taught to consider as an ordeal that must be passed through, before they can arrive at Regeneration; to satisfy such minds, it may be observed, that the slightest sorrow for Sin is sufficient, if it produce Amendment, and that the greatest is insufficient, if it do not.

Repentance. — *South.*

REPENTANCE hath a purifying power, and every Tear is of a cleansing Virtue; but these penitential clouds must be still kept dropping; one shower will not suffice; for Repentance is not one single action, but a course.

Repentance.—*Rowe.*

HABITUAL Evils change not on a sudden,
But many days must pass, and many Sorrows:
Conscious Remorse and Anguish must be felt,
To curb Desire, to break the stubborn Will,
And work a second nature in the Soul,
Ere Virtue can resume the place she lost.

Repentance.—*Shakspeare.*

REPLY not to me with a Fool-born jest;
Presume not, that I am the thing I was:
For Heaven doth know, so shall the world perceive,
That I have turn'd away my former self;
So will I those that kept me Company.

Repentance.—*Hare.*

WE look to our last sickness for Repentance, unmindful that it is during a Recovery men repent, not during a Sickness. For Sickness, by the time we feel it to be such, has its own Trials, its own selfishness: and to bear the one, and overcome the other, is at such a season occupation more than enough for any who have not been trained to it by previous Discipline and practice.

Repentance.—*La Rochefoucauld.*

OUR Repentance is not so much Regret for the Evil we have done as Fear of its Consequences to us.

Repentance.—*Shakspeare.*

O WRETCHED state! O Bosom, black as Death
O limed Soul; that struggling to be free,
Art more engaged! Help, Angels, make assay!
Bow, stubborn knees! and, Heart, with strings of steel,
Be soft as sinews of the new-born babe.

Reproof.—*Shakspeare.*

THOU hast cast away thyself, being like thyself:
A Madman so long, now a Fool: What, think'st
That the bleak air, thy boisterous Chamberlain,
Will put thy shirt on warm? Will these moss'd trees,
That have outlived the Eagle, page thy heels,
And skip, when thou point'st out? Will the cold brook,
Candied with Ice, caudle thy morning taste,
To cure thy o'ernight's surfeit? call the creatures,—
Whose naked natures live in all the spite
Of wreakful Heaven; whose bare unhoused trunks,
To the conflicting elements exposed,
Answer mere Nature,—bid them flatter thee.

Repulsion. — *Shakspeare.*

STRANGE is it, that our Bloods,
Of Colour, Weight, and Heat, pour'd all together,
Would quite confound distinction, yet stand off
In differences so mighty.

Reputation. — *Sewell.*

O REPUTATION! dearer far than Life,
Thou precious balsam, lovely, sweet of smell,
Whose cordial drops once spilt by some rash hand,
Not all the owner's care, nor the repenting Toil
Of the rude spiller, ever can collect
To its first Purity and native Sweetness.

Resentment. — *Lucian.*

EVEN the Ant has bile.

Resolution. — *Shakspeare.*

BE stirring as the time; be Fire with Fire;
Threaten the Threat'ner, and out-face the brow
Of bragging Horror: so shall inferior eyes,
That borrow their behaviours from the Great,
Grow great by your example, and put on
The dauntless spirit of Resolution.

Resolution. — *Shakspeare.*

Do not, for one repulse, forego the purpose
That you resolved to effect.

Respect. — *Greville.*

RESPECT is better procured by exacting than soliciting it.

Self-Respect. — *Shakspeare.*

To thine ownself be true;
And it must follow, as the Night the Day;
Thou can'st not then be false to any man.

Self-Respect. — *Fuller.*

BE fearful only of thyself; and stand in awe of none more than of thine own Conscience. There is a Cato in every man; a severe Censor of his Manners. And he that reverences this Judge, will seldom do any thing he need repent of.

Responsibility. — *Shakspeare.*

'TIS ever common,
That men are merriest when they are from Home.

Restlessness. — *Sir Walter Raleigh.*

'TIS plain there is not in Nature a point of stability to be found: every thing either ascends or declines: when Wars are ended abroad, Sedition begins at home; and when men are freed from fighting for Necessity, they quarrel through Ambition.

Results. — *Colton.*

TO judge by the event, is an error all abuse, and all commit; for, in every instance, Courage, if crowned with success, is Heroism; if clouded by Defeat, Temerity. When Nelson fought his battle in the Sound, it was the Result alone that decided whether he was to kiss a hand at a Court, or a rod at a Court-Martial.

Retirement. — *Goldsmith.*

SWEET was the sound, when oft at Evening's close,
Up yonder hill the Village Murmur rose:
There, as I pass'd with careless steps and slow,
The mingling notes came soften'd from below;
The Swain responsive as the Milkmaid sung,
The sober Herd that low'd to meet their young;
The noisy Geese that gabbled o'er the pool,
The playful Children just let loose from School;
The Watch-dog's voice that bay'd the whisp'ring wind,
And the loud Laugh that spoke the vacant mind;
These all in sweet Confusion sought the Shade,
And fill'd each pause the Nightingale had made.

Retirement. —*Milton.*

AND may at last my weary Age
Find out the peaceful Hermitage,
The hairy gown and mossy cell,
Where I may sit and rightly spell
Of every star that Heaven doth shew,
And every herb that sips the dew;
Till old Experience do attain
To something like prophetic strain.

Retirement. — *Spenser.*

THE Fields did laugh, the Floures did freshly spring,
The Trees did bud, and early blossomes bore,
And all the quire of Birds did sweetly sing,
And told that gardin's pleasures in their Caroling.

Retirement. — *Spenser.*

TO them that list, the World's gay showes I leave,
And to great ones such follies doe forgive,
Which oft through Pride doe their owne perill weave,
And through Ambition downe themselves doe drive
To sad decay, that might contented live:
Me no such cares nor cumbrous thoughts offend,
Ne once my Mind's unmoved Quiet grieve,
But all the night in silver Sleepe I spend,
And all the day, to what I list I doe attend.

Retirement. — *Cowper.*

THE fall of Waters and the song of birds,
And hills that echo to the distant herds,
Are luxuries excelling all the glare
The World can boast, and her chief Favourites share.

Retirement. — *Thomson.*

NO noise, no care, no Vanity, no strife:
Men, woods, and fields, all breathe untroubled Life:
Then keep each Passion down, however dear;
Trust me, the tender are the most severe.
Guard, while 'tis thine, thy philosophic Ease,
And ask no Joy but that of virtuous Peace;
That bids defiance to the storms of Fate,
High Bliss is only for a higher state.

Retirement. — *Smollett.*

NATURE I'll court in her sequester'd haunts,
By Mountain, Meadow, streamlet, grove, or cell;
Where the poised Lark his evening ditty chaunts,
And Health, and Peace, and Contemplation dwell.

Retirement. — *Pope.*

BORN to no Pride, inheriting no strife,
Nor marrying discord in a noble Wife,
Stranger to civil and religious rage,
The good man walk'd innoxious through his Age;
No courts he saw, no suits would ever try,
Nor dared an Oath, nor hazarded a Lie.
Unlearn'd, he knew no schoolman's subtle art,
No language but the language of the Heart.
By Nature honest, by Experience wise,
Healthy by Temp'rance and by Exercise;
His life, though long, to sickness pass'd unknown,
His Death was instant, and without a groan.
Oh grant me thus to live, and thus to die!
Who sprung from Kings shall know less joy than I.

Retirement. — *Thomson.*

WHAT, what is Virtue but Repose of Mind,
A pure ethereal Calm, that knows no storm;
Above the reach of wild Ambition's wind,
Above the Passions that this world deform,
And torture Man, a proud malignant worm;
But here, instead, soft gales of Passion play,
And gently stir the Heart, thereby to form
A quicker sense of joy; as breezes stray
Across th' enliven'd Skies, and make them still more gay.

Retirement. — *Southey.*

BUT peace was on the Cottage, and the fold
From court intrigue, from bickering faction far;
Beneath the chestnut tree Love's tale was told;
And to the tinkling of the light guitar,
Sweet stoop'd the western Sun, sweet rose the evening Star.

Retirement. — *Mrs. Tighe.*

HOW much they err, who to their interest blind,
Slight the calm Peace which from Retirement flows!
And while they think their fleeting joys to bind,
Banish the tranquil bliss which Heaven for Man design'd!

Retirement. — *Hammond.*

WHAT joy to hear the Tempest howl in vain,
And clasp a fearful mistress to my breast!
Or lull'd to slumber by the beating Rain,
Secure and happy, sink at last to rest!

Retirement. —*Johnson.*

COULDST thou resign the park and play, content,
For the fair banks of Severn or of Trent;
There might'st thou find some elegant retreat,
Some hireling Senator's deserted seat;
And stretch thy prospects o'er the smiling land,
For less than rent the dungeons of the Strand;
There prune thy walks, support thy drooping flow'rs,
Direct thy Rivulets, and twine thy bow'rs;
And, while thy beds a cheap repast afford,
Despise the dainties of a venal Lord:
There every bush with Nature's music rings,
There every breeze bears Health upon its wings;
On all thy hours Security shall smile,
And bless thy evening walk and morning toil.

Retirement. — *Mrs. Tighe.*

O PSYCHE, happy in thine Ignorance!
Couldst thou but shun this Heart-tormenting bane·
Be but content, nor daringly advance
To meet the bitter hour of threatened pain;
Pure spotless Dove! seek thy safe nest again;
Let true Affection shun the public eye,
And quit the busy circle of the vain,
For there the treacherous snares concealed lie;
Oh, timely warn'd, escape! to safe Retirement fly!

Retirement. — *Beattie.*

OH, how canst thou renounce the boundless store
Of charms which Nature to her votary yields!
The warbling woodland, the resounding shore,
The pomp of groves, and garniture of fields;
All that the genial ray of Morning gilds,
And all that echoes to the song of Even,
All that the Mountain's sheltering bosom shields,
And all the dread magnificence of Heaven,
Oh, how canst thou renounce and hope to be forgiven!

Retirement. — *Cowper.*

THE Statesman, Lawyer, Merchant, Man of Trade
Pants for the refuge of some rural Shade,
Where all his long anxieties forgot
Amid the charms of a sequester'd spot,
Or recollected only to gild o'er
And add a smile to what was sweet before,
He may possess the Joys he thinks he sees,
Lay his old age upon the lap of Ease,
Improve the remnant of his wasted span,
And having lived a Trifler, die a Man.

Retirement. — *Byron.*

TO fly from, need not be to hate, Mankind;
All are not fit with them to stir and toil,
Nor is it Discontent to keep the Mind
Deep in its fountain, lest it overboil
In the hot throng where we become the spoil
Of our Infection, till too late and long
We may deplore and struggle with the coil,
In wretched interchange of wrong for wrong,
'Midst a contentious World, striving where none are strong.

Retirement. — *Thomson.*

THE best of men have ever loved Repose:
They hate to mingle in the filthy fray,
Where the Soul sours, and gradual Rancour grows
Imbitter'd more from peevish day to day.
Even those whom Fame has lent her fairest ray,
The most renown'd of worthy wights of yore,
From a base World at last have stolen away.
So Scipio, to the soft Cumæan shore
Retiring, tasted Joy he never knew before.

Retirement — *Shakspeare.*

HOW Use doth breed a Habit in a man!
This shadowy desert, unfrequented woods,
I better brook than flourishing peopled Towns.

Retrospection. — *Joanna Baillie.*

FROM the sad years of Life
We sometimes do short Hours, yea, Minutes strike,
Keen, blissful, bright, never to be forgotten;
Which, thro' the dreary gloom of Time o'erpast,
Shine like fair sunny spots on a wild waste.

Retrospection. — *Shakspeare.*

ALAS, 'tis true, I have gone here and there,
And made myself a motley to the view,
Gored my own Thoughts, sold cheap what is most dear,
Made old offences of Affections new.
Most true it is, that I have look'd on Truth
Askance and strangely; but, by all above,
These blenches gave my Heart another youth,
And worse essays proved thee my best of Love.
Now, all is done, save what shall have no end:
Mine appetite I never more will grind
On newer proof, to try an older Friend,
A God in love, to whom I am confined.
Then give me welcome, next my Heaven the best,
E'en to thy pure and most most loving breast.

Retrospection. — *Horace.*

HE possesses dominion over himself, and is happy, who can every day say, "I have lived." To-morrow the Heavenly Father may either involve the World in dark clouds, or cheer it with clear Sunshine; he will not, however, render ineffectual the things which have already taken place.

Retrospection. — *Steele.*

A MAN advanced in years, that thinks fit to look back upon his former Life, and call that only Life which was passed with Satisfaction and Enjoyment, excluding all parts which were not pleasant to him, will find himself very young, if not in his Infancy.

Retrospection. — *Martial.*

OF no day can the Retrospect cause pain to a good man, nor has one passed away which he is unwilling to remember: the period of his Life seems prolonged by his good acts; and we may be said to live twice, when we can reflect with Pleasure on the days that are gone.

Retrospection. — *Southey.*

I CAN remember, with unsteady feet
Tottering from room to room, and finding pleasure
In Flowers, and Toys, and Sweetmeats, things which long
Have lost their power to please; which, when I see them,
Raise only now a melancholy wish,
I were the little Trifler once again
Who could be pleased so lightly.

Revenge. — *Bacon.*

HE that studieth Revenge keepeth his own wounds green.

Revolution. — *Colton.*

THE Mob, like the Ocean, is very seldom agitated without some cause superior and exterior to itself; but (to continue the simile) both are capable of doing the greatest Mischief, after the cause which first set them in motion has ceased to act.

Revolutionists. — *Sir T. More.*

WHO quarrel more than Beggars? Who does more earnestly long for a change than he that is uneasy in his present circumstances? And who run to create Confusions with so desperate a Boldness, as those who, having nothing else to lose, hope to gain by them?

Riches. — *Lord Bacon.*

BE not penny-wise; Riches have Wings, and sometimes they fly away of themselves, sometimes they must be set flying to bring in more.

Riches. — *Sterne.*

IF thou art rich, then show the Greatness of thy Fortune; or what is better, the Greatness of thy Soul, in the meekness of thy Conversation; condescend to men of low estate, support the distressed, and patronize the neglected. Be great.

Riches. — *Martial.*

WHAT! Old and rich, and childless too,
And yet believe your Friends are true?
Truth might perhaps to those belong,
To those who loved you poor and young:
But, trust me, for the new you have,
They'll love you dearly—in your Grave.

Riches. — *Montaigne.*

PLENTY and Indigence depend upon the opinion every one has of them; and Riches, no more than Glory or Health, have no more Beauty or Pleasure, than their possessor is pleased to lend them.

Riches. — *Young.*

MUCH Learning shows how little mortals know;
Much Wealth, how little worldlings can enjoy:
At best, it babies us with endless toys,
And keeps us children till we drop to dust.
As monkeys at a Mirror stand amazed,
They fail to find what they so plainly see;
Thus men, in shining Riches, see the face
Of Happiness, nor know it is a shade;
But gaze, and touch, and peep, and peep again,
And wish, and wonder it is absent still.

Riches. — *Sir T. Brown.*

HE hath Riches sufficient, who hath enough to be charitable.

Ridicule. — *Anon.*

EVERY age has its besetting sins; every condition its attendant evils; every state of Society its Diseases, that it is especially liable to be attacked by. One of the pests which dog civilization, the more so the further it advances, is the Fear of Ridicule; and seldom has the Contagion been so obnoxious as in England at this day. Is there anybody living, among the upper classes at least, who has not often been laughed out of what he ought to have done, and laughed into what he ought not to have done? Who has not sinned? who has not been a runagate from Duty? who has not stifled his best feelings? who has not mortified his noblest desires? solely to escape being laughed at? and not once merely; but time after time: until that which has so often been checked, becomes stunted, and no longer dares lift up its Head. And then, after having been laughed down ourselves, we too join the Pack who go about laughing down others.

Early Rising. — *Doddridge.*

THE difference between rising at five and seven o'clock in the Morning, for the space of forty years, supposing a man to go to bed at the same hour at Night, is nearly equivalent to the addition of ten years to a man's Life.

Extreme Rigour. — *Burke.*

AN extreme Rigour is sure to arm every thing against it, and at length to relax into a supine Neglect.

Rumour. — *Shakspeare.*

RUMOUR is a pipe
Blown by Surmises, Jealousies, Conjectures;
And of so easy and so plain a stop,
That the blunt Monster with uncounted heads,
The still discordant wavering Multitude,
Can play upon it.

Rumour. — *Shakspeare.*

Loud Rumour speaks:
I, from the Orient to the drooping West
Making the wind my post-horse, still unfold
The acts commenced on this ball of Earth:
Upon my tongues continual Slanders ride;
The which in every language I pronounce,
Stuffing the ears of Men with false reports.

Sacrifice. — *From the Greek.*

HE that offers in sacrifice, O Pamphilus, a multitude of Bulls and of Goats, of golden Vestments, or purple Garments, or figures of Ivory, or precious Gems, and imagines by this to conciliate the favour of God, is grossly mistaken, and has no solid understanding; for he that would sacrifice with success, ought to be chaste and charitable, no Corrupter of Virgins, no Adulterer, no Robber or Murderer for the sake of lucre. Covet not, O Pamphilus, even the thread of another man's needle; for God, who is near thee, perpetually beholds thy actions.

National Safeguards. — *Alexander Hamilton.*

SAFETY from external danger is the most powerful director of national conduct. Even the ardent love of liberty will, after a time, give way to its dictates. The violent destruction of life and property incident to war, the continual effort and alarm attendant on a state of continual danger, will compel nations the most attached to liberty to resort for repose and security to institutions which have a tendency to destroy their civil and political rights. To be more safe, they at length become willing to run the risk of being less free.

Satiety. — *Shakspeare.*

A Surfeit of the sweetest things
The deepest loathing to the Stomach brings.

Satiety. — *Byron.*

Passion raves herself to rest, or flies;
And Vice, that digs her own voluptuous tomb,
Had buried long his Hopes, no more to rise:
Pleasure's pall'd Victim! Life-abhorring gloom.

Satiety. — *Shakspeare.*

AS Surfeit is the Father of much Fast,
So every scope by the immoderate use
Turns to Restraint: Our natures do pursue
(Like rats that ravin down their proper bane)
A thirsty Evil; and when we drink, we die.

Satiety. — *Shakspeare.*

THE cloy'd Will,
(That satiate yet unsatisfied Desire,
That tub both fill'd and running,) ravening first
The Lamb, longs after for the Garbage.

Satiety. — *Steele.*

PLEASURE, when it is a Man's chief purpose, disappoints itself; and the constant application to it palls the faculty of enjoying it, though it leaves the sense of our inability for that we wish, with a disrelish of every thing else. Thus the intermediate seasons of the Man of Pleasure are more heavy than one would impose upon the vilest Criminal.

Satire. — *Pope.*

SATIRE'S my weapon, but I'm too discreet
To run a-muck, and tilt at all I meet;
I only wear it in a land of Hectors,
Thieves, Supercargoes, Sharpers, and Directors.

Satire. — *Pope.*

CURST be the verse, how well soe'er it flow,
That tends to make one worthy man my foe,
Give Virtue Scandal, Innocence a Fear,
Or from the soft-eyed Virgin steal a tear.

Saturday Night. — *Burns.*

NOVEMBER chill blaws loud wi' angry sugh;
The short'ning Winter-day draws near a close;
The miry beasts retreating frae the Pleugh;
The black'ning trains o' craws to their repose:
The toil-worn Cotter frae his labour goes,
This night his weekly moil is at an end,
Collects his Spades, his Mattocks, and his Hoes,
Hoping the morn at ease and rest to spend,
And weary, o'er the Moor, his course does hameward bend.

Saying and Doing. — *Johnson.*

IT is not difficult to conceive, that, for many reasons, a man writes much better than he lives. For, without entering into refined Speculations, it may be shown much easier to design than to perform. A man proposes his schemes of Life in a state of abstraction and disengagement, exempt from the enticements of Hope, the solicitations of Affection, the importunities of Appetite, or the depressions of Fear, and is in the same state with him that teaches upon land the art of Navigation, to whom the sea is always smooth, and the wind always prosperous.

Saving. — *From the Latin.*

NO Gain is so certain as that which proceeds from the economical use of what you have

Scepticism. — *Colton.*

AS the Man of Pleasure, by a vain attempt to be more happy than any man can be, is often more miserable than most men are, so the Sceptic, in a vain attempt to be wise beyond what is permitted to man, plunges into a Darkness more deplorable, and a Blindness more incurable than that of the common herd, whom he despises, and would fain instruct.

Scepticism. — *Greville.*

HUMAN Knowledge is the parent of Doubt

Scholastic. — *Colton.*

TO sentence a man of true Genius to the drudgery of a School, is to put a Race Horse in a mill.

School. — *Shenstone.*

WHOE'ER excels in that we prize,
Appears a Hero in our eyes :
Each Girl, when pleased with what is taught,
Will have the teacher in her thought.
When Miss delights in her spinnet,
A Fiddler may a fortune get ;
A Blockhead, with melodious voice,
In boarding-schools may have his choice ;
And oft the Dancing Master's art
Climbs from the toe to touch the heart.

Science. — *Anon.*

BACON'S prophecies of the advance of Science have been fulfilled far beyond what even he could have anticipated. For Knowledge partakes of Infinity : it widens with our capacities : the higher we mount in it, the vaster and more magnificent are the prospects it stretches out before us. Nor are we in these days, as men are ever apt to imagine of their own times, approaching to the end of them : nor shall we be nearer the end a thousand years hence than we are now. The family of Science has multiplied : new Sciences, hitherto unnamed, unthought of, have arisen. The seed which Bacon sowed sprang up, and grew to be a mighty tree ; and the Thoughts of thousands of men came and lodged in its branches : and those branches spread "so broad and long, that in the ground the bended twigs took root, and Daughters grew about the Mother Tree, a pillared shade high overarched . . . and echoing walks between," . . . walks where Poetry may wander, and wreathe her blossoms around the massy stems, and where Religion may hymn the praises of that Wisdom, of which Science erects the Hundred-aisled Temple.

The Scriptures. — *Boyle.*

A MATCHLESS Temple, where I delight to be, to contemplate the Beauty, the Symmetry, and the Magnificence of the Structure, and to increase my awe, and excite my devotion to the Deity there preached and adored.

The Sea. — *Byron.*

THOU glorious mirror, where the Almighty's form
Glasses itself in Tempests: in all time,
Calm or convulsed—in Breeze, or Gale, or Storm,
Icing the pole, or in the torrid clime
Dark-heaving;—boundless, endless, and sublime—
The image of Eternity—the Throne
Of the Invisible; even from out thy slime
The monsters of the deep are made; each Zone
Obeys thee; thou goest forth, Dread, Fathomless, Alone.

The Sea. — *Byron.*

OH, who can tell? not thou, luxurious Slave!
Whose Soul would sicken o'er the heaving wave;
Not thou, vain Lord of wantonness and ease!
Whom Slumber soothes not—Pleasures cannot please—
Oh, who can tell, save he whose heart hath tried,
And danced in triumph o'er the waters wide,
The exulting sense—the pulse's madd'ning play,
That thrills the wanderer of that trackless way?

The Sea. — *Sir A. Hunt.*

I LOVED to stand on some high beetling Rock,
Or dusky brow of savage Promontory,
Watching the Waves with all their white crests dancing
Come, like thick-plumed Squadrons, to the shore,
Gallantly bounding.

The Sea. — *Byron.*

ROLL on, thou deep and dark blue Ocean—roll!
Ten thousand fleets sweep over thee in vain;
Man marks the Earth with ruin—his control
Stops with the shore; upon the watery plain
The Wrecks are all thy deed, nor doth remain
A shadow of man's ravage, save his own,
When, for a moment like a drop of rain,
He sinks into thy depths with bubbling groan,
Without a Grave, unknell'd, uncoffin'd, and unknown.

The Sea. — *Byron.*

How happy they,
Who, from the toil and tumult of their Lives,
Steal to look down where naught but Ocean strives!

Secrecy. — *Colton.*

SECRECY has been well termed the Soul of all great designs. Perhaps more has been effected by concealing our own intentions, than by discovering those of our Enemy. But great men succeed in both.

Secrecy. — *Johnson.*

TO tell your own Secrets is generally Folly, but that Folly is without Guilt; to communicate those with which we are intrusted is always Treachery, and Treachery for the most part combined with Folly.

Secrecy. — *Massinger.*

I HAVE play'd the Fool, the gross Fool, to believe
The bosom of a Friend would hold a Secret
Mine own could not contain.

Secrecy. — *Chesterfield.*

IF a Fool knows a Secret, he tells it because he is a Fool; if a Knave knows one, he tells it whenever it is his interest to tell it. But Women and Young Men are very apt to tell what Secrets they know, from the vanity of having been trusted.

Secrecy. — *La Rochefoucauld.*

HOW can we expect another to keep our Secret if we cannot keep it ourselves?

Security. — *Colton.*

IT is fortunate for the interests of Society, that the great mass of mankind are neither Kings nor Prime Ministers, and that men are so impotent that they can seldom bring Evil upon others without more or less of danger to themselves. Thus then it is that Public Strength, Security, and Confidence grow out of Private Weakness, Danger, and Fear.

Security. — *Hume.*

SECURITY diminishes the Passions: the Mind, when left to itself, immediately languishes; and, in order to preserve its Ardour, must be every moment supported by a new flow of Passion. For the same reason Despair, though contrary to Security, has a like influence.

Seduction. — *Goldsmith.*

AH, turn thine eyes
Where the poor houseless shivering Female lies:

She, once perhaps, in Village plenty blest,
Has wept at tales of Innocence distrest;
Her modest looks the cottage might adorn,
Sweet as the Primrose peeps beneath the thorn:
Now lost to all; her friends, her Virtue fled,
Near her Betrayer's door she lays her head,
And, pinch'd with cold, and shrinking from the show'r,
With heavy Heart deplores that luckless hour,
When idly first, ambitious of the Town,
She left her Wheel and robes of country brown.

Seduction. — *Moore.*

BY Heaven! I would rather for ever forswear
The elysium that dwells in a beautiful breast,
Than alarm for a moment the Peace that is there,
Or banish the Dove from so hallow'd a nest.

Seduction. — *Shakspeare.*

THEN weigh what loss your Honour may sustain,
If with too credent ear you list his songs;
Or lose your Heart; or your chaste Treasure open
To his unmaster'd importunity.
Fear it, fear it, my dear sister;
And keep you in the rear of your Affection,
Out of the shot and danger of Desire.

Seduction. — *Burns.*

IS there, in human form, that bears a Heart—
A wretch! a villain! lost to love and Truth!
That can, with studied, sly, ensnaring art,
Betray sweet Jenny's unsuspecting youth?
Curse on his perjured arts! dissembling smooth!
Are Honour, Virtue, Conscience, all exiled?
Is there no pity, no relenting ruth,
Points to the Parents fondling o'er their Child,
Then paints the ruin'd Maid, and their distraction wild?

Seduction. — *Byron.*

SHALL Beauty, blighted in an hour,
Find joy within her broken bower?
No: gayer insects fluttering by
Ne'er droop the wing on those that die,
And lovelier things have Mercy shown
To every failing but their own,
And every woe a Tear may claim,
Except an erring Sister's Shame.

Seduction. — *Shakspeare.*

Ay, so you serve us,
Till we serve you: but when you have our Roses,
You barely leave our Thorns to prick ourselves,
And mock us with our barenness.

Seduction. — *Colton.*

WHEN Women send the Seduced to Coventry, but countenance and even court the Seducer, ought we not to wonder if Seductions were scarce?

Self-Conceit. — *La Rochefoucauld.*

THERE are few people who are more often in the wrong than those who cannot endure to be so.

Self-Control. — *Anon.*

ONE of the most important, but one of the most difficult things for a powerful mind is, to be its own master. Minerva should always be at hand, to restrain Achilles from blindly following his Impulses and Appetites, even those which are moral and intellectual, as well as those which are animal and sensual. A Pond may lie quiet in a plain; but a Lake wants Mountains to compass and hold it in.

Self-Control. — *Goethe.*

WHAT is the best Government? That which teaches us to govern ourselves.

Self-Control. — *Massinger.*

He that would govern others, first should be
The Master of himself.

Self-Control. — *English Proverb.*

HE is a Fool who cannot be angry: but he is a wise man who will not.

Self-Control. — *Seneca.*

I WILL have a care of being a Slave to myself, for it is a perpetual, a shameful, and the heaviest of all servitudes; and this may be done by moderate Desires.

Self-Control. — *La Rochefoucauld.*

THE Constancy of Sages is nothing but the art of locking up their Agitation in their hearts.

Self-Deception. — *Greville.*

No Man was ever so much deceived by another as by himself.

Self-Examination. — *Pythagoras.*

LET not Sleep fall upon thy Eyes till thou hast thrice reviewed the transactions of the past day. Where have I turned aside from Rectitude? What have I been doing? What have I left undone, which I ought to have done? Begin thus from the first act, and proceed; and, in conclusion, at the Ill which thou hast done, be troubled, and rejoice for the Good.

Self-Interest. — *La Rochefoucauld.*

OUR Virtues disappear when put in competition with our Interests, as Rivers lose themselves in the Ocean.

Selfishness. — *Sterne.*

THERE are some tempers—how shall I describe them—formed either of such impenetrable matter, or wrought up by habitual Selfishness to such an utter insensibility of what becomes of the Fortunes of their fellow-creatures, as if they were not partakers of the same Nature or had no lot or Connection at all with the species.

Selfishness. — *Young.*

THE Selfish Heart deserves the pain it feels.
More gen'rous Sorrow, while it sinks, exalts;
And conscious Virtue mitigates the pang.

Selfishness. — *Colton.*

THERE are too many who reverse both the Principles and the practice of the Apostle; they become all things to all Men, not to serve others, but themselves; and they try all things only to hold fast that which is bad.

Self-Knowledge. — *Colton.*

HE that knows himself, knows others; and he that is ignorant of himself, could not write a very profound lecture on other men's heads.

Self-Knowledge. — *Anon.*

THE first step to Self-knowledge is Self-distrust. Nor can we attain to any kind of Knowledge, except by a like process.

Self-Love. — *Colton.*

I FEAR it must be admitted that our Self-love is too apt to draw some consolation, even from so bitter a source as the Calamities of others; and I am the more inclined to think so, when I consider the converse of this proposition, and reflect on what takes place within us, with respect to our Pleasures. The sting of our Pains is diminished by the assurance that they are common to *all;* but from feelings equally egotistical, it unfortunately happens that the zest and relish of our Pleasures is heightened by the contrary consideration, namely, that they are confined to *ourselves*. This conviction it is that tickles the palate of the Epicure, that inflames the ardour of the Lover, that lends Ambition her ladder, and extracts the thorns from a Crown.

Self-Love. — *Colton.*

SELF-LOVE, in a well regulated breast, is as the Steward of the household, superintending the Expenditure, and seeing that Benevolence herself should be prudential, in order to be permanent, by providing that the reservoir which feeds should also be fed.

Self-Praise. — *Shakspeare.*

THERE'S not one Wise Man among twenty will praise himself.

Self-Pride. — *Colton.*

SELF-PRIDE is the common friend of our Humanity, and like the bell of our Church, is resorted to on all occasions; it ministers alike to our Festivals, or our Fasts; our Merriment, or our Mourning; our Weal, or our Woe.

Self-Respect. — *Shakspeare.*

CONSIDERATION like an angel came,
And whipp'd the offending Adam out of him;
Leaving his body as a Paradise,
To envelop and contain celestial spirits.

Self-Searching. — *Anon.*

IT is a strange way of showing our humble reverence and Love for the Creator, to be perpetually condemning and reviling every thing that he has created. Were you to tell a Poet that his poems are detestable, would he thank you for the compliment? The Evil on which it behooves us to fix our eyes, is that within ourselves, of our own begetting; the Good without. The half-religious are apt just to reverse this.

Self-Sufficiency. — *La Rochefoucauld.*

A MAN who shows himself too well satisfied with himself, is seldom pleased with others, and they, in return, are little disposed to like him.

Self-Torment. — *Colton.*

THERE are many moral Actæons, who are as miserably devoured by objects of their own choosing, as was the fabulous one, by his own Hounds.

Self-Worship. — *Colton.*

WERE we to say that we admire the tricks and gambols of a Monkey, but think nothing of that Power that created those limbs and muscles by which these are performed—even a Coxcomb would stare at such an asseveration; and yet he is in the daily commission of a much grosser contradiction, since he neglects his Maker, but worships himself.

Sensibility. — *Moore.*

OH! Life is a waste of wearisome hours,
Which seldom the rose of Enjoyment adorns;
And the Heart that is soonest awake to the flowers,
Is always the first to be touch'd by the thorns.

Sensibility. — *Colton.*

SENSIBILITY would be a good portress, if she had but one hand; with her right she opens the door to Pleasure, but with her left to Pain.

Sensibility. — *Rogers.*

THE soul of Music slumbers in the shell,
Till waked and kindled by the Master's spell;
And feeling Hearts—touch them but lightly—pour
A thousand melodies unheard before!

Sensuality. — *Shakspeare.*

WHAT is a Man,
If his chief good, and market of his time,
Be but to sleep, and feed? a beast, no more.
Sure, He, that made us with such large discourse,
Looking before, and after, gave us not
That capability and godlike Reason
To rust in us unused.

Sensuality. — *Seneca.*

IF Sensuality were Happiness, beasts were happier than men; but human Felicity is lodged in the Soul, not in the Flesh.

Sensuality. — *Shakspeare.*

INGRATEFUL Man, with liquorish draughts,
And morsels unctuous, greases his pure Mind,
That from it all consideration slips.

Sensuality. — *Plato.*

THOSE wretches who never have experienced the sweets of Wisdom and Virtue, but spend all their time in revels and Debauches, sink downward day after day, and make their whole life one continued series of errors. They never have the courage to lift the eye upward toward Truth, they never felt any the least inclination to it. They taste no real or substantial Pleasure; but, resembling so many Brutes, with eyes always fixed on the Earth, and intent upon their loaden tables, they pamper themselves up in Luxury and Excess.

Servants. — *Fuller.*

IF thou hast a loitering Servant, send him of thy Errand just before his Dinner.

Servants. — *Fuller.*

'TIS better that thou be rather something sparing, than very liberal, to even a good Servant; for as he grows full, he inclines either to be idle, or to leave thee: and if he should at any time murmur, thou mayst govern him by a seasonable Reward.

Servants. — *Fuller.*

IF thou employest plain Men, and canst find such as are commonly honest, they will work faithfully, and report fairly. Cunning Men will, for their own Credit, adventure without Command; and from thy business derive Credit to themselves.

Servants. — *Fuller.*

BE not too familiar with thy Servants; at first it may beget Love, but in the end 'twill breed Contempt.

Servants. — *Fuller.*

COMMAND thy Servant advisably with few plain Words, fully, freely, and positively, with a grave Countenance, and settled Carriage: These will procure Obedience, gain Respect, and maintain Authority.

Servants. — *Shenstone.*

THE trouble occasioned by want of a Servant, is so much less than the plague of a bad one, as it is less painful to clean a pair of shoes than undergo an excess of Anger.

The Sexes. — *Colton.*

NO improvement that takes place in either of the Sexes can possibly be confined to itself; each is an universal Mirror to each; and the respective Refinement of the one will always be in reciprocal proportion to the polish of the other.

Shakspeare. — *Anon.*

EVERY Age has its own peculiar forms of moral and intellectual Life; and Goethe has fully proved that an abundant store of materials for the creative powers of the Imagination were to be found, by those who had Eyes to discern them, in what might have been deemed an utterly prosaic Age. The difficulty to which I am referring, is that which he himself has so happily expressed, when in speaking of some comparisons that had been instituted between himself and Shakspeare, he said, "Shakspeare always hits the right nail on the Head at once; but I have to stop and think which is the right nail, before I hit."

Shakspeare. — *Dryden.*

SHAKSPEARE was the man who, of all modern and perhaps ancient Poets, had the largest and most comprehensive Soul. All the images of Nature were still present to him, and he drew them not laboriously, but luckily; when he describes any thing, you more than see it, you feel it too. Those who accuse him to have wanted Learning, give him the greater commendation; he was naturally learned; he needed not the spectacles of books to read Nature; he looked inward, and found her there.

Shakspeare. —*Anon.*

NO poet comes near Shakspeare in the number of bosom lines,—of lines that we may cherish in our bosoms, and that seem almost as if they had grown there,—of lines that, like Bosom Friends, are ever at hand to comfort, counsel, and gladden us under all the vicissitudes of Life,—of lines that, according to Bacon's expression, "come home to our business and Bosoms."

Shakspeare. — *Anon.*

OF the wonderful excellence of his Plays, we have no reason for believing that Shakspeare was at all aware; though Sterling does not go beyond the mark, when he says, that, "if in the wreck of Britain, and all she has produced, one creation of her spirit could be saved by an interposing Genius, to be the endowment of a new World," it would be the volume that contains them. Yet Shakspeare himself did not take the trouble of publishing that volume; and even the single Plays printed during his life seem to have been intended for playgoers, rather than to gain Fame for their Author.

Shakspeare. — *Anon.*

NO Heart would have been strong enough to hold the wo of Lear and Othello, except that which had the unquenchable elasticity of Falstaff and the "Midsummer Night's Dream." He too is an example that the perception of the ridiculous does not necessarily imply bitterness and scorn. Along with his intense Humour, and his equally intense piercing insight into the darkest, most fearful depths of Human Nature, there is still a spirit of universal Kindness, as well as universal Justice, pervading his works: and Ben Jonson has left us a precious memorial of him, where he calls him "My *gentle* Shakspeare." This one epithet sheds a beautiful light on his character: its truth is attested by his Wisdom: which could never have been so perfect, unless it had been harmonized by the gentleness of the Dove.

Shakspeare. — *Anon.*

SHAKSPEARE'S genius could adapt itself with such nicety to all the varieties of ever-varying Man, that in his "Titus Andronicus" he has portrayed the very dress of mind which the people of the declining Empire must have worn. I can conceive that the degenerate Romans would clothe their thoughts in just such words. The sayings of the free-garmented folks in "Julius Cæsar" could not have come from the close-buttoned generation in "Othello." Though human Passions are the same in all ages, there are modifications of them dependent on the circumstances of time and place, which Shakspeare has always caught and expressed. He has thus given such a national tinge and epochal propriety to his Characters, that, even when one sees Jaques in a bag-wig and sword, one may exclaim, on being told that he is a French nobleman, "This man must have lived at the time when the Italian taste was prevalent in France." How differently does he moralize from King Henry or Hamlet! although their Morality, like all morality, comes to pretty nearly the same conclusion.

Shakspeare. — *Anon.*

THE whole race of the giants would never pile an Ossa on this Olympus; their missiles would roll back on their heads from the feet of the Gods that dwell there. Even Goethe and Schiller, when they meddled with Shakspeare, and would fain have mended him, have only proved, what Voltaire, and Dryden himself, had proved before, that "Within his circle none can walk but he." Nor, when Shakspeare's genius passed away from the earth, did any one akin to him reign in his stead. Indeed, according to that law of alternation, which is so conspicuous in the whole history of Literature, it mostly happens that a period of extraordinary Fertility is followed by a period of Dearth. After the seven plenteous years come seven barren years, which devour the produce of the plenteous ones, yet continue as barren and ill-favoured as ever.

Portrait of himself. — *Shakspeare.*

THOUGH from an humble stock, undoubtedly
Was fashion'd to much Honour. From his cradle,
He was a Scholar, and a ripe, and good one;
Exceeding wise, fair spoken, and persuading:
Lofty, and sour, to them that loved him not;
But to those men that sought him, sweet as Summer.

Shame. — *Plautus.*

I CONSIDER that man to be undone who is insensible to Shame.

Sickness. — *Publius Syrus.*

THE sick man acts a foolish part, who makes his Physician his Heir.

Sickness. — *Burton.*

SICKNESS, the mother of Modesty, puts us in mind of our Mortality, and while we drive on heedlessly in the full career of worldly pomp and Jollity, kindly pulls us by the ear, and brings us to a proper sense of our Duty.

Silence. — *Shakspeare.*

THE Silence often of pure Innocence
Persuades, when speaking fails.

Silence. — *La Rochefoucauld.*

SILENCE is the safest course for any man to adopt who distrusts himself.

Silence. — *Shakspeare.*

O, MY Antonio, I do know of these,
That therefore only are reputed wise,
For saying nothing.

Silence. — *Colton.*

A MAN'S Profundity may keep him from opening on a first interview, and his Caution on a second; but I should suspect his Emptiness, if he carried on his Reserve to a third.

Silence. — *Bouhours.*

SILENCE is a Virtue in those who are deficient in understanding.

Silence. — *Burke.*

IF the prudence of Reserve and Decorum dictates Silence in some circumstances, in others prudence of a higher order may justify us in speaking our Thoughts.

Silence. — *S. T. Coleridge.*

SILENCE does not always mark Wisdom.

Simplicity. — *Shakspeare.*

WHOSE Nature is so far from doing harms,
That he suspects none.

Simplicity. — *Addison.*

WHEN a man is made up wholly of the Dove, without the least grain of the Serpent in his composition, he becomes ridiculous in many circumstances of Life, and very often discredits his best actions.

Simplicity. — *Steele.*

SIMPLICITY, of all things, is the hardest to be copied.

Simplicity. — *Shakspeare.*

HE is of a free and open nature,
That thinks men honest, that but seem to be so;
And will as tenderly be led by th' Nose,
As Asses are.

Sin. — *Barrow.*

SIN is never at a stay; if we do not retreat from it, we shall advance in it; and the farther on we go, the more we have to come back.

Sin. — *Shakspeare.*

ALL unavoided is the doom of Destiny,—
When avoided Grace makes destiny.

Sin. — *Baxter.*

USE Sin as it will use you; spare it not, for it will not spare you; it is your Murderer, and the Murderer of the World; use it, therefore, as a Murderer should be used. Kill it before it kills you; and though it kill your bodies, it shall not be able to kill your souls; and though it bring you to the grave as it did your Head, it shall not be able to keep you there. If the thoughts of Death and the Grave and Rottenness be not pleasant to you, hearken to every temptation to Sin, as you would hearken to a temptation to Self-murder, and as you would do if the Devil brought you a knife, and tempted you to cut your throat with it: so do when he offereth you the bait of Sin. You love not Death; love not the cause of Death.

Sin. — *Seneca.*

WHAT is more miserable than to see an old man only just entering on the practice of Virtue.

Sin. — *South.*

SIN is the fruitful Parent of distempers, and ill lives occasion good Physicians.

Sin. — *Shakspeare.*

SIN will pluck on Sin.

Sin. — *Tillotson.*

SHAME is a great restraint upon sinners at first; but that soon falls off: and when men have once lost their Innocence, their Modesty is not like to be long troublesome to them. For Impudence comes on with Vice, and grows up with it. Lesser vices do not banish all Shame and Modesty; but great and abominable Crimes harden men's foreheads, and make them shameless. When men have the Heart to do a very bad thing, they seldom want the face to bear it out.

Sincerity. — *Tillotson.*

SINCERITY is like travelling in a plain, beaten road, which commonly brings a man sooner to his journey's end than by-ways, in which men often lose themselves.

Sincerity. — *Shakspeare.*

HIS Words are bonds, his Oaths are oracles;
His Love sincere, his Thoughts immaculate;
His Tears, pure messengers sent from his Heart;
His Heart as far from fraud, as Heaven from Earth.

Sincerity. — *Tillotson.*

IF the show of any thing be good for any thing, I am sure Sincerity is better; for why does any man dissemble, or seem to be that which he is not, but because he thinks it good to have such a Quality as he pretends to.

Sincerity. — *La Rochefoucauld.*

WEAK persons cannot be sincere.

Sincerity. — *La Rochefoucauld.*

SINCERITY is an opening of the Heart. We find it in very few people; and that which we generally see is nothing but a subtle Dissimulation to attract the Confidence of others.

Singularity. — *Colton.*

LET those who would affect Singularity with success, first determine to be very virtuous, and they will be sure to be very singular.

Slander. — *Spenser.*

AND therein wore a thousand Tongs empight
Of sundry kindes and sundry quality;
Some were of Dogs, that barked day and night,
And some of Cats, that wrawling still did cry,
And some of Beares, that groynd continually,
And some of Tygres, that did seem to gren,
And snar at all that ever passed by;
But most of them were tongues of Mortall Men,
Which spake reproachfully, not caring where nor when.

Slander. — *Shakspeare.*

SLANDER;
Whose edge is sharper than the Sword; whose Tongue
Out-venoms all the worms of Nile; whose breath
Rides on the posting winds, and doth belie
All corners of the World: Kings, Queens, and States,
Maids, Matrons, nay, the secrets of the Grave
This viperous Slander enters.

Slander. — *Hare.*

WHEN will talkers refrain from Evil-speaking? When listeners refrain from Evil-hearing.

Slander. — *Byron.*

THE circle smiled, then whisper'd, and then sneer'd;
The Misses bridled, and the Matrons frown'd;
Some hoped things might not turn out as they fear'd;
Some would not deem such Women could be found;
Some ne'er believed one half of what they heard;
Some look'd perplex'd, and others look'd profound;
And several pitied with sincere regret
Poor Lord Augustus Fitz-Plantagenet.

Slander. — *Spenser.*

HER Face was ugly, and her Mouth distort
Foming with poyson round about her gils,
In which her cursed Tongue full sharpe and short
Appear'd like asp'is Sting, that closely kils
Or cruelly does wound whomso she wils.
A Distaffe in her other hand she had,
Upon the which she little spinnes, but spils;
And faynes to weave false Tales and leasing bad,
To throw amongst the Good which others had disprad.

Slander. — *Shakspeare.*

THE Shrug, the Hum, or Ha; these petty brands,
That Calumny doth use:—
For Calumny will sear
Virtue itself:—these Shrugs, these Hums, and Ha's,
When you have said, she's goodly, come between,
Ere you can say, she's honest.

Slander. — *Byron.*

SKILL'D by a touch to deepen Scandal's tints,
With all the kind mendacity of hints,
While mingling Truth with Falsehood, sneers with smiles,
A thread of Candour with a web of wiles;
A plain blunt show of briefly-spoken seeming,
To hide her bloodless Heart's soul-harden'd scheming;
A lip of lies, a face form'd to conceal;
And, without feeling, mock at all who feel:
With a vile mask the Gorgon would disown,
A cheek of parchment, and an eye of stone.

Slander. — *Anon.*

SLANDER meets no regard from noble minds;
Only the base believe, what the base only utter.

Slander. — *Byron.*

THAT abominable Tittle-Tattle,
The cud eschew'd by human cattle.

Slander. — *Swift.*

NOR do they trust their Tongues alone,
But speak a language of their own;
Can read a Nod, a Shrug, a Look,
Far better than a printed Book;
Convey a Libel in a Frown,
And wink a Reputation down;
Or, by the tossing of the fan,
Describe the Lady and the Man.

Slander. — *Shakspeare.*

THE jewel, best enamell'd,
Will lose his Beauty; and though Gold 'bides still,
That others touch, yet often touching will
Wear Gold; and so no man that hath a name,
But Falsehood and Corruption doth it shame.

Slander. — *Spenser.*

A FOUL and loathy Creature sure in sight,
And in conditions to be loath'd no lesse,
For she was stuft with Rancour and Despight
Up to the Throat, that oft with bitternesse
It forth would breake and gush in great excesse,
Pouring out streames of Poyson and of Gall
'Gainst all that Truth or Vertue doe professe,
Whom she with leasings lewdly did miscall,
And wickedly backbite: her name men Sclaunder call.

Slander. — *Spenser.*

SLAUNDEROUS reproches, and fowle Infamies,
Leasings, backbytinges, and vain-glorious crakes,
Bad counsels, prayses, and false Flatteries;
All those against that fort did bend their batteries.

Slander. — *Scott.*

OH! many a shaft, at random sent,
Finds mark the archer little meant;
And many a Word, at random spoken,
May soothe or wound a Heart that's broken.

Slander. — *Shakspeare.*

WE must not stint
Our necessary actions, in the fear
To cope malicious Censurers; which ever,
As ravenous Fishes, do a vessel follow,
That is new trimm'd; but benefit no farther
Than vainly longing.

Slander. — *Cowper.*

THE Man that dares traduce because he can
With safety to himself, is not a Man.

Slander. — *Byron.*

THE World, as usual, wickedly inclined
To see a Kingdom or a House o'erturn'd,
Whisper'd he had a mistress; some said *two*,
But for domestic quarrels *one* will do.

Slander. — *Spenser.*

NO wound, which warlike hand of Enemy
Inflicts with dint of sword, so sore doth light,
As doth the poysnous sting which Infamy
Infixeth in the name of noble wight:
For by no Art nor any Leeches might
It ever can recured be again;
Ne all the skill which that immortal spright
Of Podalyrius did in it retaine,
Can remedy such Hurts; such Hurts are Hellish Pain.

Slander. — *Thomson.*

THE whisper'd tale,
That, like the fabling Nile, no fountain knows.
Fair-faced Deceit, whose wily conscious eye
Ne'er looks direct. The Tongue that licks the dust,
But, when it safely dares, as prompt to sting.

Slander. — *Shakspeare.*

NO might nor greatness in Mortality
Can Censure 'scape; back-wounding Calumny
The whitest Virtue strikes: What King so strong,
Can tie the gall up in the slanderous tongue?

Sleep. — *Steele.*

IN thee, Oppressors soothe their angry brow;
In thee, th' oppress'd forget tyrannic pow'r;
In thee,
The wretch condemn'd is equal to his Judge;
And the sad Lover to his cruel fair;
Nay, all the shining Glories men pursue,
When thou art wanted, are but empty noise.

Sleep. — *Sir T. Brown.*

SLEEP is Death's younger brother, and so like him, that I never dare trust him without my Prayers.

Sleep. — *Shakspeare.*

O GENTLE Sleep,
Nature's soft Nurse, how have I frighted thee,
That thou no more wilt weigh my eyelids down,
And steep my senses in forgetfulness?
Why rather, Sleep, ly'st thou in smoky cribs,
Upon uneasy pallets stretching thee,
And hush'd with buzzing night-flies to thy slumber;
Than in the perfumed chambers of the Great,
Under the canopies of costly State,
And lull'd with sounds of sweetest Melody?
Oh thou dull God, why ly'st thou with the vile
In loathsome beds, and leavest the kingly couch
A watch-case, or a common 'larum-bell?
Wilt thou, upon the high and giddy mast,
Seal up the Ship-boy's eyes, and rock his brains,
In cradle of the rude imperious Surge;
And in the visitation of the winds,
Who take the ruffian billows by the top,
Curling their monstrous heads, and hanging them
With deaf'ning clamours in the slipp'ry shrouds,
That, with the hurley, Death itself awakes?
Canst thou, O partial Sleep, give thy repose
To the wet Sea-boy in an hour so rude?
And, in the calmest and the stillest Night,
With all appliances and means to boot,
Deny it to a King?

Sleep. — *Shakspeare.*

'TIS her breathing that
Perfumes the chamber thus: The flame o' the taper
Bows toward her; and would under-peep her lids,
To see the enclosed Lights, now canopied
Under these Windows: White and azure, laced
With blue of Heaven's own tinct.

Sleep. — *Shakspeare.*

O POLISH'D Perturbation! golden Care!
That keep'st the ports of Slumber open wide
To many a watchful night!—sleep with it now!
Yet not so sound, and half so deeply sweet,
As he, whose brow, with homely biggin bound,
Snores out the watch of Night. O Majesty!
When thou dost pinch thy bearer, thou dost sit
Like a rich Armour, worn in heat of day,
That scalds with safety.

Sleep. — *Shakspeare.*

SLEEP, that knits up the ravell'd sleeve of Care,
The Death of each day's Life, sore Labour's bath,
Balm of hurt minds, great Nature's second course,
Chief nourisher in Life's feast!

Sleep. — *Shakspeare.*

'TIS not the Balm, the Sceptre and the Ball,
The Sword, the Mace, the Crown imperial,
The enter-tissued robe of gold and pearl,
The farsed title running 'fore the King,
The throne he sits on, nor the tide of pomp
That beats upon the high shore of this world;
No, not all these thrice-gorgeous Ceremonies,
Not all these, laid in bed majestical,
Can sleep so soundly as the wretched slave;
Who, with a body fill'd, and vacant mind,
Gets him to rest, cramm'd with distressful bread;
Never sees horrid Night, the child of Hell;
But, like a lacquey, from the rise to set,
Sweats in the eye of Phœbus; and all night
Sleeps in Elysium; next day, after dawn,
Doth rise, and help Hyperion to his horse;
And follows so the ever-running year
With profitable labour to his grave:
And (but for Ceremony) such a wretch,
Winding up Days with toil, and Nights with Sleep,
Had the forehand and vantage of a King.

Sleep. — *Mrs. Tighe.*

OH! thou best comforter of that sad Heart
Whom Fortune's spite assails; come, gentle Sleep,
The weary mourner soothe! For well the art
Thou knowest in soft forgetfulness to steep
The Eyes which Sorrow taught to watch and weep;
Let blissful visions now her spirits cheer,
Or lull her cares to Peace in Slumbers deep,
Till, from fatigue refresh'd and anxious Fear,
Hope, like the Morning-star, once more shall reappear.

Sleep. — *Shakspeare.*

ENJOY the honey-heavy dew of Slumber:
Thou hast no figures, nor no fantasies,
Which busy Care draws in the brains of men;
Therefore thou sleep'st so sound.

Sleep. — *Young.*

MAN'S rich Restorative; his balmy bath,
That supples, lubricates, and keeps in play
The various movements of this nice machine,
Which asks such frequent periods of repair.
When tired with vain rotations of the Day,
Sleep winds us up for the succeeding dawn;
Fresh we spin on, till Sickness clogs our wheels,
Or Death quite breaks the spring, and motion ends.

Sleep. — *Byron.*

STRANGE state of being! (for 'tis still to be)
Senseless to feel, and with seal'd Eyes to see.

Sleep. — *Byron.*

AND she bent o'er him, and he lay beneath,
Hush'd as the babe upon its mother's breast,
Droop'd as the Willow when no winds can breathe,
Lull'd like the deep of Ocean when at rest,
Fair as the crowning rose of the whole wreath,
Soft as the callow Cygnet in its rest.

Sleep. — *Shakspeare.*

I WISH mine Eyes
Would, with themselves, shut up my thoughts: I find,
They are inclined to do so. . . . .
Do not omit the heavy offer of it;
It seldom visits Sorrow; when it doth,
It is a Comforter.

Sleep. — *Beaumont.*

HOW happy is that balm to wretches, Sleep!
No cares perplex them for their future state,
And fear of Death thus dies in senseless Sleep;
Unruly Love is this way lull'd to rest;
And injured Honour, when redress is lost,
Is no way salved but this.

Sleep. — *Shakspeare.*

O SLEEP, thou ape of Death, lie dull upon her!
And be her sense but as a Monument,
Thus in a chapel lying!

Sleep. —*Byron.*

THE crowd are gone, the Revellers at rest;
The courteous host, and all-approving guest,
Again to that accustom'd couch must creep,
Where Joy subsides, and Sorrow sighs to sleep,

And man o'erlabour'd with his being's strife,
Shrinks to that sweet forgetfulness of Life :
There lie Love's feverish hope, and Cunning's guile;
Hate's working brain, and lull'd Ambition's wile:
O'er each vain eye oblivion's pinions wave,
And quench'd existence crouches in a grave.
What better name may Slumber's bed become?
Night's Sepulchre, the universal Home,
Where Weakness, Strength, Vice, Virtue, sunk supine,
Alike in naked helplessness recline;
Glad for awhile to heave unconscious breath,
Yet wake to wrestle with the dread of death,
And shun, though day but dawn on ills increased,
That Sleep, the loveliest, since it dreams the least.

Sleep. — *Shakspeare.*

DOWNY Sleep, Death's counterfeit.

Society. — *Thomson.*

HAIL, social Life! into thy pleasing bounds
Again I come to pay the common stock,
My share of service, and, in glad return,
To taste thy Comforts, thy protected Joys.

Society. — *Byron.*

SOCIETY itself, which should create
Kindness, destroys what little we had got:
To feel for none is the true social art
Of the world's stoics—men without a Heart.

Society. — *Pope.*

HEAVEN forming each on other to depend,
A Master, or a Servant, or a Friend,
Bids each on other for assistance call,
Till one man's weakness grows the strength of all.
Wants, Frailties, Passions, closer still ally
The common interest, or endear the tie.
To these we owe true Friendship, Love sincere,
Each home-felt joy that Life inherits here.

Society. — *Milton.*

AMONG unequals what Society
Can sort, what Harmony or true delight.

Society. — *Cowper.*

MAN in Society is like a Flow'r,
Blown in its native bed. 'Tis there alone
His faculties expanded in full bloom
Shine out, there only reach their proper use.

2 Q

Society. — *Pope.*

MAN, like the generous Vine, supported lives:
The strength he gains is from th' embrace he gives.
On their own axis as the planets run,
Yet make at once their circle round the Sun;
So two consistent motions act the soul;
And one regards itself, and one the whole.
Thus God and Nature link'd the general frame,
And bade Self-love and Social be the same.

Society. — *Moore.*

THOUGH few the days, the happy evenings few,
So warm with Heart, so rich with mind they flew,
That my full Soul forgot its wish to roam,
And rested there, as in a dream at Home!

Society. — *Byron.*

SOCIETY is now one polish'd Horde,
Form'd of two mighty tribes, the Bores and Bored.

Society. — *Charron.*

GREAT towns are but a larger sort of prison to the Soul, like cages to birds, or pounds to beasts.

Softness. — *Shakspeare.*

HE hath a person, and a smooth dispose,
To be suspected; framed to make Women false.

Solitude. — *Pope.*

BEAR me, some God! oh, quickly bear me hence
To wholesome Solitude, the nurse of Sense;
Where Contemplation prunes her ruffled wings,
And the free soul looks down to pity Kings!

Solitude. — *Beattie.*

AND oft the craggy Cliff he loved to climb,
When all in mist the World below was lost.
What dreadful Pleasure! there to stand sublime,
Like shipwreck'd mariner on desert coast,
And view th' enormous waste of Vapour, tost
In billows, lengthening to th' horizon round,
Now scoop'd in gulfs, with mountains now emboss'd!
And hear the voice of mirth and song rebound,
Flocks, Herds, and Waterfalls, along the hoar profound!

Solitude. — *Deloraine.*

SOLITUDE is one of the highest enjoyments of which our Nature is susceptible. Solitude is also, when too long continued, capable of being made the most severe, indescribable, unendurable source of Anguish.

Solitude. — *Byron.*

TO sit on rocks, to muse o'er flood and fell,
To slowly trace the Forest's shady scene,
Where things that own not Man's dominion dwell,
And mortal foot hath ne'er, or rarely been;
To climb the trackless mountain all unseen,
With the wild flock that never needs a fold;
Alone o'er steeps and foaming falls to lean:
This is not Solitude; 'tis but to hold
Converse with Nature's charms, and see her stores unroll'd.
But midst the crowd, the hum, the shock of Men,
To hear, to see, to feel, and to possess,
And roam along, the World's tired denizen,
With none to bless us, none whom we can bless;
Minions of splendour shrinking from distress!
None that, with kindred Consciousness endued,
If we were not, would seem to smile the less
Of all that flatter'd, follow'd, sought, and sued;
This is to be alone; this, this is Solitude!

Solitude. — *Byron.*

IF Solitude succeed to Grief,
Release from pain is slight relief,
The vacant bosom's wilderness
Might thank the pang that made it less.
We loathe what none are left to share—
Even Bliss—'twere Wo alone to bear.
The Heart once left thus desolate,
Must fly at last, for ease—to hate.

Solitude. — *Rochester.*

DEAR solitary groves, where Peace does dwell!
Sweet harbours of pure Love and Innocence!
How willingly could I for ever stay
Beneath the shade of your embracing greens,
List'ning to the Harmony of warbling birds,
Tuned with the gentle murmur of the streams;
Upon whose bank, in various livery,
The fragrant offspring of the early year,
Their heads, like graceful swans, bent proudly down,
See their own beauties in the crystal Flood.

Solitude. — *Byron.*

I LIVE not in myself, but I become
Portion of that around me; and to me,
High Mountains are a feeling, but the hum
Of human cities Torture.

Solitude. — *Young.*

THE World's a school
Of wrong, and what proficients swarm around!
We must imitate, or disapprove;
Must list as their accomplices, or foes.
That stains our Innocence; this wounds our Peace.
From nature's birth, hence, Wisdom has been smit
With sweet Recess, and languish'd for the Shade.

Solitude. — *Milton.*

THERE in close covert by some brook,
Where no profaner eye may look,
Hide me from Day's garish eye,
While the bee with honied thigh,
That at her flowery work doth sing,
And the Waters murmuring,
With such consort as they keep,
Entice the dewy-feather'd Sleep.

Solitude. — *Byron.*

THERE is a Pleasure in the pathless woods,
There is a Rapture on the lonely shore,
There is Society, where none intrudes,
By the deep sea, and music in its roar:
I love not Man the less, but Nature more,
From these our interviews, in which I steal
From all I may be, or have been before,
To mingle with the Universe, and feel
What I can ne'er express, yet cannot all conceal.

Solitude. — *Byron.*

ARE not the Mountains, Waves, and Skies, a part
Of me and of my Soul, as I of them?
Is not the love of these deep in my heart
With a pure Passion? should I not contemn
All objects, if compared with these! and stem
A tide of sufferings, rather than forego
Such feelings for the hard and worldly phlegm
Of those whose eyes are only turn'd below,
Gazing upon the ground, with thoughts which dare not glow?

Solitude. — *Byron.*

PERHAPS there's nothing—I'll not say appals,
But saddens more by Night as well as day,
Than an enormous Room without a soul
To break the lifeless Splendour of the whole.

Solitude. — *Spenser.*

THE joyous Birdes, shrouded in chearefull shade,
Their notes unto the voice attempred sweet;
Th' angelicall soft trembling voyces made
To th' instruments divine Respondence meet;
The silver sounding instruments did meet
With the base murmure of the Waters fall;
The Waters fall with difference discreet,
Now soft, now loud, unto the Wind did call;
The gentle warbling Wind low answered to all.

Solitude. — *Young.*

O SACRED Solitude! divine Retreat!
Choice of the prudent! envy of the great!
By thy pure stream, or in thy waving shade,
We court fair Wisdom, that celestial maid:
The genuine offspring of her loved embrace,
(Strangers on earth!) are Innocence and Peace.

Solitude. — *Cowper.*

How sweet, how passing sweet, is Solitude!
But grant me still a friend in my retreat,
Whom I may whisper, Solitude is sweet.

Solitude. — *Milton.*

SOLITUDE is sometimes best society,
And short Retirement urges sweet return.

Solitude. — *Young.*

OH! lost to Virtue, lost to manly Thought,
Lost to the noble sallies of the Soul!
Who think it Solitude to be alone.

Solitude. — *Rogers.*

No, 'tis not here that Solitude is known.
Through the wide World he only is alone
Who lives not for another.

Solitude. — *Byron.*

OH! that the Desert were my dwelling-place,
With one fair spirit for my minister,
That I might all forget the Human Race,
And, hating no one, love but only her!
Ye Elements!—in whose ennobling stir
I feel myself exalted—Can ye not
Accord me such a being? Do I err
In deeming such inhabit many a spot?
Though with them to converse can rarely be our lot.

Solitude. — *Campbell.*

ENTHUSIAST of the Woods! when years apace
Had bound thy lovely waist with woman's zone,
The sunrise Path at morn I see thee trace,
To hills with high Magnolia overgrown,
And joy to breathe the Groves, romantic and alone

Sorrow. — *Shakspeare.*

THE Heart hath treble wrong,
When it is barr'd the aidance of the Tongue.
An oven that is stopp'd, or River staid,
Burneth more hotly, swelleth with more rage:
So of concealed Sorrow may be said.

Sorrow. —*Johnson.*

SORROW is a kind of rust of the Soul, which every new idea contributes in its passage to scour away. It is the putrefaction of stagnant Life, and is remedied by Exercise and Motion

Sorrow. — *Shakspeare.*

SHORT time seems long, in Sorrow's sharp sustaining,
Though Wo be heavy, yet it seldom sleeps,
And they who watch, see Time how slow it creeps.

Sorrow. — *Shakspeare.*

SORROW, like a heavy-hanging Bell,
Once set on ringing, with his own weight goes:
Then little strength rings out the doleful knell.

Sorrow. — *Shakspeare.*

GIVE Sorrow words: the Grief, that does not speak,
Whispers the o'erfraught Heart, and bids it break.

Sorrow. — *Shakspeare.*

IMPATIENCE waiteth on true Sorrow.

Sorrow. — *Shakspeare.*

OH, if thou teach me to believe this Sorrow,
Teach thou this Sorrow how to make me die;
And let belief and Life encounter so,
As doth the fury of two desperate Men,
Which, in the very meeting, fall and die.

Sorrow. — *Shakspeare.*

WE are fellows still,
Serving alike in Sorrow. Leak'd is our Bark,
And we, poor mates, stand on the dying deck,
Hearing the surges threat: we must all part
Into the Sea of Air.

Sorrow. — *Shakspeare.*

BUT he, nis own affections' Counsellor,
Is to himself, I will not say, how true;
But to himself so secret and so close,
So far from sounding and Discovery;
As is the bud bit with an envious worm,
Ere he can spread his sweet leaves to the air,
Or dedicate his Beauty to the Sun.

Sorrow. — *Shakspeare.*

AND now and then an ample Tear trill'd down
Her delicate cheek: it seem'd, she was a Queen
Over her passion, which, most rebel-like,
Sought to be King o'er her.
Patience and Sorrow strove
Which should express her goodliest. You have seen
Sunshine and rain at once:—her Smiles and Tears
Were like a wetter May. Those happiest smiles,
That play'd on her ripe lip, seem'd not to know
What guests were in her Eyes; which parted thence,
As pearls from diamonds dropt.—In brief,
Sorrow would be a Rarity most beloved,
If all could so become it.

Sorrow. — *Shakspeare.*

LO! here the hopeless merchant of this loss,
With head declined, and Voice damm'd up with wo,
With sad set eyes and wretched arms across,
From lips new-waxen pale begins to blow
The Grief away, that stops his answer so;
But wretched as he is, he strives in vain;
What he breathes out, his Breath drinks up again.
As through an arch the violent roaring tide
Out-runs the eye, that doth behold his haste;
Yet in the eddy boundeth in his Pride
Back to the strait, that forced him on so fast,
In rage sent out, recall'd in rage being past:
Even so his sighs, his Sorrows, make a saw,
To push Grief on, and back the same Grief draw.

Sorrow. — *Thomson.*

So many great
Illustrious spirits have conversed with Wo,
Have in her school been taught, as are enough
To consecrate Distress, and make Ambition
Even wish the frown beyond the smile of Fortune.

31

Sorrow. — *Shakspeare.*

I NEVER saw a vessel of like Sorrow,
So fill'd, and so becoming.

Sorrow. — *Shakspeare.*

WHEN my Heart,
As wedged with a sigh, would rive in twain,
Lest Hector or my father should perceive me;
I have (as when the Sun doth light a storm)
Buried this Sigh in wrinkle of a Smile:
But Sorrow, that is couch'd in seeming Gladness,
Is like that Mirth Fate turns to sudden Sadness.

The Soul. — *Shakspeare.*

LOOK, who comes here! a Grave unto a Soul;
Holding the eternal Spirit against her will,
In the vile prison of afflicted breath.

The Soul. — *Joanna Baillie.*

HE who will not give
Some portion of his Ease, his Blood, his Wealth,
For other's Good, is a poor frozen churl.

The Soul. — *Shakspeare.*

POOR Soul, the centre of my sinful earth,
Fool'd by those rebel powers that thee array,
Why dost thou pine within, and suffer dearth,
Painting thy outward walls so costly gay?
Why so large cost, having so short a lease,
Dost thou upon thy fading mansion spend?
Shall worms, inheritors of this excess,
Eat up thy charge? Is this thy Body's end?
Then, Soul, live thou upon thy servant's loss,
And let that pine to aggravate thy store;
Buy terms Divine in selling hours of dross;
Within be fed, without be rich no more:
So shalt thou feed on Death, that feeds on men:
And, Death once dead, there's no more dying then.

The Soul. — *S. T. Coleridge.*

EITHER we have an immortal Soul, or we have not. If we have not, we are Beasts; the first and wisest of beasts, it may be; but still true Beasts. We shall only differ in degree, and not in kind; just as the elephant differs from the slug. But by the concession of the materialists of all the schools, or almost all, we are not of the same kind as Beasts; and this also we say from our own Consciousness. Therefore, methinks, it must be the possession of a Soul within us that makes the difference.

The Soul. — *Cicero.*

IF I am mistaken in my opinion that the Human Soul is immortal, I willingly err; nor would I have this pleasant Error extorted from me: and if, as some minute Philosophers suppose, Death should deprive me of my being, I need not fear the raillery of those pretended Philosophers when they are no more.

The Soul. — *Jean Paul.*

THERE are Souls which fall from Heaven like flowers; but ere the pure and fresh buds can open, they are trodden in the dust of the Earth, and lie soiled and crushed under the foul tread of some brutal Hoof.

The Soul. — *Addison.*

THE Soul, secure in her existence, smiles
At the drawn dagger, and defies its point:
The Stars shall fade away, the Sun himself
Grow dim with age; and Nature sink in years:
But thou shalt flourish in immortal youth,
Unhurt amid the War of Elements,
The Wreck of matter, and the crash of Worlds.

The Soul. — *Armstrong.*

THERE is, they say, (and I believe there is,)
A spark within us of th' Immortal Fire,
That animates and moulds the grosser frame;
And when the Body sinks, escapes to Heaven,
Its native seat, and mixes with the Gods.

The Soul. — *Montgomery.*

THE Soul, of origin divine,
God's glorious Image, freed from clay,
In Heaven's eternal sphere shall shine
A Star of Day!
The Sun is but a spark of Fire,
A transient meteor in the sky;
The Soul, immortal as its Sire,
Shall never die.

The Soul. — *Hannah More.*

THE Soul on earth is an immortal guest,
Compell'd to starve at an unreal feast:
A spark, which upward tends by Nature's force:
A stream diverted from its Parent source;
A drop dissever'd from the boundless Sea;
A moment, parted from Eternity;
A Pilgrim panting for the rest to come;
An Exile, anxious for his native Home.

The Soul. — *Rahel.*

THE Affections and the Will know nothing of a future; the Mind—the Judgement—calls it up and gives it the force ana Life of the present. The Mind alone is free, self-acting, and directed toward the unknown; the Heart is bound to what is before it.

The Soul. — *Sterne.*

REST unto our souls!—'tis all we want—the end of all our wishes and pursuits: give us a prospect of this, we take the wings of the Morning and fly to the uttermost parts of the Earth to have it in possession: till after many miserable experiments, we have been seeking everywhere for it, but where there is a prospect of finding it; and that is within ourselves, in a meek and lowly disposition of heart.

The Soul. — *Greville.*

I HARDLY know a sight that raises one's Indignation more, than that of an enlarged Soul joined to a contracted Fortune; unless it be that so much more common one, of a contracted Soul joined to an enlarged Fortune.

Spirit. — *Byron.*

BEAUTIFUL Spirit! with thy hair of light,
And dazzling eyes of Glory, in whose form
The charms of Earth's least mortal daughters grow
To an unearthly stature, in an essence
Of purer Elements; while the hues of Youth,—
Carnation'd like a sleeping infant's cheek,
Rock'd by the beating of her mother's Heart,
Or the rose-tints, which summer's twilight leaves
Upon the lofty glacier's virgin snow,
The blush of Earth, embracing with her Heaven,—
Tinge thy celestial aspect, and make tame
The beauties of the Sunbow which bends o'er thee.

Right Spirit. — *Jonathan Edwards.*

A MAN of a Right Spirit is not a man of narrow and private views, but is greatly interested and concerned for the good of the community to which he belongs, and particularly of the city or village in which he resides, and for the true welfare of the society of which he is a member.

The Spleen. — *Pope.*

HAIL, wayward Queen!
Who rule the sex to fifty from fifteen;
Parent of vapours, and of female wit,
Who give th' hysteric, or poetic Fit,
On various Tempers act by various ways,

Make some take Physic, others scribble plays;
Who cause the proud their visits to delay,
And send the Godly in a pet to pray.

The Spleen. — *Byron.*

ONE has false Curls, another too much paint,
A third—where did she buy that frightful Turban?
A fourth's so pale, she fears she's going to faint,
A fifth's looks vulgar, dowdyish and suburban,
A sixth's white Silk has got a yellow taint:
A seventh's thin Muslin surely will be her bane,
And lo! an eighth appears—"I'll see no more!"
For fear, like Banquo's kings, they reach a score.

The Spring. — *Thomson.*

In these green days,
Reviving Sickness lifts her languid head;
Life flows afresh; and young-eyed Health exalts
The whole creation round. Contentment walks
The sunny glade, and feels an inward bliss
Spring o'er his mind, beyond the power of Kings
To purchase.

The Spring. — *Thomson.*

Wide flush the fields; the softening Air is balm;
Echo the mountains round; the Forest smiles;
And every Sense, and every Heart is Joy.

The Spring. — *Milton.*

HAIL bounteous May, that dost inspire
Mirth, Youth, and warm Desire:
Woods and groves are of thy dressing,
Hill and dale doth boast thy Blessing.

The Spring. — *Thomson.*

FROM the moist meadow to the wither'd hill,
Led by the breeze, the vivid verdure runs,
And swells, and deepens; to the cherish'd eye
The hawthorn whitens; and the juicy groves
Put forth their buds, unfolding by degrees,
Till the whole leafy Forest stands display'd,
In full luxuriance to the sighing gales.

The Statesman. — *Milton.*

With grave
Aspect he rose, and in his rising seem'd
A Pillar of State; deep on his front engraven
Deliberation sat, and public Care;
And princely counsel in his face shone
Majestic.

The Land-Storm. — *Thomson.*

ALONG the woods, along the moorish fens,
Sighs the sad Genius of the coming Storm;
And up among the loose disjointed cliffs
And fractured mountains wild, the brawling brook
And cave, presageful, send a hollow moan,
Resounding long in listening Fancy's ear.

The Land-Storm. — *Thomson.*

A BODING silence reigns,
Dread through the dun expanse; save the dull sound
That from the Mountain, previous to the Storm,
Rolls o'er the muttering earth, disturbs the flood,
And shakes the forest leaf without a breath.
Prone, to the lowest vale, aerial tribes
Descend: the tempest-loving raven scarce
Dares wing the dubious dusk. In rueful gaze
The Cattle stand, and on the scowling heavens
Cast a deploring eye; by Man forsook,
Who to the crowded Cottage hies him fast,
Or seeks the shelter of the downward Cave.

The Snow-Storm. — *Thomson.*

IN vain for him the officious Wife prepares
The fire fair blazing, and the vestment warm;
In vain his little children, peeping out,
Into the mingling storm, demand their Sire,
With tears of artless Innocence. Alas!
Nor Wife, nor Children, more shall he behold,
Nor friends, nor sacred home. On every nerve
The deadly Winter seizes; shuts up Sense,
And, o'er his inmost Vitals creeping cold,
Lays him along the Snows, a stiffen'd corse,
Stretch'd out, and bleaching in the northern Blast.

Story-telling. — *Swift.*

STORY-TELLING is subject to two unavoidable Defects; frequent repetition and being soon exhausted; so that whoever values this gift in himself, has need of a good Memory, and ought frequently to shift his Company.

Striving. — *Colton.*

HE that strives for the mastery, must join a well disciplined body to a well regulated mind; for with mind and body, as with Man and Wife, it often happens that the stronger vessel is ruled by the weaker, although in moral, as in domestic Economy, matters are best conducted where neither party is unreasonable, and where both are agreed.

Strife. — *From the Latin.*

WE hate the Hawk because he always lives in arms.

Study. — *Shakspeare.*

STUDY is like the Heaven's glorious sun,
  That will not be deep search'd with saucy looks:
Small have continual plodders ever won,
  Save base Authority from others' books.

Study. — *Shakspeare.*

CONTINUE your resolve
To suck the sweets of sweet Philosophy.
Only, while we do admire
This Virtue, and this moral discipline,
Let's be no stoics, nor no stocks, I pray,
Or so devote to Aristotle's checks,
As Ovid be an outcast quite abjured:
Talk logic with acquaintance that you have,
And practise rhetoric in your common talk;
Music and Poesy use to quicken you;
The mathematics, and the metaphysics,
Fall to them, as you find your stomach serves you:
No profit grows, where is no pleasure ta'en;—
In brief, Study what you most affect.

Study. — *Shakspeare.*

UNIVERSAL plodding prisons up
  The nimble spirits in the arteries;
As motion, and long-during action, tires
The sinewy Vigour of the Traveller.

Study. — *St. Evremond.*

STUDY has something cloudy and melancholy in it, which spoils that natural Cheerfulness, and deprives a man of that readiness of wit, and freedom of fancy, which are required toward a polite Conversation. Meditation has still worse effects in civil society; wherefore let me advise you to take care, that you lose not by it with your Friends what you think to gain with yourself.

Study.— *Seneca.*

IF you devote your time to Study, you will avoid all the irksomeness of this Life, nor will you long for the approach of Night, being tired of the Day; nor will you be a burden to yourself, nor your Society insupportable to others.

Style. — *Feltham.*

A SENTENCE well couched, takes both the Sense and the Understanding.

Style. — *Swift.*

PROPER words in proper places make the true definition of a Style.

Style. — *From the Latin.*

HIS Style shows the man. Whether in speaking or writing, a gentleman is always known by his style.

Political Subserviency. — *Calhoun.*

PIRACY, robbery, and violence of every description may, as history proves, be followed by virtue, patriotism, and national greatness; but where is the example to be found of a degenerate, corrupt, and subservient people, who have ever recovered their virtue and patriotism? Their doom has ever been the lowest state of wretchedness and misery: scorned, trodden down, and obliterated for ever from the list of nations. May heaven grant that such may never be our doom!

Success. — *Higgons.*

HAD I miscarried, I had been a Villain;
For men judge actions always by events:
But when we manage by a just foresight,
Success is Prudence, and Possession Right.

Success. — *Thomson.*

IT is Success that colours all in life:
Success makes Fools admired, makes Villains honest:
All the proud Virtue of this vaunting world
Fawns on Success, and Power, howe'er acquired.

Success. — *Colton.*

HE that has never known Adversity, is but half acquainted with others, or with himself. Constant success shows us but one side of the world. For, as it surrounds us with Friends, who will tell us only our merits, so it silences those Enemies from whom alone we can learn our defects.

Success. — *Shakspeare.*

THE great man down, you mark, his favourite flies;
The poor advanced makes Friends of enemies.
And hitherto doth Love on fortune tend:
For who not needs, shall never lack a Friend;
And who in want a hollow Friend doth try,
Directly seasons him his Enemy.

Suicide. — *Lucretius.*

OH! deaf to Nature, and to Heaven's command!
Against thyself to lift the murdering hand!
O damn'd Despair!—to shun the living light,
And plunge thy guilty Soul in endless Night!

Suicide. — *Blair.*

OUR time is fix'd; and all our days are number'd;
How long, how short, we know not: this we know,
Duty requires we calmly wait the summons,
Nor dare to stir till Heaven shall give permission.
Like sentries that must keep their destined stand,
And wait th' appointed hour, till they're relieved
Those only are the Brave who keep their ground,
And keep it to the last. To run away
Is but a Coward's trick: to run away
From this World's ills, that at the very worst
Will soon blow o'er, thinking to mend ourselves
By boldly vent'ring on a World unknown,
And plunging headlong in the dark! 'tis mad:
No Frenzy half so desperate as this.

Suicide. — *Shakspeare.*

AGAINST Self-Slaughter
There is a prohibition so divine,
That cravens my weak hand.

Mental Suicide. — *Chesterfield.*

I LOOK upon indolence as a sort of Suicide; for the Man is efficiently destroyed, though the appetite of the Brute may survive.

Summer. — *Moore.*

'TWAS noon; and every Orange-bud
Hung languid o'er the crystal flood,
Faint as the lids of maiden eyes
Beneath a Lover's burning sighs!

The Sun. — *Moore.*

AND see the Sun himself! on wings
Of Glory up the East he springs.
Angel of Light! who from the time
Those Heavens began their march sublime,
Hath first of all the starry choir
Trod in his Maker's steps of Fire!

The Sun. — *Cowley.*

THOU tide of Glory, which no rest doth know,
But ever ebb and ever flow!
Thou golden shower of a true Jove!
Who doth in thee descend, and Heaven to Earth make love!

The Sun. — *Byron.*

WOULD that yon orb, whose matin glow
Thy listless Eyes so much admire,
Did lend thee something of his Fire!

The Sun. — *Byron.*

Thou material God!
And representative of the Unknown—
Who chose thee for his shadow! Thou chief star!
Centre of many stars! which makest our Earth
Endurable, and temperest the hues
And Hearts of all who walk within thy rays!
Sire of the seasons! Monarch of the climes,
And those who dwell in them! for near or far,
Our inborn Spirits have a tint of thee,
Even as our outward aspects;—thou dost rise,
And shine and set in Glory. Fare thee well!
I ne'er shall see thee more. As my first glance
Of Love and Wonder was for thee, then take
My latest look.

The Sun. — *Southey.*

I MARVEL not, O Sun! that unto thee
In adoration Man should bow the knee,
And pour the prayer of mingled Awe and Love;
For like a God thou art, and on thy way
Of Glory sheddest with benignant ray,
Beauty, and Life, and Joyance from above.

The Sun. — *Cowley.*

ALL the World's bravery that delights our eyes,
Is but thy several liveries;
Thou the rich dye on them bestow'st,
Thy nimble Pencil paints this landscape as thou go'st

Superiority. — *Helvetius.*

TO be loved we should merit but little Esteem; all Superiority attracts awe and aversion.

Superstition. — *Colton.*

THE less we know as to things that can be done, the less skeptical are we as to things that cannot. Hence it is that Sailors and Gamblers, though not over remarkable for their devotion, are even proverbial for their Superstition; the solution of this phenomenon is, that both these descriptions of men have so much to do with things beyond all possibility of being reduced either to rule, or to reason,—the Winds and the Waves,—and the decisions of the Dice-Box.

Being Surety. — *Sir Walter Raleigh.*

IF any desire thee to be his Surety, give him a part of what thou hast to spare; if he press thee farther, he is not thy Friend at all, for Friendship rather chooseth harm to itself, than offereth it.

If thou be bound for a stranger, thou art a fool; if for a merchant, thou puttest thy estate to learn to swim; if for a churchman, he hath no inheritance; if for a Lawyer, he will find an evasion by a syllable or word to abuse thee; if for a poor man, thou must pay it thyself; if for a rich man, he needs not: therefore from Suretyship, as from a manslayer or enchanter, bless thyself; for the best profit and return will be this—that if thou force him for whom thou art bound, to pay it himself, he will become thy Enemy; if thou use to pay it thyself, thou wilt become a Beggar.

Suspicion. — *Spenser.*

HE lowrd on her with daungerous eye-glaunce,
Shewing his Nature in his countenaunce;
His rolling Eies did never rest in place,
But walkte each where for feare of hid mischaunce,
Holding a lattis still before his Face,
Through which he still did peep as forward he did pace.

Swearing. — *Hierocles.*

FROM a common custom of Swearing, men easily slide into Perjury; therefore if thou wouldst not be perjured, do not use to swear.

The Sycophant. — *Shakspeare.*

YOU are meek and humble-mouth'd;
You sign your place and calling, in full seeming,
With Meekness and Humility: but your Heart
Is cramm'd with Arrogancy, Spleen, and Pride.
You have, by fortune,
Gone slightly o'er low steps; and now are mounted,
Where powers are your retainers: and your words,
Domestics to you, serve your will, as't please
Yourself pronounce their office.

Sympathy. — *Byron.*

WHAT gem hath dropp'd and sparkles o'er his chain?
The Tear most sacred, shed for others' pain,
That starts at once—bright—pure—from Pity's mine,
Already polish'd by the Hand Divine.

Sympathy. — *Darwin.*

NO radiant pearl, which crested Fortune wears,
No gem, that twinkling hangs from Beauty's ears;
Not the bright stars, which Night's blue arch adorn;
Nor rising Sun, that gilds the vernal Morn;
Shine with such lustre as the Tear that flows
Down Virtue's manly cheek for others' Woes.

Sympathy. — *Thomson.*

THE generous Heart
Should scorn a Pleasure which gives others Pain.

Sympathy. — *Dryden.*

NATURE has cast me in so soft a mould,
That but to hear a story feign'd for Pleasure,
Of some sad Lover's death, moistens my Eyes,
And robs me of my Manhood.

Sympathy. — *Virgil.*

NOT being untutored in Suffering, I learn to pity those in Affliction

Sympathy. — *Steele.*

THERE is a kind of Sympathy in Souls, that fits them for each other; and we may be assured when we see two persons engaged in the warmths of a mutual Affection, that there are certain qualities in both their minds which bear a resemblance to one another. A generous and constant passion in an agreeable Lover, where there is not too great a disparity in other circumstances, is the greatest Blessing that can befall the person beloved, and if overlooked in one, may perhaps never be found in another.

Sympathy. — *Sterne.*

IN benevolent natures the impulse to Pity is so sudden, that like instruments of Music which obey the touch—the objects which are fitted to excite such impressions work so instantaneous an effect, that you would think the Will was scarce concerned, and that the Mind was altogether passive in the Sympathy which her own goodness has excited.

Sympathy. — *Shakspeare.*

ONE touch of Nature makes the whole world kin—
That all, with one consent, praise new-born gawds,
Though they are made and moulded of things past;
And give to Dust, that is a little gilt,
More laud than gilt o'er-dusted.

Sympathy. — *Jean Paul.*

THERE are Eyes which need only to look up, to touch every chord of a breast choked by the stifling atmosphere of stiff and stagnant Society, and to call forth tones which might become the accompanying music of a Life. This gentle transfusion of Mind into Mind is the secret of Sympathy. It is never understood, but ever felt; and where it is allowed to exert its power, it fills and extends intellectual Life far beyond the measure of ordinary conception.

Sympathy. — *Horace.*

THE Human Countenance smiles on those who smile, and weeps with those who weep.

The Syren. — *Thomson.*

WHEN on his heart the torrent-softness pours,
Then Wisdom prostrate lies, and fading fame
Dissolves in air away; while the fond soul,
Wrapt in gay visions of unreal Bliss,
Still paints the illusive form; the kindling grace;
The enticing Smile; the modest-seeming eye,
Beneath whose beauteous beams, belying Heaven,
Lurk searchless-cunning, Cruelty, and Death,
And still, false warbling in his cheated ear,
Her syren voice, enchanting, draws him on
To guileful shores, and meads of fatal Joy.

Tact. — *Anon.*

A LITTLE Management may often evade Resistance, which a vast force might vainly strive to overcome.

Tact. — *Colton.*

NEVER join with your Friend when he abuses his Horse or his Wife, unless the one is about to be sold, and the other to be buried.

Tact. — *Colton.*

GRANT graciously what you cannot refuse safely, and conciliate those you cannot conquer.

Talent. — *Colton.*

MEN may have the gifts both of Talent and of Wit, but unless they have also Prudence and Judgment to dictate the when, the where, and the how those gifts are to be exerted, the possessors of them will be doomed to conquer only where nothing is to be gained, but to be defeated where every thing is to be lost; they will be outdone by men of less brilliant, but more convertible Qualifications, and whose strength, in one point, is not counterbalanced by any disproportion in another.

Talent. — *Colton.*

DISAPPOINTED men, who think that they have Talents, and who hint that their Talents have not been properly rewarded, usually finish their career by writing their own History; but in detailing their *Misfortunes*, they only let us into the secret of their *Mistakes;* and, in accusing their patrons of Blindness, make it appear that they ought rather to have accused them of Sagacity, since it would seem that they saw too much, rather than too little; namely, that second-rate performances were too often made the foundation for first-rate pretensions.

Aristocracy of Talent. — *Thomson.*

WHOE'ER amidst the sons
Of Reason, Valour, Liberty, and Virtue,
Displays distinguish'd Merit, is a Noble
Of Nature's own creating. Such have risen,
Sprung from the dust; or where had been our honours?

Latent Talent. — *La Rochefoucauld.*

IT seems that Nature has concealed at the bottom of our minds Talents and Abilities of which we are not aware. The Passions alone have the privilege of bringing them to light, and of giving us sometimes views more certain and more perfect than Art could possibly produce.

Talking. — *Sir Walter Raleigh.*

SPEAKING much is a sign of Vanity; for he that is lavish in Words, is a Niggard in Deed.

Talking. — *Cowper.*

WORDS learn'd by rote, a Parrot may rehearse,
But talking is not always to converse;
Not more distinct from Harmony divine,
The constant creaking of a Country Sign.

Talking. — *Young.*

A DEARTH of words a woman need not fear;
But 'tis a task indeed to learn—to hear.
In that the skill of Conversation lies;
That shows or makes you both polite and wise.

Talking. — *Byron.*

BUT light and airy, stood on the alert,
And shone in the best part of Dialogue.
By humouring always what they might assert,
And listening to the topics most in vogue;
Now grave, now gay, but never dull or pert;
And smiling but in secret—cunning rogue!
He ne'er presumed to make an Error clearer,—
In short, there never was a better Hearer.

Talking. — *Sir Walter Raleigh.*

HE that cannot refrain from much speaking, is like a City without Walls, and less pains in the world a man cannot take, than to hold his tongue: therefore if thou observest this rule in all assemblies, thou shalt seldom err: restrain thy Choler, hearken much, and speak little; for the Tongue is the instrument of the greatest Good and greatest Evil that is done in the world.

Talking. —*Socrates.*

SUCH as thy Words are, such will thy Affections be esteemed; and such will thy Deeds as thy Affections, and such thy Life as thy Deeds.

Talking. —*Young.*

WINE may indeed excite the meekest Dame;
But keen Xantippe, scorning borrow'd flame,
Can vent her thunders, and her lightnings play,
O'er cooling Gruel, and composing Tea.

Talking. —*Roscommon.*

WHAT you keep by you, you may change and mend;
But Words once spoken can never be recall'd.

Talking. —*Lavater.*

HE who seldom speaks, and with one calm well-timed word can strike dumb the Loquacious, is a Genius or a Hero.

Talking. —*Shaftesbury.*

THEY who are great Talkers in company, have never been any Talkers by themselves, nor used to private discussions of our home Regimen.

Talking. —*Sir Roger L'Estrange.*

THERE are braying Men in the World as well as braying Asses; for, what's loud and senseless Talking and Swearing, any other than Braying.

Talking. —*From the French.*

A WISE Man reflects before he speaks; a Fool speaks, and then reflects on what he has uttered.

Talking. —*Selden.*

WORDS must be fitted to a Man's mouth: 'twas well said of the fellow that was to make a speech for my Lord Mayor, when he desired to take Measure of his Lordship's Mouth.

Talking. —*Plutarch.*

IF you light upon an impertinent Talker, that sticks to you like a Bur, to the disappointment of your important occasions, deal freely with him, break off the Discourse, and pursue your Business.

Talking. —*Montesquieu.*

THOSE who have few affairs to attend to, are great Speakers. The less Men think, the more they talk.

Talking. —*Terence.*

HE who indulges in Liberty of Speech, will hear things in return which he will not like.

Talking. — *Colton.*

IT has been well observed, that the Tongue discovers the state of the mind, no less than that of the body; but, in either case, before the Philosopher or the Physician can judge, the patient must open his mouth. Some men envelop themselves in such an impenetrable cloak of Silence, that the Tongue will afford us no symptoms of the temperament of the mind. Such Taciturnity, indeed, is wise if they are fools, but foolish if they are wise; and the only method to form a Judgment of these mutes, is narrowly to observe when, where, and how they smile.

Talking. — *Plutarch.*

IF any man think it a small matter, or of mean concernment, to bridle his Tongue, he is much mistaken; for it is a point to be silent, when occasion requires; and better than to speak, though never so well.

Talking. — *Socrates.*

THE Tongue of a fool is the key of his Counsel, which, in a Wise Man, Wisdom hath in keeping.

Taste. — *La Rochefoucauld.*

MEN more easily renounce their Interests than their Tastes.

Taste. — *Burke.*

IT is for the most part in our skill in Manners, and in the observances of time and place and of Decency in general, that what is called Taste by way of distinction consists; and which is in reality no other than a more refined Judgment. * * * The cause of a wrong Taste is a defect of Judgment.

Taste. — *La Bruyere.*

TALENT, Taste, Wit, Good Sense, are very different things, but by no means incompatible. Between Good Sense and Good Taste there exists the same difference as between Cause and Effect, and between Wit and Talent there is the same proportion as between a whole and its part.

Taste. — *Greville.*

MAY not Taste be compared to that exquisite sense of the Bee, which instantly discovers and extracts the Quintessence of every Flower, and disregards all the rest of it?

Taste. — *Shenstone.*

IT seems with Wit and Good-nature, "Utrum horum mavis accipe." Taste and Good-nature are universally connected.

Taxation. — *Shakspeare.*

WE must not rend our Subjects from our laws,
And stick them in our will. Sixth part of each!
A trembling Contribution!—why, we take
From every tree, lop, bark, and part o' the timber;
And though we leave it with a Root, thus hack'd,
The Air will drink the Sap.

Direct Taxation. — *Shakspeare.*

THESE exactions
Most pestilent to th' Hearing; and, to bear 'em,
The back is sacrifice to th' load: This makes bold mouths:
Tongues spit their Duties out, and cold Hearts freeze
Allegiance in them; All their curses now
Live where their Prayers did; and it's come to pass,
That tractable Obedience is a slave
To each incensed will.

Direct Taxation. — *Shakspeare.*

IT doth appear: for, upon these Taxations,
The clothiers all, not able to maintain
The many to them 'longing, have put off
The spinsters, carders, fullers, weavers, who,
Unfit for other Life, compell'd by hunger,
And lack of other means, in desperate manner
Daring the event to the Teeth, are all in uproar,
And Danger serves among them.

Temper. — *Shakspeare.*

THAT which combined us was most great, and let not
A leaner Action rend us. What's amiss,
May it be gently heard: When we debate
Our trivial difference loud, we do commit
Murder in healing Wounds: Then,
Touch you the sourest points with sweetest terms,
Nor curstness grow to the matter.

Temper. — *Shakspeare.*

WHY should a Man, whose Blood is warm within,
Sit like his Grandsire cut in Alabaster?
Sleep, when he wakes? and creep into the jaundice
By being peevish?

Temperance. — *Burton.*

TEMPERANCE is a bridle of gold; he who uses it rightly, is more like a God than a Man; the English, who are the most subject, of all other people, to Melancholy, are, in general, excellent feeders.

Temperance. — *Hesiod.*

FOOLS! not to know how far a humble lot
Exceeds abundance by Injustice got;
How Health and Temperance bless the rustic swain,
While Luxury destroys her pamper'd train.

Temperance. — *Claudian.*

MEN live best on moderate means: Nature has dispensed to all men wherewithal to be happy, if Mankind did but understand how to use her gifts.

Temperance. — *Fuller.*

MODERATION is the silken string running through the pearl-chain of all Virtues.

Temperance. — *Socrates.*

THERE is no difference between Knowledge and Temperance; for he who knows what is good and embraces it, who knows what is bad and avoids it, is learned and temperate. But they who know very well what ought to be done, and yet do quite otherwise, are ignorant and stupid.

Temperance. — *Sir Walter Raleigh.*

EXCEPT thou desire to hasten thine end, take this for a general rule, that thou never add any artificial Heat to thy body by Wine or Spice, until thou find that time hath decayed thy natural heat; and the sooner thou beginnest to help Nature, the sooner she will forsake thee, and leave thee to trust altogether to Art.

The Tempest. — *Campbell.*

HE comes! dread Brama shakes the sunless sky
With murmuring Wrath, and thunders from on high!
Heaven's fiery Horse, beneath his warrior form,
Paws the light clouds, and gallops on the Storm!
Wide waves his flickering Sword; his bright arms glow
Like Summer Suns, and light the World below!
Earth, and her trembling isles in Ocean's bed,
Are shook; and Nature rocks beneath his tread!

The Tempest. — *Byron.*

THE sky is changed!—and such a change! O Night,
And Storm, and Darkness, ye are wondrous strong,
Yet lovely in your strength, as is the light
Of a dark eye in Woman! Far along,
From peak to peak, the rattling crags among
Leaps the live Thunder! Not from one lone cloud,
But every mountain now hath found a tongue,
And Jura answers, through her misty shroud,
Back to the joyous Alps, who call to her aloud!

And this is in the night:—Most glorious Night!
  Thou wert not sent for slumber! let me be
A sharer in thy fierce and far Delight,—
  A portion of the Tempest and of thee!
  How the lit lake shines, a phosphoric sea,
And the big rain comes dancing to the earth!
  And now again 'tis black,—and now, the glee
Of the loud Hills shakes with its mountain-mirth,
As if they did rejoice o'er a young Earthquake's birth.

The Tempest.—*Byron.*

HARK, hark! deep sounds, and deeper still,
  Are howling from the Mountain's bosom:
There's not a breath of Wind upon the Hill,
  Yet quivers every Leaf, and drops each Blossom:
Earth groans as if beneath a heavy Load.

The Tempest.—*Spenser.*

SUDDEINE they see from midst of all the maine
  The surging waters like a Mountaine rise,
And the great Sea, puft up with proud Disdaine,
  To swell above the measure of his guise,
  As threatning to devoure all that his Powre despise.

The Tempest.—*Joanna Baillie.*

THE Night grows wondrous dark: deep-swelling gusts
  And sultry stillness take the rule by turn,
Whilst o'er our heads the black and heavy Clouds
Roll slowly on. This surely bodes a Storm.

The Tempest.—*Milton.*

I HEARD the wrack
As Earth and Sky would mingle; but myself
Was distant; and these flaws, though Mortals fear them
As dang'rous to the pillar'd frame of Heaven,
Or to the Earth's dark basis underneath,
Are to the main as inconsiderable,
And harmless, if not wholesome, as a sneeze
To Man.

Tempest at Sea.—*Thomson.*

THEN issues forth the Storm with sudden burst,
  And hurls the whole precipitated air
Down, in a torrent. On the passive main
Descends the Ethereal force, and with strong gust
Turns from its bottom the discolour'd deep.
Thro' the black Night that sits immense around,
Lash'd into foam, the fierce contending brine,
Seems o'er a thousand raging Waves to burn.

Temptation. — *Spenser.*

BUT all in vaine: no Fort can be so strong,
Ne fleshly Brest can armed be so sownd,
But will at last be wonne with battrie long,
Or unawares at disadvantage fownd:
Nothing is sure that growes on earthly grownd:
And who most trustes in Arme of fleshly might,
And boastes in Beautie's chaine not to be bownd,
Doth soonest fall in disaventrous fight,
And yeeldes his captive neck to Victour's most despight.

Temptation. — *Shakspeare.*

'TIS one thing to be tempted,
Another thing to fall.

Temptation. — *Thomson.*

AH then, ye Fair!
Be greatly cautious of your sliding Hearts:
Dare not the infectious Sigh; the pleading look,
Downcast, and low, in meek submission drest,
But full of Guile. Let not the serpent Tongue,
Prompt to deceive, with adulation smooth,
Gain on your purposed will. Nor in the bower,
Where woodbines flaunt, and roses shed a couch,
While Evening draws her crimson curtains round,
Trust your soft minutes with betraying Man.

Temptation. — *Pope.*

THE devil was piqued such Saintship to behold,
And long'd to tempt him, like good Job of old;
But Satan now is wiser than of yore,
And tempts by making rich, not making poor.

Temptation. — *Johnson.*

TO resist Temptation once is not a sufficient proof of Honesty. If a servant, indeed, were to resist the continued temptation of Silver lying in a window, as some people let it lie, when he is sure his master does not know how much there is of it, he would give a strong proof of Honesty. But this is a proof to which you have no right to put a man. You know, humanly speaking, there is a certain degree of Temptation which will overcome any Virtue. Now, in so far as you approach Temptation to a man, you do him an injury; and, if he is overcome, you share his Guilt.

Temptation. — *Shakspeare.*

DEVILS soonest tempt, resembling Spirits of Light.

Temptation. — *From the Latin.*

OPPORTUNITY makes the Thief.

Temptation. — *Shakspeare.*

LIE in the lap of Sin, and not mean harm?
It is hypocrisy against the Devil:
They that mean virtuously, and yet do so,
The devil their Virtue tempts, and they tempt Heaven.

Theory. — *Shakspeare.*

THOUGHTS are but Dreams till their effects be tried.

Things of the World. — *Colton.*

IT would be most lamentable if the good things of this World were rendered either more valuable or more lasting; for, despicable as they already are, too many are found eager to purchase them, even at the price of their Souls!

Thinkers. — *Dugald Stewart.*

THERE are very few original Thinkers in the world, or ever have been; the greatest part of those who are called Philosophers, have adopted the opinions of some who went before them

Thinking. — *Cicero.*

WHATEVER that be, which thinks, which understands, which wills, which acts, it is something celestial and Divine; and, upon that account, must necessarily be eternal.

Thinking. — *Lavater.*

THINKERS are scarce as Gold: but he, whose thoughts embrace all his subject, pursues it uninterrupted and fearless of consequences, is a Diamond of enormous size.

Thinking. — *Colton.*

THOSE who have finished by making all others think with them, have usually been those who began by daring to think with themselves.

Thinking. — *Johnson.*

MANKIND have a great aversion to intellectual Labour; but even supposing Knowledge to be easily attainable, more people would be content to be ignorant than would take even a little trouble to acquire it.

Thirst. — *Byron.*

TILL taught by pain,
Men really know not what good Water's worth.
If you had been in Turkey or in Spain,
Or with a famish'd boat's-crew had your berth,
Or in the Desert heard the camel's bell,
You'd wish yourself where Truth is—in a well.

Thoughts and Works. — *Hare.*

IT is much easier to think right without doing right, than to do right without thinking right. Just Thoughts may, and wofully often do fail of producing just Deeds; but just Deeds are sure to beget just Thoughts. For when the Heart is pure and straight, there is hardly any thing which can mislead the Understanding in matters of immediate personal concernment. But the clearest Understanding can do little in purifying an impure Heart, the strongest little in straightening a crooked one. You cannot reason or talk an Augean stable into cleanliness. A single day's work would make more progress in such a task than a Century's words.

Time. — *Shakspeare.*

MERRY Larks are ploughman's Clocks.

Time. — *Shakspeare.*

TIME, whose million'd accidents
Creep in 'twixt Vows, and change decrees of Kings,
Tan sacred Beauty, blunt the sharp'st intents,
Divert strong minds to the course of altering things.

Time. — *Shakspeare.*

TIME. I,—that please some, try all; both Joy and Terror,
Of Good and Bad; that make, and unfold, Error.

Time. — *Joanna Baillie.*

STILL on it creeps,
Each little moment at another's heels,
Till Hours, Days, Years, and Ages are made up
Of such small parts as these, and men look back,
Worn and bewilder'd, wond'ring how it is.
Thou trav'llest like a Ship in the wide ocean,
Which hath no bounding shore to mark its progress.

Time. — *Clarendon.*

IT is no wonder that when we are prodigal of nothing else, when we are over-thrifty of many things which we may well spare, we are very prodigal of our Time, which is the only precious Jewel of which we cannot be too thrifty, because we look upon it as nothing worth, and that makes us not care how we spend it. The Labouring Man and the Artificer knows what every hour of his time is worth, what it will yield him, and parts not with it, but for the full value: they are only noblemen and gentlemen, who should know best how to use it, that think it only fit to be cast away; and their not knowing how to set a true value upon this, is the true cause of the wrong estimate they make of all other things.

Time. — *Byron.*

THERE is a Temple in ruin stands,
Fashion'd by long-forgotten hands;
Two or three Columns, and many a stone,
Marble and Granite, with grass o'ergrown!
Out upon Time! it will leave no more
Of the things to come than the things before!
Out upon Time! who for ever will leave
But enough of the Past for the Future to grieve
O'er that which hath been, and o'er that which must be:
What we have seen, our sons shall see;
Remnants of things that have pass'd away,
Fragments of Stone, rear'd by Creatures of Clay!

Time. — *Byron.*

AND there they stand, as stands a lofty Mind,
Worn, but unstooping to the baser Crowd,
All tenantless, save to the crannying Wind,
Or holding dark communion with the Cloud.

Time. — *Shakspeare.*

THE End crowns all;
And that old common arbitrator, Time,
Will one day end it.

Time. — *Colton.*

TIME is the most subtle yet the most insatiable of Depredators, and by appearing to take nothing, is permitted to take all; nor can it be satisfied, until it has stolen the World from us, and us from the World. It constantly flies, yet overcomes all things by flight; and although it is the present ally, it will be the future conqueror of Death. Time, the cradle of Hope, but the grave of Ambition, is the stern corrector of Fools, but the salutary counsellor of the Wise, bringing all they dread to the one, and all they desire to the other; but like Cassandra, it warns us with a voice that even the sagest discredit too long, and the silliest believe too late. Wisdom walks before it, Opportunity with it, and Repentance behind it; he that has made it his friend, will have little to fear from his Enemies, but he that has made it his enemy, will have little to hope from his Friends.

Time. — *Shakspeare.*

WE see which way the stream of Time doth run,
And are enforced from our most quiet sphere
By the rough torrent of Occasion.

Time. — *Cowper.*

TIME as he passes us, has a Dove's wing,
Unsoil'd and swift, and of a silken sound.

Time. — *Young.*

THE bell strikes one. We take no note of Time,
But from its loss. To give it then a tongue,
Is wise in man. As if an Angel spoke,
I feel the solemn sound. If heard aright,
It is the knell of my departed hours:
Where are they? With the Years beyond the Flood
It is the signal that demands dispatch:
How much is to be done!

Time. — *Cicero.*

TIME destroys the speculations of Man, but it confirms the judgment of Nature.

Time. — *Shakspeare.*

TIME is the old Justice, that examines all offenders.

Time. — *Lavater.*

THE great rule of moral conduct is, next to God, to respect Time.

Time. — *Shakspeare.*

WHAT'S past, and what's to come, is strew'd with husks
The formless ruin of Oblivion.

Time. — *Shakspeare.*

TIME travels in divers paces with divers persons: I'll tell you who Time *ambles* withal, who Time *trots* withal, who Time *gallops* withal, and who he *stands still* withal. He trots hard with a young maid, between the contract of her Marriage and the day it is solemnized: if the interim be but a se'nnight, Time's pace is so hard, that it seems the length of seven years.—He ambles with a Priest that lacks Latin, and a Rich Man that hath not the Gout; for the one sleeps easily, because he cannot study; and the other lives merrily, because he feels no pain: the one lacking the burden of lean and wasteful learning; the other knowing no burden of heavy tedious penury: These time ambles withal.—He gallops with a Thief to the gallows: for though he go as softly as foot can fall, he thinks himself too soon there.—He stays still with Lawyers in the vacation; for they sleep between term and term, and then they perceive not how Time moves.

Time. — *Young.*

YOUTH is not rich in Time, it may be poor;
Part with it as with Money, sparing; pay
No moment, but in purchase of its worth;
And what it's worth, ask Death-beds; they can tell.

Time. — *Shakspeare.*

It is ten o'clock:
Thus may we see, how the world wags:
'Tis but an hour ago, since it was Nine;
And after an hour more, 'twill be Eleven;
And so, from hour to hour, we ripe and ripe,
And then, from hour to hour, we rot and rot,
And thereby hangs a Tale.

Time. — *Steele.*

IT is notorious to Philosophers, that Joy and Grief can hasten and delay Time. Locke is of opinion, that a man in great Misery may so far lose his measure, as to think a Minute an Hour; or in Joy make an Hour a Minute.

Time. — *Byron.*

"WHERE is the World," cries Young, at *eighty?* "Where
The World in which a man was born?" Alas!
Where is the World of *eight* years past? 'Twas there—
I look for it—'tis gone, a Globe of glass!
Crack'd, shiver'd, vanish'd, scarcely gazed on ere
A silent change dissolves the glittering mass.
Statesmen, Chiefs, Orators, Queens, Patriots, Kings,
And Dandies, all are gone on the wind's wings.

Time. — *Seneca.*

THE velocity with which Time flies is infinite, as is most apparent to those who look back.

Time. — *Blair.*

Time hurries on
With a resistless, unremitting Stream,
Yet treads more soft than e'er did midnight Thief,
That slides his hand under the Miser's pillow,
And carries off his Prize.

Time. — *Byron.*

There is given
Unto the things of Earth, which time hath bent,
A spirit's feeling, and where he hath leant
His hand, but broke his Scythe, there is a power
And magic.

Time. — *Shakspeare.*

LIKE as the waves make toward the pebbled shore,
So do our Minutes hasten to their end;
Each changing place with that which goes before;
In sequent Toil all forward do contend.

Time. — *Dyer.*

'TIS now the Raven's bleak abode;
'Tis now the apartment of the Toad;
And there the Fox securely feeds;
And there the poisonous Adder breeds,
Conceal'd in ruins, moss, and weeds;
While, ever and anon, there falls
Huge heaps of hoary moulder'd walls.
Yet Time has seen, which lifts the low,
And level lays the lofty brow,
Has seen the broken Pile complete,
Big with the Vanity of State;
But transient is the smile of Fate!
A little rule, a little sway,
A Sun-beam in a winter's day,
Is all the proud and mighty have
Between the Cradle and the Grave.

Time. — *Horace.*

IT flows, and it will flow uninterruptedly through every Age.

The Wrong Time. — *Zimmerman.*

THE Quarter of an Hour before Dinner is the worst suitors can choose.

Time. — *Shakspeare.*

MIS-SHAPEN Time, copesmate of ugly Night,
Swift subtle post, carrier of grisly Care;
Eater of Youth, false slave to false delight,
Base watch of Woes, Sin's pack-horse, Virtue's snare;
Thou nursest all, and murderest all, that are.
Time's glory is to calm contending Kings;
To unmask Falsehood, and bring Truth to light;
To stamp the seal of Time on aged things;
To wake the Morn, and centinel the Night;
To wrong the Wronger, till he render Right;
To ruinate proud buildings with thy hours,
And smear with dust their glittering golden Towers:
To fill with worm-holes stately monuments;
To feed Oblivion with decay of things;
To blot old Books, and alter their contents;
To pluck the quills from ancient raven's wings;
To dry the old Oak's sap, and cherish springs;
To spoil antiquities of hammer'd steel,
And turn the giddy round of Fortune's wheel:

To show the beldame daughters of her daughter;
  To make the child a man, the man a child;
To slay the Tiger, that doth live by slaughter;
  To tame the Unicorn, and Lion wild;
  To mock the subtle, in themselves beguiled;
To cheer the ploughman with increaseful crops,
And waste huge Stones with little Water-drops.
  Why work'st thou Mischief in thy pilgrimage,
Unless thou could'st return to make amends?
  One poor retiring minute in an age,
Would purchase thee a thousand thousand friends;
Lending him Wit, that to bad debtors lends.

Time. — *Mason.*

As every thread of Gold is valuable, so is every minute of Time.

Time. — *Shakspeare.*

MINUTES, Hours, Days, Weeks, and Years,
Pass'd over to the end they were created,
Would bring white hairs unto a quiet Grave.

Time. — *Franklin.*

IF Time be of all things the most precious, wasting Time must be the greatest prodigality, since lost Time is never found again; and what we call Time enough always proves little enough. Let us then up and be doing, and doing to the purpose; so by diligence shall we do more with less perplexity. Sloth makes all things difficult, but Industry all easy; and he that riseth late must trot all day, and shall scarce overtake his business at night; while Laziness travels so slowly, that Poverty soon overtakes him. Drive thy business, let not that drive thee; and early to bed, and early to rise, makes a man healthy, wealthy, and wise.

Timidity. — *Shakspeare.*

GO, prick thy Face, and over-red thy Fear,
  Thou lily-liver'd Boy. What Soldiers, Patch?
Death of thy Soul! Those linen cheeks of thine
Are counsellors to Fear.

The Tired Spirit. — *Joanna Baillie.*

FULL many a Storm on this gray head has beat;
  And now, on my high station do I stand,
Like the tired Watchman in his air-rock'd tower,
Who looketh for the hour of his Release.
I'm sick of worldly broils, and fain would rest
With those who war no more.

Titles. — *La Rochefoucauld.*

HIGH Titles debase, instead of elevating, those who know not how to support them.

Tobacco. — *Todd.*

ALL experienced people will tell you that the habit of using Tobacco in any shape will soon render you emaciated and consumptive, your Nerves shattered, your spirits low and moody, your Throat dry and demanding stimulating drinks.

Religious Toleration. — *Story.*

THERE is not a truth to be gathered from history more certain, or more momentous, than this: that civil liberty cannot long be separated from religious liberty without danger, and ultimately without destruction to both. Wherever religious liberty exists, it will, first or last, bring in and establish political liberty. Wherever it is suppressed, the church establishment will, first or last, become the engine of despotism, and overthrow, unless it be itself overthrown, every vestige of political right. How it is possible to imagine that a religion breathing the spirit of mercy and benevolence, teaching the forgiveness of injuries, the exercise of charity, and the return of good for evil; how it is possible, I say, for such a religion to be so perverted as to breathe the spirit of slaughter and persecution, of discord and vengeance, for differences of opinion, is a most unaccountable and extraordinary moral phenomenon. Still more extraordinary, that it should be the doctrine, not of base and wicked men merely, seeking to cover up their own misdeeds, but of good men, seeking the way of salvation with uprightness of heart and purpose. It affords a melancholy proof of the infirmity of human judgment, and teaches a lesson of humility from which spiritual pride may learn meekness, and spiritual zeal a moderating wisdom.

To-morrow. — *Cotton.*

To-MORROW, didst thou say?
Methought I heard Horatio say, To-Morrow!
Go to—I will not hear of it—To-morrow!
'Tis a sharper who stakes his penury
Against thy plenty—who takes thy ready cash,
And pays thee nought but Wishes, Hopes, and Promises,
The currency of idiots. Injurious bankrupt,
That gulls the easy creditor! To-morrow!
It is a period nowhere to be found
In all the hoary registers of Time,
Unless perchance in the fool's calendar.
Wisdom disclaims the word, nor holds society

With those that own it. No, my Horatio,
'Tis Fancy's child, and Folly is its father:
Wrought on such stuff as dreams are; and baseless
As the fantastic visions of the Evening.

To-morrow. — *Young.*

IN human Hearts what bolder thought can rise,
Than man's presumption on To-morrow's dawn?
Where is To-morrow? In another world.
For numbers this is certain: the reverse
Is sure to none; and yet on this "perhaps,"
This "peradventure," infamous for lies,
As on a rock of Adamant, we build
Our mountain Hopes; spin out eternal schemes,
As we the Fatal Sisters could out-spin,
And, big with Life's futurities, expire.

To-morrow. — *Johnson.*

CAN that hoary Wisdom
Borne down with years, still doat upon To-morrow?
That fatal Mistress of the young, the lazy,
The coward, and the fool, condemn'd to lose
An useless Life in wishing for To-morrow,
To gaze with longing eyes upon To-morrow,
Till interposing Death destroys the prospect!
Strange! that this general fraud from day to day
Should fill the world with wretches undetected.
The Soldier lab'ring thro' a winter's march,
Still sees To-morrow dress'd in robes of triumph;
Still to the Lover's long-expecting arms,
To-morrow brings the visionary bride;
But thou, too old to bear another cheat,
Learn, that the Present Hour alone is Man's.

Self-Torment. — *From the Latin.*

NOTHING more is wanting to render a man miserable, than that he should fancy he is so.

Tranquillity. — *Jean Paul.*

WHEN the Heart of man is serene and tranquil, he wants to enjoy nothing but himself; every movement—even corporeal movement—shakes the brimming Nectar cup too rudely.

Travelling. — *Lord Lyttelton.*

ME other cares in other climes engage,
Cares that become my birth, and suit my age;
In various Knowledge to improve my youth,
And conquer Prejudice, worst foe to Truth;

By foreign arts, domestic faults to mend,
Enlarge my notions and my views extend;
The useful science of the World to know,
Which books can never teach, or pedants show.

Trespass. — *Cicero.*

EVERY man should submit to his own Grievances, rather than trespass on the conveniences or comforts of his Neighbour.

A Troubled Spirit. — *Joanna Baillie.*

O NIGHT, when good men rest, and infants sleep!
Thou art to me no season of Repose,
But a fear'd time of waking more intense,
Of Life more keen, of Misery more palpable.

Trusting to others. — *Sir W. Temple.*

A MAN that only translates, shall never be a Poet; nor a Painter that only copies; nor a Swimmer that swims always with bladders: so people that trust wholly to others' Charity, and without Industry of their own, will always be poor.

Truth. — *Greville.*

THE mind's eye is perhaps no better fitted for the full radiance of Truth, than is the body's for that of the Sun.

Truth. — *Colton.*

THE interests of Society often render it expedient not to utter the whole Truth, the interests of Science never; for in this field we have much more to fear from the deficiency of Truth, than from its abundance.

Truth. — *Terence.*

OBSEQUIOUSNESS begets friends; Truth, hatred.

Truth. — *Paley.*

I HAVE seldom known any one who deserted Truth in trifles, that could be trusted in matters of Importance.

Truth. — *Johnson.*

ACCUSTOM your children to a strict attention to Truth, even in the most minute particulars. If a thing happened at one window, and they, when relating it, say that it happened at another, do not let it pass, but instantly check them: you do not know where deviations from Truth will end.

Truth. — *Shaftesbury.*

THE most natural beauty in the world is Honesty and moral Truth. For all Beauty is Truth. True Features make the beauty of a Face; and true proportions the beauty of Architecture: as true Measures that of Harmony and Music.

Truth. — *From the Latin.*

THERE is no doctrine so false as not to contain in it some Truth

Truth. — *Phædrus.*

TO believe is dangerous, to be unbelieving is equally so; the Truth therefore should be diligently sought after, lest that a foolish opinion should lead you to pronounce an unsound judgment.

Truth. — *Goldsmith.*

I LEARN several great Truths: as that it is impossible to see into the ways of Futurity; that Punishment always attends the villain; that Love is the fond soother of the human breast.

Truth. — *Bacon.*

CERTAINLY it is Heaven upon Earth to have a man's mind move in Charity, rest in Providence, and turn upon the poles of Truth.

Truth. — *Shakspeare.*

TRUTH'S a Dog that must to kennel; he must be whipp'd out, when Lady, the brach, may stand by the fire and stink.

Truth. — *Locke.*

TRUTH, whether in or out of fashion, is the measure of Knowledge, and the business of the Understanding; whatsoever is besides that, however authorized by consent, is nothing but Ignorance, or something worse.

Truth. — *Mackenzie.*

IT is curious to observe how the nature of Truth may be changed by the garb it wears; softened to the admonition of Friendship, or soured into the severity of Reproof; yet this severity may be useful to some tempers; it somewhat resembles a File, disagreeable in its operations, but hard Metal may be the brighter for it.

Truth. — *South.*

THE Reason of things lies in a narrow compass, if the Mind could at any time be so happy as to light upon it. Most of the writings and discourses in the world are but illustration and Rhetoric, which signifies as much as nothing to a mind in pursuit after the philosophical Truth of things.

Truth. — *Casaubon.*

THE study of Truth is perpetually joined with the love of Virtue; for there's no Virtue which derives not its original from Truth· as, on the contrary, there is no Vice which has not its beginning from a Lie. Truth is the foundation of all knowledge, and the cement of all society.

Truth. — *Colton.*

THE adorer of Truth is above all present things. Firm in the midst of Temptation, and frank in the midst of Treachery, he will be attacked by those who have prejudices, simply because he is without them, decried as a bad bargain by all who want to purchase, because he alone is not to be bought, and abused by all parties, because he is the advocate of none; like the Dolphin, which is always painted more crooked than a ram's horn, although every Naturalist knows that it is the straightest Fish that swims.

Truth. —*Milton.*

TRUTH is as impossible to be soiled by any outward touch, as the Sunbeam; though this ill hap wait on her nativity, that she never comes into the world, but like a bastard, to the ignominy of him that brought her forth; till time, the midwife rather than the mother of Truth, have washed and salted the infant, declared her legitimate, and churched the father of his young Minerva, from the needless causes of his purgation.

Truth. — *Shakspeare.*

OH, how much more doth Beauty beauteous seem,
By that sweet ornament which Truth doth give!
The Rose looks fair, but fairer we it deem
For that sweet odour which doth in it live.
The canker-blooms have full as deep a dye,
As the perfumed tincture of the Roses;
Hang on such thorns, and play as wantonly,
When summer's breath their masked buds discloses;
But, for their Virtue only is their show,
They live unwoo'd, and unrespected fade;
Die to themselves; sweet Roses do not so;
Of their sweet Deaths are sweetest odours made.

Truth. — *Cowper.*

ALL Truth is precious, if not all divine,
And what dilates the pow'rs must needs refine.

Truth. — *Colton.*

THE affairs of this world are kept together by what little Truth and Integrity still remains amongst us; and yet I much question whether the absolute dominion of Truth would be compatible with the existence of any society now existing upon the face of the Earth. Pure Truth, like pure Gold, has been found unfit for circulation, because men have discovered that it is far more convenient to adulterate the Truth, than to refine themselves. They will not advance their Minds to the Standard, therefore they lower the Standard to their Minds.

Truth. — *Ammian.*

TRUTH is violated by Falsehood, and it may be equally outraged by Silence.

Truth. — *Murphy.*

NONE but Cowards lie.

Truth. — *Shakspeare.*

IF circumstances lead me, I will find
Where Truth is hid, though it were hid indeed
Within the Centre.

Truth. — *Seneca.*

THE expression of Truth is Simplicity.

Truth. — *Cowper.*

MUCH learned dust
Involves the combatants, each claiming Truth,
And Truth disclaiming both. And thus they spend
The little wick of Life's poor shallow lamp,
In playing tricks with Nature, giving laws
To distant worlds, and trifling in their own.

Truth. — *Shakspeare.*

TRUTH needs no colour, with his colour fix'd;
Beauty no pencil, Beauty's Truth to lay;
But best is best, if never intermix'd.

Truth. — *Colton.*

TRUTH is the object of Reason, and this is one; Beauty is the object of Taste, and this is multiform.

Truth. — *Tacitus.*

TRUTH is established by investigation and delay; Falsehood prospers by precipitancy.

Truth. — *Ammian.*

TRUTH is simple, requiring neither Study nor Art.

Truth. — *Colton.*

TRUTH can hardly be expected to adapt herself to the crooked policy and wily sinuosities of worldly affairs; for Truth, like light, travels only in straight lines.

Truth. — *From the Latin.*

TRUTH, by whomsoever spoken, comes from God. It is, in short, a divine essence.

Truth. — *From the French.*

THE adherence to Truth does not produce so much good in the world, as the appearances of it do mischief.

Truth. — *Milton.*

TRUTH came once into the world with her Divine Master, and was a perfect shape most glorious to look on: but when he ascended, and his Apostles after him were laid asleep, then straight arose a wicked race of deceivers, who, as that story goes of the Egyptian Typhon with his conspirators, how they dealt with the good Osiris, took the virgin Truth, hewed her lovely form into a thousand pieces, and scattered them to the four winds. From that time ever since, the sad friends of Truth, such as durst appear, imitating the careful search that Isis made for the mangled body of Osiris, went up and down gathering up limb by limb still as they could find them. We have not yet found them all, nor ever shall do, till her Master's second coming; he shall bring together every joint and member, and shall mould them into an immortal feature of Loveliness and Perfection.

Truth. — *Colton.*

IF a man be sincerely wedded to Truth, he must make up his mind to find her a portionless Virgin, and he must take her for herself alone. The contract too, must be to love, cherish, and obey her, not only until Death, but beyond it; for this is an union that must survive not only Death, but Time, the conqueror of Death.

Truth. — *From the Latin.*

TRUTH fears nothing but Concealment.

Truth. — *Steele.*

THOUGH men may impose upon themselves what they please, by their corrupt imaginations, Truth will ever keep its station; and as glory is nothing else but the shadow of Virtue, it will certainly disappear at the departure of Virtue.

Truth. — *Anon.*

IS there less of Sincerity in Nature during her gambols in spring, than during the stiffness and harshness of her wintry gloom? Does not the bird's blithe caroling come from the Heart, quite as much as the quadruped's monotonous cry? And is it then altogether impossible to take up one's abode with Truth, and to let all sweet homely feelings grow about it and cluster around it, and to smile upon it as on a kind father or mother, and to sport with it and hold light and merry talk with it as with a loved brother or sister, and to fondle it and play with it as with a child? No otherwise did Socrates and Plato commune with Truth; no otherwise Cervantes and Shakspeare. This playfulness of truth is beautifully represented by Landor, in the Conversation between Marcus Cicero and his brother, in an allegory which has the voice and the spirit of Plato. On the other hand, the outcries of those who exclaim against every sound more lively than a bray or a bleat, as derogatory to Truth, are often prompted, not so much by their deep feeling of the dignity of the Truth in question, as of the dignity of the person by whom that Truth is maintained. It is our Vanity, our Self-Conceit, that makes us so sore and irritable. To a grave argument we may reply gravely, and fancy that we have the best of it: but he who is too dull or too angry to smile, cannot answer a smile, except by fretting and fuming.

Truth. — *Colton.*

THE greatest friend of Truth is Time; her greatest enemy is Prejudice; and her constant companion is Humility.

Truth. — *Colton.*

THE temple of Truth is built indeed of stones of Crystal, but, inasmuch as men have been concerned in rearing it, it has been consolidated by a cement composed of baser materials. It is deeply to be lamented that Truth herself will attract little attention, and less Esteem, until it be amalgamated with some particular party, persuasion, or sect; unmixed and unadulterated, it too often proves as unfit for currency, as pure Gold for circulation. Sir Walter Raleigh has observed, that he who follows Truth too closely, must take care that she does not strike out his teeth.

Truth. — *South.*

TRUTH is a great stronghold, barred and fortified by God and Nature; and Diligence is properly the Understanding's laying siege to it; so that, as in a kind of warfare, it must be perpetually upon the watch, observing all the avenues and passes to it, and accordingly makes its approaches. Sometimes it thinks it gains a point; and presently again it finds itself baffled and beaten off: yet still it renews the onset, attacks the difficulty afresh, plants this reasoning, and that argument, this consequence, and that distinction, like so many intellectual batteries, till at length, it forces a way and passage into the obstinate enclosed Truth, that so long withstood and defied all its assaults.

Truth. — *Sir T. Brown.*

EVERY man is not a proper champion for Truth, nor fit to take up the gauntlet in the cause of Verity: many, from the ignorance of these maxims and an inconsiderate zeal unto Truth, have too rashly charged the troops of Error, and remain as trophies unto the Enemies of Truth: a man may be in as just possession of Truth, as of a city, and yet be forced to surrender; 'tis therefore far better to enjoy her with Peace, than to hazard her on a battle.

Truth. — *Sir W. Temple.*

TRUTH will be uppermost, one time or other, like Cork, though kept down in the water.

Truth. — *Sir Philip Sidney.*

HE that finds Truth, without loving her, is like a bat; which, though it have eyes to discern that there is a Sun, yet hath so evil eyes, that it cannot delight in the Sun.

Truth. — *Cato.*

SOME men are more beholden to their bitterest Enemies, than to Friends who appear to be sweetness itself. The former frequently tell the Truth, but the latter never.

Truth. — *Steele.*

HUMAN nature is not so much depraved as to hinder us from respecting Goodness in others, though we ourselves want it. This is the reason why we are so much charmed with the pretty prattle of children, and even the expressions of Pleasure or uneasiness in some of the brute creation. They are without Artifice or Malice; and we love Truth too well to resist the charms of Sincerity.

Truth. — *Colton.*

NO bad man ever wished that his Breast was made of glass, or that others could read his thoughts. But the misery is, that the Duplicities, the Temptations, and the Infirmities that surround us, have rendered the Truth, and nothing but the Truth, as hazardous and contraband a commodity as a Man can possibly deal in.

Truth. — *Dryden.*

WE find but few historians of all ages, who have been diligent enough in their search for truth; it is their common method to take on trust what they distribute to the public; by which means a Falsehood once received from a famed writer becomes traditional to Posterity.

Truth. — *Hare.*

IT is a mistake to suppose the Poet does not know Truth by sight quite as well as the Philosopher. He must; for he is ever seeing her in the mirrors of Nature. The difference between them is, that the Poet is satisfied with worshipping her reflected image, while the Philosopher traces her out and follows her to her remote abode between Cause and Consequence, and there impregnates her. The one loves and makes love to Truth; the other esteems and weds her.

Self-Tyranny. — *Shakspeare.*

I CANNOT tell, what you and other men
Think of this life; but, for my single self,
I had as lief not be, as live to be
In awe of such a thing as I myself.

Tyranny. — *Milton.*

So spake the Fiend, and with Necessity,
The Tyrant's plea, excused his devilish deeds.

Tyranny. — *Shakspeare.*

AT some time, when his soaring Insolence
Shall reach the people, (which time shall not want,
If he be put upon't; and that's as easy,
As to set Dogs on sheep,) will be the Fire
To kindle their dry stubble; and their Blaze
Shall darken him for ever.

Tyranny. — *Claudian.*

HE who strikes Terror into others, is himself in continual fear.

The Unnatural. — *Shakspeare.*

THAT Nature which contemns its origin,
Cannot be border'd certain in itself;
She, that herself will sliver and disbranch
From her material sap, perforce must wither,
And come to deadly use.

The Unseen. — *From the Latin.*

EVERY thing unknown to us, we suppose to be magnificent.

Unhappiness. — *Milton.*

DID I request thee, Maker, from my clay
To mould me man? Did I solicit thee
From darkness to promote me, or here place
In this delicious Garden? As my will
Concurr'd not to my being, it were but right
And equal to reduce me to my Dust,
Desirous to resign and render back
All I received, unable to perform
Thy terms too hard, by which I was to hold
The Good I sought not.

Unconsciousness. — *Shakspeare.*

HE that is robb'd, not wanting what is stolen,
Let him not know it, and he's not robb'd at all.

Unsteadiness. — *Shakspeare.*

O PERILOUS mouths,
That bear in them one and the selfsame tongue,
Either of Condemnation or Approof!
Bidding the Law make curt'sy to their will;
Hooking both right and wrong to th' Appetite,
To follow as it draws!

The Usurer. — *Fuller.*

GO not to a covetous old Man with any Request too soon in the Morning, before he hath taken in that day's Prey: for his Covetousness is up before him, and he before thee, and he is in Ill humour: but stay till the Afternoon, till he be satiated upon some Borrower.

The Usurper. — *Shakspeare.*

A SCEPTRE, snatch'd with an unruly Hand,
Must be as boisterously maintain'd as gain'd;
And he that stands upon a slippery place,
Makes nice of no vile hold to stay him up.

Vanity. — *Anon.*

PRIDE and Vanity are for ever spoken of side by side; and many suppose that they are merely different shades of the same feeling. Yet, so far are they from being akin, they can hardly find room in the same breast. A Proud Man will not stoop to be vain; a Vain Man is so busy in bowing and wriggling to catch fair words from others, that he can never lift up his head into Pride.

Vanity. — *Colton.*

LADIES of Fashion starve their Happiness to feed their Vanity, and their Love to feed their Pride.

Vanity. — *Pope.*

EVERY man has just as much Vanity as he wants Understanding.

Vanity. — *Colton.*

IF you cannot inspire a woman with Love of you, fill her above the brim with Love of herself;—all that runs over will be yours.

Vanity. — *Greville.*

VANITY is the Poison of agreeableness; yet as Poison, when artfully and properly applied, has a salutary effect in medicine, so has Vanity in the commerce and society of the World.

Vanity. — *Anon.*

THERE are persons who would lie prostrate on the ground, if their Vanity or their Pride did not hold them up.

Vanity. — *La Rochefoucauld.*

EVERY person complains of the badness of his Memory, but none of their defective Judgment.

Vanity. — *Anon.*

PRIDE in former ages may have been held in too good repute; Vanity is so now. Pride, which is the fault of greatness and strength, is sneered at and abhorred: to Vanity, the froth and consummation of weakness, every indulgence is shown. For Pride stands aloof by itself; and that we are too mob-like to bear: Vanity is unable to stand, except by leaning on others, and is careful therefore of giving offence; nay, is ready to fawn on those by whom it hopes to be fed.

Vanity. — *La Bruyere.*

AN Egotist will always speak of himself, either in Praise or in Censure: but a modest man ever shuns making himself the subject of his Conversation.

Vanity. — *Swift.*

SOME men make a Vanity of telling their faults; they are the strangest men in the World; they cannot dissemble; they own it is a folly; they have lost abundance of advantages by it; but if you would give them the World, they cannot help it; there is something in their nature which abhors Insincerity and Constraint; with many other insufferable topics of the same altitude.

Vanity. — *Anon.*

THEY who do speak ill of themselves, do so mostly as the surest way of proving how modest and candid they are.

Vanity. — *Sterne.*

VANITY bids all her Sons be brave, and all her Daughters chaste and courteous. But why do we need her instructions? Ask the comedian who is taught a part which he does not feel.

Vengeance. — *Bonaparte.*

VENGEANCE has no Foresight.

Verbosity. — *Shakspeare.*

HE draweth out the thread of his Verbosity finer than the staple of his argument. I abhor such fanatical fantasms, such insociable and point-device companions, such Rackers of Orthography

Vice. — *Byron.*

THINK'ST thou there is no tyranny but that
Of Blood and Chains? The despotism of Vice—
The weakness and the wickedness of Luxury—
The negligence—the apathy—the evils
Of sensual Sloth—produce ten thousand tyrants,
Whose delegated cruelty surpasses
The worst acts of one energetic master,
However harsh and hard in his own bearing.

Vice. — *Colton.*

HE that has energy enough in his constitution to root out a Vice, should go a little farther, and try to plant in a Virtue in its place, otherwise he will have his labour to renew; a strong soil that has produced Weeds, may be made to produce Wheat, with far less difficulty than it would cost to make it produce Nothing.

Vice. — *Pope.*

VICE is a monster of so frightful mien,
As to be hated needs but to be seen;
Yet seen too oft, familiar with her face,
We first endure, then pity, then embrace.

Vice. — *Shakspeare.*

VICE repeated, is like the wand'ring Wind,
Blows Dust in others' eyes.

Vice. — *Byron.*

VICE cannot fix, and Virtue cannot change.
The once fall'n woman must for ever fall;
For Vice must have variety, while Virtue
Stands like the Sun, and all which rolls around
Drinks Life, and Light, and Glory from her aspect.

Vice. — *La Rochefoucauld.*

WE do not despise all those who have Vices, but we despise all those who have not a single Virtue.

Vice. — *Colton.*

VICE stings us, even in our pleasures, but Virtue consoles us, even in our pains.

Vice. —*Juvenal.*

No man ever arrived suddenly at the summit of Vice.

Vice. — *Colton.*

THE horrible catastrophes that sometimes happen to the Vicious are as salutary to others by their warning, as the most brilliant rewards of the Virtuous are by their example.

Vice. — *Sir P. Sidney.*

IN actions of Life, who seeth not the filthiness of Evil, wanteth a great foil to perceive the beauty of Virtue.

Vice. — *Colton.*

THE Good make a better bargain, and the Bad a worse, than is usually supposed; for the rewards of the one, and the punishments of the other, not unfrequently begin on this side of the grave; for Vice has more martyrs than Virtue; and it often happens that men suffer more to be lost than to be saved.

Vice. — *Shakspeare.*

BUT when we in our Viciousness grow hard,
(Oh misery on't) the wise Gods seal our eyes;
In our own filth drop our clear judgments; make us
Adore our errors; laugh at us while we strut
To our Confusion.

Vice. — *La Rochefoucauld.*

IT may be said that the Vices await us in the Journey of Life like hosts with whom we must successively lodge; and I doubt whether experience would make us avoid them if we were to travel the same road a second time.

Vice. — *Burke.*

VIRTUE will catch as well as Vice by contact; and the public stock of honest, manly principle will daily accumulate. We are not too nicely to scrutinize motives as long as action is irreproachable. It is enough (and for a worthy man perhaps too much) to deal out its Infamy to convicted Guilt and declared Apostasy.

Vice. — *Colton.*

WHEN Mandeville maintained that Private Vices were Public Benefits, he did not calculate the widely destructive influence of bad example. To affirm that a vicious man is only his *own* Enemy, is about as wise as to affirm that a virtuous man is only his *own* Friend.

Vice. — *Shenstone.*

VIRTUE seems to be nothing more than a motion consonant to the system of things; were a Planet to fly from its orbit, it would represent a Vicious Man.

Vice. — *Colton.*

THE Martyrs to Vice far exceed the Martyrs to Virtue, both in endurance and in number. So blinded are we by our passions, that we suffer more to be damned than to be saved.

Vice. — *Colton.*

IN all civilized communities, there must of necessity exist a small portion of Society, who are in a great measure independent of public opinion. How then is this seeming advantage balanced in the great account? These privileged individuals, surrounded by Parasites, Sycophants, and Deceivers, too often become the willing victims of Self-Delusion, Flattery, or Design. Such persons commence by being their own masters, and finish by being their own slaves, the automata of Passion, the Heliogaboli of Excess, and the Martyrs of Disease. Undelighted amidst all delight, and joyless amidst all enjoyment, yet sateless in the very lap of satiety, they eventually receive the full measure of the punishment of their Folly, their Profligacy, or their Vice; nay, they often suffer *more* than other men, not because they are as amenable as their inferiors, but because they go greater lengths. Experience speaks to such in vain, and they sink deeper in the Abyss, in precise proportion to the height from which they have plunged.

Vice. — *Tucker.*

THE allurements of Fancy prove the first source of wantonness, of unlucky and mischievous tricks in the earliest years, and in the riper often produce more troublesome effects; for a flow of Prosperity with continual indulgence of the desires, commonly makes men capricious, selfish, narrow-minded, intractable, contemptuous, and overbearing, until some galling Disappointment or misfortune has taught them, that there are other objects necessary to be thought of, besides that of pleasing themselves.

Vice. — *Colton.*

A SOCIETY composed of none but the Wicked, could not exist; it contains within itself the seeds of its own Destruction, and, without a flood, would be swept away from the Earth by the deluge of its own Iniquity. The moral cement of all society is Virtue; it unites and preserves, while Vice separates and destroys. The good may well be termed the Salt of the Earth. For where there is no integrity, there can be no confidence; and where there is no confidence, there can be no unanimity.

Vice. — *Shakspeare.*

ONE sin another doth provoke.

Vice. — *Pope.*

BUT when to Mischief mortals bend their will,
How soon they find fit instruments of Ill!

Vice. — *Anon.*

MANY a man's Vices have at first been nothing worse than Good Qualities run wild.

Vice. — *Colton.*

GREAT examples to Virtue, or to Vice, are not so productive of imitation as might at first sight be supposed. The fact is, there are hundreds that want Energy, for one that wants Ambition, and Sloth has prevented as many Vices in some minds, as Virtues in others. Idleness is the grand Pacific Ocean of life, and in that stagnant Abyss, the most salutary things produce no good, the most noxious no evil. Vice indeed, abstractedly considered, may be, and often is, engendered in Idleness, but the moment it becomes efficiently Vice, it must quit its cradle and cease to be idle.

Vice. — *Byron.*

NOT all that Heralds rake from coffin'd clay,
Nor florid Prose, nor honied lies of Rhyme,
Can blazon evil deeds, or consecrate a Crime.

Vice. — *Seneca.*

WHY is there no man who confesses his Vices? It is because he has not yet laid them aside. It is a waking man only who can tell his dreams.

Vigilance. — *From the Latin.*

THE Master's eye makes the Horse fat.

Villany. — *Colton.*

VILLANY that is vigilant, will be an overmatch for Virtue, if she slumber on her post; and hence it is that a bad cause has often triumphed over a good one; for the Partisans of the former, knowing that their cause will do nothing for them, have done every thing for their Cause; whereas, the friends of the latter are too apt to expect every thing from their Cause, and to do nothing for themselves.

Virtue. — *Shakspeare.*

A HEART unspotted is not easily daunted.

Virtue. — *Cowper.*

THE only amaranthine flow'r on earth
Is Virtue; the only lasting treasure, Truth.

Virtue. — *Armstrong.*

VIRTUE, (for mere good-nature is a fool,)
Is sense and spirit with Humanity:
'Tis sometimes angry, and its frown confounds;
'Tis even vindictive, but in Vengeance just.
Knaves fain would laugh at it; some great ones dare;
But at his Heart the most undaunted son
Of Fortune dreads its name and awful charms.

Virtue. — *Shakspeare.*

HOW far that little Candle throws his beams!
So shines a good deed in a naughty world.
Heaven doth with us, as we with torches do;
Not light them for themselves; for if our Virtues
Did not go forth of us, 'twere all alike
As if we had them not.

Virtue. — *Thomson.*

BELIEVE the muse, the wintry blast of Death
Kills not the buds of Virtue; no, they spread,
Beneath the heavenly beams of brighter Suns,
Thro' endless ages, into higher powers.

Virtue. — *Young.*

HIS hand the Good Man fastens on the skies,
And bids Earth roll, nor feels her idle whirl.

Virtue. — *Dryden.*

A SETTLED Virtue,
Makes itself a Judge; and satisfied within,
Smiles at that common enemy, the World.

Virtue. — *Pope.*

WHAT nothing earthly gives, or can destroy,
The Soul's calm sunshine, and the heart-felt joy,
Is Virtue's prize: a better would you fix?
Then give Humility a coach and six,
Justice a conqueror's sword, or Truth a gown,
Or public Spirit its great cure, a crown.
Weak, foolish man! will Heaven reward us there
With the same trash mad mortals wish for here?
The boy and man an individual makes,
Yet sigh'st thou now for apples and for cakes?
Go, like the Indian, in another life
Expect thy dog, thy bottle, and thy wife;
As well as dream such trifles are assign'd
As toys and empires, for a godlike mind;
Rewards, that either would to Virtue bring
No Joy, or be destructive of the thing.

Virtue. — *Pope.*

BUT sometimes Virtue starves, while Vice is fed?
What then? Is the reward of Virtue bread;
That, Vice may merit—'tis the price of toil;
The knave deserves it, when he tills the soil;
The knave deserves it, when he tempts the main,
Where folly fights for Kings, or dives for gain.

The good man may be weak, be indolent,
Nor is his claim to plenty, but content.
But grant him Riches, your demand is o'er?
No—shall the good want Health, the good want Power?
Add Health and Power, and every earthly thing,
Why bounded power? why private? why no King?
Nay, why external for internal given?
Why is not man a God, and earth a Heaven?
Who ask and reason thus, will scarce conceive
God gives enough, while he has more to give;
Immense the power, immense were the demand;
Say, at what part of Nature will they stand?

Virtue. — *Thomson.*

O VIRTUE! Virtue! as thy joys excel,
So are thy woes transcendent; the gross world
Knows not the Bliss or Misery of either.

Virtue. — *Young.*

VIRTUE, not rolling suns, the mind matures;
That Life is long, which answers Life's great end.
The time that bears no fruit, deserves no name;
The Man of Wisdom is the man of Years.

Virtue. — *Young.*

A GOOD man, and an Angel! these between;
How thin the barrier! What divides their fate?
Perhaps a moment, or perhaps a year;
Or, if an age, it is a moment still;
A moment, or Eternity's forgot.

Virtue. — *Young.*

THE man who consecrates his hours
By vig'rous effort, and an honest aim,
At once he draws the sting of Life and Death;
He walks with Nature; and her paths are Peace.

Virtue. — *Miller.*

THOU know'st but little,
If thou dost think true Virtue is confined
To climes or systems; no, it flows spontaneous,
Like Life's warm stream, throughout the whole Creation,
And beats the pulse of every healthful heart.

Virtue. — *Horace.*

LET the Wise Man be considered as a fool, the Just Man as unjust, if his rigorous adherence even to Virtue herself carries him beyond the proper bounds.

Virtue. — *Young.*

WHO does the best his circumstance allows,
Does well, acts nobly; Angels could no more.

Virtue. — *Moore.*

THE plain, good man, whose actions teach
More Virtue than a sect can preach,
Pursues his course, unsagely blest,
His tutor whisp'ring in his breast:
Nor could he act a purer part,
Though he had Tully all by heart;
And when he drops the tear on Wo,
He little knows, or cares to know,
That Epictetus blamed that tear,
By Heaven approved, to Virtue dear.

Virtue. — *Shakspeare.*

I HELD it ever,
Virtue and Knowledge were endowments greater
Than Nobleness and Riches: careless heirs
May the two latter darken and expend;
But Immortality attends the former,
Making a man a God.

Virtue. — *Cardinal Richelieu.*

A VIRTUOUS and well-disposed person, like a good Metal, the more he is fired, the more he is fined; the more he is opposed, the more he is approved: Wrongs may well try him, and touch him, but cannot imprint in him any false stamp.

Virtue. — *La Rochefoucauld.*

VANITY, Shame, and above all, Temperament, are often the causes of Courage in men, and of Virtue in women.

Virtue. — *Seneca.*

VIRTUE, like Fire, turns all things into itself: our Actions and our Friendships are tinctured with it, and whatever it touches becomes amiable.

Virtue. — *Shakspeare.*

FROM lowest place when virtuous things proceed,
The place is dignified by the doer's deed:
Where great additions swell, and Virtue none,
It is a dropsied honour: Good alone
Is good, without a name; Vileness is so:
The property by what it is should go,
Not by the Title.

Virtue. — *Shakspeare.*

VIRTUE, that transgresses, is but patched with Sin; and Sin, that amends, is but patched with Virtue.

Virtue. — *Greville.*

ONE great reason why Virtue is so *little* practised, is its being so *ill* understood.

Virtue. — *Shakspeare.*

Oh, let not Virtue seek
Remuneration for the thing it was!
For Beauty, Wit,
High Birth, Vigour of Bone, Desert in Service,
Love, Friendship, Charity, are subjects all
To envious and calumniating Time.

Virtue. — *Shakspeare.*

ALL places that the eye of Heaven visits,
Are to a wise man ports and happy havens:
Teach thy necessity to reason thus:
There is no Virtue like Necessity.

Virtue. — *La Rochefoucauld.*

IT is with certain Good Qualities as with the Senses; those who are entirely deprived of them can neither appreciate nor comprehend them

Virtue. — *Greville.*

The best judges of Pleasure are the best judges of Virtue.

Virtue. — *Colton.*

THERE are two things which speak as with a voice from heaven, that He that fills that eternal throne must be on the side of Virtue, and that which He befriends must finally prosper and prevail. The first is, that the Bad are never completely happy and at ease, although possessed of every thing that this World can bestow; and that the Good are never completely miserable, although deprived of every thing that this World can take away. We are so framed and constituted, that the most vicious cannot but pay a secret though unwilling homage to Virtue, inasmuch as the worst men cannot bring themselves thoroughly to esteem a bad man, although he may be their dearest Friend, nor can they thoroughly despise a good man, although he may be their bitterest Enemy. From this inward esteem for Virtue, which the noblest cherish, and which the basest cannot expel, it follows that Virtue is the only bond of union on which we can thoroughly depend.

Virtue. — *Sir P. Sidney.*

TO be ambitious of true Honour, of the true Glory and Perfection of our natures, is the very principle and incentive of Virtue; but to be ambitious of titles, of place, of ceremonial respects and civil pageantry, is as vain and little as the things are which we court.

Virtue. — *St. Evremond.*

VIRTUE I love, without austerity; Pleasure without effeminacy; and Life without fearing its end.

Virtue. — *Colton.*

THERE is but *one* pursuit in Life which it is in the power of all to follow, and of all to attain. It is subject to no Disappointments, since he that perseveres makes every Difficulty an advancement, and every contest a Victory: and this is the pursuit of Virtue.

Virtue. — *Shakspeare.*

IN nature there's no blemish, but the Mind;
None can be call'd deform'd, but the unkind:
Virtue is Beauty; but the Beauteous-evil
Are empty trunks, o'erflourish'd by the Devil.

Virtue. — *Seneca.*

NO man is born wise; but Wisdom and Virtue require a tutor; though we can easily learn to be vicious without a master.

Virtue. — *Shakspeare.*

SUNDRY blessings hang about his Throne,
That speak him full of Grace.

Virtue. — *Massinger.*

PRINCES can never more make known their Wisdom
Than when they cherish Goodness where they find it;
They being Men, not Gods,
They can give wealth and titles, but no Virtue;
That is without their power.

Virtue. — *Shakspeare.*

WHEN once our Grace we have forgot,
Nothing goes right.

Virtue. — *South.*

WERE there but one Virtuous Man in the world, he would hold up his head with Confidence and Honour; he would shame the world, and not the world him.

Virtue. — *Socrates.*

A HORSE is not known by his furniture, but qualities; so men are to be esteemed for Virtue, not Wealth.

Virtue. — *Cicero.*

NO man should be so much taken up in the search of Truth, as thereby to neglect the more necessary duties of active life; for after all is done, it is action only that gives a true Value and commendation to Virtue.

Virtue. — *La Rochefoucauld.*

A TRULY virtuous man is he who prides himself upon nothing.

Virtue. — *La Rochefoucauld.*

PERFECT Virtue is to do unwitnessed what we should be capable of doing before all the world.

The Volatile. — *Shenstone.*

EXTREME volatile and sprightly tempers seem inconsistent with any great Enjoyment. There is too much time wasted in the mere transition from one object to another. No room for those deep impressions, which are made alone by the duration of an Idea, and are quite requisite to any strong sensation, either of pleasure or of pain. The Bee to collect honey, or the Spider to gather poison, must abide some time upon the weed or flower. They whose fluids are mere Sal Volatile, seem rather cheerful than happy men. The temper above described is oftener the lot of Wits, than of persons of great Abilities.

Vows. — *Fuller.*

MAKE no Vows to perform this or that: it shows no great Strength, and makes thee ride behind thyself.

Wants. — *Johnson.*

WHERE Necessity ends, Curiosity begins; and no sooner are we supplied with every thing that Nature can demand, than we sit down to contrive artificial appetites.

Wants. — *Colton.*

WE are ruined, not by what we really want, but by what we think we do; therefore never go abroad in search of your wants; if they be real wants, they will come home in search of you; for he that buys what he does not want, will soon want what he cannot buy.

Wants. — *Anon.*

HOW few are our real Wants! and how easy is it to satisfy them! Our imaginary ones are boundless and insatiable.

Wants. — *Socrates.*

THE fewer our wants, the nearer we resemble the Gods.

War. — *St. Evremond.*

IN War, people judge, for the most part, by the Success, whatever is the opinion of the wiser sort. Let a man show all the good conduct that is possible, if the Event does not answer, ill fortune passes for a fault, and is justified but by a very few persons.

War. — *Addison.*

A THOUSAND glorious Actions, that might claim
Triumphant laurels, and immortal Fame,
Confused in crowds of glorious actions lie,
And troops of Heroes undistinguish'd die.

War. — *Joanna Baillie.*

WAR is honourable
In those who do their native rights maintain;
In those whose Swords an iron barrier are
Between the lawless spoiler and the weak:
But is in those who draw th' offensive blade
For added power or gain, sordid and despicable
As meanest office of the worldly Churl.

War. — *Shakspeare.*

THE Arms are fair,
When the intent of bearing them is just.

War. — *Thomson.*

BUT what most show'd the Vanity of Life,
Was to behold the nations all on fire,
In cruel broils engaged and deadly strife;
Most Christian Kings inflamed by black desire!
With honourable ruffians in their hire,
Cause War to rage, and Blood around to pour;
Of this sad work when each begins to tire,
They set them down just where they were before,
Till for new scenes of Wo Peace shall their force restore.

War. — *Shakspeare.*

TAKE heed,
How you awake our sleeping Sword of War;
We charge you in the name of God, take heed.
For never two such Kingdoms did contend
Without much fall of blood; whose guiltless drops
Are every one a Wo, a sore complaint,
'Gainst him, whose wrong gives edge unto the swords,
That makes such waste in brief Mortality.

War. — *Shakspeare.*

A VICTORY is twice itself, when the achiever brings home full numbers.

War. — *Southern.*

DOST thou not know the fate of Soldiers?
They're but Ambition's tools, to cut a way
To her unlawful ends: and when they're worn,
Hack'd, hewn with constant Service, thrown aside,
To rust in Peace, and rot in Hospitals.

War. — *Burke.*

WAR suspends the rules of moral obligation, and what is long suspended is in danger of being totally abrogated. Civil Wars strike deepest of all into the manners of the people. They vitiate their Politics; they corrupt their Morals; they pervert even the natural taste and relish of Equity and Justice. By teaching us to consider our fellow-creatures in an hostile light, the whole body of our nation becomes gradually less dear to us. The very names of Affection and Kindred, which were the bond of Charity whilst we agreed, become new incentives to hatred and rage, when the communion of our country is dissolved.

War. — *Shakspeare.*

WILL you again unknit
This churlish knot of all-abhorred War,
And move in that obedient Orb again,
Where you did give a fair and natural light;
And be no more an exhaled meteor,
A Prodigy of Fear, and a portent
Of broached mischief, to the unborn times?

The Priest Warrior. — *Shakspeare.*

IT better show'd with you,
When that your flock, assembled by the Bell.
Encircled you, to hear with reverence
Your exposition on the Holy Text;
Than now to see you here an iron man,
Cheering a rout of rebels with your drum,
Turning the Word to Sword, and Life to Death.

Waste. — *Franklin.*

WHAT maintains one Vice, would bring up two children. Remember, many a little makes a mickle; and farther, beware of little expenses; a small Leak will sink a great Ship.

Wealth. — *Colton.*

IT is far more easy to acquire a Fortune like a knave, than to expend it like a Gentleman.

Wealth. — *Propertius.*

ALL men now contend for Gold, true Piety being banished from the world. Wealth is now become the sole ground of claim to respect or consideration among men.

Wealth. — *La Bruyere.*

AS Riches and Favour forsake a man, we discover him to be a fool, but nobody could find it out in his Prosperity.

Wealth. — *Hare.*

NOTHING hides a blemish so completely as Cloth of Gold. This is the first lesson that heirs and heiresses commonly learn. Would that equal pains were taken to convince them, that the having inherited a good Cover for blemishes does not entail any absolute necessity of providing Blemishes for it to cover.

Wealth. — *Colton.*

GROSS and vulgar minds will always pay a higher respect to Wealth than to Talent; for Wealth, although it be a far less efficient source of power than Talent, happens to be far more intelligible.

Wealth. — *Horace.*

SOVEREIGN Money procures a Wife with a large fortune, gets a man Credit, creates Friends, stands in the place of Pedigree, and even of Beauty.

Wealth. — *La Bruyere.*

LET us not envy some men their accumulated Riches; their burden would be too heavy for us; we could not sacrifice, as they do, Health, Quiet, Honour, and Conscience, to obtain them: it is to pay so dear for them, that the bargain is a loss.

Wealth. — *Colton.*

IT is only when the Rich are sick, that they fully feel the impotence of Wealth.

Wealth. — *La Bruyere.*

THERE is nothing keeps longer than a middling Fortune, and nothing melts away sooner than a great one. Poverty treads upon the heels of great and unexpected Riches.

Wealth. — *Colton.*

IN proportion as nations get more corrupt, more Disgrace will attach to Poverty, and more Respect to Wealth.

Wealth. — *Colton.*

THE greatest and the most amiable privilege which the Rich enjoy over the Poor, is that which they exercise the least—the privilege of making them happy.

Wealth. — *Butler.*

MEN venture necks to gain a Fortune:
The Soldier does it every day
(Eight to the week) for sixpence pay:
Your Pettifoggers damn their souls,
To share with knaves in cheating fools.

Wealth. — *Shakspeare.*

THE aged man that coffers up his Gold,
 Is plagued with cramps, and gouts, and painful fits;
And scarce hath eyes his Treasure to behold,
 But like still-pining Tantalus he sits,
 And useless barns the Harvest of his wits;
Having no other pleasure of his gain,
But Torment that it cannot cure his pain.
 So then he hath it, when he cannot use it,
And leaves it to be master'd by his young;
 Who in their pride do presently abuse it;
Their Father was too weak, and they too strong,
To hold their cursed-bless'd Fortune long.

Wealth. — *From the Latin.*

THE acquisition of Wealth is a work of great Labour: its possession, a source of continual Fear; its loss, of excessive Grief.

Wealth. — *Johnson.*

BUT, scarce observed, the knowing and the bold
 Fall in the gen'ral massacre of Gold;
Wide wasting pest! that rages unconfined,
And crowds with crimes the records of mankind:
For Gold his sword the hireling ruffian draws,
For Gold the hireling judge distorts the laws;
Wealth heap'd on Wealth, nor truth nor safety buys,
The dangers gather as the treasures rise.

Wealth. — *Johnson.*

THE needy Traveller, serene and gay,
 Walks the wide heath, and sings his toil away.
Does Envy seize thee? crush th' upbraiding Joy,
Increase his riches, and his peace destroy.

Wealth. — *Crabbe.*

WEALTH is substantial good the Fates allot:
 We know we have it, or we have it not.
But all those graces, which men highly rate,
Their minds themselves imagine and create.

Wealth. — *Johnson.*

WHOSOEVER shall look heedfully upon those who are eminent for their Riches, will not think their condition such as that he should hazard his quiet, and much less his Virtue, to obtain it: for all that great Wealth generally gives above a moderate fortune, is more room for the freaks of Caprice, and more privilege for Ignorance and Vice, a quicker succession of Flatteries, and a larger circle of Voluptuousness.

Wealth. — *Spenser.*

ALL otherwise (said he) I riches read,
And deeme them roote of all Disquietnesse:
First got with guile, and then preserved with dread;
And after spent with Pride and lavishnesse,
Leaving behind them Grief and heavinesse.
Infinite mischiefes of them doe arize;
Strife and Debate, Bloodshed and Bitternesse,
Outrageous wrong, and hellish covetize
That noble hart in great Dishonour doth despize.

Wealth. — *Young.*

CAN wealth give Happiness? look round, and see
What gay distress! what splendid misery!
Whatever Fortune lavishly can pour,
The mind annihilates, and calls for more.

Wealth. — *Sir William Temple.*

LEISURE and Solitude are the best effect of Riches, because mother of Thought. Both are avoided by most rich men, who seek Company and Business, which are signs of being weary of themselves.

Wealth. — *Gay.*

NOW gaudy Pride corrupts the lavish age,
And the streets flame with glaring equipage;
The tricking Gamester insolently rides,
With loves and graces on his chariot sides;
In saucy state the griping Broker sits,
And laughs at Honesty and trudging wits.

Wealth. — *Johnson.*

TO purchase Heaven has gold the power?
Can Gold remove the mortal hour?
In life can Love be bought with gold?
Are Friendship's pleasures to be sold?
No—all that's worth a wish—a thought,
Fair Virtue gives unbribed, unbought.
Cease then on trash thy hopes to bind,
Let nobler views engage thy mind.

Wealth. — *Shakspeare.*

IF thou art rich, thou art poor;
For, like an ass, whose back with ingots bows,
Thou bear'st thy heavy Riches but a journey,
And Death unloads thee.

Wealth. — *Burton.*

WORLDLY Wealth is the Devil's Bait; and those whose minds feed upon Riches, recede, in general, from real Happiness, in proportion as their stores increase; as the Moon when she is fullest is furthest from the Sun.

Wealth. — *Horace.*

WHEN I caution you against becoming a Miser, I do not therefore advise you to become a Prodigal or a Spendthrift.

Weeping. — *Byron.*

SHE was a good deal shock'd; not shock'd at Tears,
For Women shed and use them at their liking;
But there is something when Man's eye appears
Wet, still more disagreeable and striking.

Wealth. — *Shakspeare.*

DESPAIR to gain doth traffic oft for gaining:
And when great Treasure is the meed propcsed,
Though Death be adjunct, there's no Death supposed.
Those that much covet are of gain so fond,
That what they have not (that which they possess)
They scatter and unloose it from their bond,
And so by hoping more they have but less;
Or gaining more the profit of Excess
Is but to surfeit, and such griefs sustain,
That they prove bankrupt in this poor-rich gain.
The aim of all is but to nurse the Life
With Honour, Wealth, and Ease, in waning Age:
And in this aim there is such thwarting strife,
That one for all, or all for one, we gage:
As Life for Honour in fell battle's rage,
Honour for Wealth, and oft that Wealth doth cost
The Death of all, and altogether lost.
So that in vent'ring all, we leave to be
The things we are for that which we expect:
And this ambitious foul infirmity,
In having much, torments us with defect
Of that we have: so then we do neglect
The things we have, and all for want of Wit,
Make something nothing by augmenting it.

The Welcome. — *Shakspeare.*

SIR, you are very welcome to our house:
It must appear in other ways than words,
Therefore I scant this breathing Courtesy.

Why and Because. — *Lavater.*

CALL him wise whose Actions, Words, and Steps are all a clear *because* to a clear *why.*

The Widow. — *Pope.*

THUS day by day, and month by month we past;
It pleased the Lord to take my spouse at last.
I tore my gown, I soil'd my locks with dust,
And beat my breasts, as wretched Widows must;
Before my face my Handkerchief I spread,
To hide the flood of Tears I did—*not* shed.

The Widow's two Mites. — *Webster.*

WHAT more tender, more solemnly affecting, more profoundly pathetic, than this charity, this offering to God, of a farthing! We know nothing of her name, her family, or her tribe. We only know that she was a poor Woman, and a Widow, of whom there is nothing left upon record but this sublimely simple story, that when the rich men came to cast their proud offerings into the treasury, this poor Woman came also, and cast in her two Mites, which made a farthing! And that example, thus made the subject of divine commendation, has been read, and told, and has gone abroad everywhere, and sunk deep into a hundred million of hearts, since the commencement of the Christian era, and has done more good than could be accomplished by a thousand marble palaces, because it was charity mingled with true benevolence, given in the fear, the love, the service, and the honour of God; because it was charity, that had its origin in religious feeling; because it was a gift to the honour of God!

The Wife. — *Milton.*

FOR nothing lovelier can be found
In Woman, than to study household good,
And good works in her Husband to promote.

The Wife. — *Shakspeare.*

MY noble Father,
I do perceive here a divided duty;
To you I am bound for Life and Education;
My Life and Education both do learn me
How to respect you; you are the lord of duty,
I am hitherto your daughter: but here's my Husband;
And so much duty as my mother show'd
To you, preferring you before her Father,
So much I challenge, that I may profess
Due to my Lord.

The Wife. — *G. H. Drummond.*

'TIS not in Hymen's gay propitious hour,
With summer beams and genial breezes blest,
That Man a Consort's worth approveth best:
'Tis when the skies with gloomy Tempests lour,
When Cares and Sorrows all their torrents pour,
She clasps him closer to her hallow'd Breast,
Pillows his Head, and lays his Heart to rest;
Drying her cheek from sympathetic shower.

The Wife. — *Pope.*

SHE who ne'er answers till a Husband cools,
Or, if she rules him, never shows she rules;
Charms by accepting, by submitting sways,
Yet has her Humour most, when she obeys.

The Wife. — *Shakspeare.*

THOU art alone,
If thy rare qualities, sweet Gentleness,
Thy meekness saint-like, wife-like government,—
Obeying in commanding,—and thy parts,
Sovereign and pious else, could speak thee out,
The Queen of earthly Queens.

The Wife. — *Milton.*

WHAT thou bid'st
Unargued I obey; so God ordains;
God is thy law; thou mine: to know no more
Is Woman's happiest knowledge, and her Praise.

The Wife. — *Hammond.*

BEAUTY and worth in her alike contend,
To charm the fancy, and to fix the mind;
In her, my Wife, my Mistress, and my Friend,
I taste the joys of Sense and Reason join'd.

The Wife. — *Milton.*

SOLE partner, and sole part, of all these Joys,
Dearer thyself than all.

The Wife. — *Prior.*

SO, if for any sins of ours,
Or our forefathers' higher powers,
Severe, though just, afflict our Life
With that prime ill, a talking Wife;
Till Death shall bring the kind relief,
We must be patient, or be deaf.

The Wife. — *Byron.*

THINK you, if Laura had been Petrarch's Wife,
He would have written Sonnets all his life?

The Wife. — *Milton.*

THY Likeness, thy fit help, thy other self,
Thy wish exactly to thy Heart's desire.

The Wife. — *Irving.*

I HAVE often had occasion to remark the fortitude with which Women sustain the most overwhelming reverses of fortune. Those disasters which break down the spirit of a man and prostrate him in the dust, seem to call forth all the energies of the softer sex, and give such intrepidity and elevation to their character, that at times it approaches to sublimity. Nothing can be more touching than to behold a soft and tender female, who had been all weakness and dependence, and alive to every trivial roughness while treading the prosperous paths of life, suddenly rising in mental force to be the comforter and supporter of her husband under misfortune, and abiding with unshrinking firmness the bitterest blast of adversity.

The Will. — *Shakspeare.*

VALUE dwells not in particular will;
It holds its estimate and Dignity
As well wherein 'tis precious of itself,
As in the prizer: 'tis mad Idolatry,
To make the service greater than the God;
And the Will dotes, that is inclinable
To what infectiously itself affects,
Without some Image of th' affected merit.
I take to-day a wife, and my election
Is led on in the conduct of my Will;
My Will enkindled by mine eyes and ears,
Two traded pilots 'twixt the dangerous shores
Of Will and Judgment: how may I avoid
(Although my Will distaste which is elected)
The wife I chose? there can be no evasion
To blench from this, and to stand firm by honour.
We turn not back the silks upon the Merchant,
When we have spoil'd them; nor the remainder viands
We do not throw in unrespective place,
Because we now are full.

The Will. — *Seneca.*

NO action will be considered as blameless, unless the Will was so, for by the Will the Act was dictated.

The Will. — *Shakspeare.*

HE wants Wit, that wants resolved Will.

The Will. — *Shakspeare.*

OUR bodies are our gardens; to the which our Wills are Gardeners; so that if we will plant nettles, or sow lettuce; set hyssop, and weed up thyme; supply it with one gender of herbs, or distract it with many; either to have it sterile with Idleness, or manured with Industry; why, the power and corrigible authority of this lies in our Wills. If the balance of our lives had not one scale of Reason to poise another of Sensuality, the Blood and baseness of our Natures would conduct us to most preposterous conclusions.

The Will. — *Fuller.*

PRESCRIBE no positive laws to thy Will: for thou mayest be forced to-morrow to drink the same Water thou despisest today.

The Will. — *Colton.*

TO commit the execution of a purpose to one who disapproves of the plan of it, is to employ but one-third of the man; his Heart and his Head are against you, you have commanded only his Hands.

The Will. — *Shakspeare.*

THE Will of man is by his Reason sway'd.

The Will. — *Dryden.*

LET Fortune empty her whole quiver on me.
I have a Soul, that like an ample shield,
Can take in all, and verge enough for more;
Fate was not mine, nor am I Fate's:
Souls know no Conquerors.

Free Will. — *Milton.*

GOD made thee perfect, not immutable;
And good he made thee, but to persevere
He left it in thy pow'r; ORDAINED THY WILL
BY NATURE FREE, not over-ruled by Fate
Inextricable, or strict Necessity.

Free Will. — *Milton.*

INGRATE, he had of me
All he could have; I made him just and right,
Sufficient to have stood, though free to fall.
Such I created all th' ethereal Powers
And Spirits, both them who stood and them who fail'd;
Freely they stood who stood, and fell who fell.

Free Will. — *Milton.*

OUR voluntary service He requires,
  NOT OUR NECESSITATED; such with Him
Finds no acceptance, nor can find; for how
Can Hearts, not free, be tried whether they serve
Willing or no, who will but what they must
By Destiny, nor can no other choose?

Making a Will. — *Osborne.*

WHAT you leave at your Death, let it be without controversy, else the Lawyers will be your heirs.

Windfalls. — *Horace.*

YOU do not value it greatly, because it came by Accident.

Winds and Waves. — *Shakspeare.*

  THIS Battle fares like to the Morning's war,
When dying Clouds contend with growing Light;
What time the Shepherd, blowing of his nails,
Can neither call it perfect Day nor Night.
Now sways it this way, like a mighty Sea
Forced by the tide to combat with the Wind:
Now sways it that way, like the self-same Sea
Forced to retire by fury of the Wind.
Sometime, the Flood prevails; and then, the Wind;
Now, one the better; then, another best;
Both tugging to be Victors, breast to breast,
Yet neither conqueror, nor conquer'd;
So is the equal poise of this fell War.

Wine. — *Milton.*

  ONE sip of this
Will bathe the drooping Spirits in delight
Beyond the bliss of dreams. Be wise, and taste.

Wine. — *Shakspeare.*

GOOD Wine is a good familiar Creature, if it be well used.

Winter. — *Spenser.*

LASTLY came Winter, cloathed all in frize,
  Chattering his teeth for cold that did him chill;
Whilst on his hoary Beard his breath did freeze,
  And the dull drops that from his purple bill
  As from a limbeck did adown distill;
In his right hand a tipped Staffe he held,
  With which his feeble steps he stayed still,
For he was faint with Cold and weak with eld,
That scarce his loosed limbes he able was to weld.

Wisdom.—*Shakspeare.*

To Wisdom he's a Fool that will not yield.

Wisdom.—*Colton.*

THERE is this difference between Happiness and Wisdom: he that thinks himself the happiest man, really is so; but he that thinks himself the wisest, is generally the greatest Fool.

Wisdom.—*Hare.*

THE intellect of the wise is like glass: it admits the Light of Heaven, and reflects it.

Wisdom.—*Anon.*

WISDOM is Alchemy. Else it could not be Wisdom. This is its unfailing characteristic, that it "finds good in every thing," that it renders all things more precious. In this respect also does it renew the spirit of Childhood within us: while Foolishness hardens our hearts, and narrows our thoughts, it makes us feel a childlike curiosity and a childlike interest about all things. When our view is confined to ourselves, nothing is of value, except what ministers in one way or other to our own personal Gratification: but in proportion as it widens, our sympathies increase and multiply: and when we have learnt to look on all things as God's works, then, as His works, they are all endeared to us. Hence nothing can be further from true Wisdom, than the mask of it assumed by Men of the World, who affect a cold indifference about whatever does not belong to their own immediate circle of Interests or Pleasures.

Wisdom.—*La Rochefoucauld.*

IT is more easy to be Wise for others than for ourselves.

Pisdom.—*From the French.*

THE strongest symptom of Wisdom in man, is his being sensible of his own Follies.

Wisdom.—*Terence.*

WISDOM consists, not in seeing what is directly before us, but in discerning those things which may come to pass.

Wisdom.—*Pliny.*

No man is at all times wise.

Wisdom.—*Grymestone.*

WISDOM is the olive that springeth from the Heart, bloometh on the Tongue, and beareth fruit in the Actions.

Wisdom.—*From the Latin.*

HE is by no means to be considered wise, who is not wise toward himself.

Wisdom. — *Colton.*

THE Wise Man has his follies, no less than the Fool; but it has been said, that herein lies the difference,—the follies of the Fool are known to the World, but are hidden from himself; the follies of the Wise are known to himself, but hidden from the World. A harmless hilarity and a buoyant cheerfulness are not unfrequent concomitants of Genius; and we are never more deceived, than when we mistake Gravity for Greatness, Solemnity for Science, and Pomposity for Erudition.

Wisdom. — *Boileau.*

THE Wisest Man is generally he who thinks himself the least so.

Wisdom. — *Fuller.*

IF thou wouldst be borne with, bear with others.

Wisdom. — *Tillotson.*

TRUE Wisdom is a thing very extraordinary. Happy are they that have it: and next to them, not those many that think they have it, but those few that are sensible of their own defects and imperfections, and know that they have it not.

Wisdom. — *Chesterfield.*

YOUNG men are as apt to think themselves wise enough, as drunken men are to think themselves sober enough. They look upon Spirit to be a much better thing than Experience; which they call Coldness. They are but half mistaken; for though Spirit without Experience is dangerous, Experience without Spirit is languid and ineffective.

Wisdom. — *Gibson.*

IT is usually seen, that the wiser men are about the things of this world, the less wise they are about the things of the next.

Wit. — *From the French.*

WIT resembles a Coquette; those who the most eagerly run after it are the least favoured.

Wit. — *Johnson.*

WIT will never make a man rich, but there are places where Riches will always make a Wit.

Wit. — *Osborn.*

LET your Wit rather serve you for a buckler to defend yourself, by a handsome reply, than the Sword to wound others, though with never so facetious a Reproach, remembering that a Word cuts deeper than a sharper weapon, and the Wound it makes is longer curing

Wit. — *South.*

AS the repute of Wisdom, so that of Wit also, is very casual. Sometimes a lucky saying or a pertinent reply has procured an esteem of Wit to persons otherwise very shallow; so that, if such a one should have the ill hap to strike a man dead with a smart saying, it ought in all Reason and Conscience to be judged but a chance-medley. Nay, even when there is a real stock of Wit, yet the wittiest sayings and sentences will be found in a great measure the issues of chance, and nothing else but so many lucky hits of a roving Fancy. For consult the acutest Poets and Speakers; and they will confess that their quickest and most admired conceptions were such as darted into their minds like sudden flashes of Lightning, they knew not how nor whence; and not by any certain consequence or dependence of one thought upon another.

Wit. — *La Bruyere.*

WIT is the god of moments, but Genius is the god of ages.

Wit. — *La Rochefoucauld.*

A MAN does not please long when he has only one species of Wit.

Wit. — *Zimmerman.*

MANY species of Wit are quite mechanical: these are the favourites of witlings, whose Fame in words scarce outlives the remembrance of their funeral Ceremonies.

Wit. — *Lavater.*

THE proverbial wisdom of the Populace at gates, on roads, and in markets, instructs the attentive ear of him who studies Man. more fully than a thousand rules ostentatiously arranged.

Wit. — *Sir Thomas Overbury.*

WIT is brush-wood, Judgment timber: the one gives the greatest Flame, the other yields the durablest Heat; and both meeting make the best Fire.

Wit. — *From the Latin.*

WITTICISMS never are agreeable, which are injurious to others.

Wit. — *Anon.*

WHAT a dull, plodding, tramping, clanking would the ordinary intercourse of Society be, without Wit to enliven and brighten it! When two men meet, they seem to be kept at bay through the estranging effects of Absence, until some sportive sally opens their hearts to each other. Nor does any thing spread cheerfulness so rapidly over a whole party, or an assembly of people however large. Reason expands the soul of the philosopher; Imagination glorifies the poet, and breathes a breath of Spring through the young and genial: but, if we take into account the numberless glances and gleams whereby Wit lightens our every-day life, I hardly know what power ministers so bountifully to the innocent pleasures of Mankind.

Woman. — *Shakspeare.*

THE venom clamours of a jealous Woman
Poison more deadly than a mad dog's tooth.

Woman. — *Anon.*

WHEN a Maiden is too forward, her admirer deems it time to draw back.

Woman. — *Shakspeare.*

PROPER Deformity seems not in the Fiend
So horrid, as in Woman.

Woman. — *Fuller.*

IF thou wouldest please the Ladies, thou must endeavour to make them pleased with themselves.

Woman. — *Shakspeare.*

How easy is it for the proper-false
In Women's waxen hearts to set their forms!

Woman. — *Sir Walter Raleigh.*

HAVE ever more care that thou be beloved of thy Wife, rather than thyself besotted on her: and thou shalt judge of her Love by these two observations: First, if thou perceive she have a care of thy Estate, and exercise herself therein: the other, if she study to please thee, and be sweet unto thee in Conversation, without thy instruction; for Love needs no teaching, nor precept.

Woman. — *Juvenal.*

FEW disputes exist which have not had their origin from Woman.

Woman. — *Colton.*

WOMEN do not like a Man the worse for having many favourites, if he deserts them all for her; she fancies that she herself has the power of fixing the wanderer; that other Women conquer like the Parthians, but that she herself, like the Romans, can not only make conquests, but retain them.

Woman. — *From the French.*

WITHOUT Woman the two extremities of this Life would be destitute of succour, and the middle would be devoid of Pleasure.

Woman. — *Shakspeare.*

Women are as Roses; whose fair flower,
Being once display'd, doth fall that very hour.

Woman. — *Shakspeare.*

Men have marble, Women waxen, minds,
And therefore are they form'd as marble will;
The weak oppress'd, the impression of strange kinds
Is form'd in them by Force, by Fraud, or Skill;
Then call them not the authors of their ill,
No more than Wax shall be accounted evil,
Wherein is stamp'd the semblance of a Devil.
Their smoothness, like a goodly champaign plain,
Lays open all the little worms that creep;
In Men, as in a rough-grown grove, remain
Cave-keeping evils that obscurely sleep:
Through crystal walls each little mote will peep:
Though Men can cover crimes with bold stern looks,
Poor Women's faces are their own faults' books.
No men inveigh against the wither'd flower,
But chide rough Winter that the flower hath kill'd!
Not that devour'd, but that which doth devour,
Is worthy blame. Oh, let it not be held
Poor Women's faults, that they are so fulfill'd
With men's abuses: those proud lords, to blame,
Make weak-made Women tenants to their Shame.

Woman. — *Shakspeare.*

A WOMAN moved, is like a Fountain troubled,
Muddy, ill-seeming, thick, bereft of Beauty;
And while it is so, none so dry or thirsty
Will deign to sip, or touch one drop of it.

Woman. — *La Rochefoucauld.*

WOMEN never have a complete severity of Demeanour except toward those whom they dislike.

Woman. — *Colton.*

PLEASURE is to Women what the Sun is to the Flower; if moderately enjoyed, it beautifies, it refreshes, and it improves; if immoderately, it withers, etiolates, and destroys.

Woman. — *Shakspeare.*

THE hand that hath made you fair, hath made you good: the Goodness, that is cheap in Beauty, makes Beauty brief in goodness; but Grace, being the Soul of your complexion, should keep the body of it ever fair.

Woman. — *Colton.*

MOST Females will forgive a Liberty, rather than a Slight; and if any Woman were to hang a man for stealing her picture, although it were set in gold, it would be a new case in Law; but if he carried off the Setting, and left the Portrait, I would not answer for his safety.

Woman. — *Shakspeare.*

I AM ashamed, that Women are so simple
To offer War where they should kneel for Peace;
Or seek for Rule, Supremacy, and Sway,
When they are bound to serve, love, and obey.
Why are our bodies soft, and weak and smooth,
Unapt to toil and trouble in the World;
But that our soft conditions and our Hearts,
Should well agree with our external parts?

Woman. — *Colton.*

THE Women are satisfied with less than the Men; and yet, notwithstanding this, they are less easily satisfied. In the first place—Preference and Precedence are indispensable articles with them, if we would have our favours graciously received; they look moreover to the mode, the manner, and the address, rather than to the value of the obligation, and estimate it more by the time, the cost, and the trouble we may have expended upon it, than by its intrinsic worth. Attention is ever current coin with the Ladies, and they weigh the Heart much more scrupulously than the Hand.

Woman. — *La Rochefoucauld.*

WOMEN can less easily surmount their Coquetry than their Passions.

Woman. — *Steele.*

IF we were to form an image of dignity in a Man, we should give him Wisdom and Valour, as being essential to the character of manhood. In the like Manner, if you describe a right Woman in a laudable sense, she should have gentle Softness, tender Fear, and all those parts of life which distinguish her from the other sex; with some subordination to it, but such an Inferiority that makes her still more lovely.

Woman. — *La Rochefoucauld.*

THERE can be no regulation in the Minds nor in the Hearts of Women, unless their temperament is in unison with it.

Woman. — *Addison.*

A VIRTUOUS mind in a fair body is indeed a fine Picture in a good light, and therefore it is no wonder that it makes the beautiful Sex all over charms.

Woman. — *Shakspeare.*

IF two Gods should play some heavenly match,
And on the wager lay two earthly Women,
And Portia one, there must be something else
Pawn'd with the other; for the poor rude world
Hath not her fellow.

Woman. — *Colton.*

WOMEN that are the least bashful are not unfrequently the most modest; and we are never more deceived, than when we would infer any laxity of Principle, from that freedom of Demeanour which often arises from a total ignorance of Vice.

Woman. — *Shakspeare.*

WHERE is any Author in the world,
Teaches such beauty as a Woman's eye?

Woman. — *Shakspeare.*

SHE is peevish, sullen, froward,
Proud, disobedient, stubborn, lacking duty;
Neither regarding that she is my child,
Nor fearing me as if I were her Father.

Woman. — *Addison.*

WIDOWS are the great game of Fortune-Hunters.

Woman. — *Herder.*

LAST among the characteristics of Woman, is that sweet motherly Love with which Nature has gifted her; it is almost independent of cold Reason, and wholly removed from all selfish hope of reward. Not because it is lovely, does the Mother love her Child, but because it is a living part of herself,—the Child of her Heart, a fraction of her own nature. Therefore do her entrails yearn over his wailings; her Heart beats quicker at his joy; her blood flows more softly through her veins, when the Breast at which he drinks knits him to her. In every uncorrupted nation of the earth, this feeling is the same; climate, which changes every thing else, changes not that.—It is only the most corrupting forms of society which have power gradually to make luxurious Vice sweeter than the tender cares and soils of Maternal Love.

Woman. — *Shakspeare.*

CONSTANT you are;
But yet a Woman; and for secrecy,
No lady closer; for I well believe,
Thou wilt not utter what thou dost not know;
And so far will I trust thee.

Woman. — *Sir Roger L'Estrange.*

HE that contemns a Shrew to the degree of not descending to word it with her, does worse than beat her.

Woman. — *Addison.*

NOTHING makes a Woman more esteemed by the opposite sex than Chastity; whether it be that we always prize those most who are hardest to come at, or, that nothing besides Chastity, with its collateral attendants, Truth, Fidelity, and Constancy, gives the man a property in the person he loves, and consequently endears her to him above all things.

Woman. — *Spenser.*

TRUST not the Treason of those smiling looks,
Until ye have their guileful trains well trode,
For they are like unto golden hooks,
That from the foolish Fish their bates do hide.

Woman. — *Greville.*

IT is perhaps true, that Women generally come into life with higher ideas of Delicacy than Men; but I believe it true also, that they generally retire from Life with lower.

Woman. — *Shakspeare.*

HER Voice was ever soft,
Gentle and low; an excellent thing in Woman.

Woman. — *Greville.*

I HAVE often thought that the nature of Women was inferior to that of Men in general, but superior in particular.

Woman. — *Shakspeare.*

I NEVER yet saw Man,
How wise, how noble, young, how rarely featured,
But she would spell him backward: if fair-faced,
She'd swear, the Gentleman should be her sister;
If black, why, Nature, drawing of an antic,
Made a foul blot; if tall, a lance ill-headed;
If low, an aglet very vilely cut;
If speaking, why, a vane blown with all winds;
If silent, why, a block moved with none.
So turns she every Man the wrong side out,
And never gives to Truth and Virtue that
Which Simpleness and Merit purchaseth.

Woman. — *Tom Brown.*

A WOMAN may learn one useful doctrine from the game of Backgammon, which is, not to take up her Man till she's sure of binding him.

Woman. — *Shakspeare.*

MISTRESS, know yourself; down on your knees,
And thank Heaven, fasting, for a good man's Love;
For I must tell you friendly in your ear,
Sell when you can; you are not for all markets.

Woman. — *Rousseau.*

THE World is the book of Women. Whatever knowledge they may possess is more commonly acquired by observation than by Reading.

Woman. — *Shakspeare.*

MAKE the doors upon a Woman's wit, and it will out at the Casement; shut that, and 'twill out at the Key-hole; stop that, 'twill fly with the smoke out at the Chimney.

Woman. — *Shakspeare.*

SHA'LL not be hit
With Cupid's arrow; she hath Dian's wit:
And, in strong proof of Chastity well arm'd,
From Love's weak childish bow, she lives unharm'd.
She will not stay the siege of loving terms,
Nor bide th' Encounter of assailing eyes,
Nor ope her lap to saint-seducing Gold.

Woman. — *La Rochefoucauld.*

WHAT causes the majority of Women to be so little touched by Friendship is, that it is insipid when they have once tasted of Love.

Woman. — *Shakspeare.*

SHE is of so free, so kind, so apt, so blessed a Disposition, she holds it a Vice in her Goodness not to do more than she is requested.

In any honest suit, she's framed as fruitful
As the free Elements.

Woman. — *Greville.*

MODESTY in Woman, say some shrewd Philosophers, is not *natural:* it is artificial and acquired; but what then, and to what end, is that *natural* Taste, that delicate Sensation, that Approbation of it, in Man?

Woman. — *Shakspeare.*

SHE hath all courtly parts more exquisite,
Than lady, ladies, Woman; from every one
The best she hath, and she, of all compounded,
Outsells them all.

Woman. — *S. T. Coleridge.*

A WOMAN'S Head is usually over ears in her Heart. Man seems to have been designed for the superior being of the two; but as things are, I think Women are generally better Creatures than Men. They have, taken universally, weaker appetites and weaker intellects, but they have much stronger Affections. A man with a bad Heart has been sometimes saved by a strong Head; but a corrupt Woman is lost for ever.

Woman. — *Shakspeare.*

ALL of her, that is out of door most rich,
If she be furnish'd with a mind so rare,
She is alone the Arabian bird.

Woman. — *Colton.*

A BEAUTIFUL Woman, if poor, should use double circumspection; for her Beauty will tempt others, her Poverty herself.

Woman. — *Shakspeare.*

SHE'S a lady
So tender of Rebukes, that words are strokes,
And strokes Death to her.

Woman. — *Shakspeare.*

ALL that life can rate
Worth name of life, in thee hath estimate:
Youth, Beauty, Wisdom, Courage, Virtue, all
That Happiness and prime can happy call.

Woman. — *La Rochefoucauld.*

COQUETTES make a merit of being jealous of their Lovers, to conceal their being envious of other Women.

Woman. — *Shakspeare.*

FOR she is wise, if I can judge of her;
And fair she is, if that mine Eyes be true;
And true she is, as she hath proved herself;
And therefore like herself, wise, fair, and true,
Shall she be placed in my constant Soul.

Woman. — *Shakspeare.*

FEAR and Niceness,
The handmaids of all Women, or more truly,
Woman its pretty Self.

Woman. — *Shakspeare.*

IF Ladies be but young and fair,
They have the Gift to know it.

Woman. — *From the Italian.*

A BEAUTIFUL Woman by her smiles draws tears from our purse.

Woman. — *Shakspeare.*

KINDNESS in Women, not their beauteous looks,
Shall win my Love.

Woman. — *Steele.*

HE that can keep handsomely within rules, and support the Carriage of a Companion to his Mistress, is much more likely to prevail, than he who lets her see the whole relish of his Life depends upon her. If possible, therefore, divert your Mistress rather than sigh for her.

Woman. — *Shakspeare.*

DUMB jewels often, in their silent kind,
More than quick words, do move a Woman's mind.

Woman. — *Simonides.*

A MAN cannot possess any thing that is better than a good Woman, nor any thing that is worse than a bad one.

Woman. — *Lavater.*

SHE neglects her Heart who studies her Glass.

Woman. — *Epictetus.*

WHEN girls are grown up they begin to be courted and caressed; then they think, that the recommending themselves to the affections of the Men is the only business they have to attend to, and so presently fall to tricking, and dressing, and practising all the little engaging Arts peculiar to their Sex. In these they place all their hopes, as they do all their Happiness in the success of them. But it is fit they should be given to understand, that there are other attractives much more powerful than these; that the respect we pay them is not due to their Beauty, so much as to their Modesty and Innocence, and unaffected Virtue. And that these are the true, the irresistible charms, such as will make the surest and most lasting Conquests.

Woman. — *Shakspeare.*

JIG off a tune at the Tongue's end, canary to it with your feet, humour it with turning up your Eyelids; sigh a note, and sing a note; sometime through the Throat, as if you swallowed Love with singing Love; sometime through the Nose, as if you snuffed up Love by smelling Love;—and keep not too long in one tune, but a snip and away: These are complements, these are Humours; these betray nice wenches.

Woman. — *St. Pierre.*

THE Christian religion alone contemplates the conjugal union in the order of Nature; it is the only religion which presents Woman to Man as a companion; every other abandons her to him as a slave. To religion alone do European women owe the liberty they enjoy: and from the liberty of Women that of nations has flowed, accompanied with the proscription of many inhuman usages diffused over all the other parts of the world, such as Slavery, Seraglios, and Eunuchs.

Woman. — *Shakspeare.*

'Tis Beauty, that doth oft make Women proud;
'Tis Virtue, that doth make them most admired;
'Tis Modesty, that makes them seem divine.

Woman. — *Plautus.*

A WOMAN'S true dowry, in my opinion, is Virtue, Modesty, and Desires restrained; not that which is usually so called.

Woman. — *Goldsmith.*

THE modest Virgin, the prudent Wife, or the careful Matron, are much more serviceable in life, than petticoated Philosophers, blustering Heroines, or virago Queens. She who makes her husband and her children happy, who reclaims the one from Vice, and trains up the other to Virtue, is a much greater character than ladies described in romance, whose whole occupation is to murder Mankind with shafts from their quiver or their eyes.

Woman. — *Shakspeare.*

A Woman impudent and mannish grown
Is not more loath'd than an effeminate Man.

Woman. — *Greville.*

WE are often governed by people not only weaker than ourselves, but even by those whom we think so.

Woman. — *Shakspeare.*

Disloyal? No;
She's punish'd for her Truth; and undergoes,
More goddess-like than wife-like, such assaults
As would take in some Virtue.

Woman. — *Butler.*

YOU wound like Parthians, while you fly,
And kill with a retreating Eye;
Retire the more, the more we press,
To draw us into Ambushes.

Woman. — *Shakspeare.*

I HAVE those hopes of her good, that her Education promises: her dispositions she inherits, which make fair gifts fairer; for where an unclean mind carries virtuous Qualities, there commendations go with pity, they are Virtues and Traitors too; in her, they are the better for their simpleness; she derives her Honesty, and achieves her Goodness

Woman.—*La Bruyere.*

WOMEN, ever in extremes, are always either better or worse than Men.

Woman.—*Shakspeare.*

THOU wilt never get thee a Husband, if thou be so shrewd with thy Tongue.

Woman.—*Pope.*

AND yet, believe me, good as well as ill,
 Woman's at best a Contradiction still.
Heaven when it strives to polish all it can
Its last best work, but forms a softer man;
Picks from each Sex, to make the favourite blest,
Your love of Pleasure, our desire of Rest.
Blends, in exception to all general rules,
Your taste of Follies, with our scorn of Fools;
Reserve with Frankness, Art with Truth allied,
Courage with Softness, Modesty with Pride;
Fix'd Principles, with Fancy ever new;
Shakes all together, and produces—YOU.

Woman.—*Lyttelton.*

ONE only care your gentle breasts should move,—
Th' important bus'ness of your life is Love.

Woman.—*Shakspeare.*

 WHO might be your Mother,
That you insult, exult, and all at once,
Over the wretched? What though you have more Beauty,
(As, by my faith, I see no more in you
Than without Candle may go dark to bed,)
Must you be therefore proud and pitiless?

Woman.—*Shakspeare.*

SHE speaks Poniards, and every word stabs: if her breath were as terrible as her terminations, there were no living near her. She would infect to the North Star. She would have made Hercules have turned spit; yea, and have cleft his Club, to make the Fire too.

Woman.—*Shakspeare.*

THE tongues of mocking Wenches are as keen
 As is the razor's edge invisible,
Cutting a smaller hair than may be seen;
 Above the Sense of Sense: so sensible
Seemeth their conference; their conceits have wings,
Fleeter than Arrows, Bullets, Wind, Thought, swifter things.

Woman.—*Moore.*

YET was there light around her brow,
  A Holiness in those dark eyes,
Which show'd—though wand'ring earthward now—
  Her spirit's home was in the skies.
Yes—for a Spirit, pure as hers,
Is always pure, even while it errs;
As Sunshine, broken in the rill,
Though turn'd astray, is Sunshine still!

Woman.—*Byron.*

SUCH was this Daughter of the southern seas,
  Herself a billow in her energies,
To bear the bark of others' Happiness,
Nor feel a Sorrow till their Joy grew less.

Woman.—*Moore.*

RAPTURED he quits each dozing Sage,
  O Woman! for thy lovelier page!
Sweet book! unlike the books of Art,
Whose errors are thy fairest part;
In whom, the dear Errata column
Is the best page in all the Volume.

Woman.—*Shakspeare.*

You seem to me as Dian in her orb;
As chaste as is the bud ere it be blown.

Woman.—*Lord Lyttelton.*

SEEK to be good, but aim not to be great;
  A Woman's noblest station is Retreat;
Her fairest Virtues fly from public sight;
Domestic worth,—that shuns too strong a Light.

Woman.—*Moore.*

O WOMAN! whose form and whose Soul
  Are the spell and the Light of each path we pursue:
Whether sunn'd in the Tropics, or chill'd at the Pole,
  If Woman be there, there is happiness too.

Woman.—*Scott.*

IN peasant life he might have known
  As fair a face, as sweet a tone;
But Village Notes could ne'er supply
That rich and varied melody;
And ne'er in cottage maid was seen
The easy Dignity of Mien,
Claiming respect, yet waving state,
That marks the Daughters of the Great.

Woman. — *Shakspeare.*

She did make defect, perfection,
And, breathless, Power breathe forth.—
Age cannot wither her, nor Custom stale
Her infinite variety.

Woman. — *Campbell.*

And say, without our Hopes, without our Fears,
Without the Home that plighted Love endears,
Without the Smile from partial Beauty won,
Oh! what were Man!—a World without a Sun.

Woman. — *Byron.*

Soft as the memory of buried Love!
Pure, as the Prayer which Childhood wafts above;
Was she.

Woman. — *Shakspeare.*

'Tis a good hearing, when Children are toward:
But a harsh hearing, when Women are froward.

Woman. — *Lamb.*

The Fair not always view with favouring eyes
The very virtuous or extremely wise,
But, odd it seems, will sometimes rather take
Want with the Spendthrift, riot with the rake.

Woman. — *Byron.*

Her eye's dark charm 'twere vain to tell,
But gaze on that of the Gazelle,
It will assist thy fancy well,
As large, as languishingly dark,
But Soul beam'd forth in every spark
That darted from beneath the lid,
Bright as the jewel of Giamschid.
Yea, Soul, and should our Prophet say
That form was naught but breathing clay,
By Alla! I would answer nay.

Woman. — *Shakspeare.*

Oh, what a Hell of witchcraft lies
In the small orb of one particular Tear!
But with the Inundation of the eyes
What rocky Heart to water will not wear?
What breast so cold that is not warmed here?
Oh, cleft effect! cold Modesty, hot Wrath,
Both fire from hence and chill extincture hath!

Woman — *Campbell.*

THE world was sad!—the garden was a wild!
The Man, the Hermit, sigh'd—till Woman smiled.

Woman. — *Shakspeare.*

SHE will outstrip all Praise,
And make it halt behind her.

Woman. — *Moore.*

NEW Eves in all her daughters came,
As strong to charm, as weak to err,
As sure of Man through praise and blame,
Whate'er they brought him, Pride or Shame,
Their still unreasoning Worshipper—
And, wheresoe'er they smiled, the same
Enchantress of Soul and Frame,
Into whose hands, from first to last,
This World with all its destinies,
Devotedly by Heaven seems cast,
To save or damn it, as they please!

Woman. — *Byron.*

FAIR as the first that fell of Womankind,
When on that dread yet lovely Serpent smiling;
Whose Image then was stamp'd upon her mind—
But once beguiled—and ever more beguiling.

Woman. — *Scott.*

O WOMAN! in our hours of ease,
Uncertain, coy, and hard to please,
And variable as the shade
By the light quivering Aspen made;
When pain and anguish wring the brow
A ministering Angel thou!

Woman. — *Shakspeare.*

SHE cannot love,
Nor take no shape nor project of Affection,
She is so self-endear'd.

Woman. — *Shakspeare.*

FIE, fie, unknit that threat'ning unkind brow;
And dart not scornful glances from those eyes,
To wound thy Lord, thy King, thy Governor:
It blots thy Beauty, as frosts bite the meads;
Confounds thy Fame, as whirlwinds shake fair buds;
And in no sense is meet or amiable.

Woman.—*Joanna Baillie.*

ZOUNDS, Lady! do not give such heavy blows;
I'm not your Husband, as belike you guess.

Woman.—*Byron.*

THE very first
Of human Life must spring from Woman's breast;
Your first small words are taught you from her lips,
Your first Tears quench'd by her, and your last Sighs
Too often breathed out in a Woman's hearing,
When men have shrunk from the ignoble care
Of watching the last Hour of him who led them.

Woman.—*Chapman.*

HE that holds religious and sacred thoughts
Of a Woman; he that bears so reverend
A respect to her, that he will not touch
Her, but with a kiss'd hand and timorous
Heart; he that adores her like his Goddess,
Let him be sure she'll shun him like her Slave.

Woman.—*Shakspeare.*

FROM Women's eyes this doctrine I derive:
They sparkle still the right Promethean fire;
They are the Books, the Arts, the Academics,
That show, contain, and nourish all the World;
Else, none at all in aught proves excellent.

Woman.—*Byron.*

WHAT they ask in aught that touches on
The Heart, is dearer to their feelings or
Their fancy, than the whole external world.

Woman.—*Shakspeare.*

WHOSE warp'd Looks proclaim
What store her Heart is made of.

Woman.—*Shakspeare.*

LADY, you have a merry heart. * * * Yea, I thank it, poor Fool, it keeps on the windy side of Care.

Woman.—*Shakspeare.*

THOU shalt be punish'd for thus frighting me,
For I am sick, and capable of Fears;
Oppress'd with wrongs, and therefore full of Fears;
A Widow, husbandless, subject to Fears;
A Woman, naturally born to Fears;
And though thou now confess, thou did'st but jest,
With my vex'd Spirits I cannot take a truce,
But they will quake and tremble all this day.

Woman. — *Milton.*

FOR Contemplation he and Valour form'd,
For Softness she and sweet attractive Grace;
He for God only, she for God in him.

Woman. — *Thomson.*

TO train the Foliage o'er the snowy lawn;
To guide the pencil, turn the tuneful page;
To lend new flavour to the fruitful year,
And heighten Nature's dainties; in their race
To rear their graces into second Life;
To give Society its highest taste;
Well-order'd Home Man's best delight to make;
And by submissive Wisdom, modest skill,
With every gentle care-eluding art,
To raise the Virtues, animate the Bliss,
And sweeten all the toils of Human Life:
This be the female Dignity and Praise.

Woman. — *Shakspeare.*

LET them anatomize her; see what breeds about her Heart: Is there any cause in Nature, that makes these hard Hearts?

Woman. — *Byron.*

OH! too convincing—dangerously dear—
In Woman's eye the unanswerable Tear!
That weapon of her weakness she can wield
To save, subdue—at once her spear and shield;
Avoid it—Virtue ebbs and Wisdom errs,
Too fondly gazing on that grief of hers!
What lost a World, and made a Hero fly?
The timid tear in Cleopatra's eye.
Yet be the soft triumvir's fault forgiven,
By this—how many lose not Earth—but Heaven!
Consign their souls to man's eternal Foe,
And seal their own to spare some Wanton's wo!

Woman. — *Spenser.*

YE gentle Ladies! in whose soveraine Powre
Love hath the glory of his Kingdom left,
And th' Hearts of men, as your eternall dowre,
In yron chaines of Liberty bereft,
Delivered hath unto your hands by gift,
Be well aware how ye the same doe use,
That Pride doe not to Tyranny you lift,
Least if men you of cruelty accuse,
He from you take that chiefdome which ye doe abuse.

Woman. — *Shakspeare.*

I GRANT, I am a Woman; but withal,
  A Woman that Lord Brutus took to wife:
I grant, I am a Woman; but withal,
A Woman well reputed; Cato's daughter.
Think you, I am no stronger than my Sex,
Being so father'd and so husbanded?

Woman. — *Lamb.*

STILL Woman draws new pow'r, new empire, still
  From every blessing and from every ill.
Vice on her Bosom lulls remorseful Care,
And Virtue hopes congenial Virtue there.
Still she most hides the strength that most subdues,
To gain each end, its opposite pursues;
Lures by Neglect, advances by Delay,
And gains command by swearing to obey.

Woman. — *Byron.*

BUT she was a soft landscape of mild earth,
  Where all was Harmony, and Calm and Quiet,
Luxuriant, budding; cheerful without mirth,
  Which if not Happiness, is much more nigh it
Than are your mighty passions and so forth,
  Which some call "The Sublime;" I wish they'd try it:
I've seen your stormy Seas and stormy Women,
And pity Lovers rather more than Seamen.

Woman. — *Pope.*

IN Men, we various ruling Passions find;
  In Women, two almost divide the kind:
Those, only fix'd, they first or last obey,
The love of Pleasure, and the love of Sway.

Woman. — *Byron.*

MAIDENS, like Moths, are caught by glare,
And Mammon wins his way where Seraphs might despair.

Woman. — *Irving.*

AS the vine which has long twined its graceful foliage about the oak, and been lifted by it into sunshine, will, when the hardy plant is rifted by the thunderbolt, cling round it with its caressing tendrils, and bind up its shattered boughs; so it is beautifully ordered by Providence, that Woman, who is the mere dependant and ornament of man in his happier hours, should be his stay and solace when smitten with sudden calamity; winding herself into the rugged recesses of his nature, tenderly supporting the drooping head, and binding up the broken heart.

Words. — *Lavater.*

VOLATILITY of Words is Carelessness in actions; Words are the wings of Actions.

Good Works. — *Fichte.*

NOT alone to know, but to act according to thy Knowledge, is thy destination; proclaims the voice of my inmost Soul. Not for indolent Contemplation and study of thyself, nor for brooding over emotions of Piety—no, for Action was existence given thee; thy Actions, and thy Actions alone, determine thy worth.

The World. — *Johnson.*

THOUGH the world is crowded with scenes of Calamity, we look upon the general mass of Wretchedness with very little regard, and fix our eyes upon the state of particular persons, whom the eminence of their qualities marks out from the Multitude; as, in reading an account of a battle, we seldom reflect on the vulgar heaps of Slaughter; but follow the Hero with our whole attention, through all the varieties of his Fortune, without a thought of the Thousands that are falling round him.

The World. —*Shakspeare.*

THAT, Sir, which serves and seeks for gain
And follows but for form,
Will pack, when it begins to rain,
And leave thee in the Storm.

The World. — *Greville.*

THE Great see the World at one end by Flattery, the Little at the other end by Neglect; the meanness which both discover is the same; but how different, alas! are the mediums through which it is seen?

The World. — *Fuller.*

TAKE this as a most certain expedient to prevent many Afflictions, and to be delivered from them: meddle as little with the World, and the Honours, Places and Advantages of them, as thou canst. And extricate thyself from them as much, and as quickly as possible.

The World. —*Shakspeare.*

YOU have too much respect upon the World:
They lose it, that do buy it with much care.

The World. — *Mackenzie.*

DELUSIVE ideas are the motives of the greatest part of Mankind, and a heated Imagination the power by which their actions are incited: the World, in the eye of a Philosopher, may be said to be a large Madhouse.

The World. — *Byron.*

I HAVE not loved the World, nor the World me;
I have not flatter'd its rank breath, nor bow'd
To its Idolatries a patient knee,—
Nor coin'd my cheeks to smiles,—nor cried aloud
In worship of an echo; in the crowd
They could not deem me one of such; I stood
Among them, but not of them; in a shroud
Of Thoughts which were not their thoughts, and still could,
Had I not fill'd my mind, which thus itself subdued.
I have not loved the World, nor the World me,—
But let us part fair foes; I do believe,
Though I have found them not, that there may be
Words which are things,—Hopes which will not deceive,
And Virtues which are merciful, nor weave
Snares for the failing: I would also deem
O'er others' Griefs that some sincerely grieve;
That two, or one, are almost what they seem,—
That Goodness is no name, and Happiness no dream.

The World. — *Buckingham.*

THE World is made up, for the most part, of fools or knaves, both irreconcilable foes to Truth: the first being slaves to a blind Credulity, which we may properly call Bigotry: the last are too jealous of that power they have usurped over the Folly and Ignorance of the others, which the establishment of the empire of Reason would destroy. For Truth, being made so plain and easy to all men, would render the designs and arts of knaves of little use in those opinions which set the World at odds, and by the feuds they maintain, enrich those who, in a charitable, peaceful World, must starve.

The World. — *Greville.*

THE World is an excellent Judge *in general*, but a very bad one *in particular*.

The World. — *Fuller.*

THOU must content thyself to see the World so imperfect as it is. Thou wilt never have any Quiet if thou vexest thyself, because thou canst not bring Mankind to that exact Notion of things and Rule of Life which thou hast formed in thy own Mind.

The World. — *Chesterfield.*

WHEN I reflect on what I have seen, what I have heard, and what I have done, I can hardly persuade myself that all that frivolous hurry and bustle of Pleasure in the world had any reality; but I look upon all that is passed as one of those romantic dreams which Opium commonly occasions, and I do by no means desire to repeat the nauseous Dose.

Lip Worship. — *Shakspeare.*

My Words fly up, my Thoughts remain below:
Words, without Thoughts, never to Heaven go.

The Worst. — *Shakspeare.*

The Worst is not,
So long as we can say, This is the Worst.

Wrong never comes Right. — *S. T. Coleridge.*

THE history of all the World tells us, that immoral Means will ever intercept good Ends.

Youth. — *Byron.*

NO more—no more—oh! never more on me
The freshness of the Heart can fall like dew,
Which out of all the lovely things we see
Extracts Emotions beautiful and new,
Hived in our bosoms like the bay o' the Bee:
Think'st thou the Honey with those objects grew?
Alas! 'twas not in them, but in thy power
To double even the sweetness of a Flower.
No more—no more—oh! never more, my Heart,
Canst thou be my sole world, my Universe!
Once all in all, but now a thing apart,
Thou canst not be my Blessing or my Curse:
The illusion's gone for ever, and thou art
Insensible, I trust, but none the worse.

Youth. — *Anon.*

BLEST hour of Childhood! then, and then alone,
Dance we the revels close round Pleasure's throne,
Quaff the bright nectar from her fountain-springs,
And laugh beneath the rainbow of her wings.
Oh! time of Promise, Hope, and Innocence,
Of Trust, and Love, and happy Ignorance!
Whose every dream is Heaven, in whose fair joy
Experience yet has thrown no black alloy;
Whose Pain, when fiercest, lacks the venom'd pang
Which to maturer ill doth oft belong,
When, mute and cold, we weep departed bliss,
And Hope expires on broken Happiness.

Youth. — *Byron.*

A lovely Being, scarcely form'd or moulded,
A Rose with all its sweetest leaves yet folded.

Youth.—*Hannah More.*

Oh! the joy
Of young Ideas painted on the mind,
In the warm glowing colours Fancy spreads
On objects not yet known, when all is new,
And all is lovely.

Youth.—*Byron.*

Her Smiles and Tears had pass'd, as light winds pass
O'er lakes, to ruffle, not destroy, their Glass.

Youth.—*La Bruyere.*

YOUNG Persons, on account of their Passion for various amusements, are less easily reconciled to Solitude than persons in more advanced life.

Youth.—*Sir W. Jones.*

THE charms of Youth at once are seen and past;
And Nature says, "They are too sweet to last."
So blooms the Rose: and so the blushing Maid.
Be gay; too soon the flowers of Spring will fade.

Youth.—*Shakspeare.*

HE hath borne himself beyond the promise of his Age; doing, in the figure of a Lamb, the feats of a Lion: he hath, indeed, bettered Expectation.

Youth.—*Byron.*

THE love of higher things and better days;
The unbounded Hope, and heavenly Ignorance
Of what is call'd the World, and the World's ways;
The moments when we gather from a glance
More joy than from all future Pride or Praise,
Which kindle Manhood, but can ne'er entrance
The Heart in an existence of its own,
Of which another's bosom is the Zone.

Youth.—*Scott.*

THE Tear, down Childhood's cheek that flows,
Is like the dew-drop on the Rose;
When next the Summer breeze comes by,
And waves the bush, the Flower is dry.

Youth.—*Byron.*

IN earlier Days, and calmer Hours,
When Heart with Heart delights to blend,
Where bloom my native valley's bowers,
I had—ah! have I now?—a Friend!

Youth. — *Moore.*

LIGHT, winged Hopes, that come when bid,
  And rainbow Joys that end in weeping,
And Passions, among pure thoughts hid,
  Like serpents under Flow'rets sleeping.

Youth. — *Rogers.*

OH who, when fading of itself away,
  Would cloud the Sunshine of his little day!
Now is the May of Life. Careering round,
Joy wings his feet, Joy lifts him from the ground.

Youth and Age. — *Cicero.*

AS I approve of a Youth, that has something of the Old Man in him, so I am no less pleased with an Old Man, that has something of the Youth.

Youth and Age. — *Shakspeare.*

YOUTH no less becomes
The light and careless livery that it wears,
Than settled Age his sables, and his weeds,
Importing Health, and Graveness.

The End.

STEREOTYPED BY L. JOHNSON & CO.
PHILADELPHIA.

www.ingramcontent.com/pod-product-compliance
Lightning Source LLC
LaVergne TN
LVHW021232110826
845150LV00002B/315

* 9 7 8 1 4 2 5 5 6 2 4 8 9 *